Rick Reynolds

HANDBOOK OF CLINICAL ASSESSMENT OF CHILDREN AND ADOLESCENTS

VOLUME II

HANDBOOK
OF CLINICAL ASSESSMENT
OF CHILDREN AND ADOLESCENTS

VOLUME II

CLARICE J. KESTENBAUM
and
DANIEL T. WILLIAMS
Editors

 NEW YORK UNIVERSITY PRESS
New York and London

Library of Congress Cataloging-in-Publication Data

Handbook of clinical assessment of children and
    adolescents.

    Includes bibliographies and index.
    1. Child psychopathology—Classification.
2. Adolescent psychopathology—Classification.
3. Mental illness—Diagnosis. I. Kestenbaum,
Clarice J., 1929–   . II. Williams, Daniel T.,
1944–   .
RJ500.5.H37   1987   618.92′89   87-20250
ISBN 0-8147-4592-X (v. 1)
ISBN 0-8147-4593-8 (v. 2)
ISBN 0-8147-4590-3 (set)

Clothbound editions of New York University Press
books are Smyth-sewn and printed on permanent and
durable acid-free paper.

Contents

VOLUME II

VII

Assessment of Children and Adolescents with Traditional Psychopathological Syndromes

25

ATTENTION DEFICIT DISORDER AND HYPERACTIVITY

Robert Hunt

The assessment and treatment of children and adolescents with attention deficit disorder and hyperactivity presents the clinician with special circumstances. The major issues to be assessed occur primarily outside the evaluation room, at home and at school, and involve behavior that the clinician may not see directly and the child may not be able to report. Thus, this assessment relies heavily on a network of collaboration with parents and teachers and on the need for descriptive quantification of the relevant behavioral data. The cognitive difficulties of these children have a distinctly subjective psychological impact on the inner life of the child and create considerable stress for the family. It requires clinical acumen to retain a sense of the child behind the symptoms and to assess the functioning of family beyond their symptomatic complaints. This process includes differential diagnosis based on a quantifiable assessment of behavior, interviews with the child and family, a medical history and exam, and perhaps specialized evaluations of cognitive and learning abilities or neurological and neurochemical status. This disorder touches a child's psychological, cognitive, and social adjustment, and hence requires a comprehensive biopsychosocial approach to assessment and treatment. It requires the full spectrum of skills of a child psychiatrist who is both a physician and therapist.

The nature of this assessment process is illustrated by the difficulties and treatment of Steven, whose story will guide the themes of this chapter.

Case History: Steven

Steven, an 8-year-old boy in the third grade, attends a special education class. Although Steven has always been distractable and overactive, his disruptive behavior recently became unmanageable. In class he is usually out of his seat, makes impulsive movements, and is excessively clownish. He has been fighting almost constantly with his classmates. He is often teased, seems to have no stable playmates, and looks sad, especially recently. Steven was placed in special education classes for reading and related subjects, and was mainstreamed in math, gym, art, and drawing. Although Steven seems to enjoy sports he has been below average in coordination and often is distracted and makes errors during games. Steven had mentioned some difficulties at home that indicated his parents have recently separated and he missed his father. The teacher recommended that Steven be evaluated for his combined behavioral, learning, and mood disorder.

DIAGNOSIS OF ATTENTION DEFICIT DISORDER

Attention Deficit Disorder with Hyperactivity (ADDH), a serious, high-incidence disorder with characteristic symptoms of impulsivity, inattention, and hyperactivity, disrupts the development of many children and frequently persists in a transmuted form into adulthood. Estimates indicate that ADDH affects over 200,000 children in the United States (Sprague and Sleator 1977; Safer and Allen 1976); it threatens academic learning, disrupts social and peer relations, and can greatly disturb functioning within the home and at school (Silver 1981; Halperin and Gittelman 1982; Cantwell 1975a; Weiss and Hechtman 1979).

The etiological roots of ADDH are both genetic and environmental. Its life course is highly affected by interpersonal relationships, life events, and treatment. The evidence of a genetic component to ADDH highlights the biological substrate of this common disturbance in attentional and behavioral modulation (Cantwell 1975b; Deutsch et al. 1982; McMahon 1981). Biochemical factors may distinguish ADDH from normal children, or there may be chemical changes that are subtype-specific and that will eventually contribute to predicting medication response.

Follow-up studies have established the persistence of this disorder into both adolescence (Lerer and Lerer 1977; Mendelson et al. 1971) and adulthood (Wender et al. 1971; Wood et al. 1976; Weiss and Hechtman 1979; Cowart 1982; Amado and Lustman 1982). Over time, ADDH children appear to be at increased risk of developing antisocial behavior (Satterfield et al. 1982), alcoholism, and substance abuse (Eyre et al. 1982).

Recent developments in neurochemistry and in cognitive psychology are beginning to clarify some of the underlying mechanisms in this disorder that affect the modulation of affect and information processing. These methods may define new dimensions of assessment and diagnosis that would allow clinicians to differentiate among possible educational and medical treatments.

The multiaxial, criterion-based classification of DSM-III has had considerable impact on research and clinical work with the hyperactive or minimal brain dysfunction child. DSM-III replaced the previous category of "Hyperkinetic Reaction of Childhood" with that of "Attention Deficit Disorder" and stated that ADD can occur either "With" or "Without Hyperactivity." It also declared that a "Residual Type" may be diagnosed in older individuals where the initial symptoms have subsided but the core dysfunction persists.

Diagnostic Criteria for Attention Deficit Disorder with Hyperactivity.

The child displays, for his or her mental age, signs of developmentally inappropriate inattention, impulsivity, and hyperactivity. The signs must be reported by adults in the child's environment, such as parents and teachers. Because the symptoms are clinically variable, they may not be observed directly by the clinician. When the reports of teachers and parents conflict, primary consideration should be given to the teacher reports because of greater familiarity with age-appropriate norms. Symptoms typically worsen in situations that require self-application, as in the classroom. Signs of the disorder may be absent when the child is in a new one-to-one situation.

The number of symptoms specified is for children between the ages of eight and ten, the peak age range for referral. In younger children, more severe forms of the symptoms and a greater number of symptoms are usually present. The opposite is true of older children.

A. *Inattention.* At least three of the following:

(1) often fails to finish things he or she starts
(2) often doesn't seem to listen
(3) easily distracted
(4) has difficulty concentrating on schoolwork or other tasks requiring sustained attention
(5) has difficulty sticking to a play activity

B. *Impulsivity.* At least three of the following:

(1) often acts before thinking
(2) shifts excessively from one activity to another
(3) has difficulty organizing work (this not being due to cognitive impairment)
(4) needs a lot of supervision
(5) frequently calls out in class
(6) has difficulty awaiting turn in games or group situations

C. *Hyperactivity.* At least two of the following:

(1) runs about or climbs on things excessively
(2) has difficulty sitting still or fidgets excessively
(3) has difficulty staying seated
(4) moves about excessively during sleep
(5) is always "on the go" or acts as if "driven by a motor"

D. Onset before the age of 7
E. Duration of at least six months
F. Not due to schizophrenia, affective disorder, or severe or profound mental retardation

Diagnostic Criteria for Attention Deficit Disorder without Hyperactivity.

The criteria for this disorder are the same as those for Attention Deficit Disorder with Hyperactivity except that the individual never had signs of hyperactivity (criterion C).

Diagnostic Criteria for Attention Deficit Disorder, Residual Type.

A. The individual once met the criteria for attention deficit disorder with hyperactivity. This information may come from the individual or from others, such as family members.

B. Signs of hyperactivity are no longer present, but other signs of the illness have persisted to the present without periods of remission, as evidenced by signs of both attentional deficits and impulsivity (e.g., difficulty organizing work and completing tasks, difficulty concentrating, being easily distracted, making sudden decisions without thought of the consequences).

C. The symptoms of inattention and impulsivity result in some impairment in social or occupations functioning.

D. Not due to schizophrenia, affective disorder, severe or profound mental retardation, or schizotypal or borderline personality disorders.

Since the formulation of these clinical diagnostic concepts, researchers and clinicians have questioned the validity of these criteria for both clinical and research purposes and the actual existence of an authentic clinical syndrome (Cantwell 1980). To what extent is this symptom cluster an authentic "illness" or just a frequently occurring mix of independent but frequently coexistent symptoms? This uncertainty has produced changes in nomenclature and prompted considerable phenomenological and genetic research. The shifting nosology has reflected changes in attributions of etiology and in our capacities for measurement. The initial concept of "minimal brain *damage*" was formulated to describe children with cognitive and behavioral problems similar to those seen in patients with known cerebral pathology; in the mid-60s the concept of "minimal brain *dysfunction*" reflected a functional rather than structural or traumatic deficit. Yet studies of the brain using CAT scan have failed to demonstrate consistent abnormalities of brain morphology, and studies of brain function and of neurophysiology show a spectrum of inconsistent and nonspecific deficits and symptoms. The extent to which ADDH is a valid syndrome with sufficient homogeneity to expect a common biological substrate remains uncertain (Rapoport and Ferguson 1981).

The recent focus on the attentional deficit as the core underlying pathological process has generated its own set of difficulties. Attention is a broad-based and complex phenomenon that is more difficult to operationalize and to measure than is either activity or impulsivity. Questions persist as to whether the children who are diagnosed ADD without hyperactivity have the same disorder as do ADD children with hyperactivity. Characteristics such as "doesn't seem to listen, easily distracted" may have different clinical significance when they are not associated with hyperactivity; indeed, such behaviors may occur in a wide variety of dysfunctional states. Thus, children who are being called ADD without hyperactivity may be inattentive for reasons quite separate from the presumed specific nervous system pathophysiology thought to underlie ADD (Gittelman 1984).

While "minimal brain dysfunction" may follow brain trauma or illness, evidence for a genetically determined disorder or syndrome is less conclusive (Rutter 1982). A large number of attentional, perceptual, and motor deficits occur in normal seven-year-olds (Gillberg and Rasmussen 1982). A naturalistic study failed to reveal a significant association among learning disabilities, hyperactivity, and soft neurological signs in affected children (Nichols and Chen 1981). Since children may have difficulties in any or all of these areas, this may not warrant the designation "syndrome." Recent developments in cognitive and neurochemical assessment may eventually define clinical populations who share more homogeneous patterns of information processing and neurotransmitter functioning.

Recent research has focused on the relationship between the symptoms of ADDH and levels of aggression or coexistence with Conduct Disorder. ADD with hyperactivity is at least twice as frequent as ADD without hyperactivity. Aggression, hyperactivity, and inattention can be reliably differentiated by teachers in the classroom (Roberts et al. 1981), and by observers of a playroom activity (Milich et al. 1982). While both hyperactive and nonhyperactive groups of ADD children are rated by peers as socially "disliked," the hyperactive group is more likely to have conduct problems as well (King and Young 1982). Children who most clearly fit the construct of ADDH are hyperactive across behavioral settings (Schachar et al. 1981). Loney et al. (1981) demonstrated that the strongest predictor of difficulty in later life is not hyperactivity per se but the combination of hyperactivity and aggression. Based on the appearance of an antisocial factor during initial evaluation, Satterfield et al. (1982) were similarly able to predict arrests for felonies in a group of hyperactives eight years later. Follow-up studies of conduct-disordered children in Kauai (Werner et al. 1971, 1977) and Robins' description of *Deviant Children Grown Up* (1966) indicate that these pernicious disorders are associated with adult outcomes that are personally painful and costly to society. Thus, a large heterogeneous group of behaviorally disturbed and dysfunctional children has not yet been successfully described by any single conceptual approach.

ADDH has been variously estimated to affect 1 to 10 percent of elementary school aged boys in the United States (Sandberg et al. 1980); a somewhat lower estimate of about 2 to 3 percent is derived from studies in England and China. This disparity suggests that differences both in cultures and in diagnostic criteria may contribute to this variability. Outcome studies of ADDH also imply that cultural and familial variables alter the risk for subsequent development of antisocial behavior. A much greater frequency of antisocial behavior was noted in follow-up studies of ADDH children in Los Angeles than in Canada (Weiss 1981). ADD with hyperactivity is more prevalent in boys than girls, by a factor estimated at five to nine fold. The attentional disturbance may be more evenly distributed across genders, but the girls' lower level of hyperactivity and behavioral disruption may diminish the likelihood of its recognition. In adults, on the other hand, symptoms of residual ADDH may be more apparent in women than men (Wood et al. 1983).

The distinction of this syndrome from the range of normal behavior or from isolated symptom areas requires careful clinical assessment. Gillberg et al. (1982, 1983) report that about one-third of the 7-year-old Swedish children with the behavioral and cognitive symptoms of ADD also had hyperactivity. Many children with coordination difficulties are cognitively intact, or in any case, exhibit no other psychiatric diagnoses (Rie et al. 1978; Shaffer 1978). "Soft" neurological signs are developmentally or age related (Adams et al. 1974) and are reliably elicited, persistent, but nonspecific; their clinical significance is not clear (Shaywitz 1982). Some motoric symptoms occur in children with no behavioral or learning difficulties. The incidence in "normal" children of dysgraphia is 10 percent; dysdiadochokinesia occurs in 8 percent, and mirror movements in 14 percent; choreiform movements were elicited in 11 percent of "normal" children (Stine et al. 1975; Shaffer 1978).

ADDH is a disorder of modulation that affects cognitive, motoric, social, and affective development. Although the behavioral manifestations are altered by life stages and events, the primary deficits may well pervade the modulation of attention, aggression, and activity during periods of stress and excitement throughout life. Monitoring of internal stimuli and feelings may be as impaired as difficulties in sustaining external attention. The problem of modulation usually affects attention to both internal and external events, and this in turn affects development of the sense of self and the internal world of object relations (Hunt and Cohen 1983; Cantwell 1975a; Cohen 1977; Lazor and Chandler 1978; Weiss and Hechtman 1979).

Steven's Development

As an infant Steven was described as colicky, irritable, and an irregular sleeper. Developmental milestones were normal; he seemed to run almost as soon as he began to walk. Since the age of two Steven has been very active and has never remained interested in anything very long. He was easily upset by minor disappointments. He seems happy when things go well, but rapidly explodes when he is excited or anticipates something special such as a birthday party. Steven has been diagnosed as having a learning disability in the first grade and a specific reading disability with tendency to reverse letters.

The untreated clinical expression of attention deficit disorder changes with development. Since the development of attention is closely linked to the emergence of attachment, a close relationship exists between a child's early cognitive behavior and his interpersonal relationships. Careful history may disclose that the ADD child was an unusual infant. He cried a lot, was irritable, and slept less than most infants. He did not sustain play or exploration with one toy or object. He destroyed or lost even the most "childproof" toy. He wore out his clothes, his toys, and his mother's patience earlier than do most toddlers. Yet other children with ADDH appear to parents to be calm and regular infants, who first became hyperactive and inattentive as toddlers or in nursery school.

By the time children attain the age of 3, parents are usually able to identify accurately those who are overactive, inattentive, and difficult to discipline. These children are also more active, impulsive, and distractable during structured laboratory tasks (Campbell et al. 1982). ADDH alters parent/child interaction. Young hyperactive children are more irritable and noncompliant toward their mothers; in turn, their mothers are more directive, negative, and less interactive than in control families (Mash and Johnson 1982).

By elementary school, ADDH children frequently exhibit learning difficulties. Some appear to have primary perceptual problems, as evidenced by a tendency to reverse letters and numbers. Others have reading difficulties (dyslexia), perhaps secondary to the impulsivity of their visual scanning. Learning difficulties also may derive from impairment in other aspects of cognition. The attentional disturbance can impair discrimination between relevant and distracting stimuli and disrupt processes of sustained vigilance or reflection. For example, the correct sequencing of information or the discrimination of a relevant pattern or concept often requires sustained focusing on subtle aspects of a stimulus, subject, or idea. Because of his distractability the impulsive child may miss sequences and patterns. Similarly, the abstract or idiomatic meaning of a word, which is partially defined by its context, may be lost to the child who processes information in rapidly shifting fragments.

In the classroom, the behavior of ADD children is characterized by restlessness, failure to finish projects, impulsivity, short attention span, defiance of authority, and distractability. If they are not treated, their school work is often sloppy and disorganized. They may forget assignments, lose papers, and neglect handing in completed work. Since the classroom is inherently a site where demands for sustained attention compete with many distractions, the symptoms of ADDH are usually most pronounced there; systematic teacher observations accordingly provide the best foundation for diagnosis. Behavior ratings from the teachers provide a standard referent for symptom quantification.

By middle childhood, attentionally impaired children are often enmeshed in conflict. Parents are unable to "make them mind"; teachers have difficulty helping them learn and behave in class; peers are annoyed by immature, attention-seeking behavior; and neighbors may complain of their negligence, destruction of property, or the "bad influence" they exert on other children. By this time children have often been diagnosed as having behavioral or learning difficulties. Many have been placed on medication and/or in special educational environments.

As the ADD child becomes aware of his learning difficulties, his social isolation, and his poor self-control, depressive or sociopathic personality features may emerge. The low self-esteem experienced frequently by these children is in part reactive—a reflection of their lack of accomplishment, social rejection, feelings of isolation, and failure to sustain attachment. Their inability to sustain attention or maintain a continuing interest leads to feelings of boredom and to a diffusion of identity. Internal disorganization parallels the symptomatic behavioral chaos. They lack a sense of commitment or direction, and they fail to channel their efforts into a meaningful sequence of accomplishment. The development of emotional continuity—the internal linking of perception and understanding to feelings—also may be difficult for children with impaired attention and impulsivity (Gardner 1979).

Adolescence. For many children, puberty becomes a crucial transition point in the manifestations of this disorder. For many, the attendant changes in hormonal status appear to increase cortical control and diminish overt hyperactivity. In some cases, medications can be discontinued at this point; clearly a drug-free or placebo trial is indicated. However, for many ADDH teenagers, their fidgetiness and impulsivity remains and is subject to the increased potential for aggressiveness and danger that characterizes adolescence.

When unmodified by appropriate intervention during adolescence, ADDH is evident in continued learning difficulties and emotional-behavioral restlessness (Hunt and Cohen 1984). Through familial, educational, and psychotherapeutic intervention, some ADDH teenagers have developed compensatory mechanisms that enable them to exercise considerable behavioral control. Others persist in stimulus-seeking and risk-taking behavior. Some studies suggest a higher incidence of mixed-substance abuse in adolescents with residual ADDH—possibly as a means of diminishing motor restlessness and subjective anxiety. A few such teenagers may continue to self-administer "uppers" for their calming effect. However, prior treatment with stimulants does not increase the risk of substance abuse. On the other hand, those ADDH adolescents with a history of childhood conduct disorder are at greater risk for subsequent antisocial and criminal behavior (Lerer and Lerer 1977; Satterfield et al. 1982). The arrest records of 110 adolescents who had childhood ADD, especially if associated with conduct disorder, demonstrated a higher incidence of serious delinquent offenses and penal institutionalization (Satterfield et al. 1982)

Outcome—Adult (Residual) ADD. As development proceeds, the motoric hyperactivity usually diminishes to manageable levels of restlessness. However, the attentional deficit and impulsivity may persist into adulthood. While some do outgrow the effects of ADD, others continue to exhibit severe impulsivity and excitability as adults. These characteristics may presently take form as excessive substance and alcohol abuse, risk taking, explosiveness or antisocial activities. ADD may be a precursor to some later forms of major affective or interpersonal disorders (Mendelson et al. 1971; Huessy et al. 1974; Cantwell 1975a; Quinn and Rapoport 1975; Wood et al. 1976; Hopkins et al. 1979; Yellin et al. 1982; Horowitz 1981; Hechtman et al. 1981, 1984; Amado and Lustman 1982; Plotkin et al. 1982).

Fragmented attention and effort may lead to a life history of poor judgment and unfinished beginnings. Marriages may be disrupted, friendships brief, parenting inconsistent, and work record unproductive. As adults, they may develop personality disorders or have substantial antisocial and legal difficulties. Psychiatric inpatients, including those with psychosis and character disorder, have reported a high incidence of symptoms of ADDH in childhood (Gomez et al. 1981).

In follow-up studies, one-third of adult male alcoholics were found to have residual ADD (Wood et al. 1983). A substantial subset of adults who had been carefully diagnosed as borderline personality gave a history of learning disabilities and ADD in childhood (Andrulonis et al. 1982). Symptoms of residual ADD coupled with complex partial seizures are frequent in adults with episodic uncontrollable rage attacks (Elliott 1982). Adults with residual ADD who exhibit antisocial behavior are those most likely to have had a conduct disorder in childhood.

DIFFERENTIAL VERSUS INCLUSIVE DIAGNOSIS OF ASSOCIATED CONDITIONS

The major assessment issues which must be addressed by the clinician are:

1. What are the child's competencies and difficulties? Are his problems serious enough to merit intervention?
2. Do these symptoms constitute the diagnosis of ADDH?
3. Are there associated symptoms such as learning disabilities, depression, aggression, conduct disorder that need separate treatment?
4. In what ways has the family contributed to the difficulties of the child?
5. How has the family been affected by problems of this child?
6. What modifications are needed in the child's life at home and at school?
7. Are medications indicated? If so, which medication and dose?
8. How will the results of intervention be monitored?

While the researcher often seeks children with maximum symptomatic homogeneity, the clinician must strive for a comprehensive evaluation of children with mixed symptomatology. Comprehensive treatment planning requires a complete survey of all related dimensions of cognition and behavior. Children often do not fit neatly or exclusively into our diagnostic specifications.

CLINICAL SUBTYPES OF ADDH

Clinical studies increasingly differentiate subcategories of children with ADDH (O'Leary and Steen 1982; Loney et al. 1978). Potential clinical subtypes have been identified on the basis of:

1) having a family history of attentional disorder, learning disability (LD), alcoholism, or affective disorder (Cantwell 1976);
2) medical history of prenatal or birth trauma or illness (Gillberg and Rasmussen 1982);
3) physical and neurological symptoms including: minor physical anomalies (Rapoport et al. 1974), presence of soft neurological signs such as delayed fine and gross motor coordination (Shaffer 1978);
4) age of onset;
5) presence of behavioral symptoms such as aggression, conduct disorder (Satterfield et al. 1981; Hechtman et al. 1981), and explosive dyscontrol (Elliott 1982);
6) cognitive difficulties such as specific learning disabilities (O'Brien 1982; August and Stewart 1982; Kupietz et al. 1982; Levine et al. 1982);
7) affective symptoms including depression and separation anxiety (Cox 1982; Gordon and Oshman 1981).

Other factors which may affect clinical outcome and medication response include:
8) family and cultural structure functioning (Idol-Maestas 1981);

9) psychophysiological variables such as abnormalities in EEG (Satterfield et al. 1973a,b), visual pursuit (Sostek et al. 1980), and electrocortical frequency response (Dykman et al. 1982). These subcategories may contribute to differential neurochemistry or response to medications (Werry 1981).

DIFFERENTIAL DIAGNOSIS

Among the possible additional diagnoses that need to be considered are: affective disorders, anxiety disorders, antisocial personality disorder, conduct disorder in its various forms, and oppositional disorder. Hyperactivity may coexist with pervasive development disorder and be remediated by methylphenidate (Geller et al. 1981). Attentional disturbance is a frequent component of more pervasive disorders such as autism, atypical development, and Tourette's Syndrome (Cohen 1980; Jagger et al. 1982). These areas include disturbances in learning, motoric skills, and social behavior.

Learning Disability. A specific learning disability exists when cognitive functioning in one modality or area is impaired relative to other more general intellectual abilities. Many children with ADD may have specific reading or arithmetic disabilities (Gittelman-Klein and Klein 1976; Harris 1976). Learning disabilities may reflect impairment in perception, cortical recognition, cross-modality integration, sequencing, abstraction, and memory storage and recall—functions that are linked by, but not confined to, attentional processes. In some cases, this attentional deficit may reflect a disturbance in attributing meaning to stimuli. Or, as was shown by recent data arising from work with developmentally delayed children, there may be a disturbance in physiological mechanisms that modulate arousal and intake of external stimuli (Kootz and Cohen 1981).

Important diagnostic and therapeutic distinctions can be drawn between children with learning or perceptual disabilities without the impulse disorder or hyperactivity of ADDH. Children with primary learning disabilities (LD) may have more difficulty with information processing (perception, sequential organization or abstraction, memory storage and retrieval), and with motor integration and output, but be less impulsive and distractable than those with ADDH. The LD child does not usually benefit from medication and is primarily in need of special education. Some but not all ADDH children are aggressive and have symptoms of conduct disorder. These distinctions are important for research and for clinical therapy.

Conduct Disorder. Children with ADDH have an increased risk for development of Conduct Disorder. Their impulsivity and propensity for action often preclude the exercise of good judgment. Their poor social skills place them at great risk of being used and scapegoated by other children to act deviantly. Family and social variables may strongly influence the likelihood of an ADDH child developing Conduct Disorder. Conduct Disorder can be reliably differentiated from "pure" ADDH (Milich et al. 1982; Roberts et al. 1981) and appears to be predictive of subsequent antisocial behavior. Many ADDH children respect the rights and property of others, exhibit personal loyalty and sustained friendships, and adhere to an organized value system.

Affective Disorder—Depression, Manic-Depression. Depression or other disorders may occur as a subjective response to these life events, or they may occur in connection with a separate primary diathesis. The incidence of depression among ADDH children has been estimated to be 30 to 50 percent depending on the clinical population and the methods and criteria utilized to determine the diagnoses.

By early adolescence many children with learning and behavioral difficulties have developed low self-esteem and symptoms of depression. By this stage, parents, teachers, and especially peers are often less sympathetic to the persisting difficulties of an older child. The adolescent himself experiences the age-appropriate desires to "fit in" and be a "normal teenager," and may feel deeply discouraged with himself. His inability to channel his efforts into a meaningful sequence of accomplishments often thwarts his achievement and gratification, despite his apparent abilities and high expectations (Das et al. 1978; Huessy et al. 1974). It is difficult to know whether depression in an adolescent with persisting symptoms of ADDH is an outcome of ADDH or whether ADDH is a phenotypic precursor of depression in many children with that genetic predisposition. A recent study of the offspring of adults with affective disorder found that a high percentage of their prepubertal children were hyperactive but not overtly depressed (Weissman et al. 1984). The finding that many ADDH children respond to tricyclics may reflect a common diathesis or the similarity in net effects on catecholamine functioning of stimulant and antidepressants. The task for the clinician is to assess carefully the mood of children presenting with behavioral problems, recognizing that conduct disorder and hyperactivity may be the obvious leading edge of an affective disorder (Puig-Antich 1982). A careful family history for symptoms of hyperactivity, learning difficulties, and affective disturbance may also aid this differentiation. However, clinicians must respect the plasticity of these symptoms in the developing child, and periodically reassess the potentially changing balance of these related disorders.

The relationship between mood and behavior was examined in three diagnostic groups of children—those with depression, those with conduct disorder and an ADDH group—by administration of a standard psychiatric interview and by asking parents, teachers, and clinicians to rate the child's mood and behavior. Considerable symptom overlap occurred across diagnostic groups. About 40 percent of subjects with ADDH had significant symptoms of depression; about 50 percent had symptoms of conduct disorder. Similarly, about a third of the depressed children gave evidence of motoric hyperactivity (Madison 1984). In another study of 178 children referred for psychiatric evaluation of school problems, 44 percent were motorically hyperactive; 75 percent of these also suffered from coexisting depression (as evidenced by sleep disturbance, somatic complaints, diminished social and academic interest, and self-deprecation) (Staton and Brumback 1981). In a study of about one hundred children with conduct disorder (many of whom may have met criteria for ADDH), Puig-

Antich (1982) identified significant depression in over one-third. When this subgroup was treated with tricyclic antidepressants, their antisocial behavior diminished.

Clinically, a primary depression is likely to be characterized by subdued affect including low self-esteem, diminished interest and involvement in activities or social events, hopelessness about the future, and some episodic alterations in energy, activity level, mood, sleep and appetite. The child's unhappy facial expression or irritable disposition may be evident in interview. Inattention is often characterized by worry and self-preoccupation and less by distractability. Early development is less likely to be characterized by severe hyperactivity and inattention. A family history of depression or of major psychological trauma, abuse, or loss is likely. Use of a depression rating scale, such as developed by Posnanski, and the depression items on the Achenbach and the standard psychiatric interviews often assists in this diagnosis. They may respond preferentially to antidepressants and require more intensive individual or family-based psychotherapy.

Atypical Personality Development of Childhood. These children are difficult to characterize because their symptoms often lie somewhat within those of children with ADDH, schizophrenia, and autism (McManus et al. 1984). Their hyperactivity, distractability, impulsivity, and short attention span all meet inclusive criteria for ADDH. However, their schizoid personality, flatness or inappropriate affect, difficulty with prosity and inflection, poor social relatedness, unpredictability of behavior, preoccupation with detail or sameness, and personality rigidity all suggest a broader base of disturbance. These children often become more disorganized or develop stereotypic behaviors on stimulant medications.

Etiology

Genetic Factors. Studies of psychopathology in families of ADDH probands, adoption studies, and twin studies suggest the presence of a genetic contribution to the illness. This is primarily evident in fathers of ADDH boys, who have an increased incidence of alcoholism, sociopathy, and a childhood history of learning and behavioral difficulties (Cantwell 1976; Wender 1981; Satterfield et al. 1974). More than half of thirty-seven hyperactive children had a first- or second-degree relative with serious legal, psychiatric, or employment difficulties (Steward et al. 1980). Nearly 25 percent of the fathers drank excessively; a similar percent had a childhood history of learning difficulties (Mendelson et al. 1971).

In response to a systematic psychiatric interview, Cantwell (1975b) found that nearly half of the parents of the hyperactive children met clinical criteria for the diagnosis of a psychiatric disorder, primarily alcoholism and sociopathy in the fathers, and hysteria in both parents. Sixteen percent of the fathers of hyperactive children gave a history of having themselves been hyperactive as children. Morrison and Stewart (1971) evaluated the parents of fifty-nine hyperactive and forty-one normal children and reported similar findings. Adoption, sibling, and twin studies have added further evidence that there is some vulnerability to this disorder that is genetically transmitted (Stewart et al. 1980; Morrison and Stewart 1973; Cantwell 1975b). A comparison of the incidence of "minimal brain dysfunction" (MBD) in full- and half-siblings of seventeen MBD children found that 53 percent of their full-siblings appeared to demonstrate MBD, while only 9 percent of their half-siblings were symptomatic (Safer 1973). When the parents of ninety-three sets of monozygotic or dizygotic twins rated the activity levels of their offspring, the ensuing comparisons suggested a substantial genetic component to activity levels (Willerman 1973). ADD children are overrepresented in studies of adoptees (Deutsch et al. 1982).

In Tourette Syndrome (TS), a genetically transmitted condition in which motor and attentional disturbances frequently coexist, recent familial studies suggest that in those probands with both ADDH and TS, the motoric and attentional dimensions segregate separately among relatives (Pauls et al. in press; Kidd et al. 1980).

Environmental Factors. The capacity to sustain an effective focus of intellect and emotion is derived at least in part from parents' reinforcing the pursuit of meaningful goals (Sandberg et al. 1978; Rollins and Thomas 1979). It is not surprising that children from chaotic homes may fail to develop this ability. A child's attention may be disrupted by a highly distracting environment or by anxiety, whether about his performance of a difficult academic task or about other issues. Disturbances of attentional mechanisms may result from internal psychological conflicts, which lead to preoccupation and to an inward shift of attention.

For some children, attentional disruption and hyperactivity may occur only in response to a particular type of task or within a given setting (Ellis et al. 1974; Barkley and Jackson 1977). Klein and Gittelman-Klein (1975) found that of 155 subjects who were hyperactive in the classroom, only 25 percent were hyperactive at home. In more severe cases, the cognitive and behavioral disturbance occurs across settings, both at home and at school.

CLINICAL ASSESSMENT OF CHILDREN WITH ATTENTION DEFICIT DISORDER

Since Attention Deficit Disorder with Hyperactivity (ADDH) is a multifaceted disorder, diagnostic process requires evaluation of the child and his environment from many perspectives. The child psychiatrist must obtain information from the parents and teachers as well as from studying the child. Collaboration with other physicians, educators, and psychologists is usually essential to effective diagnosis and treatment (Barkley 1981).

The Interview and Data Base

Rapport must be established with the parents, child, and school personnel in order to obtain an adequate data base for diagnosis and treatment planning. This requires a combination of open-ended and structured discussions, interviews, and behavior ratings.

BEHAVIOR RATING SCALES

Steven's Behavioral Ratings

On the Achenbach scales Steven exhibited symptoms of hyperactivity, conduct disorder, depression, and learning difficulties.

Parents' behavior ratings (on the Conners 48-item scale) were high for restlessness, fights, overactivity, makes noises, easily distracted, and needs frequent reminders.

Teachers' behavior ratings on the Conners 28-item scale obtained for Steven over three weeks (no medication) showed high scores for hyperactive items: restlessness, fidgety, hums, and makes noises, fails to finish tasks, demands excess attention and low frustration tolerance.

Systematic quantification of a child's symptoms requires use of standardized behavioral rating scales. The most well-standardized general behavioral rating assessment in child psychiatry is the Child Behavior Checklist developed by Achenbach (1978a, 1978b). This scale has been standardized for children of both sexes from six to fourteen; subscale norms exist for factors of internalizing (schizoid, depressed, uncommunicative, obsessive-compulsive, and systemic somatic complaints) and externalizing (social withdrawal, hyperactive aggression, and delinquent behavior). Percentile rank for social confidence reflecting activities, social involvement, and school can also be derived. Achenbach and his colleagues have recently developed and standardized a similar behavior checklist to be completed by teachers (1978a). These questionnaires are particularly useful in the identification of associated disturbances in mood, anxiety, conduct, or neurotic symptoms of childhood; they provide an index of social and intellectual competence.

Behavior ratings of hyperactivity and conduct disorder are best obtained using the behavior ratings scale developed by Keith Conners: The Parents Questionnaire, with forty-eight items, has five behavior clusters or factors: conduct problems, learning problems, psychosomatic problems, impulsivity-hyperactive, and anxiety. The Teachers Questionnaire has twenty-eight items with three factors: conduct problems, hyperactivity, and inattention-passivity (Goyette et al. 1978; Conners 1969). Behavioral factors on teachers' ratings of the Conners Scale were recently determined on a large normative population (Trites et al. 1982). A Hyperactivity Index has been developed by Barkley for use with both parent and teacher Conners questionnaires. Although many of the specific diagnostic items on DSM-III are not listed on the Conners scales, their ratings correlate highly with DSM-III diagnoses ($r = 0.95$) (Goyette et al. 1978).

These behavior ratings scales are useful for both diagnostic assessment and the monitoring and coordinating of response to medication and other interventions. A comparison of the results of both scales and ratings from parents and teachers may identify setting-specific symptoms that indicate selective areas of conflict or difficulty. Pervasive ADDH that is present in all the different settings in the child's life may be the most biologically loaded and require the most aggressive treatment.

Prior to beginning medication, the Conners scales should be repeated at least once by both parents and teachers in order to obtain a stable baseline that reflects the child's behavior over at least a two-week period. For teachers' ratings, it is useful to know the size of the class, time of day (morning or afternoon), subject matter and difficulty, and whether or not this is a regular or special educational environment. For children in middle school, ratings from more than one teacher are often necessary to reflect differences in class time, size, and academic content.

A well-standardized and computerized form for obtaining developmental history from parents, the Children's Personal Data Inventory (CPDI) is being developed by Shaywitz (Shaywitz 1982). This scale encompasses demographic information, genetic background, pre- and perinatal events, developmental and social history, educational experiences, recent life stresses, and current areas of difficulty.

PSYCHIATRIC INTERVIEW

Steven's Mental Status

Steven is alert and oriented, but appears hypervigilant, overactive, and fidgety. He touched and commented on many objects in the room, noticed outside noises, and was easily distracted. Sitting restlessly in the chair, frequently fidgeting with his fingers and pencil, he interrupted the examiner several times and changed the subject to ask about objects in the office. His mood seemed happy, almost indifferent.

He expressed sadness and fear about his parents' fights and their recent separation. He wishes they would get back together and wants to live with his father. He acknowledged feeling sad at his lack of friends and being frequently teased, but quickly changed the subject. He says that he likes his teachers but feels they pick on him unfairly and his classmates "get him into trouble and blame him for stuff." He and his younger brother fight frequently.

When evaluated in a psychiatrist's office with the exclusive attention of one adult and with few distractions, some children with ADDH may appear far less active than the description supplied by their teachers and parents. More frequently, they appear restless, fidgety, and squirmy. They may have difficulty staying seated. They frequently scan the office and are easily distracted and intrigued by what they see. They often seem oblivious to their difficulties and are inclined to report that things are going well at home and at school. Their speech may be somewhat rapid and crisp, but reflects no intrinsic difficulty with appropriate word usage or syntax. Their behavior and speech may indicate preoccupation with aggressive themes and a tendency to blame others. They frequently offer only a shallow, reflexive response to questions, with little reflectivity and insight. Some children with ADDH convey feelings of inadequacy, low self-esteem, and regret regarding their difficulties in self-control and mastery. Others externalize and project their problems. While these personality characteristics are greatly affected by the nature of the family milieu, the child's intrinsic impulsivity is a significant force in shaping his character and emotional development.

Several standard psychiatric interviews have been developed recently for children, which provide a method of confirming the diagnosis and screening for other psychiatric problems. Most of these interviews have separate schedules for parents and children. Since children often underestimate their degree of conduct and behavioral disturbance, both versions should be administered. These interviews are generally "scorable" for DSM-III diagnoses. The DICA (Diagnostic Interview for Children and Adolescents) is worded in a more literal fashion and can be used by less experienced clinicians; it consists of structured interviews that systematically survey parents and children for symptoms within the child (Reich et al. 1982). The Kiddie-SADS requires somewhat more clinical judgment. The DISC (Diagnostic Interview Schedule for Children) is being increasingly well standardized.

FAMILY HISTORY

Steven's Family History

Steven is the second of three children whose mother works as a secretary-typist. His siblings are Jennifer, age eleven, doing well in the sixth grade and very allied with mother, and Jeff, age six, anxious and enuretic. Father is a house painter, currently unemployed, with history of intermittent substance abuse and occasional gambling binges.

Steven's parents separated four months ago after an explosive argument following the father's loss of $250 betting while drinking with friends. Mother wants Steven's father to participate in Alcoholics Anonymous, but he denies he has a drinking problem. Father lives in a small apartment four miles away; he sees Steven about three times a week. Steven says he wants to live with his father. Father recalls that he had frequent difficulties in school both in behavior (was often sent to the principal's office and was suspended) and academically (repeated fifth grade, never liked reading). He dropped out of school in eleventh grade and worked as a truck driver for three years, but was laid off for having too many accidents; he has since been working for a small local painter. He has had episodes of drinking, with two arrests for drunken driving and a history of prior drug abuse, primarily amphetamines, which he says calms him down. Mother has had recurrent depressions. During these times she is less involved with Steven; his behavior often becomes more disruptive.

The development of attentional competence reflects the linkage of a child's inner life to his external environment. The normal child's acquisition of such a capacity for sustained attention is enhanced by interaction with calm and predictable parents. An environment in which affection and rules are reliably provided allows safety for a child to direct his attention to his "work" of practicing and exploration. A chaotic family, prone to explosiveness and disaster, creates an endless whirl of distraction requiring the child's continued vigilance or worry. The child may not be able to focus his energies toward the persistent pursuit of a goal—and will not be rewarded for his efforts to sustain achievement. For the ADDH child with genetically impaired modulatory capacity, familial inconsistency will augment his diffusion.

A family history of learning disability, childhood hyperactivity of the parent, or persisting symptoms of residual ADD may be obtained. These residual difficulties are characterized by persisting impulsivity; stimulus seeking and risk taking; impatience; irritability; explosiveness; disorderliness; inability to initiate, follow or execute a plan; impaired interpersonal relationships; and diminished job performance. ADDH appears to be associated with a family history of alcohol and substance abuse.

Formal assessment of family functioning can be augmented by use of a self-rating scale such as the Moos Family Environment Scale or by direct measure of parents' feelings toward a child as rated by the Expressed Emotion Scale following a five-minute uninterrupted response to the question: "Tell me about your child and your relationship with him" (Goldstein 1981).

Steven's Birth and Development

During this pregnancy mother drank to the point of intoxication about once a week. Steven was born one month prematurely and experienced some fetal distress. His birth weight was 2.5 kg (5 lbs. 9 oz.).

Maternal consumption of excessive alcohol or barbituates should be noted along with the use of other medications during pregnancy. Complications of pregnancy associated with bleeding, fetal anoxia or distress, or premature delivery should be documented. Maternal consumption of excessive alcohol may be associated with mild fetal alcohollike syndrome predominantly characterized by nonaggressive attentional disturbance (Shaywitz et al. 1980).

Psychological trauma consisting of severe emotional neglect or abuse can be a source of behavioral and attentional disturbance. Children who are continuously disrupted from tasks, or whose achievements are not appropriately praised and appreciated, may fail to develop effective task orientation. A history of psychological trauma related to severe emotional neglect or physical abuse may be obtained from a parent, relative, school, or a child protection agency.

Cognitive and behavior disturbance may follow toxic, metabolic, or traumatic damage to the brain. A childhood illness associated with high fever, encephalitis or meningitis, and seizure disorder may increase risk. Lead consumption through eating of old paint can impair cognitive development.

Transient variations in the level of the child's arousal, alertness, and motivation (his experience of the rewards and incentives for focusing on a task) may all alter attentional functioning. Seizure disorders are frequently associated with ADDH.

Physical and Neurological Exam

Steven's Medical History and Physical Examination

Past medical history includes allergies to dust, pollen, and ragweed. Mother reports that he "behaves worse" after eating candy or foods high in sugar and preservatives content.

Physical examination performed by the psychiatrist reveals Steven is of normal height and weight for his age. Some minor physical anomalies are noted: slight asymmetry of the ears, and soft cartilage, hypertelorism, moderately elevated, steepled palate, malalignment of maxillary teeth, short fifth finger, increased space between the first and second toes. Gross motor coordination is moderately "floppy." Fine motor skills are poorly developed. He is slow and awkward at rapid finger-thumb alteration and has mild left to right overflow. Laterality remains poorly defined.

A general physical exam should be performed by the psychiatrist on every child with ADDH. Measures of overall maturation, height and weight, and physical appearance are important. Visual and auditory acuity should be clinically assessed and, if questionable, followed up by laboratory measures.

The incidence of minor physical anomalies is increased in ADDH and may include: abnormal size and symmetry of head; wiry, "electric" hair; and wide-set eyes (hypertelorism) with increased epicanthal folds. Examination of the mouth may demonstrate malalignment of the teeth, a high-arched or steepled palate. The hands may have a short fifth finger; feet may exhibit irregular spacing of toes and webbing in the interdigital spaces.

The increased incidence of minor physical anomalies among attentionally impaired, hyperactive children may be evidence of a genetic disturbance or an in utero disruption of physical as well as cognitive-integrative integrity. Minor physical anomalies (stigmata) appear strongly predictive of short attention span, heightened activity level, and aggressive-impulsive behavior in the preschool years (Bell and Waldrop 1982; Waldrop and Halverson 1971; Adams et al. 1974). Rapoport et al. (1974) reported that high stigmata scores were associated with teachers' ratings of "hyperactivity" and conduct problems, and with family history of childhood behavior disorders. In addition, plasma dopamine beta hydroxylase (DBH) showed a significant positive relationship with stigmata scores. These findings suggest the possibility of a genetic disorder that may be mimicked (phenocopied) by a traumatic event in early pregnancy.

A neurological exam will assess gross and fine motor functioning and neuro-maturational development. A higher than normal overall activity level, which occurs across all settings (in free play, interview, and classroom), often is noted. Gross motor skills are assessed by comparing a child's competence to those of age-matched controls in ability to stand on one foot, to hop, skip, and stop and pivot. The ability to throw and catch a ball should be tested. Gait assessment should include tandem (heel-toe) gait and walking forwards and backwards on heels and toes. The quality of movement is assessed by noting flopping, uninhibited, poorly integrated motion. Disinhibition and overflow in latency aged children are usually suggestive of delayed maturation. A physical and neurological exam for soft signs (PANESS) appears to be a reliable indicator of neurological function and correlates well with behavioral and cognitive measures (Holden et al. 1982).

Fine motor skills may be assessed through rapid finger tap and sequential apposition of fingers and thumb, in which the rate and smoothness of performance are observed and overflow from right to left is monitored. Performance of a standard handwriting and drawing (Draw-A-Person, Bender-Gestalt) sample provides another index of fine motor control and carefulness of work. Within a neuromaturational test battery a task such as peg hole placement can be timed and compared to age-matched norms (Gardner 1979).

ADD children frequently have a delay in the development of their fine and gross motor coordination, which causes them to appear slow and awkward, loose or clumsy. Probably because of their high activity level, boys are much more likely than girls to manifest the behavioral and motoric components of this disorder (Shaffer 1978; Shaywitz 1982). Some attentionally impaired children are fidgety and impulsive; others are slow but competent in information intake and visual-motor performance, and appear grossly hypoactive. LD children may exhibit the impairment of coordination, but are less likely to be hyperactive and fidgety. Increased levels of gross motor activity, regardless of time of day or setting, were recorded in ADDH children by means of a solid-state activity-monitoring device (Porrino et al. 1983b). Treatment with d-amphetamine diminished their activity levels in the classroom (Porrino et al. 1983a).

Blood should be drawn for CBC (anemia), thyroid indices, liver function tests (if medication is prescribed), ceruloplasm and serum lead. Twenty-four-hour urinary catecholamine and copper measures may be useful.

EEGs with photic stimulation may be useful in children with ADDH. Petit mal, partial focal seizures and temporal or frontal lobe excitability may underlie symptoms of ADDH in some children.

Several investigators have reported that hyperactive children have a higher incidence of nonspecific EEG abnormalities, which are not influenced by stimulant medications (Satterfield et al. 1973a, 1974). Computer-assisted spectrum analysis of the EEG has suggested some stimulant drug effects (Itil and Simeon 1974). On a complex visual search task, the EEG spectrum 16 to 20 Hz appeared distinctive in children with hyperactivity or learning disability (Dykman et al. 1982). Methylphenidate (MPH) appears to normalize the vigilance and evoked potential of ADDH children (Michael et al. 1981). The effect of varying doses of MPH on autonomic or behavioral responses in ADD appears linear (Solanto and Conners 1982).

PSYCHOPHYSIOLOGY

Psychophysiological studies in ADD have been pursued for at least two decades; they have focused variously on both peripheral and central measures. *Peripheral measures* of autonomic nervous system activity included skin conduction, blood pressure, pulse, and pupillary dilation. Collectively these measures suggest a decrease in the orienting response and relatively lower physiological reaction to laboratory-induced stress or anxiety (Zahn et al. 1975). Central nervous system measures include power spectrum analysis and evoked response to auditory or visual stimuli. The evoked potential is the summation of EEG activity after repeated presentation of a controlled sequence of stimuli. Following the presentation of the stimulus, a mathematical summation of the electrocortical response is performed at brief intervals after the stimulus, and is monitored for about five hundred milliseconds. This technique produces a wave formation, the evoked response; a sizable set of identical stimuli produces a corresponding set of responses. These, then, can be averaged so that a single image emerges. Depending on the paradigm, the resultant wave form can be analyzed for the difference in clinical variables (age, sex, diagnosis), stimulus variables (intensity, frequency, duration, interstimulus interval), and task variables (attention to or away from the stimulus, presence of distractions).

Several earlier studies have suggested that children with ADDH had increased variability of response. In the face of increasingly intense stimuli, these children often demonstrate an enhanced or augmented response, similar to that of manic depressive individuals (Buchsbaum et al. 1976). Visual evoked potential (ERP) measures suggest that MPH acts primarily on response-related processes rather than stimulus evaluation. MPH effects were age-dependent and affected the amplitude, but not the latency, of ERP (Halliday et al. 1983). An increase in evoked potential latency seems related to a general effort at processing (Callaway and Halliday 1982; Dykman et al. 1983).

Differences in peripheral autonomic nervous system responses also may suggest a physiological basis for this disorder in some ADDH children. Investigators have reported lower levels of spontaneous skin conductance in ADD, along with increased variability and delay in reaction time, and decreased responsivity to an orienting stimulus (Porges et al. 1981).

Computerized axial tomography has not demonstrated structural abnormalities in the brains of ADD children (Caparulo et al. 1981). Studies using Magnetic Resonance Imaging (MRI) and Positron Emission Tomography (PET scan) have tremendous potential to further define brain structure, metabolism, and differentially localize neurotransmitter function.

Assessment of Learning Difficulties

Steven's Psychological Testing
Intelligence testing showed Verbal IQ of 112 and Performance IQ of 92 with a Full Scale score of 104 on the Wechsler Intelligence Scale for Children.

There was considerable scatter among subtests with low test scores in digit span, digit symbol, and coding. Highest scores were obtained on comprehension and similarities. The ITPA results suggested a specific reading disability with difficulty in visual memory and sequencing. Results of the TAT and DPA and kinetic family drawings suggested themes of helplessness, depression, and anger. Performance on the Bender-Gestalt test was 2 years below age level. The DAP finding was 1.5 years delayed. There was no suggestion of psychotic thought disorganization in spite of his low frustration level.

Clinicians can make an approximate assessment of cognitive competence and check for the presence of learning difficulties through the administration of screening tests. Visual-motor tasks might include the Draw-A-Person Test, Kinetic Family Drawing, and the Bender-Gestalt. Simple age-standardized tasks are available for sampling vocabulary, spelling, reading ability, and comprehension. Problem-solving ability can be estimated. Tasks and questions such as those derived from Piaget's studies may provide an index of reasoning and logic.

The assessment of a learning disability requires indices of overall intelligence (e.g., the WISC-R or Stanford-Binet), actual academic achievement (e.g., the WRAT, Woodcock-Johnson Psycho-Educational Battery, or Peabody Individual Achievement Test), social competence (e.g., the Vineland Social Maturity Scales), and specific areas of learning. In addition to the clinical assessment, perceptual and motor skills can be quantified through the use of tests such as the Porteus Maze, the Bender-Gestalt, or the Beery Test of Visual Motor Integration (VMI).

Tests such as the Illinois Test of Psycholinguistic Ability (ITPA) or the McCarthy aid the school psychologist in assessing the mechanisms that underlie a given learning disorder. The Detroit Tests of Learning Aptitude measure nineteen different areas of learning aptitude and cover a broad range of abilities; when scored they provide both specific subtest data and an index of general mental age. The Boehm Test of Basic Concepts yields percentile scores for a child's development of verbal concepts. The limitations of psychological tests in differential diagnosis have been discussed by Gittelman (1980).

The above are examples of standardized tests used to define overall cognitive and social competence. Other measures have been developed that sample specific steps in information processing. These tests measure reaction time, selective attention, vigilance, acquisition learning, and short- and long-term memory; they address strategies of perception, encoding, and information retrieval (Hunt and Cohen 1983; Hunt, in submission). There are suggestions they may be of value in objectively assessing these children and the effects of medication.

Steven's Diagnosis
On the basis of the comprehensive evaluation, the following diagnoses and treatment plans were devised.

Axis I.   Attention deficit disorder with hyperactivity.
           Adjustment reaction with depressed mood following parents'
           separation.
Axis II.   Specific learning disability in reading (dyslexia) with perceptual
           reversals.
Axis III. Medical: multiple allergies.
Axis IV.   Stressors: parental marital discord and separation four months prior
           to examination.
Axis V.   Highest level of function in previous year: 5.

Biochemical Factors in ADD

Given the clinical heterogeneity of ADD and the difficulty of quantifying cognition and motoric function, it is not surprising that attempts to define a common neurochemistry remain rudimentary. The neurochemical effects of stimulants suggest a possible catecholaminergic substrate for ADDH. Dopaminergic and noradrenergic mechanisms may underlie discrete components of this disorder. The possible role of other neurotransmitters has not been well studied (Young and Cohen 1979).

Normal levels of the NE-synthesizing hormone dopamine beta hydroxylase (DBH) have been found in children with ADDH (Rapoport et al. 1974; Shaywitz et al. 1982), though a possibly related group of patients with undersocialized conduct disorder had low DBH levels (Rogeness et al. 1982).

The catabolic enzyme monoamine oxidase (MAO) has been found to be normal in the platelets of ADDH children (Shaywitz et al. 1982) in spite of being a nonspecific marker of vulnerability of other major psychiatric illnesses (Murphy and Donnelly 1974). A subgroup of ADDH children may have reduced levels of platelet MAO, which return to normal after treatment with amphetamine (Shekim et al. 1982a, 1982b; Shaywitz et al. 1982).

Shetty and Chase (1976) found no difference in CSF levels of the metabolites HVA and 5-HIAA in twenty-four hyperactive children compared to six control subjects. Shaywitz et al. (1977) found no differences in CSF levels of HVA and 5-HIAA in six children diagnosed as MBD compared with sixteen controls who had other neurological difficulties. After probenecid loading, however, the ratio of HVA/probenecid was found to be lower in the MBD children.

No differences were found in the twenty-four-hour excretion of 5-HIAA, HVA, or MHPG, metanephrine, and normethanephrine between MBD and control groups (Wender 1971).

Levels of the noradrenergic (NE) metabolite MHPG, 70 percent of which may be of central origin, suggest possible inhibition of NE production. Shekim et al. (1983) reported bimodal twenty-four-hour urinary MHPG levels in untreated subjects with ADDH. Compared to controls, most ADDH children demonstrated diminished MHPG excretion; a smaller percent excreted increased MHPG. Other studies also reported decreased urinary MHPG excretion in amphetamine-responsive ADDH children

(Brown et al. 1981; Khan and Dekirmenjian 1981; Shen and Wang 1984). Those ADDH children who had a favorable clinical response to d-amphetamine developed a further reduction in urinary MHPG excretion (Shekim et al. 1982b).

In a study involving twenty-five hyperactive children, Coleman (1971) reported a decreased concentration of serotonin in the whole blood of most of the subjects. On the other hand, Rapoport et al. (1974) found the blood serotonin levels in hyperactive children to be normal. While treatment with either methylphenidate or imipramine improved behavior, only imipramine lowered blood serotonin levels. Increased whole blood serotonin (hyperserotonemia) was associated with both lower levels of plasma total protein-bound tryptophan and with a higher percentage of free tryptophan (Irwin et al. 1981). In another study, however, the plasma free and total tryptophan was found to be normal (Ferguson et al. 1981). Methodological differences in platelet preparation and assay may account for many of these discrepancies.

Challenge Studies in ADDH. By stimulating or inhibiting a selected neurochemical system at a specific point and monitoring the sequential chemical response, investigators can obtain an index of receptor responsivity. The alpha-adrenergic agonist clonidine diminishes NE and MHPG release, and prompts the release of human growth hormone (hGH) (Cedarbaum and Aghajanian 1976; Amaral and Sinnamon 1977); the alpha-2 antagonist yohimbine prompts NE release. A single acute dose of methylphenidate produces increased hGH concentrations and usually decreases prolactin (PRL) and catecholamine levels (Shaywitz et al. 1982).

Clonidine was administered as a single-dose challenge agent to ADDH boys before, during, and after treatment with methylphenidate in order to assess the effects of treatment (Hunt et al. 1984). The peak hGH level before treatment was greater than that observed following similar clonidine provocation in children with Tourette's Syndrome or with short stature. After continuing treatment with methylphenidate, the release of hGH was reduced significantly. One day following the discontinuation of MPH treatment, the hGH peak began to return toward pretreatment levels.

These results may indicate that there is a heightened noradrenergic receptor sensitivity in untreated ADDH children, and that this sensitivity decreases during treatment with MPH. Other studies also suggest that continued treatment with stimulant medication may diminish the activity and sensitivity of the noradrenergic system. A favorable response to d-amphetamine treatment was associated with a further reduction in the twenty-four-hour urinary excretion of MHPG (Shekim et al. 1983; Brown et al. 1981). Continuing treatment of ADDH with methylphenidate appears to reduce plasma DBH levels (Hunt, in submission). MPH treatment reduces plasma NE release after exercise (Nagel-Heimke et al. 1984). A low dose of clonidine that is administered continuously for eight weeks appears to be therapeutically useful in many ADDH children (Hunt et al. 1985a). Thus, the response to long-term stimulant medication may be partially mediated by a down-regulation of NE system at several sites, including the presynaptic receptor and precursor enzymes, which may reduce net NE production and release (Hunt et al. 1984). Parallel studies using yohimbine as a functionally opposite NE stimulant are in process.

The noradrenergic system has an important role in modulating neurobehavioral processes that may affect a child's affective state and his level of activity and arousal. Recent animal studies have shown that the NE Locus Ceruleus neurons are activated during transitions in behavioral states and may regulate the level of cortical and behavioral arousal (Aston-Jones and Bloom 1981; Foote et al. 1980; Foote and Bloom 1979; Bloom 1978). The pattern of behavioral and cognitive disturbance experienced by children with ADDH involves similar aspects of arousal, excitability, and distractability, which appear to be partially mediated by the noradrenergic system.

TREATMENT OF ADDH: MULTIMODAL TREATMENT

Several studies demonstrate an additive effect of combined interventions: medication, special education, and psychotherapy. Coupled with psychotherapy and special education, stimulants may improve academic adjustment and performance (Satterfield et al. 1979). However, unless accompanied by appropriate psychotherapy, family counseling, or focused educational intervention, medications alone usually do not lead to improved academic learning, higher grades, or increase in achievement scores (Quinn and Rapoport 1975; Gittelman-Klein and Klein 1976). In kindergarten aged hyperactive children there was no difference between behavior modification and methylphenidate treatment (Cohen et al. 1981). However, in older children with ADDH, methylphenidate was more effective than behavioral self-control (Anderson et al. 1981). Studies of the effectiveness of combined medication and behavioral modification suggest an additive effect of both interventions. Medication often has the most powerful short-term effect; used alone, however, it does not enhance long-term development (Gittelman-Klein and Klein 1976).

Education

Steven's Educational Treatment
Steven was placed part time in a special education program for academic subjects related to reading. He was allowed use of the school's resource room. This enabled Steven to receive individual tutoring in reading for one hour a day.

For those ADDH children with learning disabilities special education frequently is the primary treatment and it should begin early. Many ADDH children benefit from being in quieter, smaller classrooms with fewer distractions. A child should not repeat a grade unnecessarily; nor should a youngster be promoted for purely social reasons. Instead, children should receive tutoring and/or classroom education in special education programs. The major tools of special education consist of re-peated presentation of material after one-on-one teaching with few distractions and frequent reinforcement. Multisensory (visual, auditory, kinesthetic) presentation of material intensifies the learning process. Early remediation may allow a child to move back into the mainstream of education. Ignoring a problem in school in the name of mainstreaming may assure eventual failure. Specific programs for enhanc-ing motoric skills may be helpful.

Role of Family Psychotherapy in ADDH

Steven's Family Sessions

Steven's parents participated in counseling by the child psychiatrist to see if they could reconcile their differences and resume living together or proceed toward an equitable divorce. The mother was evaluated separately and began taking Elavil for depression. Counseling also focused on obtain-ing parental agreement for discipline and implementation of a behavioral program. Specific circumstances were defined for which Steven would be given added privileges and allowance; other behaviors were defined for which he would be grounded for the afternoon or for one to two days. The psy-chiatrist also suggested some activities that Steven and his mother would do together for about fifteen minutes a day and assisted Steven and his father to enrich the quality of their time together. The psychiatrist supported Ste-ven and his father in discussion of Steven's resentment of his parents' sep-aration, but Steven usually became more restless and changed the subject.

The family may need psychotherapy or counseling to help determine their be-havioral expectations for their child. Parents need to provide consequences to their ADD child's behavior rapidly, appropriately, and consistently; at the same time they must strive to avoid scapegoating, inappropriate punishment, or any tendency to indulge their impulsive child. They often need assistance in managing their guilt and embarrassment at having such a difficult child. It is easy for parents to become outraged at the child's "irresponsibility," "forgetfulness," "indifference," and his imperviousness to parental authority and sanctions. Parents complain of feeling helpless, misunderstood, and isolated. They easily become furious and blame each other for being "too strict" or "too permissive"; such experiences tend to exaggerate preexisting parental conflicts. On the other hand, they also intensify a parent's in-tolerance of personality characteristics that he sees—and resents—within himself. Both processes may require therapeutic intervention.

Role of Individual Psychotherapy in ADDH

Steven's Individual Sessions

After two months of weekly individual psychiatric sessions, Steven talked more clearly about his low self-esteem, which persisted even after his be-

havior began to improve with medication. The psychiatrist used hand puppets and mutual story-telling activities to allow Steven to portray his feelings
about his parents separating and his sense of being abandoned and angry.

Steven began to connect these feelings with his aloof and distant behavior toward his father during his visits. After talking with his therapist about
his feelings of disappointment in his relationship with his father, Steven was
able to talk more openly and directly with his father. The psychiatrist met
with the father to help him talk with his son about these feelings. Their
relationship improved after these confrontations. The therapist met with the
mother and subsequently with Steven and his mother to improve her consistency in limit setting. As Steven's feelings of blame toward his mother for
the divorce abated, he acted less defiantly at home. His attention span, grades,
and behavior began to improve at school. He felt calmer and had more self-
confidence. His prognosis has improved given his response to these multiple interventions.

Psychotherapy may change the child's self-concept from that of an inadequate
underachiever who has attempted to compensate for his deficits with clowning or
misbehavior to a sense of himself as a more competent and more consistent individual. Psychotherapy is often most effective after the ADDH child is treated with medication that increases his attention span and potential functioning. For ADDH children, psychotherapy has both educational and interpretive components. Children
can usually understand that they have a disorder that increases their distractability
and impulsivity. They must recognize these symptoms, develop internal controls,
and anticipate situations that will be stressful. Parents and children often can learn
to use medication selectively to assist them in managing circumstances that create
excessive arousal or that demand increased control.

Psychotherapy can address specific issues within the intrapsychic life of a child
with ADDH. Themes of self-esteem, self-control, the management of anxiety, and
the need to pursue and enjoy achievement become the focus of psychotherapy. These
children often experience low self-esteem due to impaired academic and social performance. Some youngsters blame themselves for their difficulties and internalize a
sense of being defective or "bad." The therapist can assist the child in understanding that his tendency to be impulsive and restless is not his fault. At the same time,
the child can exert some measure of conscious, learned control over these impulses.
The therapist must walk a fine line between freeing such a child from internalized
blame and assisting the child to maximize his self-control (Freeman and Cornwall
1980; Gardner 1979). Even after the child's ability to learn has improved, he still
must face the narcissistic injury that he is behind in academic skills and social maturity. Such children must learn to direct their increased capacity for attention and
work toward achievements that begin to close the gap. Simply being able to learn is
not identical to knowing.

These burdened children may feel envious and destructive toward others (including the therapist) who seem able without effort to act appropriately and effec-

tively. ADDH children may easily perceive the suggestions of teachers or the rules of parents as excessively critical, controlling, and rejecting. A strong therapeutic alliance may be needed to enable a child to perceive the teachers' instructions or the requirements of home (such as a behavioral shaping program) as useful rather than as threatening to his own interests. The ADDH child must also learn subtle social skills that replace his prior intrusiveness, impulsivity, and awkwardness. Psychotherapy can assist the child to counter his own tendency towards oppositional behavior.

Acting-out behavior often becomes an internalized, ego-syntonic release of anxiety for the ADDH child. His predilection toward action may thwart the development of his own potential for reflection. As the therapist encourages the child to contain his behavior and reflect upon himself, depression may surface, which had previously been defended against through bravado and stimulus-seeking behavior. The therapist's support for the child's tolerance of this depression and dysphoria without acting out can lead to an internalization of self-control, affective stability, and introspection. This depression is a developmental growth stage, not a sign of psychopathology. Psychotherapy in the context of medication and special education may help the ADDH child improve his academic skills, modulate his impulses, and develop more consistent and intimate interpersonal relationships.

Other Therapeutic Techniques in ADDH

Techniques of behavior modification or shaping have been developed for use at home and in the classroom. The underlying principles emphasize establishing clearly defined, limited goals focusing on specific behaviors addressed in terms of praise, punishment, or selective ignoring. Parents, teachers, and therapists must identify rewards that will motivate a specific child and develop a schedule of reinforcement to sustain performance on selected tasks. Behaviors to be encouraged should be specifically defined in positive terms. Prior to beginning the intervention, baseline charting of the frequency and the severity of these behaviors should be undertaken. Behavior-shaping techniques, if applied consistently, are often very useful in children with ADDH. However, difficulty of generalization from one setting to another and in sustaining the progress after the reinforcements are discontinued may limit their effectiveness (Murray 1980).

A related psychotherapeutic method relies predominantly on teaching self-monitoring and self-control and how to alter internal self-messages. This treatment is an outgrowth of the techniques of cognitive therapy. The essential intervention consists of teaching a child how to identify disruptive behaviors such as fidgetiness, talking out of turn, getting out of his seat, and using defiant or provocative speech or teasing—behaviors that are obvious to outside observers, but to which these children are often oblivious. The child is encouraged to label these actions, to identify their antecedents, and to tell himself to inhibit them before they are acted out. The child who is learning not to talk in class until called upon may be taught to notice when he feels like talking without raising his hand, and then to tell himself "I have to wait until I'm called upon," "Don't talk till teacher gives an OK." A child may learn also to substitute less disruptive behaviors: "I want to tap my pencil, but I'll chew gum instead" (Cameron and Robinson 1980).

MEDICATION FOR ADDH

Steven's Medication

Methylphenidate, 5 mg/day given before school. This was gradually increased (while monitoring of behavior ratings) to 10 mg in the morning and 5 mg at noon on schools days only. Side-effects of anorexia and insomnia prompted successful trial with clonidine, increased over two weeks to 0.05 mg q.i.d. Initial sleepiness abated after one week. Is much calmer, alert, active.

Behavior ratings were obtained from Steven's teachers and parents on a weekly basis until the dosage was stable, and then monthly.

Stimulants such as methylphenidate, amphetamine, and magnesium pemoline are useful in reducing the motor hyperactivity that frequently accompanies ADD; the medications narrow the spectrum of attention and reduce impulsivity, thus diminishing distractability in class and improving persistence in vigilance and memory or associated learning tasks. Stimulants frequently improve behavior and ease social interaction both at home and at school. Once placed on medication, many ADD children will experience an increased sense of control and mastery. The major contraindications to stimulant medication include a prior diagnosis of underlying psychosis, the presence of multiple tics, and/or a history of major side-effects with the administration of stimulants in the past (Lowe et al. 1982).

Prior to the initiation of medication, parents and teachers should be asked to complete a behavior-rating scale such as the Conners Teachers 28-Item Scale; such scales are useful in monitoring the effects of medication. These should be repeated on a weekly basis during initial treatment and monthly thereafter. Teachers should note class size, subject, and time of day. A systematic parent diary may add to the clinical assessment.

Initial choice of medication is frequently methylphenidate (MPH) at doses of approximately 0.1 to 0.2 mg/kg given before school. Medication dosage can gradually be increased toward a maximum of about 0.5 to 0.75 mg/kg, which may be given in divided doses, about 8:00 A.M. and noon. Eating meals before medication does not impair absorption of MPH. Weekly monitoring and rating of behavior by teacher and parents will assist in determining the optimal dose.

It is not yet certain whether the dosage required to produce optimal improvement in attention may be less than that needed to achieve maximal behavioral control. In a child whose primary difficulties lie in the area of attentional learning, a low dose (10 to 20 mg daily) may yield the best cognitive improvement, although some restlessness may remain.

Children can often learn to participate in the regulation of their own medication by anticipating the demands of the next four hours and altering the dosage appropriately. While medication may be needed to sustain attention and a quiet demeanor in the classroom, it may not be needed during free play or recreational activities. Medication is usually needed less consistently during the summer, allowing partial medication holidays. Except in severe cases, summer holidays are advisable and allow reassessment for continued treatment. Many ADD children can begin the academic year without medication, or the dosage can be tapered after initial adjustment to a new classroom provided behavior is monitored. The empirical trial provides an opportunity for assessing whether there is a continued need for stimulants. Some ADD children can be withdrawn from medication before puberty; some require continuous treatment on into adolescence.

Response to Stimulants

Approximately 200,000 to 400,000 children in the United States receive stimulant medication for attentional and behavioral control. For a large percent of these children, the medications produce dramatic behavioral improvement and improved self-control. However, medication alone does not improve academic grades or classroom learning, especially in children with isolated learning disabilities who are not hyperactive. Even in children with ADDH, the behavioral and educational improvements do not always coincide. Stimulants reduce motor behavior and improve reaction time, sustained vigilance, and recall of simple stimuli; however, they do not necessarily enhance many of the other processes of learning, such as identification of relevant concepts or reorganization and encoding for appropriate conceptual retrieval (Sykes et al. 1972). Improvement in cognitive laboratory measures does not always correlate with improved classroom learning. A linear dose-response relationship was found for the performance of a continuous performance task (Winsberg et al. 1982; Charles et al. 1981). In ADDH children treated for twelve weeks of flexible dose treatment with methylphenidate or thioridazine, few correlations were noted between academic progress in the classroom, scores on standard academic achievement tests, and changes in behavioral ratings or psychological test scores (Gittelman-Klein and Klein 1976). Short-term behavioral improvement on medication does not highly predict long-term outcome, although adults who were successfully treated with MPH as children recall a happier childhood than their untreated ADDH counterparts (Hechtman et al. 1984).

Stimulant medications have social effects: They decrease the number of the child's negative behaviors and reduce the teachers' need for control and use of reprimands (Whalen et al. 1981a). In a four-year follow-up, Charles and Schain (1981) reported that although stimulants successfully reduced ADDH children's hyperactivity and social difficulties, they did not substantially improve academic achievement.

Stimulant medications have multiple side-effects and some specific contraindications. Transient side-effects include anorexia, insomnia, stomach aches, afternoon withdrawal, and explosiveness (Cantwell 1975a). Long-term side-effects of stimulants may include growth suppression (Millichap 1978; Greenhill et al. 1980), although this may be transient and may depend on the dose, duration, and consistency of medication. While stimulants have been reported to induce tics (Lowe et al. 1982; Golden 1974), untreated ADDH children appear to be at increased endogenous risk for tics (Denckla and Rudel 1978). Hallucinosis and possible psychosis may follow stimulant treatment in vulnerable children (Young 1981). Children with atypical development, childhood psychosis, and multiple tic syndrome may have an exacerbation of their symptomatology while on stimulants. (Satterfield et al. 1980). Children's personalities may become more "rigid," irritable, and tense on stimulants, which may partially explain the poor compliance frequently observed with methylphenidate treatment (Firestone 1982; Kauffman et al. 1981; Sleator et al. 1982).

The dosage of stimulant medications is usually determined in relation to behavioral response, and blood level determinations are not obtained routinely; however, such measurements may have therapeutic utility in identifying children who absorb methylphenidate poorly or who excrete it rapidly and thereby fail to achieve adequate levels.

Shaywitz et al. (1982) reported that following a single oral dose of methylphenidate, the peak level was reached at 2.5 hours ($\pm$ 20 minutes). Although stable within individuals, the peak blood levels demonstrated a nearly three-fold range across subjects receiving similar methylphenidate doses. A prior breakfast does not affect absorption of MPH (Chan et al. 1983). During chronic treatment, the two-hour MPH blood levels of MPH were comparable to the levels correlated with classroom behavioral improvement as rated by teachers (Conner's APTBRS; $r = 0.5$). A minimum level of 7 ng/ml may be needed for behavioral response; however, some forms of learning may be impaired at higher doses (Sprague and Sleator 1977). The excretion half-life ($t^{1/2}$) of methylphenidate was $2.5 \pm .5$ hours. Substantial blood levels of methylphenidate persisted for up to eight hours, although the clinical effect had diminished. This lack of a simple correlation between blood level and clinical effect probably reflects methylphenidate's capacity to effect the release of stored catecholamines. These results are compatible with other pharmacological studies of methylphenidate (Hungund et al. 1979; Kupietz et al. 1982; Gualtieri et al. 1982) and are conceptually similar to the pharmacokinetic profile of d-amphetamine, which has a longer half-life (about seven hours), but a similar time of peak and duration of action (Cheng et al. 1973; Ebert et al. 1976; Brown et al. 1979). Blood levels may provide information about some children who are poor responders, and may reflect variability in absorption, binding, or excretion. Two-hour blood levels may be clinically useful in children who do not respond, who have excessive side-effects, or who suddenly require a major change in dose.

Other Medications for ADDH

Imipramine (IMI) has been administered to children for "hyperactivity," enuresis, school phobia, depression, and petit mal seizures. In the treatment of children who have symptoms of ADDH it has generally been found to be more effective than placebo but somewhat less effective than methylphenidate. Its clinical utility may be time-limited and may diminish after eight to twelve weeks. Imipramine has been found to enhance performance on cognitive tests including the Continuous Performance Test (CPT) by increasing response latency and diminishing errors. It improves performance on other measures of visual searching (MFFT), short-term memory, and perceptual-motor tasks (Gualtieri 1977).

The major side-effects of IMI consist of sedation, constipation, anorexia, and increased pulse and blood pressure; the most dangerous aspect of its use is its effect on the heart. At high doses, EKG changes occur consisting of increased PR interval; IMI toxicity may be associated with prolonged QRS interval, arrhythmias, and decreased cardiac contractility. EKG monitoring should continue on a regular basis during IMI treatment.

Some studies have shown that IMI was more useful than no treatment or placebo (Huessy and Wright 1970; Huessy 1983; Waizer et al. 1974). Response to IMI was reported better than to stimulants by Winsberg et al. (1972), whereas MPH was found better than IMI by Greenberg et al. (1974) and Quinn et al. (1974). Equivalent responses were reported by other investigators (Gross 1973; Gittelman-Klein and Klein 1976; Werry et al. 1980), but some children demonstrate preferential response to each medication.

Recent studies of the noradrenergic agonist clonidine in children with ADDH suggested its therapeutic usefulness may parallel results in subjects with Tourette's Disorder. In a twelve-week double-blind placebo-crossover study, parents' ratings on the Conners Scale showed that eight of the ten children clearly benefited from clonidine (Hunt et al. 1985). The children were neither sedated nor psychomotorically retarded; initial sleepiness diminished after two weeks of treatment. Clinically, clonidine improves frustration tolerance but is less effective than Ritalin in reducing distractability. While clonidine may be a useful alternative therapeutic agent for some children with ADDH, its relative effectiveness compared to MPH on behavioral and cognitive measures requires further study.

Other medications that have been tried in ADDH include LDOPA, Lithium, Tegretol, amitriptyline, thioridazine, haloperidol, chlorpromazine, and MAO inhibitors. Since many of these medications reduce activity, but diminish energy and blunt cognition, there is need to differentiate the behavioral and cognitive effects of these medications in order to clarify their specific indications.

Dietary Treatment of ADDH

In 1975 Feingold suggested that many ADDH children had a nonimmunological supersensitivity to food additives, coloring, and sugar. Since that time, diets restrictive of these substances have been popular. Although parental testimony has frequently supported this claim of clinical benefit from avoidance diets, controlled studies have not supported their effectiveness. The NIH consensus found the diets to be safe but not usually helpful (NIH 1983). These diets require considerable organization on the part of the family, and a significant measure of self-control and cooperation from the child. Following large doses of added food coloring versus placebo, diminished attention span and increased errors in learning were evident on the paired associate learning task (Swanson and Kinsbourne 1976). In total, controlled studies of dietary interventions suggest minimal sustained therapeutic utility (Conners et al. 1976; Williams et al. 1978; Weiss 1982; Conners 1980; Harley et al. 1978; Harner and Foiles 1980; Holborow 1981). Whether the offending dietary ingredient is a form of sugar, a food dye, or additive has been widely debated, as well as whether these ADDH children have a specific allergic or toxic response (Garfinkel et al. 1981; Wender 1980; Ferguson et al. 1981; O'Shea and Porter 1981).

SUMMARY

Attention Deficit Disorder with Hyperactivity is a serious, frequent, and long-lasting disorder. Its effects on children may persist into adulthood and create vulnerability for substance abuse, antisocial behavior, and impaired job and interpersonal performance. In childhood, ADDH is frequently associated with learning difficulties, delayed motoric development and control, disturbed interpersonal relationships at home and school, and depression and low self-esteem. Assessment requires behavioral quantification using parent and teacher rating scales, medical and neuromaturational examination, and psychiatric interview. Treatment is a collaborative endeavor requiring the coordinated skills of teachers, parents, therapist, and physician. Special education, behavioral shaping, psychotherapy, and medication all have a role in the optimal care of these children and collectively appear to improve learning, behavior, and outcome.

Advances in cognitive and in neurochemical assessment increasingly illuminate the underlying mechanisms of this disorder. ADDH children are impulsive, unreflective in their performance of cognitive tasks, and have great difficulty in organizing their work and sustaining their efforts. Research into the neurochemistry is beginning to suggest underlying mechanisms of the disorder, which may contribute to new pharmacological treatments.

ADDH often resists efforts at amelioration and continues for many years to underlie increased vulnerability to a variety of adult dysfunctions. These conditions merit the most serious kind of consideration from the clinician. They are a challenge to the child psychiatrist to exercise to the fullest all of his professional skills including diagnosis and assessment, case management and consultation, psychopharmacology, and individual and family intervention. The use of blood levels of stimulants and of new psychotherapeutic agents such as clonidine or antidepressants offers alternatives to treatment with stimulants. Improvement may be facilitated by psychotropic medication, which is often mandatory, and often requires psychotherapeutic and educational intervention to channel the child's improved potential for social and academic learning.

REFERENCES

Achenbach, T. M. (1978a). *Research in Developmental Psychology.* New York: Free Press.

————. (1978b). The child behavior profile: I. Boys aged 6–11. *J. Consult. Clin. Psychol.* 46:478–88.

Adams, R. M., Koesis, J. J., and Estes, R. E. (1974). Soft neurological signs in learning-disabled children and controls. *J. Dis. Child.* 12:614–18.

Amado, H., and Lustman, P. J. (1982). Attention deficit disorders persisting in adulthood: A review. *Comp. Psychiat.* 23(4):200–214.

Amaral, D., and Sinnamon, H. (1977). The locus coeruleus: Neurobiology of a central noradrenergic nucleus. *Prog. Neurobiol.* 9:147–96.

Anderson, E. E., Clement, P. W., and Oettinger, L. Jr. (1981). Methylphenidate compared with behavioral self-control in attention deficit disorder: Preliminary report. *J. Dev. Behav. Pediatr.* 2(4):137–41.

Andrulonis, P. A., et al. (1982). Borderline personality subcategories. *J. Nerv. Ment. Dis.* 170(11):670–79.

Aston-Jones, G., and Bloom, F. E. (1981). Norepinephrine-containing locus coeruleus neurons in behaving rats exhibit pronounced responses to non-noxious environmental stimuli. *J. Neurosci.* 1(8):887–900.

August, G. J., and Stewart, M. A. (1982). Is there a syndrome of pure hyperactivity? *Brit. J. Psychiat.* 140:305–11.

Barkley, R. A., and Jackson, T. I. (1977). Hyperkinesis, autonomic nervous system activity and stimulant drug effects. *J. Child Psychol. Psychiat.* 18:347–57.

————. (1981). *Hyperactive Children: A Handbook for Diagnosis and Treatment.* New York: Guilford Press.

Bell, R. Q., and Waldrop, M. F. (1982). Temperament and minor physical anomalies. *CIBA Found. Symp.* 89:206–20.

Bloom, F. E. (1978). Central noradrenergic systems: Physiology and pharmocology. In M. E. Lipton, K. C. Killam, A. DiMascio (Eds.). *Psychopharmacology: A 20 Year Progress Report.* New York: Raven Press, pp. 131–42.

Brown, G. L., et al. (1979). *Clinical Pharmacology of d-amphetamine in Hyperactive Children.* New York: Spectrum Publications.

Brown, G. L., et al. (1981). Urinary 3-methoxy-4-hydroxyphenylglycol and homovanillic acid response to d-amphetamine in hyperactive children. *Biol. Psychiat.* 16(8): 779–87.

Buchsbaum, M. S., Coursey, R. D., and Murphy, D. L. (1976). The biochemical high risk paradigm: Behavioral and familial correlates of low monoamine oxidase activity. *Science* 194:339–41.

Callaway, E., and Halliday, R. (1982). The effect of attentional effort on visual evoked potential N1 latency. *Psychiatry Res.* 7(3): 299–308.

Campbell, S. B., et al. (1982). A multidimensional assessment of parent-identified behavior problem toddlers. *J. Abnorm. Child Psychol.* 10(4):569–91.

Cameron, M. I., and Robinson, V. M. (1980). Effects of cognitive training on academic and on-task behavior of hyperactive children. *J. Abnorm. Child Psychol.* 8(3):405–19.

Cantwell, D. P. (1975a). *The Hyperactive Child: Diagnosis, Management, Current Research.* New York: Spectrum Publications.

———. (1975b). Genetic studies of hyperactive children: Psychiatric illness in biological and adopting parents. In R. Fieve, D. Rosenthal, and H. Brill (Eds.). *Genetic Research in Psychiatry.* Baltimore: Johns Hopkins University Press, pp. 273–80.

———. (1976). Genetic factors in the hyperkinetic syndrome. *J. Amer. Acad. Child Psychiat.* 15:214–23.

———. (1980). A clinician's guide to the use of stimulant medications for the psychiatric disorders of children. *J. Dev. Behav. Pediatr.* 1(3):133–40.

Caparulo, B. K., et al. (1981). Computed tomographic brain scanning in children with developmental neuropsychiatric disorders. *J. Amer. Acad. Child Psychiat.* 20:338–57.

Cedarbaum, J. M., and Aghajanian, G. K. (1976). Noradrenergic neurons of the locus coeruleus: Inhibition by epinephrine and activation by the alpha-antagonist piperoxane. *Brain Res.* 112:412–19.

Chan, A. U., et al. (1983). Methylphenidate hydrochloride given with or before breakfast: II. Effects on plasma concentration of methylphenidate and ritalinic acid. *Pediatrics* 72:56–59.

Charles, L., and Schain, R. (1981). A four-year follow-up study of the effects of methylphenidate on the behavior and academic achievement of hyperactive children. *J. Abnorm. Child Psychol.* 9(4):495–505.

———, Schain, R., and Zelnicker, T. (1981). Optimal dosages of methylphenidate for improving the learning and behavior of hyperactive children. *J. Dev. Behav. Pediatr.* 2(3):78–81.

Cheng, L. T., et al. (1973). Amphetamine: New radio-immunoassay. *FEBS Letters* 36:339–42.

Cohen, D. J. (1977). Minimal brain dysfunction: Diagnosis and therapy. In J. Masserman (Ed.). *Current Psychiatric Therapies, Vol. 17.* New York: Grune and Stratton, pp. 57–70.

———. (1980). The pathology of the self in primary childhood autism and Gilles de la Tourette syndrome. *Psychiatric Clin. N. Am.* 3:383–402.

———, et al. (1980). Clonidine ameliorates Gilles de la Tourette syndrome. *Arch. Gen. Psychiat.* 37:1350–57.

Cohen, N. J., et al. (1981). Evaluation of the relative effectiveness of methylphenidate and cognitive behavior modification in the treatment of kindergarten-aged hyperactive children. *J. Abnorm. Child Psychol.* 9(1):43–54.

Coleman, M. (1971). Serotonin levels in whole blood of hyperactive children. *J. Pediatrics* 78:985–90.

Conners, C. K. (1969). A teacher rating scale for use in drug studies with children. *Amer. J. Psychiat.* 126:152–56.

———. (1980). *Food additives and hyperactive children.* New York: Plenum Press.

———, et al. (1976). Food additives and hyperkinesis: A controlled double-blind experiment. *Pediatrics* 58:154–66.

Cowart, V. S. (1982). ADD: Not limited to children. *J. Amer. Med. Assn.* 16, 248(3):286.

Cox, W. H., Jr. (1982). An indication for the use of imipramine in attention deficit disorder. *Amer. J. Psychiat.* 139:1059–60.

Das, J. P., Leong, C. K., and Williams, N. H. (1978). The relationship between learning disability and simultaneous-successive processing. *J. Learn. Dis.* 19:618–25.

Denckla, M. B., and Rudel, R. G. (1978). Anomalies of motor development in hyperactive boys. *Ann. Neurol.* 3:231–40.

Deutsch, C. K., et al. (1982). Overrepresentation of adoptees in children with attention deficit disorder. *Behav. Genetics* 12(2):231–38.

Dykman, R. A., et al. (1983). Physiological manifestations of learning disability. *J. Learn. Dis.* 16(1):46–53.

———, et al. (1982). Electrocortical frequencies in hyperactive, learning-disabled, mixed, and normal children. *Biol. Psychiat.* 17:675–85.

———, Ackerman, P. T., and McCray, D. S. (1980). Effects of methylphenidate on selective and sustained attention in hyperactive, reading-disabled and presumably attention-disordered boys. *J. Nerv. Ment. Dis.* 168(12):745–52.

Ebert, M. H., Van Kammen, D. P., and Murphy, D. L. (1976). Plasma levels of amphetamine and behavioral response. In L. A. Gottschalk and S. Merlis (Eds.). *Pharmacokinetics of Psychoactive Drugs: Blood Levels and Clinical Response.* New York: Spectrum Publications, pp. 157–69.

Elliott, F. A. (1982). Neurological findings in adult minimal brain dysfunction and the dyscontrol syndrome. *J. Nerv. Ment. Dis.* 170:680–87.

Ellis, M. J., et al. (1974). Methylphenidate and the activity of hyperactives in the informal setting. *Child Dev.* 45:217–20.

Eyre, S. L., Rounsaville, B. J., and Kleber, H. D. (1982). History of childhood hyperactivity in a clinic population of opiate addicts. *J. Nerv. Ment. Dis.* 70(9):5229.

Feingold, F. (1975). *Why Your Child is Hyperactive.* New York: Random House.

Ferguson, H. B., et al. (1981). Plasma free and total tryptophan, blood serotonin, and the hyperactivity syndrome: No evidence for the serotonin deficiency hypothesis. *Biol. Psychiat.* 16(3):231–38.

———, Rapoport, J. L., and Weingartner, H. (1981). Food dyes and impairment of performance in hyperactive children (letter). *Science* 211:410–11.

Firestone, P. (1982). Factors associated with children's adherence to stimulant medication. *Amer. J. Orthopsychiat.* 52(3):47–57.

Foote, S., and Bloom, F. E. (1979). Activity of norepinephrine-containing locus coeruleus neurons in the unanesthetized squirrel monkey. In E. Usdin, I. Kopin, and J. Barchas (Eds.). *Catecholamines: Basic and Clinical Frontiers.* New York: Pergamon Press, pp. 625–27.

———, Aston-Jones, G., and Bloom, F. E. (1980). Impulse activity of locus coeruleus neurons in awake rats and squirrel monkeys is a function of sensory stimulation and arousal. *Proc. Natl. Acad. Sci. USA* 77:3033–37.

Freeman, D. F., and Cornwall, T. P. (1980). Hyperactivity and neurosis. *Amer. J. Orthopsychiat.* 50(4):704–11.

Gardner, R. A. (1979). *The Objective Diagnosis of Minimal Brain Dysfunction.* Cresskill, N.J.: Creative Therapeutics.

Garfinkel, B. D., Webster, C. D., and Sloman, L. (1981). Responses to methylphenidate and varied doses of caffeine in children with attention deficit disorder. *Can. J. Psychiat.* 26(6):395–401.

Geller, B., Guttmacher, L. B., and Bleeg, M. (1981). Coexistence of childhood onset pervasive developmental disorder and attention deficit disorder with hyperactivity. *Amer. J. Psychiat.* 38(3):388–89.

Gillberg, C., and Rasmussen, P. (1982). Perceptual motor and attentional deficits in seven-year-old children: Background factors. *Dev. Med. Child Neurol.* 24(6):752–70.

———, Carlstrom, G., and Rasmussen, P. (1983). Hyperkinetic disorders in seven-year-old-children with perceptual, motor and attentional deficits. *J. Abnorm. Child Psychol. Psychiat.* 24(2):233–46.

———, et al. (1982). Perceptual, motor, and attentional deficits in six-year-old children: Epidemiological aspects. *J. Child Psychol. Psychiat.* 23(2):131–44.

Gittelman, R. (1980). The role of psychological tests for differential diagnosis in child psychiatry. *J. Child Psychiat.* 19:413–38.

———. (1984). Hyperkinetic syndrome: Outstanding issues of treatment and prognosis. In M. Rutter (Ed.). *Behavioral Syndromes of Brain Dysfunction in Childhood.* New York: Guildford Press.

Gittelman-Klein, R., and Klein, D. F. (1976). Methylphenidate effects in learning disabilities: Psychometric changes. *Arch. Gen. Psychiat.* 33:655–64.

Golden, G. S. (1974). Gilles de la Tourette's Syndrome following methylphenidate administration. *Dev. Med. Child. Neurol.* 16:76–78.

———. (1982). Neurobiological correlates of learning disabilities. *Ann. Neurol.* 12(5):409–18.

Goldstein, M. (1981). *New Developments in Interventions with Families of Schizophrenics.* San Francisco: Jossey Bass.

Gomez, R. L., et al. (1981). Adult psychiatric diagnoses and symptoms compatible with the hyperactive child syndrome: A retrospective study. *J. Clin. Psychiat.* 42 (10):389–94.

Gordon, M., and Oshman, H. (1981). Rorschach indices of children classified as hyperactive. *Percept. Motor Skills* 52:703–7.

Goyette, C. H., Conners, C. K., and Ulrich, R. F. (1978). Normative data on revised Conners parents and teacher rating scales. *J. Abnorm. Child Psychol.* 6:221–36.

Greenberg, L. M., et al. (1974). Clinical effects of imipramine and methylphenidate in hyperactive children. In C. K. Conners (Ed.). *Clinical Effects of Stimulants in Children.* The Hague: Excerpta Medica, p. 144.

Greenhill, L. L., et al. (1980). Growth disturbances in hyperkinetic children (letter). *Pediatrics* 66(1):152–54.

Gross, M. D. (1973). Imipramine in the treatment of minimal brain dysfunction in children. *Psychosomatics* 14:283.

Gualtieri, C. T. (1977). Imipramine and children: A review and some speculations about the mechanism of drug action. *Dis. Nerv. System* 38:368–75.

———, et al. (1982). Clinical studies of methylphenidate serum levels in children and adults. *J. Amer. Acad. Child Psychiat.* 21(1):19–26.

Halliday, R., Callaway, E., and Naylor, H. (1983). Visual evoked potential changes induced by methylphenidate in hyperactive children: Dose/response effects. *Electroencephalogr. Clin. Neurophysiol.* 55(3):258–67.

Halperin, J. M., and Gittelman, R. (1982). Do hyperactive children and their siblings differ in IQ academic achievement? *Psychiat. Res.* 6(2):253–58.

Harley, J. P., Matthews, C. G., and Eichman, P. L. (1978). Synthetic food colors and hyperactivity in children: A double-blind challenge experiment. *Pediatrics* 61:975–83.

Harner, I. C., and Foiles, R. A. (1980). Effects of Feingold's K-P diet on a residential mentally handicapped population. *J. Amer. Diet Assoc.* 76(6):575–78.

Harris, L. P. (1976). Attention and learning disordered children: A review of theory and remediation. *J. Learn. Dis.* 9:100–110.

Hechtman, L., Weiss, G., and Perlman, T. (1981). Hyperactives as young adults: Past and current antisocial behavior (stealing, drug abuse) and moral development. *Psychopharmacol. Bull.* 17(1):107–10.

———, et al. (1984). Hyperactives as young adults: Various clinical outcomes. *Adoles. Psychiat.* 9:295–306.

Hopkins, J., et al. (1979). Cognitive style in adults originally diagnosed as hyperactive. *J. Psychol. Psychiat.* 20:209–16.

Holborow, P. L. (1981). Ascorbic acid, dietary restrictions, and upper respiratory infection (letter). *Pediatrics* 65(6):1191–92.

Holden, E. W., Tarnowski, K. J., and Prinz, R. J. (1982). Reliability of neurological soft signs in children: Reevaluation of the PANESS. *J. Abnorm. Child Psychol.* 10(2):163–72.

Horowitz, H. A. (1981). Psychiatric casualties of minimal brain dysfunction in adolescents. *Adoles. Psychiat.* 9:275–94.

Huessy, H. R. (1983). Imipramine for attention deficit disorder. *Amer. J. Psychiat.* 140(2):272.

———, and Wright, A. (1970). The use of imipramine in children's behavior disorder. *Acta Paedopsychiat.* 37:194.

———, Metoyer, M., and Townsend, J. (1974). An 8–10 year follow-up of 84 children treated for behavioral disorder in rural Vermont. *Acta Paedopsychiat.* 10:230–35.

Hungund, B. L., et al. (1979). Pharmacokinetics of methylphenidate in hyperkinetic children. *Brit. J. Clin. Pharmacol.* 8:571–76

Hunt, R. D. (In submission). Strategies for study of the neurochemical aspects of cognitive dysfunction: Application in attention deficit disorder.

———, and Cohen, D. J. (1983). Recognizing psychiatric problems in early and middle childhood. In H. Leigh (Ed.). *Psychiatric Problems in Primary Practice.* Menlo Park, N.J.: Addison Wesley, pp. 399–467.

———, and Cohen, D. J. (1984). Psychiatric aspects of learning difficulties. *Pediatric Clinics of North America* 31(2):471–97.

———, et al. (1984). Possible change in noradrenergic receptor sensitivity following methylphenidate treatment: Growth hormone and MHPG response to clonidine challenge in children with attention deficit disorder and hyperactivity. *Life Sciences* 35(8):885–97.

———, Minderaa, R. B., and Cohen, D. J. (1985a). Noradrenergic mechanisms in ADDH. In L. Bloomingdale (Ed.). *Attention Deficit Disorder and Hyperactivity, Vol. 3.* New York: Plenum Press.

———, et al. (1985b). Clonidine benefits children with attention deficit disorder and hyperactivity: Report of a double-blind placebo-crossover therapeutic trial. *J. Amer. Acad. Child Psychiat.* 24(5):617–29.

Idol-Maestas, L. (1981). Behavior patterns in families of boys with learning and behavior problems. *J. Learn. Dis.* 14:347–49.

Irwin, M., et al. (1981). Tryptophan metabolism in children with attentional deficit disorder. *Amer. J. Psychiat.* 138(8):1082–85.

Itil, T. M., and Simeon, J. (1974). Computerized EEG in the prediction of outcome in drug treatment in hyperactive childhood behavior disorders. *Psychopharm. Bull.* 10:36.

Jagger, J., et al. (1982). The epidemiology of Tourette's syndrome: A pilot study. *Schiz. Bull.* 8:267–78.

Johnston, M. V., and Singer, H. S. (1982). Brain neurotransmitters and neuromodulators in pediatrics. *Pediatrics* 70:57–69.

Kauffman, R. E., et al. (1981). Medication compliance in hyperactive children. *Pediatr. Pharmacol.* 1(3):2317.

Khan, A. U., and Dekirmenjian, H. (1981). Urinary execretion of catecholamine metabolites in hyperkinetic child syndrome. *Amer. J. Psychiat.* 138(1):108–9.

Kidd, K. K., Prusoff, B. A., and Cohen, D. J. (1980). Familial pattern of Gilles de la Tourette syndrome. *Arch. Gen. Psychiat.* 37:1336–42.

King, C., and Young, R. D. (1982). Attentional deficits with and without hyperactivity: Teacher and peer perceptions. *J. Abnorm. Child Psychol.* 10(4):483–95.

Klein, D. F., and Gittelman-Klein, R. (1975). Problems in the diagnosis of minimal brain dysfunction and the hyperkinetic syndrome. *Int. J. Ment. Health* 4:45–60.

Kootz, J. P., and Cohen, D. J. (1981). Modulation of sensory intake in autistic children: Cardiovascular and behavioral indices. *J. Amer. Acad. Child Psychiat.* 20:692–701.

Kupietz, S. S., Winsberg, B. G., and Sverd, J. (1982). Learning ability and methylphenidate (ritalin) plasma concentration in hyperkinetic children. A preliminary investigation. *J. Amer. Acad. Child Psychiatry* 21(1):27–30.

Lazor, A., and Chandler, D. (1978). Criteria for early diagnosis of brain dysfunction. *Can. Psychiat. Assn. J.* 23:317–23.

Lerer, R. J., and Lerer, M. P. (1977). Response of adolescents with minimal brain dysfunction to methylphenidate. *J. Learn. Dis.* 10:223–28.

Levine, M. D., Busch, B., and Aufseeser, C. (1982). The dimension of inattention among children with school problems. *Pediatrics* 70(3):387–95.

Loney, J., Langbourne, J. E., and Paternite, C. E. (1978). An empirical basis for subgrouping the hyperkinetic/MBD syndrome. *J. Abnorm. Psych.* 87:431–41.

———, Kramer, J., and Milich, R. (1981). The hyperkinetic child grows up: Predictors of symptoms, delinquency, and achievement at follow-up. In K. D. Gadow and J. Loney (Eds.). *Psychosocial Aspects of Drug Treatment for Hyperactivity*. Boulder, Colo.: Westview Press.

Lowe, T. L., et al. (1982). Stimulant medications precipitate Tourette's Syndrome. *J. Amer. Med. Assn.* 247(12):1729–31.

McMahon, R. C. (1981). Biological factors in childhood hyperkinesis: A review of genetic and biochemical hypotheses. *J. Clin. Psychol.* 37(1):12–21.

McManus, M., et al. (1984). Assessment of borderline symptomology in hospitalized adolescents. *J. Amer. Acad. Child. Psychiat.* 23(6):685–94.

Madison, R. (1984). Overlap of symptoms of depression and hyperactivity. Paper presented to the American Academy of Child Psychiatry, Toronto, Ontario, October.

Mash, E. J., and Johnson, C. (1982). A comparison of the mother-child interactions of younger and older hyperactive and normal children. *Child Dev.* 53(5):1371–81.

Mendelson, W., Johnson, N., and Stewart, M. (1971). Hyperactive children as teenagers: A follow-up study. *J. Nerv. Ment. Dis.* 153:273–79.

Michael, R. L., et al. (1981). Normalizing effects of methylphenidate on hyperactive children's vigilance performance and evoked potentials. *Psychophysiology* 18(6):655–77.

Milich, R., Loney, J., and Landau, S. (1982). Independent dimensions of hyperactivity and aggression: A validation with playroom observation data. *J. Abnorm. Psychol.* 91(3):183–98.

Millichap, J. G. (1978). Growth of hyperactive children treated with methylphenidate. *J. Learn. Dis.* 11(9):567–70.

Morrison, J., and Stewart, M. (1971). A family study of hyperactive child syndrome. *Biol. Psychiatry* 3:189–95.

———. (1973). The psychiatric status of the legal families of adopted hyperactive children. *Arch. Gen. Psychiat.* 28:888–91.

Murphy, D. L., and Donnelly, C. H. (1974). Monoamine oxidase in man. In E. Usdin (Ed.). *Neuropsychopharmacology of Monoamines and Their Regulatory Enzymes.* New York: Raven Press, pp. 71–85.

Murray, M. E. (1980). Behavioral management of the hyperactive child. *J. Dev. Behav. Pediatr.* 1(3):108–11.

Nagel-Heimke, M., et al. (1984). The influence of methylphenidate on the sympathoadrenal reactivity in children diagnosed as hyperactive. *Klin. Paediatr.* 196:78–82.

National Institute of Health consensus development conference statement: Defined diets and childhood hyperactivity. *Amer. J. Clin. Nutrition* 37(1):161–65.

Nichols, P., and Chen, T. C. (1981). *Minimal Brain Dysfunction: A Prospective Study.* Hillsdale, N.J.: Lawrence Erlbaum.

O'Brien, J. (1982). School problems: School phobia and learning disabilities. *Psychiat. Clin. N. Amer.* 5(2):297–307.

O'Leary, S. G., and Steen, P. L. (1982). Subcategorizing hyperactivity: The Stony Brook Scale. *J. Consult. Clin. Psychol.* 50(3):426–32.

O'Shea, J. A., and Porter, S. F. (1981). Double-blind study of children with hyperkinetic syndrome treated with multi-allergen extract sublingually. *J. Learn. Dis.* 14(4):189–91.

Pauls, D. L., et al. (In press). Evidence against a genetic relationship between Tourette's syndrome and attention disorder with hyperactivity. *Arch. Gen. Psychiat.*

Plotkin, D., Halaris, A., and Demet, E. M. (1982). Biological studies in adult attention deficit disorder: Case report. *J. Clin. Psychiat.* 43(12):501–2.

Porges, S. W., et al. (1981). The influence of methylphenidate on spontaneous autonomic activity and behavior in children diagnosed as hyperactive. *Psychophysiology* 18(1):42–48.

Porrino, L. J., et al. (1983a). A naturalistic assessment of the motor activity of hyperactive boys, II: Stimulant drug effects. *Arch. Gen Psychiat.* 40(6):688–93.

———, et al. (1983b). A naturalistic assessment of the motor activity of hyperactive boys, I: Comparison with normal controls. *Arch. Gen. Psychiat.* 40(6):681–87.

Puig-Antich, J. (1982). Major depression aond conduct disorder in prepuberty. *J. Amer. Acad. Child Psychiat.* 21(2):118–28.

Quinn, P. O., and Rapoport, J. L. (1975). One year follow-up of hyperactive boys treated with imipramine and methylphenidate. *Amer. J. Psychiat.* 132:241–45.

———, et al. (1974). Imipramine and methylphenidate treatments in hyperactive boys: A double-blind comparison. *Arch. Gen. Psychiat.* 30(6):789–93.

Rapoport, J. L., and Ferguson, H. B. (1981). Biological validation of the hyperkinetic syndrome. *Dev. Med. Child Neurol.* 23(5):667–82.

Rapoport, J. L., Quinn, P. O., and Lamprecht, F. (1974). Minor physical anomalies and plasma dopamine-beta-hydroxylase activity in hyperactive boys. *Amer. J. Psychiat.* 121:386.

———, et al. (1980). Dextroamphetamine: Its cognitive and behavioral effects in normal and hyperactive boys and normal men. *Arch. Gen. Psychiat.* 37:933–43.

Reich, W., et al. (1982). Development of a structured psychiatric interview for children: Agreement on diagnosis comparing child and parent interviews. *J. Abnorm. Child Psychol.* 10(3):325–36.

Rie, E. D., et al. (1978). An analysis of neurological soft signs in children with learning problems. *Brain and Language* 6:32–46.

Roberts, M. A., et al. (1981). A multi-trait multi-time analysis of teachers' ratings of aggression, hyperactivity, and inattention. *J. Abnorm. Child Psychol.* 9(3):371–80.

Robins, L. N. (1966). *Deviant Children Grown Up: A Sociological and Psychiatric Study of Sociopathic Personality.* Baltimore: Williams and Wilkins.

Rogeness, G. A., et al. (1982). Biochemical differences in children with conduct disorder socialized and undersocialized. *Amer. J. Psychiat.* 139(3):307–11.

Rollins, B. C., and Thomas, D. L. (1979). Parental support, power and control techniques in the socialization of children. In W. Burr (Ed.). *Contemporary Theories About the Family, Vol. 1.* New York: Free Press, pp. 317–64.

Rutter, M. (1982). Syndromes attributed to "minimal brain dysfunction" in childhood. *Amer. J. Psychiat.* 139(1):21–33.

Safer, D. J. (1973). A familial factor in minimal brain dysfunction. *Behav. Genetics* 3:175–86.

———, and Allan, R. P. (1976). *Hyperactive Children: Diagnosis and Management.* Baltimore: University Park Press.

Sandberg, S. T., Rutter, M., and Taylor, E. (1978). Hyperkinetic disorder in psychiatric clinic attenders. *Developm. Med. and Child. Neurol.* 20:279–99.

———, Wieselberg, M., and Shaffer, D. (1980). Hyperkinetic and conduct problem children in a primary school population: Some epidemiological considerations. *J. Child Psychol. Psychiat.* 21(4):293–311.

Satterfield, J. H., Cantwell, D. P., and Satterfield, B. T. (1974). Pathophysiology of the hyperactive child syndrome. *Arch. Gen. Psychiat.* 31:839–44.

———, Cantwell, D. P. and Satterfield, B. T. (1979). Multimodality Treatment: A one-year follow-up of 84 hyperactive boys. *Arch. Gen. Psychiat.* 36:965–74.

———, Schell, A. M., and Barb, S. D. (1980). Potential risk of prolonged administration of stimulant medication for hyperactive children. *J. Dev. Behav. Pediatr.* 1(3):102–7.

———, Satterfield, B. T., and Cantwell, D. P. (1981). Three-year multimodality treatment of 100 hyperactive boys. *J. Pediatr.* 98:650–55.

———, Hoppe, C. M., and Schell, A. M. (1982). A prospective study of delinquency in 110 adolescent boys with attention deficit disorder and 88 normal boys. *Amer. J. Psychiat.* 139(6):795–98.

Satterfield, J. H., et al. (1973a). Response to stimulant drug treatment in hyperactive children: Prediction from EEG and neurological findings. *J. Autism Child. Schiz.* 3:36–48.

———, et al. (1973b). EEG aspects in the diagnosis and treatment of minimal brain dysfunction. *Ann. N.Y. Acad. Science* 205:274–82.

Schachar, R., Rutter, M., and Smith, A. (1981). The characteristics of situationality and pervasively hyperactive child syndrome: A retrospective study. *J. Child Psychol. Psychiat.* 22(4):375–92.

Shaffer, D. (1978). Longitudinal research and the minimal brain damage syndrome. *Adv. Biol. Psychiat.* 1:18–34.

Shaywitz, S. E. (1982). The Yale neuropsychoeducational assessment scales. *Schiz. Bull.* 8(2):360–424.

———, Cohen, D. J., and Bowers, M. B., Jr. (1977). CSF monoamine metabolites in children with minimal brain dysfunction: Evidence for alteration of brain dopamine. *J. Pediatrics* 90:67–71.

———, Cohen, D. J., and Bowers, M. B., Jr. (1980). Cerebrospinal fluid monoamine metabolites in neurological disorders of childhood. In J. H. Wood (Ed.). *Neurobiology of Cerebrospinal Fluid, Vol. 1.* New York: Plenum Press, pp. 219–36.

Shaywitz, et al. (1982). Psychopharmacology of attention deficit disorder: Pharmacokinetic, neuroendocrine, and behavioral measures following acute and chronic treatment with methylphenidate. *Pediatrics* 69:688–94.

Shekim, W. O., et al. (1982a). Platelet MAO in children with attention deficit disorder and hyperactivity: A pilot study. *Amer. J. Psychiat.* 139(7):936–38.

———, et al. (1982b). Effects of d-amphetamine on urinary metabolites of dopamine and norepinephrine in hyperactive boys. *Amer. J. Psychiat.* 139(4):485–88.

———, et al. (1983). Urinary MHPG and HVA excretion in boys with attention deficit disorder and hyperactivity treated with d-amphetamine. *Biol. Psychiat.* 18(6):707–14.

Shen, Y. C., and Wang, Y. F. (1984). Urinary 3-methoxy-4-hydroxyphenylglycol sulfate excretion in 73 school children with minimal brain dysfunction syndrome. *Biol. Psychiat.* 19:861–70.

Shetty, T., and Chase, T. N. (1976). Central monoamines and hyperkinesis of childhood. *Neurology* 26:1000–1006.

Silver, L. B. (1981). The relationship between learning disabilities, hyperactivity, distractibility and behavioral problems: A clinical analysis. *J. Amer. Acad. Child Psychiat.* 20(2):385–91.

Sleator, E. K., Ullman, R. K., and Von Neuman, A. (1982). How do hyperactive children feel about taking stimulants and will they tell the doctor? *Clin. Pediatr.* 21(8):474–79.

Solanto, M. V., and Conners, C. K. (1982). A dose-response and time-action analysis of autonomic and behavioral effects of methylphenidate in attention deficit disorder with hyperactivity. *Psychophysiology* 19(6):658–67.

Sostek, A. J., Buchsbaum, M. S., and Rapoport, J. L. (1980). Effects of amphetamine on vigilance performance in normal and hyperactive children. *J. Abnorm. Child Psychol.* 9:491–500.

Sprague, R. L., and Sleator, E. K. (1977). Methylphenidate in hyperactive children: Differences in dose effects on learning and social behavior. *Science* 198:1274–76.

Staton, R. D., and Brumback, R. A. (1981). Non-specificity of motor hyperactivity as a diagnostic criterion. *Percept. Motor Skills* 52(1):323–32.

Stewart, M. A., Deblois, C. S., and Cummings, C. (1980). Psychiatric disorder in the parents of hyperactive boys and those with conduct disorder. *J. Child Psychol. Psychiat.* 21(4):293–311.

Stine, O. C., Saratosioter, J. M., and Mosser, R. S. (1975). Relationships between neurological findings and classroom behavior. *Amer. J. Dis. Child.* 129:1036–40.

Swanson, J., and Kinsbourne, M. (1976). Stimulant related state-dependent learning in hyperactive children. *Science* 192:1254–56.

Sykes, D. H., Douglas, V. I., and Morgenstern, G. (1972). The effect of methylphenidate (ritalin) on sustained attention in hyperactive children. *Psychopharmacologia* 25:262–74.

Trites, R. L., Blouin, A. G., and Laprade, K. (1982). Factor analysis of the Conners Teacher Rating Scale based on a large normative sample. *J. Consult. Clin. Psychol.* 50(5):615–23.

Waizer, J., et al. (1974). Outpatient treatment of hyperactive school children with imipramine. *Amer. J. Psychiat.* 131:587.

Waldrop, M., and Halverson, C. F. (1971). Minor physical anomalies and hyperactive behavior in young children. In J. Hellmuth (Ed.). *Exceptional Infant, Vol. 11: Studies of Abnormalities.* New York: Brunner/Mazel, pp. 343–89.

Weiss, B. (1982). Food additives and environmental chemicals as sources of childhood behavior disorders. *J. Amer. Acad. Child. Psychiat.* 21(2):144–52.

Weiss, G. (1981). Controversial issues of the pharmacotherapy of the hyperactive child. *Can. J. Psychiat.* 26(6):385–92.

———, and Hechtman, L. (1979). The hyperactive child syndrome. *Science* 205:1348–53.

Weissman, M. M., et al. (1984). Onset of major depression in early childhood—increased familial loading and specificity. *Arch. Gen. Psychiat.* 41(12):1136–43.

Wender, P. H. (1971). *Minimal Brain Dysfunction in Children.* New York: Wiley-Interscience.

———. (1980). New evidence on food additives and hyperkinesis: A critical analysis. *Amer. J. Dis. Child.* 134(12):1122–25.

———. (1981). Psychiatric genetics and the primary prevention of psychiatric disorders. *Bibl. Psychiat.* 160:7–14.

———, et al. (1971). Urinary monoamine metabolites in children with minimal brain dysfunction. *Amer. J. Psychiat.* 127:1411–15.

Werner, E., and Smith, R. (1977). *Kauai's Children Come of Age.* Honolulu: University of Hawaii Press.

————, Berman, J., and French, F. (1971). *The Children of Kauai: A Longitudinal Study from the Prenatal Period to Age Ten*. Honolulu: University of Hawaii Press.

Werry, J. S. (1981). Drugs and learning. *J. Child Psychol. Psychiat.* 22:283–90.

————, Aman, M. G., and Diamond, E. (1980). Imipramine and methylphenidate in hyperactive children. *J. Child Psychol. Psychiat.* 21:27–35.

Whalen, C. K., Henker, B., and Dotemoto, S. (1981a). Teacher response to the methylphenidate (ritalin) versus placebo status of hyperactive boys in the classroom. *Child Dev.* 52(3):1005–14.

————, Henker, B., and Finck, D. (1981b). Medication effects in the classroom: Three naturalistic indicators. *J. Abnorm. Child Pychol.* 9(4):419–33.

————, et al. (1979). A social ecology of hyperactive boys: Medication effects in structured classroom environments. *J. Appl. Behav. Analysis* 12:65–81.

Willerman, L. (1973). Activity level and hyperactivity in twins. *Child Dev.* 44:288–93.

Williams, J. I., et al. (1978). Relative effects of drugs and diet on hyperactive behaviors: An experimental study. *Pediatrics* 61:811–17.

Winsberg, B. G., et al. (1972). Effects of imipramine and dextroamphetamine on behavior of neuropsychiatrically impaired children. *Amer. J. Psychiat.* 128:1425.

————, et al. (1982). Methylphenidate oral dose plasma concentrations and behavioral response in children. *Psychopharmacology* 76(4):329–32.

Wood, D. R., et al. (1976). Diagnosis and treatment of minimal brain dysfunction in adults. *Arch. Gen. Psychiat.* 33:1453–60.

————, Wender, P. H., and Reimherr, F. W. (1983). The prevalance of attention deficit disorder, residual type, or minimal brain dysfunction, in a population of male alcoholic patients. *Amer. J. Psychiat.* 140(1):95–98.

Yellin, A. M., Hopwood, J. H., and Greenberg, L. M. (1982). Adults and adolescents with attention deficit disorder: Clinical and behavioral responses to psychostimulants. *J. Clin. Psychopharmacol.* 2(2):133–36.

Young, J. G. (1981). Methylphenidate-induced hallucinosis: Case histories and possible mechanisms of action. *Dev. Behav. Pediatr.* 2(2):35–37.

————, and Cohen, D. J. (1979). The molecular biology of development. In J. D. Noshpitz (Ed.). *Basic Handbook of Child Psychiatry*. New York: Basic Books, pp. 22–62.

Zahn, T. P., et al. (1975). Minimal brain dysfunction, stimulant drugs, and autonomic nervous system activity. *Arch. Gen. Psychiat.* 32:381–87.

26

CONDUCT DISORDER

William H. Kaplan

INTRODUCTION

This chapter will examine the degree to which the DSM-III classification of conduct disorder meets requirements for a psychiatric disorder. Is it more than a clustering of items? Do we understand its etiology? Does it have a characteristic clinical picture? Can it be delimited from other psychiatric disorders? Is it a stable diagnosis or one that changes to become another disorder over time? What are the psychosocial correlates, and how specific are they to conduct disorder? What is the mode of transmission? What can we say about the prognosis of antisocial behavior in childhood and adolescence? What are the treatments available for this disorder, and how well can we predict response to the treatment?

Clearly, there are not wholly satisfying answers to all of the above questions, but the issue that must be resolved is whether current epidemiological data and clinical wisdom provide a sufficient foundation on which to base the concept of a discrete disorder of conduct. This chapter will examine the subject from the epidemiological, clinical, and research perspectives.

NOSOLOGY

The current DSM-III classification represents the distillation of clinical experience and statistical methods, such as factor analytic techniques. The approach is highly phenomenological, but without clear guidelines for determining the quality and quantity of a particular deviant behavior. In fact, DSM-III does not take note of particular developmental phases in which certain disturbances of conduct such as stealing, lying, fighting and verbal aggressiveness might not be considered pathological.

There are four subclassifications of conduct disorder: (1) undersocialized and aggressive; (2) socialized and aggressive; (3) undersocialized and nonaggressive; and (4) socialized and nonaggressive. For an aggressive disorder, one must exhibit a repetitive and persistent pattern in which the basic rights of others are violated, as evidenced by either physical violence against persons or property, or thefts outside the home involving confrontation with the victim. For a nonaggressive conduct disorder, a repetitive and persistent pattern must occur in which either basic rights of others or major age-appropriate societal norms or rules are violated, as manifested by any of the following: chronic violations of important rules, such as persistent truancy and substance abuse; running away from home overnight; persistent lying in and out of the home; and stealing not involving confrontation with a victim.

There are several problems with this classification system. There is empirical evidence for separating aggressive and nonaggressive antisocial behavior based on many statistical analyses. Based on the factor analysis of the Child Behavior Checklist, Achenbach (1978) found separate factors for aggressive and nonaggressive antisocial behavior. Loeber (1982) identified a continuum for antisocial behavior, with covert behaviors corresponding to a nonaggressive category at one end of the spectrum and overt behaviors corresponding to a category of aggression at the other end of the spectrum. Loeber found a clustering at the covert end of the pole, made up of behaviors such as lying, stealing, drug use, vandalism and fire setting, and examples of overt behavior such as aggression, excessive quarreling, disobedience, and fighting. It is important to note that two behaviors found by the Achenbach Child Behavior Checklist and the work by Loeber—fire setting and vandalism—fall into a nonaggressive category, in contradistinction to the DSM-III nomenclature. Such a situation creates confusion for the clinician and researcher who are trying to make an assessment and who are interested in the differences in the clinical course, prognosis, and response to treatment of two supposedly distinct subcategories of the same disorder.

The examples given in DSM-III for aggression are specific acts that correspond to legal definitions of delinquency and criminality. These are in contrast to the antisocial behaviors identified by Loeber, Achenbach and many other studies, thirty-seven of which have been reviewed by Quay (1979), which refer to nondelinquent antisocial behaviors. Thus, benchmarks provided by DSM-III leave the clinician in a quandary because rape, mugging, and gas station robberies are rarely seen in the vast majority of children and adolescents labeled as aggressive. For egregious antisocial acts, one hardly needs a psychiatric classification system distinct from a sociolegal one, if the nosology of the psychiatric system consists of specific criminal offenses and does not meet criteria for a true psychiatric disorder.

However, even though aggressive delinquent acts are subsumed under the DSM-III system, this is hardly what is meant by aggression or overt antisocial behaviors. If one examines the twenty-two items that cluster under the heading of an aggressive syndrome for boys ages 12 to 16 in the Achenbach Child Behavior Checklist, one sees many behaviors that cannot be easily operationalized, and that certainly are highly nonspecific to a conduct disorder. Many of the items cluster with other diagnostic categories. A sampling of items includes the following: argumentative, hyperactive, demanding, disobedient at home, jealous, impulsive, nervous, stubborn, moody, sulky, excessively talkative, given to temper tantrums, and raucous. Loeber includes disobedience in overt antisocial behaviors (his aggressive category). One can easily see the striking difference between what is intended in DSM-III and the pattern of aggressive behavior identified in clinical psychiatric settings and found to cluster consistently.

There are four points about the above items that raise serious questions as to whether they can be part of a distinct clinical syndrome. First, several of these items overlap with symptoms identified with attention deficit disorder, with or without hyperactivity. The strong correlation between antisocial behavior and attention deficit disorder with hyperactivity has been firmly established and reviewed by Rutter and Gould (1985). Second, many of the items are affect-laden and conjure up the concept of a masked depression or a coexistent depressive disorder. This interface between depression and antisocial behavior will be discussed below; but suffice it to say here that in the Achenbach Child Behavior Checklist taxonomy, distinct syndromes appear that combine factors of depression and disorders of conduct (Achenbach and Edelbrock 1983). Third, judgments about the pathology of these behaviors rest strongly upon an understanding of child development and the context in which the behaviors occur. Fourth, these symptoms and behaviors are extremely difficult to operationalize and place the clinician in the difficult position of trying, on his own, to set anchors. This introduces unacceptable biases. As an example of the diagnostic problems facing the clinician using DSM-III, one must determine whether or not the disturbances of conduct fall in the category of a true conduct disorder or in what appears to be the milder form of a conduct disorder: the oppositional disorder of childhood or adolescence, characterized by violations of minor rules, temper tantrums, argumentativeness, provocative behavior, and stubbornness.

Another problem area for the clinician, once he has established whether the conduct disorder fits in the aggressive or nonaggressive camp, is the categorization of the child as socialized or undersocialized, a distinction that remains controversial (Rutter et al. 1975). On the one hand remains the controversy about the validity of the socialized concept, but on the other hand is the problem of how to determine reliably its presence or absence. The clinician, with only five broad criteria as a guide, must make highly value-laden decisions about "a normal degree of affection, empathy or bond with others." Can one determine these factors in a single interview? Can they be known without direct observation in a naturalistic setting, or without the aid of a reliable informant? How well do observers differentiate attachment behaviors from the social context in which they occur; for example, is there a risk of discounting bonds and signs of affection in situations and with individuals found to be objectionable?

A further difficulty for the clinician arises with the nonaggressive behavior of substance abuse. Use of alcohol constitutes a status offense in our society because of legal constraints against minors' use of this substance. In the 1981 National Co-hort of High School Seniors, lifetime prevalence rates were 93 percent for alcohol, 71 percent for smoking cigarettes, and 60 percent for marijuana use. Among young adults 18 to 25 years of age in a national survey in 1978, 33 percent used an illicit substance other than marijuana, and 23 percent experimented with cocaine. In the same survey, 38 percent of the boys and 26 percent of the girls in high school were considered problem drinkers (Kandel 1982). With such high base rates and the influ-ence of societal mores, a clinician cannot be left without more precise information about what constitutes substance abuse in a conduct disorder.

The clinician cannot rely on the DSM-III criteria alone. It is mechanical and shortsighted to deny the importance of dynamics, antecedents, and stressors that relate to the problem behaviors. Often the symptoms appear situation-specific and reactive, even though they meet the minimum duration requirements of six months. It can be difficult to differentiate problem behaviors of a conduct disorder from an adjustment disorder with disturbance of conduct.

I will offer some brief examples from my own clinical work to highlight diag-nostic problems.

Case #1

A 15-year-old girl came before the family court because of chronic truancy; she had missed over one year of school. She had no meaningful peer rela-tionships and spent her time at home, venturing out only occasionally with her mother. The girl had deteriorated since the remarriage of her mother and the estrangement from her biological father. At home she was sullen, withdrawn, negativistic, argumentative, and stubborn. She appeared to be suffering from a major depressive disorder with agoraphobic features. How-ever, to the probation department, family court judge, school authorities, and even a clinician at the community mental health center who had evalu-ated the girl, this adolescent had a disturbance of conduct.

The chronic truancy and attendant behavior problems obscured from the view of important adult authority figures an underlying mood disorder. How could this happen? One reason seems to be a reliance on a behavior such as truancy or on a group of deviant behaviors as indicative of a disorder, when in fact these are highly nonspecific behaviors that could suggest a wide range of pathology. The truancy, which became the preoccupation of those in-volved with the girl, should have been seen in a broader context that con-sidered the behaviors and affects from a child-centered view sensitive to the interplay with the environment, stressors, development, personality, and biology of the individual.

Case #2

A 14-year-old boy came before the Family Court with a third felony charge brought against him within the last year. This mandated him as a desig-nated felon and meant that he would be placed in a restricted residential facility. He had stolen valuable property, lied chronically, and acted impulsively, jumping out of a second-storey window while already handcuffed by the police who had arrested him. He had shown a quick and violent temper, destroyed property in a rage on several occasions, and had been physically and verbally abusive. Despite this strong case for a diagnosis of an aggressive conduct disorder, a curious aspect was that all of the antisocial behavior had begun in the last eighteen months, during which time his mother, divorced since the boy was five years old, formed a relationship with a man who himself had some antisocial features. This man tried to impose discipline and structure on the adolescent, who resented and resisted his involvement.

Further, the mother, despite her protestations and anger at his delinquent behavior, seemed to derive vicarious pleasure from her son's deviance. She seemed to fuel his antisocial behavior through her own highly inconsistent parenting, at times being overly indulgent, and at other times extremely angry and punitive with him. She seemed to fit the model of the superego lacunae described by Johnson & Szureck (1952). The mother, a most attractive and seductive woman, eroticized the relationship with her son. She vacillated between overstimulation and rejection of him. She admired his physical development and prowess, yet derided his preoccupation with weight lifting. The mother put him in his place when she felt so inclined, either through her own direct actions or through delegating the responsibility to her male companion. The adolescent seemed determined to establish his turf and win an oedipal victory over his mother's current suitor.

This youth became absorbed not only in weight lifting, but even had begun to take steroids, which he had obtained illicitly, to enhance his physique. His bravado, muscle development, impulsivity, rage, and antisocial behavior all seemed to be evidence of his commitment to preserve his identity and maintain a special dyadic and now eroticized relationship with his mother. The stealing, destruction of property, and the rage were directed almost exclusively toward the mother: He destroyed her bedroom, stole her credit cards and jewelry, and his assaultive behavior occurred entirely within their household, directed at the mother.

At a six-month follow-up of this youngster, following his placement in a residential facility for delinquent boys, it appeared that this adolescent had made an excellent adjustment. None of the antisocial behavior persisted, and he told me that he liked all the rules and structure because the staff was fair and he always knew where he stood.

The diagnostic problem in this case would seem to be that although the youth met criteria for an aggressive conduct disorder, the antisocial behaviors arose within the confines of his home, with his rage directed almost exclusively at his mother. It occurred at a time when his adolescent sexuality both stressed and overwhelmed the coping strategies and defenses of the mother and adolescent. He had become in a year's time a designated felon because of his repeated court involvement. Yet placement in a well-run residential facility allowed not only for a quick reduction in his impulsivity and antisocial behavior, but also for a less intense and volatile relationship with his mother. She remained concerned and involved in his life, but at a much safer distance for both. In this example, one again sees the limitation of using a diagnosis that ignores the context in which these behaviors occur and the dynamics that fueled them, both of which played a vital role in terms of treatment strategies and prognosis.

Case #3

A 16-year-old girl had been picked up three times for shoplifting in the last year. She had also become a chronic truant and a frequent runaway. Her parents considered her a pathological liar, and they reported that she had stolen money and property from them.

Most upsetting to these middle-class parents was the fact that their daughter was not only sexually active, but also highly promiscuous. She chose males several years her senior whom the parents described as high school dropouts, known drug users, and delinquents. The parents were devastated because they had seen their daughter as a model child with much promise. She had been a proficient cellist and honor student up to her fourteenth birthday. Both parents described her as outgoing, good-natured, and obedient. The dramatic change in behavior occurred at age fourteen, upon return from camp, when the teenager told her parents that she had her first boyfriend. The parents were shocked to discover that the boyfriend had been a high school dropout, five years older than the girl, and someone whom the parents considered a most unsavory character. The parents took a strident position that their daughter could have no contact with this youth. This led to a cascade of events in which the girl not only disregarded the dictum of her parents, but seemed to abandon most age-appropriate rules set by the parents and school. She lost her ambition to play the cello and she became frequently truant and unmotivated with respect to school, and her grades plummeted. The relationship with her parents became increasingly polarized and conflictual.

Important in this case are the facts that the father had been suffering from a chronic depression that had gone untreated, and the parents had serious marital difficulties, having grown apart from and resentful of one another. The adolescent sexuality of this girl appeared to trigger an intensely rigid reaction by both parents, who seemed to displace negative feelings relating to years of marital strife onto a preoccupation with the sexual exploits of their daughter. They persisted in making impossible demands on the girl, which she initially agreed to follow, only to disregard flagrantly and impulsively. The mother gained some insight into the role that family dynamics played in the antisocial behaviors of this girl; however, the father's approach remained inflexible and he persisted in a futile attempt to control his daughter's life. For example, the father continued to insist that he interview, or, as the patient put it, "interrogate" her male friends. He drove his daughter to and from her nightly social activities, and he made surprise visits to places where this youth liked to "hang out." The father justified his intrusive behavior as necessary in order to know if his daughter spent time in activities and places that met his standards. This enraged the girl, who seemed driven to an escalation of her antisocial behavior and promiscuity in order to frustrate the will of her parents.

The three examples show a weakness in the system of classification. The emphasis on nonspecific antisocial behaviors puts the onus on the child and often ignores other important considerations relating to the familial, developmental, and environmental factors. These deviant behaviors also tend to arouse such frustration and negative reactions in the natural authority figures in the child's life, that parents and teachers tend to ignore coexistent emotional problems and the possibility of intrapsychic conflict. For example, a clinician may be struck by the irritation or protestation shown by a parent or teacher when he observes that a conduct-disordered youth suffers from depression. Too often, the concept of conduct disorder permits the natural raters in the child's life to focus attention and responsibility for the problem behaviors onto the youngster, when in a more objective light, one sees the behaviors to be reactive to and understandable in the full context of the youth's life.

EPIDEMIOLOGY

The reported prevalence rates for antisocial behavior in this country have varied between 3 and 25 percent. It is a serious problem that spares no locality or group. Robins (1981) called antisocial behavior the single most costly childhood disorder to society. Rates vary depending on the area studied and the methodology used. One will find higher rates of antisocial behavior based on self-report measures than by use of official delinquent contacts. Nevertheless, in official delinquent arrest rates used in a longitudinal sample by West and Farrington (1973, 1977), 25 percent of a working-class cohort in London had been classified as delinquent, defined as a conviction for an offense involving aggression. Prevalence rates are also influenced by the cohort effect, in which assessments of more recent teenage cohorts yield higher rates of antisocial behavior. The disorder has risen steadily over the last fifty years, and the absolute numbers are staggering.

Arrest and conviction rates raise several problems as measures of antisocial behavior. Not only do they underrepresent the true number of antisocial activities, but the results are also skewed because of sociodemographic biases. There is a great deal of discretion about who gets referred for legal action, who is arrested, and what kind of disposition is to be made. School officials have latitude about whom and when to refer to court for the status offense of chronic truancy. The police maintain discretion about whom to arrest, and once having arrested, when to drop the case, file a station adjustment, or remand for court action. Robins (1966) observed that social status is an important variable that predicts which youth, once arrested by police, will go to court and from court be institutionalized. The relationship is an inverse one in which members of the higher socioeconomic stratum are less likely to receive court action and confinement for a particular offense. Lewis et al. (1980)

concluded that black adolescents who are violent and seriously disturbed psychiatrically were more likely to be channeled through a correctional facility than were their aggressive, white male counterparts, who were more likely to be directed toward psychiatric facilities. Rutter and Madge (1976) also concluded that low socioeconomic status blacks received more court appearances and harsher punishments compared to middle-class white offenders.

The disorder occurs about five times as frequently in males as in females. Despite the disparity, young females have been closing the gap. In the United Kingdom, for example, the ratio in 1957 was 11 to 1, male to female (Rutter 1981). One theory advanced to explain the female predominance for unipolar depression beginning in adolescence and the male predominance of antisocial behavior, which mushrooms in the teenage years, is the depressive spectrum hypothesis by Winokur (1979). He proposed that alcoholism and sociopathy may represent alternate pathways for a depressive diathesis in males.

Urban areas have the highest prevalence rates. The urban poor from disadvantaged minority groups are at greatest risk for disorders of conduct (Robins 1981). The peak age range appears to be between 15 and 18 years (Rutter 1981). In the Isle of Wight Study (Rutter 1970), involving a nonurban population, one finds among the latency age children a lower prevalence rate of antisocial behavior; among ten- and eleven-year-old children the rate of nonaggressive conduct disorder was 4 percent, and of aggressive conduct disorder, 1.1 percent. Another important finding was that 39 percent of the conduct-disordered group had a coexistent affective or emotional disturbance. The latter finding raises the possibility that an underlying mood disorder may include antisocial features in adolescents. Kandel and Davies (1982) asserted that antisocial behavior precedes drug use, and that a depressive mood is a predictor for marijuana initiation and use. One-fourth of daily marijuana users among high school seniors reported that they use the drug to escape from their problems. Kandel believed that the use of illicit drugs among adolescents may be a form of self-medication to cope with depression.

CLINICAL FINDINGS

The most common symptoms of childhood antisocial behavior, according to Robins (1981), are as follows: incorrigibility, theft, running away, truancy, school failure, failure despite adequate intelligence, curfew violations, fighting, early sexual activity, and early substance abuse. There appears to be a sequential nature to the antisocial behavior, with truancy and school failure first, followed by drinking and sexual activity and later, illicit drug use and theft. The stages of disturbances of conduct give important information about the natural course of the disorder and have implications for prevention.

One area of vital importance for early prevention of antisocial behavior is the school. Robins (1966), Rutter (1979), and West and Farrington (1977) have shown the importance of school maladjustment, school failure, truancy, and learning disability as predictors for later delinquency. What early, nondelinquent emotional and behavioral traits have predictive value for antisocial behavior? Based on the Woodlawn longitudinal study of inner-city black children followed from first grade through adolescence, Ensminger et al. (1981) found that for males in the first grade, aggression predicted for later delinquency, and shyness against it. Similarly, West and Farrington (1973) found that boys rated as withdrawn rarely become delinquent, even when antisocial behavior occurred frequently in siblings and parents. West and Farrington (1973) found that by the age of 10 those who later became delinquent were less popular than their peers, had somewhat lower IQs, more clumsiness, and more evidence of psychopathology. It is also believed that the delinquent will experience lower self-esteem and early rejection by peers.

ENVIRONMENTAL FACTORS

As Rutter (1981) noted, with psychosocial disorders, multifactorial causation is the rule. There will be no single causative agent, and risk factors will often be nonspecific for the disorder under investigation. Background factors will not affect all youth the same way. Constitutional factors such as temperament and cognitive skills, acquired habit patterns such as coping strategies and defense mechanisms, and mediating factors such as the social support system all influence the outcome and thus preclude a single common pathway leading to antisocial behavior. In spite of the obstacles, how well can we predict those at risk for delinquent behavior?

West and Farrington (1973) derived five significant background factors for antisocial behavior: low family income, large family size, parental criminality, low intelligence, and poor parental behavior (defined as a global impression of family conflict and unsatisfactory parental attitudes and discipline). West and Farrington designated boys with three or more of these adversities as the most vulnerable group for future delinquent behavior. At follow-up, approximately 50 percent had indeed become juvenile delinquents and one-third had become recidivists. They established that these adversities had a cumulative effect, whereby the presence of any of the factors resulted in a one-third future delinquency rate, but if three particular factors were present (parental criminality, low family income and poor parental behavior) the rate of future delinquency was 71.4 percent. Robins (1966) found a cumulative effect for educational delay, truancy and low socioeconomic status in association with antisocial behavior before the age of 15. When none of these factors was present, only 3 percent became delinquent, in contrast to 36 percent if all three were present.

Rutter (1981) proposed that an additional critical psychosocial risk factor is the quality of school. Rutter demonstrated that characteristics of the school itself affected student adjustment and motivation. Further, within a school district with common socioeconomic factors, considerable differences could be noted in student behavior and achievement among the schools. The school characteristics predictive of good student behavior can be seen as a paradigm for a social learning theory approach to behavior. The factors include ample use of rewards and praise; pleasant and comfortable school environment; opportunities for children to assume responsibilities in school; emphasis on academic matters; accessible teachers to handle problems; well-organized teachers who are firm and consistent but focus their attention on good, rather than disruptive behavior; and a consensus among the school staff about academic matters and discipline.

Although the correlations between delinquency and preexisting risk factors seem compelling, a caveat is in order when one considers early labeling of high-risk children, implementation of an early prevention program, and public policy decisions. In the West and Farrington study (1973), sixty-three boys were placed in the most vulnerable group based on their aforementioned risk factors. Of the original sixty-three, thirty-one went on to future delinquent activity. Of the eighty-four boys who did become delinquents, fifty-three came from the nonvulnerable group. The 2×2 table below summarizes the findings:

	Future Delinquent	Not Future Delinquent	
Risk Factors Present	a 31	b 32	False Positives
Risk Factors Absent	c 53	d 295	

False Negatives

$$\text{Sensitivity} = \frac{a}{a+c} = \frac{31}{84} = .37$$

$$\text{Specificity} = \frac{d}{b+d} = \frac{295}{327} = .90$$

The high number of false negatives and low sensitivity manifest the imprecision of the associational links. Even the 90 percent specificity remains problematic because this is a disorder with a high prevalence rate, which will create a large, absolute number of false positives. Further, these false positives will be children incorrectly labeled and perhaps stigmatized as future delinquents. Each background factor embodies a complex set of variables and each factor interacts with others. In some, a host of family factors plays a critical role in the formation of a conduct disordered youth. In the Runaway Project in the Division of Child Psychiatry at Columbia University, 83 percent of the youth evaluated cited serious family problems as the primary reason for running away from home. Parental disharmony, divorce (Rutter 1981), parental sociopathy, alcohol and substance abuse (Robins 1966), rejection and hostility of parents toward the child (Rutter 1981), parental cruelty and abuse, and disinterest and inconsistency with respect to parenting and discipline (McCord and McCord 1969) all portend for a youth at high risk for subsequent delinquency and conduct disorder.

NATURE VERSUS NURTURE

Clearly we are dealing with a multifactorial etiology in which the environment interacts with genes and temperament. It is difficult to differentiate nongenetic and genetic factors. Is the strong association between antisocial fathers and their delinquent male offspring a congenital vulnerability or exposure to similar child-rearing practices and socioeconomic deprivations? Genetic factors seem to influence antisocial behavior, but not in an ineluctable fashion. An extra Y chromosome in a male affects height (taller), IQ (lower), and perhaps emotions (less stable), but it does not predict strongly for antisocial behavior (Shields 1979). In other words, the premature assumption that the extra Y chromosome in the male was a biological marker for sociopathy was based on limited and faulty data.

A sample from the Stockholm adoption study (Bohman et al. 1982; Cloninger et al. 1982), which included 862 men born out of wedlock from 1930 to 1949 and adopted at an early age by nonrelatives, showed the following results:

1. The adopted-away sons had 1.6 times the risk of alcohol abuse if either biological parent had abused alcohol.
2. The adopted-away sons had 1.9 times the risk of criminality if either biological parent had a history of criminality without the presence of alcohol abuse.
3. Low social status of the adoptive or biological parents alone did not increase the risk of antisocial behavior, but either did increase the risk of criminality in the adopted offspring of biological parents who were petty criminals.
4. Of the explainable variability of criminality unrelated to alcoholism, genes alone explain the majority of the variance.
5. The congenital antecedents of criminality were the same regardless of sex, but the genetic factor had to be more pronounced in women to have a manifest effect.
6. Postnatal antecedents to criminality were gender-specific, that is, prolonged institutional care and urban rearing increased the risk of criminality in females but not in males; and multiple temporary placements and low social status of the adoptive home increased the risk in men but not in women.

It is important to note that although the genetic factor is present and statistically significant in both male and female delinquents, the relative risk is not overwhelming. In the Stockholm adoption study, even though the genetic factors alone accounted for 60 percent of the explainable variability among criminal, alcoholic, and unaffected (nondelinquent and nonalcoholic) men, this represented only 14 percent of the total variability.

COEXISTENT DISORDERS

Given the dearth of successful treatment for antisocial behavior, one area of investigation has been the treatment of concomitant neuropsychiatric disorders with the hope that a causal link exists and that the treatment of the coexistent disorder will have impact upon the antisocial behavior. Problems have arisen in such investigations because studies have tended to look at highly skewed populations, those already delinquent and/or with signs of major psychopathology, and studies have tended to be retrospective, anecdotal, and without adequate controls for comparison. A further difficulty has been a lack of consensus about diagnostic criteria for neuropsychiatric disorders, although this has improved immensely in recent years.

Lewis and Balla (1976) concluded that 6.3 percent of court-referred delinquent children met their criteria for psychomotor epilepsy. Their criteria were clinical and did not require a positive EEG. A child required four out of six symptoms to receive a positive diagnosis. The symptoms included auras of fear, visceral symptoms, alterations of consciousness, automatic behaviors, visual, auditory, or tactile hallucinations, episodes of déjà vu, frequent visual distortions, and complex and sometimes aggressive behaviors of which the child had little or no memory. The prevalence rate of 6.3 percent of the studied children exceeds the prevalence in the general population by about twenty times. Lewis and Balla noted that fifteen out of the eighteen children with psychomotor epilepsy and delinquency had a history of perinatal problems and/or head injury. This suggests that the covariation between a seizure disorder and delinquency is mediated by the antecedent variable of head trauma.

Chadwick et al. (1981) established that head injury does increase the risk of psychopathology, including conduct disorder. Their design overcame flaws in earlier work reporting the link between brain injury and psychopathology. Their sample consisted of children with head injuries that resulted in posttraumatic amnesia for at least one week. The individually matched control group consisted of children with orthopedic injuries that involved no head injuries and no loss of consciousness. The results showed that the two groups had similar rates of psychiatric disorder prior to injury, but by four months later the head-injured group had almost four times the prevalence rate of psychopathology, and the strong differential persisted at the two-year follow-up. Since they knew that the head injuries were accidents outside the control of the child, that is, not an accident related to a preexisting disorder, such as attention deficit disorder with hyperactivity, they convincingly established that it was the head injury that increased the risk of later psychopathology.

Lewis et al. (1984) reported that among psychiatrically hospitalized adolescents who had been diagnosed as conduct-disordered, the most common discharge diagnosis was schizophrenia. Of the sample studied, those boys given a diagnosis of conduct disorder had also shown high rates of paranoid ideation (50 percent) and psychotic symptoms (55.9 percent). A caveat here would be the possibility of Berkson's bias, in which the selection of a hospitalized population could lead to a spurious association, for example, between conduct disorder and schizophrenic spectrum disorders. There does appear to be an increased risk of schizophrenia in adult life in those diagnosed as having a conduct disorder in adolescence. Robins (1966) found 7 percent of the youth originally referred to a child guidance clinic for disturbances of conduct to be schizophrenic by mid-life.

The relationship between attention deficit disorder with hyperactivity and conduct disorder would seem to be a plausible association, given the overlap of symptoms such as impulsivity, poor judgment, and school-related learning and behavior problems. Maletzky (1974) treated delinquent adolescents with a psychostimulant (d-amphetamine) and reported improvement in disturbances of conduct, which correlated with a reduction in attentional and hyperactive scores. However, longitudinal studies failed to show long-term benefits for children treated with a psychostimulant (Satterfield et al. 1982; Riddle and Rapoport 1976). In the retrospective study by Satterfield et al. (1982), boys between the ages of 6 and 12 were treated with psychostimulants and other standard treatments for attention deficit disorder with hyperactivity. At follow-up eight years later, the ADDH subjects were far more likely to have become delinquent. Comparing the cases and controls by socioeconomic status, the ADDH group in the upper class was five times, middle class four times, and lower class twenty-six times more likely to have committed a serious delinquent offense.

Finally, is there a causal link between depression and antisocial behavior? As Puig-Antich (1982) observed, it is only in the last decade that advances in our understanding and diagnosis of childhood depression allow for a differentiation between an affective disorder and conduct disorder. There does appear to be at least an association between disturbances of conduct and depression.

Chiles et al. (1980) interviewed 120 consecutive admissions (adolescent boys and girls ages 13 to 15) to a correctional facility. They found that 23 percent met Research Diagnostic Criteria for depression. This is a surprisingly high prevalence rate for depression, compared to a general population survey: Rutter and Madge (1976) found in their Isle of Wight Study a depression rate of approximately 1.5 percent among 14-year-old adolescents. The Chiles study gives a point prevalence, which does not permit insight into the causal relationship between depression and antisocial behavior. Second, it says nothing about the natural course of concomitant disorders. Further, 96 percent of the adolescents studied had spent approximately four weeks at a previous diagnostic center, deprived of their freedom prior to transfer to the correctional facility. To what extent did that previous detention influence the emergence of an affective disorder, and thereby become an antecedent psychosocial stressor?

In the Chiles study, the groups were divided as depressed and nondepressed based on a psychiatric interview. The self-rating scale, using the Beck Depression Inventory, failed to differentiate the two groups at day 1 when the psychiatric interview was conducted and at day 15. Also, the blind observer ratings of depression failed to differentiate the two groups at day 8, although there was a statistically significant difference at day 15.

One problem with this study of antisocial youth is the lack of equivalence between a diagnostic interview and self-report or other psychometric measures for a mood disturbance. The use of the Beck Depression Inventory has been found to yield a high rate of false positives for depression when given to a group of normal young teenagers; 33 percent scored in the moderate-to-severe depression range (Albert and Beck 1975). It is important when assessing antisocial youth who may be under great stress and reactively dysphoric to ascertain what one means by depression—a depressed mood, a cluster of depressed symptoms, or a depressive syndrome (Kandel and Davies 1982; Weissman and Klerman 1977; Cantwell and Carlson 1979). Shaffer and Caton (1984) found high rates of depressed mood in runaway youth, with 85 percent of the females and 56 percent of the males reporting sadness in the last year severe enough to impair functioning. It is puzzling that in the Chiles study, the Beck Depression Inventory revealed low mean scores in both the depressed and nondepressed groups, when one would predict relatively high rates for both, given the stressful predicament of the youngsters. It appears essential that the valid assessment of depression among antisocial youth must be based on clinical interviews using well-operationalized criteria. Further, assuming the lability of mood and high degree of reactivity to environmental stressors, repeat clinical interviews over relatively short time intervals become imperative.

Puig-Antich's (1982) pilot data show that over one-third (sixteen out of forty-three) of prepubertal boys who met criteria for a major depressive disorder also met criteria for a conduct disorder. Treatment of the depressed boys with tricyclic antidepressant medication and a psychosocial intervention resulted in remission of the conduct disorder, which did not return except with the reemergence of the depression. It must be borne in mind that Puig-Antich found this association unexpectedly in his child depression clinic, where the reason for referral had been depression, not conduct disorder.

Finally, as noted earlier, among the several symptom clusters identified by Achenbach through multivariate analysis, depression and disorders of conduct have combined to form discrete syndrome profiles. A similar finding was made using the Achenbach Child Behavior Checklist in a study investigating delinquent adolescents referred to a family court (Kaplan et al. 1984). The following is a list of the most significant interfactor correlations in the family court study.

Among the females:
1. Depressive-withdrawal factor correlated with the immature-hyperactive factor, $r = 0.64$, $p < .03$;
2. Depressive-withdrawal factor correlated with the delinquent factor, $r = 0.61$, $p < .040$;

3. Depressive-withdrawal factor correlated with the aggressive factor, $r = 0.65$, $p < .028$.

Among the males:

1. Uncommunicative factor correlated with the delinquent factor, $r = 0.70$, $p < .001$.

In this sample of consecutive delinquent referrals to a family court, 51.5 percent at the time of the initial assessment met research diagnostic criteria for either a major or minor depression based on the Kiddie-SADS structured interview.

The delinquent youth were followed over a two-month period of time through to adjudication. Not only did 71 percent of the depressed group show remission, but significant improvement in school behavior, attitudes, attendance, and performance was noted. Family relationships, especially with respect to mother, showed dramatic improvement in the depressed group who exhibited remission over the two-month study period. This reinforces the possibility that among a select group of delinquent adolescents, the state of dysphoria correlates positively with disturbances of conduct, and that a successful intervention with one disorder affects the other one. The possibility that a family court intervention could at least temporarily be therapeutic for both antisocial behavior and depression will be discussed below in the treatment section.

ASSESSMENT

Whether the clinician follows a highly structured format such as the Kiddie-SADS or a semistructured interview that taps the areas required by DSM-III, a true understanding of the conduct disorder cannot be obtained simply through a phenomenological or checklist approach.

One must understand the context of the antisocial behaviors. Is it situation-specific? Does it fit into a developmental paradigm? What are the familial, genetic, intrapsychic, and reactive factors that contribute to the cause of the antisocial behavior? Is there a coexistent neuropsychiatric or medical disorder that causes or exacerbates the conduct disorder? What role do sociocultural and peer factors play in the emergence of the antisocial behavior? The following is a list of suggestions for the evaluation of conduct disordered youth.

It is important to obtain information from several sources and to try not to rely solely on the youth and a parent informant. The youth may be too distrustful or manipulative to give reliable information. A parent may be ignorant about the situation of the youth or conspire with the youth in deceit. Objective information from school, recreational programs, and the police can be invaluable. I encountered an adolescent male who denied any significant antisocial behavior, and a separate interview with the mother fully corroborated the youth's position. However, while the interview with the mother was proceeding, the adolescent was observed to leave the office of a colleague. An expensive dictating machine was noted to be missing. The youth became indignant at the accusation, and the mother fully supported her son. Police and school records later substantiated the fact that this was a serious sociopathic adolescent. At times, the clinician certainly can appreciate the absurdity of asking a pathological liar whether, in fact, he is a pathological liar!

It is important to meet with the youth on more than one occasion before making a determination of conduct disorder. Too often, an initial interview highlights deviant socialization with insolence, noncompliance, negativism, hostility, or bravado. Certain delinquent behaviors may be denied by subjects in the first interview, only to be revealed in subsequent assessment periods when the youngster may be more trusting and comfortable with the clinician. In a study of delinquent youth referred to a family court (Kaplan et al. 1984), 60 percent of the delinquent youth who showed severe cruelty to animals and 40 percent who had set property damaging fires denied such activities in the first interview session, but did admit to them in subsequent meetings.

It is important to be sensitive to the context in which the antisocial behavior occurred. Even if it does not influence the clinician's judgment about the diagnosis, it may be important in terms of treatment and prognosis. Two brief clinical vignettes help make the point. Two boys, both age 14, were referred to a family court for juvenile delinquent petitions. Both met criteria for conduct disorder, one an aggressive type and the other nonaggressive. The first boy had caused serious head injuries to two classmates in separate incidents. In both assaults, the boy used a heavy metal object. Although teasing may have preceded both episodes, school officials were convinced that they were unprovoked and vicious. The boy was sullen, socially isolated, and highly negativistic. In a separate interview with the mother, she informed me that the boy had had brain surgery for a nonmalignant condition eight months ago, prior to both assaults. The neurosurgeon was confident that the assaultive behavior did not have an organic basis.

The other 14-year-old boy was arrested for a home burglary in which he had stolen valuable coins. The boy was secretive, depressed, and paranoid. He had a highly strained relationship with his father. In a separate interview with the father, it was learned that he had tolerated the boy stealing money from him for many years. The father himself was an ardent coin collector. Further, the boy, who had passed his other school subjects, had failed woodworking class. His father made his living as a carpenter. In both examples, the diagnosis by itself would not be meaningful in terms of understanding the psychodynamics and planning an appropriate treatment strategy.

As mentioned earlier, it is important to look for conduct disorders in the context of other neuropsychopathology to be certain that a treatable coexistent disorder such as depression may not be a causal factor in the antisocial behavior.

TREATMENT

Since antisocial behavior stems from a multiplicity of antecedent factors, it is clearly not a disorder that corresponds well to a singular treatment modality. Conduct disorder also has certain salient characteristics that are often antithetical to psychotherapeutic approaches. The youth often exhibit difficulty with compliance, control of aggressive and sexual impulses, and the formation of attachments. This triad of factors undermines most traditional psychotherapy approaches, which require the patient to come regularly and promptly to a clinic setting, obey basic rules of conduct, and allow the development of a therapeutic alliance. In the Runaway Project in the Division of Child Psychiatry at Columbia University, the team abandoned attempts to set up appointments with conduct-disordered adolescents in a child psychiatry clinic, but rather provided psychiatric services to them in the runaway shelters that housed the youngsters. The Runaway Project team has experienced frustration familiar to all clinicians who work with antisocial youth; hours of wasted time waiting for youth to keep an appointment; theft of property from the offices of clinicians; and problems with an alliance that can either be too quickly eroticized or intensified by the youth, or at the other end of the spectrum, can involve a youth who remains so highly resistant and distrustful that he refuses to share anything of himself or acknowledge any value in the therapist.

The clinician needs to have a broad repertoire of approaches, and will be most effective working on a team that shares expertise. In the initial assessment of antisocial youth in the Runaway Project, we have developed a comprehensive screening instrument that allows us to identify the areas of most concern to the youth. This can lead to the establishment of trust and cooperation when the adolescent sees the clinician's willingness to understand him, accept him on his own terms, and propose help that the youth sees as relevant. The initial work could involve provision of medical and dental services, escorting the youth to a store to replace broken eyeglasses, or locating decent clothing. As contact with the youth increases and his needs are better understood, the clinician may direct his attention to stabilization of the living situation, identification of recreational and vocational opportunities, and placement in an educational program that the youth finds nonthreatening.

The clinician must understand well the psychodynamics of the antisocial behavior. He must know the stressful life events; the family, peer, and school status of the youth; problems with the law; sociocultural factors; history of abuse and neglect; and not only the deficiencies and psychopathology in the youth, but also ego strengths and coping skills. When a family situation is viable, Patterson (1974, 1982) has shown the benefits of the behavioral approach, in which the parents are trained how to become effective in social reinforcement. However, with runaways and youth with serious conduct disorders, it is often impossible or inappropriate to attempt either to reconstitute the family or to work with the parents, whose very psychopathology precludes such a program. Yet, social reinforcement techniques need not be confined to a nuclear family. Group homes, residential facilities, and schools can effectively employ such methods. In his identification of healthy school environmental factors, Rutter (1981) suggested the vital need to revamp approaches to antisocial youth in school, where they quickly develop low self-esteem, discouragement, poor academic performance, and deviant behavior. This need was reemphasized in a demonstration by Becker et al. (1967) of the efficacy of regular positive reinforcement in the classroom, combined with nonreinforcement of negative behaviors.

Shaffer (1984) cautioned that psychotherapy has the potential for making delinquent children worse. He cites the following study of the Cambridge-Somerville intervention project of children at high risk for delinquency, in which McCord (1978) found that those youth who received the intervention did worse on most outcome measures. Further, one observation of the Runaway Project at Columbia University has been that conduct-disordered youth, who are among the most challenging to treat, too often are assigned to inexperienced therapists and caseworkers who quickly become overwhelmed with the intensity of feelings these youngsters stir up. In the Runaway Project, the team has repeatedly observed situations where an inexperienced primary therapist has responded to an adolescent's idealization by promising more than can be delivered, only to terminate the relationship because the youth eventually devalues the relationship or the therapist becomes burdened by the profound needs and deficits of the youth.

There is evidence to support the approach that emphasizes structure and firmly establishes contingencies. Berg et al. (1978) discovered that chronically troubled youths did better with a process called "judicial adjournment" than with assignment to a social caseworker for a psychotherapeutic intervention. Judicial adjournment simply meant that the judge deferred sentencing and had the youth make regular contact with him to monitor school attendance. The duration between judicial visits depended upon compliance with school attendance, and failure to attend meant that eventually the youth would be placed outside of the home.

A similar finding occurred in the family court study (Kaplan et al. 1984) mentioned earlier, in which the active participation by probation services and the judge stabilized the school and home situation in most instances. These authority figures imposed a nonambivalent, fair but firm structure on what had generally become a demoralizing and chaotic situation in which the youth appeared beyond the control of both parents and teachers.

PROGNOSIS

In the seminal work by Robins, *Deviant Children Grown Up* (1966), the true tragedy of antisocial behavior in youth becomes apparent. The antisocial youth cannot be seen as experiencing an adolescent rebellion that can easily be shed in early adult life. Rather, the picture is a bleak one. The youths referred to the child guidance clinic for antisocial behavior grew into adults with high rates of poverty and social alienation, frequent hospitalizations for psychiatric and medical reasons, and subjective feelings of poor health. For the antisocial boys, the risk of future arrests was 71 percent, with almost half having frequent arrests and almost half having been imprisoned. Half of the antisocial youth grew into problem drinkers. The antisocial youth were at high risk for failed relationships and marriages and for job instability. Only 15 percent of the highly antisocial youth group ever entered high school, and only one-third completed the eighth grade.

CONCLUSION

The diagnosis of conduct disorder, for all of its limitations such as its poor delimitation from other psychiatric disorders and the too heavy reliance on poorly defined discrete behaviors, does seem to be an important classification in child psychiatry. As a disorder concept, it does meet basic criteria for having psychosocial correlates, a characteristic clinical picture, familial factors, and prognostic value. Where the disorder concept seems most vulnerable is in the area of a predictable response to treatment. Despite the high prevalence rate, clinicians often shun these youth as too difficult and unrewarding to treat and beyond the pale of most psychotherapeutic approaches. I would argue that the discouragement about the value of the psychiatrist or other mental health professional is unwarranted. I have tried to show that a careful assessment, a high degree of flexibility with respect to the use of psychotherapeutic, behavioral, and psychopharmacological treatment strategies, and a willingness to work closely in concert with vocational, recreational, and educational authorities, social service agencies, court officials, and other health care providers give reason for some optimism. Finally, if this most costly of all childhood disorders, with its poor prognosis, is to be successfully treated, one must recognize the grossly inadequate funding for research and clinical services and the fact that the least experienced clinician is often expected to carry the brunt of the workload.

REFERENCES

Achenbach, T. M. (1978). The Child Behavior Profile, I. Boys Age 6 to 11. *J. Consult. Clin. Psychol.* 46:478–88.

———, and Edelbrock, C. (1983). *Manual for the Child Behavior Checklist and Revised Child Behavior Profile.* Burlington: Department of Psychiatry, University of Vermont.

Albert, N., and Beck, A. T. (1975). Incidents of depression in early adolescence: A preliminary study. *J. Youth Adolesc.* 4:301–8.

Becker, W. C., et al. (1967). The contingent use of teacher attention and praise in reducing classroom problems. *J. Special Ed.* 1:287–307.

Berg, I., et al. (1978). A rare controlled trial of two court procedures in truancy. *Brit. J. Criminology* 18:232–44.

Bohman, M., et al. (1982). Predisposition to petty criminality in Swedish adoptees, I. *Arch. Gen. Psychiat.* 39(11):1233–41.

Cantwell, D. P., and Carlson, G. (1979). Problems and prospects in the study of childhood depression. *J. Nerv. Mental Dis.* 167(9):522–29.

Chadwick, O., et al. (1981). A prospectus study of children with head injuries, II. *Psychol. Med.* 11:49–61.

Chiles, J. A., Miller, N. L., and Cox, D. B. (1980). Depression in an adolescent delinquent population. *Arch. Gen. Psychiat.* 37(10):1179–86.

Cloninger, C., et al. (1982). Predisposition to petty criminality in Swedish adoptees, II. *Arch. Gen. Psychiat.* 39(11):1242–47.

Ensminger, M. K., Kellam, S. G., and Rubin, B. R. (1981). School and family origins of delinquency. Paper presented at the Conference of Society for Life History Research, Monterey, Calif, November 25.

Johnson, A. M., and Szurek, S. A. (1952). The genesis of antisocial acting out in children and adults. *Psychoanalytic Quart.* 21:323–43.

Kandel, D. B. (1982). Epidemiological and psychosocial perspectives on adolescent drug use. *J. Amer. Acad. Child Psychiat.* 21(4):328–47.

Kandel, D. B., and Davies, M. (1982). Epidemiology of depressive mood in adolescence. *Arch. Gen. Psychiat.* 39:1205–12.

Kaplan, W. H., et al. (1984). The relationship between depression and antisocial behavior among a court referred adolescent population. Paper presented at American Academy of Child Psychiatry annual meeting in Toronto, Canada, October 10.

Kaplan, W. H., and Canino, I. A. (1985). New York State Runaway Project: First status report. Division of Child Psychiatry, New York State Psychiatric Institute, September 17.

Lewis, D. L., et al. (1980). Race bias in the diagnosis and disposition of violent adolescents. *Amer. J. Psychiat.* 137(10):1211–16.

———, et al. (1984). Conduct disorder and its synonyms: Diagnoses of dubious validity and youthfulness. *Amer. J. Psychiat.* 141:514–19.

———, and Balla, D. A. (1976). *Delinquency and Psychopathology.* New York: Grune and Stratton.

Loeber, R. (1982). The stability of antisocial and delinquent child behavior: A review. *Child Development* 53:1431–46.

McCord, J. (1978). A thirty-year follow-up of treatment effects. *Amer. J. Psychol.* 33:284–89.

McCord, W., and McCord, J. (1969). *Origins of Crime.* New York: Columbia University Press.

Maletzky, B. M. (1974). D-amphetamine and delinquency: Hyperkinesis persisting? *Dis. Nerv. System* 35:543–47.

Patterson, G. R. (1974). Interventions for boys with conduct problems: Multiple settings, treatments and criteria. *J. Consult. Clin. Psychol.* 4:471–81.

———. (1982). *Coercive Family Process.* Eugene, Oreg.: Castalia Publishing.

Puig-Antich, J. (1982). Major depression and conduct disorder in prepuberty. *J. Amer. Acad. Child Psychiat.* 21(2):118–28.

Quay, H. C. (1979). Classification. In H. C. Quay and J. D. Werry (Eds.). *Psychopathological Disorders of Childhood.* 2d Ed. New York: Wiley, pp. 1–42.

Riddle, K. P., and Rapoport, J. L. (1976). A two-year follow-up of 72 hyperactive boys. *J. Nerv. Ment. Dis.* 162:126–34.

Robins, L. N. (1966). *Deviant Children Grown Up.* Baltimore, Md.: Williams and Wilkins.

———. (1981). Epidemiological approaches to natural history research: Antisocial disorders in children. *J. Amer. Acad. Child Psychiat.* 20(3):566–80.

———, and Hill, S. Y. (1966). Assessing the contribution of family structure, class and peer groups to juvenile delinquency. *J. Criminal Law, Criminology Police Sci.* 57:325–34.

Rutter, M. (1970). A children's behavior questionnaire for completion by parents. In M. Rutter, J. Tizard, and K. Whitmore (Eds.). *Education, Health and Behavior.* London: Longman, pp. 412–32.

———. (1979). *Changing Youth in A Changing Society.* London: Nuffield Provincial Hospital Trust.

———. (1981). Epidemiological/longitudinal studies in causal research in child psychiatry. *J. Amer. Acad. Child Psychiat.* 20:513–44.

———, and Gould, M. (1985). Classification. In M. Rutter and L. Hersov (Eds.). *Child and Adolescent Psychiatry: Modern Approaches.* London: Blackwell Scientific Pubs.

———, and Madge, N. (1976). *Cycles of Disadvantage.* London: Heinemann.

———, Shaffer, D., and Shepherd, M. (1975). A multi-axial classification of child psychiatric disorders. World Health Organization.

Satterfield, J. H., Hoppe, C. M., and Schell, A. M. (1982). A prospective study of delinquency in 110 adolescent boys with attention deficit disorder and 88 normal boys. *Am. J. Psychiat.* 139:795–98.

Shaffer, D. (1984). Notes on psychotherapy research among children and adolescents. *J. Am. Acad. Child Psychiat.* 23(5):552–61.

———, and Caton, C. (1984). Runaway and homeless youth in New York City. A report to the Ittleson Foundation, New York.

Shields, J. (1979). Genetic and mental development. In M. Rutter (Ed.). *Scientific Foundations of Developmental Psychiatry.* London: Heinemann.

Weissman, M., and Klerman, G. (1977). Sex differences and the epidemiology of depression. *Arch. Gen. Psychiat.* 34:98–111.

West, D. J., and Farrington, D. P. (1973). *Who Becomes Delinquent?* London: Heinemann.

———. (1977). *The Delinquent Way of Life.* London: Heinemann.

Winokur, J. (1979). Unipolar depression. *Arch. Gen. Psychiat.* 36:47–56.

27

LATE ONSET PSYCHOSES OF CHILDHOOD AND ADOLESCENCE

William J. Chambers

INTRODUCTION

Since the time of Kraepelin, the concept of the illness schizophrenia has been associated with onset at puberty. However, both Kraepelin (1919) and Bleuler (1950) reported a small incidence of cases in which the illnesses of their patients, diagnosed as suffering from dementia praecox or schizophrenia, began in the preadolescent years. The concept that psychotic disorders can have their onset in childhood is generally agreed to have begun with deSanctis's description in 1906 of "dementia praecoxissima," a designation that now appears to include many cases of mental retardation and neurological dysfunction.

In the past, many investigators described psychotic disorders occurring in childhood and adolescence according to several traits: mode of onset, symptomatology, course, global severity of disorder, and a presumed encephalopathy. In contrast to these authors, the classification and diagnosis of psychotic conditions in childhood and adolescence took a great step forward with Kanner's (1943) delineation of the syndrome of infantile autism. He described this disorder as a syndrome defined by multiple parameters. Kanner's description of infantile autism was the first demonstration that the childhood psychoses, previously diagnosed as the unitary condition "childhood schizophrenia," may rather be composed of a heterogeneous group of disorders each with its own psychopathology and pathogenesis.

At the same time that Kanner was defining infantile autism, Lauretta Bender (1947, 1952, 1953, 1970) collected at Bellevue Hospital the largest sample of psychotic children in the country. She described a unitary condition "childhood schizophrenia" that, in contrast to the view of Kanner, included all of the psychotic disorders of childhood, including infantile autism. She characterized this disorder as a "diffuse encephalopathy" with pathology reflecting a failure of integration of functions within the central nervous system. The criteria require the diagnostician to infer the presence of an encephalopathy from diverse and nonspecific clinical phenomena. While these criteria have been criticized as too vaguely defined (Eisenberg 1957), Bender's major contribution in focusing attention on the neurological, intellectual, developmental, and prognostic aspects of the psychopathology of psychotic children is generally acknowledged.

The study of the childhood psychoses continued largely without focus through the 1940s and 1950s. A review by Eisenberg (1957) appears to have stimulated a good deal of empirical research into the psychotic disorders of childhood. In the decade of the 1960s, Kolvin conducted at Oxford and Newcastle what would prove to be the definitive study into the psychopathology of the childhood psychoses up to that time. Because of a catchmented system of public provision of health care services, Kolvin (1971a) and Kolvin et al. (1971b-f) were able to obtain an approximately epidemiological sample of children who experienced the onset of a psychotic disorder before the age of 15 years. Then, the age of onset of psychosis, an admittedly difficult determination to make (Annell 1963), was plotted against the incidence of psychosis at that age. Kolvin found, as did Makita (1966) and Vrono (1973/4) in similar studies in divergent cultures, a bimodal distribution. There is a group of children with the onset of psychosis at age 3 or below; a very small group with the onset of psychosis between the ages of 3 and 6; and a second large group with the onset above the age of 7. When the early (3 years and before) and late (above 7 years) onset psychotic groups are compared, Kolvin and subsequent researchers have found that the two groups form quite distinct disorders on a number of important parameters. The early onset group ("infantile psychosis") is composed of children with infantile autism and other related severe developmental disabilities. The late onset group is composed of children who manifest the productive symptoms generally associated with the severe psychotic disorders in adults: hallucinations, delusions, and formal thinking disorders. Furthermore, the late onset group does not have the kind of severe developmental disorders as are found in the infantile group; and, when members of the infantile group grow into middle childhood and adolescence, most investigators agree that they do not manifest the productive symptoms of adult psychoses: hallucinations and delusions. In instances in which autistic or autisticlike children are diagnosed on follow-up as schizophrenic, their symptoms generally resemble the simple schizophrenic form. When psychoses with more productive symptoms of schizophrenic psychoses develop in previously autistic individuals, this has not been shown to occur at a frequency greater than the approximately one percent of autistics expected to develop schizophrenia purely by chance. Thus, the conclusion is that the late onset psychoses are a disorder or a group of disorders distinct from the infantile psychoses.

DIAGNOSTIC APPROACH TO PSYCHOTIC CHILDREN AND ADOLESCENTS

The concept of the multiaxial diagnostic approach, reviewed elsewhere in this volume (Cantwell, Chapter 1) and which forms the foundation of DSM-III, was initially developed by a group of child psychiatrists (Rutter et al. 1973). The necessity for this change in the diagnostic nomenclature became clear when one attempted to classify in children and adolescents disorders of the severe sort, such as the psychotic disorders. A review of Bender's diagnostic scheme, for example, reveals that data from a number of diverse axes, (descriptive, psychopathological, vegetative, motor, perceptual, intellectual, emotional, and social) are all included in a single diagnostic entity. The possibility for a confounded and complex diagnostic system, which would be impossible to administer reliably, is virtually certain unless the different axes are considered separately. Thus, in this chapter, Axis I of DSM-III will be addressed separately in discussing the diagnostic assessment of children and adolescents with late onset psychoses.

DIAGNOSIS OF PSYCHOSIS

The literature on the historical progression of thinking on psychotic disorders proceeded largely with a presumption that the issue of what constituted a psychosis in children and adolescents was clear. A review of the diagnostic criteria of the nine cited studies of the childhood psychoses (Chambers 1986) reveals a wide diversity of criteria. As early as 1963, however, the Swedish child psychiatrist Annell reported her difficulty in deciding precisely what constitutes a psychotic disorder in childhood. The issue has not been the study of much systematic research to guide the clinician, however.

As early as 1911, Bleuler equated normal childhood fantasy play, with its momentary suspension of a reality sense, as a "normal" variant of the same autistic thinking that he considered to be pathognomonic of schizophrenia in adults. Similarly, Piaget (1951) reported that "a child replaces his own individual and egocentric point of view by the point of view of others and the reciprocity existing between them" and "[this process] begin[s] very early . . .[is] very slow . . . remain[s] uncompleted at the close of childhood and survive[s] throughout the intellectual development of the adult."

Thus, there is a question as to whether one is able to draw a clear line of distinction between phenomena in children that represent manifestations of psychotic processes and those that are merely variations of normal behavior with little negative psychopathological import (Chambers 1986). This hypothetical continuum is ordered along an axis of progressively severe distortions in the capacity to interpret reality correctly.

Systematic research in recent years has investigated whether such a continuum exists in schizophrenic disorders in adults. Strauss (1969) studied a group of adult schizophrenic subjects who were assessed using the PSE (Wing et al. 1974) as part of the International Pilot Study of Schizophrenia. The subjects were all diagnosed as schizophrenic by the participants in the pilot study. In this group of patients, the characteristics of the hallucinations and delusions were then studied, again using the rating scales of the PSE. Hallucinations can be rated in the PSE as either "definite," "?" or "absent." The "?" designation referred to experiences that were of an intermediate degree of severity. In the one hundred nineteen patients in the schizophrenic group, twelve patients diagnosed as schizophrenic had only "?" hallucinations and no definite hallucinations. Forty-one hallucinations were rated as "?" while thirty-eight were rated as "definite." Similarly, there were twenty-three patients reporting "?" delusions and not reporting any "definite" delusions. There were seventy-four "?" delusions reported as compared to ninety-one "definite" delusions. The conclusion is thus clear: In adults diagnosed as schizophrenic, the productive symptoms of the psychosis can be rated along a continuum according to the degree of disturbance of the function of reality testing.

Koehler (1979) has taken the Schneiderian first-rank symptoms (Schneider 1959) and organized them as points along three hypothetical continua. Koehler hypothesized that these represent degrees of severity of more basic deranged functions.

Their validity has not as of this time been demonstrated. Chapman and Chapman (1980) have, in contrast to Koehler, constructed a single scale of eleven points representing degrees of severity of an impairment of reality testing. This scale was derived from a clinical interview study of college students who were asked to describe certain experiences that they had. From these descriptions, the scale was constructed. The presumption of the existence of a continuum has been incorporated into the SADS (Schedule for Affective Disorders and Schizophrenia) developed for the NIMH Collaborative Study on the Psychobiology of Depression. Here, hallucinations and delusions are rated along continua of "severity," representing degrees of disturbance of the reality function.

CRITERIA FOR THE DIAGNOSIS OF SCHIZOPHRENIA

In DSM-III, the same diagnostic criteria apply to children as apply to adults. In order to be diagnosed as schizophrenic, a child must manifest at least one of the described productive symptoms; have had a deterioration from a previous level of psychosocial functioning; show signs of illness for at least six months, though not necessarily of psychosis; and show absence of the depressive or manic syndrome. Since the symptoms present during the six-month duration of disorder can be prodromal to psychotic symptoms, and since the productive symptoms can be "auditory hallucinations on several occasions with content of more than one or two words having no relation to depression or elation," a child could be diagnosed as schizophrenic with a six-month period of withdrawal and drop in school grades, and hear voices on several occasions in the period of several days and be diagnosed as schizophrenic. This appears to be too liberal a criterion, when one considers the fact that children may be more predisposed to hallucinate than adults. This is attested to by the fact that, in the sample of late onset psychoses diagnosed by Lutz and followed up by Eggers (1978) fifteen years later, 51 percent of the patients had good or excellent social functioning at follow-up, as opposed to the deteriorating course one would expect were the diagnosis schizophrenia.

DIAGNOSTIC EXAMINATION

The author's approach to the diagnosis of children and adolescents is guided by three general principles that, I believe, represent the most responsible and prudent reading of the current literature. These principles are:

1. The diagnosis of schizophrenia is to be avoided, except as a diagnosis of exclusion. All effort must be made to rule out the presence of treatable Axis I disorders other than schizophrenia, which may have psychotic forms. This is most important for two reasons: First, the possibility of developing tardive dyskinesia is great when the diagnosis of schizophrenia is made in childhood or adolescence, because the patient will likely be exposed to the neuroleptic drugs for decades. Thus, if a disorder can be identified in which the treatment can both alleviate the symptoms of psychosis and prevent the development of the social apathy, withdrawal, and oddity seen in chronic schizophrenics, without the use of neuroleptic drugs, a great service may be done for patients.

2. The precise psychopathological significance of psychotic and psychoticlike phenomena in childhood and adolescence is at the moment unclear, as has been briefly reviewed above.

3. Our knowledge of the pathogenesis of psychotic disorders is presently quite incomplete. We do not know, for instance, which of three possibilities account for the development of a psychotic form of a disorder in one individual and a nonpsychotic form in another. Here are the three possibilities: (1) the psychotic form of a disorder may represent a more severe form of the disorder than the nonpsychotic form; (2) the psychotic form represents a completely different disorder, with a different and distinct pathophysiology from the nonpsychotic form of what is at this stage of our knowledge considered the same disorder; (3) the psychotic form may represent the end result of an interaction between the pathophysiology and pathogenesis of the nonpsychotic disorder and a second separate factor, possibly in the neurological or cognitive sphere. It is thus recommended that all three be considered in performing the diagnostic evaluation. Practically, this means that the neurological and cognitive spheres especially should be investigated fully in all patients.

HOSPITALIZATION DECISION

The decision as to whether to hospitalize children and adolescents with psychotic disorders is made on consideration of two factors: the safety of the child, either because of dangers he or she may pose to him or herself, or the incapacity of the family structure to provide the necessary supports; or the need to clarify the diagnosis in a controlled environment. Children appear to be far more vulnerable than are adults to external influences in the genesis and maintenance of psychiatric disorder. These influences can be either psychosocial or biological, including illicit drugs. In order to clarify a diagnosis, it may be necessary to place the child in a controlled environment.

SEMISTRUCTURED DIAGNOSTIC INTERVIEW

The Kiddie-SADS approach to the diagnosis of psychotic disorders in children and adolescents parallels our diagnostic approach to the nonpsychotic disorders. In this, we use a semistructured diagnostic interview with the parents and with the child or adolescent patient, and we incorporate information from any other relevant source or informant (school teacher, pediatrician, relatives, etc.). We have developed the Kiddie-SADS for this purpose. The principles by which the author believes the diagnostician must be guided in the diagnostic assessment of psychotic disorders are as follows:

1. Preadolescent children are likely, as the preceding review has suggested, to be more susceptible to hallucinate than are adolescents or adults. We have documented the reporting of an unusually high incidence of phenomenologically typical hallucinations in a high proportion of children with otherwise typical affective disorders (Chambers et al. 1982).

2. If it is true that depressed and manic disorders can manifest hallucinations and delusions then other typical disorders, when occurring in children, may similarly manifest hallucinations and/or delusions.

3. Children will not report hallucinations and delusions spontaneously in a high proportion of cases. Parents were shown to be unaware of their children's hallucinations in two-thirds of the cases in our study (Chambers et al. 1982). These symptoms must be inquired for in a systematic way in all child and adolescent patients.

4. The precise demarcation between pathological symptoms of psychosis, particularly hallucinations and delusions in children and adolescents, and normal phenomena involving a suspension of consensual reality is not clear. Rather, psychotic children and adolescents, as is true for adults as well, are likely to report psychotic phenomena along a continuum defined by the relative deficit in the capacity to interpret reality correctly. How one defines with validity that a condition is psychotic remains problematic. The diagnostician must thus be cautious in declaring a condition to be a psychotic one and in drawing therapeutic or prognostic implications from this. The research that would allow one to do this has not yet been performed.

It has not been demonstrated that psychotic symptoms portend an ominous prognosis when they occur in childhood and adolescent disorders (Chambers 1986).

Based on the above considerations, the author recommends that symptoms of psychotic disorders and of certain similar phenomena (imaginary companions, illusions, etc.) should be inquired of in all children and adolescents being evaluated; and that data relevant to the diagnosis of all possible Axis I psychiatric disorders must be inquired of in every child being evaluated, including those who manifest psychotic symtomatology or appear quite psychotic. Evaluators must be sure to inquire of hallucinations and delusional beliefs in children and adolescents even when they are not reported spontaneously and consider the remainder of Axis I symptomatology once hallucinations and delusional beliefs are reported. Without attention to these areas, nonschizophrenic children and adolescents may be diagnosed as schizophrenic, solely on the basis of hallucinations and delusions, and the presence of treatable Axis I disorders may be overlooked. Similarly, if hallucinations, delusions, and certain hallucination-like phenomena are not inquired of in every child being evaluated, then important diagnostic information may be lost. While it may not be clear what the diagnostic significance of these data may be, they may provide important clues for the diagnostic evaluation, as will be discussed later.

THE SEMISTRUCTURED INTERVIEW

The use of the semistructured interview in child psychiatric diagnosis is being presented elsewhere in this volume (see Chapters 2 and 3). The Kiddie-SADS was developed specifically for use in studies of children and adolescents with affective and psychotic disorders. The procedures for the conduct of the semistructured interview are as follows: First, all available information from schools, counselors, other physicians, and so on, is reviewed before the start of the formal interview. It is very useful at the same time to have the parents and teachers complete a standardized general questionnaire for symptomatology, such as the Achenbach Child Behavior Checklist (Achenbach 1982). This affords the examiner a broad overview of the child's symptomatology before he embarks on a focused investigation of symptomatology. It provides a perspective to guard against the examiner's taking too narrow a focus and overlooking important information. Knowledge of the broad scope of symptomatology and behavior, which might otherwise not be available until after the conclusion of the formal interview, can be a valuable guide in the interview with the parents and child.

COURSE OF DISORDER

Before the start of the semistructured interview, an unstructured interview is performed. This has been adapted for the Kiddie-SADS from the interview developed by Rutter and Graham (Graham and Rutter 1968; Rutter and Graham 1968).

We first perform an unstructured interview with the parents, inquiring as to the range of symptomatology and symptomatic behaviors of which they are aware, and of the time course and evolution of these in the current episode of the disorder. This is a crucial segment of the diagnostic assessment, as it is used to ascertain the relevant aspects of the course of the disorder. It is left to the clinical skill of the interviewer to elicit the relevant data on the evolution of symptomatology. Initially, this is performed in an interview with the parents who are generally more aware than the patient. This is especially true of younger children, because of their immaturity and any interference of the disorder itself on recall.

At the conclusion of the unstructured interview with the parent, the interviewer should have a reasonably clear picture of the following: the major symptoms of the current or index episode of disorder; the dated time of onset of the current episode of disorder; the mode of onset of the current episode of disorder, whether acute, insidious, or a combination of these; and the course of major symptomatology manifested by a patient as observed by the parent over the course of the child's lifetime. This latter factor may involve a discrete episode of a specific disorder, as a depressive or separation-anxious disorder; a disorder that continuously evolved over a long time period, possibly the entire lifetime of the child, as in an attention deficit disorder; or a succession of disorders that evolve into each other, such as a phobic or separation-anxious disorder that evolves into a depressive disorder, an attention deficit disorder that evolves into an affective disorder, or a cyclical manic-depressive illness in which different affective states alternate with each other.

The semistructured interview with the parent follows the unstructured interview. In this, the broad range of child and adolescent psychiatric symptomatology is investigated in a systematic manner. Following the semistructured interview with the parent, the interviewer conducts an unstructured interview with the child. By this time, the basic developmental course of the present psychiatric disorder should be quite clear. The formulation as to the course of the disorder, which was made after the unstructured parent interview, may be modified on the basis of subsequent information obtained in the parent semistructured interview or the child unstructured interview. By this time, the the course of the disorder should be clear.

The validity the examiner can attribute to both the unstructured and semistructured child interviews will depend to a large extent on the age of the patient. In general, one tends to place greater weight on the reports of adolescents and intelligent children than on those of prepubertal children and those of low intelligence. In the assessment of children and adolescents with psychotic symptomatology or disorders, one must obviously be more cautious because of the impact of the psychosis on the interview.

Child psychiatric disorders tend to follow a rather characteristic course for that disorder or class of disorders. Affective and emotional disorders can occur in the same individuals, and conduct disorder is often preceded by an attention deficit disorder. However, psychotic disorders often do not follow a simple or characteristic course, and it is necessary to plot the course of the illness meticulously.

At times when the course of a disorder is complex, one can use a time plot chart to track fluctuating symptomatology. The time periods recorded on the horizontal axis of the chart are those derived from the unstructured interview(s). The symptoms listed along the vertical axis are those that either were derived from the unstructured interview or are included in the diagnostic criteria for the disorders being considered in the differential diagnosis. Since the diagnostic process typically follows a decision tree approach, the symptoms included along the vertical axis can be modified as the diagnostic interviews proceed.

The semistructured interview with the child and parent focuses on the present episode of the disorder. In instances where there has been a fluctuating course of the disorder, the current episode must be chosen carefully. Prior periods of disorder can be separately assessed using the Lifetime version of the Kiddie-SADS (Kiddie-SADS-L).

SEMISTRUCTURED INTERVIEWS

The semistructured interview section of the Kiddie-SADS is organized according to the major groups of child psychiatric disorders. A general description of the instrument and the interviewing procedure for affective disorders is published elsewhere (Puig-Antich et al. 1983; Chambers et al. 1985). In this section, I will focus on the assessment procedures for psychotic symptomatology.

The universe of symptoms and behaviors and their characteristics, which are obligatory inquiries in the Kiddie-SADS and which are described in detail in the interview protocol, is as follows:

1. Hallucinations
   a. Nonverbal (noises).
   b. Name being called.
   c. Command.
   d. Commentary: Patients hear a voice that comments on his or her actions, thoughts, or feelings as they occur.
   e. Conversing: The patient hears two or more voices carrying on a conversation. This may also be a commentary hallucination if the conversation is about the child.
   f. Persecution: These voices criticize, threaten, or insult the child.
   g. Religious: The patient hallucinates voices he or she believes to be those of religious figures. This includes the Devil.
   h. Thoughts aloud: The patient hears his or her own thoughts spoken aloud as they are thought. The patient believes that a person standing next to the patient could actually hear the patient's thoughts being spoken.
   i. Other verbal hallucinations spoken directly to the patient: This category includes any hallucinated speech more complex than one or two words, which does not fit into the categories just enumerated.
   j. Visual hallucinations.

k. Tactile or somatic hallucinations: This category involves hallucinations either of the skin being stimulated by touch, or of unusual sensations within the patient's own body.

l. Olfactory hallucinations.

2. Other perceptual phenomena frequently confused with hallucinations

a. Hypnagogic or hypnopompic hallucinations: True hallucinations occurring only when the patient is either falling asleep or waking, not merely lying in the dark before falling asleep. This is at times a difficult distinction to make on a number of counts. First, children have a difficult time distinguishing when they are falling asleep. Secondly, children seem to hallucinate more frequently when alone in bed with the lights out; this is likely due either to the sensory deprivation or to the fact of being alone and lonely. The distinction is an important one, as hypnagogic and hypnopompic hallucinations have no psychopathological importance.

b. Illusions: False perceptions stimulated by a real perception that is momentarily transformed. Illusions frequently occur due either to inattention or to reduced orienting stimuli and are immediately corrected when attention is focused on the external sensory stimulus.

c. Eidetic imagery: Some children have the ability to voluntarily produce vivid and almost perfect visual images that are never confused with reality.

d. Imaginary companions: Normal children frequently describe a clear image of another child or living creature in external objective space, which they treat as real, with complex interactions. Most of the time, the children will acknowledge that this is only in their imaginations, but at times they will insist on the reality of the imaginary companion. The psychopathological importance of this insistance is not known.

e. Elaborated fantasies: These are experiences typical of normal childhood fantasy play, which most children readily admit are fantasies, but which a few children reiterate with apparent belief. They are distinguished from delusions by their generally benign content, the lack of conviction in their reality, and their generally egosyntonic nature.

3. Delusions

a. Reference: Delusional beliefs that seemingly insignificant remarks, objects, or events refer to the child himself.

b. Control or influence: The belief or experience that the patient's feelings, impulses, thoughts, or actions are not his own and are imposed on him by some external force. This does not include the mere conviction that he is acting as an agent of God, or has had a curse placed on him. The essential aspect is that the child has the experience that his will, thoughts, or feelings are under the control of an external force.

c. Mind being read: The conviction that other people can know the patient's thoughts without their being spoken.

d. Thought broadcasting: Belief or experience that the patient's thoughts are broadcast from his head into the external world so that others can hear them. This can be a delusion or the delusional elaboration of an hallucination of thoughts aloud.

    e. Thought insertion: The belief or experience that thoughts that were not his own are inserted into his mind by external sources.

    f. Thought withdrawal: The belief that thoughts have been removed from his head, reducing the number of his thoughts.

    g. Persecution: The delusional belief that the patient or people close to him have been attacked, harassed, cheated, persecuted or conspired against.

    h. Guilt or sin: The delusional belief that the patient has done something terrible or is responsible for some event or condition that has had terrible consequences.

    i. Grandiose delusions.

    j. Somatic delusions.

    k. Nihilism.

4. Formal thinking disorder
    a. Loosening of associations.
    b. Illogical thinking.
    c. Poverty of content.
    d. Neologisms.
    e. Flight of ideas.

5. Affective and behavioral disturbance: These parts of the behavior rating section relate to psychotic conditions and are rated from observed behavior during the interview:
    a. Inappropriate affect.
    b. Blunted affect.
    c. Catatonic motor behavior.
    d. Bizarre behavior.

These symptoms represent the most common and relevant productive symptoms of psychotic disorders found in adults, which have been reported in the late onset group of psychotic disorders in the studies reviewed above. In our study of prepubertal depressive disorder (Chambers et al. 1982), the majority of parents were unaware that their children experienced hallucinations and delusions; direct questioning of the children is essential. Our experience is that one must meticulously inquire of each specific symptom because children, particularly prepubertal children, do not spontaneously report such experiences. Children can be quite suggestible, and it requires considerable clinical skill to ensure that the child is reporting his experiences as they occurred.

Several characteristics of psychotic symptoms, particularly hallucinations and delusions, are important to assess. These are included in the Kiddie-SADS protocol and are:

    a. Severity: The severity rating of the Kiddie-SADS is the same scale as is used in the adult SADS (Endicott and Spitzer 1978). It is a semiquantitative continuous scale of six defined points of increasing severity, representing two parameters on a single scale: the degree of conviction in the verity of the abnormal experience; and the degree to which this symptom interferes with the patient's life or psychosocial adaptation.

b. Thematic consistency with prevailing mood disorder: The concept has evolved over the past decade that what had been thought to represent in adults symptoms that were pathognomonic of schizophrenia could be found in otherwise typical affective disorders. The courses and responses to treatment were more similar to those of affective disorders than of schizophrenia. Thus, the Research Diagnostic Criteria for psychiatric disorders (Spitzer et al. 1978) specify that thematic consistency with a prevailing mood disorder of hallucinations and delusions determines whether the diagnosis is of pure affective disorder or of schizoaffective disorder. The presumption was that these "pathognomonic" symptoms indicate a schizophrenic process with a more ominous prognosis. The more modern view (Pope and Lipinski 1978), reflected in DSM-III, is that thematic consistency with mood disorder is less important than temporal consistency. However, the relationship of the childhood and adolescent affective disorders to those occurring in adults is still being investigated. It might also be found that thematically inconsistent psychotic symptoms may have psychopathological importance.

c. Temporal consistency with prevailing mood disorder: The correlation of a period of hallucinations and delusions with the time period of an episode of affective disorder is now believed to have greater psychopathological import than does the thematic consistency with the prevailing mood disorder. This conclusion has been incorporated into DSM-III; in instances where psychotic symptoms occur only within the period of an episode of affective disorder, the diagnosis is of affective disorder, psychotic type, whatever the content of the symptoms may be. In instances in which the psychotic symptoms occur outside the time period of an affective disorder, the diagnosis of schizoaffective disorder is made. Thus, this is a crucially important diagnostic point. The problem, obviously, is to make a valid assessment of the times at which both an affective disorder and a period of hallucinations and delusions may have begun. The sources of inaccuracy are multiple and problematic, but the attempt at assessment should be made.

d. Frequency of hallucinations: The frequency with which certain hallucinations occur is presumed to have psychopathological import. One is able to diagnose schizophrenia, in addition to the presence of social dysfunction and a duration criterion, by the presence of auditory hallucinations heard throughout the day, a frequency criterion. Presumably, a voice heard only once does not qualify for this diagnosis.

e. Location of experienced origin of hallucinated voices: The concept of pseudohallucinations is one that has had a long history in psychopathological research. For Bleuler, a pseudohallucination was one in which the conviction in its reality was not absolute, that is, the "severity" rating was in the intermediate range. However, some modern researchers such as Wing (Wing et al. 1974) regard a pseudohallucination as one that has its experienced origin within the subject's head. Whichever of these concepts one uses, the belief is that pseudohallucinations represent symptoms of less psychopathological import than do "true" hallucinations. This conclusion has not been established by systematic research in adults. In children, in whom the diagnosis of psychosis can be so problematic, this is even less certain. It is thus important that the parameter be assessed and recorded systematically.

f. Degree of familial and subcultural fostering of the experience: In addition to their physical and cognitive immaturity, children are also immature in their psychosocial functioning. By virtue of the prolonged period before children in western cultures are expected to assume adult responsibilities, they are quite dependent on the adults in their families and cultural group for emotional and physical sustenance. As a result, the extent to which a child's caretaking environment fosters the development or maintenance of psychotic and psychoticlike phenomena must be assessed. The situations that could fall into this category are a folie à deux with a psychotic parent, or the religious encouragement of certain hallucinatory experiences. This is recorded on Axis IV.

DIAGNOSTIC ASSESSMENT: THE CLINICAL INTERVIEW

The semistructured interview with the parent and child follows the format outlined above for the Kiddie-SADS interview in general. Both interviews follow an identical format and generally represent a relatively straightforward collection of information. The semistructured interview with the child requires special considerations and greater care and precision than does the inquiry for other symptoms in the Kiddie-SADS. Most symptoms of child psychiatric disorder have behavioral referents that indicate to the parent the presence of the symptom, or they are such that children will talk with their parents about them. Such is evidently not the case with the majority of children manifesting symptoms of psychosis. This puts a greater burden on the interview with the child. Secondly, as the interview with the child is so important for the diagnosis of psychotic disorders, the child's language abilities become increasingly important. In Kolvin et al. (1971c) series of children and adolescents with late onset psychoses, 15 percent of the children manifested unequivocal evidence of structural brain dysfunction, and another 15 percent showed less clear evidence of neurological dysfunction. This is a higher proportion than would be found in other psychiatric disorders. Mean tested IQ was 85.9. While the presence of language disorder was not assessed, it is likely that some of the group had a language disorder that would have made diagnostic interview by semistructured interview difficult. Furthermore, preadolescent children's language development is immature; and in this group the diagnostic interview for psychotic symptoms is more difficult and requires special care. Thirdly, the line between pathological and normal phenomena is probably less clear for psychotic symptoms than for symptoms of other disorders. The clinician must thus exercise greater care in making this assessment.

The interviewing clinician should first relieve any discomfort that the child might feel, explaining that many children have experiences that frighten them and that they do not understand. He should then inquire as to the presence of any frightening or unusual experiences the child may have had. The examiner must be certain not to introduce suggestion to the child as to the symptoms in which he is interested. It is thus imperative to begin with general and broad questions as to "unusual experiences," "strange things," and so on, before going on to inquire more specifically for individual symptoms. Children appear to hear voices more frequently when they are alone. They appear to be able to understand and respond to the idea of frightening experiences in the context of being alone, when they often feel frightened.

At the completion of the interview, the examiner must decide whether certain phenomena reported by the patient qualify as positive symptoms of psychosis. In our study of prepubertal depressive disorder, the severity ratings of hallucinations were spread over the entire range of degree of conviction in the reality of the experience. We have chosen the minimal levels in the Kiddie-SADS protocol severity scales for positive ratings, as follows: For hallucinations, this is the level at which hallucinations are definitely present, but the patient is usually aware that they are in his imagination and is able to ignore them. For delusions, this is at the level at which the patient generally has conviction in the false belief. The validity of these as relevant cutoff points for children and adolescents has not been established, but it conforms to general clinical practice.

After the interview is completed, the symptoms are applied to the diagnostic algorithm and a diagnosis is made.

AXES II, III, IV, V

The rigorous assessment of the Axes II to V is essential for a thorough diagnosis. Axis II (Specific Developmental Disorders) records disorders of neurocognitive development. The study of Kolvin et al. (1971e) reported some signs of cerebral dysfunction in 31 percent of the children in their late onset psychosis (LOP) sample, with signs of severe dysfunction in 15 percent. They also found IQ under 90 in 43 percent of the LOP children tested (Kolvin et al. 1971f). Since the principal psychopathological symptoms involve the perceptual and cognitive spheres of function, the precise assessment of cognition and its component functions is essential.

Axis III records neurological and other medical disorders. The Kolvin data on cerebral dysfunction previously discussed relates here as well. Research into late onset childhood psychoses is at a rudimentary level compared with research into adult psychoses. Nevertheless, recent findings of structural brain disease in adult schizophrenics mandate the assessment of the structural aspects of the brain. Similarly, Kolvin et al. (1971e) found abnormal EEGs in one-third of LOP cases, with a preponderance of temporal lobe epilepsy. Thus, electroencephalography with deep electrodes and activation procedures must be performed on all cases of LOP.

Axis IV records the severity of psychosocial stressors related to the onset of the disorder. There is a literature (Wilking and Paoli 1966; Eisenberg 1962) reporting the onset of hallucinations in children who are undergoing acute stress. The hallucinations resolve when the children are removed from the stressful environment. Both the severity and the type of psychosocial stressor being experienced by the children must thus be assessed and relieved wherever possible.

Axis V records the highest level of adaptive functioning in the past year. The data of Eggers (1978) reveal good or better psychosocial functioning in over 50 percent of his sample of LOP. Since in adults the level of premorbid social functioning appears to predict social functioning on follow-up, this is probably an important predictor variable for outcome.

The descriptive case report that follows is of a boy who presented with what was initially diagnosed as an acute schizophrenic psychosis. On further examination, the Axis I diagnosis was changed to a nonpsychotic one and was treated successfully without the use of neuroleptic drugs.

CASE VIGNETTE

M. was a 7-year-old righthanded adopted black boy admitted to the hospital for a multitude of behavioral difficulties with which his foster parents were unable to cope. These included violently assaulting familiar people and strangers without provocation; attempting to stab his foster mother and foster sister with knives and forks; destroying property in the home without provocation; setting many dangerous fires in the home; running away, either from school, the home, or the playground, at virtually any time he was left unattended, and at times taking a several hour subway trip to another borough, necessitating calls to the police; suicidal and dangerous behavior: one month before admission, M. stood at a window as if to jump, saying that he wanted to fly and also that he knew he would die, and "that's what I want," and he repeatedly ran recklessly into traffic, saying that "I want a car to flatten me"; and being refractory to discipline in all areas of his life.

When asked for his reasons for such behavior, M. said on one occasion that "James made me do it," explaining that James is "a person in my head who told me to do it." On other occasions he told his foster parents that a voice inside his head told him to run away and to hit people. For the two years preceding admission the foster parents describe M. as sitting alone for periods of up to an hour talking to himself.

M. was born out of wedlock to a 13-year-old girl described as having severe mental illness of unknown type, which necessitated placement at an early age. She was in placement at the time of his birth. The father is unknown. M. was hospitalized for three months following his birth because of

an operation to relieve an intestinal obstruction. He was taken into his current foster home at three months and has been raised as if this were his
permanent home. The foster parents were in the middle of adoption proceedings at the time of admission.

The foster parents report that M.'s developmental milestones involving
sitting, eating, language and toilet training were within normal limits. Phi-
mosis was present and surgery was not contemplated. M. has been hyperactive since his earliest days. He walked unsupported at one year, at 18
months he started to run, and "he's been running ever since." He has a
very short attention span, typically jumping from one activity to another,
and will watch television or play for only from five to fifteen minutes before
getting up. At 14 months M. became terrified of triangles. When he saw a
triangle or when the Sesame Street teacher would show this shape he "went
into a fit." At no time in his life did M. appear autistic or withdrawn, and
he never appeared sad or depressed.

At the time of admission to the hospital, two aspects of M.'s behavior
were striking. First was his hyperactivity. He was at times constantly in
motion, rarely staying at one activity for longer than a few minutes. He
provoked and fought with other children, and frequently ran. He derived a
great deal of pleasure from flushing the toilet so that it overflowed onto the
floor. The second striking aspect of his behavior was his intense fantasy life,
which preoccupied him for large portions of the day, with resultant avoidance of other social activities. He reported elaborately constructed imaginary
companions to whom he sometimes talked for hours at a time, remaining
stationary for one of the few times on the unit. At these times he was frequently not able to admit that these companions were products of his imagination. At such times he also reported auditory hallucinations, which he
described as coming from the air and which were unrelated to the imaginary
companions. During these times he appeared absorbed in this activity and
was not at all responsive to the events going on around him. However,
when directly questioned as to what he was doing, he replied "talking to
my friends," would talk freely to the staff, then return to his talking when
left alone. At these times he was quiet, not at all fidgety, and totally involved in this activity, in striking contrast to the other times, when he was
inattentive, impulsive, excitable, and overactive. Such "fantasy" activity had
become increasingly prominent in the year preceding admission and became
more so in the first three weeks of hospitalization.

When M's foster mother visited, he would speak with her for a very brief
period, eating whatever she had brought him; as soon as the food was finished, he would stand and say "Mommy, I love you and Daddy very much.
What I'm telling you goes for both of you. I can't be bothered to tell Daddy
too." He would run off, not to return. One day, the staff prevented his
leaving. He then said to his mother "Did you hear that?" (she heard nothing). He later explained that he had heard a voice coming from another
room that was not that of an imaginary companion, saying: "M., if you have
a toy and the man lets you have it, will you let me hold it?" He said he did
not recognize this voice. As his departure from the foster mother continued

to be blocked, M. became progressively more agitated, circling around her, rolling on a sofa, spilling out soda and sucking it up through a straw until after forty minutes he asked to go to his rest period.

In his therapy sessions M. showed none of the above behavior. He was eager and warmly related. There were no persistent or intensively experienced emotional themes. Rather, he preferred painting with watercolors, dashing off five in forty-five minutes, then pouring water all over them, gleefully likening this to his flooding the bathrooms at home.

M. told freely of his imaginary companions: Badman was with him all the time preceding entry into the hospital, save at night, when he left to sleep with Badlady. Badman lived in the back of M.'s head and told him to "jump out the window," which scared M. and to "follow that boy," a command he is more comfortable with; this command caused his running away. Badman went away when M. entered the hospital, to be replaced by NeeNee, a small man living outside his head. M. told of auditory hallucinations (in clear consciousness) of God telling him to "do good things" such as "don't hit somebody." He heard "rattles like a skeleton" under his bed; he once saw the skeleton and hit it and it did not bother him any more. M.'s affect was at times flat while he was with his mother (except when discussing food) and during his periods of talking with his "friends." At all other times on the unit, he appeared cheerful and well-related and showed a range of affect—though sadness was notably absent. At times his associations became loose and tangential, though these occurrences were infrequent. M. denied any paranoid ideas, ideas of reference, grandeur, nihilism, thought interference, or other possibly delusional ideas. There was no evidence of any depressive, manic, or hypomanic symptomatology, nor of neurotic symptoms involving separation anxiety, phobias, depersonalization, derealization or obsessive-compulsive phenomena. M. was oriented in three spheres, and was right-dominant for hand, foot, and eye. EEG was diffusely and mildly abnormal for his age. All laboratory tests were within normal limits. Neurological examination revealed only moderately poor dysdiadochokinesis bilaterally and mild overflow from the left to the right hand. WISC-R testing revealed a verbal score of 118, a performance score of 91, and a full scale score of 105.

Despite M.'s psychotic symptomatology, the unit staff was not convinced of a diagnosis of schizophrenia: M. was generally well related and cheerful, with only brief periods of schizoid withdrawal. Furthermore, his thinking disorder was not particularly prominent, and there was no interference by cognitive deficits or symptomatology in his schoolwork; in a classroom of six children he functioned normally and in keeping with his IQ. Furthermore, the childhood history had been consistent with a DSM-III diagnosis of severe attention deficit disorder; when he was five, this was complicated but not replaced by symptoms of a schizophreniform psychosis, which further developed within the confines of the hospital. Because of these considerations and a reluctance to begin a child on neuroleptic drugs, M. was given increasing doses of dextroamphetamine, with careful monitoring for signs of exacerbation of symptoms. With each increase in dose, M. became progressively less symptomatic in all his presenting symptoms and aberrant ward behaviors. The imaginary companion went away. Home passes, during which he received 25 mg of dextroamphetamine at breakfast and 15 mg at lunch, went without incident. On one occasion when he did not receive the medication, he did poorly, with the prior symptoms returning. On two occasions when the medication was discontinued for side-effects, he reported that "NeeNee came back" only to disappear when the medication was restarted. At the time of last contact three years later, Mrs. T. reported that M. was doing very well in a regular school, taking the dextroamphetamine, and having no behavior problems. The T.'s had in the interim legally adopted M.

SUMMARY

Many of the unknown factors in the diagnosis of psychotic children and adolescents are similar to issues that are unresolved in the study of the adult psychoses. These are: (1) the relationship of the productive symptoms of psychosis (hallucinations, delusions) to the negative symptoms (apathy, dullness) that impact so heavily on prognosis; (2) the relationship of the group of psychotic affective disorders to the group of "pure" schizophrenias; (3) the heterogeneity of the schizophrenic disorders, either in terms of physiological and psychopathological factors, or in a complex interaction of numerous pathogenic factors; (4) the factors that promote or protect against the development of schizophrenic psychoses and the progression to defect states, both those that occur naturally and those that relate to treatment.

The study of psychotic disorders in children and adolescents, especially in preadolescent children, involves many problems, among them the following: (1) psychoses occurring in childhood are quite rare, so it takes a long time to assemble suitable sized research samples. The result is that the available data are rudimentary relative to that available for adults; (2) the factor of the cognitive immaturity of children may predispose them to manifest productive symptoms of psychosis that may have less psychopathological import than the same symptoms would if they occurred in adults; (3) similarly, children are immature in their psychosocial development and are thus more vulnerable to stress, which may again predispose them to manifest psychotic symptoms more readily than would adults experiencing similar stressors. The result may be that children under stress who manifest hallucinations have been described as having essentially benign courses.

Since research data on children manifesting symptoms of psychosis are quite sparse, diagnostic conclusions based upon these symptoms should, in this author's view, be interpreted conservatively. Suggested guidelines for the diagnostic assessment of such children are presented in the text.

REFERENCES

Achenbach, T. (1982). *Developmental Psychopathology.* New York: Wiley.

Annell, A-L. (1963). The prognosis of psychotic conditions of childhood. *Acta Psychiat. Scand.* 39:235–97.

Bender, L. (1947). Childhood schizophrenia: Clinical study of one hundred schizophrenic children. *Amer. J. Orthopsychiat.* 17:40–56.

————, et al. (1952). Schizophrenia in childhood: A confirmation of the diagnosis. *Proceed. Amer. Neurol. Assoc.* 77:67–73.

————. (1985). Childhood schizophrenia. *Psychiat. Quart.* 27:663–81.

————. (1970). The life course of schizophrenic children. *Biolog. Psychiat.* 2:165–72.

————, and Lipkowitz, H. H. (1940). Hallucinations in children. *Amer. J. Orthopsychiat.* 10:471.

————, and Vogel, B. F. (1941). Imaginary companions in children. *Amer. J. Orthopsychiat.* 11:56–65.

Bleuler, E. (1950). *Dementia Praecox or the Group of Schizophrenias.* New York: International Universities Press.

Cantor, S., Trevenen, R., and Postuma, R. (1979). Muscle biopsy in hypotonic schizophrenic children: A preliminary report. *Schiz. Bull.* 5:616–22.

————, et al. (1980). Is childhood schizophrenia a cholinergic disease? I. Muscle morphology. *Arch. Gen. Psychiat.* 37:658–67.

————, et al. (1981). The group of hypotonic schizophrenics. *Schiz. Bull.* 7:1–11.

Chambers, W. J. (1986). Hallucinations in psychotic and depressed children. In D. Pilowsky and W. J. Chambers (Eds.). *Hallucinations in Childhood and Adolescence.* Clinical Monograph Series. Washington, D.C.: American Psychiatric Association.

————, et al. (1982). Psychotic symptoms in prepubertal major depressive disorder. *Arch. Gen. Psychiat.* 39:921–31.

————, et al. (1985). The assessment of affective disorders in children and adolescents by semistructured interview. *Arch. Gen. Psychiat.* 42:696–702.

Chapman, L. J., and Chapman, J. P. (1980). Scales for rating psychotic and psychotic-like experiences as continua. *Schiz. Bull.* 6:476–89.

DeSanctis, S. (1906). On some varieties of dementia praecox, trans. M. L. Osborn, from the original, published in 1906 in *Rivista Sperimentale di Freniatria* 32:141–65 and reprinted in J. G. Howells. *Modern Perspectives in International Child Psychiatry.* Edinburgh: Oliver and Boyd, 1969, pp. 590–609.

Eggers, C. (1978). Course and prognosis of childhood schizophrenia. *J. Autism Child. Schiz.* 8:21–36.

Endicott, J., and Spitzer, R. L. (1978). A diagnostic interview. The schedule for affective disorders and schizophrenia. *Arch. Gen. Psychiat.* 35:837.

Eisenberg, L. (1957). The course of childhood schizophrenia. *Arch. Neurol. and Psychiat.* 78:69–83.

————. (1962). Hallucinations in children. In L. J. West (Ed.). *Hallucinations.* New York: Grune and Stratton.

Graham, P., and Rutter, M. (1968). The reliability and validity of the psychiatric assessment of the child. II. Interview with the parent. *Brit. J. Psychiat.* 114:581–92.

Green, W. H., Campbell, M., and Hardesty, A. S. (1984). A comparison of schizophrenic and autistic children. *J. Amer. Acad. Child Psychiat.* 23:399–409.

Kallman, F. J., and Roth, B. (1956). Genetic aspects of preadolescent schizophrenia. *Amer. J. Psychiat.* 112:599.

Kanner, L. (1943). Autistic disturbances of affective contact. *Nervous Child* 2:217–50.

———. (1971). Follow-up study of eleven autistic children originally reported in 1943. *J. Autism Child. Schiz.* 1:119–45.

Koehler, K. (1979). First rank symptoms of schizophrenia: Questions concerning clinical boundaries. *Brit. J. Psychiat.* 134:236–48.

Kolvin, I. (1971a). Studies on the childhood psychoses: I. Diagnostic criteria and classification. *Brit. J. Psychiat.* 118:381–84.

———, et al. (1971b). II. The phenomenology of childhood psychoses. *Brit. J. Psychiat.* 118:385–95.

———, et al. (1971c). III. The family and social background in childhood psychoses. *Brit. J. Psychiat.* 118:396–402.

———, Garside, R. F., and Kidd, J. S. H. (1971d). IV. Parental personality and attitude and childhood psychoses. *Brit. J. Psychiat.* 118:403–6.

———, Ounsted, C., and Roth, M. (1971e). V. Cerebral dysfunction and childhood psychoses. *Brit. J. Psychiat.* 118:407–14.

———, Humphrey, M., and McNay, A. (1971f). Cognitive factors in childhood psychoses. *Brit. J. Psychiat.* 118:415–19.

Kraepelin, E. (1919). *Dementia Praecox and Paraphrenia.* (Trans. R. M. Barclay, from 8th Ed. of *Psychiatrie.* Liepzig: Barth). Edinburgh: Livingstone.

Makita, K. (1966). The age of onset of childhood schizophrenia. *Folia Psychiat. Neurol. Japon.* 20:111–21.

Piaget, J. (1951). *The Child's Conception of Physical Causality.* London: Routledge and Kegan Paul.

Pope, H., and Lipinski, J. (1978). Diagnosis in schizophrenia and manic-depressive illness. *Arch. Gen. Psychiat.* 35:811.

Puig-Antich, J., Chambers, W. J., and Tabrizi, M. A. (1983). The clinical assessment of current depressive episodes in children and adolescents: Interviews with parents and children. In D. Cantwell and G. Carlson (Eds.). *Childhood Depression.* New York: Spectrum.

Rutter, M., and Graham, P. (1968). The reliability and validity of the psychiatric assessment of the child: I. Interview with the child. *Brit. J. Psychiat.* 114:563–79.

———, Shaffer, D., and Shepherd, M. (1973). An evaluation of the proposal for a multiaxial classification of child psychiatric disorders. *Psychol. Med.* 3:244–50.

Schneider, K. (1959). *Clinical Psychopathology.* New York: Grune and Stratton.

Spitzer, R., Endicott, J., and Robins, E. (1978). Research diagnostic criteria: Rationale and reliability. *Arch. Gen. Psychiat.* 35:773–82.

Strauss, J. S. (1969). Hallucinations and delusions as points on continua function. *Arch. Gen. Psychiat.* 21:581.

Vrono, M. (1973/4). Schizophrenia in childhood and adolescence. *Intl. J. Mental Health* 2:8–11.

Wilking, V., and Paoli, C. (1966). The hallucinatory experience. *J. Amer. Acad. Child Psychiat.* 5:431.

Wing, J. K., Cooper, J. E., and Sartorius, N. (1974). *The Measurement and Classification of Psychiatric Symptoms.* London: Cambridge University Press.

28

CHILDREN WITH BORDERLINE PERSONALITY ORGANIZATION

Paulina F. Kernberg

GENERAL DIAGNOSTIC CONSIDERATIONS

Recently, various authors have focused on the descriptive symptomatology of the borderline personality organization in children (Bemporad et al. 1982; Aarkrog 1981; P. Kernberg 1983; Kestenbaum 1983; Leichtman and Nathan 1983; Pine 1983; Rinsley 1980b; Vela et al. 1983).* But a descriptive picture alone does not suffice for understanding the childhood syndrome (Gualtieri et al. 1983).

A systematic study of the descriptive validity of borderline children was undertaken by Verhulst (1984). He used a set of twenty-eight items obtained from the literature to differentiate borderline children from neurotic and psychotic children. Several items proved to be highly sensitive and specific in the differentiation from neurotic children: primitive anxiety context, primary process thinking, shifting levels of ego functioning, identity disturbance, primitive defense mechanisms, micropsychotic states, ineffective superego functioning, oddities of motor functioning, marked fantasy activity, and discrepancy between interest or talent and actual functioning. The item "withdrawal" and its opposite—demanding, clinging, and unpredictable relationship—reflect the typical fluctuation of the borderline child's relationships to others.

Identity disturbance was considered the best discriminating item between borderline children, in whom it is present, and neurotic children, in whom it is absent. In contrast, feelings of loneliness, separation anxiety, and hyperactivity did not distinguish borderline children from the neurotic group.

The gap between the borderline and the psychotic group of children was narrower. Items that differentiated more frequently borderline from psychotic children

---

*Earlier writings have also contributed to this portrait of the borderline child (see Ekstein and Wallerstein 1954; Frijling-Schreuder 1969; Geleerd 1958; Mahler and Kaplan 1977; Rosenfeld and Sprince 1963; Weil 1953).

were: demanding, clinging unpredictable relationships, primitive defense mechanisms, shifting levels of ego functioning, micropsychotic states, and feelings of loneliness, whereas psychotic children presented more frequently and typically withdrawn and aloof contact with others, need-fulfilling relationships, language and speech peculiarities, special interest of talent in one area, and resistance to change in the environment.

In their discussion, Verhulst et al. concluded that demanding, clinging and unpredictable relations, primitive defense mechanisms, shifting levels of ego functioning, micropsychotic states and suspicious, paranoid, and marked fantasy activity were mostly sensitive and specific of borderline children. Indeed, borderline children can be distinguished from neurotic children. However, no single item is pathognomonic of them. Characteristically, borderline children show a variety of symptoms covering every area of psychological functioning, including motor functioning, although to a lesser extent. Neurotic children rate high, primarily on the level of emotions and affects.

Psychotic children seem to have a more predictable overall functioning, despite their impairment in social and cognitive functioning, which is quite in contrast to the marked fluctuation presented by borderline children and considered almost pathognomonic by Bemporad et al. (1982). This study observed that borderline children present with symptoms taken initially for mild or moderate disturbances; only after prolonged diagnostic evaluations or during the course of psychotherapy does the severe pathology emerge. In 42 percent of cases with the diagnosis "borderline" the psychiatrist needed more time for his diagnosis, as opposed to 16 percent of neurotic children and 26 percent for the diagnosis of psychotic children.

Rubin, Lippman, and Goldberg (1984) were also able to delineate systematically borderline levels from neurotic children from a behavioral and structural perspective. They showed that ego function disturbances, distortions in affect, and disturbances in attention and concentration significantly differentiated their group of borderline children from neurotics, whereas anxiety and impulsivity did not show discriminatory power.

We need not only to take into account symptoms presented across various diagnostic categories within Axis I of *Diagnostic and Statistic Manual-III*, but also to include a structural and developmental perspective of these children. Such a viewpoint leads us to consider characteristics that correspond closely to those in Axis II of DSM-III, the axis encompassing personality traits, personality disorders, and specific developmental disorders. Here it is important to note that the child's response to psychological treatment and specific medications will be codetermined by the descriptive syndrome and the underlying personality or developmental learning disorder (Axis II). The prognosis will be more guarded if borderline personality organization is diagnosed as the underlying personality disorder.

Specifically, what are we looking for? First, in terms of the Axis I diagnosis or descriptive syndrome, we would suspect borderline personality organization in children in the following categories: (1) attention deficit disorder with hyperactivity; (2)

conduct disorder, undersocialized, aggressive; (3) conduct disorder, undersocialized, nonaggressive; and (4) conduct disorder, socialized aggressive. Yet borderline personality organization may also appear in separation anxiety disorders, overanxious disorders, schizoid disorders of childhood, elective mutism, identity disorders, and eating disorders such as anorexia nervosa and bulimia. In addition, specific developmental disorders, such as reading disorders, arithmetic disorders, or developmental language disorders with or without attention deficit disorder, have all been found in a significant percentage of borderline adolescents and young adults (Andrulonis et al. 1980).

But how do we arrive at the diagnosis "borderline" in children? Until relatively recently, the term "borderline" was not even applied to children, as it was generally believed that personality disorders did not exist in children between 6 and 12 years. Children of that age were considered to be neurotic, psychotic, suffering from a behavioral disorder, or presenting an organic disorder of some sort. Nor does DSM-III contain a specific category for borderline personality disorder in children. It is, however, assumed that if children meet the criteria for a personality disorder of adulthood, they can be diagnosed in that way. Indeed, both Petti and Law (1981) and Liebowitz (1981) have demonstrated the applicability of the DSM-III diagnosis of adult borderline personality disorder to children in inpatient and outpatient settings respectively. Using DSM-III, at least five of the following criteria are required: (1) impulsivity or unpredictability; (2) a pattern of unstable and intense interpersonal relationships marked by shifts of attitude; (3) inappropriate intense anger or lack of control of anger; (4) identity disturbance, manifested by uncertainty about several issues relating to identity; (5) affective instability, marked by shifts from normal mood to depression, irritability, or anxiety; (6) intolerance of being alone; (7) physically self-damaging acts, suicidal gestures, self-mutilation, etc.; (8) chronic feelings of emptiness or boredom.

Turning to a list of symptoms compiled by Vela et al. (1983) from the work of numerous authors, we find that only one reference—Rosenfeld and Sprince (1963)—includes identity disturbance. I emphasize this because, in my opinion, a disturbed sense of identity is a crucial diagnostic criterion for borderline personality organization. Indeed, I believe the most reliable criteria for making this diagnosis in children are a disturbed sense of identity and sudden shifts in level of functioning, an assumption substantiated by Verhulst in 1984. The exclusion of identity disorder as a criterion in children may well be due to the assumption that "identity" is achieved only in adolescence. Strictly speaking this may be true. But children between ages 6 and 12 *do* have a sense of "me-ness." They know who they are and which gender they are. They have a sense of community and group relatedness, as well as a clear idea of their own continuity through various activities and in time. Their awareness of themselves encompasses both objective attributes and subjective experience. Simply put, they know what they can do, what they like, and what they are like.

A DEVELOPMENTAL PERSPECTIVE

In assessing borderline personality organization in children, it is crucial to consider age-appropriate developmental achievements. We find that preschool borderline children have not accomplished certain tasks expected at this age. They cannot tolerate separation from mother, lack established standards for bad and good, show an inability to express a wide variety of modulated feelings, and are uncertain about sexual distinctions. Latency-age borderline children are also behind in their developmental achievements. They do not maintain a sense of sex and role identity through play, fantasy, and learning tasks. Impulse control remains poor, with unpredictable states. These children do not show enjoyment of peer interactions and increased independence from parents; nor do they have a sense of belonging to an extended community. Finally, they have not yet resolved the Oedipus complex through sublimatory channels and repression. Turning to developmental achievements expected for preadolescents and adolescents (Senn and Solnit 1968), we see that borderline patients have not acquired a sense of identity or developed age-appropriate abstract thinking. There is little indication of a struggle for emancipation and autonomy from the family, and perceptions of the family tend to be unrealistic. Sex-role identity, with capacity for intimacy and heterosexual adjustment, is not established, and masturbatory fantasies are primarily connected with pregenital themes.

A developmental perspective bears on any evaluation of descriptive symptomatology. Various authors point to a characteristic multiple symptomatology, with obsessions, phobias, compulsions, and hysterical traits. (Schizoid personality as well as paranoid personality traits have also been noted in borderline children, but they are relatively less fixed.) It is not, however, the neurotic and behavioral symptoms per se that typify borderline children. What is more characteristic is the reemergence of symptoms that should have been outgrown. Preschool fears and phobias or compulsive behaviors typically found in 2- to 3-year-olds persist, with increasing intensity, beyond these developmental stages. The shifting levels of functioning further confuse the picture, necessitating careful assessment of overall behavior. A good example is Jane, a 9-year-old I shall describe in detail later. At age 7 she had seen the movie *Jaws* and now had difficulty using the toilet. She was afraid "Jaws" would appear and bite her. Finally, she tested her fear by putting her hand in the toilet; "Jaws" did not appear. She then stopped being afraid, indicating her capacity to test reality.

A STRUCTURAL EVALUATION

The anchoring criteria I mentioned—identity disorder and shifting levels of ego organization—reflect the application of Otto Kernberg's (1978) concept of adult borderline personality organization to children. Such a structural perspective enables us to understand better the varied symptomatology these children present, both cross-sectionally and in longitudinal studies (Aarkrog 1981; Kestenbaum 1983). The disturbed sense of identity contributes to these children's lack of a sense of "me-ness," unclear gender identity, and incapacity to be alone. Their shifting levels of ego function, with abrupt regressions, account for their lack of judgment and their impulsivity, as well as their disturbed relationship to reality (although they can test reality). Finally, the use of primitive defenses, particularly splitting, relates to their difficulties in assuming responsibility for their actions, in other words, their shifting level of superego functioning.

Splitting features prominently in the borderline child's object relations. The relationship to the mother is characterized by either primitive idealization or extreme devaluation, while there is an inability to relate to the parents as a couple. The child tends to relate to either mother (to the exclusion of father), or to father (to the exclusion of mother). Anna Freud (1969) pointed to the child's inability to accept comfort from others. There is also an inability to deal with sibling rivalry and envy, often with expressions of intense hostility against siblings and even outright sibling abuse.

On another level, clinical observation of borderline children suggests that transitional objects are absent or acquire a bizarre quality. The existence of a transitional object presupposes some internalization of a positive object relation with the mother, so that the child's relations to this internalized object can be reproduced in an intermediate world of experience. Borderline children, however, have not developed a positive sense of self in relation to a positive object (in the context of soothing, pleasurable experience with mother). It is thus not surprising that they lack a transitional object at the appropriate age (8 to 24 months), or one of the usual quality (such as a soft toy). Instead, these children tend to cling directly to the mother, possibly searching for symbioticlike experiences or positive feelings. Or they may represent their relationship to the bad mother by attaching themselves to a mechanical object. One child, for instance, used a robot as a transitional object, taking this with him wherever he went. Moreover, if the borderline child does have a transitional object, it tends to portray a part of the child's self (e.g., a hat), rather than to reflect the gestalt of the experience with mother (e.g., through texture or smell).

The defects of these children's internal object relations can be seen in their use of others as part-objects or outright self-objects. The other person's individual characteristics are completely missed. Instead, these children seem to live in a world where the other is only a vehicle for their own projections—a "thing" to be leaned upon, controlled, idealized, or devalued. These interactions are poignantly expressed in their relationships to peers. They fluctuate from apparent sociability to withdrawal from others. They seem indiscriminate and too possessive, or they shadow their friends' sadistic behavior with other children. Ninety percent of borderline children have poor peer relations (Bentivegna et al. 1985). In spite of social skills they seem unable to maintain friendships, ending in a chronic sense of isolation.

But what about the relation to self. As noted, borderline children do not convey a distinct sense of "me-ness." They may perceive themselves as different, without continuity, from one situation to the next. They fail to anticipate gratification or even to show it. Nor do they evidence enjoyment in their activities, especially in play. Also missing is an age-appropriate capacity for realistic self-esteem or mastery. Overall, the feeling tone is one of apathy and anhedonia, of worthlessness. Moreover, their chronic depression is often compounded by parental and peer rejection as well as by academic problems.

The disturbances in the sense of self indicate certain developmental fixations or regression points. Frequently, one finds a pervasive feeling of anxiety in close interactions with mother, suggesting an inability to enter or come out of an intimate relationship. The perception may be of an either-or situation—either they are locked in tight with the mother or they are dropped completely, into a vaccum. The fears of merger, then, are not so much fears of loss of boundaries as fears of this threatening experience with "the other."

Other experiences also reflect these children's unstable self-concept and their difficulties in their separation-individuation process. They may feel that they cannot survive without the other, as if they were hooked to this other person. Mother or "another" person has to stand by on an ongoing basis, always there. They feel like toddlers whose mother is permanently out of the room, to paraphrase Frijling-Schreuder (1969). Or they may indicate that they do not need anybody and are beyond danger. At other times they try to control others totally or submit entirely to another's control in order to gain some sense of themselves (P. Kernberg 1983). As Ekstein and Friedman (1967) have described, these children may reverse self and object, much as adult borderline patients do. In treatment these patients may take on the role of therapist, attributing the role of patient to the therapist; this may be done so vividly that the therapist literally feels as the patient does.

Christenson and Wilson (1985) have developed a questionnaire for adults assessing the above interactions based on the theory that borderline patients have disturbances in their separation-individuation process. DSM-III borderline personality disorders scored significantly higher than a random university employee control group in this preliminary study. It is hoped that such an instrument could be developed for children.

Most authors agree that the borderline patient's anxiety is of an intense, diffuse nature, without the signal quality found in neurotics (Geleerd 1958; Pine 1974; Rosenfeld and Sprince 1963). Rage is prevalent with tantrum-proneness (Mahler et al. 1949). Aggression may reach dangerous proportions, and in general there is a lack of modulation of affects, seen in abrupt mood changes and an all-or-nothing quality. Marked fluctuations occur between elation with coercive attempts and depressive helplessness.

The high incidence of associated depression in these patients deserves further comment. In adults, there is increasing evidence of a strong association between borderline personality organization and major affective disorders, as if the major affective disorder preserved and maintained borderline personality organization. Here, genetic aspects are important (Pope et al. 1983). As noted, the child's sense of worthlessness and helplessness is compounded by difficulties in object relations. These children do not derive gratification from mutuality and reciprocity in maternal, paternal, or peer relations. To the contrary, they are rejected and disliked for their primitive ways of relating to others. In addition, children are persecuted by terrifying superego forerunners, as in the case of the girl who was afraid of being eaten up by "Jaws." Their inability to derive pleasure from play, or to use play to neutralize frustration and aggression, adds to their helplessness, leading to chronic depressive affect. Lastly, the frequent coexistence of organicity makes for difficulties in learning and social interaction, again compounding their inability to cope and hence worsening depression. This multidetermined depression combines with impulsivity (determined either by the borderline personality organization itself or by organicity), so that suicidal attempts are a frequent cause for hospitalization (Pfeffer 1983). In adolescent borderlines, the tendency to react severely to loss, poorly controlled anger, and self-defeating impulsivity were characteristically associated with suicidal attempts (Cramley 1981).

Looking at specific ego functions, it is important to note that these children generally function below their academic potential. Because this lag may be due in part to developmental learning disabilities or minimal brain dysfunction, neuropsychological testing is recommended. The same is true of motoric functioning. Often one finds poor patterning in these children's developmental history, including erratic eating and cleaning habits. Incoordination may make them accident-prone. Yet, whatever the role of organicity, as psychological functioning improves with treatment, so can motoric functioning (P. Kernberg 1983).

Although borderline children often report visual and auditory hallucinations, kinesthetic and tactile hallucinations are rather rare. Visual and auditory hallucinations may be fostered if children are unable to express their aggression because their parents cannot contain or handle it. Moreover, the parents are frequently poor models for reality testing (Pine 1974). All the authors concur that contact with reality is present in borderline children but that this contact may be lost at times, as if the reality span were brief (Geleerd 1958). The preservation of the capacity for reality testing can be assessed by observing the child's capacity to bounce back from paranoid ideas, as in Jane's case. One should also note if these children seek or accept clarification of their distortions. Another indication that loss of reality testing is only transitory can be found in cases where, despite a high incidence of play disruption, the child can reassume the play activity with therapeutic intervention. A similar indication is given in the child's ability to come back to everyday life on termination of a session whose content was of a primitive nature.

Borderline children's play shows several important characteristics. These children do not play normally or age-appropriately, and they are addicted to pretend play (Weil 1953). Their play has a compulsive, static quality, with little evidence of enjoyment, resolution of conflict, or elaboration of fantasy. These children, according to Bemporad et al. (1982), "are unable to control the progression of their thinking from neutral themes to those of mutilation and death." Games may be tonelessly repeated, or the child may enter into an elementary fantasy play more typical of much younger children, playing at eating or flying and falling. The incidence of play disruption is higher than in neurotic children. Aggressive and sexual impulses infiltrate the play so that intense anxiety follows; the child is unable to continue playing because the margin between play and the direct expression of drive—the space of make-believe—has collapsed. In fantasy life, including masturbatory fantasies, themes of omnipotence and oral and anal sadism predominate.

Borderline children suffer from poor tolerance for anxiety, frustration, and depression. They fail to engage in goal-directed activities, and even if their perceptual, motor, and intellectual capacities are intact, they do not use them creatively or effectively. Overall, then, there is a deficit in adaptation (Leichtman and Nathan 1983).

These children's defenses have a rigid, yet tenuous, quality. This general constriction can lead to more primitive defenses, such as projective identification, splitting, withdrawal into fantasy, denial, primitive idealization, and devaluation. These children may even have brief psychotic episodes related to stress, with paranoid symptoms, depersonalization, derealization, dissociation, and suicidal attempts, lasting a few hours to a day or two.

Yet it is important to distinguish a failure of defenses or brittle defenses from a lack of psychological differentiation and structure. Clinical experience suggests that structured, although primitive, forms of defense *are* present in borderline states. A problem is that these defense mechanisms may in themselves be ego-weakening (O. Kernberg 1978); they should not be confused with real ego deficits, which these children may also have. The differential diagnosis depends on the child's ability to reconstitute at a higher level when these defense mechanisms are clarified and verbalized in the clinical interaction (P. Kernberg 1983).

OTHER EVALUATION MEASURES

A common battery for psychological assessment includes the Weschler Intelligence Scale for Children (Revised), Wide Range Achievement Test, Benton Visual Memory Test, Draw-A-Person, Illinois Test of Psycholinguistic Abilities, Ravens Progressive Matrices, Thematic Apperception Test, Rorschach and Neuropsychological Screening Tasks (time orientation, sequencing, laterity, motor functioning, visuomotor functioning, sensory processing, memory functioning, and general academic functioning). In both structured and unstructured tests, borderline children show fluidity of associations, peculiar logic, and flights into fantasy. Engel (1963) emphasized the particular intense involvement that borderline children develop with the examiner. In contrast to psychotic children, borderline children are able to portray their massive anxiety in "realistic fantasies and stories." According to Leichtman and Shapiro (1980b), these children have no expectation of themselves and no motivation to give a right answer. There is a lack of phase-dominance in terms of drives, and in the Rorschach one frequently finds inanimate movement responses and sexualization of responses as a counterphobic maneuver. Fear of the ink blobs and anxiety reactions may be extreme, with concerns about survival, separation, and destruction. Anxiety easily escalates to panic. In terms of thought disorder, one sometimes encounters strange associations and perseveration with little tendency to reality adherence. There is also a quality of playing "crazy" when people appear.

Object representations within the Rorschach seem to be unrealistic and unidimensional. The few human percepts tend to split into all good or bad figures (grandiose/impotent, idealized/malevolent). One sees a regressive experience of merger, or rather partial merger, in the sense of one person being attached to another. Leichtman and Shapiro (1980b), for instance, report two-headed people, Siamese twins, two Martians fused together, two elephants joined together at the tail, or two women chanting in unison. Also present are themes of loss, separation, and abandonment with helplessness and primitive aggression. The tenuous sense of identity is illustrated by body-image distortions showing a strong identification with extraterrestrial beings, anxiety about disappearance, and visions of people about to explode.

Only recently the MMPI has been studied in relation to borderline personality disorder. Although this has been tried with an adolescent population, it is mentioned here because the MMPI serves as an independent validation of the diagnosis. Archer, Ball, and Hunter (1985) studied 146 inpatient adolescents between 12 and 18 years of age: 82 percent white, 11 percent black, 7 percent other ethnic backgrounds, from lower- to middle-class socioeconomic status, consecutively admitted. They were selected according to DSM-III diagnostic criteria. Norm conversions for the MMPI in adolescent populations were applied.

Borderline personality disorder had significantly higher MMPI mean scores on the following scales: (Hs) Hypochondria, (D) Depression, (Sc) Schizophrenia, (F) Feminity-Masculinity, and (Pd) Psychopathic Deviation than the comparison groups: conduct disorders, dysthymic, and other personality disorders. The combination of the MMPI scales (F, Pa, Pd, D, Pt, K, and Sc) accounted for 59 percent of the variance in discriminating between borderline personality disorder and the group including all other diagnostic categories (dysthymic disorders, conduct disorders, and other personality disorders). The MMPI should be used in addition to other tests and not by itself.

The similarity of MMPI found in adolescent and adult personality disorders points to the congruence of the clinical symptomatology of these two age groups.

Blotcky (1984) offered a practical application of the Rorschach tests in anticipating transference developments of borderline adolescents, specifically in their use of primitive idealization and devaluation. These examples also illustrate the frequent responses of paired figures in these patients, such as of two ugly men or women in negative interactions, two monsters or two people or animals stuck together—ugly, hating each other versus extremely positive context of twosomes—two really happy heroes, two great human giants, two angels who are very happy with each other.

Biological assessment of borderline patients has not been conclusive. However, a prospective electroencephalographic sleep study by Reynolds et al. (1985) points out the similarity of REM latency between borderlines and depressed patients. Moreover, this short-term REM latency is independent of the level of depressive symptoms as assessed by the Hamilton Scales. In addition to abbreviated REM sleep latency, there is shifting REM sleep time to the first half of the night and difficulty in sleep initiation; all these findings are common with nonborderline major depressives.

There is a suggestion of an intrinsic relationship between borderline and affective illness. This has been further pursued by Schubert, Sacuzzo, and Braff (1985) in their comparative study of information processing among normal controls, borderlines, major and minor depressives, manic, and schizoaffective patients.

Borderline patients showed no difference from normals and controls; their visual information processing in turn was distinct from the group of psychotic disorders. Moreover, schizophrenic patients and schizotypal patients have a similarly impaired visual information processing. This supports the separation of schizotypal from borderline personality disorders.

One frequently finds pervasive pathological interactions within the families of borderline adolescents (Shapiro et al. 1975) and children. The family situation tends to maintain borderline functioning. There is anxiety about supporting the child's autonomy and a denial of his or her dependence. Parents may use the child narcissistically, and dyadic relations between the child and each parent predominate. Bemporad et al. (1982) remarked on the chaotic nature of parent-child interaction, often reflecting abuse, neglect, and bizarre behaviors on the part of the parents, as well as inconsistent care. Ten out of twenty-four children in his sample were physically abused. Further reference to family dynamics will be seen in the following discussion of etiology.

Soloff and Millward (1983) have presented an excellent outline of the developmental (sometimes overlapping) hypothesis for borderline disorder. What follows is a summary of their research, in which the developmental histories of borderline patients with affective and schizophrenic patients are compared in an attempt to validate the borderline personality disorder.

The neurobiological model refers to the frequent association of borderline personality disorder with impaired central nervous system functioning. The various deficits affect the child's internal and external world of experience, the relationship to the mother, and the interpersonal world. These deficits refer to impulsivity, low frustration tolerance, controls over cognition, attention, and affect; they put the child at risk for borderline ego development and defensive structure and behavior, based on an organic pathway. Substance abuse, alcoholism, and histrionic and sociopathic behaviors are concomitant phenomena in these behaviors.

Complications of pregnancy were significantly higher for borderline patients as was a tendency for prematurity and low birth weight. A continuum of learning difficulties was found, from most severe in schizophrenics, to intermediate in borderlines and least among depressed patients. Temper tantrums, head banging, and rocking were highly prevalent in borderline patients versus the other two groups, as was a strikingly high use of alcohol and drugs in borderlines and schizophrenics, as compared with depressed controls.

Andrulonis et al. (1980) provided further contributions to understanding a neurobehavioral basis; among male patients 53 percent presented with minimal brain dysfunction or learning disability, compared with 13.5 percent of female patients.

The "organic" borderline pattern presents an early childhood onset of impulsive acting out, drug abuse, and mild depression. In contrast, the predominantly female "nonorganic" borderlines had a typical adolescent onset of more depression and family history of affective disorder.

FAMILY STUDIES

According to Dahl (1985), the 38 percent of borderline patients who have a relative with a depressive disorder is probably a low estimate, because patients and informants tend to underreport when compared to direct examination of the relatives.

Moreover, Loranger et al. (1982) have found that first-degree relatives of borderline personality disorders have nearly a tenfold morbid risk for borderline personality disorder over the relatives of bipolar and schizophrenic probands. The risk for unipolar depression in borderline personality disorder relatives is similar to the risk for bipolar disorder relatives. However, there doesn't seem to be an increased risk for bipolar disorders in relatives of borderline personality disorder probands. Pope et al. (1983) also found increased prevalence of borderline personality disorder in first-degree relatives of borderline personality disorder probands.

Although various studies have indicated the high incidence of depression among the relatives of borderline personality disorder patients, I would agree with McGlashan (1983) that depression may be a nonspecific response secondary to any psychiatric disorder, which has to be differentiated from major unipolar and bipolar disorders. In this connection, there is no higher incidence of borderline personality disorder among the close relatives of affective disorder probands.

Torgersen (1984) studied sixty-nine same-sex twins in Norway with borderline disorders, using DSM-III criteria. He found forty-four schizotypal twins, ten with borderline personality disorder, and fifteen with borderline personality disorder and schizophrenic personality disorder. A matched control group had major depression and anxiety disorders. The Axis I diagnosis did not differentiate between the two. Seven out of twenty-one monozygotic cotwins had schizotypal personality disorders, compared with one of twenty-three dyzogotic twins. In the pure borderline personality disorder group only two out of seven dizygotic twins also had borderline personality disorder, and none of the monozygotic twins had. Thus there was no support for a genetic factor in the etiology of borderline personality disorder. The same applied for the mixed schizotypal personality disorder-borderline personality disorder group.

Studies of twins with affective disorders have not been reviewed for borderline disorders among twins.

The separation hypothesis suggests the important role of separation and loss or the threat of loss through withdrawal of parental affection. The separation-individuation process is affected, producing a developmental arrest characterized by the persistence of primitive defenses and a failure to achieve object constancy.

Soloff and Millward (1983) assessed borderline patients in terms of the intactness of their families. They suffered a significantly greater incidence of paternal loss by death or divorce compared with controls. Separation here is taken as severance from an important parental figure.

According to Soloff and Millward (1983), borderline patients showed problems in more areas of developmental separation than the other groups, especially as they grew into adulthood: 64 percent borderlines, 37 percent depressed, and 3 percent schizophrenics. This study demonstrates increased separation experiences and increased sensitivity for separation in borderline patients.

Rinsley (1981) summarized his conception of the developmental arrest that borderlines present in terms of their separation-individuation failure, beginning at the practicing subphase and, I would add, the differentiation subphase (P. Kernberg 1979), and reaching its peak during the rapprochement subphase.

Shapiro et al. (1975) indicated that primitive defenses such as splitting, good/bad, and projective identification operate equally at the level of the family group, namely, the child reenacts the role as parent and the parent reenacts the role as child. Independence and separation from family is taken as devaluation of family values, or dependency is experienced as an overwhelming and dangerous burden on the family.

Fathers of borderline patients contribute to the risk of borderline personality disorder in their offspring either by being passive and/or noninvolved, or through hostile rejection, a pattern commonly observed in father-son relationships or mother-daughter relationships. Sexual abuse seems to be more prevalent than in other patient populations. Soloff and Millward's findings (1983) illustrated that among borderline patients' families the overall pattern is one of severe familial pathology, with intrusive controlling mothers, distant or hostile fathers, and conflictual marital relationships.

How stable is the diagnosis of borderline personality disorder over time?

The predictive validity of the diagnosis is relatively low. Fifty percent of the borderlines followed up by McGlashan retained their original diagnosis, 20 percent got a diagnosis of schizophrenia or schizoaffective disorder, and only a few had developed major affective disorders.

Borderline personality disorder overlaps with histerics, antisocial, or narcissistic personality disorders, which points to the usefulness of a personality organization concept (O. Kernberg 1975). Schizotypal personality can be considered a prepsychotic personality disorder, a stable one evolving into schizophrenia or a residual state of schizophrenia. Prospective studies are needed to study this problem.

Suicidal attempts in borderlines are less than 10 percent, no different from that found in affective psychosis and schizophrenia. Criminal substance abuse is more common in borderline personality disorders and indicates a worse outcome.

Functional Outcome. Pope et al. in their four- to seven-year follow-up study, showed that 26 percent of their patients had good global outcome and 48 percent had poor global outcome. In contrast, McGlashan's study, which is a longer follow-up study (fifteen years), indicates that the borderline personality disorder group did significantly better than Pope's groups, and that depression makes the outcome somewhat worse, rather than better, as Pope indicated in his study.

Case #1

The case of Jane, a 9-year-old outpatient with organicity, highlights some of the characteristics outlined in this chapter. Jane, who lived with her parents and two older siblings (ages 11 and 12), came to the outpatient department because of attentional problems, awkwardness, and some "social problems." Her teachers were concerned about her poor academic progress, her isolation from her peers, who did not include her in games, and her tendency to give either incorrect or seemingly unrelated answers to questions in class. Jane had become increasingly reluctant to go to school because she said the other children made fun of her and called her names.

At home, Jane was afraid to be alone. She had nightmares and was terrified of the dark, fearing monsters would enter her room. For two months preceding the evaluation, she had slept in the same bed with her father. (Earlier, she had slept in her mother's room.) She was preoccupied with fears that her parents or her pet guinea pig would die.

Sometimes Jane talked with people "who were not there," although her mother indicated that these were not clearly distinct characters. Frequently, she mumbled or made up words. She had temper tantrums and was very jealous of her sisters, fighting a great deal both verbally and physically. She liked to wear boys' clothing, particularly Cub Scout uniforms, and wanted to wear exactly the same clothing after school every day.

Born by Cesarean section, Jane was described as a difficult baby who cried, "never slept," and spit up frequently. Yet she liked to be held. She sat at 6 months, walked at 11 months, and spoke single words at 8 or 9 months and sentences at 1 year. She was easily toilet trained by 2 years. Beginning nursery school presented difficulties because Jane was afraid of her teacher. Although she adjusted to school, she was frequently absent for illness. In the third grade she began to say she did not want to go to school.

Jane's mother was described as having the same fears as her daughter. She was, for instance, fascinated by monster movies and watched them frequently. When her husband had to work at night, she would take the children and sleep at the maternal grandmother's because she did not like to stay alone overnight—indicating a confusion of generational boundaries. The marriage was described as "working well," although father and mother slept in different quarters, with the patient sleeping with one or the other parent.

Clinically, Jane seemed of normal intelligence even though she was functioning 6 months below grade level. With the interviewer, she talked continually and showed a full range of affect, but her speech was tangential. Although she knew the names of the days of the week, she did not know how many days there were in a week. In listing the months of the year, she skipped one month and was once out of sequence. She was aware that she tended to mix up days, months, and years, but blamed her classmates for her shortcomings. Nevertheless, there were no loose associations, nor was there evidence of delusions or hallucinations.

Jane described herself as small and ugly and complained that other children picked on her. Her use of primitive defense mechanisms was illustrated in her comment that she was angry with a classmate and wanted to bite him. "But," she added, "I don't want bite marks." When asked how she would get bite marks, she explained that biting people leaves marks. She denied that she thought her classmate would bite her in return. Although she was patient with the interviewer's questions, she was unable to clarify how she instead of her classmate would end up with bite marks.

At another point Jane explained that for a while she was afraid most of her dreams would come true, but that she learned that this was not so. Once she dreamed that a monster would attack her house and waited the following day in terror for the monster to appear. When this didn't happen, she concluded that monster dreams did not come true. She also remembered her mother telling her that these dreams were not real. I have already described her ability to test reality in relation to her fears of "Jaws."

In the family diagnostic interview, it was apparent that the family behaved in an enmeshed way with little distinction of generational boundaries. Jane seemed to be used as the joker in the family, to divert the focus on any emotionally charged topic. She also tended to cling to her mother and allowed herself to be treated as the baby in the family.

Psychological test reports indicated a full IQ of 96 on the WISC-R (Verbal IQ, 90; Performance IQ, 105). Jane's language problems were particularly evident in word-finding difficulties. Her tendency to be concrete appeared to be a manifestation of a language-related cognitive defect. She also showed problems with auditory memory, having trouble remembering the questions. (The impairment in auditory memory was also seen in the Auditory Sequential Memory Test of the Illinois Test of Psycholinguistic Abilities, on which she scored 8.8 age level.)

The overall diagnostic impression from neurological and psychological testing was of temporal parietal lobe left hemisphere dysfunction, characterized by short-term auditory memory, word-finding difficulties, letter and number sequence reversals, and trouble with borrowing and carrying in arithmetic. There was the suggestion of a mild right-sided involvement of the left-hand side. In addition, in some of her verbalizations, Jane seemed to confuse active and passive. She also showed trouble following directions, apparently due to attention difficulties and problems expressing herself verbally.

On projective testing, Jane relied heavily on projection as a defense, indicating, for example, that her mother was a "murderous person." Love and acceptance could never be obtained from mother, who preferred boys and kids who never fought. Jane's protocol was filled with a sense of bleakness, inner impoverishment, and helplessness. Fantasies of running away from the bad mother were intense, as were death fantasies.

Jane had a core female gender identity, but showed considerable gender identity confusion. Her wish to be a boy was related to her belief that her mother valued boys but felt girls were useless. In addition, her boyishness seemed to be a defense against very intense and exciting sexual feelings for her father, who was seen as a good person but unavailable to her.

A reason for Jane's distancing herself from people could be discerned in intense aggressive impulses that threatened to overwhelm her and destroy the object. On the Rorschach, for instance, she saw two women who were on the verge of ripping apart a crab, but were kept from doing so by a butterfly. The butterfly seemed to symbolize the weakness of her ego to defend against the aggressive impulses. Other responses on the projective tests were not well related to the percepts on the cards. Her protocol suggested a chronic borderline structure, with a longstanding withdrawal into an idiosyncratic world. There were many peculiar verbalizations, a tendency toward contamination, and a few instances of loss of reality testing when she felt overwhelmed by aggression.

Following DSM-III, Jane was given a diagnosis of separation anxiety disorder and Axis II mixed personality disorder with borderline personality disorder, developmental disorder. The underlying borderline personality organization can be seen in a number of areas. Jane clearly showed the poor peer relations, uneven early development, and deficits in academic performance described in borderline children. Difficult sibling relationships were also present. Her dyadic relationship with her parents could be seen in her sleeping habits. Particularly telling was the uncertain identity and unstable self-concept evident in Jane's inability to be alone, her dressing in boys' clothing, and her confusion about whether to play the baby or the clown in the family. She also showed a tendency to paranoid ideation, as well as the persistence of fears and symptoms beyond the age-appropriate stage. Yet her capacity to test reality was preserved. Finally, it is important to note the role of organicity in complicating Jane's problems. Her problems in word finding, spatial sequencing, and short-term auditory memory may have contributed to frustrating experiences with the mother, increasing aggression and interference with her process of separation-individuation.

The case of Jane underlines the need to assess the borderline personality organization descriptively, developmentally, and structurally. Most characteristic are signs of identity disorder and shifting ego states. Organicity and depression are also frequently present, complicating the picture. The importance of a thorough assessment cannot be stressed enough, for it helps significantly in clarifying the overall prognosis. It will indicate whether long-term psychological intervention is needed, with medication for target symptoms such as depression, and if educational learning approaches are indicated.

Case #2

Rita was a 10-year-old borderline outpatient girl with no organicity. She had no serious illnesses, although she had a lifelong history of obesity. There was no history of psychiatric illness in any family member. She had run away from her fifth-grade classroom twice during the month of June and was behaving strangely after sniffing perfume. The patient presented with a three-year history of interpersonal difficulty with peers. She had been "bossy" and controlling with peers since the age of 7 (around the time her father had a cardiac by-pass operation). She forced other children to play her games, ended up fighting with them, and then lost them as friends. Rita was especially sensitive to their taunts and teasing about her obesity. As a result, she had become socially isolated and played alone with her dolls, describing them as her only friends.

Coincident with deteriorating peer relations, Rita became nervous and overexcited. She calmed herself with constant eating and at the time of interview was thirty-seven pounds overweight. When not fed, she became especially nervous. The parents had not succeeded in controlling her eating, and the father, who was the primary caretaker, did not have the energy or will power to discipline her.

The patient exhibited no vegetative signs or apparent depressive symptomatology, although she had once stated, when in an otherwise happy mood, that she wished she were dead. Approximately one year prior to presentation, the father had recommended that Rita be brought in for a psychiatric evaluation; the parents reported that at that time treatment had not been recommended. In June, the patient had acted strangely on two occasions, with inappropriate laughter. The father suspected that Rita had been inhaling perfume and cologne, which she denied. On another occasion, she drank some alcohol after watching a soap opera in which a drunk man killed a baby, and was unable to explain why she had succumbed to this irresistible impulse. These incidents prompted the mother to appear with Rita at a child outpatient clinic.

The patient was the product of an unplanned pregnancy when her mother was 40, her father was 50, and her brother was 21; it was a Cesarean birth. Rita reported that she had almost killed her mother due to her large size at birth. The mother described Rita as an active infant in terms that made it apparent that she had been tired out trying to keep up with her. Rita was bottle-fed until the age of 8 months, and she had had a reversed sleep-wake cycle—a problem that the mother felt helpless about changing until her pediatrician recommended restricting Rita's daytime sleep. Rita walked at 9 months; talked at 1 year; was toilet trained at 2 years; and went to kindergarten at 4 years. She had a history of nightmares about monsters, which caused her to sleep with her mother from the ages of 3 to 8.

Rita's parents were born in Salvador. They married when the mother was 15 and the father was 26. The father had been disabled throughout the patient's life. He had developed a heart condition that required him to stop working when Rita was 1 year old. When Rita was 7, he had his by-pass operation. The mother was a practicing Catholic who brought Rita to mass each week. There was a large family support system in the vicinity but the family was isolated from unrelated neighbors. The mother appeared to be a tired, helpless, and disorganized woman who was evidently quite intelligent. She was out of the house when Rita was home and consequently expected her husband to discipline the child. The mother had given up hope of controlling Rita and did not restrict her eating. The father's illness obviously limited the attention he could give Rita. In addition, he was reluctant to discipline her, since he felt that she would have enough unhappiness in her life when he had died. Unlike the mother, the father seemed to recognize that Rita's behavior indicated an emotional disturbance.

Both parents treated Rita as an adult. They tried to convince her rationally why she shouldn't overeat, but they were unwilling to enforce the rules. By virtue of their advanced ages, they seemed out of touch with Rita's childishness and did not support it. Similarly, they were unwilling to play the parental role in controlling her behavior. Instead, she was seen as a miniature adult who did not respond to action. As a result, the patient had an air of pseudomaturity about her.

Rita was a large, overweight girl with a cheerful mood, above-average intelligence, and the ability to relate well to adult interviewers. Her speech tone and pattern were wide-ranging and appropriate except during the play group, when she began to giggle expansively and was on the verge of losing control. The patient was not in the least constricted and, in fact, could move easily between fantasy and rationality. Her reality testing seemed generally intact, with occasional elaborations of fact or intermingling of fact with fantasy. Her general intelligence seemed strong, although her verbal facility was markedly better than her abstract skills. While her insight was good, it was more difficult to evaluate her thinking and judgment. When she was calm, her thinking was logical; however, when stimulated she was vulnerable to poor judgment.

She was a good student who was concerned about making a good impression on her teachers. However, with peers her inability to compromise and her disagreeableness made social contacts volatile. School information corroborated the high quality of school work and her difficulty with peers. Psychological testing of WISC totaled 110; her verbal score was 115; and her performance score was 105.

The patient exhibited marked strengths in ego functioning and superego development. She was heavily defended against the experience of depressive affect and a sense of emptiness; her overall character style contained features of a cheery, hysterical personality and an entitled self-gratifying narcissistic personality. Significant pockets of ego weakness were present, and her impulse control deteriorated in the face of stimulation. She tried to regulate her affective experience by gratifying herself and by controlling others. Consequently, she spent her time in solitary activities. This compromise solution seemed to be breaking down, as was indicated by the use of alcohol and perfume.

Rita's conflicts and her identity problems revolved around themes of oral aggression. She identified with Bunnicula, the vampire bunny, and allegedly recalled biting down on the nurse's finger with her one tooth, shortly after birth. These cannibalistic themes reflected her preoccupation with being dangerous to others—a ritual she acted out constantly with food and peers. Rita was struggling with her aggressive impulses. She believed that she had almost killed her mother by being born and worried that she would kill her father. Both Rita and her mother felt that they had to constrain their aggressive impulses around the father for fear they would kill him. By controlling her friends, which is an aggressive act, and by eating uncontrollably Rita was acting out her aggressive impulses in the least dangerous way. At one point, Rita had said that she would "kill Menudo with kisses." For her, love and aggression had become intermingled.

Overall Assessment

Axis II: Mixed personality disorder. 301.89 Borderline Personality Disorder with histrionic features.
Axis III: Obesity
Axis IV: 4
Axis V: 4

Overall Treatment Considerations

The assessment of the borderline child involves a comprehensive biopsychosocial examination. The importance of this diagnosis is reflected in an appropriate treatment plan, which includes a combination of the following categories:

1) A particular type of supportive-expressive psychotherapy, with a minimum of twice weekly sessions, alerting the therapist to the particular transference and countertransference issues (P. Kernberg 1983).

2) A crucial involvement of both parents, and the intensive work with the family system.

3) The role of group therapy to compensate for lags in social skills and friendships.

4) The role of long-term therapeutic milieu (hospital, day hospital, or residential setting). Bentivegna et al. (1985) indicated that the mean length of treatment for borderline children who improved was 3.8 years versus 2.2 years for those who showed no change. Moreover, 34 percent of those who improved had some form of residential treatment, as compared to only approximately 15 percent for those who did not change, and to no residential treatment for those who became worse.

5) Medication, primarily used for target symptoms. Impramine has proved beneficial for depression in borderline children; ritalin for attention deficit

disorders, or antipsychotic drugs for acute disorganization. Medication for adults may eventually be tried on children.

In adults, the pure borderline personality disorders have not responded favorably to drug treatment. However, Alprazolam (Faltus 1984), Levodopa (Bonnet and Redford 1982), Thiotixene, and Haloperidol (Serban and Siegel 1984) have been tried. The positive effects were on anxiety, cognitive disturbances, paranoid ideation, and depression, including a significant reduction of negative self-image.

SUMMARY

The borderline syndrome in childhood continues to be a complex riddle. There has been definite progress in its descriptive validity, especially in its delineation from neurosis in children. Follow-up studies indicate several outcomes, which do not detract from the current value of the borderline diagnosis in prognosis and treatment planning. Biological markers may still be found in future research, but genetic studies seem at this point negative. Environmental and constitutional factors are most crucial and should be part of a thorough assessment. The association with affective disorders may be overrepresented, due to the fact that the borderline personality disorder is frequently associated with various kinds of depression (e.g., characterological), not only with major depression.

The diagnosis should not be given in the presence of acute Axis I diagnosis. The main characteristics are identity diffusion, shifting ego states, disturbed peer relationships, and the disturbance in play.

Prospective studies in children, taking into account the role of organicity, the type of treatment interventions, and naturalistic studies should further our current knowledge.

REFERENCES

Aarkrog, T. (1981). The borderline concept in childhood, adolescence and adulthood: Borderline adolescents in psychiatric treatment and five years later. *Acta Psychiat. Scand.* Suppl. 293:1–300.

Andrulonis, P. A., et al. (1980). Organic brain dysfunction and the borderline syndrome. *Psychiatric Clinics of North America* 4(1):47–66.

Archer, R. P., Ball, J. D., and Hunter, J. A. (1985). MMPI characteristics of borderline psychopathology in adolescent inpatients. *J. Personality Assess.* 49:1.

Asarnow, J. R., et al. (1982). Family interaction and the course of adolescent psychopathology: An analysis of adolescent and parent effects. *J. Abnor. Child Psychol.* 10(3):427–42.

Bemporad, J., et al. (1982). Borderline syndromes in childhood: Criteria for diagnosis. *Amer. J. Psychiat.* 139(5):596–602.

Bentivegna, S. W., Ward, L. B., and Bentivegna, N. P. (1985). Study of a diagnostic profile of the borderline syndrome in childhood and trends in treatment outcome. *Child Psychiat. Human Devel.* 15:3.

Blotcky, A. D. (1984). Early use of the Rorschach in anticipating the transference of borderline adolescents. *Dynamic Psychother.* 2(2):157.

Bonnet, K. A., and Redford, H. R. (1982). Levodopa in borderline disorders. *Arch. Gen. Psychiat.* 39:862.

Christenson, R. M., and Wilson, W. P. (1985). Assessing pathology in the separation-individuation process by an inventory: A preliminary report. *J. Nerv. Mental Dis.* 173(9):561–65.

Crumley, F. E. (1981). Adolescent suicide attempts and borderline personality disorder. *Southern Med. J.* 174(5):546–49.

Dahl, A. A. (1985). Borderline disorders: The validity of the diagnostic concept. *Psychiatric Developments* 2:109–52.

———. (1985). Borderline patients: A comparative study of adult hospitalized cases. Oslo, unpublished monograph.

Ekstein, R., and Friedman, S. (1967). Object constancy and psychotic reconstruction. *Psychoanal. Study Child* 22:357–74.

———, and Wallerstein, J. (1954). Observations on the psychology of borderline and psychotic children: Report from a current psychotherapy research project at Southard School. *Psychoanal. Study Child* 9:344–69.

Engel, M. (1963). Psychological testing of borderline psychotic children. *Arch. Gen. Psychiat.* 8(196):426–34.

Faltus, F. S. (1984). The positive effects of alpiazolam in the treatment of three patients with borderline personality disorder. *Amer. J. Psychiat.* 141:802–3.

Freud, A. (1969). *The assessment of borderline cases in the writings of Anna Freud*, Vol. 5. New York: International Universities Press.

Frijling-Schreuder, E. C. M. (1969). Borderline states in children. *Psychoanal. Study Child* 24:307–27.

Geleerd, E. R. (1958). Borderline states in childhood and adolescence. *Psychoanal. Study Child* 13:279–95.

Gualtieri, C. T., Komath, U., and Bourgondien, M. E. (1983). *J. Autism and Devel. Disorders* 13:1.

Kernberg, O. (1975). *Borderline Conditions and Pathological Narcissism*. New York: Jason Aronson.

———. (1978). The diagnosis of borderline conditions in adolescence. In S. Feinstein and P. Giopacchini (Eds.). *Adolescent Psychiat.* Vol. 6. Chicago: University of Chicago Press.

Kernberg, P. F. (1979). Psychoanalytic profile of the borderline adolescent. *Adolescent Psychiat.* 8:234–56.

———. (1983). Borderline conditions: Childhood and adolescent aspects. In K. S. Robson (Ed.). *The Borderline Child—Approaches to Etiology, Diagnosis, and Treatment*. New York: McGraw-Hill, pp. 101–19.

Kestenbaum, C. J. (1983). The borderline child at risk for major psychiatric disorder in adult life. In K. S. Robson (Ed.). *The Borderline Child—Approaches to Etiology, Diagnosis, and Treatment*. New York: McGraw-Hill, pp. 49–82.

Leichtman, M., and Nathan, S. (1983). A clinical approach to the psychological testing of borderline children. In K. S. Robson (Ed.). *The Borderline Child—Ap-

proaches to Etiology, Diagnosis, and Treatment. New York: McGraw-Hill, pp. 121–70.

———, and Shapiro, S. (1980a). An introduction to the psychological assessment of borderline conditions in children: Borderline children and the test process. In J. S. Kwawer, et al. (Eds.). *Borderline Phenomena and the Rorschach Test.* New York: International Universities Press, pp. 343–66.

———, and Shapiro, S. (1980b). An introduction to the psychological assessment of borderline conditions in children: Manifestations of borderline phenomena on psychological testing. In J. S. Kwawer, et al. (Eds.). *Borderline Phenomena and the Rorschach Test.* New York: International Universities Press, pp. 367–94.

Liebowitz, J. H. (1981). Descriptive aspects and clinical features of borderline children and adolescents: An empirical study. Presented at the American Orthopsychiatric Association, New York City, March.

Loranger, A. W., Oldham, J. M., and Tulis, E. H. (1982). Familial transmission of DSM-III borderline personality disorder. *Arch. Gen. Psychiat.* 39:795–99.

McGlashan, T. H. (1983). The borderline syndrome. II. Is it a variant of schizophrenia or affective disorder? *Arch. Gen. Psychiat.* 40:319–23.

Mahler, M. S., Ross, J. R., Jr., and DeFries, Z. (1949). Clinical studies in benign and malignant cases of childhood psychosis (schizophrenia-like). *Am. J. Orthopsychiat.* 19:295–305.

———, and Kaplan, L. (1977). Developmental aspects in the assessment of narcissistic or so-called borderline personalities. In P. Hartocollis (Ed.). *Borderline Personality Disorders: The Concept, the Syndrome, the Patient.* New York: International Universities Press, pp. 71–85.

Perry, J., and Klerman, G. (1980). Clinical features of the borderline personality disorder. *Amer. J. Psychiat.* 137:165–73.

Petti, T. A., and Law, W. (1981). Abrupt cessation of high-dose imipramine treatment in children. *J. Amer. Med. Asso.* 246:768–81.

Pfeffer, C. R. (1983). Clinical observations of suicidal behavior in a neurotic, a borderline, and a psychotic child: Common processes of symptom formation. *Child Psychiat. Human Devel.* 13(2) (in press).

Pine, F. (1983). A working nosology of borderline syndromes in children. In K. S. Robson (Ed.). *The Borderline Child—Approaches to Etiology, Diagnosis, and Treatment.* New York: McGraw-Hill, pp. 83–100.

———. (1974). On the concept "borderline" in children: A clinical essay. *Psychoanal. Study Child* 29:391–68.

Pope, H. G., et al. (1983). The validity of DSM-III borderline personality disorder. *Arch. Gen. Psychiat.* 40:23–30.

Reynolds, C. F., III, et al. (1985). Depression in borderline patients: A prospective EEG sleep study. *Psychiat. Research* 14:1–15.

Rinsley, D. B. (1980a). The developmental etiology of borderline and narcissistic disorders. *Bull. Menninger Clinic* 44:127–34.

———. (1980b). Diagnosis and treatment of borderline and narcissistic children and adolescents. *Bull. Menninger Clinic* 44:147–70.

———. (1981). Borderline psychopathology: The concepts of Masterson and Rinsley and beyond. *Adolescent Psychiat.* 9:259–74.

Rosenfeld, K., and Sprince, M. (1963). An attempt to formulate the meaning of the concept "borderline." *Psychoanal. Study Child* 18:603–35.

Rubin, S. S., Lippman, J., and Goldberg, H. (1984). Borderline and neurotic children: What's the difference anyhow? *Child Psychiat. Human Devel.* 5(1):4–20.

Schubert, D. L., Sacuzzo, D. P., and Braff, B. L. (1985). Information processing in borderline patients. *J. Nerv. Mental Dis.* 173(1):26–31.

Senn, M. J. E., and Solnit, A. J. (1968). *Problems in Child Behavior and Development*. Philadelphia: Lea and Febiger.

Serban, G., and Siegel, S. (1984). Response of borderline and schizotypal patients to small doses of thiotixene and haloperidol. *Amer. J. Psychiat.* 141:1455–58.

Shapiro, E. R., et al. (1975). The influence of family experience on borderline personality development. *Int. Rev. Psychoanal.* 2:399–412.

Smith, F. H., Bemporad, J. R., and Harrison, G. (1982). Aspects of the treatment of borderline children. *Amer. J. Psychother.* 36:2.

Soloff, H. P., and Millward, J. W. (1983). Developmental histories of borderline patients. *Comprehensive Psychiat.* 24(6):574–88.

Stone, M. H. (1983). Special problems in borderline adolescents from wealthy families. *Adolescent Psychiat.* 11:163–76.

Torgersen, S. (1984). Genetic and nosological aspects of schizotypal and borderline personality disorders: A twin study. *Arch. Gen. Psychiat.* 141:546–54.

Vela, R., Gottlieb, E., and Gottlieb, H. (1983). Borderline syndromes in childhood: A critical review. In K. S. Robson (Ed.). *The Borderline Child—Approaches to Etiology, Diagnosis, and Treatment*. New York: McGraw-Hill, pp. 31–48.

Verhulst, F. C. (1984). Diagnosing borderline children. *Acta Paedopsychiat.* 50:161–73.

Weil, A. P. (1953). Certain severe disturbances of ego development in childhood. *Psychoanal. Study Child* 8:271–86.

29

AFFECTIVE DISORDERS

Jules R. Bemporad and Kyu Won Lee

In dramatic contrast to the paucity of literature on childhood affective disorders prior to the 1970s, the last fifteen years have witnessed a massive outpouring of articles, chapters and books on this form of pediatric disturbance. Despite this wealth of information, basic questions regarding diagnosis, assessment, and etiology remain. Some researchers believe that childhood depression is essentially the same as the adult form of the disorder, while others insist that there are important differences that reflect the social and cognitive developmental immaturity of children.

Until quite recently, the overwhelming clinical dogma was that depression simply did not occur in children, or that if it did, depression assumed myriad forms devoid of sad affect or other cardinal diagnostic features of adult depressions. These latter alleged manifestations were termed "depressive equivalents," meaning that the manifest nondepressive symptom was a sort of substitute for the more familiar affective disturbance. On this basis, numerous symptoms, from colic and headbanging (Toolan 1962) to sleep disorders (Sperling 1962), have been suggested as childhood equivalents of depression. While it may be that depression is expressed and experienced differently at various stages of development, it does not follow that any symptom can be labeled as depression in disguise unless there is some logical link between the symptom and depression itself. In a cogent review of depressive equivalents, Rie (1966) concluded that just such a logical relationship is missing and that the term has been extended beyond usefulness. More recently, Carlson and Cantwell (1980) have reported that one can penetrate beneath so-called masked depression by careful interviewing and find a depressive symptom complex coexisting with other complaints. Concurrently, Cytryn et al. (1980) have renounced their earlier use of masked depression or depressive equivalents as diagnostic labels on the basis of further work with depressed children. Today there is general agreement that depression does occur in children before puberty and that dysphoria is a major characteristic of the disorder. (The case is not so decided for manic-depressive or bipolar disorders in childhood. Scattered case reports of childhood manic episodes have been criticized as diagnostically vague, unreliable, and lacking follow-up that would confirm the diagnosis [Anthony and Scott 1960].)

This newer characterization and acceptance of childhood affective disorders may be due in part to a major alteration of the general theoretical interpretation of depression. One aspect of this alteration was a simplification of the psychodynamic view of depression in the course of the evolution of general psychoanalytic theory, resulting in less stringent criteria that would apply to children as well as to a greater number of adults. This change in the conceptualization of depression began with the work of Bibring (1953), who suggested that depression be viewed as a basic state of the ego that is automatically experienced in particular circumstances, rather than as the result of complex intrapsychic struggles such as aggression directed at a pathognomonic introject or the ego being punished by an excessively severe superego. Sandler and Joffee (1965) further developed this simplified view of depression, suggesting that dysphoria be viewed as a basic affect, much like anxiety, which accompanied the loss of a prior sense of well-being. Sandler and Joffee added two other theoretical refinements that have particular importance to childhood and adolescent depression. They suggested that the loss of a prior sense of well-being is a sufficient cause of depression and that the role of object loss, which had been seen as a significant factor in depression since Freud's original contribution (1917), was causative only insofar as the lost object had supplied the individual with a sense of well-being. Therefore, object loss per se might not cause a depressive response, while the loss of gratifying activities or status could result in depression.

The other pertinent observation of Sandler and Joffee was the differentiation of two forms of depression: an immediate and ubiquitous "psychobiological" reaction and a later, less frequent clinical depressive episode. The former state is a reaction to the abrupt loss of well-being and autonomously arises in everyone. In time, most individuals will be able to overcome this sense of loss by substituting other activities, objects, or goals and by removing dysphoria. However, some individuals, due to personality deficits or particular external circumstances, are not successful in finding alternate substitutes for their loss of well-being; this perpetuates and intensifies the initial reaction into a clinical episode. The separation of depression into these forms is especially relevant, for it may be questioned whether the initial "psychobiological" reaction should be called depression at all or whether it is to be viewed as a justifiable and self-limited response to frustration. This lack of agreement is apparent in the works of Arieti (1978), who has also greatly shaped our current concepts of depression. Arieti, like Bibring and Sandler and Joffee, considered depression as a basic affect that arises in situations that deprive the individual of needed self-esteem and meaning. He also differentiated an initial reaction that, if not remedied, escalated into clinical depression. However, for Arieti the initial reaction was best described as *sadness*, a normal emotion rather than depression, which he considered as a pathological state. In fact, depression revealed its pathological nature by arising only in those individuals whose psychological limitations prevent their adequately responding to initial sadness, which should be seen as an alarm signal much like physical pain, calling for its removal by changes in activity and modes of being.

This less complex formulation of depression would more easily lend itself to the possibility of true affective disturbances in childhood, although variations in clinical presentation would still be subject to differences in levels of development.

An equally strong motive for the documentation of depression in childhood may be the impressive advances achieved in the study of adult affective disorders in the past few decades. Pharmacological treatments such as lithium carbonate, tricyclic, and MAO inhibiting antidepressants have been introduced, with great success, for particular forms of adult affective disorders. Concurrently, heuristic and synthesizing theories of etiology, such as the catecholamine hypothesis, have raised hopes of discovering an underlying metabolic defect in affective illness, possibly resulting from a more basic genetic abnormality. This search for an etiological agent has given rise to large-scale epidemiological and genetic studies. A related avenue of research has been the investigation of possible biological markers representing coexisting clinical, or even pathognomonic, signs of affective disorders that are accessible to laboratory confirmation.

Current advances in the understanding of central nervous system neurotransmission have provided a framework for identifying biological markers in the assessment of affective disorders in adults. In the past decade, results of similar efforts made in child psychiatry began to appear in the literature when psychobiological research conducted on adult affective disorders was replicated in children, investigating "biological markers" such as urinary MHPG level, growth hormone response, sleep EEG, and Daxamethasone Suppression Tests (DST). Although very limited in quantity compared to the volume of neurohormonal research of affective disorders in adults, the reports on prepubertal and adolescent depressed patients largely, though not uniformly, parallel the findings in their senior counterparts.

McKnew and Cytryn (1979) reported a significantly lowered urinary MHPG level in depressed prepubertal children compared with the level found in normal controls. However, these depressed children secreted more MHPG in their urine compared to the age-matched orthopedic inpatients without depression. Hyposecretion of growth hormone in response to insulin-induced hypoglycemia found among the adults with endogenous depression was replicated with the depressed children. Subsequent studies by Puig-Antich and Chambers (1978) also demonstrated that prepubertal depressed children secreted more growth hormone during sleep than did their normal controls. Disordered REM sleep, one of the documented sleep disturbances in adults with endogenous depression, was also studied in depressed children, with inconsistent findings. One study of depressed adolescents showed shortened REM sleep paralleling the findings of adults with endogenous depression. On the other hand, prepubertal depressed children did not reveal any deviation in REM latency from that of normal controls; however, they did show a significantly shorter first REM period after they had been fully recovered from depression and were drug-free. Studies of DST reported the same positive results as in depressed adults in both prepubertal and adolescent children with depression.

There is great promise in the emerging knowledge of neuroendocrinology and its possible application to diagnostic and therapeutic sophistication in dealing with depressed children. It suggests the possibility of a much-desired integration of neurochemical, genetic, and psychosocial data. However, none of these tests has yet been established as a stable biological marker for childhood depression. Nor are such tests as easily accessible at this point as a diagnostic tool in everyday child psychiatry practice. Furthermore, care should be exercised in interpreting the results of biochemical tests in one's appraisal of the childhood depression. Cohen and Young (1977) aptly made this point in a broader context, noting that finding a deviation in catecholamine metabolism, thus, does not necessarily imply that this precedes or causes a child's difficulties; it may result from his experience (e.g., the stress of chronic perceptual problems, social isolation, or hospitalization). In order to perform such studies, valid, reliable and preferably rapid evaluation of childhood affective disorders becomes mandatory and necessitates the creation of objective assessment instruments. In turn, these assessment techniques require agreed upon criteria for diagnosis and some fundamental system of classification.

DIAGNOSTIC CRITERIA

The third edition of DSM-III does not list separate diagnostic characteristics for affective disorders in childhood, stating that the major symptoms are the same for infants, children, adolescents, and adults. However, the DSM-III does recognize the existence of developmental differences. The classification of affective disorders in the DSM-III consists of 1) major affective disorders, which are divided into bipolar disorder and major depression; 2) other specific affective disorders, which include cyclothymic disorder and dysthymic disorder (depressive neurosis); and 3) atypical affective disorders, which are specified as atypical bipolar disorder and atypical depression. In addition, adjustment disorder with depressed mood is listed under the category of adjustment disorders. The criteria for major depressive disorder are listed below with the modifications allowed for different age groups:

A) Dysphoric mood or loss of interest or pleasure in all or almost all usual activities and pastimes. (For children under 6, dysphoric mood may have to be inferred from a persistently sad facial expression.)

B) At least four of the following symptoms have been present nearly every day for a period of at least two weeks (in children under 6, at least three of the first four).
   i) poor appetite or significant weight loss (when not dieting) or increased appetite or significant weight gain (in children under 6, failure to make expected weight gains);
   ii) insomnia or hypersomnia;
   iii) psychomotor agitation or retardation (but not merely subjective feelings of restlessness or being slowed down) (in children under 6, hypoactivity);

iv) loss of interest or pleasure in usual activities, or decrease in sexual drive (not limited to a period when delusional or hallucinating) (in children under 6, signs of apathy);

v) loss of energy; fatigue;

vi) feelings of worthlessness, self-reproach, or excessive or inappropriate guilt (either may be delusional);

vii) complaints or evidence of diminished ability to concentrate, such as slowed thinking, or indecisiveness not associated with marked loosening of associations or incoherence;

viii) recurrent thoughts of death, suicidal ideation, wishes to be dead, or suicide attempt.

In addition, the DSM-III lists possible age-associated features for major depressive episode, which in the case of children include intense anxiety symptoms (for prepubertal children) and various antisocial or negativistic behavior for adolescent males.

The major features for dysthymic disorder are a chronic disturbance of mood or lack of interest in activities that is not of sufficient severity to meet criteria for major depressive disorder. For adults, a two-year duration of chronic dysphoria is required, while for children and adolescents only one year duration is required. The only other diagnosis with affective symptomatology likely to be found in children is adjustment disorder with depressed mood, for which no specific modifications are given for different age groups. The essential feature of adjustment disorders is a maladaptive reaction to an identifiable psychosocial stressor. The maladaptive nature of the response is shown by impairment in occupational or social functioning or by symptoms that exceed a normal and expected reaction.

In essence, the criteria for affective disorder in childhood as presented in DSM-III are quite similar to those indicated for adults. The appropriateness of these criteria for prepubertal individuals, and particularly for young children, is still controversial. Hodges and Siegel (1985) commented that there is a paucity of information available about the reliability or validity of the diagnostic categories listed in DSM-III. Published field trials on interrater reliability for affective disorder categories showed good agreement for adult individuals but generally poor agreement for child and adolescent subjects. Some researchers (Puig-Antich 1982; Kovacs et al. 1984) have utilized DSM-III categories with children over age six with apparent ease. Others (Kashani et al. 1984) have found the categories difficult to employ with preschool children. Therefore, despite the recommendations of DSM-III, there is still a lack of consensus on the criteria for diagnosis of childhood affective disorder, although much progress has been made.

The continuing difficulties revolve around whether the essential features of affective disorders are the same in children and adults and whether there are age-specific features of affective disorders that parallel the developmental process. The lack of overall agreement has led individual researchers to propose their own list of diagnostic criteria that they feel are more appropriate for use with children. Generally, all these schemata include mood changes and lack of interest in activities, as does DSM-III, but substitute items such as poor school performance or somatic complaints (rather than vegetative symptoms), which are more typical of the child's social and psychological experience. Much of the impetus to develop valid and reliable criteria is the need for an accurate method of assessment in order to pursue research studies on other variables, such as family history, biological markers, environmental and personality characteristics, or response to treatment, which would aid in uncovering the etiology and prognosis of childhood affective disorders. Often, diagnostic criteria have been proposed in order to construct an assessment scale that would identify the presence of affectively ill children in research populations. Numerous assessment instruments have appeared in the last ten years and, while still in the early stages of development, are being used in a variety of research studies.

A recent review by Hodges and Siegel (1985) divide those assessment instruments into the following: 1) self-rating scales; 2) clinician rating scales; 3) diagnostic interviews; 4) peer interviews; and 5) parent scales. Among the self-report scales, the Children's Depression Inventory (CDI) (Kovacs and Beck 1977) and the Children's Depression Adjective Checklist (C-DACL) (Brewer and Lubin 1983) were modified from adult measures. The Children's Depression Scale (CDS) (Land and Tisheria 1978) and the Self Rating Scale (SRS) (Birleson 1981) were developed by selecting relevant diagnostic items from the literature. These scales all ask the child to respond in terms of presence, absence, or frequency of symptom items, but they differ in the selection of items. For example, the C-DACL centers on dysphoric mood, the CDI includes items of major depressive disorder such as vegetative symptoms, and the CDS queries more socially related areas such as family relationships and mother's health.

The clinician rated scales include the Bellevue Index of Depression (BDI) (Petti 1978) and the Children's Depression Rating Scale (CDRS) (Poznanski et al. 1979). The former is based on diagnostic criteria for childhood depression formulated by Weinberg et al. (1973), and the latter is modeled after the Hamilton Depression Scale used with adults. These scales are scored by the interviewer, who judges the presence or severity of symptoms, based on the client's answers on selected items.

The Diagnostic Interviews include the Interview Schedule for Children (ISC) (Kovacs 1983) and the Kiddie Schedule for Affective Disorders and Schizophrenia (Puig-Antich and Chambers 1978), both of which are aimed at assessing depression in children. The procedure for these scales consists of a semistructured interview that forms the basis for a scored rating of depression. These instruments seem closer to general clinical practice; they allow a more naturalistic exchange between interviewer and child as well as the opportunity to clarify responses.

A novel approach to the assessment of childhood depression is the Peer Nomination Inventory for Depression (PNID) developed by Lefkowitz and Tesing (1980). This measure asks children in a group questions about their peers, such as "who doesn't have much fun?" Each child nominates other children for each of the questions. Those children who are nominated for a substantial number of selected questions are assumed to be depressed. This instrument, like other peer rating methods, is based on the belief that psychopathology may be most readily noticed by peers who interact in an everyday setting.

Each of these instruments shows promise for an objective and reliable assessment of childhood depression, free of clinical bias and subjectivity. However, reviewers (Kazdin 1981; Hodges and Siegel 1985) have commented that much work still remains to be done in establishing reliability and validity of the instruments. Each method presents its own advantages and limitations. Self-reports seem to be the most direct manner of obtaining information, yet seem to be prone to a good deal of error. Other methods utilize a rater or interviewer who may introduce his own biases into the scoring. Other difficulties include the selection of items, the ages of the children for whom the test items are appropriate, and the setting in which the information is obtained. A particularly pertinent question is the validity of information obtained at one instance, particularly in younger children who may be changeable from one day to the next. Other difficulties are the measures' ability to distinguish between depression and general unhappiness or transient sadness, the inclusion of relevant data from all sources (parents, school, etc.), and the assessment of relative causative factors in the environment (child abuse, for example) in order to arrive at a comprehensive understanding of the child in his or her social and developmental context.

A more profound question into methods of assessment regards the basic nature of affective disorders. The DSM-III, as well as numerous clinical and research papers, adopts the medical model, implying that depression is an illness that has a consistent causative agent, course, prognosis, and response to specific treatments. An alternate view is that depressive phenomena are part of the human being's repertoire of possible responses to stressful events and do not represent evidence of an illness in the medical sense. Some individuals, because of life experiences that shape the personality and its ability to cope in adverse circumstances, may be more prone than others to react to stress with affective disturbances, but the difference is more a matter of degree than of exclusionary categories. The following pages will adopt this latter view, which is still far from validated, but which may give a more comprehensive clinical picture of depressivelike phenomena in children. These phenomena will be examined against a framework of development, in keeping with the observation that the process of cognitive and social maturation affects markedly the manifestation of any psychological disturbance. It is assumed that the child's psychological equipment will color the manner in which he can adapt to or respond to stressful events. As Anthony (1975) has indicated, depression itself undergoes development commensurate with the overall development of the child.

DEPRESSION AND DEVELOPMENT

Despite the unlikelihood of depression being found in the earliest developmental stage because of the great immaturity of the child, the earliest reports of childhood depression concerned infants. Rene Spitz's pioneer studies of the 1940s (Spitz 1946) documented the reactions of 6-month-old children who were separated from their mothers. Spitz found that the infants appeared sad, weepy, and apathetic. They seemed to lose interest in their surroundings, moved slowly, and showed disturbances in eating and sleeping. If the children were reunited with their mothers within three to five months, further deterioration could be averted; if not, according to Spitz, the children grew up retarded and prone to infection and death. Spitz named the syndrome "anaclictic depression" and felt that its major features—sadness, withdrawal, and lethargy—closely resembled symptoms of depression seen in adults.

Depressionlike syndromes have also been described in older infants. Engel and Reichsman (1956) reported the case of Monica, a 15-month-old girl, who had an esophageal atresia and had been neglected severely by her mother. The child exhibited muscular inactivity, hypotonia, a sad facial expression, and eventually, a withdrawn, sleepylike state. These symptoms disappeared when Monica was reunited with a familiar person. Engel and Reichsman concluded that their patient presented an infantile form of depression as well as a basic conservation-withdrawal reaction. The latter response was utilized to exclude a painful psychological environment and to preserve the integrity of the psyche.

Finally, Bowlby (1960) has mentioned symptoms that are suggestive of depression in his elucidation of the separation process. After abnormal separation from the mother, the infant first exhibits the stage of protest characterized by loud crying and thrashing about. The stage of despair follows, during which the infant becomes quieter, shows less movement, and is listless. Finally, the infant appears to defend against his loss and in the last stage, called detachment, becomes cheerful again and reacts to new maternal substitutes. The second stage of despair shows some similarity to the depressive syndromes described by Spitz and by Engel and Reichsman.

A summary of the clinical presentation of the dysphoric infant would include sad faces, listlessness, a lack of responsiveness to the environment, and possibly disturbances in eating and sleeping. The interpretation of this state is that the infant is withdrawing from a world made painful by the absence of the mother. There is little doubt that infants do present with such a clinical picture; however, the inference that this presentation represents an infantile form of depression has come under repeated criticism. The same withdrawal-like state has been observed in children who lacked cognitive stimulation (Dennis and Najarian 1957) or were malnourished (Malmquist 1977) and who had not been subjected to an abrupt separation or loss. This syndrome is being reevaluated as the result of deprivation of needed environmental supplies—cognitive, emotional, and nutritive—rather than a reactive depression. Poznanski (1979) criticized Spitz's conclusions by emphasizing: 1) that only 15 percent of the children who underwent separation showed the "anaclitic depressive" syndrome, so that factors other than maternal separation could have been causative; and 2) that subsequent to depression the infants were placed in a deprived environment, so that their reaction may have been to overall current and continuing multiple deprivations rather than solely to the past loss of the mother.

A similar criticism has been leveled at Bowlby's conclusions, since the children he studied were not simply separated from their mothers but were often put into painful, deprived environments such as hospitals or institutions. It is questionable if the dull withdrawal state would have emerged if the children had been transferred to lively, warm, and gratifying environments.

Therefore, the depressionlike picture of infants may be interpreted as at least influenced by deprivation of needed environmental stimulation. The infant may become unreactive because there is little in the environment to react to or because he is in physical pain secondary to hunger or other problems. These statements are not meant to underplay the importance of the role of the mother figure in normal development during infancy. The mother satisfies most of the infant's needs; for food, physical comfort, reciprocal interaction, and stimulation. Her loss leaves the child in a deprived environment that, if continued without compensation, produces the syndrome described. This syndrome may be the product of having matured in a barren environment at a stage of life when external response is necessary for normal psychological growth.

An interesting parallel finding of depressionlike syndromes comes from experiments with infant monkeys who have been separated from their mothers (see McKinney and Moran 1982, for a review). Separated infant monkeys go through a protest-despair-detachment sequence similar to that described in humans by Bowlby. The degree of this basic response, however, has been found to be influenced by a number of factors, including the age at separation, the nature of the preseparation relationship, the species of monkey, and the degree of surrogate mothering or stimulation available. For example, separated infants housed in pairs were less "depressed" than those housed alone. Similarly, separated monkeys who were raised with younger peers showed little abnormality. The extent to which peer contact can negate or greatly ameliorate effects of maternal separation in infant monkeys raises again the question of what the nature of deprivation really is in these monkeys. Researchers have found that the same separation sequence can be observed in infant monkeys who were separated from mothers at birth and reared together and then were removed from the peer group. In this case, the loss of stimulation and rupture of attachment bonds to peers provokes an equal reaction to separation from the mother. A more provocative study was reported by Mason and Berkson (1974), who showed that the behavior ascribed to maternal separation in infant monkeys raised in isolation may have been due to stimulus deprivation. They found that if mobile, rocking, terrycloth surrogate mothers were substituted for the stationary ones traditionally used in isolation experiments, the expected self-rocking and lack of play activities were not observed. These results suggest the absence of vestibular stimulation on an isolated infant monkey may determine aspects of its later behavior as much as maternal separation.

These animal studies, much as observations on human infants, document that separation from the mother is a highly stressful event that elicits a basic separation sequence in the infant, part of which resembles a depressive state. It is still unknown what the actual inner experience of these infants may be beyond the clear indication that it is highly unpleasant, and may have long-term consequences. It may be that such experiences represent a primal psychobiological state of discomfort produced by various factors. The protest observed after separation appears to be an attempt to call the mother, while the despair stage will elicit caregiving behavior from mother surrogates, if available. These behaviors can be conceptualized in ethological terms as ensuring the helpless primate infant of continued care necessary for further development.

Early Childhood

The preschool period, when the child is roughly 2½ to 6 years of age, is notable for the paucity of reports describing depression. The lack of sustained dysphoria in early childhood is exemplified by Poznanski and Zrull's (1970) search through the charts of 1,788 children who had been outpatients at the Children's Psychiatric Hospital of the University of Michigan from 1964 to 1968. They could find only one child under the age of 5 who could be considered as showing some evidence of depressive symptoms. This child was a 3-year-old girl who had been neglected by her mother and exhibited failure to thrive, fear of abandonment, and quiet withdrawal. The authors commented that they were greatly aided in their diagnosis of this child by a reevaluation when she was 5 years old. In general, other authors also have not found depression to be manifested in children below school age. Kovacs and Beck (1977) summarized these reports as follows: "Our initial period of perusal of the literature disclosed a prevalent opinion that among children under five or six years of age, depressive disorders either do not exist or are exceedingly difficult to recognize" (p. 2).

The reasons for the rarity of depression in the preschooler may be found in the developmental characteristics of this stage. Children at this age do not sustain moods for long periods of time but are exquisitely reactive to changing situations. During the first half of this stage the child delights in activity and obtains gratification from doing rather than passively receiving. This is the era of normal oppositionalism, with the typical testing of the will and autonomy. Fears and inhibitions are overruled by a delight in exploring and manipulating the physical world. This is not fertile soil for the generation of depressive disorders.

Some children in the early preschool period, however, present with a lack of the expected exuberance and willfulness that we have come to expect from toddlers. Mahler (1961) described these children as clingy and whiny, particularly in the presence of their mothers, from whom they find it difficult to separate. It would appear that the normal push to individuation has for some reason threatened the mother, who responds to the child's burgeoning attempts at mastery with psychological abandonment. The toddler may then perceive his newly acquired strivings for satisfaction as jeopardizing his older, established security needs. He may inhibit his seeking pleasure in autonomous doing, presenting an overly controlled, pseudomature child who needs to be reassured that his mother will continue her nurturance. These children do not present with depression or even periods of sadness, but may be at grave risk for later depressive illness when they have begun to suppress their inborn sense of gratification through independent activity in order to ensure a tenuous flow of narcissistic supplies from needed others.

As the child progresses beyond the "typical" toddler stage to nursery school age, the early manifested exuberance becomes overshadowed by a normal renewed need for parental support. Mahler (1968) called this period the "rapprochement" phase of the separation-individuation process, during which the child lessens his sense of invulnerability and realizes he needs the mother and others for protection and support. If these "older" preschool children are subjected to repeated separations or deprivations, they may manifest symptoms of profound unhappiness as a direct reaction to the lack of a needed emotional reassurance from significant others. These periods of dysphoria are typically accompanied by anger and fears of abandonment, as well as occasional phobias and sleeping and eating disorders. The following clinical vignette is illustrative of the depressionlike disorders seen in this age group.

Jean

Jean was first seen at age 6 years and 10 months for a diagnostic evaluation following possible sexual abuse by her uncle. Jean was described as being frequently sad, with prolonged episodes of crying, alternating with numerous temper tantrums. The mother was only 13 years old when Jean was born, but was able to care for her throughout her early infancy. For the past two years, however, the mother had been addicted to heroin and supported her habit through prostitution. Along with the addiction, the mother had become increasingly unstable in her general functioning, showing periods of erratic and aggressive behavior. Jean was cared for by her maternal grandmother and aunt, while her mother became an inconsistent figure in the household. After being away for weeks, she would return home and be quite loving and affectionate toward Jean, only to disappear again. In recent months, the mother's condition had deteriorated and she was openly psychotic and bizarre during her unpredictable visits to the household. Jean reacted to her mother's decompensation with temper tantrums, a refusal to eat, quiet withdrawal, and self-injury. Once the mother was gone a few days, Jean seemed to improve, only to become symptomatic again when the mother reappeared. During these times, Jean's daycare teacher noticed that the child would not play with her peers and often sat alone scratching herself to the point of bleeding.

On evaluation, Jean was responsive and friendly, although in her diagnostic doll play session she produced stories of crying babies and of dangers in the environment. During these play sessions Jean was manifestly sad and unhappy, although she could quickly become cheerful again if distracted.

Jean's behavior appeared to be the result of repeated disappointments and rejections by a needed mother who was insensitive to the child's needs because of her own difficulties. The recurrent separations, interspersed with periods of affectionate care, and the eventual decompensation of the mother undermined Jean's embryonic sense of security. Her reaction was one of anger and defiance but also of sadness and apathy in the face of being psychologically deprived of her former "good" mother.

In summary, depressive symptoms are extremely rare in the preschool child. Infrequently, children are seen who respond to almost constant frustration with withdrawal, sadness, and fear of abandonment. Other children display a serious precociousness and a lack of spontaneity, and cling to the parent. While this latter type of child does not exhibit dysphoria, he may be at risk for later depressive episodes for he has learned to inhibit normal avenues of satisfaction for the security of a continued relationship with the parent.

Middle Childhood

Longer and more profound periods of genuine sadness may be observed as the child grows to school age. For example, Bierman, Silverstein, and Finesinger (1961) reported the case of a 6-year-old boy who was hospitalized with poliomyelitis, which had caused limb paralysis. After two months of this illness, the boy developed an almost adultlike depression. He seemed profoundly sad, withdrew from others, and cried frequently. The illness caused him to be deprived of his usual gratifying everyday activities. His mother visited him regularly but her presence could not compensate for his loss of the ability to play games, be with peers, attend school, and so on. Fortunately, with recovery from poliomyelitis, his depression disappeared. It is significant that, although appearing profoundly depressed in terms of depth of affect, this boy did not exhibit lowered self-esteem or a concern with the future. Rather, he was reacting to two months of confinement, deprivation of gratifying activities, and isolation.

This case is instructive, for it shows that children at this age may show severe depressive affect, but do so mainly in response to gross environmental deprivation. They react directly to their surroundings and do not appear to generate feelings of depression based on judgments about themselves or others. Their thinking is "intuitive" in the Piagetian (1952) sense, meaning that they base their conclusions on intuition rather than on looking beyond their immediate situation for logical underlying reasons. Feelings are tied to a concrete, immediate present environment. If that environment is punitive or depriving, the child will become sad or angry, with little change in his estimation of himself. McConville et al. (1973) illustrated the superficial aspects of dysphoria at this developmental stage by describing depression in a group of 6- to 8-year-olds as being an almost pure feeling state with few cognitive components in terms of reason or judgment.

Those situations that provoke a dysphoric response are those that deprive the child of stage-appropriate gratifications, such as chronic illness as in the case of the child described above. Much more frequent, however, is the deprivation of needed consideration and appreciation by the parent, concurrent with enforced restriction from obtaining these satisfactions from others. During this phase of development the child normally idealizes the parents, and their positive response is needed for him to feel good about the environment in general. The child has not as yet begun to find increasing satisfaction from peers or from influential extrafamilial figures, such as teachers or older children who later replace the parents as idealized models. However, even during the oedipal years, nurturing adults or friends may do much to make up for lack of parental care. We (Bemporad and Lee 1984) have found that children at this stage who present with chronic depressionlike episodes have undergone a period of rejection or abandonment by a parent with whom they had a significant emotional tie and are for a variety of reasons prevented from receiving substitute care from others. The children present with a sad demeanor, loss of interest or pleasure in their usual activities, and complaints of feeling lonely and unloved. They may have difficulty falling asleep as well as problems with appetite. A not unusual finding is the blatantly stated threat of suicide. Although they complain of their circumstances, there is little in the sense of dissatisfaction with themselves or of lowered self-esteem. This "externally" caused unhappiness often results in concomitant aggressive outbursts and fights with siblings or peers.

Carol

A typical dysphoric child of this age group was Carol, who was seen at age 6 because of suicidal threats. At evaluation, Carol was sad, quiet, and generally inhibited. In her diagnostic doll play, she eventually loosened up and described a young girl named Hazel who was abused by her mother and who was often alone at home and frightened. On further investigation, Carol said the mother doll abused the Hazel doll because the former was drunk and Hazel was "bad"; however, being bad meant only being called "bad" by the mother doll. As represented by her doll play, Carol felt frustrated, abused, and lonely, and was appropriately saddened by her situation. However, she could give no reasons beyond her concrete experience for feelings; there was no real estimation of herself or others.

Carol had been born to a 16-year-old girl who was currently in prison. In early infancy she was given over to her grandmother, who was only 28 at the time. The grandmother died shortly thereafter and Carol was taken in by her great-grandmother, who was in her fifties. This woman tried her best to raise Carol, but resented having to care for yet another child. She was often out drinking, leaving Carol home alone and not allowing her to leave the apartment. When drunk, the great-grandmother was both verbally and physically abusive toward Carol, although when she was sober she was a diligent, if not loving, caretaker. Carol threatened to kill herself in a jealous rage when the great-grandmother fussed over a visiting neighbor's child. The older woman seemed to take advantage of the incident to seek aid in ridding herself of the child. Carol has since done well as a result of therapy and placement in a good foster home.

Dysphoric episodes at this stage may still be considered as reactive disorders despite the occasional profundity of sad affect, suicidal preoccupations, and aggressive symptoms. Even in the midst of feeling terribly sad, a child of this age may respond cheerfully if his attention is distracted by enjoyable circumstances such as games and treats. However, as the child begins to interpret his environment through the use of deeper categories of meaning involving estimations of himself and others, the dysphoria loses its situation-specific characteristics. At this more mature phase, the child will respond to punishment or criticism from others as implicit of some defect within himself rather than simply as an externally frustrating situation. Older depressed children begin to blame themselves if they cannot meet the demands of their parents, and they react with inner dissatisfaction where previously there may only have been fear of punishment.

Late Childhood

As the child approaches puberty, he begins to evolve a system of thought that includes evaluations of himself as well as others. At the same time, familial values have been firmly internalized and characteristic, consistent modes of dealing with stress become gradually crystallized. The child is more stable over time and situations in terms of his personality patterns, responsivity to stimuli, and basic moods. Following the either gradual or abrupt loss of sources of well-being, the child will respond with a dysphoric affect, but in addition will give reasons for his distress that go beyond the immediate environmental events. He will reveal a sense of personal failure or disappointment with others. The individual in late childhood has become able to view himself more objectively and at the same time in terms of judgments that are no longer intuitive but correspond to a rudimentary set of values and aspirations. Therefore, in addition to a long-standing dysphoric affect, these children will verbalize a sense of worthlessness or will blame themselves for their predicament. They also present a clinical picture of social isolation, but now justify their loneliness by saying that others could not like them or want to be with them. They will express dissatisfaction with themselves if they cannot meet parental or societal standards rather than show anger at having expectations imposed upon them. Other findings are boredom, decreased interest in activities, declining academic performance, and occasional angry, provocative behavior with peers or siblings.

A type of child who frequently presents with depression is one who has had to inhibit his own means of gratification to such a degree in order to please the parent that he finds little pleasure in living. Such a child seems to derive his major source of satisfaction in pleasing the parent, so that he does not master the significant task of latency, namely to enjoy his cognitive and social accomplishments, to find extra-familial ideal models, and to become part of a peer society. These children have been prevented, for a variety of reasons, from emotionally breaking away from the familial orbit. Often the parent may be demanding and critical; equally pernicious is the chronically depressed parent who lays the burden of being cheered up and cared for onto the child's precarious shoulders. The following case history illustrates this form of depression.

Carl

Carl, a 10-year-old boy, was seen in emergency consultation after he had expressed suicidal ideation to his school psychologist. He had been seen for counseling for three months because of changes noted in his behavior. Carl, who used to be a good student, had become less interested in academic achievement, was aggressive with other children, and stole money at school. One week prior to an emergency evaluation, he had been expelled from his afterschool program for aggressive and disruptive behavior.

Prior to Carl's evaluation, there had been several precipitating events that involved actual and threatened losses. In the month previous, his oldest brother, whom he respected, had been arrested for stealing and consequently had been placed in a Division of Youth Services facility. Around the same time, the next older brother, who used to help Carl be with children outside the family, began to spend less time with Carl as he started working after school. Following one week of Carl's stealing attempts, his mother threatened to poison herself and her children.

While the mother was pregnant with Carl, his father left the family. Three years later, the mother gave birth to his half-sister, whose father had lived with them since. This man had threatened to leave the family for the year prior to evaluation and appeared uninvolved with the children, as did their mother, who had been chronically depressed. Carl's mother and older sister had made numerous suicidal threats. The mother had recently buried herself in her work as a lab technician in a local hospital, and spent her evenings drinking at home. In the past, Carl tried very hard to be good so that he could make his mother feel better, but recently gave up on his efforts.

Carl, a slim boy dressed neatly in a three-piece suit, was very polite and controlled, with a frail, depressed, old man quality about him. He was intelligent, articulate, and cooperative with the interviewer. He spoke of feeling sad, bored, and lonely, especially after school; everyone at home was "coming and going and gone." Questions about his suicidal thoughts elicited various fantasies of self-injury, ranging from hurting his knee on purpose by jumping to stabbing himself in the heart to kill himself.

This child was hospitalized because of his suicidal potential. His therapy sessions revealed that he was constantly worried about his mother and felt he had to take care of her. He blamed himself for her depression, believing he had failed to make her happy.

Finally, children at this stage of development may become depressed because of difficulties outside the home. Some children feel rejected by their peers because of poor athletic or social skills and retreat into their households, often magnifying their alleged inferiorities. Children who have learning disabilities and are pressured to achieve academically are at risk for feelings of inadequacy and worthlessness. Often these children are called lazy by their parents and internalize the belief that if only they tried harder, they could do well, only to find they cannot. They fail at a most important activity of late childhood, and are unfairly blamed by their parents, penalized by the school system, and ridiculed by peers. It is not difficult to understand why this group should be particularly vulnerable to depression, or why a significant number turn to acts of delinquency in order to achieve respect in the eyes of their friends and to express their anger at what appears to them an unjustly punitive society.

In summary, the presenting picture of depressed older children consists of persistent sadness, inhibition, verbalized expressions of low self-esteem, and isolation from peers. Often these children are forced to strive for some goal that they are incapable of attaining, either because the goal is unreasonable for their developmental stage or because personal deficiencies preclude success. While their depressions are often severe and do not always respond rapidly to intervention, they are different from the melancholia seen in adults, for these children still lack an accurate sense of continuity between the present and the future. The depressed prepubertal child does not complain of an empty life ahead or an inability to face tomorrow. It is not that he defensively denies the future; rather, he does not think of it because he does not as yet have sufficient cognitive ability. Rie (1966) stressed this difference, finding that hopelessness and despair are absent in depression before adolescence. He argued that these two cardinal features of an adult melancholia depend on cognitive abilities such as the relationship of long-range goals to present strivings, the meaning of infinity, and the absolute permanence of a loss or disappointment, conceptualizations that he believed are too sophisticated for the prepubertal child. Therefore, while exhibiting many features of adult depressions, the dysphorias of older children still show specific characteristics of their developmental immaturity.

Adolescence

With the onset of adolescence, the clinical aspects of depressive disorders truly resemble those of an adult and may surpass the melancholia of maturity in the depth of despair, hopelessness, propensity for suicide, and accompanying anxiety and agitation. Adolescents often view themselves and their world in black and white categories. This all-or-nothing approach is manifested in the depressions of adolescents, during which they view themselves as totally worthless, forever unlovable, or unredeemable failures. Adolescents lack the moderation in thought and action that appears to come with greater life experience and the repeated getting over losses, humiliations, and frustrations that normally occur in the course of growing up. For some adolescents, failing a quiz means certain academic failure, or being stood up for a date means a life of eternal loneliness. Therefore, the depressions of adolescence appear to be provoked easily, present dramatically, and often, but not always, pass quickly.

Those adolescents who present with more sustained dysphoria that goes beyond the immediate reaction to a narcissistic blow are often those who, for one reason or another, are finding it difficult to adjust to life outside of their nuclear families. The reasons for this failure are multiple. The youngster may carry within himself unrealistic expectations that represent the earlier parental ideals; he may be tied to familial mores that are at odds with the values of his peer group; or he may be unprepared for the increased demands made upon individuals at this time of life. It may often happen that parental demands sabotage normal individuation and the shift of interests outside the family group.

We have found that adolescents who experience prolonged and profound depressions often have been relatively isolated from peers and tied emotionally to their families, or have put great demands upon themselves that they could not fulfill. There is usually a history of prior unsatisfactory adjustment, although some form of precarious adaptation may have been achieved in childhood through securing gratification within the family circle, obtaining good grades, or exhibiting some special talent. During adolescence these older gratifications no longer suffice to ensure self-worth, and the youngster perceives himself as somewhat deficient or inferior vis-à-vis his contemporaries. Following some trivial humiliation or frustration, he becomes convinced that he will be a misfit forever or that he is totally worthless, and his sense of self-esteem collapses, producing a profound depression. The dysphoria is felt acutely; depressed adolescents emit a desperate sense of urgency and an apparent inability to tolerate dysphoria. These characteristics may lead to suicidal gestures, use of drugs, or antisocial acts committed in an atmosphere of despair. Other youngsters may seek out faddish groups or cults in the hope of gaining acceptance or a feeling of worth from parent surrogates. Some youngsters feel paralyzed at the prospect of making their own life decisions and defend against the guilt or sense of failure that would arise from acting on their own will by following the orders of some charismatic leader. Still others retreat into further isolation, feel cheated by life, and develop cynical or angry facades that drive others, who are so desperately needed, further away.

Vegetative symptoms, typical of some adult depressions, begin to be clinically significant in adolescence. Decreased or increased appetite may be found, as well as insomnia or excessive sleeping. We have also found that some adolescents react to their feelings of worthlessness and deprivation with antisocial or destructive acts as if to punish an ungratifying world. Many are hostile and uncommunicative during psychiatric evaluation; they sense their being seen by a clinician as a further indignity that confirms their inadequacy, or they perceive the interviewer as yet another adult who will make demands of them.

The following clinical excerpt illustrates some aspects of depression in adolescence.

Joe

Joe was a 16-year-old junior referred by his high school counselor because of deterioration in his academic performance, disruptive behavior in class, and an insolent and provocative attitude toward his teachers. He had recently been caught stealing, smoking, and drinking. Because of his poor grades he had been dropped from the basketball team.

On evaluation, Joe presented as a tall, well-dressed youngster who looked anxious and depressed. He reluctantly followed the interviewer into the office and during ensuing sessions volunteered little information and was restrained in his communications. Beneath his defensiveness, he continued to look sad and demoralized. He said he found little enjoyment in anything and didn't care much about most things.

For the past five years, Joe had been caught in an escalating problem between his parents. His father had started drinking and gradually withdrew emotionally from his family. More recently, the father had become physically abusive to his wife, who in turn relied on Joe, who was over six feet tall, to protect her. Joe felt obligated to protect his mother and be furious at his father, but mostly he was disgusted with both of them and saw them as excessively relying on him. His role as protector prevented him from appropriately finding his extrafamilial activities as satisfying and meaningful. He gradually withdrew from social contacts, started drinking, and felt that nothing in life should matter to him.

While Joe's depressive picture showed obvious elements of self-defeating aggression and distancing provocation, other adolescents may manifest a picture of depression together with depersonalization and an almost schizoid withdrawal into an agonizing fantasy world of self-hatred. In these cases, it is often difficult to rule out a possible incipient schizophrenic disorder. The following young girl illustrates this particularly alarming presentation of depression.

Betsy

Betsy was seen at age 16 for insomnia, weight loss, headache, and social withdrawal. During the initial interview, she complained that she could not concentrate and was terribly worried about her grades as a result. She stated that she felt she was different from other children her age and that she was "uncomfortable with herself." Sometimes she felt apart from the world and "frozen," with her mind a blank. At other times, she was overwhelmed with self-hatred, blaming herself for not fitting in with her peers, for being "strange," a failure, and a disappointment to her parents.

Betsy was the youngest of four children from an upper-middle-class family. She was described as always being a shy, poetic "dreamer" who demonstrated advanced intellectual abilities and poor social skills. During her early teens, she had started to come out of her shell and had made two close friends and participated in extracurricular activities at her private school; with the departure from home of her older siblings, she began to be more outspoken with her parents.

The summer before her depressive episode she had gone overseas on a student exchange visit. This trip proved to be a disaster for her; she did not get along with the family with whom she was placed, and she lived in an isolated area so she had few other contacts. Throughout the summer, she gradually withdrew back to her older isolated self and counted the days until she would return home. When she was reunited with her family, she felt traumatized but basically optimistic about her continued happiness now that she was back among family and friends.

She soon found, however, when she started her junior year, that social demands had changed greatly. Most of the class was involved in dating and some were drinking or taking drugs. Betsy recoiled from both activities, feeling unprepared for dating and scared of experimenting with alcohol or illicit drugs. She was content to go back to being with her two friends and devoting herself to getting good grades. Her close friends, however, had also changed; they were now interested in boys and wanted to be accepted by the "in crowd." They essentially abandoned Betsy after she proved unwilling to join in the social activities that frightened her. Eventually, Betsy found herself once again alone in what she perceived as an environment to which she could not belong because of her inadequacies. She recalled her isolation of the previous summer and the longer periods of estrangement during her earlier childhood. She convinced herself she would always be different from others, always an outcast and alone.

The presentation of depression in adolescence is quite variable, depending on the individual's goals and aspirations, adaptive strengths, defenses, and actual social situation. The hallmarks of depression in this age group are a sense of urgency and great despair together with an unrealistic sense of finality about one's future. There is also a great need to act either in terms of impulsive hurting of the self or in angry outbursts toward others. Feelings of shame play a large role in the depression of adolescents, and the social isolation of these youngsters may point to their fear of appearing weak or foolish in the eyes of others. In general, adolescence is too often a time when self-esteem seems to depend too greatly on external daily experiences. During this psychologically shaky time, those youngsters who have not been able to form a satisfactory sense of their worth, still rely too heavily on the security of their family, or believe they have to achieve unrealistic goals are prone to depressive episodes.

TREATMENT

The controversy regarding the characteristics, diagnosis, and etiology of juvenile affective disorders is equally applicable to the area of treatment. The literature on psychotherapy consists mainly of anecdotal case reports or clinical guidelines (Bemporad 1982; Glaser 1978; Bowerman and French 1979). While these publications suggest that psychotherapy is an effective treatment for child and adolescent depression, they are not a substitute for large-scale research studies on psychotherapy, which would be more convincing.

Early studies of drug treatment of juvenile affective disorders, while closer to a research format, were flawed by methodological difficulties: No control groups were used, diagnostic criteria were not stated, dosages of medication were variable, and the length of therapeutic trials was inconsistent (see Weller and Weller 1984, for a review). The majority, however, did report clinical improvement with tricyclic antidepressants. Recently, Puig-Antich (1982) conducted a series of carefully designed studies on the effects of imipramine on prepubertal depressed children. Puig-Antich utilized an objective assessment of depression in a five-week, double-blind, placebo-controlled trial of imipramine up to doses of 5 mg/kg/day. Plasma drug levels were also monitored. Results showed that 60 percent of the imipramine-treated group and 60 percent of the placebo group demonstrated clinical improvement. However, all of the children who showed plasma imipramine levels over 155 ng/ml improved, while only one-third of the imipramine-treated children with plasma levels below 155 ng/ml were affected. Puig-Antich argued that if proper blood levels had been reached in all imipramine-treated children, a significant difference from the placebo group might have resulted. Nonetheless, the substantial figure of 60 percent improvement on placebo may question the need for medication, or if medication was the active therapeutic agent. It could be that the attention given these children, the change in the environment, or other by-products of the research protocol could have had a beneficial effect on the children or on their families, producing an improvement.

Management for manic episodes is much less controversial, with lithium carbonate recommended as the treatment of choice. However, there is some question whether true bipolar illness occurs prior to adolescence (Anthony and Scott 1960, Youngerman and Canino 1978). Clinical reports of alleged manic behavior in young children have appeared, but a lack of diagnostic rigor and of adequate follow-up puts these reports in doubt. When bipolar illness occurs in adolescence, the treatment appears identical to that for adults.

In view of the lack of certainty in the treatment of juvenile affective disorders, clinical common sense might serve as the best guide at present. Very young children appear to respond best to beneficial changes in those environmental stressors that are responsible for experiences of deprivation and frustration. The improvement of the psychological quality of daily experience through parental counseling, family therapy or placement in a therapeutic setting, and psychotherapy should be sought in order to protect the child from continued dysphoria and the internal structuralization of depressogenic patterns of thought and reactions.

Older children who generate depressive states as the consequence of internal beliefs, habitual interpersonal modes of relating, and self-evaluation appear to require more intensive therapy to alter these ingrained patterns of processing experience. However, treatment of the family and alterations in the environment also remain important factors in effecting clinical outcome.

The treatment of depressed adolescents requires both individual and environmental attention but may also necessitate the use of medication, particularly when vegetative signs form a predominant part of the clinical picture. These simple guidelines, based on a comprehensive understanding of each particular patient in his or her specific context and in light of his or her own experiences, may be the best that can be offered until definitive studies have shown the specific efficacy of any treatment modality.

CONCLUSION

In this chapter we have emphasized developmental factors in the clinical presentation of depressed children. It is our belief that as the individual's abilities increase through childhood and adolescence, psychopathology becomes more complex, mirroring continuous growth in all areas. This developmental framework is helpful not only in understanding the differences in the expression and experience of depression at different stages of development, but also in appreciating the particular needs of the child at each stage so that appropriate intervention and therapy can be offered.

REFERENCES

Anthony, E. J. (1975). Childhood depression. In E. J. Anthony and T. Benedek (Eds.). *Depression and Human Existence.* Boston: Little Brown.

————, and Scott, P. (1960). Manic-depressive psychosis in childhood. *Child Psychol. Psychiat.* 1:53–72.

Arieti, S. (1978). The psychology of sadness. In S. Arieti and J. R. Bemporad. *Severe and Mild Depression.* New York: Basic Books.

Bemporad, J. (1982). Management of childhood depression: Developmental considerations. *Psychosomatics* 23:272–79.

————, and Lee, K. W. (1984). Developmental and psychodynamic aspects of childhood depression. *Child Psychiat. Human Devel.* 14:145–57.

Bibring, E. (1953). The mechanism of depression. In P. Greenacre (Ed.). *Affective Disorders.* New York: International Universities Press.

Bierman, J., Silverstein, A., and Finesinger, J. (1961). A depression in a six-year-old boy with acute poliomyelitis. *Psychoanal. Study Child* 13:430–50.

Birleson, P. (1981). The validity of depressive disorder in childhood and the development of a self-rating scale: A research report. *J. Child Psychol. Psychiat.* 22:73–78.

Bowerman, H., and French, A. P. (1979). Treatment of the depressed child. In A. P. French and I. N. Berlin (Eds.). *Depression in Children and Adolescents.* New York: Human Sciences Press.

Bowlby, J. (1960). Grief and mourning in infancy and early childhood. *Psychoanal. Study Child* 15:9–52.

Brewer, D., and Lubin, B. (1983). Adjective checklists for the measurement of depressive mood in children and adolescents. Unpublished manuscript.

Carlson, G. A., and Cantwell, D. P. (1980). Unmasking masked depression in children and adolescents. *Am. J. Psychiat.* 137:445–49.

Cohen, D. J., and Young, J. G. (1977). Neurochemistry and child psychiatry. *J. Am. Acad. Child Psychiat.* 16:353–411.

Cytryn, L., McKnew, P. H., and Bunney, W. E. (1980). Diagnosis of depression in children: A reassessment. *Am. J. Psychiat.* 177:22–25.

Dennis, W., and Najarian, P. (1957). Infant development under environmental handicap. *Psycholog. Monograph* 71:1–13.

Engel, G., and Reichsman, F. (1956). Spontaneous and experimentally induced depression in an infant with gastric fistula. *J. Am. Psychoanal. Assoc.* 4:428–56.

Freud, S. (1917). Mourning and melancholia. In *Collected Papers*, Vol. 4. New York: Basic Books, 1960.

Glaser, K. (1978). Treatment of depressed and suicidal adolescents. *Am. J. Psychother.* 32:252–67.

Hodges, K. K., and Siegel, L. (1985). Depression in children and adolescents. In E. E. Beckham and W. R. Leber (Eds.). *Handbook of Depression*. Homewood, Ill.: Dorsey Press, pp. 517–55.

Kashani, J. H., Ray, J. S., and Carlson, G. A. (1984). Depression and depression-like states in pre-school children in a child development unit. *Am. J. Psychiat.* 141:1397–1401.

Kazdin, A. E. (1981). Assessment techniques for childhood depression: A critical appraisal. *J. Am. Acad. Child Psychol.* 20:358–75.

Klee, S. H., and Garfinkel, B. D. (1984). Identification of depression in children and adolescents: The role of the Dexamethasone Suppression Test. *J. Am. Acad. Child Psychiat.* 23:410–15.

Kovacs, M. (1983). The interview schedule for children (ISC): Interrater and parent-child agreement. Unpublished manuscript (cited in Hodges and Siegel).

——, and Beck, A. (1977). An empirical-clinical approach toward a definition of childhood depression. In J. Schutlerbrandt and A. Raskin (Eds.). *Depression in Childhood*. New York: Raven Press, pp. 1–26.

——, et al. (1984). Depressive disorder in childhood: A longitudinal prospective study of characteristics and recovery. *Arch. Gen. Psychiat.* 41:229–37.

Land, M., and Tisheria, M. (1978). *Children's Depression Scale*. Victoria, Australia: Australian Council for Education Research.

Lefkowitz, M. M., and Tesing, E. P. (1980). Assessment of childhood depression. *J. Consult. Clin. Psychol.* 48:43–50.

Lahmeyer, H. W., Poznanski, E., and Buller, S. N. (1983). EEG sleep in depressed adolescents. *Am. J. Psychiat.* 140:1150–53.

McConville, B., Boag, P., and Purohit, A. (1973). Three types of childhood depression. *Can. Psychiatric Assoc. J.* 18:133–38.

McKinney, W. T., and Moran, E. C. (1982). Animal models. In E. S. Paykel (Ed.). *Handbook of Affective Disorder*. New York: Guilford Press, pp. 202–11.

McKnew, D. H., Cytryn, L., and White, I. (1974). Clinical and biochemical correlates of hypomania in a child. *J. Am. Acad. Child Psychiat.* 13:576–85.

———, and Cytryn, L. (1979). Urinary metabolites in chronically depressed children. *J. Am. Acad. Child Psychiat.* 18:608–15.

Mahler, M. (1961). Sadness and grief in childhood. *Psychoanal. Study Child* 16:332–51.

———. (1968). *On Human Symbiosis and the Vicissitudes of Individuation.* New York: International Universities Press.

Malmquist, C. (1977). Childhood depression: A clinical and behavioral perspective. In J. Schulterbrandt and A. Raskin (Eds.). *Depression in Childhood.* New York: Raven Press, pp. 33–60.

Mason, W. A., and Berkson, G. (1974). Effects of maternal mobility on the development of rocking and other behaviors in rhesus monkeys: A study with artificial mothers. *Devel. Psychobiol.* 8:197–211.

Petti, T. A. (1978). Depression in hospitalized child psychiatry patients. Approaches to measuring depression. *J. Am. Acad. Child Psychiat.* 17:49–59.

Piaget, J. C. (1952). *The Origins of Intelligence in Children.* New York: International Universities Press.

Poznanski, E. O. (1979). Childhood depression: A psychodynamic approach to the etiology and treatment of depression in children. In A. French and I. Berlin (Eds.). *Depression in Children and Adolescents.* New York: Human Sciences Press.

———, and Zrull, P. (1970). Childhood depression. *Arch. Gen. Psychiat.* 239:8–15.

———, Cook, S. C., and Carroll, B. J. (1979). A depression rating scale for children. *Pediatrics* 64:442–50.

———, et al. (1982). The Dexamethasone Suppression Test in prepubertal depressed children. *Am. J. Psychiat.* 139:321–24.

———, and Zrull, P. (1970). Childhood depression. *Arch. Gen. Psychiat.* 239:8–15.

Puig-Antich, J. (1982). Psychobiological correlates of major depressive disorder in children and adolescents. In L. Grinspoon (Ed.). *American Psychiatric Association Annual Review,* Vol I. Washington, D.C.: American Psychiatric Press.

———, and Chambers, W. J. (1978). Schedule for Affective Disorders and Schizophrenia for School-Age Children (6–16 yrs.)-Kiddie-SADS. Unpublished manuscript, New York State Psychiatric Institute, New York (cited in Hodges and Siegel).

———, et al. (1981). Prepubertal response to insulin induced hypoglycemia. *J. Biolog. Psychiat.* 16:801–18.

———, et al. (1983). Sleep architecture and REM sleep measures in prepubertal major depressives. *Arch. Gen. Psychiat.* 40:187–92.

———, et al. (1984). Growth hormone secretion in prepubertal children with major depression. *Arch. Gen. Psychiat.* 41:443–60.

———, et al. (1984). Growth hormone secretion in prepubertal children with major depression. II. Sleep-related plasma concentration during a depressive episode. *Arch. Gen. Psychiat.* 41:463–66.

Rie, H. (1966). Depression in childhood: A survey of some pertinent contributions. *J. Am. Acad. Child Psychiat.* 5:653–85.

Sandler, J., and Joffee, W. G. (1965). Notes on childhood depression. *Int'l. J. Psychoanal.* 46:80–96.

Sperling, M. (1962). Equivalents of depression in children. *J. Hillside Hospital* 8:138–48.

Spitz, R. (1946). Anaclitic depression. *Psychoanal. Study Child* 5:113–17.

Toolan, J. (1962). Depression in children and adolescents. *Am. J. Orthopsychiat.* 32:404–15.

Weinberg, W. A., et al. (1973). Depression in children referred to an educational diagnostic center: Diagnosis and treatment. *J. Pediatrics* 83:1065–72.

Weller, E. B., et al. (1984). The dexamethasone suppression test in hospitalized prepubertal depressed children. *Am. J. Psychiat.* 141:290–91.

———, and Weller, R. A. (1984). *Current Perspectives on Major Depressive Disorders in Children*. Washington, D.C.: American Psychiatric Press.

Youngerman, J., and Canino, I. A. (1978). Lithium carbonate use in children and adolescents. *Arch. Gen. Psychiat.* 35:216–24.

30

CHILDREN AT RISK FOR PSYCHOTIC DISORDER IN ADULT LIFE

Leo Kron and Clarice J. Kestenbaum

INTRODUCTION

During the past twenty-five years there has been a vast increase in research efforts focused on individuals with a high probability of developing a psychotic disorder in adult life. These studies are subsumed under the rubric "risk research" and have been directed for the most part toward determining which children are most vulnerable to eventual psychotic illness. Most of the "risk" studies deal with the schizophrenic syndromes (for literature reviews see Kety et al. 1968; Erlenmeyer-Kimling 1975; Kestenbaum 1980; Gottesman and Shields 1972). Only recently have affective disorders been studied in similar fashion.

"Risk" is a statistical concept and refers to the greater possibility that certain individuals will develop an unfavorable outcome compared with others selected at random from the same community (Garmezy 1974). For example, the children of diabetics are at greater statistical risk for developing diabetes than the general population. "Vulnerability" implies that each individual is endowed with a specific vulnerability to illness that under certain circumstances will become manifest. Few but not all children of diabetic parents are constitutionally vulnerable, but not all of these children will actually develop diabetes; genetic loading, environmental stress, and dietary regulation are all contributing elements.

Numerous factors, including genetic, physiological, and neuropsychological, increase the risk of a severe psychiatric disorder in adult life. The question still unanswered is whether a given deficit in premorbid adjustment is enough for psychotic breakdown to occur later on, or if a particular environmental stress is necessary for the development of the illness.

Most researchers in schizophrenia risk research adopt the view that schizophrenic breakdown will occur when genetic factors interact with a particular kind of family functioning and abnormal social relationships. High-risk researchers have studied the development of the natural history of the disorder and have attempted to identify vulnerable children. Particular attention has been given to the determination of early predictors of the disorder, particularly those predisposing factors indicative of underlying biological deficits, and to examination of the environmental features that may enhance the development of the disorder as well as those that may be protective. If one could detect the vulnerable child and provide preventive interventions, could subsequent psychotic breakdown be avoided?

One of the major difficulties inherent in risk research is the fact that predictive validity is almost nonexistent. To date we have no biological markers or laboratory tests that will predict with certainty which children will eventually develop schizophrenia or manic-depressive disorder. Moreover, because the child is a developing organism, illness patterns of prepsychotic children may be different from similarly affected adults. The question linking clinical studies within the same diagnostic category is the issue of continuity versus discontinuity of schizophrenia or affective disorders in children and adults.

In the absence of a biological marker investigators have relied on data from retrospective studies, single-case follow-up studies of symptomatic children, longitudinal family studies of children at risk, and most recently, the study of personality and its relationship to psychotic disorders.

PRECURSORS OF SCHIZOPHRENIC ILLNESS

It is well known that the schizophrenic syndromes include a range of symptom complexes, ages of onset, and outcome. Bleuler (1950) specified certain fundamental characteristics present in every case and at every point in time. These included cognitive symptoms, such as disturbance of association, ambivalence, and autism (detachment from the outer world and predilection for fantasy as against reality) as well as disturbances of affect. He considered the "accessory symptoms"—hallucinations and delusions—to be secondary manifestations of the underlying condition. Like Bleuler, Rado (1953) was convinced of the presence of a pathological core in schizophrenia, whether or not the individual ever became actively psychotic, and he believed that the etiology was an inherited predisposition. An inherent incapacity to experience pleasure—anhedonia—is central to his conceptual framework.

Numerous researchers during the past decade have agreed with Rado that the hedonic deficit is of central importance. Physiological explanations abound. Some researchers speculate that the schizophrenic's deficient pleasure resource may stem from dysfunction of noradrenergic pathways. Meehl (1972) contends that anhedonia along with certain core characterological traits (shyness and eccentricity) is central to schizophrenia.

In Meehl's model, genetic error leads to biochemical endophrenotype, to neurophysiological endophrenotype, to abnormal behavioral disposition, and then to the learned maladaptive behavior of the schizophrenic. Behaviors are not inherited. What is inherited, Fish (1975) agreed with Meehl, is a subtle neurointegrative deficit. Meehl's term for this basic core is "schizotaxia," with the implication that the schizotaxic individual develops a schizophrenic organization. If the basic core concept of schizophrenia is valid, it should be a testable hypothesis. One should be able to ascertain which individuals are predisposed to schizophrenic illness and which premorbid characteristics indicate vulnerability to breakdown under stress. Regarding current views on the strength of the genetic factor in schizophrenia and the mode of transmission, the best available evidence points to the likelihood that for the unmistakable cases of schizophrenia, a genetic factor constitutes a necessary though not sufficient antecedent. It is still not certain whether the predominant mode of transmission is polygenic or that of a single major locus gene. Heterogeneity is likely, probably involving a common neurobiological pathway (Erlenmeyer-Kimling 1968; Matthysee and Kidd 1976).

Although there are some proponents of a psychogenic theory, in which abnormal patterns of family life are held to be specific for the pathogenesis of schizophrenia (Wynne and Singer 1964; Lidz 1973), most recent researchers favor a diathesis-stress model. Genetic research, dating from Kallmann's 1946 twin studies, points to a hereditary hypothesis: The more closely related an individual is to a schizophrenic relative, the greater the likelihood of his becoming schizophrenic. Morbidity-risk studies have shown that in contrast with schizophrenia-risk figures for the general population (approximately 1 percent), the adult offspring of one schizophrenic parent have an increased risk of 11 to 12 percent, while the offspring of two schizophrenic parents have a 36 to 40 percent likelihood of developing schizophrenia in adult life (Gottesman and Shields 1972).

The twin study method has been widely used since the inception of high-risk studies; despite differences in the concordance rates of the various studies, all show at least a three-to-one ratio of monozygotic compared with dizygotic twin concordance for schizophrenia (Kallmann 1946; Kringlen 1968). Gottesman and Shields, using sophisticated techniques and blind raters, achieved a concordance rate of 42 percent for monozygotic twins as against 9 percent for dizygotic twins (the same as sibling rates concordant for schizophrenia). The Danish adoption studies of Kety et al. (1968) are also very striking. They corroborate Heston's finding (1966) that the incidence of schizophrenia among the biological relatives of adopted-away schizophrenics was six times as high as the incidence noted for the relatives of control adoptees (Rosenthal 1975).

The prospective longitudinal model for high-risk research in schizophrenia was first proposed by Pearson and Kley in 1957; several follow-back and follow-up clinical studies produced some interesting findings regarding the premorbid functioning of schizophrenic adults. Watt (1972) systematically examined teachers' adlibbed comments in the cumulative school records of fifty-four children who were hospitalized for schizophrenia as adults and 143 matched control subjects. The results demonstrated that the children destined to become schizophrenic behaved differently in school from other children. Almost half of them were deviant prior to psychotic decompensation. The preschizophrenic boys demonstrated primary evidence of unsocialized aggression and secondary evidence of internal conflict and depression; the girls, on the other hand, were overly sensitive and extremely introverted. In another landmark study of 18,000 children seen at the Judge Baker Child Guidance Clinic in Massachusetts, 175 adult schizophrenics were found and matched for age, sex, class, IQ, and ethnicity (Waring and Ricks 1965). The schizophrenics were divided into two groups, those with nonremitting chronic illness and those who had been hospitalized intermittently for schizophrenia. Normal births were noted in fewer than 40 percent of the preschizophrenics, and many were noted to have slower motor development, poorer coordination, and more speech anomalies than the controls. The chronic group was much sicker than the intermittently hospitalized group and had more disturbed mothers (psychotic, schizoid, or borderline), a family history of schizophrenia, and extremely poor social adjustment (no peer relations); many were noted to be symbiotically attached to their mothers.

In a subsequent study, Ricks and Berry (1970) believed that the chronic schizophrenic has biological and social equipment that offers a small margin for error in development. They hypothesized that IQ, social and vocational success, a reasonably receptive home environment, and the presence or absence of biological handicaps are all relevant predictive factors in determining which high-risk children would become overtly schizophrenic.

The follow-up and follow-back studies produced interesting hypotheses that could subsequently be tested in a prospective longitudinal research design. Mednick and Schulsinger (1970), two of the originators of the longitudinal method, believed that the offspring of schizophrenic mothers show a particular vulnerability to schizophrenic illness that is a joint function of genetic loading and pregnancy and birth complications. This combined liability results in an infant who demonstrates a labile pattern of autonomic responsiveness. Fish (1975) believed from her longitudinal study of infants of schizophrenic mothers that a "pan-developmental retardation," a transient dysregulation of motor, visuomotor, and physical development noted between birth and two years predicts vulnerability to schizophrenia.

Another group of investigators (Marcus et al. 1985) compared neurological functioning in children at risk for schizophrenia from samples recruited in Israel and Denmark. In both samples neurological signs were assessed in school age children with one schizophrenic parent and a matched group of children with no mentally ill parents. A subgroup of the offspring of schizophrenics, but not the controls, showed multiple signs of neurological dysfunctioning that varied in pattern among individuals.

The New York High-Risk Project

The New York High-Risk Project was initiated in 1971 at the New York State Psychiatric Institute under the direction of Dr. L. Erlenmeyer-Kimling (Erlenmeyer-

Kimling et al. 1979). The project consists of two groups, the original study group and a replication sample. Sample A initially consisted of 205 subjects between the ages of seven and twelve years: sixty-three children of one or two schizophrenic parents, and two comparison groups consisting of forty-three children of parents with an affective disorder necessitating hospitalization and ninety-seven children of parents without psychiatric disorder. The replication sample (Sample B) consists of 150 children: forty-six children of one or two schizophrenic parents, thirty-nine whose parents have affective disorders, and sixty-five with "normal" parents. The comparison groups are matched for age, sex, ethnicity, and social class. The parents were selected in accordance with strict diagnostic criteria.

It was assumed that a certain percentage of these children would experience psychotic decompensation in later life, and that careful assessment of these children at regular intervals would reveal pathology in *status nascendi,* in other words, permit the identification of vulnerable individuals within the high-risk group.

The study focuses on neurological, psychophysiological, psychiatric, psychological, and social measures. Home interviews and laboratory testing include a structured home rating scale, behavior rating scale, neurological examination, and psychological tests such as the WISC, Bender-Gestalt, and projective tests. Data from school records were collected. Since hypotheses regarding psychobiological dysfunction in adult schizophrenics suggest that schizophrenics may have difficulty processing stimuli, tests were selected that would measure attentional dysfunction and distractability (Erlenmeyer-Kimling 1968). Therefore, EEG measures of auditory and visual evoked potentials were taken as well as a variety of cognitive, attentional, and distractibility measurements. The continuous performance test (CPT) is a test of sustained visual attention in which the subject is required to respond whenever the stimulus is identical to the one immediately preceeding it, and the attention span task (ATS) requires subjects immediately to recall a series of either three or five letters presented by tape recorder, with or without distraction.

A videotaped psychiatric semistructured interview (Mental Health Assessment Form, or MHAF, Kestenbaum and Bird 1978) was developed especially for the project. The interviewer is blind as to a child's parental background, as are two raters who independently rate the videotapes for psychopathology and possible diagnosis.

RESULTS

In addition to corroboration of positive neurological findings in the index cases consistent with those of other investigators, a study of attentional tasks has emerged that differentiates the high-risk group from the controls. Sample A has been tested on four occasions over a twelve-year period. Consistent group differences were found on the CPT and ATS. The high-risk subjects made significantly fewer correct responses and more random commission errors than the normal comparison group with and without distraction. The index subjects also scored lower on the Bender-

Gestalt, and some showed unusual patterns of auditory and visual evoked potentials, particularly when attention was required at a task.

Behavioral disturbances are measured according to a Behavior-Global Adjustment Scale (B-GAS) developed by Dr. Barbara Cornblatt (Cornblatt and Erlenmeyer-Kimling 1984), which relies heavily on parents' information. Three major areas of functioning are taken into consideration in assigning the ratings: 1) family relationship, 2) peer interactions, and 3) school functioning. High-risk subjects were significantly more disturbed than normal comparison subjects. It is noteworthy that when the later B-GAS scores are compared with each subject's deviance score on the laboratory measures taken at the first round of testing, the high-risk subgroup that is deviant on the laboratory measures shows an increasing overlap with the subjects who demonstrate subsequent behavior problems. Thus it seems that Sample A subjects who show early deficits on laboratory measures exhibit increasingly deviant behavior as they get older—a finding that supports the hypothesis that attentional dysfunctions serve as early predictors of later pathology.

CLINICAL STATUS

To date, ten study children in Sample A have been hospitalized for a psychiatric disorder, seven in the high-risk group (12 percent), two from the psychiatric comparison group (5 percent), and one from the normal comparison group (1 percent).

The children later hospitalized for schizophrenia had lower IQ scores at first testing, particularly in the verbal subtests, compared to the high-risk group as a whole. (The Mean Full Scale IQ score was 93 for the hospitalized subjects versus 104 for the total high-risk group.) Most of the hospitalized subjects had poor Bender-Gestalt results, poor total scores on the pediatric neurological scores, and poor CPT scores. On the composite attentional indices (CPT, ATS, and WISC Digit Span), the hospitalized high-risk and treatment high-risk subjects were among the worst performers on the composite score compared to the high-risk group as a whole.

In summary, the data on the subjects who have been hospitalized suggest a pattern for the high-risk subjects in which lower IQ (particularly verbal IQ) and poor performance on the Bender-Gestalt, neurological examination, and attentional indices at a young age may be indicative of later psychopathology (Erlenmeyer-Kimling et al. 1984).

The Mental Health Assessment Form (MHAF) also demonstrated significant differences among the groups. The individual items included hyperactivity, negative verbal behavior, impression of deficits in intelligence (memory, conceptualization, vocabulary, abstractions), loose associations, distractibility, hostile fantasies, and nightmares.

In essence the results suggest that some of the children of schizophrenic parents demonstrate early neurophysiological deviance, particularly in measures of attention and cognition, maturational lag on neuropsychological functions, and later behavioral deviations—in other words, *vulnerability* to schizophrenia. The attentional dysfunction is not found in the majority of siblings of the vulnerable children and seems to rule out the possibility that this deficit is of strictly environmental origin as a result of living with a schizophrenic parent. It is assumed that most of the children who demonstrate early neurophysiological deviance, including the children from the comparison groups, will not become clinically schizophrenic.

Judging from clinical impression of the Sample A cohort, four main clinical patterns are discernable thus far in the high-risk group:

> (1) children who displayed early neurophysiological deviance who either experienced psychotic decompensation or are considered severely disturbed along the continuum of schizophrenic spectrum disorders; (2) children who displayed early neurophysiological deviance and are functioning relatively well without manifestations of schizophrenia; (3) children who did not display neurophysiological deviance and are functioning poorly in terms of school and work performance and interpersonal relationships but who do not appear to show signs of a schizophrenic spectrum disorder; (4) children who did not display neurophysiological deviance and are functioning well. The third group could be exhibiting symptoms resulting from the stress of having a mentally ill parent, multiple separations, and chaotic home environment. The fourth group has not succumbed to the stress of living with an ill parent and has coped with the situation, often with extraordinary fortitude. Statistical analysis of data concerning the four clinical patterns and the effects of environmental stressors is currently underway (Kestenbaum 1986).

Thus far seven of the high-risk study children from Sample A have had subsequent psychotic decompensation necessitating hospitalization. All were among the group demonstrating early deviance. Four percent of the high-risk cohort from Sample B have been hospitalized thus far. They are only now approaching the age of risk for schizophrenic decompensation. Some may become psychotic as they approach late adolescence, but most will undoubtedly not experience psychotic breakdown. In-depth studies are in progress of those nonspecific environmental variables that enhance the likelihood that vulnerable individuals will decompensate as well as of those that are protective.

Billy B. (Adult Diagnosis: Schizophrenia, Paranoid Type)

Presenting Symptoms. Billy B. was first evaluated at age 7 because of reading failure, short attention span, an articulation problem (a lisp), and severe temper tantrums.

Family History. Mr. B., Billy's father, a 43-year-old truck driver of Irish descent, was a seventh-grade dropout. An alcoholic, he was abusive toward his wife and children. The paternal grandfather had died in an institution (diagnosis unknown), and the paternal grandmother was said to be "simple or retarded."

Mrs. B. was the granddaughter of a physician and the daughter of a Protestant minister. She too dropped out of high school prior to graduation. Billy's three older brothers were known as the "neighborhood hoodlums," either suspended from school or in trouble with the law. Home was chaotic; the parents were constantly quarreling or physically fighting.

Developmental History. Billy was the product of a full-term normal delivery. Pathological developmental features included difficulty in sucking, projectile vomiting until 14 months, food allergies until age 2, headbanging until age 2½, and hospitalization for asthma at age 3. Developmental milestones were normal except for delay in sitting up (9 months) and the presence of a lisp when he began to talk (22 months). Although he was toilet trained at 18 months, Billy was enuretic until age 7. A sister died from apparent crib death during the time Billy was hospitalized, and Mrs. B. reported being depressed for six months.

Billy was noted to be more clinging and fearful than his siblings. He refused to go to kindergarten and had to be threatened with force. He needed to have a favorite pillow with him at all times. Terrifying nightmares began when Billy was 4, which resulted in punitive threats from Mr. B. Tantrums could last for an hour.

Clinical Course. The initial consultation resulted in Billy's receiving speech therapy for his articulation problems; the only recommendation the family would accept. Billy was reevaluated at age 11, once again referred by the school principal for severe academic and social problems. He was found to be anxious and immature, inattentive in class, and deeply preoccupied by his inner world. He had developed a handwashing compulsion that resulted in twelve to fifteen trips to the sink each day. A quiet loner, Billy had no friends and was frequently called "crybaby." He was often in trouble for truancy and failure to do his homework. Psychological tests revealed a full-scale IQ of 115, with much subtest scatter. According to the psychologist, extreme anxiety interfered with his performance. Moderately poor graphomotor skills were also noted, along with a "fair-to-poor" Bender-Gestalt test. No EEG abnormalities were detected.

Psychotherapy was begun despite his suspiciousness and projective trend. He was inordinately fearful of being alone, of being mugged, knifed, bombed. He half believed in the late-night television monsters that invaded his dreams, but he denied ever having had hallucinations. His dreams were filled with violence and death. "I was embalmed in a glass case, on exhibition," he once reported. "Another corpse rose up and came toward me. It was my father. He was dead, decomposing. I could smell his body even in the dream. He touched me and I died. The whole street was covered with arms and legs and blood."

During the six months of treatment, Billy was at times clinging and childishly demanding; at other times he expressed hatred and rage toward his therapist for seeing other patients or going on vacation. He was doing better in school, however, and his parents decided that he had had enough therapy when the school year ended.

When Billy was 16 he was once again brought for psychiatric evaluation, but this time he was admitted to the Adolescent Inpatient Unit. A high-school dropout with a police record for assaultive behavior, he was hospitalized for suicidal and homicidal preoccupation, with the diagnosis "borderline adolescent." A trial of phenothiazine medication was unsuccessful in curbing his instigation of fist fights on the unit, and he was sent to a state hospital. Released after one year, he was readmitted at age 19 with a history of auditory hallucinations that were persecutory in nature. He believed that people were trying to kill him. He was diagnosed "schizophrenia with an affective component." A trial of lithium was unsuccessful. During the next seven years, Billy was hospitalized nine times with the diagnosis "schizophrenia, paranoid type." He was never able to complete high school, hold a job, or form an intimate relationship (Kestenbaum 1982).

PRECURSORS OF BIPOLAR AFFECTIVE DISORDER

As with schizophrenia, there is consistent evidence supporting the prominent role of a genetically transmitted vulnerability to affective and especially bipolar illness (Tsuang 1978). The weight of the genetic factor in bipolar disorder is revealed by average concordance rates for bipolar illness in monozygotic twins of 72 percent, as opposed to only 14 percent in dizygotic twins (Allen 1976). Family studies have found that morbidity risk rates for affective illness in the first-degree relatives of bipolar probands are between 10 percent and 40 percent, with more than one-third of these at risk for bipolar illness (Smeraldi, Negri, and Melicaam 1977). In addition to bipolar illness, offspring have been found to be at an increased risk for the development of cyclothymia, dysthymia, sociopathy, and alcoholism (Winokur et al. 1969).

The genetic mode of transmission of manic-depressive illness is still unclear. Angst et al. (1980) concluded that unipolar and bipolar illnesses are genetically different entities. Genetic heterogeneity and multiple threshold models have been postulated (Gershon et al. 1971). These investigators believe that unipolar and bipolar illnesses represent positions on a continuum of liability. Greater liability tends to manifest itself as bipolar, less liability as a unipolar disorder.

The average age of onset of bipolar illness is over 30 years, although one-fifth to more than one-third of bipolar cases have an early onset between the ages of 10 and 19 (Winokur et al. 1969). A causal relationship between genetic loading and clinical severity is suggested by findings that bipolar probands with a positive family history of bipolar illness are more likely to have an early onset and a greater number of hospital admissions for mania. Also, significant stressful life events are less likely to precede the affective episodes of early onset than late-onset bipolars, suggesting a greater endogenous component in the former.

Familial aggregation of bipolar spectrum disorders does not necessarily imply a genetic transmission of disorder. Even in those studies most supportive of a genetic hypothesis, significant environmental factors are also implicated to explain, for example, those monozygotic twins who are discordant for bipolar illness. Environmental factors vary qualitatively and quantitatively and in their importance relative to the genetic factors with which they interact. It is this complex gene-environment interaction that accounts for the clinical picture at any one point in the life history of the manic-depressive.

The search for markers that would identify future manic-depressives has led to investigations in biological, environmental, and clinical spheres.

Biological Factors

In order to elucidate the biological underpinnings of affective disorders in childhood, research strategies similar to those used with adults have been applied. No proven biological markers have as yet been discovered. This research is still in the earliest phases of its development and has been directed at the following areas.

Pituitary/Adrenal Axis. Abnormalities of cortisol secretion are found in a significant subgroup of adults with endogenous depressions, in whom this finding represents a marker of the acute depressive episode—a marker of state rather than trait. Studies of endogenously depressed prepubertal children have found that approximately 20 percent, a rate about half that found in adults, are cortisol hypersecretors (Puig-Antich 1983).

The Dexamethasone Suppression Test (DST) has been used to identify a group of adult depressives who fail to show normal pituitary suppression after its administration. Similar findings have been reported in endogenously depressed prepubertal children. However, the diagnostic value of the DST in children and adolescents is limited because of an apparent lack of specificity (Shaffer 1985).

Growth Hormone Secretion. Abnormal secretion of growth hormone has been found in some endogenously depressed children (Puig-Antich 1983). Both hyposecretion in response to the insulin tolerance test and hypersecretion during sleep were presumed to result from a disturbance of hypothalamic serotonin mechanisms. The fact that these abnormalities were also found to be present after recovery from the acute depressed episodes suggests that they could represent a marker of "trait," as well as "state."

Biogenic Amine Metabolism. Putative abnormalities of central biogenic amine systems figure prominently in current biological models of the pathophysiology of affective disorders. Similar to findings in adults, chronically depressed children have been found to excrete lower levels of MHPG (3-methoxy, 4 hydroxy phenylglycol) in their urine than controls (Cytryn et al. 1984).

The tendency for some depressed adults and adolescents to reverse polarity and exhibit a hypomanic response to the administration of amines and tricyclics is consistent with the biogenic amine hypothesis of affective disorders. That this response may represent a trait marker for bipolar illness is supported by the finding that pharmacologically induced hypomania was found to be 100 percent specific in identifying those depressed adolescents who would later go on to show a bipolar course

(Akiskal et al. 1985). Similar responses to tricyclics and stimulants are well known in childhood, but no follow-up studies of these children have been reported.

Disturbance of Cerebral Laterality. Disturbances of cerebral laterality have been implicated in adult affective disorders. In studies of bipolar offspring, an overrepresentation of left-handed children and a WISC-R profile with significantly higher verbal than performance IQs differentiated them from normal controls (Kestenbaum 1979; Decina et al. 1983). These findings are consistent with those in adults and suggest a disturbance and/or imbalance of lateralized brain function in some children at risk for bipolar illness.

Environmental Factors

Organic. Evidence implicates organic factors in the etiology of many cases of bipolar illness in which a family history of affective disorder is lacking. Also, early bipolar onset is found to be associated with a greater frequency of gestational and perinatal complications, more neuropsychiatric dysfunction, and lower IQ (Waters et al. 1983).

Interpersonal. Bipolar offspring are in double jeopardy. In addition to a possible genetic predisposition for affective illness, they must contend with the complex impact of bipolar illness on the family unit, on the parent-child relationship, and on their own ego development, with its implications for the development of defenses and coping mechanisms.

At its worst, during acute affective episodes that threaten familial disintegration, the family's resources are the most strained. The unpredictable chaotic bipolar environment, characterized during mania by magical wish fulfillment, euphoria, and a delusional omnipotence, is bolstered and eventually undermined by psychotic denial. Not surprisingly divorce is a frequent consequence. The resourcefulness of the "well" parent, older siblings, and other family members is critical in minimizing the traumatic effect on young children. Manic episodes are the most anxiety producing and disruptive, so that a chronic depressive state is better tolerated and often preferred by other family members.

Between episodes the family unit and the bipolar parent may appear to function in a normal and unremarkable manner. Manic-depressives can be productive, creative, and sociable. They seek to conform to conventional social standards but often set unrealistic goals for themselves and their children (Cohen et al. 1954). Excessive attention to superficial appearances of success and well-being is one expression of the massive denial apparent in the bipolar family's attitudes and communications (Davenport et al. 1979), which is central to the manic-depressive's intrapsychic defensive makeup.

Denial is used, not only to ward off depressive affects associated with loss, grief, and anger, but often to avoid completely the awareness of a parent's illness. Frequently found fears, regarding the recurrence of affective episodes or the heritability of the disorder, remain unspoken. As a result children are deprived of an important protective factor that the open recognition and discussion of parental illness could afford them (Morrison 1983). Parents tend also to deny affective disturbance in their children, who in turn suppress the expression of painful affects. This interferes with the timely detection and treatment of affective disorders in these at-risk offspring.

The direct pathogenic effect of parental bipolarity on offspring is not limited to the acute states of mania or depression. Anthony (1975) described the "manic-depressive environment" between episodes as one in which each family member is to some extent affected as he is more or less brought within the "orbit" of influence of the bipolar parent and his subclinical fluctuations in mood and behavior. Each child in a family adopts his own idiosyncratic role vis-à-vis the ill parent, as part of the family's attempt to cope and survive. Those offspring who are able to remain relatively uninvolved in the parent's disorder, and are able to find partial surrogates, seem to fare better than those who are more closely bound up with a labile and at times psychotic parent. The latter share in the euphoria and omnipotence of their hyperthymic parent and then in disillusionment, guilt, and hopelessness when that parent becomes depressed.

The pathogenic impact of parental manic-depressive illness on the affective development of their offspring seems to be influenced by several additional variables. These include the clinical type and severity of the parental illness; the need for and frequency of hospitalization; the role of the "well" parent, siblings, and other family members; and the relationship between the parent's bipolar course and the child's development. Recent studies have found the degree of affective psychopathology in bipolar offspring to be greater in those whose mother, rather than father, is bipolar; who are younger at the time of the first exposure to the parental illness; whose parent's illness is chronic and requires prolonged separation; whose nonbipolar parents fail to have a protective influence due to their own psychological disturbance or functional absence as a result of marital discord or parental divorce (LaRoche et al. 1985).

The impact on an infant of a mother with an affective postpartum psychosis can be developmentally disastrous and even life-threatening. However, even at subpsychotic levels the depressed or hypomanic mother is self-involved and often deficient in her ability to empathize. Unable to respond appropriately to her infant's cues, she cannot take part in the reciprocal mutuality that characterizes a healthy mother-infant dyad. The infant may, in turn, respond to his mother's uninvolvement by his own withdrawal or the development of an intensely ambivalent attitude, which Benedek (1956) described as part of the "depressive constellation." A. Freud (1966) explained the presence of a depressive tendency in children of depressed mothers as resulting partly through identification, whereby the infant attempts to achieve a sense of unity and harmony with the mother by reproducing the mother's depressed mood in himself. This phenomenon is limited neither to infants nor to depressive affects. For example, older children may identify with the hypomanic parent and join in his euphoria and his magical wishes for merger and omnipotence.

CLINICAL CHARACTERISTICS

Depression in childhood, once unappreciated, has been the focus of much recent research. As with adults, the diagnosis of childhood depression probably covers a heterogeneous group of children in which some are more severely affected than others or where some may be more clearly "reactive" or "endogenous" than others. A group of children has been identified fitting adult criteria and demonstrating biological characteristics found in some endogenously depressed adults (i.e., abnormalities of hormonal and biogenic amine systems).

Interest in the prepubertal expression of bipolar illness has until recently been quite limited, although its importance in adolescence has long been appreciated. Kraeplin (1921) noted that with each year into adolescence the frequency of manic-depressive onset increases. Nevertheless adolescents with affective disorders, unipolar and bipolar, frequently go unrecognized and are misdiagnosed as adjustment disorders, behavior disorders, narcissistic personalities, borderline personalities, substance abuse disorders, or schizophrenics (Akiskal et al. 1985; Kestenbaum 1982). Diagnostic imprecision, shifting diagnostic biases, and specific developmental characteristics of adolescence help account for this. For example, behavioral manifestations such as delinquency, promiscuity, or drug abuse might deflect attention from a history and symptomatology otherwise indicative of affective disorder. The frequent misdiagnosis of schizophrenia might be due to the finding that psychotic symptoms (mood-congruent and incongruent) are seen much more frequently in the adolescent, as compared to the older onset bipolar, and decrease with subsequent episodes.

Many adolescents who present initially with depressive episodes will subsequently exhibit a bipolar course. These adolescents have been found to differ from future unipolar depressives by the acute onset of symptoms; the prominence of psychotic symptomatology; the prominence of psychomotor retardation and hypersomnia; the presence of bipolar disorder in parents, siblings, and transgenerationally in the family tree; the precipitation of depression by childbirth; and especially by the finding of pharmacologically induced hypomania, which seems convincingly specific for an eventual bipolar course (Akiskal et al. 1983).

In contrast to prepubertal depression, mania or hypomania in childhood, conforming to adult diagnostic criteria is extremely rare. Anthony and Scott (1960) reviewed the world literature from 1896 to 1960 and found only twenty-eight reports of manic-depressive illness in individuals below the age of 12. Only three cases, all 11 years old, fulfilled their exacting criteria for manic-depressive illness resembling the familiar adult form of the disorder. Even in populations where future manic-depressives are presumed to exist, such as in the offspring of adult bipolars, no cases of prepubertal mania or hypomania have been found.

Most case reports of so-called childhood variants of bipolar disorder are of children showing severe and often pervasive but nonspecific disturbances in which periodic hyperactivity, impulsivity, and affective symptoms (often aggressive) are prominent. Of particular interest are recent case reports showing good lithium response. For example, Feinstein and Wolpert (1973) reported the case of a girl whose intermittent impulsivity, distractability, hyperactivity, and destructive behavior first brought her to treatment at the age of 3. Affective swings continued with increasing severity until she was placed on lithium at age 6 and maintained for twelve years with good clinical response. The same authors report the case of a 10-year-old girl treated successfully with lithium until she was 16. At that time she removed herself from the medication, with a consequent full-blown manic episode. These and other case reports of atypical childhood onset bipolar illness may represent particularly severe genetic variants of the disorder. Sometimes, however, as frequently seems the case, they involve situations where the inherited vulnerability is stressed and compounded by particularly adverse environmental and organic factors. However, for the most part this is not the way that future adult bipolars appear in childhood— even those with heavy familial loading.

Clinical investigations designed to reveal a premorbid picture have taken the form of retrospective studies of diagnosed bipolar adults and adolescents, cross-sectional and prospective studies of bipolar offspring, and studies of personality as a subsyndromal expression of affective disorder.

Retrospective accounts by adult bipolars do not reveal a consistent premorbid picture in childhood, although characteristics related to affective vulnerability are common. However, often no overt psychiatric disturbance is revealed. Instead they are often portrayed in childhood as highly functioning, extraverted, ambitious, and sociable, although having superficial relationships with unmet dependency needs and a rigid adherence to conventional values and achievement (Cohen et al. 1954).

The reliability of premorbid reconstruction is greater when young adolescents presenting in their first bipolar episodes are studied, rather than adults. More often in these accounts there is clear evidence in childhood of unrecognized affective episodes or periodicity, which undoubtedly represented the prepubertal expression of overt bipolar illness (Esman et al. 1983; Anthony and Scott 1960).

Kraeplin (1913) and several investigators since have formulated relationships between personality type and later developing affective subtypes, such that diluted forms characterized as hypomanic, depressive (dysthymic), and cyclothymic are found premorbidly in those who later become manic, depressed, and bipolar. Akiskal et al. (1985) supported the contention of continuity between cyclothymia and bipolar disorder. They found that cyclothymic patients were like bipolar controls in demonstrating similar patterns of familial affective illness, hypomanic responses to antidepressants, and positive responses to lithium. Follow-up after a relatively short time period showed that one in three cyclothymics had gone on to develop distinct affective episodes of hypomania or depression. These findings support the view of personality configuration as an attenuated expression of affective disorder. In some cases, cyclothymia is transitional between a chronic, relatively stable premorbid personality configuration and an affective decompensation. In these cases it is an expression of the bipolar pathology in *status nascendi.*

The literature pertaining to personality traits associated with depression is remarkably consistent. Traits repeatedly found in depressives suggest that between episodes and premorbidly they lack self-confidence and demonstrate deficiencies of social adroitness, nonassertiveness, worry, and pessimism. They tend to be rigid, obsessive, inhibited, dependent, and insecure. In addition, introversion and neuroticism scores are higher in depressed than control groups in studies using self-rating questionnaires and personality inventories (Von Zerssen 1977).

However, the presence of distinct personality traits during states of remission does not prove their premorbid existence. They could also be explained as characterological scarring resulting from acute affective episodes rather than preceding or predisposing to them. However, observations made on bipolar offspring and siblings prior to the occurrence of distinct affective episodes support the view that some of these traits seen in remission precede rather than result from the full expression of the affective disorder.

Data regarding the premorbid and interepisodic characteristics of bipolar patients, as gathered by personality inventories, is less voluminous but reveals that bipolars score significantly higher than unipolars on scales of extraversion, sociability, and activity. But except for higher scores on scales of obsessionality, bipolars studied between episodes are indistinguishable from the general population (Von Zerssen 1977). This finding is consistent with the retrospective clinical accounts of grossly normal functioning before and between episodes.

Bipolar spectrum disorders can be expected in about 27 percent of bipolar offspring. Several recent studies have been based on the hypothesis that in childhood these offspring will be at an early, yet discernible stage in the development of their bipolar pathology (reviewed in Kron et al. 1982). Most of these are cross-sectional, and those with a prospective design have been initiated too recently to provide as yet much longitudinal data.

Cytryn et al. (1984) compared seven male infant bipolar offspring to matched controls and followed them until age 3. Disturbances in the development and regulation of anger, distress, and pleasure were noted. Associated were disturbances in behavior, attachment, and peer relations.

Several studies of juvenile and adolescent bipolar offspring have been reported, but differing methodologies makes comparison and summary of these studies difficult. All report very high rates of psychopathology, ranging from 33 to 52 percent, in bipolar offspring. In those studies where children were assessed indirectly via parental report, pathology was not easily categorized and included diverse personality, behavior and learning disorders, and some depression. On the other hand, in those studies where children were examined directly, depressive disorders constituted by far the most common diagnosis. Several cases of severe depression were unreported by parents, reflecting the unreliability of parents as historians and the prominence of parental denial in these disorders.

Restricting their sample to the prepubertal offspring of rigorously diagnosed bipolars and using a control group for comparison, Decina et al. (1983) confirmed the high incidence of psychopathology and particularly depression in these children. In addition, their findings supported Kestenbaum's hypothesis (1979) that bipolar offspring differ from control children by a pattern on the WISC-R in which verbal scores are significantly higher than performance scores. Also found were higher ratios of color determinants to movement determinants on the Rorschach and an overrepresentation of left-handedness in the bipolar sample. These findings are similar to characteristics described in adult bipolars and are consistent with theories attributing affective pathology to disturbances of cerebral laterality.

Examining these same bipolar offspring for developing patterns of personality traits, Kron et al. (1982) discerned four groupings of children. Two of these, an "inhibited" and an "extraverted" group, demonstrated features akin to those traits associated with depression and hypomania respectively, supporting the view that these traits may precede acute affective episodes. Of particular interest were the findings related to the "extraverted" group, which was characterized by traits at a subclinical level of extroversion, expansiveness, exhibitionism, egocentrism, dependency, and separation anxiety. It was this "extraverted" group of children that primarily accounted for the psychometric characteristics that differentiated the entire group of bipolar offspring from controls (i.e., their verbal/performance discrepancies were approximately three times larger than other experimental children and they showed higher color to movement ratios). In addition, this "extraverted" group of experimental children were significantly more likely to have Bipolar I parents, in whom the manic component is relatively more pronounced. The authors hypothesized that this "extraverted" group of children would contain future adult-onset bipolars in whom the manic element was relatively prominent. Likewise, LaRoche et al. (1985) found a cyclothymic group among their bipolar offspring.

Akiskal et al. (1985) were able to follow a group of bipolar offspring and siblings already manifesting disturbance sufficient to warrant psychiatric referral. Eighty-five percent presented with affective illness including mania. None of the ten prepubertal presentations was of mania, but all had affective disorders—five dysthymias, one cyclothymia, one hyperthymia, and two atypical bipolar disorders. Of those presenting at intake with affective disorders, a large number had received psychiatric diagnoses previously, but none of an affective disorder even though abundant affective symptomatology appeared in their records. All manner of personality and behavioral disorder was diagnosed instead, presumably because the pathoplastic effects of adolescent development and the acute situational context distracted from the total clinical picture. This was especially demonstrated with regards to patients previously diagnosed as substance abuse disorders, all of whom eventually showed a typical affective course. During a mean prospective follow-up period of three years, several subjects demonstrated a reversal of affective polarity or pharmacologically induced hypomania, such that at time of follow-up 68 percent of the original sample were considered bipolar.

To summarize, these clinical studies show an alarmingly high rate of diagnosable psychopathology in bipolar offspring, some of which represents the earliest expressions of manic-depressive illness. Especially prominent are depressive disorders, both major and minor, while mania is not found. However, some children who are not diagnosable by DSM-III criteria show traits at a subsyndromal level which are related to affective disorders. These have been variably referred to as inhibited, introverted, and dysthymic, or hyperthymic, cyclothymic, and extraverted. Perhaps because of its essential periodic nature, no one consistent premorbid personality configuration has been identified.

Some future manic-depressives presumably have sufficient psychological resources to cope with the biopsychosocial stressors of adolescence and do not decompensate until later on in life. Others show increasing polymorphous affective symptomatology in childhood and adolescence, which represents the emergence of an early-onset bipolarity. Often, an increasingly distinct and intense cyclothymia heralds the approaching affective decompensation. Intervention at this time may avert psychosis and hospitalization and their sequelae.

CASE VIGNETTES

Two clinical vignettes are presented to illustrate the clinical course of a case of early-onset bipolar disorder and the extraverted, hyperthymic traits found in some bipolar offspring.

Chris M.

The first case illustrates the not unusual history and clinical course of an adolescent manic-depressive. Chris, a bright premed student who was hospitalized in a psychotic mania at age 21, had presented to the student health service six months previously with complaints of anxiety, fear of failure, low self-esteem, and sexual inhibition. Psychotherapy was begun, with apparently good early results. What in retrospect was a depressive phase of a worsening cyclothymia gradually lifted. The news that he had been accepted to the medical school of his choice was followed by further elevation of mood and self-confidence. Hyperthymia turned to hypomania as the summer approached, and just prior to his planned trip to Europe, a full mania developed. The florid psychotic presentation, along with visual hallucinations and messianic delusions, prompted the early misdiagnosis of schizophrenia. Fortunately, once he was hospitalized the bipolar disorder was recognized and quickly stabilized with lithium carbonate. A few weeks later, Chris was able to begin his first year of medical training and was functioning well at a short-term follow-up.

Had the index of suspicion for major affective disorder been higher when he initially presented to the health service, and had it led to a more thorough history taking and psychiatric examination, the following findings may have led to an earlier diagnosis of affective disorder and the prophylactic administration of lithium carbonate. Family history revealed the presence of affective disorder on both sides of the family. The father had had an agitated depression when he was 19. The mother suffered from depressions, and a grandparent was manic-depressive.

Detailed history revealed a psychiatric evaluation at age 7 because of withdrawal, shyness, poor social relations, and low self-esteem. Psychotherapy was instituted, with good results. Chris became superficially more confident and socially extraverted, but remained oversensitive to the opinions of others. Criticisms, real or imagined, resulted in self-doubt and depression. For the most part, however, he functioned very well academically and socially until college. In high school he was active in athletics, was quite popular, and was elected the president of his class.

In the summer following his second year of college he decided to tour Europe with a friend. While there he experienced in rapid succession a hyperthymic episode and then a depressive one from which it took several months to recover. It was thereafter, while still moderately depressed, that Chris sought treatment at the student health service.

Had Chris's family and personal psychiatric history been known and understood as a manifestation of affective disorder, the switch from depression to hypomania in the period prior to the manic episode might have alerted the health service psychiatrist to the fact that he was witness to the evolution of a manic-depressive disorder and that he could, with lithium, abort it.

Fred T.

Fred, an 11-year-old whose father had a bipolar I disorder, was evaluated as part of a study of manic-depressive offspring. He is presented as an example of an apparently well-functioning and asymptomatic child who nevertheless, at closer look, showed extraverted, hyperthymic personality traits and affective patterns akin to those found in adult hypomania but at a subclinical level of expression.

Fred related warmly and was eager to please. Bright, articulate, and dramatic, he gestured with his hands and spoke in a somewhat pressured manner. He functioned well in school and out. He filled his time with numerous interests. He liked to draw and paint, play the trombone, collect comic books, lift weights, and hold down a paper route. He was quite exhibitionistic, liking nothing more than the attention he got riding down the street on his unicycle. He performed for audiences, seeing himself as somewhat of a clown. His parents described him as good-natured, smart, funny, alive, and always on the go, although also "overconfident," "egocentric," unempathic, and manipulative.

Underlying his exhibitionism and grandiosity there was a very low self-esteem. He felt stupid and like a "schlepp." Fred was sure that others didn't like him and thought him foolish, laughing at him rather than with him. He consciously avoided sad affects, especially through activity. He noted, in this context, his curious reaction to his mother's recent surgery. At first he felt "scared," but then reacted to it and her absence with an energetic feeling of well-being and "high spirits." He was aware of the inappropriateness of this reaction.

Overtly Fred was mildly symptomatic. He was occasionally enuretic, overate, and suffered from frequent "stomach aches." When his parents were away he became overly preoccupied with their safety. He was also anxious in large crowds, with the irrational idea that he might get lost.

Psychological testing found a verbal IQ on the WISC-R 25 points higher than the performance IQ, with a full-scale score in the superior range. Projectives revealed "a pervasive sense of vulnerability" with a "poor self-esteem . . . defended by exhibitionism." On the Rorschach, there was a very high ratio of color to movement determinants.

Fred does not currently warrant a DSM-III diagnosis. Were he an adult, he would satisfy criteria for a narcissistic personality disorder. He is extraverted, exhibitionistic, expressive, egocentric, and expansive, traits unlikely to cause great concern as they are consistent with parental expectations and parental denial. That these traits are used defensively to ward off depressive affects was most evident in Fred's hypomanic reactions to feared loss and threats to his self-esteem—reactions quite typical of the adult bipolar. Children such as Fred, who appear on the surface to be happy and well adjusted, nevertheless warrant regular follow-up to detect the possible emergence of an overt bipolar disorder.

CONCLUSION

The accurate identification of those children and adolescents who will later become overtly schizophrenic or bipolar would constitute a major advance toward the primary prevention of these often devastating psychiatric disorders. Unfortunately, the reliable, specific, and easily detectable biological marker that is needed for this purpose has not yet been found. However, several characteristics have been described in association with those who will later become psychotic.

Evidence of familial loading is the major risk factor for the development of both schizophrenia and manic-depressive illness. A history of these disorders in family members, especially parents, should always alert the clinician to their potential presence in young patients being assessed regardless of the presenting complaint, which may vary greatly. In addition, the high risk of psychiatric morbidity in their offspring justifies the recommendation that all children of schizophrenic or bipolar parents be routinely evaluated.

With regards to schizophrenic offspring, the following characteristics have been associated with those who will later develop schizophrenia themselves: a history of perinatal insult and of early lags in neuropsychological development; neurological "soft" signs and low Bender-Gestalt scores, reflecting disturbances of neural integration and coordination; cognitive difficulties as manifest in relatively lower IQ scores, with verbal scores lower than performance scores, and disturbances of attention; behavioral disturbances at home, in school, and with peers, especially unsocialized aggression in boys and extreme shyness and withdrawal in girls; clinical evidence of loosening of associations, distractability, hyperactivity, and cognitive impoverishment (of conceptualization, abstract thinking, and vocabulary).

Characteristics that have been reported in association with those bipolar offspring who will later develop manic-depressive illness are: a history of affective lability, periodicity or impulsivity; evidence of discrete depressive episodes in childhood and adolescence; cyclothymia; the presence of prominent personality traits associated with extraversion (hyperthymia) or chronic dysthymia; findings on psychological testing of verbal IQ scores significantly higher than performance scores and high color to movement ratios on the Rorschach; reactions to antidepressants or stimulant medications characterized by hypomania, hyperthymia, hyperactivity, or agitation.

In order to assess the presence of these characteristics, comprehensive evaluations are required including a detailed family genetic history, developmental history—including details of affective development, a thorough psychiatric examination, neurological assessment, and psychological testing. Most important is a heightened degree of clinical suspicion, informed by an awareness of the natural history of these disorders and of the variations created by the effects of the developmental process on the clinical picture.

The characteristics listed above do not predict schizophrenia or bipolar illness. They can serve only as a preliminary guide toward identifying those offspring who warrant periodic reassessment and follow-up. Among them will be those who will show an increasingly symptomatic course preceding decompensation—a time during which preventive interventions can be initiated. These would be comprehensive in nature, including medications, supportive psychotherapy, educational planning, and parental counseling.

REFERENCES

Allen, M. (1976). Twin studies of affective illness. *Arch. Gen. Psychiat.* 33:1476–78.

Akiskal, H., et al. (1983). The relationship of personality to affective disorders: A critical review. *Arch. Gen. Psychiat.* 40:801–10.

———, et al. (1985). Affective disorders in referred children and younger siblings of manic-depressives. *Arch. Gen. Psychiat.* 42:996–1005.

Angst, J., et al. (1980). Bipolar manic-depressive psychoses: Results of a genetic investigation. *Human Genetics* 55:237–54.

Anthony, E. J. (1975). The influence of a manic-depressive environment on the developing child. In E. J. Anthony and T. Benedek (Eds.). *Depression and Human Existence*. Boston: Little Brown.

———, and Scott, P. (1960). Manic-depressive psychosis in childhood. *J. Child Psychol. Psychiat.* 1:53–72.

Benedek, T. (1956). Toward the biology of the depressive constellation. *J. Amer. Psychoanal. Assoc.* 4:389.

Bleuler, E. (1950). *Dementia Praecox or the Group of Schizophrenias*. J. Zinkin (trans.). New York: International Universities Press. (Originally published 1917).

Cohen, M., et al. (1954). An intensive study of twelve cases of manic-depressive psychosis. *Psychiatry* 17:103–37.

Cornblatt, B., and Erlenmeyer-Kimling, L. (1984). Early attentional predictors of adolescent behavioral disturbances in children at risk for schizophrenia. In N. F. Watt, et al. (Eds.). *Children At Risk for Schizophrenia: A Longitudinal Perspective.* New York: Cambridge University Press, pp. 198–211.

Cytryn L., et al. (1984). A developmental view of affective disturbances in the children of affectively ill parents. *Amer. J. Psychiat.* 141(2):219–22.

Davenport, Y., et al. (1979). Multi-generational families. *Amer. J. Orthopsychiat.* 49:24–35.

Decina, P., et al. (1983). Clinical and psychological assessment of children of bipolar probands. *Amer. J. Psychiat.* 140:548–53.

Erlenmeyer-Kimling, L. (1968). Studies on the offspring of two schizophrenic parents. In D. Rosenthal and S. S. Kety (Eds.). *The Transmission of Schizophrenias.* New York: Pergamon Press.

———. (1975). A prospective study of children at risk for schizophrenia. In R. Wirt, G. Winokur, and M. Rolf (Eds.). *Life History Research In Psychopathology.* Minneapolis: University of Minnesota Press, pp. 22–46.

———, Cornblatt, B., and Fleiss, J. (1979). High-risk research in schizophrenia. *Psychiatric Annals* 9:79–110.

———, et al. (1984). Assessment of the New York high-risk project subjects in sample A who are now clinically deviant. In N. F. Watt, et al. (Eds.). *Children At Risk for Schizophrenia: A Longitudinal Perspective.* Cambridge: Cambridge University Press, pp. 227–39.

Esman, A., et al. (1983). Juvenile manic-depressive illness: A longitudinal perspective. *J. Amer. Acad. Child Psychiat.* 22:302–5.

Feinstein, S. C., and Wolpert, E. A. (1973). Juvenile manic-depressive illness: Clinical and therapeutic considerations. *J. Amer. Acad. Child Psychiat.* 12:123–36.

Fish, B. (1975). Biologic antecedants of psychosis in children. In D. X. Freedman (Ed.). *Biology of the Major Psychoses.* New York: Raven Press, pp. 49–80.

Freud, A. (1966). *Normality and Pathology in Childhood.* London: Hogarth Press.

Garmezy, N. (1974). Children at-risk: The search for the antecedents of schizophrenia. Part 1. Conceptual models and research methods. *Schiz. Bull.* 8:14–90.

Gershon, E. S., Dunner, D., and Goodwin, R. (1971). Toward a biology of affective disorders. *Arch. Gen. Psychiat.* 25:1–15.

Gottesman, I. I., and Shields, J. (1972). *Schizophrenia and Genetics: A Twin Study Vantage Point.* New York: Academic Press.

Heston, L. L. (1966). Psychiatric disorders in foster home reared children of schizophrenic mothers. *Brit. J. Psychiat.* 112:819–25.

Kallmann, F. J. (1946). The genetic theory of schizophrenia: An analysis of 691 schizophrenic twin index families. *Amer. J. Psychiat.* 103:309–22.

Kestenbaum, C. J. (1979). Children at risk for manic-depressive illness: Possible predictors. *Amer. J. Psychiat.* 136:1206–8.

———. (1980). Children at risk for schizophrenia. *Amer. J. Psychother.* 34(2):164–77.

———. (1982). The borderline child at risk for major psychiatric disorder in adult life. In K. S. Robson (Ed.). *The Borderline Child.* New York: McGraw-Hill, pp. 49–82.

————. (1986). Precursors of affective and cognitive disturbance in schizophrenia. In D. Feinsilver (Ed.). *Towards a Comprehensive Psychoanalytic Psychotherapy for Schizophrenic Disorders*. Hillsdale, N.J.: Analytic Press, pp. 211–36.

————, and Bird, H. R. (1978). A reliability study of the mental health assessment form for school-age children *J. Amer. Acad. Child Psychiat.* 17(2):338–47.

Kety, S. S., et al. (1968). Mental illness in the biological and adoptive families of adopted schizophrenics. In D. Rosenthal and S. Kety (Eds.). *Transmission of Schizophrenia*. Oxford: Pergamon Press, pp. 345–62.

Kraeplin, E. (1913). *Psychiatrie*. Vol. 3. Leipzig: Barth.

————. (1921). *Manic-Depressive Insanity and Paranoia*. Edinburgh: Livingstone.

Kringlen, E. (1968). An epidemiological-clinical twin study on schizophrenia. In D. Rosenthal and S. Kety (Eds.). *Transmission of Schizophrenia*. Oxford: Pergamon Press, pp. 49–63.

Kron, L., et al. (1982). The offspring of bipolar manic-depressives: Clinical features. In S. Feinstein, et al. (Eds.). *Adolescent Psychiatry*, Vol. 10. Chicago: University of Chicago Press.

LaRoche, C., et al. (1985). Psychopathology in the offspring of parents with bipolar affective disorders. *Can. J. Psychiat.* 30:337–43.

Lidz, T. (1973). *The Origin and Treatment of Schizophrenic Disorders*. New York: Basic Books.

Marcus, J., et al. (1985). Neurological dysfunctioning in offspring of schizophrenics in Israel and Denmark. A replicational analysis. *Arch. Gen. Psychiat.* 42:753–61.

Matthysee, S., and Kidd, K. K. (1976). The biology of attention. *Schiz. Bull.* 3:370–72.

Mednick, S. A., and Schulsinger, F. (1970). Factors related to breakdown in children at high risk for schizophrenia. In M. Roff and D. F. Ricks (Eds.). *Life History Research in Psychopathology*. Vol. 1. Minneapolis: University of Minnesota Press, pp. 51–93.

Meehl, P. E. (1972). A critical afterward. In I. I. Gottesman and J. Shields (Eds.). *Schizophrenia and Genetics*. New York: Academic Press, pp. 367–415.

Morrison, H. (1983). Risk factors in children of depressed parents. In H. L. Morrison (Ed.). *Children of Depressed Parents*. New York: Grune and Stratton.

Pearson, J. S., and Kley, I. B. (1957). On the application of genetic experiences as age-specific base rates in the study of human behavior disorder. *Psychol. Bull.* 54:406–20.

Puig-Antich, J. (1983). Neuroendocrine and sleep correlates of prepubertal major depressive disorder: Current status of the evidence. In D. Cantwell and G. Carlson (Eds.). *Affective Disorders in Childhood and Adolescence*. New York: Spectrum Publications.

Rado, S. (1953). Dynamics and classification of disorder behavior. *Amer. J. Psychiat.* 110:406–16.

Ricks, D. I., and Berry, J. C. (1970). Family and symptom patterns that precede schizophrenia. In M. Roff and D. F. Ricks (Eds.). *Life History Research in Psychopathology*. Minneapolis: University of Minnesota Press, pp. 31–50.

Rosenthal, D. (1975). The spectrum concept in schizophrenic and manic-depressive disorders. In D. X. Freedman (Ed.). *Biology of the Major Psychoses*. New York: Raven Press, pp. 19–25.

Shaffer, D. (1985). Depression, mania and suicidal acts. In M. Rutter and L. Hersov (Eds.). *Child and Adolescent Psychiatry*. Oxford: Blackwell Publications, pp. 698–719.

Smeraldi, E., Negri, F., and Melicaam, A. (1977). A genetic study of affective disorder. *Acta Psychiat. Scand.* 56:382–98.

Tsuang, M. T. (1978). Genetic counseling for psychiatric patients and their families. *Amer. J. Psychiat.* 135:1465–75.

Von Zerssen, D. (1977). Premorbid personality and affective psychoses. In G. D. Burrows (Ed.). *Handbook of Studies on Depression*. New York: Excerpta Medica.

Waring, M., and Ricks, D. F. (1965). Family patterns of children who became adult schizophrenics. *J. Nerv. Ment. Disease* 140:351–64.

Waters, B., Marchenko, I., and Smiley, D. (1983). Affective disorder, paranatal and educational factors in the offspring of bipolar manic-depressives. *Can. J. Psychiat.* 28:527–31.

Watt, N. F. (1972). Longitudinal changes in the social behavior of children hospitalized for schizophrenia as adults. *J. Nerv. Ment. Disease* 155:42–54.

Winocur, G., Clayton, P., and Reich, T. (1969). *Manic-Depressive Illness*. St. Louis: Mosby.

Wynne, L. C., and Singer, M. T. (1964). Thought disorder and family relations of schizophrenics. *Arch. Gen. Psychiat.* 12:201–12.

31

CHILD AND ADOLESCENT SUICIDE RISK

Cynthia R. Pfeffer

Epidemiological data offer dramatic proof that suicidal behavior in the young is a major mental health problem. Suicidal behavior follows only accidents and homicide as the leading cause of death in teenagers (Monthly Vital Statistics 1984). In 1981, there were 27,596 suicides in the general population in the United States; of these, 5,161 were of adolescents and young adults who were 15 to 24 years old. Furthermore, although preadolescents have the lowest number of suicides of all age groups (there were 167 suicides among 5- to 14-year-olds in 1981), nonfatal suicidal behavior among children who are less than 12 years old is relatively common (Pfeffer et al. 1980, 1982, 1984; Cohen-Sandler et al. 1982; Myers et al. 1985). These facts highlight the urgent need to focus attention on effective prevention of suicidal behavior among young people.

Early recognition and appropriate intervention for suicidal behavior are some of the most important prevention approaches known. Yet a large number of clinicians are not sufficiently skilled to carry out these prevention methods effectively. For example, Holmes and Howard (1980) found that when a variety of clinicians, including physicians, psychologists, and social workers, were polled about their knowledge in evaluating adult suicidal risk, many believed that they were not adequately knowledgeable about treating a suicidal individual. Furthermore, it appeared that the psychiatrists and physicians from other medical specialties were significantly better than the other groups of clinicians in evaluating suicidal risk. It is not surprising that even less is known about the skills of clinicians who work with suicidal children and adolescents. It can be assumed that there is a need to help clinicians enhance their skills in working with suicidal young people. With this in mind, this chapter will review recent information about suicidal behavior in children and adolescents in order to provide information that will be helpful in assessing suicidal risk. In addition, this chapter will discuss technical approaches to interviewing and suggest a schema for implementing suicidal risk assessment and planning treatment.

CLINICAL VIGNETTES

Allen, age 6 years, was brought to a psychiatric clinic by his frightened mother on the same day that he suddenly ran to his fourth-floor apartment window and feverishly struggled to open it in an attempt to jump out. He had just been reprimanded by his mother for hitting and punching his 4-year-old brother.

Debbie, age 8 years, was psychiatrically hospitalized after threatening to kill her mother and herself with a kitchen knife during an argument with her mother. Debbie had a stormy relationship with her mother that was exaggerated just after her parents divorced two years before this frightening episode with the knife.

Calvin, age 10 years, was referred for psychiatric consultation by his pediatrician, who was worried about Calvin's inability to pay attention in school, his impulsively aggressive behavior, and his vivid fantasies about enemies attempting to invade Earth from foreign planets. Calvin's parents were deeply concerned about his repeated statements that he wished to die.

Sandra, age 12½ years, was transferred from a residential treatment center to a child psychiatric hospital for intensive evaluation of her anger and sadness, which had intensified before she jumped out the second-story window of her classroom. Fortunately, she landed unharmed in bushes below.

Katherine, age 15 years, was transferred from a pediatric unit to a psychiatric hospital after being medically cleared of the effects of an overdose of Tylenol. Katherine refused to talk to her pediatrician about her motivation to take such large quantities of the drug.

Barry, age 17 years, was brought for emergency psychiatric evaluation by his parents, who were frightened by his written note to his mother, expressing his desire to kill himself. In the note, he described feeling deeply despondent. Barry was an excellent student at school, but in the weeks preceding his note, he withdrew from friends and school activities.

These six brief vignettes vividly portray the alarming realities of children and adolescents who contemplate and carry out serious life-threatening behaviors. These children were intensely preoccupied by a desire to end their lives.

These six children represent the lucky ones whose behavior served as a signal of intense distress; a signal that was appropriately heeded so that they were able to receive adequate psychiatric assessment and intervention. Unfortunately, many more children and adolescents are not recognized as being potentially suicidal. This may be due to lack of adequate evaluation of distressed children and adolescents and to the minimization of the seriousness of their behaviors.

DEFINITION OF TERMS

In order to approach adequately the assessment of suicidal behavior, it is necessary to define the parameters being considered. It is crucial to define what is meant by suicidal behavior, especially among children and adolescents, and to delineate the factors that ought to be assessed.

A useful definition was proposed by Shneidman (1985): "Currently, in the Western world, suicide is the conscious act of self-induced annihilation, best understood as a multidimensional malaise in a needful individual who defines an issue for which the suicide is perceived as the best solution" (p. 203). This definition implies that a variety of factors require evaluation, among them the types of family and other environmental stresses that may stimulate unbearable pain and frustration.

With regard to childhood suicidal behavior, *The Suicidal Child* (Pfeffer 1986) discussed the dilemmas inherent in arriving at an adequate definition of suicidal behavior in children. These dilemmas center on distinguishing developmentally normative self-injurious behaviors from suicidal behavior, the difficulty in delineating children's intent to die, and the influence of children's concepts of death. Having considered these issues, Pfeffer proposed that the definition of suicidal behavior for children is similar to that for adolescents and adults. It involves the child's intent to kill himself in response to a perceived state of unbearable suffering. Therefore, the assessment of suicidal risk necessitates evaluating the youngster's thoughts about life-threatening actions as well as those risk factors that raise the level of the child's distress to sufficient levels to make suicidal behavior likely. Furthermore, it is recognized that the suicidal state is usually not longstanding; in contrast to this, the effects of risk factors are usually operative for a chronic period of time.

A CLINICIAN'S RESPONSES TO A SUICIDAL YOUNGSTER AND ORGANIZING THE THERAPEUTIC FORMAT

Suicidal behavior is a symptom whose expression waxes and wanes depending on a youngster's current psychological state and immediate interactions with others (Pfeffer 1986). This means that suicidal behavior may be expressed suddenly and may last for a short time. A suicidal youngster by definition is in a state of extreme crisis. Such a state generates high levels of anxiety in those who are involved in helping the youngster and is especially felt by a clinician during the process of initial evaluation of suicidal behavior.

A clinician's anxiety is specifically stimulated by the realization that at any moment a suicidal youngster may be injured or killed. Nevertheless, the clinician must be able to be objective and to respond with empathy. This is exemplified by Stone's (1980) suggestion that "it is important that the therapist not become engulfed in the suicidal patient's protestations about the helplessness of the situation less the therapist come to agree with him" (p. 58).

In addition to arousing anxiety, a suicidal youngster's crisis may stimulate other conscious and unconscious reactions in a clinician. Intense emotions associated with death, violence, and helplessness constantly impinge upon a clinician. Fantasies about loss, annihilation, and injury, ethical questions, and the fulfillment of wishes can increase the clinician's anxiety too. These reactions may make the clinician feel ineffective and alone in trying to help a suicidal youngster. A clinician's anxiety also may stem from situational concerns about whether there are appropriate resources to call upon if a youngster requires emergency hospital admission or other emergency life-saving measures.

At least two important factors can alleviate a clinician's anxiety. First, it is essential that a clinician be protected from becoming overwhelmed by a suicidal youngster's plight. This can be accomplished by collegial supervision and discussion of the types of problems encountered during an assessment. In addition, it may be necessary for a clinician to gain insight into his own personal conflicts through psychotherapy or psychoanalysis.

Another safeguard against becoming overwhelmed by a patient's suicidal phenomena is to limit the number of such patients being evaluated or treated at a given time. The emotional energy needed to work with a suicidal child or adolescent is enormous. Lesse (1975) realized that this work requires a therapist to be very active as a means of stimulating hope. Therefore, a therapist must not be exhausted or emotionally depleted.

An unfortunate situation can arise if a therapist is psychologically compromised. Maltsberger and Buie (1974) described this and proposed that certain intense responses of a therapist, especially involving anger, may provoke a suicidal patient to commit suicide. A therapist must be acutely aware of his or her responses and careful that such responses not be perceived by the patient as a rejection. In fact, a therapist's responses may be particularly problematic when working with a suicidal child or an adolescent. Such youngsters, because of their developmental immaturities, become intensely attached and dependent on a therapist. Perceptions of rejection can be excessively felt by children and adolescents.

Another way to diminish a therapist's anxieties is to use time effectively. An assessment of a suicidal youngster requires much highly focused time. Therefore, it is essential to plan an assessment so that ample time is allotted to each interview. Specifically, it is unwise to schedule an appointment when the therapist is compelled to end the interview at a specific time. Interviews must allow several hours to evaluate a patient's clinical condition so that dynamic interactions between patient and therapist can be observed and the effects of initial interventions evaluated. This is especially important in testing whether a youngster can form the therapeutic alliance that ensures successful work. Whether a patient can delay acting upon suicidal impulses must be determined immediately.

The therapist must be very available to a suicidal patient. Stone (1980) noted that "just as one must be 'there' for the suicidal patient in the office—to a greater extent than is necessary for many other sorts of patients—one must continue to be available outside the appointed hours as well" (p. 68). This means that phone calls and frequent office visits must be feasible. Furthermore, an assessment of a suicidal child or adolescent dictates that a patient be seen at closely spaced intervals. During the early phases of assessment, it is essential to see a patient the next day or within a few days of a first visit. Only when it is clear that risk of suicidal behavior has diminished can longer intervals between sessions be considered.

Finally, the format for assessment should include a network of people who can observe a youngster and communicate with the therapist if a life-threatening situation arises. Among key people to be included in this network are the youngster's family, peers, school personnel, and others who have regular contact with him. This feedback system should be explained to a child or adolescent in order to help him realize that any time he feels upset, he or she should try to communicate with one of the individuals in the network.

FACTORS FOR CLINICAL ASSESSMENT

Suicidal behavior in children and adolescents is a complex symptom that is determined by the interplay among intrapsychic, developmental, environmental, and biological forces (Pfeffer 1986). Ackerly (1967) listed an intricate interplay of factors associated with suicidal behavior that included aggressive drives, narcissistic expectations, superego functioning, withdrawal of interest from the world, state of the child's identifications, disappointment at not achieving hoped-for aspirations, loss of a sense of well-being, concepts of death, attempts to overcome helplessness, and the wish for a reunion with an all-giving parent.

Several recent empirical studies substantiate Ackerly's assertions and show that suicidal behavior occurs in youngsters of varying ages. For example, among preschool children, suicidal behavior is associated with nonsuicidal self-directed aggression, loss of interest, morbid ideas, depression, impulsivity, hyperactivity, running away, and being unwanted and abused by parents (Rosenthal and Rosenthal 1984). In preadolescent psychiatric inpatients and outpatients as well as in nonpatients, depression, preoccupations with death, and depression and suicidal behavior in the family are specifically associated with suicidal risk (Pfeffer et al. 1979, 1980, 1982, 1984). Furthermore, other factors, such as family turmoil and school problems, are associated with psychological problems that raise risk for suicidal behavior in a less direct way. Finally, studies of adolescent populations point out the varied components of suicidal behavior, which include depression, aggression, psychiatric disorders, substance abuse, family disruption, and peer relations (Garfinkel et al. 1982; Inamdar et al. 1982; Friedman et al. 1983; Alessi et al. 1984). Therefore, no child or adolescent is immune from the potential occurrence of suicidal behavior. It follows from these observations that *all children and adolescents who are evaluated psychiatrically should be evaluated for suicidal risk.*

Although it is necessary to focus on a broad array of factors during an assessment of suicidal risk, there are factors more highly associated with suicidal risk, which require an extensively detailed assessment. The following brief vignettes illustrate some of the multiple factors evident among suicidal preschoolers, preadolescents, and adolescents.

Case #1

Sandy, a 3½-year-old boy, was brought to the pediatric emergency room after he ingested twelve aspirins. The suicide attempt occurred when Sandy hid in the bathroom at home after he was reprimanded by his stepfather. Sandy climbed up to the medicine cabinet, found the aspirins, and ingested them. He was hospitalized on a pediatric unit for observation. He told the child psychiatrist who evaluated him that he "wanted to die. No one loves me. They only yell at me and hit me." Sandy's physical examination revealed that he had the marks of three old bruises on his thighs. Sandy told the doctor that he was hit with a belt by his stepfather, who often drank wine.

Sandy's mother corroborated that her husband used excessive methods of punishment and that her marriage was in jeopardy of a breakup. She was seriously depressed, cried throughout much of the interview, and acknowledged thoughts of suicide. She was told that the bureau of child protective services would be notified about her husband's severe punishment of Sandy and that Sandy and the family would need extensive help.

This example points out the serious environmental disorganization; parental problems of alcohol abuse, physical abuse, and depression; and the heightened state of depression and anxiety in this overwhelmed suicidal preschooler. Extensive assessment of environmental and intrapsychic factors was necessary.

Case #2

Rebecca, age 10 years, was psychiatrically hospitalized because she "wanted to kill herself." She burned her legs with matches and heard voices telling her she was "a bad person." She wanted to die so that she could be with her dead grandmother. She had been in outpatient psychiatric treatment and was treated with a neuroleptic medication until she attempted to burn herself. At that time, hospital admission was recommended.

Rebecca had a chronic history of learning problems and poor attention span. She lived with her mother, two older brothers, and her grandmother. Four months before Rebecca's hospitalization, her grandmother died suddenly while in the house. Although Rebecca had not witnessed the death, she spoke vividly about how her grandmother died of a sudden heart attack. Rebecca became overly anxious after her grandmother's death. She had been very close to her grandmother and depended on her for companionship and guidance. Shortly after the death, Rebecca reported that the auditory hallucinations that had bothered her before had intensified. She was placed on Haldol by her psychiatrist. However, Rebecca continued to feel very frightened. She worried that she might be kidnapped from school and that she might be sexually molested by men. She reported that she thought her teacher hated her.

This example depicts the psychological difficulties of a psychotic young-ster, which were exaggerated after the child's grandmother died. The loss of support and the close relationship with her grandmother increased the child's anxiety. Intense wishes to rejoin her grandmother motivated Rebec-ca's self-destructive actions and suicidal preoccupations.

Assessment of this child involved an extensive evaluation of her psycho-logical state, which included exploration of mourning responses and delin-eation of how external support could be offered to compensate for this child's realistic loss of environmental support.

Case #3

Richard, age 16 years, had repetitious thoughts of wanting to kill him-self. He had recently withdrawn from activities with friends and in school. Often, he became irritable and angry at his parents. He did not know why he felt like this but tried to alleviate these uncomfortable feelings by drink-ing beer. He consulted a psychiatrist at the suggestion of his parents.

Richard talked with the psychiatrist of his worries about what to do after he graduated from high school. He believed his father wanted him to join the family business, but this did not appeal to Richard. Instead, he loved music, was a talented guitarist, and wanted to form a folk music group. His parents were vehemently opposed to this. Richard felt angry, frustrated, and helpless in being unable to get his parents to understand his wishes. Numerous family arguments occurred, during which Richard became more and more suicidal.

Richard's psychiatric evaluation involved assessing his depression and his family's style of communicating. While his parents were very concerned about Richard's current distress, they were rigid in their beliefs about his future. Assessment of the meaning for each family member of Richard's fu-ture plans was crucial in decreasing his suicidal preoccupations.

In each of these examples, individual and family assessment was indicated. These examples suggest another principle for assessment of suicidal risk in children and adolescents. *The family should be interviewed during the early phase of assessment.* Fur-thermore, other factors that are associated with suicidal risk must be specifically evaluated; these are described in the next sections.

Suicidal Tendencies

Suicidal behavior can be classified according to a spectrum of severity with des-ignations of nonsuicidal behavior, suicidal ideas, suicidal threats, suicidal attempts and suicide (Pfeffer et al. 1979, 1980). Furthermore, it is known that previous history of nonfatal suicidal behavior is associated with higher risk for suicide (Weissman 1974) and that the number of suicidal attempts far outweighs the frequency of suicide (Eisenberg 1984). This suggests that it is essential *to take seriously and evaluate carefully any suicidal idea or action by a child or adolescent.* Unfortunately, many parents minimize the seriousness of their youngster's suicidal communications and thereby deprive the child of appropriate interventions. Some clinicians also avoid direct assessment of suicidal tendencies. Usually, such avoidance is associated with the anxiety of discovering a suicidal condition or with a clinician's lack of skill in speaking with children and adolescents about suicidal impulses. To emphasize another principle: *Assumptions should not be made about the severity of suicidal tendencies without a satisfactory assessment.* Assessment of this symptom involves estimating a youngster's intent to kill himself and the lethality of the consequences if the behavior is fully enacted.

Assessment of suicidal tendencies should always be done through direct discussion. Such discussion requires that a clinician specifically ask a patient about suicidal ideas or actions. Examples of questions to be asked are: Have you felt so bad that you wanted to harm or kill yourself? Did you ever try to kill or injure yourself? Have you considered committing suicide? Did you ever hurt yourself purposely or attempt to commit suicide?

It is apparent that children of all ages can talk about death and suicidal impulses. For example, Rosenthal and Rosenthal (1984) offered an example of a 2½-year-old girl who talked with her therapist about the ingestion of pills. "When asked where she found the pills she said, 'It was in the closet.' 'What will happen to the baby now?' asked the therapist. 'Baby is going to die.' The therapist asked, 'What is going to happen?' Elizabeth replied, 'Ambulance is going to come and take baby to the hospital and then the doctor will fix her and she will be all right' " (p. 522). Pfeffer (1986) collected statements of suicidal preadolescents. One 7-year-old girl stated, "Sometimes I want to kill myself. When my stomach hurts I say, God I will kill myself because I feel so bad. This year I thought of it" (p. 179). Adolescents, too, are capable of talking about their suicidal tendencies. Robbins and Alessi (1985) noted that "adolescents appear to be reliable reporters of their suicidal feelings when they are interviewed directly by someone with whom they have some degree of rapport" (p. 592). A dramatic example of suicidal statements was offered by Vivienne, a 14-year-old who committed suicide by hanging herself. In the book *Vivienne—The Life and Suicide of an Adolescent Girl* (Mack and Hickler 1981), she described her suicidal preoccupations in a letter to her teacher: "I took out the scarf and wrapped it tightly around my neck and pulled as hard as I could. . . . Finally I got it so I was cutting off the air completely and not just the blood. But then my lungs would just about burst and I would let it go" (p. 116).

It is obvious that a clinician should ask questions relating to suicidal behavior in language appropriate to the developmental level of a youngster. Furthermore, the questioning should be done at various times during an interview in order to elicit as much information as possible and to allow an opportunity to intervene if necessary. A clinician ought not assume that denial of suicidal impulses in the early phases of an interview is a true response or an absolute commentary on the child's suicidal level. As a youngster develops trust in a clinician, he may be more able to speak about suicidal tendencies. However, a youngster who can talk about suicide logically, distinctly, and openly, and who denies suicidal tendencies consistently, may be assumed to be nonsuicidal. In contrast, one who denies such tendencies and is guarded in discussion cannot be assumed to be devoid of suicidal tendencies. Thus, the assessment of the severity of suicidal behavior requires that the process of interaction between therapist and patient be evaluated. The assessment of suicidal behavior requires a dynamic approach whereby the therapist repeatedly checks for the patient's suicidal tendencies.

It follows from this that throughout any psychotherapeutic interaction, whether it be psychiatric assessment or psychiatric treatment, a clincian must continually monitor the potential for suicidal behavior. Especially in the treatment of a suicidal youngster, the therapist must evaluate the patient's suicidal urges during each session.

Depression

Studies of suicidal behavior indicate that there is a direct association between depression and the severity of suicidal behavior (Carlson and Cantwell 1982; Pfeffer et al. 1979, 1980, 1982, 1984; Robbins and Alessi 1985). However, not all youngsters who are depressed become suicidal. Therefore, the clinical assessment of suicidal risk involves assessment of the severity of depression within the context of other factors. Cohen-Sandler et al. (1982) pointed this out in their study of psychiatrically hospitalized preadolescents. They determined that certain factors distinguish depressed nonsuicidal youngsters from depressed suicidal ones. Their study determined that suicidal children experience more chronic and severe environmental stresses than do nonsuicidal depressed youngsters. These findings suggest that while it is necessary to evaluate the severity of depression, other factors, such as the quality of environmental stresses, are instrumental in creating suicidal risk. Nevertheless, the assessment of suicidal risk requires a detailed assessment of the severity of depression.

DSM-III criteria are appropriate indicators of a depressive constellation in a child or an adolescent. Such factors as depressed mood; changes in eating, sleeping, activity level, and concentration; and social withdrawal are usually associated with severe depression. These factors should be specifically addressed during the assessment of suicidal risk. In fact, empirical research supports this contention. In a study of sixty-four psychiatrically hospitalized adolescents, Robbins and Alessi (1985) interviewed these adolescents with the Schedule for Affective Disorders and Schizophrenia, a standardized semistructured interview format. They found that there was an association between suicidal preoccupation and such factors as depressed mood, feelings of worthlessness, anhedonia, insomnia, poor concentration, indecisiveness, lack of reactivity, and psychomotor disturbance.

From a psychodynamic perspective, depression is associated with actual or fantasied loss. The meaning of loss must be addressed during the evaluation of depression. Depressed children often feel rejected, abandoned, worthless, and hopeless. In fact, research evidence suggests that the most important component of depression associated with suicidal risk is hopelessness (Kazdin et al. 1983; Beck et al. 1985). Assessment of whether hope can be generated is best done within the context of interaction with the youngster. Therefore sufficient time for discussion of the issues must be allotted in the assessment. However, it must be remembered that while the psychodynamics of depression are similar for mild or severe depression, the assessment of severity of depression must include measurement of such criteria as eating and sleep problems, activity level, withdrawal, and so on.

Depressed children have chronic social problems, especially with parents, peers, and siblings (Puig-Antich et al. 1985). Such youngsters' verbal and affective communications with parents and siblings are highly problematic. Risk for suicidal behavior can be increased by the chronic problematic psychosocial functioning of a depressed child, especially when the child or adolescent feels isolated, misunderstood, and alienated. In fact, suicidal risk can be reduced if a youngster develops trust and hope that positive personal relationships are possible. Furthermore, a positive interaction between the child and therapist may be a model to help that child develop better social relationships.

Preoccupations with Death

Fantasies, fears, and preoccupations with death can be the earliest signs of suicidal tendencies in a child or an adolescent (Pfeffer 1986). Many clinicians are not aware of these indicators of suicidal risk, and as a result do not attempt to gather information about them. Often clinicians shy away from speaking with children about death because they worry that such talk may frighten the child. In contrast, studies have demonstrated that children are capable of talking about death and that they have distinct concepts about death (Koocher 1974; Nagy 1948; Orbach and Glaubman 1978; Pfeffer et al. 1979, 1980, 1982, 1984). As long as a child has a concept of death, he is capable of having suicidal ideas (Pfeffer 1986).

Clinicians may not fully appreciate that many adolescents do not have a mature understanding of death. For example, a study of 598 children and adolescents who were 13 to 15 years old pointed out that 50 percent of the adolescents believed in spiritual continuation after death, 20 percent had doubts about the finality of death, and over 20 percent believed in complete cessation of life (McIntire and Angle 1972). Furthermore, the suicidal youngsters in this study significantly more often denied that death was final. Thus, as with younger children, realistic concepts of death seem to be less critical an issue in defining suicidal behavior than whether a teenager has a distinct intent to die.

It is mandatory to determine what experiences a patient has had with death and the degree of preoccupation with death. Suicidal youngsters often have excessive fantasies about death (Pfeffer 1986). They worry about their own death and that of others; they dream about people dying or getting killed; they feel both anxious and fascinated with death. Some suicidal teenagers are preoccupied with extensive thoughts of death by violent means, while others worry about illness or accidents. Few suicidal children are devoid of such preoccupations.

Any child who is preoccupied with death should be questioned about suicidal tendencies. In fact, death preoccupations may be the first manifestations of suicidal tendencies even before a youngster is aware of suicidal thoughts. Therefore, the clinician should be alert to the possibility of suicidal behavior in any child or adolescent who exhibits excessive death preoccupations.

Family Factors

Studies suggest that family influences are associated with suicidal behavior in children and adolescents (Garfinkel et al. 1982; Pfeffer et al. 1979, 1980, 1982, 1984; Tishler and McKenry 1982). Among important family factors are parental physical abuse (Green 1978); parental depression and suicidal behavior (Garfinkel et al. 1982; Pfeffer et al. 1979, 1980, 1982, 1984); and parental alcoholism (Tishler and McKenry 1982). In assessing a child or adolescent for suicidal risk, it is essential to gather information about family history of these problems. To reduce the child's suicidal risk necessitates interventions that will decrease these parental problems. Most youngsters who have parents with these problems feel abandoned, confused, angry, and bad about themselves; they wish to die. Bender and Schilder, as long ago as 1937, recognized that a child may react to an intolerable family situation by experiencing suicidal behavior.

Interactions between family members must be evaluated. Case reports have suggested several types of problematic family dynamics. For example, Aleksandrowicz (1975) described a case of a 7½-year-old girl who jumped out the third-floor window of her apartment and survived. Aleksandrowicz proposed that the child's suicidal proclivities were enhanced by a chronic mismatch between the mother's personality and behavioral characteristics of the child. Another family dynamic, proposed by Sabbath (1969), is the the expendable child concept. This concept involves conflicted family interactions that create a situation in which there is "presumed a parental wish, conscious or unconscious, spoken or unspoken, that the child interprets as their desire to be rid of him, for him to die" (p. 273). Parents in such families find it difficult to offer empathy, support, and objective counseling to their child. This type of dynamic must be evaluated, because without parental support, a youngster is at high risk for suicidal behavior. Pfeffer (1981) also hypothesized a relevant schema of family functioning. This schema has five features: 1) there is a lack of generational boundaries; 2) there is a severe inflexible spouse relationship; 3) parental conscious and unconscious feelings are projected onto the child; 4) a symbiotic parent/child relationship persists; and 5) family members relate in a rigid way and any change is felt as a threat. When these factors occur in combination, a probable suicidal state can arise in a child or an adolescent. The clinician must judge whether there is a potential to effect reasonable change in such family interactions.

Unlike many other psychiatric symptoms, assessment of suicidal risk requires that the family be involved immediately. The purpose of including the family is that a clinician can observe communication patterns and behaviors of family members. Without adequate family support, the child may need to be removed from the family and placed in a supportive setting such as a psychiatric hospital unit. Another important issue for evaluation is whether the family can change sufficiently to promote the hope that they can work together to help a suicidal youngster.

Other Environmental Factors

School activities and peer relations are significant factors that may stress a youngster and increase suicidal risk. Although these factors are important for pre-adolescents, adolescents are particularly responsive to extrafamilial influences. Separation from family and reattachments to peers are potentially traumatic stresses for an adolescent. In fact, it has been suggested that family life is a potentially protective influence against suicidal behavior in preadolescents (Shaffer and Fisher 1981), but that this protective influence diminishes for adolescents.

During the assessment process, it is necessary to determine whether there is difficulty in school or whether there are stresses in peer relationships. Of prime importance is the assessment of substance abuse among peers and whether an adolescent participates in this with friends. Finally, it is essential to evaluate whether a youngster is able to talk about these problems with the family or other supportive people.

OTHER ASSESSMENT TECHNIQUES

Thus far, we have explored only a verbal interactive approach for assessment of suicidal risk. While such a format has advantages of focusing directly on the serious nature of suicidal behavior, other techniques can be valuable, especially for preadolescents. Many children are not able to communicate primarily within such a mode—especially young children or those who are developmentally immature. Therefore, other techniques should be incorporated into the schema of assessment.

Since play is one of the most developmentally expressive forms of communication for children, a play period should be included in the evaluation format. This format provides an opportunity to observe conscious and unconscious factors that can be expressed in play. Furthermore, play may evince specific clues to potential suicidal behavior.

For a suicidal child, observation of play may provide early clues to suicidal behavior even before suicidal impulses are obvious. Factors leading to expression of suicidal behavior are being dealt with through play, in order to alleviate stress, to master traumatic situations, and to gain mastery over conflicted feelings. However, when the functions of play can no longer bind these factors, expression of suicidal impulses may be evident in a direct form.

There are at least four features of play that are associated with childhood suicidal behavior (Pfeffer 1979). One characteristic is related to the processes of separation from parents. This is expressed by throwing objects, jumping off high places, and falling and wishing to be caught. Such play is seen normally among preschool children, but it is a possible indicator of suicidal behavior in preadolescents. Sandy, age 9 years, illustrated this in sessions with his therapist. He repeatedly depicted play scenes in which his house was on fire and a boy jumped out the window and was caught by a fireman. This play represented the child's suicidal incident, which occurred after he had a violent fight with his father and then attempted to jump out the third-floor apartment window. The wish to be rescued was vividly depicted in his play and was a hopeful sign that indicated Sandy's wish to be rescued from his intolerable family problems, especially with his father.

A second characteristic of play involves the manner in which play objects are handled. Suicidal children often abuse play objects, throw them away, or otherwise use them violently. Adam, age 8 years, was psychiatrically hospitalized after he threatened to stab himself in the chest. He had been repeatedly teasing his 4-year-old sister and was punished harshly by his mother. On an occasion after he had punched his sister in the eye, he ran to the kitchen with the intent of killing himself. He felt very bad about himself and knew his mother would be very angry at him. Alerted by the sister as to what had happened, his mother quickly went to locate Adam. She found him looking through the kitchen cabinets searching for a large knife with which to stab himself. While in the hospital, his play revealed that Adam had dolls beat each other up. He threw dolls on the floor or pounded their heads against the wall. He enacted many battle scenes in which soldiers were captured by enemies and brutally punished. These play events symbolized Adam's fantasies about himself and his belief that he is bad and deserves punishment. Adam attempted to injure the dolls in as violent a fashion as he threatened to end his life.

Another feature of play of suicidal children is the expression of reckless behavior. Many suicidal children place themselves in dangerous situations while playing. One suicidal child rode on the back of buses and another suicidal child jumped from fire escapes of apartment buildings. This play is similar to the abuse of play objects, except that in this case the child *is* the play object. The child places himself in as dangerous a situation as is depicted in the way toys are used. The boundaries between what are and are not safe limits are often so thin that the child may actually get hurt. In fact, such injuries may appear to have occurred accidentally.

A fourth sign in play of potential suicidal behavior involves identification with superheros, such as Superman, Batman, and the Bionic Woman. The child's play involves dangerous situations that the superhero has to resolve. However, this play has a different quality from the play of nonsuicidal children, who also commonly enact superhero themes. The play of suicidal children is more violent and dangerous than that of nonsuicidal children. For example, suicidal children play out intense scenes in which someone may actually get hurt.

While the four characteristics of the play of suicidal children may be similar to that of nonsuicidal children, the qualities of these characteristics are unique. Suicidal children's play is more out-of-control, has less protection from realistic dangerous situations, and is repetitive. Suicidal children often are unable to respond to interpretations or to stop enactments of play. They seem to lose their identity and assume roles of the characters in the play. In fact, often the boundary between the child and what is enacted in play becomes indistinguishable. Parents should also be asked how their child plays. Detailed questions should be asked about the types of play that are repeatedly enacted, how toys are used, and whether excessive violence or danger is present. Such information should be gathered from the child as well as others who know the child. In this way, early clues to suicidal risk may be discovered even before suicidal behavior is overtly manifest.

SUMMARY

This chapter focused on techniques of evaluating suicidal risk in children and adolescents. An interactive format between the patient, the family, and the therapist makes it possible to observe conscious and unconscious factors associated with suicidal risk. Treatment, therefore, is guided by diagnosing which factors promote suicidal risk; it must use approaches to decrease depression and other self-destructive behaviors, such as alcohol or drug abuse. It must aim to diminish family conflicts. Parental psychopathology, involving serious depression, alcoholism, and violent abuse, must be treated.

The format of monitoring suicidal risk proposed in this chapter should be utilized throughout the psychiatric treatment of any suicidal child. The assessment, as outlined in this chapter, is not a static event to be used only during the initial phases of interaction with a youngster. Continued use of this assessment format, with its purpose of elucidating suicidal risk indicators, can serve as a mechanism to monitor objectively the outcome of treatment. When no evidence of suicidal indicators is present, a clinician can assume that treatment has been successful.

The assessment format presented here is based on a verbal, interactive approach. Direct inquiry about suicidal ideas and/or actions is required, and detailed evaluation of the severity of depression, presence of death preoccupations, and parental psychopathology and family problems is necessary. A verbal format is advocated, regardless of whether a patient is a preadolescent or an adolescent. Assessment is based on a flexible structural format that includes the parents. Direct observation of family patterns of communication, empathy, and support point out how effective the family can be in providing necessary stability for a distressed suicidal child or adolescent. Play observation for children is valuable, too, in enhancing the process of assessment. Play may provide clues to suicidal tendencies even before suicidal behavior is evident.

The assessment may stimulate intense anxiety in a clinician. Anxiety can be decreased by having peer supervision or personal psychotherapy. In all cases, a clinician should limit the number of suicidal patients seen within a given time period.

Finally, it is commonly recognized that any approach that can highlight early warnings of suicidal risk has value for suicide prevention. Therefore, it is necessary to promote opportunities for ongoing education of clinicians and to teach new techniques of evaluating suicidal risk among young patients.

REFERENCES

Ackerly, W. C. (1967). Latency age children who threaten or attempt to kill themselves. *J. Amer. Acad. Child Psychiat.* 6:242–61.

Aleksandrowicz, M. D. (1975). The biological strangers: An attempted suicide of a 7½-year-old girl. *Bull. Menninger Clinic* 39:163–76.

Alessi, N. E., et al. (1984). Suicidal behavior among serious juvenile offenders. *Amer. J. Psychiat.* 141:286–87.

Beck, A. T., et al. (1985). Hopelessness and eventual suicide: A 10-year prospective study of patients hospitalized with suicidal ideation. *Amer. J. Psychiat.* 142:559–63.

Bender, L., and Schilder, P. (1937). Suicidal preoccupations and attempts in children. *Amer. J. Orthopsychiat.* 7:225–35.

Carlson, G. A., and Cantwell, D. P. (1982). Suicidal behavior and depression in children and adolescents. *J. Amer. Acad. Child Psychiat.* 21:361–68.

Cohen-Sandler, R., Berman, A. L., and King, R. A. (1982). Life stress and symptomatology: Determinants of suicidal behavior in children. *J. Amer. Acad. Child Psychiat.* 21:178–86.

Eisenberg, L. (1984). The epidemiology of suicide in adolescents. *Pediat. Annals* 13:47–54.

Friedman, R. C., et al. (1983). History of suicidal behavior in depressed borderline inpatients. *Amer. J. Psychiat.* 140:1023–26.

Garfinkel, B. D., Froese, A., and Hood, J. (1982). Suicide attempts in children and adolescents. *Amer. J. Psychiat.* 139:1257–61.

Green, A. (1978). Self-destructive behavior in battered children. *Amer. J. Psychiat.* 135:579–82.

Holmes, C. B., and Howard, M. E. (1980). Recognition of suicide lethality factors by physicians, mental health professionals, ministers, and college students. *J. Consult. Clin. Psychol.* 48:383–87.

Inamdar, S. C., et al. (1982). Violent and suicidal behavior in psychotic adolescents. *Amer. J. Psychiat.* 139:932–35.

Kazdin, A. E., et al. (1983). Hopelessness, depression, and suicidal intent among psychiatrically disturbed inpatient children. *J. Consult. Clin. Psychol.* 51:504–10.

Koocher, G. P. (1974). Talking with children about death. *Amer. J. Orthopsychiat.* 44:404–11.

Lesse, S. (1975). The range of therapies in the treatment of severely depressed suicidal patients. *Amer. J. Psychotherapy* 29:308–26.

McIntire, M. S., and Angle, C. R. (1972). Psychological biopsy in self-poisoning of children and adolescents. *Amer. J. Diseases Children* 126:420–26.

Mack, J. E., and Hickler, H. (1981). *Vivienne—The Life and Suicide of an Adolescent Girl*. Boston: Little Brown.

Maltsberger, J. T., and Buie, D. H. (1974). Countertransference hate in the treatment of suicidal patients. *Arch. Gen. Psychiat.* 30:625–33.

Monthly Vital Statistics Report of the National Center for Health Statistics (1984).

Myers, K. M., Burke, P., and McCauley, E. (1985). Suicidal behavior by hospitalized preadolescent children in a psychiatric unit. *J. Amer. Acad. Child Psychiat.* 24:474–80.

Nagy, M. (1948). The child's theories concerning death. *J. Genetic Psychol.* 73:3–27.

Orbach, I., and Glaubman, H. (1978). Suicidal, aggressive, and normal children's perception of personal and impersonal death. *J. Clin. Psychol.* 34:850–57.

Pfeffer, C. R. (1979). Clinical observations of play of suicidal latency age children. *Suicide and Life-Threatening Behavior* 9:235–44.

———. (1981). The family system of suicidal children. *Amer. J. Psychother.* 35:330–41.

———. (1986). *The Suicidal Child*. New York: Guilford Press.

———, et al. (1979). Suicidal behavior in latency-age children: An empirical study. *J. Amer. Acad. Child Psychiat.* 18:679–92.

———, et al. (1980). Suicidal behavior in latency-age children: An outpatient population. *J. Amer. Acad. Child Psychiat.* 19:703–10.

———, et al. (1982). Suicidal behavior in latency-age psychiatric inpatients: A replication and cross validation. *J. Amer. Acad. Child Psychiat.* 21:564–69.

———, et al. (1984). Suicidal behavior in normal school children: A comparison with child psychiatric inpatients. *J. Amer. Acad. Child Psychiat.* 23:416–23.

Puig-Antich, J., et al. (1985). Psychosocial functioning in prepubertal major depressive disorders: I and II. *Arch. Gen. Psychiat.* 42:500–17.

Robbins, D. R., and Alessi, N. E. (1985). Depressive symptoms and suicidal behavior in adolescents. *Amer. J. Psychiat.* 142:588–92.

Rosenthal, P. A., and Rosenthal, S. (1984). Suicidal behavior by preschool children. *Amer. J. Psychiat.* 141:520–25.

Sabbath, J. C. (1969). The suicidal adolescent: The expendable child. *J. Amer. Acad. Child. Psychiat.* 5:272–89.

Shaffer, D., and Fisher, P. (1981). The epidemiology of suicide in children and young adolescents. *J. Amer. Acad. Child Psychiat.* 20:545–65.

Shneidman, E. (1985). *Definition of Suicide*. New York: Wiley.

Stone, M. H. (1980). The suicidal patient: Points concerning diagnosis and intensive treatment. *Psychiatric Q.* 52:52–70.

Tishler, C. L., and McKenry, P. C. (1982). Parental negative self and adolescent suicide attempts. *J. Amer. Acad. Child Psychiat.* 21:404–8.

Weissman, M. M. (1974). The epidemiology of suicide attempts, 1960 to 1971. *Arch. Gen. Psychiat.* 30:737–46.

32

THE CLINICAL MANAGEMENT OF BEDWETTING IN CHILDREN

David Shaffer

EPIDEMIOLOGY AND NATURAL HISTORY

Approximately a quarter of 3-year-olds wet their beds at least once a week. One in five of these will have become dry by the following year, but if they are still wetting at age 4 or thereafter, their prognosis will be less good. Only 6 percent of enuretic 4-year-olds will be dry by their fifth birthday, and the rate of spontaneous acquisition of continence stays at this low level throughout childhood and adolescence. By age 7 approximately 7 percent of boys and 3 percent of girls are wet more often than once a week (Rutter et al. 1973), and at age 18 approximately 1 percent of males are still incontinent.

Enuresis in children and adolescents is a chronic condition with an excellent long-term but poor short-term prognosis. Unfortunately, there is little useful information in the literature about the clinical features that could enable a clinician to predict when a child will become dry. In a longitudinal study, Miller et al. (1960) noted that very few children became dry abruptly and most went through a period of wetting with decreasing frequency, often when febrile or during cold weather. However, when faced with a child who is wetting frequently, the clinician cannot reasonably advise a parent to temporise before starting what is a somewhat demanding but nevertheless highly effective course of treatment, because the child is likely to "grow out of it." The child will grow out of it, but the clinician cannot know when.

> Paul H., 10 years old, had always been wet at night. He had been distressed by this and his parents had first sought advice on treatment when he was 5. They were told by the pediatrician that bedwetting at that age was normal and that he could be expected to grow out of it. Thereafter he was taken by his parents to a succession of pediatricians and child psychiatrists at annual intervals. On each occasion until he was 9 his parents were given the same advice, sometimes coupled with a suggestion that they restrict his

fluid intake in the evenings or that they wake him before they went to bed. Paul's parents had tried these methods many times since he was 5, never with any success. Shortly after his ninth birthday he was referred to a child psychotherapist who saw him weekly and his parents every two weeks. After ten months of psychotherapy his wetting frequency was unchanged, and the parents sought referral elsewhere. He responded well to treatment with the bell and pad and was fully continent after a course of treatment lasting ten weeks.

By no means all enuretics seek treatment. Those who do will often wet frequently and most will have been wet all of their lives. However, a small proportion of so-called *"secondary"* or *"onset"* enuretics will have started to wet after a period of initial dryness. Secondary enuresis is usually reported to have its onset between the ages of 5 and 7 and is more common in boys (Oppel et al. 1968; Miller 1973; Essen and Peckham 1976).

Clinicians often believe that secondary enuresis indicates a psychological basis for the symptom. While it appears that the start of wetting frequently coincides with some stressful event such as the birth of a sibling, being admitted to a hospital, or starting school (Werry and Cohrssen 1965), studies comparing primary and secondary enuretics (Rutter et al. 1973; Fritz and Anders 1979; Shaffer et al. 1985) suggest that despite an element of stress or disturbance at the time of onset, secondary enuretics have the same rate of emotional or behavioral problems as primary enuretics.

Sex. In older children enuresis is more common in boys. However, epidemiological studies (Rutter et al. 1973) show that before the age of six years enuresis is as common in girls as in boys. It seems that the later male excess is in part because they are slower to become dry spontaneously and in part because they are also more likely to develop secondary enuresis (Oppel et al. 1968; Miller et al. 1960).

CLINICAL FEATURES

Urinary Symptoms. A high proportion of enuretic children experience frequency and urgency during the day. This is not necessarily indicative of urinary tract infection, but is more likely to be a sign of low *functional bladder volume* (see below). These symptoms will often be reported by the children, although they may not have been noticed by the parent.

John V. was an enuretic aged 11. His parents were interviewed first and denied that he had ever experienced symptoms of frequency or urgency. However, on direct questioning John said that at school he often felt an urgent need to empty his bladder and that sometimes he could not control this and he would pass a small amount of urine in his pants. This also happened during a baseball game and when he went for a long car ride with his parents. On investigation there was no evidence of urinary tract infection or anatomical abnormality of his genitourinary tract. However, after a fluid load the maximum volume of any micturition was 150 ml., which was less than would be expected for a boy of his age.

Situation Specificity. Many enuretic children are dry when they sleep away from home, as when they are on vacation, during a hospital admission, or when staying with a friend. Careful history taking from older, more articulate, enuretics suggests that this temporary continence is usually bought at the cost of disturbed sleep. The child may be dry but repeatedly wakens spontaneously to check himself. This feature does not appear to have any prognostic significance, but it is worth noting, because parents of children who wet only at home often feel either that the child is being incontinent on purpose and could do something about it if only he tried, or that the enuresis is a sign of family disturbance. Some clinicians will therefore mistakenly view the phenomenon as a reason to direct treatment to the parents or family, rather than to the child.

> Peter B.'s parents reported that he was wet nearly every night at home, but that whenever he went to spend a night with his cousin he was dry. His parents felt that his being wet only at home was his way of telling them that they were doing something wrong. They had sought family counseling for this and the whole family had been in therapy for the past six months. When Peter was spoken to alone he admitted that he would be very anxious when he spent a night with his cousin because they did not know that he wet the bed. When he stayed there he would always empty his bladder before going to sleep and would often wake two or three times during the night. He would then check to see if he had been wet and would often get up to go to the toilet. He also recalled a stressful two-week vacation he had spent with relatives and how although he had been dry for the first week, he had wet the bed again at the start of the second week.

ASSOCIATED CONDITIONS

Daytime Wetting. Among 5-year-old nocturnal enuretics, approximately 16 percent of boys and 30 percent of girls are also wet during the day. These rates fall 50 percent by age 7 (Hallgren 1957). Conversely, 60 to 80 percent of daytime wetters are also enuretic at night (Bloomfield and Douglas 1956). Both psychiatric problems (Rutter et al. 1973) and associated urinary tract infections are more common in children with a combination of day and nighttime enuresis.

Urinary Tract Abnormalities and Infections. Epidemiological surveys (Meadow et al. 1969; Dodge et al. 1970) of young school children indicate that urinary tract infections occur several times more often in enuretics than in nonenuretics. The asso-

ciation is stronger in female enuretics than in males, and this has led to the suggestion that the enuresis may itself predispose to ascending infection. Support for this
notion is drawn from a follow-up study (Dodge et al. 1970) that showed that recurrence of urinary tract infection is more common in enuretic girls than in nonenuretics.

The frequency and urgency described by many enuretics may be due to the fact
that a high proportion of enuretics also have a low *functional bladder volume* (Starfield
1967; Shaffer et al. 1985). That is to say, a micturition contraction occurs and is
sensed by the individual as urgency when the bladder contains a lesser amount of
urine than in normals. The cause of this functional abnormality is not clear, but
cystometric studies under anesthesia (Troup and Hodgson 1971) indicate that
the abnormality is likely to be a functional one and not caused by an anatomically
smaller bladder.

Associated Psychiatric Symptoms. Population surveys show that psychiatric symptoms are more common among children who wet the bed than among those who
do not. Rutter et al.'s 1973 epidemiological study showed that disturbed behavior or
emotions are present up to three times more often in enuretics than in nonenuretics.
However, the large majority of enuretics *do not* show other types of disturbed behavior.

Psychiatric disorder is more common in enuretic girls than boys, but is no com-
moner in older enuretics than younger ones, nor in children with secondary enuresis. Enuretic patients with associated psychiatric symptoms are clearly more likely
to be referred to child psychiatrists for treatment, and this may give psychiatrists
and other mental health professionals a misleading impression about the relationship between psychiatric disorder and bedwetting.

A number of possible reasons explain the significant association between enuresis and behavior disturbance.

1) Enuresis is a distressing condition, and it might be that any associated disturbance results directly from the bedwetting itself. However, clinical observations suggest that when enuresis is successfully treated in a child with significant psychiatric
disturbance, the disturbance will rarely abate.

> Leonard H., age 11, had never done well at school and was currently
> more than two grades behind in his reading scores. He had always been
> enuretic. He had one enuretic sibling, and his mother gave a history of en-
> uresis as a child. He was referred to the clinic because of disobedience, per-
> sistent truancy, and stealing. His parents punished him harshly when he
> wet the bed. An attempt was made to treat him with the bell and pad but it
> was difficult to obtain his parents' cooperation. They continued to punish
> him when he was wet even though they had been told that the treatment
> would take many weeks before it became effective. Because of this, condi-
> tioning treatment was discontinued and he was treated with imipramine.
> This resulted in a reduction in the number of wet nights for as long as he
> took his medication, but his aggressive and truant behavior persisted. The
> enuresis recurred when treatment with imipramine was discontinued.

Anna G. was a 12-year-old, overweight, withdrawn girl. She would binge on food and would then feel remorseful and depressed. She had few friends and once when tense had slashed at her wrists with a knife. She, like her three sisters, had always wet the bed. She responded rapidly to treatment with the bell and pad, becoming completely dry within six weeks of starting treatment. Although she expressed pleasure at this change there was little perceptible change in her mood, adjustment at school, or her social relationships.

By contrast, treating enuresis in the better adjusted child often results in a marked improvement in self-confidence, assertiveness, and good mood.

Robert D., 10 years old, had always wet the bed. His performance at school was uneven and he was found to have a marked verbal/performance IQ discrepancy on psychometric testing, with an average performance IQ score but a verbal score twenty-five points higher. He had one close friend, whom he had known for many years. He was reluctant to participate in sports and was generally thought to be unadventurous. Although he was known to be bright, he rarely spoke up in class. At home he was often pushed around by his older brother, who also teased him about his bedwetting. However, his mood was generally normal, there was no history of antisocial behavior, and he had no manifest anxiety symptoms. He responded rapidly to treatment with the bell and pad and his parents noticed an almost immediate change in other aspects of his behavior. He no longer accepted being pushed around by his brother and retaliated when teased. His school teachers noted that his performance had improved. He was more outspoken and he started to join in activities with more enthusiasm. He signed up for a school trip, something he had always avoided in the past. He invited a few friends over for the day for the first time that anyone could recall.

2) The psychodynamic literature has suggested that enuresis is itself a sign of psychopathology. A common theory is that it is a covert manifestation of aggression in children with a passive-dependent character disorder (Michaels 1961). However, a systematic analysis of case records obtained in a psychoanalytically oriented child psychiatric clinic (Achenbach and Lewis 1971) showed no specific association between character type and enuresis; epidemiological surveys show that when the two conditions coexist it may be with a range of different psychiatric problems, and there do not appear to be any specific deviant behavioral correlates (Rutter et al. 1973).

Other evidence points to the importance of biological rather than psychodynamic factors as a cause of enuresis. Thus, family history studies show that about 75 percent of enuretics have a first-degree relative who was enuretic, and comparisons between monozygotic and dizygotic twins indicate that concordance for enuresis is greater in monozygotic than dizygotic twins (Bakwin 1961).

3) A third possibility is that the excess of psychiatric disorder found in enuretics is caused by some common antecedent factor that predisposes separately to both

wetting and disturbed behavior. In support of this explanation, a detailed comparison of disturbed and nondisturbed enuretics (Shaffer et al. 1985) indicated that enuretics with psychiatric problems are more likely to have other developmental problems such as speech difficulty, neurological signs, and a low functional bladder volume.

AN EXPLANATORY MODEL FOR ENURESIS
AND ITS VALUE IN TREATMENT PLANNING

Clearly, biological factors are extremely important in determining whether or not a child wets the bed. These have been outlined above. However, it is also likely that certain experiences predispose a child to become or remain incontinent.

Children who are hospitalized between the ages of 1 and 3 have a higher likelihood of later enuresis than children of similar background who have not been hospitalized (Douglas 1973); children who are residents of institutions have a high prevalence of enuresis (Stein and Susser 1965) and children who are toilet trained later rather than earlier also are more likely to become enuretic (Kaffman and Elizur 1977) (in contrast to the common belief that enuresis arises as a reaction to very *early* toilet training). Enuresis has been reported to occur more commonly in children reared under unfavorable social and family circumstances (Miller et al. 1960). All of these conditions or circumstances have in common an interruption of or inadequate social learning opportunities.

It is reasonable to believe that bladder continence requires both bladder competence, which is biologically determined, and adequate and effective social learning experiences that place value on continence and disapproval of incontinence.

Social learning experiences are likely to be inadequate in the presence of significant familial stress and ineffective when the symptom is tolerated. Tolerance of wetting occurs when families choose to delay toilet training usually because of inaccurate advice from child development "experts" who have accepted unproven theoretical models. Tolerance also occurs when children are reared in an institutional or group setting. This may be because responsibility is divided among multiple caretakers with no one clearly responsible for praising or disapproving of incontinence, or because of compassion for a child faced with a multitude of social and environmental problems. Some child-care workers in a group setting take the view that enuresis is a symptom of inner distress and are reluctant to comment negatively on it or to expect continence because of the child's other problems. Tolerance of enuresis may also occur in families where one of the parents was himself enuretic. The parents who themselves wet the bed as children may choose to minimize the importance of enuresis, either because of a feeling that they are responsible for passing on the symptom or, if they did not receive effective treatment in early childhood, through feelings of helplessness over a problem that in their experience was untreatable.

This model for enuresis can be restated as *"Some children have a difficult bladder to train and others don't receive enough training.''* A rider would be that *"a given amount of training may suffice for an 'easy' bladder but may be inadequate for a difficult to train bladder.''*

Although this model does not consider enuresis as an act of metaphorical or symbolic significance, it should not be overlooked that any behavior can assume some function within the family economy (Winnicott 1953). For example, the child who is developmentally immature, with perhaps a mild speech articulation disorder, may well elicit a more caring and closer dependent relationship with his parents. In such children enuresis may originate as a developmentally or biologically determined symptom, but may come to serve mutually satisfying dependent relationships between parent and child. As long as the child wets the bed it will be reasonable to defer expectations of independence, for the parent to provide extra care and for the child to receive it. The need and expectations for cure may be low in such a relationship and may work against effective behavior therapy treatment (see below).

Donald J., age 12, was referred for conditioning treatment of his long-standing enuresis. He was an intelligent boy who had a history of early speech difficulties and who still spoke with a persistent dyslalia. He was clumsy and socially anxious. Despite his intelligence, his performance at school was moderate. He had a very close relationship with his mother, who admitted that she did not think there was anything too terrible about bed-wetting and who had agreed to come for treatment only because of pressure from her husband. The prescribed treatment required that mother come into Donald's bedroom after the alarm had sounded to make sure that he went through the necessary procedures, changing the bed, emptying bladder, disconnecting alarm, and so on. (Most parents and children find this noxious and it may well be that some avoidant learning plays a part in the efficacy of the treatment.) Donald's progress was unusual. He showed *no* diminution in the number of wet nights, but did not appear to be at all distressed by the lack of progress. After several months it was suggested that treatment be discontinued and tried again six months later. However, both Donald and his mother resisted this. They insisted that they found the visits and the treatment helpful. It was then suggested that they could continue to attend, but that the alarm procedure be discontinued because, although it was clearly ineffective, it did represent an intrusion on the family's previous routines. This suggestion too was resisted. Both mother and son felt that it was helpful.

At this point a closer history was taken about what actually took place at night when the alarm sounded. It emerged that after going through the prescribed procedures, the mother would sit at her son's bedside and they would talk about the previous day's events. It seemed likely that far from being a noxious event, night waking was a structured, sanctioned, and enjoyable opportunity for mother and son to be close together. Procedures were then changed. It was left that the father would do whatever nocturnal supervision was necessary, that parental intervention would be confined to ensuring that procedures were followed and would involve a minimum of verbal communication and no direct touching. Initially this change of treatment seemed promising. Dry nights were experienced for the first time in many years. However, after about three weeks the father said that he could no longer afford to have his sleep disturbed, and responsibility for the treatment fell back to the mother. Improvement was lost and the symptom persisted unaltered by the treatment.

INVESTIGATIONS

Urinary Tract Investigations. All enuretic children should have a routine physical examination and should have a clean catch specimen of urine cultured and examined microscopically. This examination should be repeated at least once. A detailed uroradiological medical examination is indicated only if significant bacteriuria is present; if there is a history of episodic enuresis associated with dysuria, urgency, or frequency; a clear history of polyuria; or if any congenital malformations are noted on examination (American Academy of Pediatrics, Committee on Radiology 1980).

Taking a History. In the author's view, the most effective treatment available for enuresis is behavior (conditioning) therapy, details of which are given below. In order to implement behavior therapy, some specific information is required, and a guide to this is included in this section.

Enuresis, like many psychiatric problems that arise in childhood, is a chronic disorder. The wise child psychiatrist will always inquire why the parent of a child with such a long-standing disorder has decided to seek help at one particular time rather than at any other. A common reason in the case of enuresis is that the child is planning to take a vacation away from home or wants to go to camp, and the symptom is a deterrent to doing so. If this is the case, then clearly it would be inappropriate to suggest any period of prolonged baseline observations, or to prescribe a method that may take weeks or months to become effective. If the referral was precipitated by some unrelated family or child crisis, that will need attention quite independently of the enuresis.

The clinician should inquire about what types of management have been used in the past. There are certain commonsense approaches such as limiting fluids at night before going to bed, offering rewards and punishments, and waking the child at night before the parent retires. These are ideas which parents have probably used before coming to get professional help and which by definition have been ineffective. Treatment involving rewards or punishments will often have been inappropriate. Rewards are commonly of a material nature, such as cash for a certain number of dry nights or the delayed promise of a gift or the withholding of an allowance if dryness is not maintained. Delayed reinforcements of this sort are rarely effective because they are noncontingent. The parents may have tried a variety of social punishments, such as scolding or shouting, but this will have been done inconsistently and will often have been followed by apologies. Not only will these approaches have been ineffective, but they will contribute to a feeling of pessimism in both the parents and the child.

Clinicians should also inquire about any unusual parenting practices, such as the use of physical punishment or the opposite, an excessively solicitous or sympathetic approach. The punitive parent will have difficulty going along with the demands of a complex behavior therapy program, and the punished child is likely to have other psychiatric problems that may require separate interventions. The problems of the oversolicitous or oversympathetic approach have been outlined above. Such parents may find it especially difficult to comply with a behaviorally oriented treatment that focuses only on the wetting behavior. Other parents may have been advised by therapists to avoid becoming overly involved in the management of the enuresis, and if a behaviorally oriented program is decided upon (which *will* require a good degree of involvement by the parents) these strictures will have to be taken into account before the parent can play the active role that may be required.

Previous treatment may have been inadequate. Conditioning treatment may have been used without adequate instruction or guidance, such as using an appliance purchased by mail order or prescribed by a professional who was unfamiliar with the many practical problems that arise during treatment (see below). Before accepting that a previous trial of conditioning treatment has failed, make sure that it was applied adequately; that is, it should have been given for a duration of no less than eight weeks, and it should have been established that the child woke with the alarm or that the treatment was not discontinued prematurely because of false alarms. Often the treatment will have been abandoned by parents or children who, unaware that the average duration of treatment before cure is several weeks, expect the bell to lead to immediate dryness. Sometimes an initial cure may have been achieved but the child then relapsed. When this happens parents may feel negatively about the value of the treatment and may decline to provide a further course even though this is the recommended procedure.

If medication has previously been used, inquire about its nature, the dosage, duration, efficacy, and side-effects. If it has not been used previously, ascertain the parents' attitude toward pharmacological treatment.

As indicated above, a premise in this chapter is that behavior therapy is the only known effective remedy. Medical treatments have a place in the short-term management of the condition, but do not produce a permanent cure of the condition. In taking a history it is therefore important to obtain information useful in planning a behavior therapy program. Inquire about whether the child sleeps alone or with siblings, where the child sleeps relative to the parents' bedrooms, and the relative time of going to bed for the parent and the child. Effective management of conditioning treatment requires some direct intervention from the parent both in the early and in the latter part of the evening.

Find out what the child knows of the treatment and prognosis of enuresis. Does the child feel the bedwetting is his/her own fault? How common does he understand the problem to be among other children? Many children feel that they are unique in being enuretic and anticipate that treatment will involve injections or surgical operations on their genitalia.

Determine how concerned the child is about the bedwetting or how much he wants to be cured in a "three wishes" type probe; for example, "If you could have three wishes come true, which would they be?" Many parents misinterpret their child's embarrassment or denial as a sign of indifference to the symptom. This may affect the parent's attitudes to the problem and treatment. If it can be demonstrated that the child does care about being wet, parents' motivation to become involved in the treatment program may improve.

TREATMENT

Nonspecific Treatments

General Reassurance and Record Keeping. About 10 percent of enuretic children will wet significantly less often after an initial visit to a practitioner who has done nothing more than provide reassurance and request that they systematically record how often they are dry over a two-week period (Shaffer et al. 1968).

Reassurance is addressed to both the child and the parent. It should be made clear that enuresis is a biologically based condition that may be made worse by stress, and that it will often cause adverse psychological consequences or be associated in a noncausal way with other psychiatric problems. It should be stated very explicitly that enuresis is not a willful behavior under the child's conscious control. Younger children should be told that they are not alone in wetting the bed and that it is common in their age group. Both parent and child should be told of the excellent prognosis that can be expected from satisfactory treatment.

The record keeping is usually done by maintaining a "star chart," which records with a star or other sticker if the child was dry on the previous night. Many parents will say that their child is too old to use stars or stickers, but even youngsters in their early teens appear to obtain satisfaction and social reinforcement from a graphic display of their progress.

It is important to stress that children should keep and complete the star chart themselves, but that they should show it to the parent each day. The parent should then offer appropriate praise if there has been a dry night. If the parent decides to keep the chart ("in the interest of accuracy"), then the child will have a reduced sense of participation. If the child keeps the chart and does not show it on a daily basis to the parent, the opportunity for social reinforcement for success is reduced.

Night Waking and Fluid Restriction Before Bed. Waking a child during the night and restricting fluids before bedtime are commonsense measures that many parents adopt of their own accord. However, they appear to do little to increase the chances of a dry night (Roberts and Schoellkopf 1951). In a controlled study into night lifting and fluid restriction in older children with other psychiatric problems, Hagglund (1965) found that although they led to an initial reduction in the frequency of wetting, any improvement was short lived, and within three months the treated group was wetting as often as the untreated control group.

Surgical Treatment. Urethral dilatation, meatotomy, and bladder-neck repair have all been advocated for the treatment of enuresis (Mahoney 1971). The rationale for surgical treatment is that many enuretics have a subcritical obstructive lesion of the urinary outflow tract. But the basis for this view is uncertain (Manley and French 1970; Cendrion and Lepinard 1972), and surgical intervention to relieve purported obstruction is now out of favor. Attempts to modify the neurological control of the bladder by division of the sacral nerves (Torrens and Haldt 1979) or the detrusor by bladder transection have also been disappointing (Jankneget et al. 1979). No surgical treatment has been subject to controlled trial, although the hazards of surgical intervention are well documented (Smith 1969) and include urinary incontinence, recurrent epididymitis, and aspermia.

Psychotherapy. Controlled studies show that psychotherapy alone is not an effective treatment for enuresis (Werry and Cohrssen 1965; DeLeon and Mandell 1966). However, as indicated above, associated psychological problems occur commonly with enuresis and may independently call for psychotherapeutic approaches.

Hypnosis. Uncontrolled studies have suggested that hypnotherapy may be an effective treatment (Bauman and Hinman 1974; Olness 1975), although the duration of improvement after hypnosis has not been documented.

Drug Treatment. The use of modern pharmacotherapeutic agents to treat enuresis began when anticholinergic atropine and belladonna derivates were used to increase bladder tonicity and decrease upsical capacity. Since then a wide range of drugs has been tested for their clinical efficacy (see Blackwell and Currah 1973, for a review). However, only the tricyclic antidepressants (TCAs and more recently the vasopeptide DDAVP) have been shown in methodologically adequate studies to be superior to placebo.

Tricyclic Antidepressants. Imipramine was the first TCA to be shown effective in childhood enuresis (Maclean 1960). The initial case report was subsequently replicated in many well-conducted double-blind studies, and the TCAs seem to be effective in all types of enuresis, including those with associated psychiatric disturbance (Shaffer et al. 1968; Mikkelson et al. 1980), urological abnormality (Kunin et al. 1962; Petersen et al. 1973), and even mental retardation (Milner and Hills 1968).

Most of the currently available tricyclics have been tried in double-blind studies, and all seem equally effective regardless of whether they are classified as primary or secondary amines or if their predominant pharmacological effects are to inhibit the reuptake of norepinephrine or serotonin. However, no controlled study has yet compared the efficacy of TCAs with differing pharmacological profiles directly in the same patient.

The response of enuresis to treatment with TCAs follows a consistent pattern. Tricyclics generally reduce the frequency of enuresis within the first week of use and at a constant dose level there is no cumulative effect, providing that the initial dose is adequate and all children who respond do so within the first week (Korczyn and Kish 1979; Rapoport et al. 1980).

Between 20 and 50 percent of children will become completely dry while they are receiving the TCA (Blackwell and Currah 1973), and most of the others will show a significant reduction of wetting frequency, usually on the order of 50 percent (Bindelglas et al. 1968; Forsythe and Merrett 1969; Leiderman et al. 1969).

However, treatment with TCAs does not cure enuresis. Initial improvement may not be sustained; tolerance frequently develops between the second and sixth week of treatment even if plasma tricyclic levels remain stable (Rapoport et al. 1980), and wetting will nearly always recur rapidly after medication has been discontinued regardless of whether it is withdrawn abruptly or tapered off over weeks (Shaffer et al. 1968). All improvement is usually lost within two weeks of discontinuing medication.

Although tricyclic antidepressants are the most common pharmacological agents used to treat enuresis, their mode of action remains obscure. Enuresis is generally nonepisodic, by no means always associated with psychiatric disorder, and cannot reasonably be regarded as a "depressive equivalent." This suggests that the effects are not brought about by any effect on mood; moreover the antienuretic effect of the TCAs occurs rapidly in contrast to its delayed antidepressant activity (Rapoport et al. 1980), and as indicated above, the drugs are equally effective in enuretics with or without an associated psychiatric disorder.

It is unlikely that the TCAs work through their marked effect on sleep architecture (TCAs decrease the number of wakenings and the time spent in rapid eye movement [REM] sleep and increase stage four sleep [Baldessarini 1980]), because enuretic events are not confined to any one sleep stage (Mikkelson et al. 1980).

It also seems unlikely that the TCAs work through their anticholinergic and antiadrenergic properties. Tricyclics with no anticholinergic activity (Petersen et al. 1973) are effective in enuresis, while primary anticholinergics (Wallace and Forsythe 1969) and antiadrenergic agents (Shaffer et al. 1978) are not. In summary, none of the known effects of the TCAs—antidepressant activity, their effect on levels of sleep and arousal, their anticholinergic and adrenolytic effects on bladder function—seems likely to be the effective mechanism.

Other Pharmacological Agents. Other pharmacological agents that have shown some promise in the treatment of enuresis include DDVP, oxybutinin, chlordiazepoxide, and amantadine hydrochloride.

In a double-blind study, Aladjem et al. (1982) found 40 percent of children ceased wetting completely and a further 40 percent showed a satisfactory response in a double-blind clinical trial of the vasopeptide *Desamino-D-Arginine Vasopressin (DDVP)*. These findings are comparable to those noted with the tricyclic antidepressants. However, as with the TCAs, when medication was discontinued, most children reverted to their pretreatment wetting frequency. The treatment did not appear to have been mediated by the drug's antidiuretic effect because urine osmolality was unchanged.

Oxybutinin is an antispasmodic that reduces uninhibited detrusor contraction and increases the vesical volume at both the first reflex contraction and at the first desire to void (Thompson and Lauvetz 1976; Koff et al. 1978). In an uncontrolled study of imipramine resistant primary enuretics, wetting frequency was significantly reduced in a large majority of cases on a dose of 5 mg three to four times daily (Buttarazzi 1977).

The minor tranquilizer *chlordiazepoxide* has been reported to reduce enuresis by Salmon (1973) and Noark (1964). Salmon noted a significant reduction in wetting frequency when administering 10 mg of chlordiazepoxide three times per day in a double-blind placebo-controlled study. Werry et al. (1977) found chlordiazepoxide ineffective in comparison to imipramine.

In an uncontrolled study, *Amantadine hydrochloride,* an antiviral agent and dopamine agonist, reduced wetting frequency significantly when given at an average dose of 150 mg/day in divided doses.

Behavioral Treatments (Conditioning)

In the author's view this is the preferred treatment. Unlike medication, it offers a good prospect of permanent cure. This must weigh heavily in its choice as the most appropriate treatment, even though it is more time-consuming and demanding of the patient, the family, and ultimately the therapist, who must familiarize himself with a new therapeutic skill. A detailed description of exactly how the device is used with a patient is provided in the appendix at the end of this chapter.

History and Description. Pfaundler (1904) devised an alarm system that alerted nurses after their medical patients had wet the bed. He noted that when this was used many children stopped wetting. Despite this early report of a successful treatment for enuresis, the method was not generally applied for another thirty years, when Mowrer and Mowrer (1938) described a similar device. The Mowrer apparatus (known as bell and pad), with some technical refinements, has continued in use and constitutes the most effective form of therapy now available. Most devices consist of an auditory signal linked to two electrodes, either in the form of perforated metal or foil sheets separated by an ordinary cotton sheet, or metallic strips placed on a single plastic sheet arranged in a parallel spiral pattern. Urine bridges the two electrodes and triggers an alarm. The theoretical basis for the treatment has been described elsewhere (Shaffer et al. 1985).

It is unlikely that Pavlovian conditioning is the only learning process involved when the bell and pad are used. The "gadget effect," in which the child becomes dry when the apparatus is placed on the bed but not switched on (DeLeon and Mandell 1966), suggests that *avoidance learning,* a form of operant conditioning, may also be important. The effectiveness of the twin-signal apparatus, designed by

Lovibond (1964) and Hansen (1979), lends support to this. The apparatus emits a moderate volume auditory signal when micturition is first detected and a second, much louder aversive noise several seconds later. This device is effective in enuretic children who do not respond to conventional bell-and-pad treatment and suggests that avoidance learning (to avoid the second loud, aversive noise) may be coupled with classic conditioning to result in a cure. This is important, because it provides a rationale for the rather elaborate and presumably inconvenient nighttime ritual that is usually recommended for the child after he has been waked by the bell.

Turner (1973) has pointed out that when the bell and pad are used the family's attention is directed to the wetting habits of the child, so that dry nights are more likely to be noted and rewarded by praise. In his view, *social learning* contributes an important component to the efficacy of the treatment program.

Efficacy. Cure rates vary in different studies from 60 to 90 percent. Acceptable success rates have been reported among the retarded (Sloop and Kennedy 1973; Smith 1981) and nonretarded institutionalized children.

Duration of Treatment. "Cure," defined as fourteen nights of continuous dryness, is usually reached during the second month of treatment (Kolvin et al. 1972), although in retarded patients cure may be expected after a longer period of initial treatment (Smith 1981). If stimulant drugs such as methylamphetamine (Young and Turner 1965) are given at the same time as the bell and pad, the response time taken until cure can be reduced, but this also increases the likelihood of relapse. The time taken until cure is reached may also be reduced by increasing the intensity of the auditory stimulus of the alarm itself (Finley and Wansley 1977).

Young and Morgan (1973) and Dische et al. (1983) have found that maternal anxiety, disturbed home background, and a failure of the child to waken with the alarm are all associated with a delayed response to treatment. Age of the child and initial wetting frequency are *not* significantly related to delay.

Noncompliance with Treatment. Many families discontinue treatment before the child is dry. Factors likely to lead to discontinuing treatment are: (1) failure to understand or to follow instructions; (2) failure of the apparatus to waken the child; (3) irritation at false alarms (Turner 1973); (4) unrealistic expectations about the length of time usually required for treatment. These are all more likely when the treatment is unsupervised, as when the apparatus is purchased by mail order, when the treatment is not fully understood by the prescribing therapist, or when the time taken to provide instructions is inadequate.

Duration of "Cure." Relapses within a year of completing treatment that resulted in an initial cure occur in about one-third of all children (Turner 1973). They are usually treated successfully in the same way as the first course of treatment. Young and Morgan (1973) found that relapse is more likely in older children, but no other factors have been found to be associated with the phenomenon.

Two techniques appear to reduce the relapse rate. These are:

1) Intermittent reinforcement, using special apparatus designed to waken the patient contingently (shortly after wetting) after only a proportion of enuretic events

(Finley et al. 1973). Such apparatus is not readily available, and the treatment requires a great deal of parental cooperation. Lovibond (1964) suggested that by using conventional apparatus only three or five days each week, similar results may be obtained. It should be noted that if that approach is used, the time taken to reach initial cure may be lengthened.

2) Overlearning. Young and Morgan (1973) found that if children who have been dry for fourteen consecutive nights are then given a fluid load of two pints before retiring (designed to reinduce wetting and with it the triggering of the bell), the relapse rate is reduced from 35 percent to 11 percent. This approach has the advantage of not delaying the initial "cure."

Despite these problems, the bell and pad offer an opportunity of cure to the great majority of bedwetters. However, its successful use requires that the therapist be acquainted with practical problems that are likely to arise during treatment and that he be available for support and guidance during the early stages of treatment.

Other Behavioral Approaches. Azrin, Sneed, and Foxx (1974) reported that treatment time with the bell and pad could be shortened by a number of other procedures grouped under the name of the "dry-bed" program. These include: (a) retention-control training (see below), (b) training the child to waken rapidly, and (c) giving reinforcement for appropriate micturition during the day. Although Ballard and Woodroofe (1977) and Azrin and Thienes (1978) have suggested that these procedures could be modified to make the use of the bell and pad unnecessary, other reports (Nettelbeck and Langeluddecke 1979) indicate that without the simultaneous use of an alarm apparatus these procedures are no better than placebo.

The dry-bed procedure (Azrin and Thienes 1978) is complicated. On the first afternoon a variation of retention training is carried out. The child is encouraged to drink large quantities of a favorite beverage to increase the frequency of micturition and with it the number of opportunities for learning. When the child feels the need to urinate, he or she is asked to hold for increasingly longer periods of time; when urination is necessary, the child is asked to lie on the bed as if asleep and then to get up to go to the bathroom, role-playing what he will have to do at night. This is rewarded with praise and more fluid.

Just before bedtime, the child is asked to role-play a self-correction procedure that will have to be carried out in the middle of the night—taking off pajamas, removing sheets, and putting them back on. There is a discussion about the rewards for being dry. Fluids continue to be given until the child falls asleep. Once asleep, the child is wakened hourly until 1 A.M. Additional fluids are given on each awakening until 11:00 P.M. If dry, the child is asked to rehearse yet again what will have to be done if he or she feels the need to pass urine; and if the child urinates, he or she is praised for correct toileting. If incontinent, the child is awakened by the parent, reprimanded for wetting, directed to the bathroom to finish urination, and asked to repeat the self-correction procedure. If dry the next morning, the child is allowed to stay up for an extra hour the next night and other social reinforcement is offered. If wet the next morning, the child is once again required to change his bed and pajamas and to do a number of positive practices in correct toileting, both in the morning and one-half hour before bed the following night.

Mattsson and Ollendick (1977) have reported adverse affects from this very intensive approach, stating that preschool children may react to such methods with temper tantrums or withdrawing behavior, and that the parents may also become upset and need support. Given that the simultaneous use of the bell and pad is essential to achieve cure, it is questionable whether its use can be justified in enuresis, although a brief trial in the younger, presumably normal child may be a useful approach to toilet training.

Retention-Control Training. In 1948 Smith suggested that enuresis could be treated by training children to defer micturition during the day. Paschalis et al. (1972), Stedman (1972), and Miller (1973) have described a treatment procedure whereby enuretic children were instructed to delay micturition by increments of two to three minutes each day after feeling the urge to void. Tokens were provided each time this was done, just *before* use of the toilet (the token after micturition might have the effect of reinforcing rather than deferring micturition). This continued for twenty days, by which time the children were deferring micturition for forty-five minutes on each occasion. In a controlled treatment study, half the children adopting this procedure (and none of the controls) became dry at night (Paschalis et al. 1972).

However, these positive findings have not been confirmed by others (Harris and Purohit 1977; Fielding 1980). In Fielding's study comparisons were made between treatment with the bell and pad only (see later) and four weeks of retention-control training, *followed by* the bell and pad. The bell-and-pad procedure was far superior to retention-control in reducing night wetting in both nocturnally and diurnally enuretic children. Functional bladder capacity was measured before and after treatment, and no significant increase was noted among the night wetters regardless of treatment mandated or whether or not cure had been achieved. Retention control is a time-consuming and questionably effective treatment, and there is at present no clear indication for its use alone or in combination with other procedures.

Treatment Summary

Treatment should be preceded by a period of observation. During this period it may be found that the child is wet only very infrequently, or the child may in fact stop altogether. Observation can be carried out by using a simple star chart. The child sticks in a star whenever he has a dry night. If this is displayed for the rest of the family to see, the social rewards for being dry may themselves have a therapeutic effect. During this period of baseline observation, which should last for at least two weeks, various simple interventions, such as lifting or fluid restriction, can be assessed.

Every effort should then be made to treat the child with the bell and pad. This is a safe, relatively brief form of treatment and is more likely to result in a permanent cure than any other. Ideally, instruction on how to fit the bell and pad on the patient's bed should be given with an accompanying demonstration on a clinic couch made up for this purpose. Initial follow-up should take place a few days after the bell and pad have been supplied, to deal with any difficulties that the patient or parents might experience.

Many children are not waked by the alarm, and parents should be warned of this possibility before treatment is started. Sleeping arrangements may need to be altered so that the parent can hear the bell and wake the child after it has sounded. Booster alarms of differing volumes and tones are available and are often helpful. Some children will turn the bell off before going to be bed, and parents should be advised to place it as far from the child's bed as possible so that it is out of reach. They should also check that the switch is still on before they retire to bed.

Once the bell has rung, the child should get up, turn off the alarm, and empty his bladder in the toilet. He should then be encouraged to remove the wet sheets, replacing them with dry ones. The bell is switched back on and the child will in almost all cases return to sleep without delay. If a second micturition should occur during sleep, it is reasonable to advise parents not to reset the alarm for a third time.

False alarms are a source of irritation to the family and may be due to contact between the clips or metal sheets through movement or else through a worn intervening sheet. Both the top sheet and intervening sheet should be large enough to be tucked in under the mattress, thus securing the electrode sheets in position. In her excellent review of the practical aspects of treatment with the bell and pad, Dische (1973) has pointed out that another cause of false alarms may be inadequate laundering of the intervening sheets. Urinary electrolytes deposited in the soiled sheet may facilitate conduction by perspiration.

After the child has been dry for two continuous weeks, the parent should be told that the chances of relapse can be reduced by continuing with the bell and pad for a further two weeks, during which time the child is encouraged to drink up to two pints of fluid at night before retiring. In a very few cases, this will result in a complete breakdown of continence and the procedure should then be abandoned; however, in most cases continence at night is maintained despite this stress.

Drug Treatment. The bell-and-pad method can result in a permanent cure in a high proportion of cases and is therefore the treatment of choice. Nevertheless, there are a number of situations in which treatment with imipramine or other tricyclic drugs might seem appropriate. Such situations would include: when it is important to obtain an immediate short-term effect, as when the child is first seen just before going away on holiday; when the wetting has become the focus of aggressive and hostile behavior on the part of parents or siblings. A rapidly effective treatment may serve to reduce the stresses in the family until such a time as the bell and pad can be used. Often, conditions for the use of the buzzer are likely to improve in the near future; for example, in a family living in overcrowded conditions but anticipating rehousing, or a family living in an inadequately heated house presenting for treatment in the winter months (treatment with the bell and pad will be more acceptable in warmer weather). Some apparently disorganized and inadequate families seem able to use the bell and pad successfully in the most unpromising circumstances, even, for example, when the enuretic child is sharing the bed with a sibling, or after failure of conditioning treatment.

TABLE 32.1   Problem Checklist for Conditioning Treatment

Problem	Solutions
1. "The bell doesn't work."	a. Check batteries and apparatus.
	b. Check that porous separating sheets are being used.
	c. Make sure that child is not turning off alarm before going to sleep or immediately after sounding. Get parent to check if alarm is on after child is asleep and place alarm out of easy reach.
2. "The bell goes off but does not wake the child."	a. Increase the volume of the alarm by placing it on an empty can or other resonating surface.
	b. Rearrange sleeping arrangement so that parent can wake the child.
3. "The bell goes off and the child wakes, but no cure."	a. Check on consistency of treatment.
	b. Check for possible reinforcing factors in night waking, e.g., mother doing all the work, with no tasks left for the child.
	c. Check on delay between alarm sounding and child rising. Should not exceed thirty minutes.
	d. Prescribe d-amphetamine 5 mg at night.
4. "False alarms."	a. Check that separating sheets are: 1. not threadbare; 2. rinsed through each day; 3. big enough to prevent slippage.
	b. Add a second separating sheet.
5. "The child is cured but relapses."	a. Repeat treatment.

TABLE 32.2   Overlearning Instructions for Patients Who Have Completed Initial Course of Behavior Therapy

1. Approximately thirty minutes before you plan to be asleep drink 1½ pints of fluid over a period of ten to fifteen minutes.
2. Go to bed with the alarm set up and on.
3. Don't worry if you wet—that is the idea.
4. If the bell goes off, carry out the usual procedure, i.e., get up, turn bell off, and empty bladder.
5. Carry on for fourteen nights, unless: You have more than three wet nights in the space of seven nights. If you have that many wets, stop extra fluids, and carry on with the bell until the next appointment.

REFERENCES

Achenbach, T., and Lewis, M. A. (1971). A proposed model for clinical research and its application to encopresis and enuresis. *J. Amer. Acad. Child Psychiat.* 10:535–54.

Aladjem, M., et al. (1982). Desmopressin in nocturnal enuresis. *Arch. Disease in Childhood* 57:137–40.

American Academy of Pediatrics—Committee on Radiology. (1980). Excretory urography for evaluation of enuresis. *Pediatrics* 65:644–45.

Azrin, N. H., Sneed, T. J., and Foxx, R. M. (1974). Dry bed: A rapid method of eliminating bed-wetting (enuresis) of the retarded. *Behavior Research Therapy* 11:427–34.

———, and Thienes, P. M. (1978). Rapid elimination of enuresis by intensive learning without a conditioning apparatus. *Behavior Research Therapy* 9:342–54.

Bakwin, H. (1961). Enuresis in children. *J. Pediat.* 58:806–19.

Baldessarini, R. J. (1980). Drugs and the treatment of psychiatric disorders. In A. G. Gilman, L. S. Goodman, A. Gilman (Eds.). *The Pharmacological Basis of Therapeutics.* New York: Macmillan, pp. 391–447.

Ballard, R. J., and Woodroofe, P. (1977). The effect of parent administered dry-bed training on nocturnal enuresis in children. *Behavior Research Therapy* 15:159–65.

Bauman, F. W., and Hinman, F. (1974). Treatment of incontinent boy with non-obstructive disease. *J. Urol.* 3:114–16.

Bindelglas, P. M., Dee, G. H., and Enos, F. A. (1968). Medical and psychosocial factors in enuretic children treated with imipramine hydrochloride. *Amer. J. Psychol.* 124:1107–12.

Blackwell, B., and Currah, J. (1973). The psychopharmacology of nocturnal enuresis. In I. Kolvin, R. MacKeith, and S. R. Meadow (Eds.). *Bladder Control and Enuresis.* London: Heinemann, pp. 231–57.

Bloomfield, J. M., and Douglas, J. W. B. (1956). Bedwetting—Prevalence among children aged 4–7 years. *Lancet* i:850–52.

Buttarazzi, P. J. (1977). Oxybutynin chloride (Ditropan) in enuresis. *J. Urol.* 118:46.

Cendrion, J., and Lepinard, V. (1972). Maladie de col vesical chez l'enfant. *Urol. Int.* 27:355–60.

DeLeon, G., and Mandell, W. (1966). A comparison of conditioning and psychotherapy in the treatment of enuresis. *J. Clin. Psychol.* 22:326–30.

Dische, S. (1973). Treatment of enuresis with an enuresis alarm. In I. Kolvin, R. MacKeith, and S. R. Meadow (Eds.). *Bladder Control and Enuresis.* London: Heinemann.

———, et al. (1983). Childhood nocturnal enuresis: Factors associated with outcome of treatment with an enuresis alarm. *Devel. Med. Child Neurol.* 25:67–82.

Dodge, W. F., et al. (1970). Nocturnal enuresis in 6- to 10-year-old children. *Amer. J. Disabled Children* 120:32–35.

Douglas, J. W. B. (1973). Early disturbing events and later enuresis. In I. Kolvin, R. MacKeith, and S. R. Meadow (Eds.). *Bladder Control and Enuresis.* London: Heinemann, pp. 109–17.

Essen, J., and Peckham, C. (1976). Nocturnal enuresis in childhood. *Devel. Med. Child Neurol.* 18:577–89.

Fielding, D. (1980). The response of day and night wetting children and children who wet only at night to retention control training and the enuresis alarm. *Behavior Research Therapy* 18:305–17.

Finley, W. W., et al. (1973). The effect of continuous, intermittent and placebo reinforcement on the effectiveness of the conditioning treatment for enuresis nocturna. *Behavior Research Therapy* 11:289–97.

———, and Wansley, R. A. (1977). Auditory intensity as a variable in the conditioning treatment of enuresis nocturna. *Behavior Research Therapy* 15:181–85.

Forsythe, W. I., and Merrett, J. D. (1969). A controlled trial of imipramine (Tofranil) and nortriptyline (Allergon) in the treatment of enuresis. *Brit. J. Clin. Pract.* 23:210–15.

Fritz, G. K., and Anders, T. F. (1979). Enuresis: The clinical application of an etiologically based classification system. *Child Psychiat. Human Devel.* 10:103–13.

Hagglund, T. B. (1965). Enuretic children treated on fluid restriction or forced drinks. A clinical and cystometric study. *Ann. Paediat. Fenn.* 11:84–90.

Hallgren, B. (1957). Enuresis: A clinical and genetic study. *Acta Psychiat. Neuro. Scand.* 32(suppl.):114.

Hansen, G. D. (1979). Enuresis control through fading, escape, and avoidance training. *J. Applied Behavior Anal.* 12:303–7.

Harris, L., and Purohit, A. (1977). Bladder training and enuresis: A controlled trial. *Behavior Research Therapy* 15:485–90.

Jankneget, R. A., Moonen, W. A., and Schrienemechars, L. M. H. (1979). Transection of the bladder as a method of treatment in adult enuresis nocturna. *Brit. J. Urol.* 51:275–77.

Kaffman, M., and Elizur, E. (1977). Infants who become enuretics: A longitudinal study of 161 kibbutz children. *Monogr. Soc. Res. Child Dev.* 42(2):170.

Koff, S. A., et al. (1978). Uninhibited bladder in children: Causes for urinary obstruction infection and reflux. In J. Hodson and P. Kincaid-Smith (Eds.). *Reflux Nephropathy*. New York: Masson, pp. 161–70.

Kolvin, I., et al. (1972). Enuresis: A descriptive analysis and a controlled trial. *Dev. Med. Child. Neurol.* 14:715–26.

Korczyn, A. D., and Kish, I. (1979). The mechanism of imipramine in enuresis nocturna. *Clin. Exp. Pharmacol. Physiol.* 6:31–35.

Kunin, C. M., Zacha, E., and Paquin, A. J., Jr. (1962). Urinary tract infections in school children: An epidemiologic, clinical, and laboratory study. *New Engl. J. Med.* 266:1287–96.

Leiderman, P. C., Wasserman, D. H., and Leiderman, V. R. (1969). Desipramine in the treatment of enuresis. *J. Urol.* 101:314–16.

Lovibond, S. H. (1964). *Conditioning and Enuresis*. Oxford: Pergamon Press.

Maclean, R. E. G. (1960). Imipramine hydrochloride and enuresis. *Amer. J. Psychiat.* 117–551.

Mahoney, D. T. (1971). Studies of enuresis. I. Incidence of obstructive lesions and pathophysiology and enuresis. *J. Urol.* 106:951–58.

Manley, C. B., and French, R. S. (1970). Urinary tract infection in girls: Prevalence of spina bifida occulta. *J. Urol.* 103:348–51.

Mattsson, J. L., and Ollendick, T. H. (1977). Issues in training normal children. *Behavior Therapy* 8:549–53.

Meadow, S. R., White, R. H. R., and Johnston, N. M. (1969). Prevalence of symptomless urinary tract disease in Birmingham school children. *Brit. Med. J.* 3:81.

Michaels, J. J. (1961). Enuresis in murderous aggressive children and adolescents. *Arch. Gen. Psychiat.* 5:490–93.

Mikkelson, E. J., et al. (1980). Childhood enuresis I. Sleep patterns and psychopathology. *Arch. Gen. Psychiat.* 317:1139–45.

Miller, F. J. W., et al. (1960). *Growing up in Newcastle-upon-Tyne*. London: Oxford University Press.

Miller, P. M. (1973). An experimental analysis in retention control training—The treatment of nocturnal enuresis in two institutionalized adolescents. *Behavior Therapy* 288–94.

Milner, G., and Hills, N. F. (1968). A double-blind assessment of antidepressants in the treatment of 212 enuretic patients. *Med. J. Aust.* 1:943–47.

Mowrer, O. H., and Mowrer, W. M. (1938). Enuresis: A method for its study and treatment. *Amer. J. Orthopsych.* 8:436–59.

Nettelbeck, T., and Langeluddecke, P. (1979). Dry-bed training without an enuresis machine. *Behavior Research Therapy* 17:403–4.

Noark, C. H. (1964). Enuresis nocturna: A long-term study of 44 children treated with imipramine hydrochloride (Tofranil) and other drugs. *Med. J. Aust.* 1:191–92.

Olness, K. (1975). The use of self-hypnosis in the treatment of childhood nocturnal enuresis. *Clin. Pediat.* 14:273–79.

Oppel, W. C., Harper, P. A., and Rider, R. V. (1968). Social, psychological and neurological factors associated with enuresis. *Pediat.* 42:627–41.

Paschalis, A. P., Kimmel, H. D., and Kimmel, E. (1972). Further study of diurnal instrumental conditioning in the treatment of enuresis nocturna. *J. Behavioral Research Exper. Psych.* 3:253–56.

Petersen, K. E., Anderson, O. O., and Hansen, T. (1973). The mode of action of imipramine and related drugs and their value in the treatment of different categories of enuresis nocturna. *Acta Paed. Scand.* 236(suppl):63–64.

Pfaundler, M. (1904). Demonstration eines Apparetes zur selbstatig Signalisierung stattgehabter Bettnassung. *Verhandlungen der hesellschuft Kinde. heilkd.* 21:219–20.

Rapoport, J. L., et al. (1980). Childhood enuresis. II. Psychopathology, tricyclic concentration in plasma, and antienuretic effect. *Arch. Gen. Psychiat.* 37:1146–52.

Roberts, K. E., and Schoellkopf, J. A. (1951). Eating, sleeping, and elimination practices in a group of 2½ year olds. *Amer. J. Disabled Children* 82:144–52.

Rutter, M. L., Yule, W., and Craham, P. J. (1973). Enuresis and behavioural deviance: Some epidemiological considerations. In I. Kolvin, R. MacKeith, and S. R. Meadows (Eds.). *Bladder Control and Enuresis*. London: Heinemann, pp. 137–47.

Salmon, M. A. (1973). The concept of day-time treatment for primary nocturnal enuresis. In I. Kolvin, R. MacKeith, and S. R. Meadow (Eds.). *Bladder Control and Enuresis*. Philadelphia: Lippincott, pp. 189–94.

Shaffer, D., Costello, A. J., and Hill, J. D. (1968). Control of enuresis with imipramine. *Arch. Disabled Children* 43:665–71.

————, Hedge, B., and Stephenson, J. D. (1978). Trial of an alpha-adrenolytic drug (Indoramin) for nocturnal enuresis. *Devel. Med. Child Neurol.* 20:183–88.

————, et al. (1985). Behavior and bladder disturbance of enuretic children: A rational classification of a common disorder. *Devel. Med. Child Neurol.* 26:781–92.

Sloop, E. W., and Kennedy, W. A. (1973). Institutionalized retarded nocturnal enuretics treated by a conditioning technique. *Amer. J. Ment. Def.* 77:717–21.

Smith, D. R. (1969). Critique of the concept of vesical neck obstruction in children. *J. Amer. Med. Assoc.* 207:1686–92.

Smith, L. J. (1981). Training severely and profoundly mentally handicapped nocturnal enuretics. *Behavior Research Therapy* 19:67–74.

Starfield, S. B. (1967). Functional bladder capacity in enuretic and nonenuretic children. *J. Paediat.* 70:777–81.

Stedman, J. M. (1972). The extension of the Kimmel treatment method for enuresis to an adolescent: A case report. *J. Behavior Therapy Experi. Psych.* 3:307–9.

Stein, Z. A., and Susser, M. W. (1965). Socio-medical study of enuresis among delinquent boys. *Brit. J. Prev. Soc. Med.* 19:174–81.

Thompson, I. M., and Lauvetz, R. (1976). Oxybutynin in bladder spasm, eneurogenic bladder and enuresis. *Urology* 8:452–54.

Torrens, M., and Haldt, L. (1979). Bladder denevation procedures. *Urol. Clin. North. Amer.* 6:283–93.

Troup, C. W., and Hodgson, N. B. (1971). Nocturnal functional bladder capacity in enuretic children. *J. Urol.* 105:129–30.

Turner, R. K. (1973). Conditioning treatment of nocturnal enuresis: Present studies. In I. Kolvin, R. MacKeith, and S. R. Meadow (Eds.). *Bladder Control and Enuresis.* London: Heinemann, pp. 195–210.

Wallace, I. R., and Forsyth, W. I. (1969). The treatment of enuresis: A controlled clinical trial of propantheline, propantheline and phenobarbitone, and placebo. *Brit. J. Clin. Pract.* 23:207–10.

Werry, J. S., and Cohrssen, J. (1965). Enuresis: An etiologic and therapeutic study. *J. Ped.* 67:423–31.

————, et al. (1977). Imipramine and chlordiazepoxide in enuresis. *Psychopharmacol. Bull.* 13:38–39.

Winnicott, M. (1953). Symptom tolerance in paediatrics. *Proc. Royal Soc. Med.* 46:675.

Young, G. C., and Turner, R. K. (1965). CNS stimulant drugs and conditioning treatment of nocturnal enuresis. *Behavior Research Therapy* 3:93–101.

————, and Morgan, R. T. T. (1973). Overlearning in the conditioning treatment of enuresis. *Dev. Med. Child Neurol.* 15:488–96.

33

ENCOPRESIS

Gary A. Pawl

DEFINITION

The term encopresis was first used by Weissenberg in 1926 to connote a descriptive similarity to enuresis. Encopresis can be defined as disorders effecting normal bowel function and control in the absence of organic pathology, beyond the age at which a child is expected to be toilet-trained. In DSM-III, the term functional encopresis is used as a subcategory of disorders of elimination for such disorders. Several other terms have also been utilized: fecal soiling and fecal incontinence are general terms used to describe a variety of etiological factors. Psychogenic megacolon is properly used to define abnormal bowel function where excessive retention has resulted in an enlarged colon. There has been disagreement in accurately defining associated factors, frequency, duration, and age of occurrence of encopresis. Most recently in DSM-III(R), the diagnostic criteria for functional encopresis are described as: repeated passage of feces of normal or near-normal consistency into places not appropriate for that purpose, whether voluntary or involuntary; at least one such event a month for a least six months; chronological and mental age of at least 4; and not due to a physical disorder, such as aganglionic megacolon.

EPIDEMIOLOGY

The age at which a child is expected to have achieved voluntary and involuntary bowel control varies among authors. Early studies assigned the limit at 2 years of age (Berg and Jones 1964). Other studies have noted that the age at which bowel control is attained in different cultures varies widely (Anthony 1957). Cultural expectations affect the age at which bowel control is attained (Brazelton 1962), as well as other factors including depth of sleep, seasonal variation, birth order, family size, and socioeconomic status (Stein and Susser 1967).

The prevalence of fecal soiling at various ages has been studied by several authors more recently. Bellman's 1966 study of 8,863 Swedish children by parent questionnaire found the prevalence of fecal soiling to decrease as a function of age. She noted that 8.1 percent of 3-year-olds, 2.8 percent of 4-year-olds, and 2.2 percent of 5-year-olds had symptoms of encopresis. Stein and Susser (1967), in a study of 671 British preschool children, found that more than 50 percent had achieved bowel control by 24 months and almost 100 percent by 48 months. By age 16 the occurrence of abnormal bowel control was practically zero. In general, fecal soiling after 4 years of age is accepted as abnormal.

Numerous studies have noted a higher rate of encopresis in boys than girls (Anthony 1957; Olatawura 1973; Berg and Jones 1964). Bellman (1966) found the prevalence of fecal soiling in boys at age 8 was 2.3 percent compared to 0.7 percent for girls. Rutter et al. (1970) reported that 1.2 percent of males and 0.3 percent of females on the Isle of Wight ages 10 to 12 were encopretic. Davie et al. (1972) found daytime soiling in 5-year-olds to be 1 percent of their cohort. Soiling was found three times more often in boys than in girls. Levine (1975) examined 102 encopretics from a pediatric clinic, reporting that 88 percent were between the ages of 4 and 13; 85 percent were male.

Several studies have reported a high rate of fecal soiling following a period of fecal continence. Levine (1975) classified 40 percent of encopretic subjects as continuous, having never been symptom-free for more than one month. This is in keeping with other studies, in which it was found that 50 to 60 percent of encopretics developed symptoms secondary to an interval of normal bowel control (Bellman 1966). Other studies have reported an association between enuresis and encopresis (Bellman 1966; Stein and Susser 1967; Levine 1975; Rutter et al. 1970). There is incomplete evidence for a familial component to encopresis; Bellman (1966) found that 15 percent of fathers of encopretics had themselves been encopretic. In general social class has not been found to contribute significantly to successful toilet training (Stein and Susser 1967; Rutter et al. 1970).

PHYSIOLOGY

The physiology of bowel control is a complex interaction of voluntary and involuntary responses (Anthony 1963; Nixon 1973). The process of defecation is initiated reflexively by rectal stimulation caused by peristalsis of feces out of the colon into the rectum. On contact and distention of the rectal mucosa, receptors stimulate increased colonic peristalsis, relaxation of the internal sphincter, pelvic floor discomfort, and a sense of urgency. Voluntary relaxation of the external anal sphincter and voluntary increase of intraperitoneal pressure by abdominal and thoracic muscle contraction lead to completion of normal defecation. If voluntary delay of defecation is to occur, the striated external sphincter can maintain contractions up to thirty seconds, during which time urge to defecate and reflex peristalsis diminish. During periods of relative colonic inactivity the internal sphincter and the wall of the anal canal maintain constant tonic pressure, preventing small quantities of feces from passing through the rectum. Recurrence of colonic peristalsis initiating another bowel movement may not occur for several hours, during which time colonic mucosal absorption of water from feces may promote a hard, difficult to eliminate stool. Excessive retention of feces can lead to distention of the rectum and compromise of anal sphincter control. In cases of overflow incontinence, loose, watery stool may then leak through the anal sphincter without elimination of retained feces. It is also evident that anxiety in relation to bowel function may lead to disordered voluntary muscle control and consequently to problems with retention or adequate voluntary delay of defecation.

In addition to the normal physiological response of defecation, factors of motivation and social learning interact with successful bowel control. Gesell et al. (1974) have described some of the developmental milestones frequently observed. By 15 months the child is usually standing and may squat to defecate. He may enjoy going to the toilet, with positive attention given by parents, but cannot voluntarily delay defecation. When speech begins, the child is able to communicate the need for toileting verbally, but he may still have difficulty "learning" that soiling outside of the toilet is socially unacceptable. He may enjoy playing with feces. By age 3 the child usually has developed the ability to postpone defecation voluntarily and can ask for help in toileting. By age 4 toilet training is generally complete and autonomous, no longer requiring parental assistance. Although adultlike toileting behavior usually occurs by 4 years, interest in size, color, shape, and consistency of fecal productions frequently remains high.

CLASSIFICATION

Several systems of classification have been employed in the literature to characterize encopretic children. Most schemes have used primary versus secondary or continuous versus discontinuous, in parallel with enuresis (Anthony 1957; Easson 1960; Bellman 1966). In DSM-III, there is no provision for recording primary versus secondary; but the term primary encopresis is used if soiling occurs after the child has reached 4 years of age and if it had not been preceded by a period of rectal continence for at least one year. Conversely, encopresis would be secondary if it had been preceded by a period of fecal continence for at least one year. Authors have also attempted to differentiate encopretics on the basis of current symptomatology: a) constipation versus not constipation; b) normal versus abnormal bowel habits; and c) soiling of normally formed stool versus excessively fluid feces. Others have also suggested differentiating those encopretics responsive to bowel catharsis and laxatives from those unresponsive to similar treatment. Hersov (1985) has suggested classification of encopretics into four categories based on the child's physical and psychological ability to control bowel movements.

In the first case the child has never been able to control soiling, and bowel movements are involuntary. Soiling in such cases tends to occur randomly in multiple situations and locations. History is often suggestive of poor learning as a result of faulty toilet training. Inability to learn to control toileting behavior may be evidence of mental retardation or neurological disorder. Significant social immaturity may be present, as evidenced by symptoms associated with conduct disorder, learning disability, or attention deficit disorder. There may be evidence of excessive chronic environmental stress resulting in inadequate or coercive social training.

In the second case soiling is known to be under physiological control, but feces are passed in socially inappropriate settings. In such cases feces are usually normally formed. There is frequently a discernable pattern to soiling behavior, often occurring in specific settings where there is a high level of social unacceptability. There may be gross denial of behavior. Recent onset or increase of stress, such as birth of a sibling, entering school, divorce of parents, admission to a hospital, or death of a family member, may be present. Coercive toileting practices with punitive training may be evident. In some cases there is a lack of distress in the child regarding encopresis, which is inconsistent with his capacity to understand socially determined behavior.

In the third case there is passage of watery stools secondary to physical disease, excessive anxiety, or overflow incontinence with chronic retention of feces. Most frequently, soiling of diarrhea or loose stools is associated with the latter, overflow incontinence. Often a history of constipation with painful defecation is present. Soiling is often frequent and of small quantity. There may be a history of reluctance to defecate when toileted by parents. If no evidence of fecal masses is evident on physical evaluation, symptoms of excessive anxiety may be present. Thorough medical evaluation must be done to rule out the presence of bowel disorders, including irritable bowel syndrome, allergies, and Crohn's disease.

In a fourth type of encopresis, less common in children, cases exhibit excessive fears of toileting, termed phobias by some authors (Ashkenazi 1975). There may be a history of trauma associated with toileting or toilet training. Often other phobic behavior exists concomitantly.

ETIOLOGY AND ASSOCIATED FACTORS

Numerous explanations for encopresis have been set forth, in general appealing to three major theoretical orientations: psychogenic, developmental/physical, and social learning/behavioral. Psychogenic explanations focus on psychological conflict leading to delayed or otherwise abnormal toileting. Developmental/physical formulations focus on neurological immaturity and poor physiological functioning of the defecatory response. Social learning/behavioral theories emphasize disordered training with inadequate or inappropriate reinforcements.

Psychogenic theories of encopresis were systematically formulated first by Freud, who coined the phrase "anal period" to denote a psychosexual stage in which the 2-year-old child for the first time develops some control over his body (Freud 1905). Freud described the so-called "battle of the pot," a struggle between the mother and child over timing of bowel functioning. Issues of compliance versus opposition were assumed to be more pronounced with a coercive-intrusive mother. Subsequently, underlying conflicts such as pregnancy wishes, guilt, aggression, fear of loss of self, and separation anxiety were elaborated as significant psychological determinants of successful toilet training. Other authors attributed psychogenic factors to a limited group of cases in which there was evidence of normally formed stools and patterns of fecal soiling apparently maximizing the level of social unacceptability. Extensive study of the mother-child relationship in regard to encopresis has concentrated on the quality of toilet training and the mother-child interaction. Several authors have described coercive toilet training in encopretics. Bellman (1966) and Easson (1960) have noted ambivalence in maternal attitudes toward toilet training, evidenced by indulgent, intrusive interactions contrasted with angry, punitive reactions to soiling behavior of their children.

Developmental/physical factors have also been implicated in the etiology of encopresis. From this theoretical orientation, cortical immaturity and inadequate physiological functioning of defecation are considered contributing factors in the genesis of encopresis. Organic disorders such as Hirschprung's disease can clearly cause disordered ability to control defecation. However, in encopretics without a demonstrable organic component, the developmental/physical contribution is less clear. It is difficult to determine whether social withdrawal or anxiety disorder reported by some authors (Bellman 1966) are primary or secondary to encopresis. Language delays, low intelligence, and/or neurological impairment reported by others (Bemporad et al. 1971; Olatawura 1973) in association with encopresis are more suggestive of a primary contribution to abnormal bowel control. Constitutional and dietary factors have not been well studied. Encopresis in association with marked mental retardation and severe developmental disorders is common but poorly defined.

Social learning/behavioral approaches attribute disordered or insufficient learning to the etiology of encopresis. Faulty learning can occur prior to correct toilet training, and/or encopresis can be maintained by inappropriate reinforcers. In the absence of reinforcement to mold proper toileting behavior, encopresis continues as a learned response often with built-in secondary gains. Social learning/behavioral approaches rely heavily on functional analysis of stimulus-response cycles. Primary encopresis may develop as a result of a lack of prerequisite toileting skills or an inadequate ability to discriminate the need to defecate. Teaching such skills will enable the child to recognize the need to defecate and respond appropriately. Secondary encopresis with retention may be learned avoidant behavior, reinforced by delay of painful defecation. Relief of pain on defecation with laxatives, combined with positive reinforcement for acceptable toileting, will allow the child to learn alternative behavior. Where parental attention is maintaining soiling, alteration of parental response patterns is used to change encopretic behavior. Behavioral approaches have proven very powerful in treatment of encopresis of diverse etiologies.

ASSESSMENT

Having established a history of encopretic behavior, a thorough evaluation is necessary prior to undertaking treatment. It is apparent that successful treatment of encopresis will be effected by accurate understanding of medical, developmental, and psychological factors associated with specific cases. In general, classifying the type of encopresis (continuous, discontinuous, retentive, or other), identifying associated characteristics, and ruling out organic causes will guide the clinician in differential application of treatment. Comprehensive evaluation should include a medical evaluation, psychiatric interview, family assessment, and behavioral records.

Medical evaluation should include medical history, review of systems, physical examination, and appropriate laboratory tests. The differential diagnosis of organic causes of encopresis without retention includes diarrheal disorders (irritable bowel syndrome, Crohn's disease), CNS diseases, and sensory motor deficits of anorectum or pelvic floor muscle. Organic causes of encopresis associated with retention include Hirschprung's disease, neurogenic megacolon, intestinal pseudo-obstruction syndrome, hypothyroidism, hypercalcemia, chronic codeine or phenothiazine use, disease of intestinal smooth muscle and anal/rectal stenosis or fissure (Fleisher 1976). Physical evaluation should include careful abdominal and rectal exam to determine if fecal masses are present. Levine (1982) has recommended an X ray of the abdomen for detection of fecal masses in the rectum. Barium enemas and other bowel contrast studies are not indicated unless there is further evidence of bowel-related disease. Medical history and blood tests should be aimed at ruling out the physical disorders already mentioned.

The psychiatric interview should be aimed at defining the type of encopresis, elucidating emotional determinants of behavior, and identifying behavioral contingencies relating to encopretic behavior. Psychiatric assessment should include a developmental history with a thorough history of encopretic behavior and previous treatment. Associated factors, such as developmental delays in other areas or family dysfunction, would indicate differing treatment approaches. It is important to determine the child's ability to sense urgency and the need to go to the toilet, as this would indicate level of maturity and social learning. Associated psychopathology in the encopretic child may be more highly suspected where there is a history of previous normal bowel control, identified stressors, and onset beyond age 8. Excessive anxiety or refusal of toileting may indicate toileting phobias, coercive toilet training, or a history of painful defecation resulting from constipation.

Detailed records of soiling and toileting behavior can help define existing environmental reinforcement for soiling behavior, as well as establish a baseline for evaluating treatment response. Family evaluation will help clarify motivation, attitudes, and the family's ability to follow through on treatment recommendations as well as aid in identifying existing pathology. Diagnostic evaluation should continue throughout treatment as new information is obtained and treatment outcome is assessed.

TREATMENT

Appropriate treatment of encopresis is determined by a thorough assessment. Characterization of etiological factors, including possible organic causes, psychological conflict, and/or environmental factors call for differing treatment strategies. A developmental history clinical interview will differentiate between the need for toilet training in cases where appropriate toileting has never been achieved and cases where the child has learned toileting but has regressed to fecal soiling secondary to psychiatric disorders, parent-child difficulties, or other environmental stresses. In both cases contingencies reinforcing soiling behavior may be identified and modified, allowing the child more acceptable alternatives to soiling. Often the support and management alternatives provided by the clinician can lessen parental pressure on the child, thus reducing parent-child stress and promoting a familial atmosphere more conducive to learning appropriate behavior.

In cases of soiling usually seen in younger children, where toilet training has never been achieved, a systematic program designed to reinforce appropriate toileting behavior should be initiated. Therapy will focus on teaching practical toileting skills, including regular visits to the toilet after meals; how to identify the need for toileting; how to disrobe and sit on the commode; and how to increase abdominal pressure to promote defecation. Positive reinforcement of appropriate toileting through use of verbal praise, simple "star charts," or more complex systems of material or social rewards will encourage the desired behavior. At the same time care must be taken to eliminate parental reinforcement of soiling, which is most frequently seen as negative parental attention or other secondary social gain. Since encopresis engenders a variety of negative responses from parents, orientation counseling to alleviate unrealistic expectations and reduce punishment strategies will lessen the pressure on the child as well as the family. Attention to broader pathological family functioning will frequently be needed where the encopretic child represents only one of several social and familial problems. Doleys (1983) has detailed psychosocial/behavior approaches as outlined above. Where more intensive behavioral techniques have been required, other authors have used mechanical devices to detect soiling episodes (Foxx and Azrin 1973) and to monitor defecation in a commode (Cheney 1973). Once desired behavior is identified, rewards for proper toileting are utilized. Olness et al. (1980) have used biofeedback devices for training sphincter control in difficult cases, with some success. In cases where encopresis is secondary to retention with overflow incontinence, there is usually a history of painful defecation and/or marked struggle between parent and child over toileting. Initial treatment should consist of alleviating retention through the use of enemas and maintaining soft, painless stools by laxative administration (Berg and Jones 1964). Involvement of parents in treatment is indicated where coercive or other negative interactions exist between parent and child (Levine 1982). Behavioral techniques to increase the frequency of acceptable toileting should be utilized as part of the training process.

In encopretic cases where bowel control has been achieved previously, treatment is more problematic. Often secondary encopresis is part of more extensive psychopathology in the child or deviance in family functioning. Frequently a varied approach, including relief of constipation, individual psychodynamic therapy, and family treatment, is required. Where encopresis appears secondary to severe environmental stress, amelioration of the stressor may bring rapid remission. High levels of anxiety, guilt, anger, or depression in the child are often successfully treated by verbal or play therapies in combination with family counseling and appropriate medical management of constipation. Kestenbaum (1985) offered a case vignette in illustration of the use of multiple strategies.

CASE VIGNETTE

George W. was a 6½-year-old boy referred for a psychiatric evaluation because of a five-month history of fecal soiling. George had a history of severe constipation since age 3 and had been evaluated at that time for possible megacolon, with a negative result. His first-grade teacher reported that he was teased by other children, nicknamed "Stinky," and was spending more and more time away from any group activity. He was an excellent student, meticulous about his workbook, his drawings, and the order of his desk; he had always been shy and quiet in class.

George was the younger of two boys, children of an electronics engineer and a former grade school teacher. The family was well-to-do, but the father had been fired from his last position because of his alcohol problem and was currently unemployed. George had been exposed to loud family quarrels and a stiff upper lip approach on the part of the mother, who constantly reproached the father with the admonition "not in front of the children."

The examiner found George to be a small, anxious, quiet child, clearly intelligent but totally lacking in spontaneity. He admitted feeling ashamed about his inability to control his bowels but refused to elaborate further.

It was evident that the family style was noncommunicative; problems were not dealt with but suffered in silence.

The evaluation included a pediatric and psychological evaluation. The pediatrician noted that physical examination revealed fecal masses in the lower left quadrant of the abdomen. On rectal examination a large fecal plug was encountered, occupying the rectum up to the anal canal. Liquid stool was leaking around the plug. He diagnosed George as having encopresis resulting from functional constipation. The doctor ordered an initial Fleets enema followed by a mineral oil regimen in an attempt to regulate George's bowel habits. Psychological examination revealed a Stanford-Binet Score of very superior IQ (164) and superb productions in the Draw-A-Person test commensurate with the general level of endowment.

The psychiatrist recommended family counseling, a program for alcohol-abusing families, and psychodynamically oriented psychotherapy for George.

George spent his sessions painting, working with clay (he constructed over many weeks an aquaduct that could actually transport water), and writing stories. The themes usually concerned small forest animals who didn't like to go to animal school, particularly gym class. George's own fear of swimming, group activities, and rough-and-tumble play was evident. Therapy dealt with these fears, family conflict, and George's inability to control his world as well as his body; withholding the stool was equated with withholding in other areas.

Within six weeks the encopresis was under control. Within six months George had made two friends, had overcome some of his fears, and was more open and spontaneous. Alcoholics Anonymous and family therapy were extremely beneficial to the W.'s. Individual treatment was discontinued after nine months. A ten-year follow-up revealed that George had done brilliantly in high school, had friends, was accepted into a prestigious college, and plans to become an architect. The encopresis has never recurred.

Finally, in cases of "toilet phobias" where the child is fearful of approaching or sitting on the commode, behavior regimens designed to reinforce successive approximations to sitting on the commode have been successful (Ashkenazi 1975). As with all cases of encopresis, attention must also be given to treatment of retention, individual psychological conflict, and environmental stress, if present.

Although numerous studies of varying treatment strategies exist in the literature, there are few well-controlled treatment trials; it is thus difficult to evaluate the effectiveness of specific treatments. Comparison of studies is further complicated by differences in study population and the use of multiple treatment procedures and measurements of treatment outcomes. Nevertheless, it is clear that improvement or cure in the treatment of encopresis can be expected in the majority of cases.

In a two-year follow-up study of 186 clinic cases with encopresis, Bellman (1966) found that about 50 percent of children had spontaneously remitted and that practically all had remitted by age 16. Several studies have reported high success rates in treatment of encopresis using verbal and play therapy. Improvement or complete remission from encopresis in 60 to 90 percent of cases has been reported by Berg and Jones (1964) and Gavanski (1971), using psychotherapy alone or in combination with laxatives where constipation coexisted with soiling. Others have reported cure or improvement in up to 90 percent of their cases where laxatives and enemas were used to treat fecal retention. Behavior approaches in treatment of encopresis have reported high success rates as well. In a double-blind randomly controlled trial using the laxative Senokot and behavioral therapy to treat forty cases of persistent encopresis, Berg et al. (1983) reported significant improvement after three months of treatment. Numerous other studies have reported similarly high rates of remission from encopresis using various combinations of reinforcement and punishment schedules supplemented with the use of laxatives where appropriate. Finally, it should be noted that treatment interventions in encopretics with developmental disorders and mental retardation have not been well studied.

SUMMARY

Although recently defined in DSM-III, encopresis remains a descriptive diagnosis of a disorder of multiple etiologies including constitutional, psychological, and environmental factors. Classification of encopresis has undergone numerous revisions but continues to be unsettled. It is clinically useful to define primary versus secondary encopresis in the presence or absence of fecal retention. Assessment requires a thorough evaluation of the child's development, environment, and psychological state. Behavioral, medical, psychodynamic, and family-oriented treatment approaches must be combined to accommodate the characteristics of each individual case. Further research is needed to define more accurately etiological, diagnostic, and treatment factors; nevertheless, there is abundant literature demonstrating favorable prognosis in the treatment of encopresis. The clinician utilizing individualized treatment strategies can anticipate eradication of encopretic behavior in the majority of cases.

REFERENCES

Anthony, C. P. (1963). *Textbook of Anatomy and Physiology*. 6th ed. St. Louis: Mosby.

Anthony, E. J. (1957). An experimental approach to the psychopathology of childhood: Encopresis. *Brit. J. Med. Psychol.* 30:146–75.

Ashkenazi, Z. (1975). The treatment of encopresis using a discriminative stimulus and positive reinforcement. *J. Behav. Ther. and Exper. Psychiat.* 6:155–57.

Bellman, M. (1966). Studies on encopresis. *Acta Paediat. Scand.* Suppl. 170.

Bemporad, J. L., et al. (1971). Characteristics of encopretic patients and their families. *J. Amer. Acad. Child Psychiat.* 10:272–92.

Berg, I., and Jones, K. V. (1964). Functional fecal incontinence in children. *Arch. Dis. Child.* 39:465–72.

———, et al. (1983). A controlled trial of "Senokot" in fecal soiling treated by behavioral methods. *J. Child Psychol. Psychiat.* 23:543–49.

Brazelton, T. B. (1962). A child-oriented approach to toilet training. *Pediatrics* 29:121–28.

Cheney, C. D. (1973). Mechanically augmented human toilet training or the electric potty chair. In R. L. Schwitzgebel and R. H. Schwitzgebel (Eds.). *Psychotechnology: Electronic Control of Mind and Behavior*. New York: Reinhart and Winston.

Davie, R., Butler, N., and Goldstein, H. (1972). *From Birth to Seven*. London: Longman.

Doleys, D. M. (1983). Enuresis and encopresis. In T. H. Ollendic and M. Hersen (Eds.). *Handbook of Child Psychopathology*. New York: Plenum Press.

Easson, R. I. (1960). Encopresis-psychogenic soiling. *Canad. Med. Assoc. J.* 82:624–28.

Fleisher, D. (1976). Diagnosis and treatment of disorders of defecation in children. *Pediatr. Ann.* 5:72.

Foxx, R. M., and Azrin, N. H. (1973). *Toilet Training the Retarded*. Champaign, Ill.: Research Press.

Freud, S. (1905). *Three Essays on the Theory of Sexuality*. Standard Edition, Vol. 7. New York: Norton.

Gavanski, M. (1971). The treatment of nonretentive secondary encopresis with imipramine and psychotherapy. *Canad. Med. Assoc. J.* 104:227–31.

Gesell, A., Ilg, F. L., and Ames, L. B. (1974). *Infant and Child in the Culture of Today*. New York: Harper and Row.

Hersov, L. (1985). Fecal soiling. In M. Rutter and L. Hersov (Eds.). *Child Psychiatry: Modern Approaches*. Philadelphia: Blackwell.

Kestenbaum, C. J. (1985). The creative process in child psychotherapy. *Amer. J. Psychother.* 3A:479–89.

Levine, M. D. (1975). Children with encopresis: A descriptive analysis. *Paediatrics* 56:412–16.

———. (1982). Encopresis: Its potentiation, evaluation, and alleviation. *Ped. Clin. North Amer.* 29:315–30.

Nixon, H. (1973). Sphincter cripples. *Proc. Roy. Soc. Med.* 66:575–78.

Olatawura, M. (1973). Encopresis: A review of thirty-two cases. *Acta Paediat. Scand.* 62:358–64.

Olness, K., McParland, F. A., and Piper, J. (1980). Biofeedback: A new modality in the management of children with fecal soiling. *J. Pediatr.* 96:505–9.

Rutter, M., Tizard, J., and Whitmore, K. (Eds.). (1970). *Education, Health, and Behavior*. London: Longman.

Stein, Z., and Susser, M. (1967). Social factors in the development of sphincter control. *Develop. Med. Child. Neurol.* 9:692–706.

Weissenberg, S. (1926). Uber enkopresis. *Z. Kinderheilk.* 40:67.

34

CHILDHOOD ANXIETY DISORDERS

Rachel Gittelman Klein

This chapter will provide a brief overview of approaches relevant to the clinical assessment of childhood anxiety disorders. It is intended for clinicians and school personnel who deal with anxious children rather than for scientists concerned about technical aspects of assessment. Anxiety, a normal psychological phenomenon, leads to marked impairment when it assumes certain forms or becomes severe. Means of assessing anxiety, for the most part, have been devised for normal variations of anxiety, rather than for pathological forms.

Anxiety has been conceptualized as both a trait and a state. As a trait, it is viewed as an enduring characteristic occurring in varying degrees of intensity—a stable personality feature that is thought to be relatively independent of circumstances. Therefore, someone with a trait of high anxiety would experience a relatively marked level of anxiety even if his immediate experiences were innocuous and not particularly stressful. Thus, a trait is conceived as an intrinsic personality feature that does not require provocation to occur. The origin of the trait may well lie in some previous experiences, but it becomes an integral part of one's personality and does not require external events to become manifest.

In contrast, a state refers to a transient phenomenon that occurs in conjunction with some identifiable event or experience, often a life stress such as an examination, divorce, illness, or other trauma.

The everyday anxiety we experience may well be appropriately conceived in the above way, but pathological anxiety does not fit well either the trait or the state model. Anxiety disorders cannot be viewed as the extreme manifestation of traits, since they (unlike traits) can be finite; nor are they well accounted for by the concept of a state, since disorders can also be chronic. Unlike both the anxiety trait and state, anxiety disorders always impair adaptive function and are associated not only with dysfunction, but also with psychic pain. Moreover, even when anxiety disorders are chronic, they do not necessarily represent excessive trait anxiety, because the anxiety symptoms may be quite specific, experienced about certain events only (as for example, in social phobias), and may not be pervasive, generalized anxiety symptoms. From these comments, it is apparent that I am not impressed by the contribution that the state/trait concepts of anxiety can make to our understanding of psychopathology. However, these notions have been influential in the assessment of anxiety and therefore deserve attention.

CLASSIFICATION OF CHILDHOOD AND ADOLESCENT ANXIETY DISORDERS

The way in which we conceptualize the anxiety disorders has been shaped by the DSM-III classification and modified slightly in DSM-III-R. The recent nomenclature does not conform to the preexisting classification that did not provide special nosological grouping for children's anxiety disorders. The current diagnostic schema is reviewed briefly.

Separation Anxiety Disorder of Childhood

Abnormal separation anxiety manifests itself in multiple ways. The child's distress upon separation, which in the severe form of the disorder becomes panic, is the most evident symptom. In addition, morbid worries about dangers to the integrity of the family are also frequent. Finally, severe homesickness and yearning to be reunited with parents to a degree beyond what is usual are signs of the disorder. These features may occur concurrently or independently. They are considered pathological when they restrict the child's activities or interfere markedly with his emotional well-being.

Many theories of separation anxiety have been proposed. In Freud's view, as illustrated in the case of Little Hans, the separation anxiety represented a libidinal longing for the mother (Freud 1909). It was coupled with castration anxiety, which Hans viewed as imminent retaliation by the father. The phobia of horses is derived from the fear of the father, a good example of symbolic representation of an unconscious conflict. Thus, two forms of anxiety are noted, each with its own dynamic process (for a full discussion see Trautman 1986).

All theories of child and personality development have a model for the development of separation anxiety in young children. Operant and classical conditioning paradigms in learning theories postulate that the child is reinforced by the mother's response to cries of distress, or that the child learns to associate the absence of the mother with an increase in physiological drives and her presence with the reduction of discomfort associated with these drives. As a result, the mother's presence is experienced as pleasurable and her absence then triggers anxiety (Shaffer 1986). In Piaget's theory, the mother's presence becomes incorporated in the child's schema and disturbance of that schema is anxiety provoking. Other views include ethological models, in which separation anxiety is conceptualized as an evolutionarily adaptive behavior repertoire whose initial elicitation does not require learning by the infant. When the newly mobile infant separates from its mother, it experiences acute discomfort and emits cries of distress that elicit maternal care. If the infant is lost, its cries guide the mother to the stranded offspring, optimally before biological impairment occurs. In this formulation, it is also assumed that the child's distress triggers retrieval and caretaking behavior in the parent. Therefore, the most efficient evolutionary relationship is one in which both the young child *and* the mother are subject to separation anxiety. This formulation is supported by much animal observation; for example, the distress of mother cats, dogs, monkeys, and so on, when their infants are removed or are heard crying, followed by searching and retrieval behavior on the mother's part.

The ethological view has been influential, and a great number of theoreticians have come to believe that there is a predisposition in the human infant to develop separation anxiety. This occurrence is related to the process of attachment, the groundwork for which is also likely to be built-in, requiring no complicated learning experience or unconscious conflict to occur.

The theoretical notions briefly mentioned above have also been applied to other forms of anxiety. For example, in the classical psychoanalytic view, all fears and anxieties represent an unconscious wish, no matter the content of the symptom. Within learning theory, all symptoms are learned either through operant or associative mechanisms.

Overanxious Disorder

The diagnosis of overanxious disorder includes children who have multiple anxieties and worries, including public speaking and performance anxiety, at times accompanied by perfectionism and overly great attention to details of one's work. Children with inordinate concern about visits to doctors and dentists are also included in this diagnosis. Fear of ridicule, easy embarrassment, and a general self-conscious attitude are psychological concerns considered part of overanxious disorders; however, separation worries are excluded, though the two disorders can coexist.

Simple Phobia

Phobias of specific objects are common in young children. The severity of functional impairment that they cause determines diagnostic standards. If a child is so frightened of dogs that he resists going outside or visiting friends who have a dog, he deserves professional attention. Irrational fears of unthreatening situations or objects can lead to considerable impairment. A case in point is that of Little Hans, described by Freud over a half-century ago (Freud 1909). The child's fear of horses made him extremely uncomfortable when out of the house. Although the condition is well known as a clinical entity, its scarcity among patient groups has rendered its study difficult.

Obsessive-Compulsive Disorder

Although categorized as an anxiety disorder by DSM-III, obsessive-compulsive disorder is not given separate consideration under the heading of Anxiety Disorders of Childhood and Adolescence, apparently reflecting the relative rarity of this disorder early in life. Furthermore, recent work has raised serious question regarding whether this disorder should be considered under the rubric of anxiety disorder, at least as far as childhood is concerned (Berg et al. 1986). Consequently, further discussion of obsessive-compulsive disorder will be deferred to another chapter (pharmacotherapy).

The above classifications are probably not exhaustive of all forms of childhood anxiety. However, they most likely encompass the great majority of the anxiety states found in children. (For further discussion of these issues see Gittelman 1985.)

It would be truly extraordinary to have assessment techniques applicable to the new diagnostic schema, given its recency. It would be futile to attempt a review of measures for the DSM-III childhood anxiety disorders, which include separation anxiety disorder and overanxious disorder, as well as several conditions listed in the adult section of the manual, especially simple phobia, which is common in childhood. Finally, the adjustment disorder with anxious mood also belongs among the anxiety disorders. In fact, none of the systematic assessments devised has been tied to diagnostic schemas, except for the recent development of structured clinical interviews specifically designed to generate DSM-III diagnoses. The assessment of anxiety has a surprisingly long history, emerging as an active endeavor with the advent of sophisticated statistical measures such as factor analysis. This led to the development of the early personality measures, many of which include an anxiety factor. Subsequently, probably because of the central role attributed to anxiety for all types of psychopathology, special scales to quantify anxiety were constructed. Finally, as noted previously, the interest in psychiatric diagnosis fostered by the DSM-III stimulated the development of structured diagnostic interviews. The various approaches are summarized.

PERSONALITY ASSESSMENT

Many of the personality scales developed for children have anxiety items and generate scores for anxiety scales. Because they were devised as overall personality tests, they are long; but in spite of their length they do not provide a comprehensive assessment of the various forms of anxiety. They can be used only with children who have good reading skills; otherwise they must be read to the children. Probably the most widely used personality tests in the United States are the California Tests of Personality. Four forms are available for different ages: from kindergarten to third grade (Primary Form) (Thorpe et al. 1953a); from fourth to sixth grade (Elementary Form) (Thorpe et al. 1953b); from seventh to tenth grade (Clark et al. 1953); and from ninth grade to college (Secondary Form) (Tiegs, Clark, and Thorpe 1953). They include a scale called "Freedom from Nervous Symptoms," which can be construed as a measure of anxiety. It is heavily weighted for somatic complaints such as headaches, stomachaches, frequent colds, sneezing spells, and eyes hurting. Therefore, the content does not reflect the manifold aspects of pathological anxiety, rendering the scales inappropriate for the quantification of anxiety.

The Eysenck Personality Questionnaire has a version for children that includes a neuroticism scale, but its item content is not designed to reflect the presence of worries, fears, and anxiety (Eysenck and Eysenck 1975). It also lacks norms and has no demonstrated validity for measuring anxiety.

Cattell, an early pioneer in the development of personality questionnaires, has devised several measures for self-ratings of anxiety in children of ages 6 to 8 (The Early School Personality Questionnaire) (Cattell and Coan 1979), ages 8 to 12 (The Children's Personality Questionnaire) (Porter and Cattell 1979), and for adolescents (The High School Personality Questionnaire) (Cattell and Cattell 1979). A videocassette is available to facilitate oral administration at early ages. These generate scores for thirteen or fourteen personality traits, several of which seem related to the child's anxiety experiences. For example, the questionnaires include scores for shy versus venturesome, self-assured versus apprehensive, and relaxed versus tense. However, the advantages of providing comprehensive measures are lost to those who wish detailed descriptive coverage of a specific area of function, such as anxiety. As stated by Thorndike (1978), "Cattell has tended to emphasize breadth of coverage at the expense of precision in single scores" (p. 766).

The personality tests are self-report measures that require the child to indicate whether he experiences various fears. One of the problems is that different standards are applied by each child to judge his own level of anxiety. Children who experience the same discomfort might judge it quite differently. Some might minimize its personal significance, whereas others might exaggerate it. As a result, similar ratings cannot be conceived as indicating identical personality features. In addition, the ratings do not require an indication of how the fear affects the child's life; they thereby provide another source of confusion, since children whose ratings are identical might adapt quite differently. For example, some might expose themselves to the phobic situation and others not. For these reasons, the utility of personality tests to assess anxiety in children is very limited, and their use cannot be recommended.

The development of personality tests has been an active enterprise whose onset dates back a half-century. Although the paper and pencil personality tests generated much research, they never became popular for the assessment in the clinical setting. There are probably several reasons for the lack of interest evinced by clinicians in these sophisticated instruments. For one, they approached behavior in an objective fashion that did not fit well the clinical models of psychopathology prevalent at the time, which were on the whole psychoanalytically oriented. Therefore, straightforward descriptive reporting was viewed as superficial and trivial to the concerns of clinicians.

In spite of the lack of reciprocity between the personality test developers and the clinicians, they shared the basic view that anxiety was a characteristic intrinsic to the individual—that is, a trait. The notion that behavior could be understood as the expression of pervasive tendencies subsequently became controversial. Social learning theorists suggested that behavior could be understood only if one identified the stimulus content that provoked it, and that emotions reflected responses to specific environmental conditions rather than the expression of an organismic stable personality trait. Therefore, even when the shift came from psychodynamic theories to behaviorally oriented theories, personality scales that were based on a trait model of behavior continued to be ignored by clinicians whether they were dynamically or behaviorally oriented.

ANXIETY SCALES

Unlike the personality tests that provide an evaluation of multiple aspects of personality, the content of anxiety scales, as their name indicates, is limited to items that reflect fears and worries.

The group led by Cattell extracted a forty-item anxiety scale, the IPAT Anxiety Scale, from a broad-based adult personality questionnaire (Cattell et al. 1976). It provides norms for high school age; it has been reported to have demonstrated construct validity (McReynolds 1978).

The field of childhood assessment is not rich in anxiety scales. The State-Trait Anxiety Inventory for Children (Spielberger 1973) attempts to distinguish the two types of anxiety. To do so, the child is asked to rate himself as he feels right now (state), and in general (trait); it does not elicit information about situations that trigger anxiety temporarily. However, it is most doubtful that it succeeds in assessing state anxiety. The clinical significance of self-ratings of anxiety at the time of test administration is very likely to be minimal. It is probably judicious to regard this scale as similar to the other anxiety scales in providing self-ratings of general anxiety. It may not be possible to construct a self-rated instrument that can reliably reflect important but complicated distinctions in the various forms of anxiety. It probably requires a clinically trained evaluator to differentiate phenomenological variations in anxiety.

In 1956, a child version of the adult Taylor Manifest Anxiety was published (Castaneda et al. 1956). The scale for adults had been extracted from the MMPI (Minnesota Multiphasic Personality Inventory) (Hathaway and McKinley 1951). The Children's Manifest Anxiety Scale consists of forty-two anxiety items and also includes a "lie" scale to provide some indication as to whether the child has replied honestly. The child is required to indicate by a "yes" or "no" whether each item applies to him. The score is simply the sum of items scored "yes." Subsequently, the scale was rewritten, some items deleted, others added, to generate a thirty-seven-item scale, twenty-five of which were from the original list and nine of which made up the new lie scale (Reynolds and Richmond 1978). The content of the revised Children's Manifest Anxiety Scale, renamed "What I Think and Feel," is listed in Table 34.1. The reading level is pegged to the average third grader; therefore, except for precocious readers, the scale must be administered orally to first and

TABLE 34.1   Revised Children's Manifest Anxiety Scale and its Factor Structure

Factor*	Item
1	I have trouble making up my mind.
2	I get nervous when things do not go the right way for me.
3	Others seem to do things easier than I can.
L	I like everyone I know.
1	Often I have trouble getting my breath.
2	I worry a lot of the time.
3	I am afraid of a lot of things.
L	I am always kind.
1	I get mad easily.
2	I worry about what my parents will say to me.
3	I feel that others do not like the way I do things.
L	I always have good manners.
1	It is hard for me to get to sleep at night.
2	I worry about what other people think about me.
3	I feel alone even when there are people with me.
L	I am always good.
1	Often I feel sick in my stomach.
2	My feelings get hurt easily.
3	My hands feel sweaty.
L	I am always nice to everyone.
1	I am tired a lot.
2	I worry about what is going to happen.
3	Other children are happier than I.
L	I tell the truth every single time.
1	I have bad dreams.
2	My feelings get hurt easily when I am fussed at.
3	I feel someone will tell me I do things the wrong way.
L	I never get angry.
1	I wake up scared some of the time.
2	I worry when I go to bed at night.
3	It is hard for me to keep my mind on my schoolwork.
L	I never say things I shouldn't.
1	I wiggle in my seat a lot.
2	I am nervous.
3	A lot of people are against me.
L	I never lie.
2	I often worry about something bad happening to me.

*L = Lie Scale item
Factor 1: Physiological anxiety
Factor 2: Worrying, oversensitivity
Factor 3: Fear/Concentration

second graders (and to older poor readers). The new scale was constructed to provide descriptors that were internally consistent for ratings provided by several hundred grade school children from grades one through twelve. Reynolds and Richmond (1979) conducted a factor analytic study of the revised Children's Manifest Anxiety Scale and reported three factors: Factor 1, which they judged to reflect physiological signs of anxiety; Factor 2 they considered to indicate worry and oversensitivity; and Factor 3 is labeled Fear/Concentration. Mean scores and standard deviations are provided for each factor, so that children who rate themselves relatively anxious can be identified. If the criteria for "highest anxiety" scores are one standard deviation above the mean, they will identify 15 percent of children as anxious; if more rigorous standards are applied and only scores two standard deviations above the mean are selected as deviant, about 2 percent of the general school population would be considered to be highly anxious. In Table 34.2, the mean and standard deviation values are presented so that the threshold for selecting high scores can be individualized. However, it would be erroneous to view scores that are only one standard deviation above the mean as indicating disabling high anxiety.

The factors generated by the revised scale are very similar to those from a previous factor analysis of the original scale (Finch et al. 1974); therefore, it is likely that the scale taps meaningful aspects of children's emotional state. Further support for the construct validity of the scale was obtained by Reynolds (1980), who found it to correlate highly with the scores for trait anxiety on the State-Trait Anxiety for Children by Spielberger (1973). In contrast, the revised manifest anxiety scale scores and the state anxiety ratings did not correlate significantly. It would seem reasonable to assume that the revised manifest anxiety scale reflects relatively stable attitudes rather than current feelings at the time the children complete the scale. However, several words of caution are in order. In the above correlational study by Reynolds (1980), a sample of referred children was utilized, yet their scores were not deviant. This is surprising, since almost one-third were diagnosed as having emotional disorders, and one would expect children with disorders other than emotional disorders as well to be more anxious than normals, especially at the time of referral. Others who have studied the original scale have not found it to distinguish groups. Therefore, one must be cautious in drawing clinical conclusions from scores obtained on either version of the Children's Manifest Anxiety Scale. Finally, the notion that the lie scale does what it is claimed to do has been pointedly critiqued (Sarason 1966).

TABLE 34.2   Means and Standard Deviations of Three Factors of the Revised Children's Manifest Anxiety Scale*

Factor	Mean	S.D.
1. Physiological	4.57	2.14
2. Worry and Oversensitivity	5.39	2.34
3. Fear/Concentration	3.88	2.14

*From Reynolds and Richmond (1979)

To evaluate children's fears in a number of contexts, Scherer and Nakamura (1968) devised an eighty-item scale, the Fear Survey Schedule for Children, modeled after a similar adult questionnaire (The Wolpe-Lang Fear Survey) (Wolpe and Lang 1964). Each item is rated on a five-point scale, from none to very much. It is applicable to children ages 9 through 12. Several factors were generated from its item content. However, it was done with a sample too small to permit the confident use of the factor scores. Using the fear survey to contrast school-phobic and normal children, Ollendick (1983) reported very adequate score consistency ($r = .82$) over brief time (one-week test-retest). Not surprisingly, the test-retest reliability was less satisfactory after a three-month interval ($r = .55$). The scores on the survey correlated only moderately with the trait measure of the State-Trait Anxiety Inventory ($r's = .46$ and .51); we must therefore conclude that, though the two scales tap some common characteristic, they cannot be viewed as interchangeable instruments that measure the same psychological process. This finding is different from the reported very high relationship between the manifest anxiety scale and the trait anxiety measure of the State-Trait Inventory (Reynolds 1980). Encouragingly, Ollendick (1983) found that school-phobic children referred for treatment obtained significantly higher scores than controls, though considerable overlap between the two groups occurred. This overlap precludes using the scale scores to classify children as anxious versus non-anxious. However, as Ollendick noted, the survey could be used to identify children with relatively elevated scores in case-finding procedures, in which one is interested in identifying children for further study.

All the above anxiety scales for children are self-rating scales. Therefore, they incur the same concerns as the personality tests. There are no standards provided for evaluating the severity of a fear, and individuals will vary in their thresholds for reporting anxiety; in addition, the degree of functional impairment is not obtained. The Children's Manifest Anxiety Scale and the State-Trait Anxiety Inventory for Children have a two-point scoring, requiring a yes or no choice. In contrast, the Fear Survey Schedule for Children provides gradations of scoring, which make it far more useful for detecting change over time.

Behavior Rating Scales

For the purpose of obtaining a large amount of behavioral information in a rapid, economical way, behavior rating scales filled out by parents and teachers have been devised. As is the case for the personality tests, they aim to sample a broad spectrum of psychopathology; consequently, they do not provide a full assessment for each type of dysfunction. All the scales have been factor analyzed, and some provide an anxiety scale.

One of the oldest parent rating scales, the Louisville Behavior Checklist (Miller 1967a, 1967b), has eleven items in the anxiety factor (see Table 34.3). This factor structure was obtained from parental ratings (yes/no) of boys between 6 to 12 years of age whose parents were applying to a clinic for treatment for their children. The anxiety factor represents the types of parent-perceived behaviors that cluster together in patient groups; it cannot be understood as reflecting the way the items would sort themselves in a normal population. Therefore, it could be used to evaluate how anxious a child is rated compared to patients, but not compared to normals. As can be seen from the item content, the multiforms of anxiety are poorly reflected in the anxiety factor. Furthermore, several items (phobic, afraid at night, fearful), which clearly reflect anxiety, loaded on factors other than the anxiety factor.

The anxiety scale was revised to provide better internal consistency and better face validity, so that the modified scale reflects important clinical aspects of childhood anxiety and appears much more satisfactory than its predecessor (Miller et al. 1971a). This is a good example of how a statistically or empirically derived anxiety factor is irrelevant to clinical reality, and how further improvements are possible. The renamed Fear Scale, also presented in Table 34.3, has eighteen items that include specific fears (trains, loud noises) as well as general anxiety and separation anxiety.

The scores obtained for boys and girls (five hundred school children, grades two to seven) were very similar (Miller et al. 1971b). A child whose parent endorsed twelve or more scale items would fall in the top percentile of the general population. On average, the normal children received positive scores on somewhat fewer than two items, and about 50 percent were rated "yes" on three items.

The same investigators developed a parent-rated fear questionnaire. The Louisville Fear Survey is a list of sixty fears—scored no, normal, or excessive—that can be given to parents or children (ages 4 to 18). The list was derived from clinical judgments and other fear inventories (Miller et al. 1972). The parent ratings of normals and of a clinical group of phobic children were subjected to factor analysis. Three factors emerged: Factor 1 includes items related to separation, such as threats to the well-being of the family or child; Factor 2 reflects fear of natural events, such as lightning, thunder, and so on; and Factor 3 concerns mostly anxiety about performance and social ridicule. None of these is pure with regard to the type of anxiety it reflects; furthermore, it should not be assumed that these factors represent discrete clinical characteristics. It is very likely that fearful children obtain high scores on all three or on two of the three factors, rather than only one of the three. In other words, it would be erroneous to conclude from the factor analysis that it has identified separate syndromes of anxiety. However, it could be a helpful measure to identify specific sources of difficulty. It could also be administered directly to children. It is quite similar to the Fear Survey Schedule mentioned above but has the marked advantage of being applicable to a wider age group. For unknown reasons, this scale never became popular and it has not been used widely. Perhaps it is because it never provided for a teacher-rated version. It is generally felt that teachers provide more reliable and valued information about children's behavior than parents do, since they are able to judge children with a built-in standard for average behavior for the child's age and sex. Yet, when assessing affective states such as anxiety and depression, parents are felt to be critical sources of information.

TABLE 34.3   Item Content of Anxiety Factors on Major Behavior Rating Scales

Scale: Louisville Behavior Check List
Raters: Parents
Scoring: Yes/No
Items: Headaches; Migraine headaches; Stomachache-somatic; Fear of school; Worries—guilty; Complains not loved easily; Feels pain more; Says "picked on"; Feels inferior; Cries

Scale: Louisville Behavior Check List Fear Scale
Raters: Parents
Scoring: Yes/No
Items: Dependent on others/unable to do things for himself; Tosses and turns in sleep, rolls, gets up often at night, etc. (poor or restless sleeping); Demands special attention or fusses at bedtime; Says he's not as good as others; feels inferior; Afraid of such things as the dark, thunderstorms, domestic animals; Wants or demands that someone sleep with him; Always worrying that he or someone else is going to die; Fearful, constantly afraid; Worries all the time or feels very guilty; Worries that parents may get hurt or sick or die; At times afraid he is going to die; Is afraid that he will see or hear something frightening at night; Complains of bad dreams or nightmares; Very much afraid of loud noises; Afraid of being in cars, or trains, or airplanes, or elevators; Takes things in stride, not easily upset; Becomes "jittery," builds up tension, becomes "wound up"; Worries about disasters such as hurricanes, wars, fires at school, air raids

Scale: Personality Inventory for Children (PIC)
Rater: Parent
Scoring: Yes/No
Items (Positive): My child worries about things that usually only adults worry about; My child is worried about sin; My child has little self-confidence; Thunder and lightning bother my child; My child often asks if I love him (her); My child seems too serious minded; Often my child is afraid of little things; My child worries about talking to others; My child frequently has nightmares; My child seems fearful of blood; My child is easily embarrassed; My child will worry a lot before starting something new; My child often has crying spells; My child broods some; My child is afraid of dying; My child seems unhappy about our home life; Others often remark how moody my child is; My child insists on keeping the light on while sleeping; My child is afraid of the dark
Items (Negative): My child is as happy as ever; My child is usually in good spirits; My child usually looks at the bright side of things; Usually my child takes things in stride; My child takes criticism easily; Nothing seems to scare my child

Scale: Child Behavior Checklist
Rater: Parent
Scoring: Not true, Somewhat or sometimes true, Very true or often true
Items:
Girls 4–5
Obsessions; Clings to adults; Cries much; Demands attention; Fears; Feels persecuted; Hears things; Nervous; Anxious; Sees things; Sleeps little; Strange behavior; Can't sleep; Whining
Boys 4–5
None
Girls 6–11
None
Boys 6–11
Clings to adults; Fears; Fears school; Hears things that aren't there; Overconforms; Anxious; Sleeps in class; Sees things that aren't there; Shy, timid
Girls 12–16
Obsession; Lonely; Cries much; Jealous; Fears; Fears school; Fears own impulses; Needs to be perfect; Feels unloved; Feels persecuted; Feels worthless; Nervous; Nightmares; Anxious; Feels guilty; Self-conscious; Sleeps little; Can't sleep; Worrying
Boys 12–16
None

Scale: Child Behavior Checklist
Raters: Teachers
Scoring: Not true, Somewhat or sometimes true, Very true or often true
Items:
Girls 6–11
Clings to adults;* Fears; Fears own impulses;* Needs to be perfect;* Feels worthless;* Nervous; Overconforms;* Anxious;* Feels guilty;* Self-conscious;* Shy, timid;* Feels hurt when criticized;* Too neat;* Sad; Anxious to please;* Fears mistakes;* Worrying*
Boys 6–11
Starred items (*) of anxiety factor in Girls 6–11, plus Secretive
Girls 12–16
Clings to adults;× Cries; Fears;× Fears own impulses;× Needs to be perfect;× Feels worthless;× Nail biting; Nervous;× Overconforms;× Anxious;× Feels guilty;× Self-conscious;× Shy, timid; Feels hurt when criticized;× Anxious to please;× Fears mistakes;× Whining; Worrying×
Boys 12–16
Crossed items (x) of anxiety factor for Girls 12–16, plus Lonely; Jealous; Feels unloved; Feels persecuted; Easily frustrated; Too neat; Sad

Taking inspiration from the well-established MMPI, a group of investigators developed a similar instrument to be filled out by parents about their children. The Personality Inventory for Children, known as PIC, includes six hundred items rated true/false. It is possible to select parts of the schedule so that one can tailor the questionnaire to particular interests. The factors were not derived from statistical investigation only, but also relied on the judgments of clinicians. The content of the anxiety factor is presented in Table 34.3. It has good internal reliability, and good short-term test-retest consistency. Extensive work has been done with the scale and it provides norms for children of preschool age through adolescence (Lachar 1982; Wirt et al. 1977). More recently, the scale has also been used with teachers. Although considerable evidence has been accumulated concerning the validity of many aspects of the scale, it has never been studied in relationship to anxiety disorders in children, and its usefulness in this limited area is in question.

Some of the most widely used rating scales are the Conners Parent and Conners Teacher Rating Scales (Goyette et al. 1978). These have been shown to be extremely helpful for the assessment of hyperactive children and for detecting treatment effects among these children. The parent, but not the teacher, scale provides an anxiety factor; the scales have not been used in groups where their usefulness for the detection of anxiety and its reduction with treatment can be assessed. Because of their very limited sampling of anxiety, it must be concluded that the Conners scales are not suitable for the assessment of anxiety in children.

Achenbach has carried out a major effort to provide norms for parent- and teacher-rated behavior of boys and girls, aged 6 through 16 (Achenbach 1978; Achenbach and Edelbrock 1979). As does the PIC, Achenbach's Child Behavior Profile provides very well-established norms for each sex at each age, enabling a relatively confident judgment as to the degree of deviance. However, the checklist has real limitations with respect to the assessment of anxiety. An anxiety factor was obtained for girls 4 to 5, and 12 to 16, but not for the 6- to 11-year-olds. Yet there is no reason to believe that anxiety is not a relevant aspect of function in 6- to 11-year-old girls.

For boys, the picture is equally puzzling; an anxiety factor was obtained for 6- to 11-year-olds only (the age group in which no anxiety factor was obtained in girls), but not for the 4- to 5-year-old and 12- to 16-year-old boys. Yet from many other surveys, the nature of fears and anxiety does not appear very different between boys and girls (though their magnitude differs between them). The age and sex asymmetry of the CBC anxiety factor, as well as the inconsistencies in the items that make up the anxiety factors (when they are derived), preclude comparisons between boys and girls and across age groups within and between genders. The scale seems awkward for the assessment of anxiety in children, and its utility is thereby limited. A complicating factor in the early application of the scale is the divergent content of the anxiety factor for boys and girls of the same ages, and for each sex at different ages. These differences are readily observable from a perusal of the item content of the anxiety scores presented in Table 34.3. The age and sex differences raise questions concerning the construct validity of the anxiety factors (i.e., what do they really measure?), since it is generally observed that there are no qualitative differences between boys and girls in the nature of the anxieties they experience. As is the case for other rating scales, the Child Behavior Profile does not allow important decisions and clinical judgments to be reached about specific children. The PIC and the Child Behavior Profile are probably best seen as ways of identifying major areas of difficulty and as signals to look further, through careful clinical assessment, for specific dysfunctions. Both these instruments have the shortcoming of requiring two or three point decisions for item ratings. For clinical purposes, this is a disadvantage, since it limits the possibility of subtle rankings and of detecting change over time without treatment. However, the scales have many other virtues, such as well-established reliability, a number of data concerning validity (but not for anxiety), and acceptability by parents and teachers. They represent a major advance in the assessment of childhood psychopathology.

STRUCTURED DIAGNOSTIC INTERVIEWS

The clinical structured interviews have all been devised to detect the presence of a number of disorders, and not for the assessment of anxiety disorders specifically. As a result, they provide a rough screen for the presence of anxiety disorders, but lack sufficient detail to qualify as thorough investigations of anxiety symptoms. Nevertheless, they can help guide the initial inquiry into the presence of anxiety states, leaving the clinician latitude to explore further to fill in the clinical picture. All the clinical interviews include a version for interview with the child and another to be used with the parent. Though it has been argued that the interview with the child provides no information above and beyond what is obtained from the parent (Rutter 1976), this observation cannot be assumed to be true for all types of psychopathology. For the assessment of anxiety, which represents an internal state, the child's report may provide information that the parent does not. Furthermore, the degree to which parents' and children's reports overlap depends not only on the type of information asked about, but also the age of the child. At all ages, a proper evaluation demands that information be inquired from multiple sources.

The first clinical interview (Graham and Rutter 1968; Rutter and Graham 1968) provides a single overall category for anxiety disorders. The more recent interviews appeared after the DSM-III classification and therefore provide diagnoses for the anxiety disorders included in the manual. The three elaborate structured interviews in use with children all include an assessment of anxiety. The Diagnostic Interview Schedule for Children (DIS-C) (Costello et al. 1983); the Diagnostic Interview for Children and Adolescents (DICA) (Reich et al. 1982); and the Schedule for Affective Disorders and Schizophrenia for School-Age Children (the Kiddie-SADS or K-SADS) (Chambers et al. 1985). If they are administered in their entirety, they are very time-consuming. However, for purposes of assessing the presence of anxiety disorders, one could select specific sections. Doing so is difficult in the case of the Diagnostic Interview Schedule for Children, since the interview focuses on functioning within settings (school, home, etc.), rather than on the clinical content of each disorder. Therefore, the items pertaining to a specific disorder are not always grouped together. In the case of the other two diagnostic interviews, the Diagnostic Interview for Children and Adolescents (DICA) and the Kiddie-SADS, questions are organized around disorders, so that it is a simple matter to select sections pertinent to one's clinical goals. To illustrate the approaches used in these assessments, Table 34.4 presents the section on separation anxiety from the DICA.

TABLE 34.4 Inquiry for Separation Anxiety Disorder in DICA

	Code 1 = No
Anxiety Disorders	2 = Yes

Separation Anxiety Disorder

Some children (adolescents) worry a great deal about being away from their parents or from home.

(USE PAST TENSE WITH CHILDREN AGE 13 OR OVER, WHEN APPROPRIATE.)

158. When you are not with your parents do you worry a lot about something bad happening to them (like they might get sick or hurt or die)? _____

159. Do you worry a great deal that something bad might happen to you (like getting kidnapped or killed), so that you couldn't see your parent(s) (or loved ones) again? _____

160. Do you ever refuse to go to school (or try to stay home), because you are afraid that something bad (like sickness, accident, or death) might happen to your parent(s) (or loved person)? _____

IF NO TO Q. 158 + 159 + 160, SKIP TO Q. 174.

IF YES TO ANY, ASK:

161. Do you have to have your mother or dad (or another adult) stay close to you in order to go to sleep at night? IF CHILD IS UNCERTAIN, ASK:

Does_____(mother, father, grandparent—INSERT APPROPRIATE WORD) lie down on the bed with you when it's time to go to bed? _____

162. Does it upset you to be left in a room by yourself at home? _____

TABLE 34.4   (continued)

	Code
	1 = No
Anxiety Disorders	2 = Yes

Separation Anxiety Disorder

163. Have you ever had a chance to go away to camp or to visit someone and refused to go, because you were afraid to leave home? _____

164. Have you ever gone away from home for a few days, like going to camp, and been so upset and worried that you went back home right away? _____

165. Do you often have bad dreams about losing your parent(s) or other loved person? IF YES, Do these bad dreams come as often as 2 or 3 times a month?
SCORE AS POSITIVE ONLY IF YES TO SECOND QUESTION. _____

166. When you have to leave home to go to school or some place else, do you get stomachaches or headaches or do you feel nauseated or vomit? _____

167. Do you throw tantrums or cry and beg your parents to stay home when they plan to go somewhere? _____

168. Do you feel so sad when your mother (father or loved adult) is not around that you don't want to play or do your school work? _____
IF LESS THAN 3 YES ANSWERS IN Q. 158–168, SKIP TO Q. 174.
IF 3 OR MORE YES ANSWERS, ASK:

169. Did that worry you had about not being with your parent(s) stay with you for as long as 2 weeks (or more)? _____

170. Did you ever miss 2 weeks of school in one school year, because you didn't want to leave your parents or leave home?
(DO NOT COUNT REFUSAL TO GO TO SCHOOL DUE TO OTHER REASONS.) _____

171. A. How old were you when you first remembered being unable to leave your parents, because of your worries? _____

    B. How old were you the last time that happened?

172. When did you last have problems in being away from your parents?

	CODE
WITHIN LAST 2 WEEKS	1
WITHIN LAST MONTH	2
WITHIN LAST 6 MONTHS.	3
WITHIN LAST YEAR	4
MORE THAN 1 YEAR AGO	5	_____

173. Did you ever have to see a doctor because of that problem?
IF NO, SKIP TO C.
IF YES, ASK:
A. Did you stay in the hospital? _____
IF YES, ASK:
B. How many times? CODE NO. TIMES
                          NONE = 0
                          7 +   = 7 _____

C. Did you take any medicine for this problem of being scared to leave home? _____
IF NO, SKIP TO Q. 174.
IF YES:
D. Do you know the name of the medicine? _____

E. Do you still take it? _____
IF NO:
F. How old were you when you stopped taking medicine for these worries? _____

Some investigation has been conducted regarding the validity of the clinical interviews of children in the general population. So far, little work has been done to validate the diagnoses of anxiety disorders in clinical groups. Nevertheless, these interviews can help one approach children to assess the presence of an anxiety disorder.

PSYCHOLOGICAL TESTS

The structured tests, such as the individual intelligence tests, and the unstructured or projective tests, have been used to infer the presence of pathological level of anxiety in children. Other measures as well that were not designed to assess personality constructs, such as the Bender-Gestalt and the Draw-A-Person tests, have been used for similar purposes. All the work done with these measures occurred before the current standard for diagnosing anxiety disorders. Therefore, it is completely obscure to what extent the inferences about anxiety derived from these test results reflect the presence of anxiety disorders. In the adult literature it has often been claimed that relatively low scores on the arithmetic and coding subtests of the Wechsler Intelligence scales reflect anxiety. These same tests are used to infer impaired attention such as is present in children with attention deficit disorder with hyperactivity. The Wechsler Intelligence Scale for Children has had such a poor record for purposes of clinical diagnosis that it would be most surprising if it offered any help in the assessment of anxiety disorders. As noted in previous reviews (Gittelman 1980; Gittelman-Klein 1978), the tests have been shown to distinguish children referred to psychiatric clinics from normals. However, there is no evidence that the tests are useful in discriminating among different types of psychopathology. Sadly, it must be concluded that at this time the psychological tests do not offer a useful addition to the diagnosis of children. Whether they can be applied to generate more subtle inferences about children's psychological adjustment is not clear. Anxiety has not been researched; the only personality traits that have been studied are aggression, self-esteem, and concern about loss (Gittelman 1980).

OTHER ASSESSMENTS

Because the behavioral therapeutic approaches require detailed assessment of function before treatment, many techniques have been developed by behaviorally oriented therapists and researchers to observe children's fearful behavior. However, these procedures are complicated and are best undertaken by experts; they are cumbersome and are relevant largely to assessment for research purposes. Those interested in this specialized area of assessment may refer to an excellent review by Barrios et al. (1981).

Physiological Assessment

The physiological assessment of any psychological state is an important source of information that can elucidate the biological correlates of human behavior. Once that is accomplished, we can examine the mechanisms under which these psychological functions are regulated and can determine the mechanisms that may lead to their dysregulation. Because the subjective experience of anxiety, at least in its extreme form, has long been known to be associated with activation of the autonomic nervous system, a great deal of work has been done to document the specific changes in physiology that accompany the experience of anxiety. Several measures have been used, but mostly in adults. Among the changes in cardiovascular function noted are increased pulse, increased blood pressure, and peripheral vasoconstriction. Pupillary changes such as increased dilation, muscular changes such as tremor, alteration in skin conductance with increased palmar sweating, and endocrine changes including increased cortisol and catecholamines secretion have all been noted. However, as mentioned, these have been conducted almost exclusively with adults. One of the difficulties in drawing clear interpretations from results obtained is that there does not seem to be a unique pattern of autonomic response to anxiety. Much the same pattern of change occurs with other forms of emotional arousal or other stress experiences.

For the clinician, the use of psychophysiological measures holds no promise and cannot be used as an adjunct to other diagnostic procedures. They are mentioned here because they represent a legitimate approach to the assessment of anxiety, but only for researchers in the context of experimental investigations.

It is not a mere coincidence that the physiological indices that have been studied correspond to the somatic complaints that patients often report, such as a rapid heartbeat, shakiness, sweating, and feeling cold or warm. Indeed, these clinical somatic complaints reported by anxious individuals represent the subjective symptoms caused by some of the autonomic changes that have been studied.

Sex Differences

All surveys, regardless of the instruments used, have reported that girls obtain higher scores on anxiety measures than boys do. This difference is important in the school setting, where ratings may be made in large groups of children. Should the instruments be used to assess anxiety, some adjustment is necessary to estimate deviance in girls and boys. In the clinical setting this problem is not as critical, since the child is already identified as experiencing problems. Furthermore, anxiety differs between girls and boys in the general population, but not in clinical groups with anxiety disorders. Werry (1986) has noted that since the number of girls referred for anxiety problems does not exceed the number of boys, we cannot equate relatively high anxiety on parental scales with the presence of anxiety disorders.

Treatment

Leading modalities in the contemporary treatment of childhood anxiety disorders include pharmacotherapy (Gittelman and Koplewicz 1986), behavior therapy (Carlson et al. 1986), and psychodynamically oriented psychotherapy (Lewis 1986). It should be noted that while each of these approaches has been based on a combination of clinical experience and a plausible conceptual rationale, supporting empirical evidence from controlled studies has been sparse. Consequently, the eclectically trained clinician faced with a child manifesting anxiety disorder will often justifiably draw from the contributions of each of the above approaches to foster symptom alleviation and improved adaptation in the patient.

CONCLUSION

There are several approaches to the systematic assessment of anxiety in children, but within each there are limited options. It is hoped that this brief review will make it clear that none of the assessments or instruments reviewed provides a complete or adequate evaluation of childhood anxiety disorders. This restriction does not preclude their use. Many of the measures discussed can be applied to obtain a quick survey whose results can be followed by a fuller clinical assessment. The overriding merit of the self-rating scales and other behavior rating scales is that they are cheap, rapid, and convenient. However, for the assessment of anxiety disorders, the old cliché "You get what you pay for" is appropriate. Even the clinical interviews do not appear to provide sufficient coverage to be altogether satisfactory to the diagnosis of anxiety disorders in children. For adults, a recent elaborate interview has been devised specifically to assess anxiety disorders (Fyer et al. 1985). Such a detailed clinical evaluation of anxiety for children has not yet been done. Until then, the best strategy is to view current available techniques as means to signal the possible presence of pathological levels of anxiety, with the expectation that further investigation is called for.

The clinician need not feel limited by the formal aspects of the available scales. For example, for our childhood anxiety clinic, we have developed a parent form of the Children's Manifest Anxiety Scale to obtain simultaneous children and parent perceptions of anxiety in the child. Moreover, we have modified the scores to provide gradations in severity rather than the yes-no stipulated by the authors. In this way, we are deviating from the standard generated by normative studies, and we will not be able to compare our scores to those from the general population. But the modifications suit our purposes better, since we are dealing with seriously anxious children. As long as one understands that rules are not being adhered to and how doing so affects the interpretations one can derive from the instruments, there is no reason why a clinician cannot tailormake his anxiety scales. For example, the clinician might select the most promising items from factors in different scales to con-

struct a more elaborate anxiety scale. Researchers will probably balk at this suggestion, since idiosyncratic procedures preclude comparing results among investigators.
However, the clinician has different goals and there is no reason why he cannot
behave accordingly.

REFERENCES

Achenbach, T. M. (1978). The child behavior profile: 1. Boys aged 6–11. *J. Consult.
Clin. Psychol.* 46:478–88.
Achenbach, T. M., and Edelbrock, C. S. (1979). The child behavior profile: 2. Boys
aged 12–16 and girls aged 6–11 and 12–16. *J. Consult. Clin. Psychol.* 47:223–33.
Barrios, B. A., Hartmann, D. P., and Shigetomi, C. (1981). Fears and anxieties in
children. In E. J. Mash and L. G. Terdal (Eds.). *Behavioral Assessment of Childhood
Disorders.* New York: Guilford Press, pp. 259–304.
Berg, C. J., et al. (1986). Childhood obsessive-compulsive disorder: An anxiety dis-
order? In R. Gittelman (Ed.). *Anxiety Disorders of Childhood.* New York: Guilford
Press, pp. 126–35.
Carlson, C. L., Figueroa, R. G., and Lahey, B. B. (1986). Behavior therapy for child-
hood anxiety disorders. In R. Gittelman (Ed.). *Anxiety Disorders of Childhood.*
New York: Guilford Press, pp. 204–32.
Castaneda, A., McCandless, B., and Palermo, D. (1956). The children's form of the
Manifest Anxiety Scale. *Child Devel.* 27:317–26.
Cattell, R. B., and Cattell, M. D. (1979). *High School Personality Questionnaire.* Cham-
paign, Ill.: Institute for Personality and Ability Testing.
———, and Coan, R. W. (1979). *Early School Personality Questionnaire.* Champaign,
Ill.: Institute for Personality and Ability Testing.
———, Krug, S. E., and Scheier, I. H. (1976). *IPAT Anxiety Scale.* Champaign, Ill.:
Institute for Personality and Ability Testing.
Chambers, W. J., et al. (1985). The assessment of affective disorders in children and
adolescents by semistructured interview. *Arch. Gen. Psychiat.* 42:696–702.
Clark, W. W., Tiegs, E. W., and Thorpe, L. P. (1953). *California Test of Personality:
Intermediate Form AA.* Monterey, Calif.: McGraw-Hill.
Costello, A. J., et al. (1983). *Diagnostic Interview Schedule for Children.*
Eysenck, H. J., and Eysenck, S. B. G. (1975). *Eysenck Personality Questionnaire (Ju-
nior).* San Diego, Calif.: Educational and Industrial Testing Service.
Finch, A. J., Kendall, P. C., and Montgomery, L. E. (1974). Multidimensionality of
anxiety in children: Factor structure of the Children's Manifest Anxiety Scale. *J.
Abnorm. Child Psychol.* 2:331–36.
Freud, S. (1909). Analysis of a phobia in a five-year-old boy. In E. Jones (Ed.). *The
Life and Work of Sigmund Freud,* Vol. 3. London: Hogarth Press, 1957, pp. 149–
287.
Fyer, A. J., et al. (1985). Schedule for Affective Disorders and Schizophrenia-Life-
time Version. Modified for the study of anxiety disorders (SADS-LA). New York:
New York State Psychiatric Institute.
Gittelman, R. (1985). Anxiety disorders in children. In B. B. Lahey and A. E. Kazdin

(Eds.). *Advances in Clinical Child Psychology*, Vol. 8. New York: Plenum Press, pp. 53–79.

———. (1980). The role of psychological tests for differential diagnosis in child psychiatry. *J. Amer. Acad. Child Psychiat.* 19:413–38.

———, and Koplewicz, H. S. (1986). Pharmacotherapy of childhood anxiety disorders. In R. Gittelman (Ed.). *Anxiety Disorders of Childhood.* New York: Guilford Press, pp. 188–203.

Gittelman-Klein, R. (1978). Validity of projective tests for psychodiagnosis in children. In R. L. Spitzer and D. F. Klein (Eds.). *Critical Issues in Psychiatric Diagnosis.* New York: Raven Press, pp. 141–66.

Goyette, C. H., Conners, C. K., and Ulrich, R. F. (1978). Normative data on the revised Conners parent and teacher ratings scales. *J. Abnorm. Child Psychol.* 6:221–36.

Graham, P., and Rutter, M. (1968). The reliability and validity of the psychiatric assessment of the child. II. Interview with the parents. *Brit. J. Psychiat.* 114:581–92.

Hathaway, S. R., and McKinley, J. C. (1951). *The Minnesota Multiphasic Personality Inventory Manual*, Rev. ed. New York: Psychological Corporation.

Lachar, D. (1982). *Personality Inventory for Children (PIC) Revised Format Manual Supplement.* Los Angeles: Western Psychological Services.

Lewis, M. (1986). Principles of intensive individual psychoanalytic psychotherapy for childhood anxiety disorders. In R. Gittelman (Ed.). *Anxiety Disorders of Childhood.* New York: Guilford Press, pp. 233–55.

McReynolds, P. (1978). IPAT Anxiety Scale. In O. K. Buros (Ed.). *The Eighth Mental Measurements Yearbook.* Lincoln: University of Nebraska Press, p. 859.

Miller, L. C. (1967a). Louisville behavior checklist for males, 6–12 years of age. *Psycholog. Reports* 21:885–96.

———. (1967b). Dimensions of psychopathology in middle children. *Psycholog. Reports* 21:897–903.

———, et al. (1971a). Revised anxiety scales for the Louisville Behavior Checklist. *Psycholog. Reports* 29:503–11.

———, et al. (1971b). Children's deviant behavior within the general population. *J. Consult. Clin. Psychol.* 37:16–22.

———, et al. (1972). Factor structure of childhood fears. *J. Consult. Clin. Psychol.* 39:264–68.

Ollendick, T. H. (1983). Reliability and validity of the revised Fear Survey Schedule for Children (FSSC-R). *Behav. Research Ther.* 21:685–92.

Porter, R. B., and Cattell, R. B. (1979). *Children's Personality Questionnaire.* Champaign, Ill.: Institute for Personality and Ability Testing.

Reich, W., et al. (1982). Development of a structured psychiatric interview for children: Agreement on diagnosis comparing child and parent interviews. *J. Abnorm. Child Psychol.* 10:325–36.

Reynolds, C. R. (1980). Concurrent validity of what I think and feel: The revised Children's Manifest Anxiety Scale. *J. Consult. Clin. Psychol.* 48:774–75.

———, and Richmond, B. O. (1978). What I Think and Feel: A revised measure of children's manifest anxiety. *J. Abnorm. Child Psychol.* 6:271–80.

————, and Richmond, B. O. (1979). Factor structure and construct validity of "What I Think and Feel": The revised children's manifest anxiety scale. *J. Person. Assess.* 43:281–83.

Rutter, M. (1976). Research report: Institute of Psychiatry, Department of Child and Adolescent Psychiatry. *Psycholog. Med.* 6:505–16.

————, and Graham, P. (1968). The reliability and validity of the psychiatric assessment of the child. I. Interview with the child. *Brit. J. Psychiat.* 114:563–79.

Sarason, S. B. (1966). The measurement of anxiety in children: Some questions and problems. In C. D. Spielberger (Ed.). *Anxiety and Behavior.* New York: Academic Press, pp. 63–79.

Scherer, M. W., and Nakamura, C. Y. (1968). A Fear Survey Schedule for Children (FSS-FC): A factor analytic comparison with manifest anxiety (CMAS). *Behav. Research Ther.* 6:173–82.

Shaffer, D. (1986). Learning theories of anxiety. In R. Gittelman (Ed.). *Anxiety Disorders of Childhood.* New York: Guilford Press, pp. 157–67.

Spielberger, C. D. (1973). *State-Trait Anxiety Inventory for Children.* Palo Alto, Calif.: Consulting Psychologists Press.

Thorndike, R. L. (1978). Critique. In O. K. Buros (Ed.). *The Eighth Mental Measurements Yearbook.* Lincoln: University of Nebraska, p. 766.

Thorpe, L. P., Clark. W. W., and Tiegs, E. W. (1953a). *California Test of Personality: Primary Form.* Monterey, Calif.: McGraw-Hill.

————. (1953b). *California Test of Personality: Elementary Form.* Monterey, Calif.: McGraw-Hill.

Tiegs, E. W., Clark, W. W., and Thorpe, L. P. (1953). *California Test of Personality: Secondary Form.* Monterey, Calif.: McGraw-Hill.

Trautman, P. (1986). Psychodynamic theories of anxiety and their application to children. In R. Gittelman (Ed.). *Anxiety Disorders of Childhood.* New York: Guilford Press, pp. 168–87.

Werry, J. S. (1986). Diagnosis and assessment. In R. Gittelman (Ed.). *Anxiety Disorders of Childhood.* New York: Guilford Press, pp. 73–100.

Wirt, R. D., et al. (1977). *Multidimensional Description of Child Personality: A Manual for the Personality Inventory for Children.* Los Angeles: Western Psychological Services.

Wolpe, J., and Lang, P. J. (1964). A fear survey schedule for use in behavior therapy. *Behav. Research Ther.* 2:27–30.

35

THE SOMATIZING DISORDERS: SOMATOFORM DISORDERS, FACTITIOUS DISORDERS, AND MALINGERING

Daniel T. Williams and Glenn Hirsch

Somatization is the term used here to describe physical symptoms or abnormal bodily sensations that are not directly related to a physically based disease process. Somatization includes the use of the body as a coping mechanism for expression of an emotional state or for personal gain. It is a common phenomenon, probably utilized to some degree by everybody at some time or other. However, some individuals become symptomatically bogged down in a pattern of repetitive use of somatization. This may occur either acutely, in response to overwhelming immediate stresses, or chronically, when it may become integrated into one's basic personality style of coping and hence may become a way of life (Ford 1983). Much more has been written regarding the syndromes subsumed under this heading as they present during adulthood than in childhood and adolescence. However, there is a consensus that the propensity to somatization often has its etiological roots in these early formative periods. It is an important responsibility of the well-trained child and adolescent psychiatrist to be sensitive and informed about the complexities of this group of disorders, so that appropriate evaluation and intervention at an early stage can minimize or prevent a progression toward chronic somatization.

Somatoform disorders, factitious disorders, and malingering share the common features of somatization delineated above. They are individually distinguished from each other by two key parameters: 1) the question of conscious versus unconscious intentionality on the part of the patient with regard to symptom formation; and 2) the question of whether the ostensible goal of the symptom formation is readily recognizable in terms of evident external incentives. Judgment regarding these differentiating characteristics often involves inference on the part of the clinician. In the absence of objective, measurable parameters to buttress one's clinical judgment in this domain, there is clearly significant opportunity for error and disagreement among different clinicians. Nevertheless, the distinctions have been found to be clinically useful over time, so that the effort seems justified to refine the differential diagnostic sensitivity as a guide to appropriate treatment intervention in these three separate but at times overlapping clinical entities.

CLINICAL ENTITIES

Somatoform Disorders

Somatoform disorders are characterized by physical symptoms suggesting physical disorder for which there are no demonstrable organic findings or known physiological mechanisms, and for which there is positive evidence, or a strong presumption, that the symptoms are linked to psychological factors or conflicts. The symptom production in somatoform disorders is *not under voluntary control*, hence implying an unconscious mechanism in symptom formation. The following subdivisions of somatoform disorders are most commonly encountered among children and adolescents.

CONVERSION DISORDER

Conversion disorder is characterized by a loss or alteration of physical functioning that suggests physical disorder, but that instead is apparently an expression of a psychological conflict or a need. After appropriate investigation, the disturbance cannot be explained by any physical disorder or known pathophysiological mechanism. Psychological factors may be judged to play a primary etiological role in a variety of ways. Thus, a temporal relationship may exist between the onset or worsening of the symptom and the presence of an environmental stimulus that activates a psychological conflict or a need. Alternatively, the symptom may be noted to free the patient from a noxious activity or encounter. Finally, the symptom may enable the patient to get help from others that might otherwise not be forthcoming. The most common conversion symptoms are those suggesting neurological disease, but virtually any known bodily disease may be unconsciously mimicked in a conversion disorder. Some of the common clinical features of conversion disorders are outlined below (Nemiah 1985).

Motor Disturbances. Conversion symptoms presenting as abnormal movements may take many forms, including seizures, coordination difficulties, and movement disorders. Conversion paralysis and weakness most often affect the extremities, either singularly or in combination. However, any body part may be affected, ranging from the vocal cords (leading to aphonia); to the trunk, leading to hysterical scoliosis (lateral curvature of the spine), camptocormia (forward flexion of the upper body on the hips), or other variations on this theme.

Sensory Disturbances. Conversion disturbances of skin sensation may occur in any location and pattern, but are found most often in the extremities. Disorders of motor function are often accompanied by diminished or totally absent sensation, often involving all modalities. As with motor disturbances of conversion etiology, the distribution of sensory disturbance follows a pattern determined by the patient's conception of the anatomic abnormality, rather than the actual pattern of nerve innervations. Hence, the frequently encountered postinjury pattern of glove and stocking anesthesia of the hands and feet and other clearly nonphysiological patterns of deficit that are commonly observed. The special organs of sense may also be affected, leading to impairment of hearing and vision to varying degrees. Sensory hallucinations are sometimes encountered, occasionally including auditory or visual components. Finally, pain may accompany other sensory and motor disturbances in many patients with conversion disorders.

Symptoms Simulating Physical Illness. The symptoms of conversion disorder may simulate physical disease so closely that diagnosis is difficult to establish. A common pattern here may involve an identification with the symptoms of the illness of a person with whom the patient has had a special relationship. A parent or close friend who has recently died, for example, may engender conversion symptoms in a vulnerable individual as one manifestation of a pathological grief reaction.

Symptoms Complicating Physical Illness. Symptoms of bonafide physical illness may be protracted or complicated by secondary conversion symptoms. Thus, limb weakness or disuse that begins after an injury may be prolonged as a conversion symptom long after the initial physical injury has subsided. A patient with bonafide neurogenic seizures may develop secondary conversion seizures that can be difficult to differentiate from the neurogenic ones. Symptoms in this category often present challenging problems of differential diagnosis.

Lateralization of Conversion Symptoms. Conversion disorders in adults have been more frequently reported to occur on the left side of the body (Flor-Henry 1983). In contrast, Regan and LeBarbera (1984) reported a predominance of the lateralization of conversion symptoms in children and adolescents to the right side of the body. The basis of this intriguing difference remains to be further clarified.

IDIOPATHIC PAIN DISORDER

Idiopathic pain disorder was previously combined with conversion disorders in DSM-II under the rubric of hysterical neurosis, conversion type. In DSM-III and DSM-III-R it is given an independent status. The characteristic feature is the complaint of pain in the absence of adequate physical findings to explain the pain in physiological terms and in the presence of positive evidence of the etiological role of psychological factors. Psychogenic pain disorder will be considered here conjointly with conversion disorder, as the two appear to be closely linked and there is insufficient data regarding differences between the two among children and adolescents to discuss them separately.

SOMATIZATION DISORDER

Somatization disorder (formerly called hysteria or Briquet's syndrome) most often has its onset in adolescence. The essential features include recurrent multiple somatic complaints of several years duration beginning before the age of 30. Medical attention is sought repeatedly, but the symptoms are not found to be due to any physical disorder. Complaints of at least thirteen symptoms from the list of thirty-five enumerated in DSM-III-R must be elicited in order to establish the diagnosis. These include gastrointestinal symptoms, pain symptoms, cardiopulmonary symptoms, conversion symptoms, psychosexual symptoms, and female reproductive system symptoms.

It has been estimated that approximately 1 percent of the adult female population has this disorder (Ford 1983), while it is rarely diagnosed in males. There is a higher incidence of antisocial personality disorder among family members of those with somatization disorder than in the general population. The clinical course tends to be chronic but fluctuating, with extensive utilization of medical services over time and with rare incidence of spontaneous remission. As will be noted later, a clinically important question is the possibility that untreated, protracted or recurrent episodes of conversion disorder or psychogenic pain disorder in childhood or adolescence may predispose to the subsequent development of somatization disorder.

HYPOCHONDRIASIS

Hypochondriasis (or hypochondriacal neurosis) is characterized by an unrealistic interpretation of physical signs or sensations as abnormal, leading to preoccupation with the fear or belief of having a serious disease. A thorough physical evaluation does not support the diagnosis of any physical disorder that can account for the physical symptoms or sensations or for the individual's unrealistic interpretation of them. The unrealistic fear or belief of having a physical disease persists despite medical reassurance and has a duration of at least six months.

The disorder is equally common in males and females. Common associated features include anxiety, depression, compulsive and narcissistic personality traits, and a history of many medical consultations. The age of onset is commonly in adolescence. The course is often chronic with waxing and waning of symptoms. This disorder is commonly seen in general pediatric and medical practice, yet such patients often resist a psychological interpretation of their symptoms and consequently often decline referral for psychiatric treatment.

From the above description, it is clear that there is an overlap in phenomenology in somatization disorder and hypochondriasis. In addition to the quantitative distinction between the two, having to do with symptom enumeration and duration, there is a qualitative difference in the mode of presentation. Patients with somatization disorder tend to be more dramatic and extroverted in style, while those with hypochondriasis tend to be more obsessive and introverted. Similar questions arise with hypochondriasis, as with somatization disorder, regarding the possible role of early, extended experience with conversion symptoms in childhood and adolescence as a predisposing factor to the development of a hypochondriacal lifestyle.

Factitious Disorders

Factitious disorders are characterized by physical or psychological symptoms that are intentionally produced or feigned, hence being by definition *under voluntary control*. The sense of voluntary control is subjective and can only be inferred by an outside observer, giving rise to ready diagnostic confusion with somatoform disorders. The judgment that symptoms are voluntarily produced is based on observations of behavior suggesting dissimulation or concealment, after excluding all other possible causes of the behavior. However, it should be noted that this behavior has a compulsive quality and hence is voluntary in the sense of being deliberate and purposeful, while implying a lack of full control that is an inherent feature of a compulsive behavior. Another essential feature is the psychological need to assume the sick role, as evidenced by the absence of external incentives for the behavior, such as economic gain, avoidance of onerous responsibilities, or attaining more comfortable circumstances via the sick role. This is important in distinguishing factitious disorders from malingering. An illustrative example of a factitious disorder would be a child with a spiking fever of unknown etiology who is admitted to the hospital and is subjected to numerous and sometimes painful diagnostic procedures, who is eventually found by unobtrusive observation to be surreptitiously rubbing the thermometer against the bedsheets to generate an elevated temperature reading. In its more chronic forms, factitious disorder may be associated with either physical symptoms (Munchausen syndrome) or psychological symptoms (Ganser's syndrome, pseudopsychosis, or pseudodementia). These manifestations are generally associated with severe dependent, masochistic, or antisocial personality disorders.

MUNCHAUSEN SYNDROME BY PROXY

This variant of factitious disorder was first reported by Meadow (1982). He reported on nineteen children under 7 years of age, from seventeen families, whose mothers consistently gave fraudulent clinical histories and fabricated signs that led to needless and harmful medical investigations, hospital admissions, and treatment over a period of time ranging from a few months to four years. Episodes of bleeding, neurological abnormality, rashes, fevers, and abnormal urine were commonly simulated. Often the mothers had previous nursing training and some had a history of fabricating symptoms or signs relating to themselves. Two of the nineteen children died. One 6-year-old child spent five months in a hospital, had thirteen procedures, 120 venipunctures, and was prescribed more than twenty-five medications. Meadow's study of these children and their families led to a list of warning signs to consider, together with recommendations for dealing with suspected acts. He noted the need to separate the mother and child in suspect circumstances to confirm the fabrication and emphasized the subsequent need to confront the families with the deception when it was confirmed. Of the seventeen survivors in his series, eight children were taken into protective care and the other nine remained at home after the arrangements were made for augmented supervision. In the four years since Meadow's influential 1982 article, there have been no fewer than twenty-eight publications in various pediatric, psychiatric, and other medical publications on this special form of child abuse that requires augmented vigilance and circumspection on the part of clinicians.

Malingering

Malingering is not considered to be a mental disorder. It is characterized by the voluntary production and presentation of false or grossly exaggerated physical or psychological symptoms. In contrast to factitious disorder, the symptoms in malingering are produced in pursuit of a goal that is readily recognizable with an understanding of the individual's circumstances rather than his or her individual psychology (Yudofsky 1985). Examples of such readily understandable goals include the avoidance of school or work, the securing of financial compensation, the evasion of criminal prosecution, or the acquisition of drugs.

As with somatoform disorders and factitious disorders, the determination of a patient's volitional intent is often not possible with certainty by the clinician. The particular characteristic of the malingerer, namely that of deceiving and manipulating the physician into unwitting compliance with a goal of the malingerer's choosing, is particularly likely to elicit strong countertransference feelings on the part of the physician when this diagnosis is suspected. Because the confrontational presentation of such suspicion to a child or adolescent will irremediably sabotage any prospects of a therapeutic relationship and inevitably transform it into a hostile, adversarial one, it is particularly important to refrain from such confrontation until all other differential diagnostic possibilities have been adequately considered and explored. It is important to note that somatoform disorders may include "secondary gains," which may falsely lead to the presumption of malingering. It is therefore best in ambiguous cases to give the patient the benefit of the doubt, so as to preserve the clinician's therapeutic leverage with a view to symptom alleviation.

EPIDEMIOLOGY

Literature on the epidemiology of somatizing disorders in childhood and adolescence is sparse. Confusion is engendered by frequent use in the older literature of the term "hysteria," with imprecise or variable definition by different authors. Robins and O'Neal (1953) studied the incidence of childhood hysteria at St. Louis Children's Hospital over a fifteen-year period (1935–1950) and found forty-one cases, which constituted 4 percent of all cases with a psychiatric diagnosis exclusive of mental retardation. Proctor (1958) reviewed twenty-five cases of childhood hysteria encountered in a rural setting in North Carolina and reported a total incidence of 13 percent among child psychiatry referrals, of which 10 percent were defined as conversion reactions and the other 3 percent either dissociative reactions or combined disorders. Proctor speculated on the role of a more rural and repressive "Bible Belt" mentality as possibly contributing to the higher incidences of such disorders in his outpatient population as compared to the generally lower incidence of such disorders previously reported. Rock (1971) found the overall incidence of conversion reactions to be 4 percent of children receiving psychiatric treatment at a general hospital in Honolulu. Herman and Simmonds (1975) also found an overall incidence rate of 4 percent of conversion symptoms among pediatric patients referred to both inpatient and outpatient child psychiatry consultation at the University of Missouri School of Medicine. Yet, in this study, conversion reactions were found to have an incidence of only 1.3 percent in the child psychiatry outpatient clinic but of 22 percent among psychiatric consultations on the pediatric inpatient service.

British authors have generally reported lower rates of somatoform disorder. Caplan (1972) found only twenty-eight patients with a diagnosis of "hysteria" in a review of the charts of prepubertal children referred to the child psychiatry department of the Maudsley Hospital over a twenty-two-year period, representing 0.3 percent of all referrals. Rutter et al. (Hersov 1977) found no cases of conversion hysteria among 10- and 11-year-olds on the Isle of Wight, nor were there any new cases seen in a similar general population study of 14-year-olds in London. In a retrospective review of 3,000 cases over a twelve-year period, Goodyear (1981) found only fifteen cases of hysterical conversion reactions among pediatric inpatients at Park Hospital for Children, Oxford, representing 0.5 percent of the total inpatient population during that time. The author does not say what proportion of patients receiving psychiatric consultation this represented. By contrast, an American study by Maloney (1980) found 105 cases of hysterical conversion reactions among pediatric inpatients at the Cincinnati Children's Hospital Medical Center over a 3-year period, representing 16.7 percent of the pediatric inpatients receiving child psychiatry consultation during that time. The incidence relative to the total inpatient population during that period is not indicated. One is tempted to speculate that cultural factors influencing either the pediatric population or their psychiatric diagnosticians or both may play some role in these disparities.

It is sometimes contended that conversion disorders are less frequent currently than they were in the last century, yet how much of this reflects a true change in incidence and how much a change in diagnostic propensity over time is difficult to ascertain. An example of the mutability of these judgments is a study by Rae (1977), who found that the incidence of childhood conversion disorder at three medical settings ranged from 5 percent to 24 percent of psychiatric referrals. Furthermore, the incidence of conversion disorder increased threefold over three years at one setting. This was attributed by Rae to greater education and sensitization of the medical staff to the presence of conversion phenomena, probably leading eventually to their overdiagnosis. The majority of studies, dating from the ninety-seven cases reviewed by Sheffield (1898) to the thirty cases reviewed by Volkmar et al. (1984), have noted a preponderance of somatoform disorders among girls in comparison to boys. The sex differences tend to be small to negligible in early childhood, become more prominent during adolescence, and then apparently remain so in adulthood, as reflected by the overwhelming preponderance of somatization disorder among women, noted above.

Epidemiological studies on the incidence or prevalence of factitious disorders and malingering among children and adolescents are unavailable. This is probably due in part to the relatively more recent refinement of differential diagnostic criteria within the larger spectrum of the somatizing disorders.

DIFFERENTIAL DIAGNOSIS

In addition to the complex and subtle discriminations required on the part of the clinician in distinguishing among the various somatizing disorders outlined above, the following two categories require special consideration.

Undiagnosed Physical Illness

This is probably the most common and certainly the most important source of differential diagnostic error in the diagnosis of the somatizing disorders. Of the twenty-eight cases reviewed by Caplan (1972) with a diagnosis of "hysteria," a minimum of thirteen were found on follow-up to have an organic illness related to the presenting symptom either by the time of discharge from the hospital or at follow-up from four to eleven years later. In his comparison between the thirteen ultimate "organic" patients and the fifteen probably "hysteric" patients, Caplan found that a family history of hysterical conversion symptoms occurred only in the "hysterics." Furthermore, a history of severe physical illness, especially in a site related to that of the child's symptoms, was more common in the first-degree relatives of the "hysterics."

It should be emphasized that diagnosing a somatizing disorder requires more than simply the inability to find an organic basis for a given physical symptom on the initial medical evaluation. Many medical disorders such as multiple sclerosis, lupus erythematosus, and dystonia musculorum deformans may present with initially subtle, fluctuating, and insidiously progressive physical symptoms that are frequently misdiagnosed early in their course as "functional," or more specifically, as somatizing disorders. Furthermore, it should be noted that patients with true medical disorders may develop secondary somatizing disorders as a reactive way of dealing with their anxiety about what they subliminally perceive to be an underlying physical derangement, about which they have difficulty communicating directly with those in their environment. The best defense against this common and sometimes treacherous source of diagnostic error is maintaining close contact between a consulting mental health practitioner and a coevaluating pediatrician or other examining physician, while keeping in mind the possibility during ongoing assessment and treatment that undiagnosed physical illness may exist.

Psychological Factors Affecting a Physical Condition

This category is used in DSM-III and DSM-III-R to describe not only disorders that have in the past been referred to as psychosomatic or psychophysiological, but more broadly, to delineate any physical condition in which psychological factors are judged to have a contributory role. This judgment requires evidence that psychologically meaningful environmental stimuli are temporally related to the initiation or exacerbation of a physical condition. Furthermore, the physical condition must have either demonstrable organic pathology (e.g., ulcerative colitis) or a known pathophysiological process (e.g., migraine headache).

To illustrate the differential diagnostic complexity that may pertain, consider a child or adolescent with uncontrolled seizures who is referred by a neurologist for psychiatric consultation because of apparent emotional precipitants of at least some of the seizures. The referring and consulting clinicians must discern what proportion of the seizures represent uncontrolled neurogenic seizures, a somatoform disorder, a factitious disorder, malingering, or psychologically precipitated neurogenic seizures (psychological factors affecting a physical condition). Furthermore, they must consider whether some undiagnosed physical condition (e.g., CNS infection, tumor, or degenerative disease) may be contributory. Implicit in the above, they must be aware that two or more of the above conditions may coexist in the same patient. The result can be and often is a diagnostic challenge that taxes the resources of even the most seasoned neurologists and psychiatrists (Williams et al. 1978, 1979; Williams and Mostofsky 1982).

ETIOLOGY

The following is a brief review of some of the main contemporary conceptual formulations of the genesis of the somatizing disorders having relevance to the clinician working with children and adolescents. It should be noted that these formulations are not mutually exclusive, but rather may be viewed as elucidating different possible contributions to the development of somatizing disorders in different individuals.

Somatoform Disorders

PSYCHOANALYTIC THEORY

Using conversion disorder as a paradigm of the somatoform disorders, a fixation is postulated in early psychosexual development at the level of the Oedipus complex (Adams 1979). A failure to relinquish the incestuous tie to the loved parent leads to intrapsychic conflict over the sexual drive because it retains its forbidden incestuous quality. This drive is therefore repressed, and the energy associated with the drive is *converted* into a psychologically determined physical symptom. The symptom not only protects the patient from conscious awareness of the repressed drive but simultaneously often provides a psychologically significant symbolic expression of it.

In addition to this *primary gain* there are often *secondary gains* of the symptom that contribute to its retention. These include the attention, sympathy, and support often provided to an individual as a result of the conversion symptoms. The associated disability may also excuse the individual from onerous tasks and responsibilities, thus gratifying dependency needs and reinforcing the perpetuation of the symptom.

GRATIFICATION OF DEPENDENCE NEEDS

For some patients, gratification of dependency needs may be a primary rather than a secondary determinant of conversion symptoms (Nemiah 1985). Experiences with psychiatric combat casualties during the world wars disclosed many conversion disorders where the primary motivation of the symptoms appeared to be self-preservation rather than oedipal sexual drives. In these situations, the symptoms enabled the individual to escape a dangerous situation and to receive protection and support under the rubric of the patient role, which could not honorably be requested directly.

Among children and adolescents, physical illness often is perceived unconsciously as an accessible route of escape from the onerous burdens of school or other competitive social situations about which the youngster feels anxious or inadequate. When a child is faced with a conflict between unconscious dependency needs on one hand and idealized demands of conscience to be persevering and productive on the other, conversion symptoms can provide a temporary, albeit maladaptive escape hatch. Since the physical symptom is perceived by both the patient and others as an affliction over which he or she has no control, it brings relief of school and/or other social burdens and legitimizes the unconsciously coveted dependency status the youngster cannot honorably request directly.

REACTION TO ENVIRONMENTAL STRESS

Another perspective on the phenomena of conversion disorder as a paradigm of somatoform disorders is offered by learning theory. From this perspective, behavior can be reinforced by reduction of the intensity of an inner painful psychological drive, whose reduction predictably follows the behavior. For example, a conversion symptom may result in a reduction of the painful drive of fear and anxiety, such as that associated with being at school. The relief obtained in this manner reinforces the conversion symptom that generated the relief and predisposes to a repetition of the same symptom each time the anxiety is experienced. In this manner, a pattern of behavior is reinforced repetitively and may eventually become chronic.

This learning theory approach to understanding human behavior shifts the focus of attention away from unconscious psychic forces and onto the observable contingencies of reinforcement that influence behavior. Some of the differences between learning theory and psychodynamic theory seem to be more conceptual than operational when the actual implications for clinical application are scrutinized (Sloane et al. 1975). Yet, insofar as learning theory emphasizes the systematic review of reinforcing contingencies that affect conversion symptoms, this often has pragmatic benefit in formulating treatment strategies with patients and their families.

THE PHENOMENON OF DISSOCIATION

Janet and Freud used the term *dissociation* in describing hysteria to refer to the splitting off from consciousness of painful affects and associated ideas (Frankel 1976). Insofar as our contemporary definition of somatoform disorders continues to emphasize that symptom production is not under voluntary control, there remains an intrinsic presumption that the phenomenon of dissociation plays a central role in these disorders. Thus, the curious phenomenon of a conversion paralysis that is mediated by the "voluntary" musculature, whose innervation is intact yet *not* under the conscious voluntary control of the patient, presents a conceptual paradox that is best understood in terms of the experience of dissociation.

Freud's early interest in the study of hysteria was integrally related to his interest in hypnosis, which is also characterized by the phenomenon of dissociation (Spiegel and Spiegel 1978). Contemporary studies of the phenomenon of dissociation, as exemplified by the hypnotic trance state, thus provide a useful route of inquiry that can help us better understand the phenomenology of somatoform disorders. Concomitantly, such inquiry may be useful in delineating systematic approaches to assessment and treatment (see Chapter 54).

SYMPTOMS AS COMMUNICATION

This perspective views the conversion symptoms as a nonverbal communication in body language that serves to influence or coerce another person to some action, such as helping or paying attention to the person who is communicating the symptom (Nemiah 1985). According to this view, somatoform disorder is not an illness but a game played in conformity with certain rules of communication that determine the form of the behavior. This perspective, a variation on the theme of learning theory, with a particular emphasis on the symbolic and communicative aspects of conversion symptoms and their function as a means of expressing dependency needs, has some limitations. Specifically, it lends itself to the reductionist approach that has simplistically equated somatoform disorders with factitious disorders and malingering.

NEUROPHYSIOLOGICAL PREDISPOSITION

Flor-Henry (1983) marshaled three lines of evidence to support the contention that a particular pattern of cerebral disorganization is fundamental to the most severe of the somatoform disorders, somatization disorder (hysteria). First, he undertook an historical reinterpretation of the case of Anna O., based on recently disclosed medical data that he felt supported the contention that a subacute limbic encephalitis is a more convincing explanation of her variegated symptomatology than the purely psychological theory advocated by Freud. He further cited a controlled neuropsychological investigation on ten adult patients with the stable syndrome of "hysteria," who were matched for sex, handedness, and full-scale IQ with ten normal controls, ten psychotic depressives, and ten schizophrenics. The findings were interpreted to suggest that dominant hemisphere dysfunction is fundamentally related to the syndrome of hysteria and that dysfunction of the nondominant hemisphere is brought about by the associated features of the syndrome. He further posited, citing genetic studies, that hysteria in the female is a syndrome equivalent to psychopathy in the male insofar as psychopathic fathers tend to produce daughters with hysteria. He contended that in hysteria the defect in the understanding of endogenous somatic signals and sensorimotor integration is the consequence of altered dominant hemisphere systems, and produces, when it occurs in the female, a secondary disorganization of the contralateral hemisphere that determines the flamboyant facade of feminine hysteria. The possible relevance of this perspective with respect to somatoform disorders in children and adolescents remains to be explored.

THE ROLE OF DEPRESSION

Klerman (1982) noted that although the evidence is inconclusive, there appears to be a moderate overlap between the components of somatoform disorder and the clinical phenomenon of depression. Whether viewed from the vantage point of somatoform disorder or from that of depression, moderate percentages of patients with both disorders have manifestations of the other disorder. Klerman noted, based on a review of the adult literature, that the presence of conversion symptoms and other hysterical symptoms appears to be associated with less intensity of the manifest affective and mood component of the depressive syndrome. This may be so dramatic that the patient's depression may be almost completely masked by the bodily symptoms and behavior. He noted that it may require skillful interviewing and clinical experience to help the patient become aware of his or her sadness and melancholic feelings so as not only to confirm the diagnosis but to make the treatment process more meaningful and effective for the patient. The extent to which depression plays a role in somatoform disorders in childhood and adolescence has not been systematically explored. Clinical experience suggests, however, that this issue is frequently pertinent, particularly when the symptoms have become chronic.

THE ROOTS OF SOMATIZATION DISORDER

A clinically important question, in view of the chronic and disabling nature of somatization disorder, pertains to the predisposing factors to its development. It seems plausible to suggest that untreated, protracted, or recurrent episodes of conversion disorder or idiopathic pain disorder in childhood or adolescence would be likely predisposing factors. Supporting this postulation are the observations that conversion disorders are more commonly diagnosed in children and adolescents than in adults, while the reverse is true for somatization disorder. Additional supportive evidence for this developmental transformation is presented by the work of Ernst et al. (1984). In a retrospective study of children with abdominal pain seen in a multi-specialty medical clinic, those with organic findings were compared to those whose physical examinations were negative (the functional pain group). For children with functional abdominal pain (but not for the others), the number of symptoms of somatization disorder was significantly related to the chronicity of the child's condition. Thus, the longer the duration of functional pain, the greater the number of symptoms reported. These findings are strongly supportive of the above-noted hypothesis.

Factitious Disorders

The crucial distinction between somatoform disorders and factitious disorders, as noted above, resides in the issue of conscious versus unconscious intention regarding symptom formation. Insofar as conscious versus unconscious intent is frequently difficult to establish, there is often empirically a blurring of the overall diagnostic distinction. This is particularly true in more chronic forms of both of these illnesses, where associated personality disorders commonly color the presentations of each. In a developmental sense, one should consider the possibility that a child's early experience with conversion disorder that is inappropriately handled by parents or others may predispose not only to somatization disorder as suggested above, but also to factitious disorder, when there is a more conscious and intentional secondary elaboration of symptoms by the child.

If the above postulate is true, then some of the previously outlined etiological considerations regarding somatoform disorders would also pertain to factitious disorders. Some additional etiological considerations regarding factitious disorders are outlined below (Ford 1983).

Family histories of patients with factitious disorder frequently yield reports of parental abuse, neglect, or abandonment. One or both parents are usually seen as rejecting figures who are unable to form close relationships. These observations have led to psychological models suggesting that patients with factitious disorder have been unable to achieve a necessary sense of acceptance by an early love object such as a parent, consequently leaving their dependency needs inadequately satisfied. The resulting personality of such persons is viewed as vulnerable to subsequent life events that produce persistent medical and hospital-seeking behavior.

The medical setting and hospital staff are perceived by these patients as a potential source of security and response to unmet dependency needs. An institutional dependency is created in which the hospital and staff become a surrogate home and family. However, by virtue of the pathological severity of the dependency needs, the resources of the hospital and staff are soon exhausted, leading to alienation and eventual rejection.

The inherent masochism of submitting to innumerable procedures is often interpreted as an attempt to relieve unconscious guilt. Alternate views of mutilating and self-destructive behavior have led to the idea that they can be equated with acts of suicide, representing aggression against the rejecting parent or family.

A history of work in the health profession is recorded in over 50 percent of recognized adult cases, while there are also numerous reports of patients whose fathers or other relatives are either physicians or other health-related practitioners, which may play a role in the problematic identity formation of youngsters with factitious disorder.

DIAGNOSIS

As already noted, the absence of readily diagnosable physical illness at the time of initial medical evaluation is not by itself enough to establish the diagnosis of a somatizing disorder. The evaluating psychiatrist must be convinced first of all that undiagnosed physical illness as well as psychological factors affecting a physical illness have been effectively ruled out. In addition, however, there must be convincing positive evidence that a somatizing disorder exists. If the presenting symptom includes features that are clearly nonphysiological (e.g., the patient talking during an apparent grand mal seizure), the presence of a somatizing disorder is clearly established. Such documentation, however, clearly does not rule out the possible coexistence of either an undiagnosed physical illness or of psychological factors affecting a bonafide physical condition. Adequate diagnostic assessment and treatment plan formulation clearly require a thorough review of the patient's history, physical examination, and current psychological status. Direct communication by the psychiatrist with the referring pediatrician or other primary medical practitioner is a crucial component of this diagnostic process.

History

Information supporting the impression that a given symptom is a manifestation of a somatizing disorder would include the following:

1) The historical data regarding the symptom are compatible with the primary diagnosis of a somatizing disorder.
2) There is a history of other symptoms (past or current) that clearly have the characteristics of a somatizing disorder, such as unexplained paralysis or anesthesia. Inquiry on such matters should apply not only to the patient, but also to family members, who are a ready source of identification for the patient.
3) There is a history of other overt emotional or behavioral symptoms, such as anxiety, depression, obsessions, phobias, school avoidance, or separation anxiety disorder. As above, inquiry with regard to such symptoms in other family members is also of relevance.
4) There is a history of a recent death or other loss of a person important to the patient, or some other major psychological stress, temporally related to the onset of the presenting symptom or symptoms.
5) There is a history of a relative, friend, or acquaintance who has had a physical symptom similar to that which the patient now presents and the patient may have plausible reason to affiliate with this symptom by identification.
6) There is a history of sexual seduction or abuse (Herman and Hirschman 1981).

The above enumerated historical features are suggestive but by no means exhaustive of the variety of life stresses and predisposing factors that should lead the clinician to consider the diagnosis of a somatizing disorder.

One's tactical approach to the patient and family is of importance in establishing an appropriate rapport that is crucial for effective diagnostic assessment and treatment for all somatizing disorders. The patient with a somatoform disorder, for example, is by definition unaware of the relationship between environmental stress or intrapsychic conflict and the appearance of the presenting symptoms. In such a setting, a confrontational approach with the patient or parents during the initial assessment is clearly counterproductive. Any inquiries that are perceived by the patient or parents as seeking to establish such etiological connections in an accusatory tone are likely to be met with denial or distortion. A preferable approach for all somatizing disorders is to begin by explaining supportively to both the patient and parents that psychiatric consultation has been sought by the referring physician because of the possibility that psychological factors may be playing some role in the patient's presenting symptom, as they do in many commonly encountered medical problems. This opens the way for a collaborative dialogue in which the patient and parents will be helping the psychiatrist with two difficult tasks: first, understanding the genesis of the symptom and then, one hopes, enabling the patient to overcome it. If available medical information at the time of psychiatric referral is not conclusive regarding the presence or absence of physical disease, it is important to clarify that issue with the patient and family. It should also be explained that ongoing contact will be maintained with the primary referring physician, as physical and psychiatric assessments proceed concurrently.

Psychiatric assessment should yield a detailed picture of the patient's individual strengths and weaknesses, social relationships, school functioning, and pattern of family interaction. The process of exploring these areas will often yield additional clues as to whether there exists a combination of intrinsic vulnerabilities in the patient and cumulative stressors in his or her environment that would predispose to the development of a somatizing disorder.

Physical Examination

Although physical examination is not generally the primary province of the psychiatrist in evaluating somatizing disorders, it is relevant to highlight some illustrative findings regarding physical diagnosis in this area to facilitate communication with one's medical colleagues (Weintraub 1977).

SENSORY DISTURBANCES

As noted above for somatoform disorders, but applicable to somatizing disorders generally, disturbances of sensation generally follow the patient's lay concept of anatomy rather than known neuroanatomic patterns of sensation. In this context, most patients are unaware that in organic loss there are gradual borders of sensory change at anatomic sites because of the interdigitation of the peripheral nerves. Thus, they are unaware that paramedian sparing occurs in organically based hemianesthesia. Further, unilateral loss of vibration sensation when tested over the frontal bone of the sternum generally points to a somatizing disorder, since this sensation is ordinarily bilateral due to bone conduction if the bony skeleton is intact.

In cases of complete loss of sensation in an extremity, the examiner can have the patient perform the finger-to-nose or heel-to-shin task. In true sensory damage, there is a disequilibrium of the fingers or feet, as the patient does not perceive their position in space. In the somatizing disorders, the patient is able effectively to touch the designated target.

It should be noted, however, that despite the presence of numerous sensory complaints and the initial absence of neurological findings indicative of organic disease, the presence of some serious organic illnesses cannot be ruled out except by repeated physical examinations. Peripheral neuropathies, such as Guillain-Barré syndrome, provide striking examples of how many medical practitioners can be diagnostically fooled by an insidiously progressive organic disease.

MOTOR DISTURBANCES

The physician can employ numerous tests based on physiological principles to detect latent strength in cases of apparent paralysis. For example, contraction of agonist and antagonist muscles can be tested and the response observed when resistance is suddenly withdrawn or increased. Different responses, indicating residual weakness in organically based disorders and residual strength in the case of somatizing disorder, can be diagnostic.

Patients with suspected somatizing disorders can also be observed while eating, dressing, or performing other activities. The patient may then be seen to use the affected limb in a way that would be impossible if it were truly paralyzed. These observations may be additionally helpful; hospitalized patients can be observed to move "paralyzed" limbs in their sleep, either spontaneously or in response to a noxious stimulus.

The Hoover test of unilateral leg paresis is based on the principle that when a person in a supine position attempts to lift one leg against resistance, there is normally an associated downward thrust of the other leg to provide counterbalancing leverage. In the Hoover test, the examiner places one hand under the heel of the weak leg and with the other hand, presses down on the unaffected leg. As the patient attempts to raise the unaffected leg, the examiner's hand under the heel of the weak leg detects pressure. This associated pressure occurs when the paralysis is "functional" but not when it is organic. Conversely, in attempting to raise the weak leg against resistance, a motivated patient with organic deficits will exert downward pressure with the unaffected leg in an effort to implement the requested response. In a patient with a somatizing disorder, by contrast, no downward pressure with the unaffected leg will be detected during this maneuver, as there is no volitional effort at compliance. Once again, as with sensory disturbances, it should be emphasized that some motor disturbances, particularly movement disorders, may present with initially subtle, fluctuating, and clinically unsubstantiatable neurological findings that only declare themselves more definitely over time. Thus, Lesser and Fahn (1978) reported that thirty-seven out of a series of eighty-four patients who had idiopathic torsion dystonia had been misdiagnosed originally as having primary psychiatric illness.

For discussion of specific differential diagnostic tests in disturbances of gait, coordination, vision, and other cranial nerve disturbances, the reader is referred to Weintraub (1977). A discussion of differential diagnostic approaches to patients with suspected pseudoseizures is presented by Williams and Mostofsky (1982).

Mental Status Evaluation

Children and adolescents with somatoform disorders are generally alert, oriented, and in effective communication with the examiner. It is advisable for the clinician to make specific inquiry about feelings of depression and associated vegetative signs, though these are often not present. Thought content is generally not grossly abnormal, nor is there evidence of a primary process thought disorder or bizarre behavior.

The most frequently described abnormality in the mental status of patients with conversion symptoms is "la belle indifference." This refers to the patient's attitude toward the symptom, which suggests a relative lack of concern out of keeping with the significant nature of the impairment. This feature has little diagnostic value, however, since it is also encountered in some seriously ill medical patients who are stoic about their conditions. Furthermore, it has been observed that many patients with conversion symptoms often experience diffuse anxiety and other painful affects concomitant with those symptoms, while remaining indifferent in regard to the conversion symptoms themselves. Finally, histrionic personality traits may or may not coexist with either a somatoform disorder or an organic illness.

If a documented psychosis is present, coexisting conversion symptoms should be considered secondary to the underlying psychotic or schizophrenic process. However, in patients with recent onset of psychotic behavior associated with severe environmental stress, rapid decompensation, and other conversion symptoms or histrionic personality features, the diagnosis of historical psychosis should be considered (Spiegel and Fink 1979). In such cases, differential diagnosis can be facilitated by using a standardized measure of hypnotic trance capacity. Patients with hysterical psychosis are generally highly hypnotizable, while those who are schizophrenic or otherwise psychotic have low to zero hypnotizability.

It should be emphasized that in all cases where a somatizing disorder in a child or adolescent is being evaluated, the securing of additional information from the parents and other potentially relevant informants is often as important as interviewing the patient. This is obviously related to the patient's consciously or unconsciously withholding relevant historical and/or motivationally important information that others may be more willing or able to address. It is clearly important for the clinician to define this exploration in supportive terms, so that potentially helpful informants do not become alienated by what they perceive as an attempt to stigmatize or dismiss the patient's symptoms.

Characteristic behavioral features of patients with both factitious disorders and malingering include evasiveness, truculence, and manipulativeness. In the hospital setting one may observe a propensity for splitting, as manifested by playing on the sympathies of some staff members while angrily denigrating or threatening others. These features often become more pronounced as patients sense that their fabrications have been recognized.

In cases of malingering, the somatizing behavior tends to clear as soon as the recognizable goal is either attained for finally perceived by the patient to be clearly unattainable. With factitious disorders, by contrast, somatizing behavior tends to persist or recur independent of immediate consequences or irrefutable confrontation regarding the fabrications involved.

Psychometric Evaluation

Learning disabilities or other intellectual limitations that may not have been previously recognized by parents, teachers, or the evaluating clinician can be documented by formal psychometric testing. Delineation of such learning difficulties can be extremely helpful, both in understanding the evolution of the somatizing disorder and in formulating an appropriate treatment plan.

Projective tests, such as the Rorschach and the Thematic Apperception Test, may add observations that reinforce the clinician's own impressions, since they represent a standardized, structured form of clinical interview. In comparison with patients having other "neurotic" syndromes, those with somatoform disorder tend to give test responses that are freer and more imaginative, accompanied by more labile affect and a tendency toward impulsiveness. In the case of factitious disorders, projective tests have commonly yielded profiles suggestive of borderline personality organization.

Some psychological tests, such as the MMPI, have "lie scales" that may support clinical suspicions in cases of factitious disorders and malingering. Again, however, these scales might also implicate patients with somatoform disorders, who commonly make use of denial as a defense mechanism.

TREATMENT

Many different treatment approaches have been used with children and adolescents with somatizing disorders. As with most psychotherapeutic interventions (Frank et al. 1978), controlled studies are extremely difficult to implement, and such studies are simply not available for this group of disorders. Those therapeutic approaches that clinical experience has found useful will be considered here. Each of these treatment approaches has some potential value for some patients. Often, different treatment approaches can be effectively combined in the management of a given patient. It is consequently advantageous for the clinician to be as well informed about as many of these approaches as possible, to be able innovatively to structure a treatment plan that most effectively meets the unique needs of each patient.

Reassurance, Placebo, and Suggestion

Variations on this theme have been used throughout history, sometimes quite successfully, by religious healers, physicians, and others, as a way of relieving the symptoms of somatizing disorders. This approach involves the use of reassurance, placebo, and/or suggestion to foster symptom relinquishment without generating a sophisticated grasp, by contemporary psychiatric standards, of the symptom's psychogenic determinants. Traditionally, this has involved the invocation of supernatural healing forces and/or the exorcism of nefarious illness-producing forces so as to restore the patient to health. Frequently, the use of prayer or an associated religious ceremony is involved, for which the patient and/or family makes some monetary or other contribution as part of a process of expiation of sin or appeasement of the deity. In a more secular context, the use of placebo can serve a comparable function in mobilizing the positive expectation and belief of the patient that relief of illness will be forthcoming thanks to the powerful forces of pharmacological intervention that the scientific revolution has generated. It should be noted in passing that more recent studies have clarified the capacity of placebo to affect neurophysiological functioning by activating the release of endorphins within the central nervous system, so that dismissing this process as "merely suggestion" is unwarranted. The use of these nonspecific modalities often employed by pediatricians and other medical practitioners prior to referral for psychiatric consultation may be effective for the relief of acute conversion symptoms that arise in response to a short-term and self-limited environmental stress. When used supportively and sensitively in such a setting, this approach may be not only effective in symptom relief but also judicious in sparing the patient and family an expensive involvement in unnecessary psychotherapy.

Complications arise, however, when this treatment approach is used indiscriminately for all somatizing disorders, including those symptoms with complex, sustained intrapsychic determinants and/or in the presence of continuing, unmanageable environmental stress. In such situations, this approach is counterproductive. Here, it will be either totally ineffective or of only short-term benefit, with prompt emergence of symptom recurrence or substitution. Furthermore, there is a loss of confidence by the patient and family in the clinician who takes such an approach. This is so because an attempt has been made to remove a symptom that has been serving a defensive function, albeit maladaptively, without an effort to alleviate the patient's underlying sources of distress.

Individual and Family Therapies

Only brief discussion of these approaches can be outlined here. It should be noted, however, that they draw primarily on the conceptual frameworks outlined earlier in this chapter in the section dealing with etiology. Since a myriad of intermingling etiological factors may pertain, it behooves the clinician to address as many of the pertinent issues as possible in the course of history taking. Based on a thorough exploration of relevant factors in this context, a working hypothesis regarding the evolution of the somatizing disorder is likely to emerge. With this working hypothesis in mind, the clinician's next task is to explore possible ways to alleviate pathogenic environmental influences impinging on the patient and/or to augment the patient's capacity for mastering ongoing intrapsychic distress.

Alleviating environmental stress often involves working with the patient's immediate family and significant others, such as teachers. If marital conflict between the parents is apparently contributing to the youngster's somatization, for example,

direct counseling of the parents should be considered regarding their marital adjustment and more appropriate ways of communicating with their child about it. Similarly, if a "valedictorian syndrome" exists whereby parents, teachers, and/or the
patient himself have generated excessive demands for academic achievement relative to the youngster's actual intellectual capacity, then direct, supportive counseling
of both the patient and family as well as communication with teachers may be needed
in order to alleviate this frequent contributant to somatization. As another example,
if sexual abuse or seduction has occurred as a precipitating factor, clearly the protection of the patient from the perpetrator as well as supportive alleviation of associated feelings of guilt and/or violation are essential ingredients in the treatment plan.

Dealing with the apparent dynamics of intrapsychic conflict in youngsters with
somatizing disorder requires tact and sensitivity. It is useful to view the somatizing
symptom as a makeshift refuge to which the patient has intuitively and sometimes
unconsciously retreated under duress. The clinician is challenged to formulate for
the patient and family a safe and honorable route by which the symptom can be
understood as a maladaptive defense encumbrance that can be relinquished with
dignity in favor of a more effective coping method. There are many ways to do this,
but the clinician commonly presents some version of his working hypothesis to the
patient and the parents to aid the process of cognitive, emotional, and behavioral
reorientation. The extent to which this process can be "worked through" with the
patient and parents in terms of conscious understanding of the relevant dynamics
is variable.

In the pursuit of the above noted therapeutic goals, several specialized treatment approaches are often helpful in the context of individual and/or family therapy. Some of these will be briefly noted.

PSYCHOANALYSIS

From the time of Freud's initial exploration of the dynamics of hysteria until
recently, it was believed by many that psychoanalysis or intensive long-term dynamic psychotherapy were the specific treatments of choice for both somatoform
disorders and, presumably, factitious disorders as well. It is now apparent that only
a minority of the total number of patients with these disorders are candidates for
such therapy. This is true in part because of the combined demands of time, money,
and intellectual investment, which most patients and families simply do not have.
Equally important, however, is the fact that for many patients, other approaches
can achieve therapeutic results more rapidly and with much less expense.

In treating somatoform disorders, the psychoanalytic approach advocates uncovering the presumed neurotic conflict that led to the disorder and, as a result of
this uncovering, helping the patient to reconvert (Anthony 1975). In the case of
conversion symptoms, the decoding of the unconscious meaning of the symptom
through interpretation is said to induce progressive alterations in the transference
relationship and in the symptoms, until the work of reconstruction pieces together

the historical development of the symptom, making use of dreams and fantasies as an adjunct.

Clearly, psychiatrists who work with children and adolescents having somatizing disorders must have a sophisticated grasp of the subtle and complex factors involved in the diverse intrapsychic, interpersonal, and environmental fields that impinge on these patients. It is not necessary, however, for each patient to attain a full level of insight in order to achieve effective and sustained symptom relief. Extended analytic work can certainly add new dimensions of self-understanding for those with the resources to use this approach. Yet for the many who for various reasons cannot or do not wish to do so, more supportive and directive methods of treatment are more appropriate.

HYPNOSIS

Freud's interest in developing the technique of psychoanalysis was heavily influenced by the limitations he observed both in his colleagues and his own use of hypnosis to treat hysteria (Freud 1955a). These limitations included the narrow use of abreaction and suggestion without benefit of the dynamic understanding of symptom formation that Freud was subsequently to develop. Freud himself in later years foresaw how public health needs would rekindle a need for hypnosis to enable more widespread therapeutic application of psychoanalytic insights in a more expeditious manner (Freud 1955b).

Further considerations regarding the use of hypnosis with children and adolescents having somatoform disorders are outlined in Chapter 54. Admonitions sometimes expressed against the use of hypnosis with such youngsters are based on the erroneous assumption that hypnosis necessarily involves the simplistic and heavy-handed use of direct suggestion that was the usual mode of Freud's contemporaries. Furthermore, there are some positive benefits to enabling a patient and family to learn that the patient's capacity for dissociation can be elicited under controlled therapeutic conditions. In this context, the dissociation that is an essential ingredient in the symptom formation of somatoform disorders can be clearly understood by the patient and family as a manageable psychological attribute that can be channeled, under therapeutic auspices, in the service of symptom alleviation. Teaching the patient a self-hypnosis exercise can help shift the youngster's and family's attention away from preoccupation with the sick role and toward the mastery experience of returning to normal functioning.

BEHAVIOR MODIFICATION

Therapeutic strategies geared to symptom alleviation in the somatizing disorders must deal with the "secondary gain" features of the symptoms. (In the case of malingering, these are equivalent to the primary gain features.) With children and adolescents especially, the long-range benefits of a therapeutic endeavor may be difficult for the patient to appreciate if the immediate benefits of the symptom constitute a substantial deterrent to symptom relinquishment. It is therefore essential that any ongoing secondary gain features of a symptom be diminished or eliminated. Indeed, this is crucial if the symptom's removal is to be sustained. Chapter 53 of this text illustrates a number of ways in which behavior modification strategies can be formulated, taking into account the existing contingencies of reinforcement that impinge on the patient.

PHYSICAL THERAPY

Although physical therapy does include some features of reassurance, placebo, and suggestion when used in treating patients with somatizing disorders, it does have noteworthy benefits in clinical practice, particularly for patients where motor deficits are involved. This is especially true if the somatizing symptom arises as a complication of an actual illness or injury. Obviously, to be most effective such physical therapy should be combined with a psychological strategy that addresses pertinent psychodynamic issues and external contingencies of reinforcement that affect the symptoms. When this is done, however, physical therapy often provides a face-saving maneuver that the youngster can use as a supportive bridge to honorable resumption of normal functioning.

MEDICATION

As implied above, medications have frequently been used as the key element in a placebo-based treatment approach to the somatizing disorders. There are, however, situations in which medication can have a specific role to play when somatizing disorders arise in conjunction with associated psychiatric conditions for which medication is particularly indicated. One such condition is school refusal (or other variants of separation anxiety disorder), in which case imipramine or other tricyclic antidepressant medication is often effective as a key component of the treatment plan (Wiener 1985). As noted above, other conditions that may predispose to and/or accompany the somatizing disorders are depression and pathological grief reactions. In these instances, tricyclic antidepressant medication should also be considered when initial psychotherapeutic efforts are ineffective. The merits of minor tranquilizers for the adjunctive treatment of associated generalized anxiety disorders should also be noted.

There is no rational basis for using neuroleptic medications in the treatment of somatizing disorders in the absence of psychotic symptoms. If there is clearly documented evidence that a youngster has a schizophrenic disorder or other psychotic disorder upon which substrate somatizing symptoms may be secondarily superimposed, the psychotic disorder itself becomes the primary focus of therapeutic concern, with the somatizing symptoms being treated as a secondary manifestation.

SUPPORTIVE REALITY TESTING

Even the most patient of clinicians will encounter some patients and families where extensive supportive therapeutic endeavor geared toward symptom alleviation is defeated by the tenacious investment the patient and/or family have made in the reality and sometimes the incurability of the presenting symptoms. Clinical experience suggests that this is more commonly the case when a somatizing disorder has become chronic and has gone through a long series of extensive medical evaluations and interventions, sometimes also accompanied by unavailing psychotherapeutic interventions. In these cases, the somatizing disorder often appears to be interwoven with an associated personality disorder, variably involving dependent, histrionic, antisocial, masochistic, or borderline features. In such situations the degree of family psychopathology is often greater, frequently constituting a substantial source of resistance to treatment. These circumstances are particularly common in patients with somatization disorder, factitious disorder, and malingering. In such circumstances, one clearly must take cognizance of an associated personality disorder as part of one's clinical assessment and treatment planning. Such patients, initially unwilling to explore somatizing aspects of their illness, may be willing to address features of anxiety, depression, or other dysphoric symptoms that can be the starting point for therapeutic work. Some patients and families will, however, be unengageable in treatment despite the most flexible and extended efforts. If parental mistreatment and/or unengageability in treatment is documented, court action and/or the involvement of child welfare services may be necessary.

CONCLUSION

The somatizing disorders, under a variety of diagnostic labels and viewed through a variety of theoretical frameworks, have presented challenges in both diagnosis and treatment to physicians and psychotherapists throughout the ages. Evidence available to date suggests that these are a multidetermined set of disorders, with the consequent need for a sophisticated assessment by the clinician of both the patient's psychological state and coexisting family and other environmental stresses. Of necessity, effective treatment requires that the clinician have a capacity to integrate several therapeutic avenues of approach so as to meet most effectively the unique needs of each patient and family. There is substantial basis to advocate strongly early intervention with children and adolescents manifesting any of the somatizing disorders, as chronicity can breed intractability in the conscious or unconscious devotion to illness as a way of life.

REFERENCES

Adams, P. L. (1979). Psychoneuroses. In J. Noshpitz (Ed.). *Basic Handbook of Child Psychiatry*, Vol 2. New York: Basic Books, pp. 194–234.

Anthony, E. J. (1975). Neurotic disorders in children. In A. M. Freedman, H. I. Kaplan, and B. J. Sadock (Eds.). *Comprehensive Textbook of Psychiatry*, Vol. 2. Baltimore: Williams and Wilkins.

Caplan, H. L. (1972). A study of hysteria in childhood. M. Phil. dissertation, University of London.

Ernst, A. R., Routh, D. K., and Harper, D. C. (1984). Abdominal pain in children and symptoms of somatization disorder. *J. Ped. Psychol.* 9:77–86.

Flor-Henry, P. (1983). *Cerebral Basis of Psychopathology.* Boston: John Wright.

Ford, C. V. (1983). *The Somatizing Disorders: Illness as a Way of Life.* New York: Elsevier Biomedical.

Frank, J. D., et al. (1978). *Effective Ingredients of Successful Psychotherapy.* New York: Brunner/Mazel.

Frankel, F. H. (1976). *Hypnosis: Trance as a Coping Mechanism.* New York: Plenum Press.

Freud, S. (1955a). An autobiographical study. In J. Strachey (Ed.). *The Standard Edition of the Complete Psychological Works of Sigmund Freud*, Vol 20. London: Hogarth Press, pp. 3–74.

———. (1955b). Lines of advance in psychoanalytic therapy. In J. Strachey (Ed.). *The Standard Edition of the Complete Psychological Works of Sigmund Freud*, Vol 17. London: Hogarth Press, pp. 159–68.

Goodyear, I. (1981). Hysterical conversion reactions in childhood. *J. Child Psychol. Psychiat.* 22:179–88.

Herman, J., and Hirschman, L. (1981). Families at risk for father-daughter incest. *Amer. J. Psychiat.* 138:967–70.

Herman, R. M., and Simmonds, J. R. (1975). Incidence of conversion symptoms in children evaluated psychiatrically. *Missouri Med.* 72:597–604.

Hersov, L. (1977). Emotional disorders. In M. Rutter and L. Hersov (Eds.). *Child Psychiatry—Modern Approaches.* Oxford: Blackwell Scientific Pubs.

Klerman, G. L. (1982). Hysteria and depression. In A. Roy (Ed.). *Hysteria.* New York: Wiley, pp. 211–28.

Lesser, R. P., and Fahn, S. (1978). Dystonia: A disorder often misdiagnosed as a conversion reaction. *Amer. J. Psychiat.* 135:349–52.

Maloney, M. J. (1980). Diagnosing hysterical conversion reactions in children. *J. Pediatrics* 97:1016–20.

Meadow, R. (1982). Munchausen syndrome by proxy. *Arch. Dis. Child.* 57:92–98.

Nemiah, J. C. (1985). Somatoform disorders. In H. I. Kaplan and B. J. Sadock (Eds.). *Comprehensive Textbook of Psychiatry.* 4th Ed. Vol. 2. Baltimore: Williams and Wilkins, pp. 924–41.

Proctor, J. (1958). Hysteria in childhood. *Amer. J. Orthopsychiat.* 23:394–406.

Rae, W. A. (1977). Childhood conversion reactions: A review of incidence in pediatric settings. *J. Clin. Child Psychol.* 6:69–72.

Regan, J., and LaBarbera, J. D. (1984). Lateralization of conversion symptoms in children and adolescents. *Amer. J. Psychiat.* 141:1279–80.

Robins, E., and O'Neal, P. (1953). Clinical features of hysteria in children with a note on prognosis. *Nervous Child* 10:246–71.

Rock, N. L. (1971). Conversion reactions in childhood: A clinical study on childhood neuroses. *J. Amer. Acad. Child Psychiat.* 10:65–93.

Sheffield, H. B. (1898). A contribution to the study of hysteria in childhood (as it occurs in the U.S.A.). *N.Y. Med. J.* 412–16.

Sloane, R. B., Stapes, F. R., and Cristol, A. H. (1975). *Psychotherapy vs. Behavior Therapy.* Cambridge: Harvard University Press.

Spiegel, D., and Fink, R. (1979). Hysterical psychosis and hypnotizability, *Amer. J. Psychiat.* 136:777–81.

Spiegel, H., and Spiegel, D. (1978). *Trance and Treatment: Clinical Uses of Hypnosis.* New York: Basic Books.

Volkmar, F. R., Poll, J., and Lewis, M. (1984). Conversion reactions in childhood and adolescence. *J. Amer. Acad. Child Psychiat.* 23:424–30.

Weintraub, M. I. (1977). Hysteria: A clinical guide to diagnosis. *Clin. Symptosia* (Vol. 29, No. 6). Summit, N.J.: CIBA.

Wiener, J. M. (Ed.). (1985). *Diagnosis and Psychopharmacology of Childhood and Adolescent Disorders.* New York: Wiley.

Williams, D. T. (1985). Somatoform disorders. In D. Shaffer, A. Ehrhardt, and L. Greenhill (Eds.). *The Clinical Guide to Child Psychiatry.* New York: The Free Press, pp. 192–207.

———, Spiegel, H., and Mostofsky, D. I. (1978). Neurogenic and hysterical seizures in children and adolescents: Differential diagnostic and therapeutic considerations. *Amer. J. Psychiat.* 135:82–86.

———, et al. (1979). The impact of psychiatric intervention on patients with uncontrolled seizures. *J. Nerv. Mental Dis.* 167:626–31.

———, and Mostofsky, D. I. (1982). Psychogenic seizures in children and adolescents. In T. Riley and A. Roy (Eds.). *Pseudoseizures.* Baltimore: Williams and Wilkins, pp. 169–84.

Yudofsky, S. (1985). Malingering. In H. I. Kaplan and B. J. Sadock (Eds.). *Comprehensive Textbook of Psychiatry.* 4th Ed., Vol 2. Baltimore: Williams and Wilkins, pp. 1862–64.

36

PSYCHOLOGICAL FACTORS INFLUENCING MEDICAL CONDITIONS

Boris Rubinstein

INTRODUCTION

The interaction between psychological factors and medical conditions has captured the interest of psychiatrists for many years. More recently, increased attention has been given to the interactions between psychological and biological conditions, highlighting the need to understand disorders in both of these areas through a comprehensive approach. A case in point is discussed by Graham (1985a), who pointed out that although there is a clear association between smoking and heart disease and smoking and lung cancer, both illnesses are biological events, whereas the antecedent, smoking, is a psychologically based event. Thus, the study of smoking behaviors is relevant to the understanding of both illnesses, to their prevention, and perhaps ultimately to their treatment. On the other side of the spectrum lies a disorder such as delinquency, in which social and environmental factors appear to play a major role. More recent work, however, suggests the presence of biological factors associated with delinquency, as evidenced by the high incidence of delinquency in adoption studies where the determinant of delinquency in the offspring was not the adoptive family but the biological family: Children of delinquent parents tended to become delinquent even when reared apart (Crowe 1974). Thus, the understanding of both psychological and biological factors is relevant to the understanding of disease.

The clinical assessment of psychological factors that influence medical conditions needs to consider the child, his illness, and the social milieu in which the child lives: his family, his school, and his particular medical environment.

PSYCHIATRIC DISORDERS IN MEDICALLY ILL CHILDREN

Children with chronic physical illnesses have been reported to have higher rates of psychiatric disorder than children without a chronic handicap. The data to support this assumption come from several epidemiological surveys (Pless and Roghmann 1971; Haggerty et al. 1975; Rutter et al. 1970). The first of these surveys, the British National Survey of Health and Development (Douglas and Blomfield 1958) is a prospective study of a representative sample of five thousand children born in the United Kingdom during the first week in March of 1946. The subjects were studied every two years and systematic information was collected on educational progress, behavior in and out of school, parental attitudes, home circumstances, and hospital admissions. They observed that 25 percent of the physically ill children under the age of 15 had two or more symptoms of behavior disorder, compared to 17 percent in the healthy population. The second of the surveys, the Rochester Child Health Survey (Haggerty et al. 1975; Pless and Douglas 1971), looked at a representative sample of children under the age of 18 years living in an upstate New York county. Through parent interviews and later through professional assessment, they identified two hundred six children who had chronic physical disorders and matched them with healthy controls. The rates of behavior deviance in the chronically ill children were consistently higher and were reflected in behaviors such as poor attitudes toward school and truancy. The third of these epidemiological surveys, the Isle of Wight Study (Rutter et al. 1970), is a total population survey of 9- to 10-year-olds in a defined geographic area. The children were interviewed by psychiatrists, assessed by pediatricians, and subjected to a battery of psychological tests. The parents were systematically assessed regarding behavioral symptoms in the children and the presence of marital dysfunction. The teachers were requested to fill out behavioral questionnaires. Rutter and his colleagues (1970) found that 6 percent of the population suffered from a chronic physical illness. The prevalence rate of psychiatric disorder in the general population was approximately 7 percent. They also found that the prevalence rate of psychiatric disorder in children with chronic physical illness but without brain lesions was about 12 percent, and the rate of behavior deviance in children with brain damage was three times higher: 34 percent. From these surveys we can conclude that children with physical illnesses have higher rates of behavior deviance than healthy controls and that central nervous system involvement significantly increases the likelihood of a psychiatric disorder. Further support for this notion comes from other studies such as the findings of Cantwell et al. (1980) that 53 percent of children with language disorders had a psychiatric diagnosis and those of Birch et al. (1970) suggesting that children with psychiatric abnormalities had high rates of neurological findings.

These studies clearly suggest that as a group chronically ill children, particularly those with central nervous system (CNS) pathology, are more likely to suffer from psychiatric disorders; however, there are other aspects of chronic illness that can have an impact on the *individual child:* stressful life events, repeated separations from home, lengthy hospitalizations, parental overprotectiveness, and frequent school absences. Often children can be isolated from peers because of feelings of embarrassment due to their illness or their physical appearance (e.g., facial disfigurement in burns or baldness after chemotherapy in leukemia) or can be limited in peer activities because of fatigue (e.g., chronic renal failure or cardiac diseases) or the scheduling of courses of treatment (e.g., chemotherapy or dialysis).

PSYCHOLOGICAL FACTORS INFLUENCING PHYSICAL CONDITIONS

The notion that specific types of psychological conflicts are expressed through characteristic physical symptoms, much in vogue in the early history of psychosomatic medicine, is not a widely held belief today. The more contemporary view, reflected in the current diagnostic classification of DSM-III (1980), is that in the presence of a physical illness, or when there is a biological predisposition for such a disorder, psychological factors may precipitate, worsen, or modify the expression of such an illness. This formulation moves away from the concept of the specific "psychophysiological disorders" that was reflected in the old diagnostic classifications—such as DSM-II—and broadens the psychiatric concept of the interaction between "psyche" and "soma." This approach has some theoretical as well as practical implications. Theoretically, one does not have to invoke psychodynamic mechanisms that cannot be empirically validated. Similarly, the search for "the unconscious meaning" of psychosomatic symptoms, not necessarily a productive therapeutic endeavor, can be abandoned in order to explore, in an empirical and open-minded fashion, the way in which psychological factors may affect a physical illness.

In medically ill children, psychological factors may influence their physical condition in two ways: by maintaining maladaptive illness behaviors or by exacerbating physical symptoms. In a study of pain in children, Oster (1972) pointed out how "pain behavior" is learned and subsequently reinforced in social situations. The child in pain may learn patterns of behavior or coping strategies that may provide immediate relief of suffering or help obtain attention or sympathy. These behaviors, however, may be counterproductive to long-term recovery.

CASE VIGNETTE

A.B., an 8-year-old girl, was admitted to the hospital with severe abdominal pain of two months duration. The pain was so severe that she stopped attending school, refused to sleep alone and spent nights in her parents' bed, slept poorly even with them, and was unable to participate in any age-appropriate activities. The pain started after several environmental stresses: Grandfather developed a painful back condition, grandmother was diagnosed as having breast cancer, and a close uncle died suddenly at home.

The medical work-up failed to disclose any organic cause for the pain, but any suggestion that there could be a psychological factor affecting the experience of pain was quickly dismissed by A.B., though not by her parents.

After a child psychiatrist explained to the parents that the clinical picture was compatible with separation anxiety and described the many affective components to her pain, he presented A.B. the following idea: Whatever had caused the onset of her pain had now disappeared. The pediatricians did not find any evidence that a "bad disease" was lingering on. However, she was told, pain fibers are "dumb" and once they become activated it is hard for them to stop. A rationale was given to her for the need to "break the vicious cycle," and a treatment program was developed using relaxation training for pain control, gradually increasing her physical activity and tolerance for exercise, family therapy to discuss the many stresses the family was experiencing, and tricyclic antidepressants to control her anxiety symptoms. As her pain began to remit, she was able to participate fully in the family discussions and to understand the connection between her psychological state and her physical symptom. After one week the pain decreased in intensity and by the fourth week the pain had completely disappeared. At a six-month follow-up, she remained free of pain and was back in school.

A similar pattern can be observed frequently in many medical conditions that are characterized by periodic exacerbations. Thus, a symptom that was originally produced by a pathophysiological event may be maintained by a different set of stimuli that may include its psychological antecedents or its psychological consequences.

CASE VIGNETTE

J.K. was a 15-year-old adolescent boy with juvenile diabetes mellitus who had been admitted to the hospital on numerous occasions because of diabetic ketoacidosis. He lived with his 20-year-old sister and a younger brother. His sister was the family's caretaker as his mother had died of cancer the year before. The father had deserted the family when J.K. was a young child and saw them sporadically. J.K. appeared as a chronically depressed boy with many thoughts and feelings of unresolved grief.

During his many hospital admissions, his diabetes was always easily controlled. J.K. had developed many attachments to the hospital and its staff. After a few days in the hospital he seemed happier, more relaxed, and able to participate in recreational activities. However, every time his discharge became imminent, he would start spilling ketones and would develop ketoacidosis. This pattern was evident regardless of the length of time in the hospital and apparently was not related to compliance with diet or his insulin regimen.

In cases similar to this one, Baker and Barcai (1970) reported on a small group of girls with "super-labile" diabetes. In these patients it appeared that "emotional arousal'' led easily to recurrent episodes of diabetic ketoacidosis (DKA). They suggested that those patients experienced augmented ketones in response to their endogenous catecholamines. Therefore, stress or emotional arousal would increase pituitary ACTH as well as catecholamine excretion. As a consequence, there would be a decrement in insulin production and a rise in free fatty acids. Support for this possibility was found when beta adrenergic blocking drugs appeared to inhibit this process. Even though biological explanations have a certain appeal, it is important to remember that noncompliance with insulin treatment is the single most important cause of diabetic ketoacidosis (Wilkinson 1981).

The child psychiatrist working in a medical setting needs to be alert to the many factors that can influence the course of a physical disorder.

SPECIFIC CONDITIONS

Noncompliance

Noncompliance with medical treatments, including not taking medications as prescribed, failure to return for follow-up visits, or failure to follow a diet or a therapeutic exercise program, is a serious problem in medicine and specifically in the care of children with chronic illness. Estimates in adults suggest that the rates of noncompliance range from 33 percent to 82 percent depending on the nature of the medical intervention (Dunbar and Agras 1980). In pediatrics noncompliance with medical regimen appears to be a frequent reason for recurrence of asthmatic attacks or seizures and perhaps an important determinant in some cases of recurrent hospitalizations.

The clinician needs to take into account several variables that affect compliance: personal characteristics of the primary care physician, such as warmth and empathy; the manner in which appointments are made; the seriousness and length of the illness; the complexity of a medication regimen; the manner in which patient and family understand the illness and its treatment; the level of intelligence of the patient and his caretakers.

CASE VIGNETTE

P.M., the 9-year-old daughter of a Spanish-speaking immigrant, suffered from intractable asthma. Shortly after every admission for severe status asthmaticus, P.M.'s lungs cleared rapidly; in the hospital her asthma appeared easy to manage and after a few days she seemed to experience no respiratory discomfort. However, a few days after discharge she would start wheezing again and would require admission to the hospital for control of her respiratory distress. A psychiatric examination of P.M. was requested by the treating pediatrician to explore the psychological factors affecting the physical illness. During the interview, P.M. appeared as a pleasant, engaging child showing only mild symptoms of separation anxiety. The most striking finding during the interview was P.M.'s lack of understanding of her disease. When P.M.'s mother was interviewed, she appeared as a simple but caring woman, who had no understanding of P.M.'s disease. Because of language difficulties, she did not understand that asthma was a chronic illness that needed long-term medications. She believed asthma was a transitory condition "like a cold," and eventually P.M. would "grow out of it." It took several sessions to explain to P.M.'s mother the meaning of the illness and the role that breathing exercises and compliance with the medical regimen have in the treatment of asthma. After this explanation, there was a reduction in the number of P.M.'s admissions to the hospital. This case illustrates the complex interactions between the course of an illness, the family's understanding of that illness, and their compliance with treatment.

When evaluating noncompliance, the clinician assumes that the conditions needed to maintain adherence to a medical regimen are not present, and he has to restructure the environment so that it supports appropriate behaviors (Hovanitz et al. 1984). Compliant behaviors, however, are often negative and punishing in their immediate outcome—the pain associated with self-injections for diabetics, the exercise and physical therapy for cerebral palsy, or the dietary restrictions for end-stage renal disease, to name just a few. Although the long-term effects may be rewarding, it is difficult for some children to maintain these behaviors without some supportive intervention. In some cases, the supportive intervention may be tailoring the child's medication regimen so that normal daily activities serve as cues for appropriate treatment behaviors. In others, disease-related cues, such as tightness of the chest or the aura of a seizure, signal the need for early intervention; this requires extensive patient training so that therapeutic maneuvers (i.e., relaxation or self-hypnosis) can be instituted at the early signs. In other children positive reinforcers such as verbal feedback or a token economy (Magrab and Papadopoulou 1977) will be needed to increase the child's cooperation.

In summary, noncompliance with medical treatments is a common occurrence in the treatment of physically ill children. The clinician has to evaluate the child, his family, and the circumstances in which noncompliance occurs to arrive at an appropriate treatment strategy.

Asthma

Asthma is one of the most common chronic illnesses in childhood. It occurs in about 2 percent of the population, and is more common in children than adults and in boys than girls. Asthmatic children should not be viewed as a homogeneous population. Graham and his colleagues (1967) analyzed the data from the Isle of Wight Study and provided some epidemiological evidence for the association of asthma and psychiatric disturbances. They identified 66 children with asthma and compared them with 38 physically handicapped children, 126 children known to have behavioral maladjustment, and a group of healthy controls. There was a striking overrepresentation of asthmatic children in families from higher socioeconomic classes. The rate of psychiatric disturbance was slightly higher in the asthmatic group (11 percent) than in the general population (7 percent). However, children with other physical disorders not involving the central nervous system had rates similar to those of the asthmatic children. There is suggestive evidence that although in its milder forms asthma will not produce serious psychological sequelae, children with severe asthma can experience a high frequency of behavioral difficulties (McNichol et al. 1973).

Asthmatic children have been described as having a defined personality pattern: dependent, sensitive, shy, tense, and inhibited. Neuhaus (1958) compared the personality characteristics of asthmatic, cardiac, and normal children. He found that asthmatics were significantly more maladjusted than normal controls, and their personality traits included anxiety, insecurity, and dependence. However, there were no differences in the personality traits between children with asthma and children with cardiac disease; there were also no differences between the traits exhibited by physically ill children and their normal siblings. This finding casts some doubts on the idea that a characteristic personality pattern is linked to a specific "psychosomatic" disease and also suggests that familial and environmental factors may play a more important role in determining personality traits. Kim et al. (1980) studied the temperamental characteristics of asthmatic children ages 3 to 7. Children with asthma were characterized by lower rhythmicity, lower adaptability, lower intensity of reaction, lower mood, and lower persistence, as compared to normal children and to children with allergies but without asthma. This suggests that children with asthma can be more difficult to manage and to parent.

The role of emotional tension associated with family interactions precipitating asthmatic attacks in susceptible children was studied by Purcell and colleagues (1969). A group of asthmatic children was left at home (thus ensuring continued exposure to the same allergens) while the parents were removed to a different location. Many children showed a definite improvement in their asthma following this "parentectomy." Kanner et al. (1983) described a group of children chronically hospitalized for asthma who experienced wheezing only on weekends during home visits with parents. This suggests that in many children with asthma, an attack can be precipitated by excitement or anxiety.

To clarify further the role of mother-child interaction in the genesis of asthma, Gauthier et al. (1978) studied thirty-five preschool children with milder forms of asthma. At the time of the initial evaluation, the children were 14 to 30 months of age. They were found to be developing normally in all areas, and specifically in areas of autonomy and self-assertion. When they were studied again at 4 to 6 years of age, the majority of mother-child pairs were coping well with the stresses of chronic illness, but a number of conflictual mother-child interactions began to appear. Mrazek et al. (1985) reported on a sample of twenty-six severely asthmatic preschool children compared to twenty-two healthy controls. One-third of the asthmatic children were found to have significant emotional disturbance, with depressive mood, fearfulness, and sleep disturbances as the most predominant characteristics. A number of mothers described the asthmatic children as being difficult to handle and as having temper tantrums. During observation sessions, asthmatic children were found to be confrontive and persistently noncompliant. These two studies suggest that the difficulties that asthmatic children experience and the family's response are secondary to the presence of a chronic illness, and that asthmatic children may benefit form early intervention to help the parents provide consistent and sensitive support for their child. Whether these findings are illness-specific or typical for all chronic illnesses requires further investigation.

Severe asthma can be fatal. The mortality rate among children with severe chronic asthma is high: 1 to 2 percent. To understand the physiological and psychological characteristics associated with death in asthmatic children, Strunk et al. (1985) studied twenty-one patients with severe asthma who died and compared them with twenty-one asthmatics matched for age at the time of hospitalization, sex, and severity of illness. They found that psychological variables such as conflicts between the patient's parents and hospital staff regarding medical management of the patient; self-care of asthma while in the hospital that was not appropriate for the child's age; depressive symptoms; and disregard for asthmatic symptoms played an important role as determinants of mortality risk. Other important physiological factors included history of seizures associated with an asthma attack; prednisone dosage having been decreased by more than 50 percent during the course of hospitalization; and inhaled beclomethasone dipropionate required for treatment. This study indicates that psychological risk factors were prominent in severely asthmatic children who subsequently died of an asthmatic attack. The mechanisms by which these variables lead to death are not clearly understood. However, the variables defined by the study may be important in identifying patients who are at high risk for dying of asthma and in developing appropriate treatment interventions to prevent death in this population.

Chronic Abdominal Pain

Abdominal pain is a very common childhood complaint. Apley (1975) suggested that it affects 10 to 15 percent of schoolchildren at any given time. The presence of abdominal pain does not necessarily reflect gastrointestinal pathology; abdominal pain is a common occurrence in children with emotional disorders and depression. Children with school refusal seem particularly prone to experience recurrent abdominal pain. Rarely, neurological conditions can present with abdominal pain. For instance, episodic abdominal pain associated with nausea, vomiting, other sensory disturbances, and a family history of migraine has been termed "abdominal migraine." Also, the occurrence of recurrent abdominal pain in epileptic children accompanied by an aura, nausea, and vomiting, and followed by somnolence should raise the possibility of "abdominal epilepsy," a rare condition indeed. Children with lactose intolerance or chronic constipation can also present with abdominal pain.

Of interest to the child psychiatrist is the child with chronic abdominal pain where no known organic disease entity can be found to explain the symptoms. Many of these children undergo extensive medical evaluations and hospitalizations, as well as medical and on occasion even surgical treatments. Hughes (1984) reported on twenty-three children hospitalized with recurrent abdominal pain and suggested that the abdominal pain is the manifestation of childhood depression. Hughes used many clinical vignettes to describe his patients. Although there were many depressive themes in the description of these children, it is not clear that they suffered from a major depressive disorder or were experiencing many depressive symptoms. However, equally, if not more prominent, was the presence of separation anxiety themes in the clinical description of the children. To further our understanding of the psychiatric correlates of this syndrome, Hodges et al. (1985), using standardized interviews and questionnaires, studied twenty-five children with recurrent abdominal pain and compared them with sixty-seven behaviorally disordered children and forty-two healthy controls. The children with recurrent abdominal pain did not report any more depressive symptoms than healthy children. Unfortunately, there was no mention in the report of the presence or absence of symptoms of separation anxiety.

Ernst et al. (1984) studied retrospectively the charts of 149 children seen by a pediatric group for complaints of abdominal pain. Of those, 108 children were found to have no significant medical findings. These cases were further subdivided according to the duration and onset of the abdominal pain. The charts were reviewed to determine the presence of other physical symptoms that required a separate medical examination but resulted in no organic findings. For children with functional abdominal pain, symptoms of somatization disorder were found and were correlated with the chronicity of the abdominal pain. Children with functional pain of recent onset had two other symptoms, while children with complaints for more than one year since age 6 had four other symptoms. Similarly, in a long-term follow-up study of children with chronic abdominal pain, Apley and Hale (1973) suggested that between one-third and one-half persist with such pain well into adulthood. These findings are suggestive that recurrent abdominal pain may represent a distinct, chronic polysymptomatic somatization disorder beginning in childhood. Further work is needed to support this conclusion.

It is likely that family factors may play a role in this disorder. Hodges et al. (1985) found that the mothers of children with recurrent abdominal pain reported more depressive symptoms than the mothers of healthy children, with 25 percent of these mothers indicating the presence of at least a mild degree of depression as measured by the Beck Depression Inventory. Hughes (1984) reported that five of the twenty-three mothers he interviewed had a major depressive disorder, and when discussing the child's health, most mothers became anxious, sometimes to the point of panic. Hughes (1984) and Christensen and Mortensen (1975) reported a high frequency of concurrent abdominal symptomatology in the parents of children with chronic abdominal pain. This suggests the possibility that parent-child communication of anxiety and bodily symptoms can play an important role in the causation of this illness (Routh and Ernst 1984).

Renal Disease

Recent advances in medical technology, such as the introduction of hemodialysis and renal transplantation for the treatment of children with end-stage renal disease, have created a new set of problems for the child psychiatric consultant. Korsch et al. (1971) provided a useful clinical description of the psychological experiences of children and families during hemodialysis and kidney transplantation: During the period of renal decompensation the child experiences periods of denial, physical malaise, and depressive affect. The family experiences denial, mourning, and depression. With the onset of hemodialysis, the child and his family experience renewed hope as well as increased well-being and activity levels. The family needs to undergo a period of adaptation to a new lifestyle, since dialysis can last several hours and can occur up to three times in a week. When the possibility of transplantation appears, the family needs to deal with questions about the future and the uncertainties about the suitability of donors. The child fears pain and complications. Transplantation also appears to bring another set of difficulties, from the fear of kidney rejection to complications from the drugs needed to prevent such a rejection. Throughout this time the child and family need guidance and support.

To explore the effects of transplantation in children, Lilly et al. (1971) studied fifty-seven children who underwent renal transplantation. They found that twenty-three children who had a kidney transplant before the age of 12 years suffered no psychiatric sequelae, while two of the thirty-four children transplanted after the age of 12 years committed suicide. Three out of forty survivors had academic difficulties that predated the transplant. Further evidence of a relatively high prevalence of psychiatric disorder in these children comes from Khan et al. (1971). They studied fourteen children with end-stage renal disease, using a semistructured interview. Isolation was a prominent symptom in this sample, as reflected by withdrawal, little contact with peers, and problems with school attendance. Twelve children were depressed, even though their parents thought they were happy, suggesting either denial on the parents' part or poor communication in the family system. Support for this last possibility comes from the same study, in which ten of the families were seen as overprotective, while two were rejecting. There were many problems in the relationships with siblings.

Kaplan De-Nour (1979) reported on eighteen adolescents in chronic hemodialysis and compared them with a group of adult renal patients. As a group, the adolescents were less compliant with medical regimens and more resistant to becoming engaged in vocational rehabilitation. They were more difficult to interview; they did not talk spontaneously, appeared withdrawn and sullen, refused to discuss their illness, and were more preoccupied with their appearance. During dialysis they talked little and slept more than their adult counterparts. Ten adolescents experienced moderately severe depression and anxiety, and two also had suicidal ideations.

Children with end-stage renal disease can have impaired cognitive functioning.

Rasbury et al. (1983) studied children before and after successful transplantation and found that before transplantation, children appeared to have the most difficulty with tasks that involved complex or difficult problem solving. They did not seem to have problems with simple learning tasks or with the ability to pay attention. Successful transplantation resulted in improved problem-solving behavior, most evident in the performance section of the Wechsler Intelligence Scale for Children and the Halstead Reitan Category Test.

Life Events

Greene and Miller (1958) studied the association that stressful life events, such as experiences of separation and loss, played in the development of leukemia in children. They discovered that children with leukemia experienced frequent losses in the two-year period preceding the onset of their disease; half of these experiences occurred in the six months prior to the diagnosis.

This finding led other investigators to ask whether life events were specific for the production of malignancies or whether stress acted as a nonspecific etiological factor in this as well as in other conditions. To answer this question in part, Coddington (1972) studied the effects of stress on children at varying ages. He was able to derive a Life Event Score that gives a numerical value (from 0 to 100) to different stressful events, taking into account the developmental stage of the child. Thus, the loss of a job by a parent carries a score of twenty-three for a preschool child, but a score of forty-eight for a young adolescent in junior high school. This life events scale has been shown to have a high degree of interrater agreement for the occurrence of such events. Heisel and associates (1973) looked at the association of life events and the onset of juvenile rheumatoid arthritis, admission to a general pediatric inpatient ward, admission for appendectomy and herniorrhaphy, and admission to the child psychiatry outpatient service. In all of those groups, the children experienced two to three times as many stressful life events as did their healthy peers. Life events have also been found significant in other studies. Jacobs and Charles (1980) showed that certain life events occurred with greater frequency in the year prior to the discovery of malignancy in children as compared to controls, and Morillo and Gardner (1979) suggested that bereavement may play a role as an antecedent in children with thyrotoxicosis.

There are several difficulties in the interpretation of these studies (Graham 1985b). First, the retrospective assessment of life events may induce an element of bias. As a person tries to integrate and adjust to a catastrophic event such as cancer or a hospital admission, he may try to find an explanation of its occurrence by focusing on other determinants such as life stresses; while a person who is not in need of a major psychological adaptation may not recall otherwise "important" life events. Second, although the Life Event Score assigns an absolute numerical value to an event, it is conceivable that the relative value is more important in the production of psychophysiological derangements in the organism that may contribute to the production of a disease state. Thus, we need to take into consideration the personal meaning and significance of the event for the child. For instance, divorce or separation, which carries a score of 78 for a nonabused child in elementary school, would be experienced differently in a family where there is child abuse and the marital separation brings about an end to the situation of abuse. Third, the retrospective assessment could induce some confusion between very early clinical manifestations of a disease and an antecedent life event. For instance, if a child fails in school because of severe misbehavior and later on is found to have a metabolic disorder, could the decrement of school performance be a consequence of his metabolic abnormality instead of an antecedent?

A pioneer study by Meyer and Haggerty (1962) lends evidence to the notion that there may be a link between stress and the onset of medical illnesses. They studied prospectively one hundred children from sixteen families for one year. Every two weeks they cultured the children's throats for streptococci, and the families kept a diary of upsetting events. In the two weeks before an infection there was a marked increase of upsetting events; although only one-quarter of streptococcal infections were preceded by stressful events, the risk of an infection increased severalfold after a stress. Although further work is needed in this area, it appears to be a very fruitful avenue for further research.

FAMILY INFLUENCES

It has been well established that family factors are important in the production of psychiatric disorders in children. Similarly, the presence of a medical illness in a child, specifically a chronic disease, can decrease the family's tolerance for social stress and increase the risk for the development of psychiatric disorder.

Parental reactions to handicapping conditions can influence the child's psychiatric state and his adjustment to a physical illness. Solnit and Stark (1961) described the reaction of parents to the birth of a handicapped child. The similarities of this reaction to bereavement are striking. After an initial period of shock and denial, the parents go through a period of guilt, anger (often directed at the medical staff), and sadness, followed by adaptation and reorganization. Even though these reactions were described after the birth of a handicapped infant, similar reactions occur in parents of children who develop either a catastrophic or a chronic illness later in life (Friedman et al. 1963).

The adaptation of parents to a handicap in their child is not an event that occurs only once in a lifetime. A birthday or the anniversary of the original diagnosis or hospitalization, as well as transitions, such as a second child moving from kindergarten to grade school or from high school to college, or a wedding will evoke in the parents the feelings and memories of the original traumatic event. The parents will need to mobilize their psychological resources each time to enable them to go through another adaptive cycle of guilt, sadness, anger, and resolution, whose intensity may vary depending on the life circumstances of the family.

The psychosocial factors that contribute to disharmony and breakdown in the families of ill children are not completely understood. Dorner (1975) studied the families of sixty-three children with myelomeningocele and found that marital disharmony and breakdown did not occur more frequently than in the general population. In the five cases where the marriage broke up, the mothers did not consider that the presence of the handicapped child had brought about difficulties with the husband. On the other hand, Gath and Gumley (1984) found that marital disharmony and breakdown were more frequent in the families of children with Down syndrome than in a group of normal controls. Whether the disharmony is related to the severity of the handicap or to chronicity is not clear. Dorner (1975) found no correlation between severity of the handicap and poor marital relations. However, Hoare (1984) found an association between psychiatric disturbance in the child and increased psychiatric morbidity in the mothers of children with chronic epilepsy. This suggests the possibility of a transactional model where chronicity of a condition may have an adverse effect on the family's psychological health and in turn will affect the child's behavior and adaptation. Further elucidation of the factors that play a role in marital breakdown is necessary.

Family factors may play an important role in the course of a medical illness. Depression, isolation, and the ability of parents to cope play a significant role in the production of psychiatric disorders among children with medical illnesses. This transactional effect seems evident in several studies. Gath and associates (1980) found high rates of family disharmony in a group of diabetic children whose diabetes was out of control. This group of children had higher rates of psychiatric disorder as compared to children with stable diabetes. Fishman and Fishman (1971) found striking correlations between self-esteem and adjustment in young adolescents with birth defects and the mothers' ability to cope with their children's handicaps. This transaction affects not only the children, but the parents as well. Dorner (1975) found that mothers of adolescents with spina bifida had more depressive symptoms than mothers of normal children, and Minde (1978) found that parents and siblings of cerebral-palsied adolescents tended to withdraw from them. Hoare (1984) showed a similar association with psychiatric disturbance in the parents of children with chronic epilepsy. Haggerty (1980) reported on the positive effects of parental counseling on the psychological health of the child; the study suggests that the brain-injured child is unusually sensitive to his parents' emotional state. The temperamental characteristics of the child may also adversely influence the parents' reactions in such a way as to increase further its disadvantage. Diamond and Jaudes (1983) found that children with brain damage constitute a high-risk group for child abuse. In summary, children with brain damage may be more susceptible to social stresses and family disharmony.

The siblings of chronically ill children seem to be more at risk for the development of emotional disorders. Hoare (1984) showed that siblings of children with chronic epilepsy had higher rates of psychiatric disturbance than either those of newly diagnosed epileptic children or of children in the general population. In their study of families in which there were children with Down syndrome, Gath and

Gumley (1984) found that older sisters were more disturbed than the general populations. Breslau and colleagues (1981) studied siblings of chronically handicapped children and found them to have mentation difficulties as well as a higher frequency of behaviors such as fighting and delinquency than a group of controls. The reasons for the increased rates of emotional disturbance in the siblings of handicapped children is not yet clear. The need to develop adaptive coping mechanisms to deal with chronic stress, an inability to tolerate the increased parental attention that chronically ill children receive, feelings of guilt and shame, and the effects of parental psychopathology may all contribute to this increased rate.

PSYCHOLOGICAL EFFECTS OF HOSPITALIZATION

The notion that separations from caretakers can affect the psychological development of children captured the interest of the child-care community during World War II, spurred by the effects of the war on the integrity of families. In the years that followed, claims were made that prolonged separation from parents was an important cause of delinquency, and that daycare centers caused psychological damage. This alarmist view, held by the World Health Organization in 1951, had no support in empirical evidence. Indeed, there are many factors that can determine the appearance of psychiatric disorder following separations from caretakers: the age of the child and the length of the separation, the quality of family life preceding the separation, the presence of alternate caretakers who are warm and responsive to the child's needs, and the child's innate ability to deal with separations.

Robertson (1958), studying the effects of hospitalization in children, and Bowlby (1965), looking at the effects of separations of children from caretakers, concluded that during these events children experience a phenomenon characterized by different phases. Upon separation, children go through a phase called protest, in which they show emotional upset with crying and fear. This is followed by despair, in which the child appears to withdraw from his environment. Then detachment takes place, in which the child settles down in his new environment, the intensity of the emotional reaction decreases, and he becomes again engaged in his environment. For a variable period after returning home, the child may experience sleep difficulties as well as negativism, usually considered a period of testing out parental permanence. Play behavior sometimes displays a reemergence of interest in variants of a "peek-a-boo" game, as if the child begins to master the experience of appearing and disappearing.

To clarify further the long-range effects of hospitalizations, Douglas (1975) used the data from the National Health Survey to study the effects of hospitalization in children. He reported that single hospital admissions of one week or less were not associated with behavior difficulties during adolescence. On the other hand, prolonged or repeated hospitalizations in childhood were associated with an increased risk of behavior disturbance ten years later. Quinton and Rutter (1976) replicated

Douglas's findings using the data from their epidemiological surveys and reached similar conclusions.

It is of course appropriate to consider whether recurrent hospitalizations and psychiatric disturbance are the result of family disadvantage. Quinton and Rutter (1976) found that children who experienced recurrent hospitalizations were more likely to come from disadvantaged homes and that the risk of disturbance arose more from chronic family stress than the admission itself. They also suggested that chronic family stress may increase the child's susceptibility to the pathogenic effects of recurrent hospitalizations. Douglas (1975) also found that although chronic illness as well as recurrent hospitalizations were independently associated with psychiatric disability, the association with recurrent hospitalizations was stronger. In summary, the findings reported strongly suggest that there is a statistically significant association between recurrent hospitalizations and later behavior disturbance.

A recent study by Shannon et al. (1984) appears to contradict earlier reports. They reported on hospital admissions and subsequent psychiatric disability, studying children who were admitted to the hospital in the preschool period and followed at age 6. They found no increase in the rates of behavioral deviance in the study children as compared to a group of controls. There are many possible reasons for the lack of association. For example, the follow-up period is too short—only two years, as compared to up to ten years in the Douglas series. On the other hand, the years that followed the appearance of Douglas's and Quinton and Rutter's findings saw many changes in the care of children in hospitals. Specifically, the tendency toward shorter hospital stays, the liberalization of visitation, where parents can now stay with their children in the hospital around the clock, the availability of playrooms and child-life programs, and better preparation for admissions may all have contributed to make the hospital experience less pathogenic than in years past. If this is the case, it would be an example of scientific research that has had an impact not only in clinical care but also in the administrative practice of pediatric medicine.

THE MEDICAL ENVIRONMENT

The clinician evaluating children with medical illnesses should be conversant not only with those aspects of the consultation related to specific disease entities, such as psychiatric and pediatric syndromes, as well as basic aspects of child development, but also with some general principles of liaison psychiatry. These principles should include knowledge of general systems theory as well as an understanding of small group dynamics.

Child psychiatry consultation work follows the request of a pediatrician that a child psychiatrist see a particular child (Anders and Niehans 1982; Mrazek 1985). The pediatrician may have concerns about the child's mental state, his response to his illness, or the contribution of psychological factors to his medical difficulties.

This consultation is goal oriented and designed to answer a set of predetermined questions.

On the other hand, liaison child psychiatry is a broader concept that calls for a special type of collaborative work between pediatricians and psychiatrists designed to provide integrated medical and psychological care to children (Anders 1977; Mrazek 1985; Rothenberg 1968, 1979). The objectives of liaison child psychiatry include teaching psychiatric principles in the care of children; helping to set up environmental support programs to aid children during their hospital stay, and helping the staff to deal with their own feelings in caring for severely ill children or with the stresses of providing intensive care (Petrillo and Sanger 1980; Frader 1979).

Liaison Services

Liaison child psychiatry, with its emphasis on teaching and collaborative work, has often encountered resistance on the part of the pediatricians recipient of such services (Sperling et al. 1978). In contrast with liaison psychiatry in general medicine, which has recently been criticized because it seems to reinforce the concept of psychiatry as separate from the mainstream of medicine (Hackett 1985), liaison child psychiatry is within the mainstream of modern pediatric medicine, and at least in this author's experience, an invaluable prerequisite for successful consultation work.

Karasu et al. (1977) surveyed departments of medicine, surgery, gynecology and obstetrics, rehabilitation medicine, and pediatrics in order to answer two questions: 1) What aspects of psychiatric consultation are valued by physicians of different departments? and 2) What aspects of psychiatric consultation are valued by physicians of different levels of experience and responsibility? The findings support the notion of a division between patient-centered consultation and liaison psychiatry. The activities valued most by the pediatricians were the child psychiatrist's work directly with the families of the patients and his follow-up visits with them. Other aspects of the consultation work that were also highly valued included the psychiatrist's aid in evaluating the contribution of psychological factors to somatic illnesses as well as the psychological aspects of a patient's illness. The activities that were rated least important by all the departments surveyed included those in which the staff members were the recipients of the consultant's services. Such activities included teaching interviewing techniques, resolving conflicts among ward staff, helping staff deal with the stress generated by patients' behavior, and helping the staff to deal with their reactions to individual patients.

This survey points out some of the difficulties one encounters in liaison work; it could raise serious questions as to the validity of this activity. From another perspective, it is a common impression of psychiatrists in child psychiatric consultation-liaison services that liaison work is an important component of the service. The pediatrician might not request a clinically indicated psychiatric consultation unless he is somewhat knowledgeable in basic aspects of child psychiatry and development. To address this problem, Lewis and Colleti (1973) integrated teaching of child psychiatry into the pediatric residency by using a weekly study group in which pediatric trainees met with a senior child psychiatric consultant to learn child development and psychiatry. In our training program, we use a weekly meeting with the pediatric trainees, a pediatric attending, and a senior child psychiatrist to discuss current cases from the pediatric service, and we use the conference as a springboard for teaching child psychiatry and development. Although both experiences suggest that benefits ensue, further studies are still needed to assess the optimal manner in which liaison services should be provided.

Consultation Services

To understand the functions of consultation we should turn to several reports on the activities on consultation services. Taken together, these reports suggest a pattern of problems encountered by the child psychiatric consultant in a pediatric setting. At the same time, they suggest that liaison services should be an integral part of a consultation service (Lewis 1978).

Fritz and Bergman (1985) reported the results of a survey of the attitudes of pediatricians toward child psychiatrists. In this survey, twenty-two percent of the respondents had no access to child psychiatrists; from these, 60 percent wished they had such access and 40 percent were satisfied without it. An important finding was that the more pediatric-psychiatry contacts occurred during training, the higher the interest in collaborating with psychiatrists. Depression and anorexia nervosa were seen as disorders within the realm of competence of child psychiatrists, but hyperactivity, learning disorders, child abuse, and family crises were more often seen as within the realm of competence of behaviorally trained pediatricians. Although in general pediatricians rated psychiatrists positively, there were no rave reviews, and many expressed criticism of the psychiatrists' poor follow-up, low level of interest, and lack of competence in the care of the chronically medically ill.

Monelly et al. (1973) reported that in a 165-bed children's hospital, requests for consultation occurred in about 1 percent of admissions. The most frequent reasons for referral were: (1) to determine the role of emotional factors in the etiology of physical symptoms (30 percent); (2) evaluation of depression (19 percent); (3) behavior problems in the ward (13 percent); (4) evaluation of specific symptoms (10 percent); and (5) evaluation of a parent with psychiatric problems (9 percent).

Mattson (1976) described the use of ward rounds as an effective vehicle to teach and consult in a sixty-four-bed inpatient pediatric unit. Of the first 125 patients presented, 35 percent had to do with the psychological reactions of children with chronic physical illness; 15 percent had to do with reactions of children and staff to fatal illnesses; 12 percent was ward management of children with acute physical illness complicated by behavior difficulties; 30 percent had to do with the psychosocial determinants or organic etiology of various psychosomatic disorders; and 8 percent were discussions around legal issues including child abuse.

Wrate and Kolvin (1978) described the patterns of referrals to a consultation service from the pediatric outpatient service and the inpatient wards. They received 218 referrals over 3½ months. Sixty-two percent of the children were referred for assessment of overt psychological disturbances; 20 percent for advice on the psychological management of severe medical disorders; 14 percent for opinion following a suicide attempt; and 14 percent because of lack of an organic basis for the presenting symptoms.

Jellinek et al. (1981) described the consultation service in an eighty-three-bed inpatient pediatric unit. In the nine-month study period, there were seventy-two requests for consultation: 38 percent were concern for the child's reaction to his illness and hospitalization; twenty-eight percent were to determine whether psychological factors had caused the child's illness; 14 percent were to assess suicidal gestures; and 15 percent were to help with ward management.

In summary, pediatricians often request psychiatric consultations centered around the effects and consequences of physical illness. Active contact with child psychiatrists during pediatric training increases the likelihood of collaborative work with child psychiatrists after training. Child psychiatrists need to increase their expertise in the diagnosis and treatment of the chronically medically ill and concomitantly the psychiatrically disturbed child. Joint clinical research in this area can be a marvelous vehicle to foster collaboration and dialogue.

THE ELEMENTS OF A CONSULTATION

There are no studies that have systematically assessed the elements of a successful consultation, but most of the descriptions of consultation services convey similar ideas when describing the consultation process. Anders and Niehans (1982) wrote an excellent description of the different elements of a successful consultation; many of their ideas have been incorporated in this section.

The request for a consultation is an important event that sets in motion the consultation process. The initial request may take place formally either via telephone or in writing, and may be first received by a physician, by a member of the consultation and liaison service, or by a secretary. Often the initial request may be informal. In those settings where child psychiatrists are routinely present in the pediatric services, a request may come as a "curbside" consultation. It is helpful for consultation services to develop guidelines on how to request a consultation and to distribute those guidelines to the pediatric staff.

Regardless of how the initial contact took place, the request for a consultation must be initiated by a physician and received by another physician. In teaching hospitals, it is a common occurrence that requests for consultation often come from a concerned medical student, a social worker, or a staff nurse. Proceeding with a consultation before discussing it with the physician in charge of the patient will, in the majority of the cases, render the consultation useless. It is important in all those cases to contact the physician in charge to formalize the request for consultation. In all instances it is useful to discuss the request not only with the pediatric house staff but with the attending physician in charge of the case as well.

Once the child psychiatric consultant has made contact with the responsible physician and has clarified where the request originated, he can discuss the goals of the consultation. It is best if the request for consultation can be formulated and defined as a problem or a series of problems that need to be answered. In this manner, the process can be useful for the referring physician, the patient, and the family. The answers to the problem can fall in several categories: Does the consultation involve a problem of differential diagnosis, the management or treatment strategies of certain behavioral difficulties, assessing the appropriateness of a child's behavior in the context of an illness, assessing and resolving a therapeutic impasse between the family and the treating physician, or evaluating parental behavior?

The urgency of the consultation must also be determined. Pediatricians differ from child psychiatrists in their conception of the time frame for an evaluation. This is especially true in an acute care inpatient setting, where patients are admitted and discharged fairly rapidly, and where the clinical condition of a patient may change with unusual speed. Thus, it is important for the psychiatric consultant to work in collaboration with the pediatrician to carry out the consultation within an appropriate time frame. The child psychiatric consultant also must evaluate whether the referring physician wants him to take over the case, to arrange for a disposition, to provide only a diagnostic opinion, or to help arrange a referral to someone else.

Child-Centered Consultation

Once the initial request for consultation has been clarified, it is important to prepare the child and his family for the event. One of the most common causes of failures in child psychiatric consultations is the lack of adequate preparation of the patient and his family by their primary physician. Without adequate preparation, parents are more likely to feel labeled as psychologically inadequate, and the child is apt to think that the doctors perceive his medical problem as "not real" or that he is psychologically disturbed. This range of misunderstandings can seriously jeopardize not only the psychiatric consultation but also the alliance between the pediatrician and the family. The procedure for preparing the patient and his parents for the consultation should be discussed with the referring physician. This way he can sensitively discuss with the child and his family the reasons for and the expectations of the consultation. Similarly, it is useful for the pediatrician to prepare the ward staff to minimize misunderstandings as to the reasons for the consultation.

Scheduling appointments in a busy pediatric ward can prove difficult. There are very few things more irritating than appearing in the ward and not having a patient to see. The patient may be away from the ward, involved in medical, surgical, or rehabilitation procedures, in the hospital's classroom or playroom. The child may be recovering from anesthesia or involved in a consultation with another specialist. The child psychiatric consultant has to be aware of the many hospital routines and of the priorities in the care of medically ill children; he needs to be flexible enough to adapt to them. It is useful to call the ward and talk to the responsible nurse to ensure that the patient is in the ward when the consultant comes.

Once the consultant is on the ward, he should be introduced to the staff if he is not a permanent part of the pediatric unit; he should review the medical record and should be introduced to the patient and his family, preferably by the pediatric physician. The staff who work with the child usually have useful and valuable clinical information. Discussion with the ward staff allows the consultant to evaluate the child's behavior as perceived by other significant caretakers, including nurses, members of the child life program, teachers, and occupational and physical therapists. Often parents or patients may not disclose relevant information to the consultant out of embarrassment, guilt, or a belief that some details of the development of the child's illness may be irrelevant. It is important to include other staff in the assessment of the child not only because of the valuable insights they can provide, but also because those staff members can help to implement treatment programs that include behavior management techniques. The consultant must review thoroughly the medical chart, including the nurses' notes, and pay close attention to the clinical history, the descriptions of behavior, the chronology of the different procedures the child has had, and the type and dosage of the medications that he may be taking.

It is useful, but not essential, for the child psychiatrist to be introduced to the family by the referring pediatrician or by another member of the staff with whom the family is particularly involved. The psychiatrist should discuss with the family and the child their understanding of the reasons for the consultation to ensure that their understanding is correct and realistic. The psychiatrist should outline his understanding of the objectives and expectations of the consultation.

As with any other psychiatric assessment, the child psychiatrist obtains information and analyzes it for the purposes of making a diagnosis and developing a treatment plan. It is essential for the consultant to meet with the parents of the child to obtain the necessary background and historical information that will allow him to arrive at a correct diagnostic assessment and to formulate a sensible treatment plan. Furthermore, involvement of the parents at the early stages of the consultation ensures better cooperation and fosters the development of a therapeutic alliance. On occasion it will be difficult to assess the parents before proceeding with the assessment of the child; this often occurs when evaluating children in the hospital. On those occasions, the parents should be seen as soon as possible after evaluating the child. A different situation pertains in the case of teenagers, where in certain instances, assessment of the adolescent should take place before talking to the parents. This may promote an alliance between the consultant and the teenager and allow for the development of a sense of trust. At other times, however, it will make more sense to interview the parents before the teenager or initially to see the whole family together and then decide on the sequence of subsequent contacts. The child psychiatric consultant must be flexible with his schedule and in his approach to properly evaluate a child and his family in an inpatient medical setting.

Hovanitz et al. (1984) described the importance of understanding the behavior of medically ill children by looking at the following categories: given a behavior, (a) what are the antecedents that elicit or set the stage for the maladaptive behavior? (b) what are the physiological variables that have an impact on the behavior (i.e., side effects of medication, energy level or fatigue, etc.)? (c) to what extent do consequences play a minimal role in maintaining the behavior, and is the maladaptive behavior mostly a consequence of an emotional state such as a depression, anxiety, or fear? and (d) in what way do consequences play a major role in maintaining a behavior? As expected, in the majority of situations that involve physically ill children, there will be elements of all the above components. This functional assessment of a child's behavioral difficulties can provide the basis for the development of a treatment plan. On occasion, the variables that contribute to the development of a behavior problem in a medically ill child may not be available for change by the psychiatrist. For instance, when the child's erratic behavior is the result of a brain lesion, the psychiatrist cannot change the lesion, but may help develop an intervention program to redirect the child's behavior. At other times the variables that contribute to the development of a behavior problem will not be directly relevant to the choice of therapy.

When interviewing medically ill children, the first visit is particularly important. Often, this first visit will set the tone for subsequent contacts. Due to the nature of hospital treatments and the child's physical state in some medical conditions, the sessions with the child may not be as long as those we are used to in the office. At times it is appropriate to carry on the evaluation over several short sessions. In the case of a short hospital stay, the first session with the child may be a short one designed exclusively to clarify the objectives of the evaluation; the assessment can then proceed in the office. In the hospital, every attempt should be made to encourage the child's independence as well as to respect his need for privacy and sense of decorum. If the child is mobile and can leave his bed, it is important to encourage the patient to move and accompany the consultant to a private office. At times, this may mean moving an IV pole or some other piece of equipment the child is dependent on for treatment. The discussion around the need for this equipment can provide a convenient and fruitful way to start a dialogue with the child. When the child cannot be mobilized, he should be made as comfortable as possible by raising the bed to a sitting position or by having him sit next to the bed. Particularly with teenagers, some privacy should be afforded by closing the curtains around the bed. The clinical interview can then proceed along the lines of any other assessment. When the child is in pain, frightened, or has fluctuating levels of alertness, the assessment will have to be modified accordingly.

With young children it is often helpful to use play therapy techniques for the interview. For instance, the use of a toy bag that the consultant can carry with him to the ward will help to develop a play interview. A doctor's bag with medical equipment such as stethoscope, syringes, flashlight, bandaids, and tongue blades, as well as "nurse and doctor" puppets, can help a young child describe the hospital experience and express emotions and conflict. Drawing and coloring can help to establish communication and a relation of trust. Physically ill children can be asked to draw a picture of what they look like "inside"; this can be helpful not only to establish communications, but to assess the child's cognitive development, his conception of the illness and its etiology, and his understanding of medical procedures.

The child psychiatrist needs to discuss his findings with the parents and the child. This is clearly important when, based on an initial psychiatric assessment, psychological factors appear to influence a medical condition. It is best done, however, after discussing the diagnostic impression first with the referring physician so that a coordinated approach to the patient is achieved. The child psychiatrist should convey to the family his understanding of the child's illness and the contribution of the different psychological factors. This should be done in a supportive manner and in language they can understand. It is essential not to use psychiatric jargon and to be careful not to scapegoat the child or a family member. Parents can be so anxious that they may not hear the explanation of the illness the first time it is presented. The consultant must be prepared to meet with the parents several times to ensure a clear understanding of the child's condition. The use of euphemisms to describe a clinical condition can, at times, make the difference between acceptance and cooperation from the parents or anger and rejection of the consultant's suggestions (Sherman 1982). The description of a child as "developmentally deviant" instead of "mentally retarded" can help some parents cope better with the impact of this diagnosis. However, some parents can use this type of euphemism to avoid dealing with the severity of a condition. When working with such patients in ongoing treatment, the consultant should meet regularly with the referring physician and the hospital staff to discuss respective impressions and to coordinate treatment plans.

In spite of the guidelines just described, there is little empirical data on the most effective techniques for assessing physically ill children. Only isolated reports in the literature (Hodges et al. 1985; Kashani et al. 1981) describe the use of structured interviews in the assessment of medically ill children. Further elucidation of the systematic assessment of these children is needed to determine the most effective ways of obtaining clinically useful and relevant information.

WRITING A CHILD PSYCHIATRIC CONSULTATION REPORT

Writing a psychiatric note in the medical chart should be an integral part of the psychiatric consultation. This serves not only to communicate with the staff and to record clinical findings, but also to document and explain the needs of the patient. Garrick and Stotland (1982) reported their thoughts on the appropriate elements of writing a consultation for adult patients, but very little has been written on the contents of a child consultation note. The main reason to write such a note is to respond to those questions that were raised by the referring pediatrician; it should be identified with a heading as a psychiatric note and should be written without psychiatric jargon. Although the consultant may not be able to obtain all the necessary information at the first contact with the patient, it is appropriate to write an initial short note and to wait for more information before writing a lengthy consultation report.

The initial history should contain information regarding the current medical condition and the reason the referral was made at this time. Next should follow a detailed account of the symptoms or incidents about which the staff and the parents are concerned; this should note the frequency, duration, and progression of those behaviors or symptoms. The setting in which the symptoms or behaviors occur as well as the temporal relationships between their onset and life events, medical illnesses, and exposure to different medications, should be recorded. Many behaviors tend to be maintained or reinforced by their consequences; therefore, the child psychiatrist has to assess the parental and staff responses to the child's difficulties, as well as previous attempts at seeking help. These will provide clues to the pitfalls and difficulties of treatment. The absence of deviant behaviors can provide as much of a clue to the nature of the disorder as their presence. Therefore it is important to undertake a systematic review of deviant and prosocial behaviors very much as a pediatrician elicits a review of systems. Because problem behaviors can manifest themselves differently in different settings, an account of the problem should be sought from other informants, such as the nursing staff, the teacher, and other members of the medical staff, including medical students as well as physiotherapists or dietitians.

It is important to describe parental symptoms such as alcoholism, phobias, depression, and suicidal thoughts or behaviors, as well as parental history of abuse or maltreatment and medical conditions in the parents or in other family members. Metabolic disorders or chronic pain syndromes can influence the parents' ability to care for a child or the child's psychological state. A note should be made as to the parental support systems such as religious affiliations, extended family, and close friends, as well as social stressors such as divorce, single-parent family, elderly caretaker, or economic difficulties.

The report should also contain details of the child's psychosocial background, such as school performance, grade, special class placement, peer relations, and the use of leisure time. The consultant should describe the child's developmental and medical background as well as the child's current medications with names, dosages, and side-effects. A note should be made regarding problems with compliance, as they will have an impact on the child's medical and psychiatric condition. A report of the child's mental status examination, including a description of behavior, appearance, mood and affect, use of language, and the presence of both appropriate and abnormal thought processes, as well as a systematic review of psychiatric symptoms has to follow all the historical information.

Toward the end of the report the consultant should formulate his understanding of how symptoms or behaviors have developed to the present time. Sherman (1982) described the difficulties that the liaison psychiatrist faces in communicating with nonpsychiatrists. This formulation must be written in clear and concise language, avoiding psychiatric jargon or foggy terms that can be misinterpreted or misunderstood. The different diagnostic possibilities should be described as well as the reasons why one diagnosis is favored over another. The child psychiatric consultant should point out what additional information may influence the direction of the diagnostic thinking.

A comprehensive treatment plan should contain a statement of the goals of treatment and the means to achieve them. In order for a treatment plan to be successfully implemented, it must reflect a common understanding of the nature of the problem by the psychiatrist and the referring physician as well as an agreement between them as to the optimal treatment strategies. The same principle is valid when arranging a disposition for a patient after discharge from a pediatric unit.

When a treatment plan has been implemented, the psychiatric consultant should write frequent progress notes. The notes should be clearly identified as psychiatric progress notes and could follow the model of a problem-oriented medical record. The note should contain information on the child's current symptoms and behaviors as well as on his treatment and the changes that have occurred since the last note. A brief description of the child's mental state and the main themes in therapy is a useful addition to the progress notes. A current diagnostic impression and a restatement of the treatment plan should follow, in particular when changes have occurred since the original psychiatric note.

TREATMENT

The psychiatric treatment of children in whom psychological factors influence medical conditions should take into account not only the nature of the psychiatric disability and the effects of the medical condition but also the many indirect ways in which familial, social, and educational difficulties contribute to the production of psychopathology.

Preparation of children for hospitalization may help alleviate some of the distress caused by the separation and medical or surgical procedures. Skipper and Leonard (1968) reported on the effects of preparation in children admitted for tonsillectomy. The experimental group received an explanation of the surgery and the effects of the anesthetic, as well as emotional support by a staff nurse; the control group received routine medical care. The children in the intervention group experienced fewer postoperative complications: less vomiting, reduced use of pain medications, and, on follow-up, experienced less sleep disturbance than the control group. In another experiment, Ferguson (1979) compared the effects of preparation carried out (a) by a nurse at home and (b) by a film modeling sequence shown on admission, with a group of controls who experienced neither method. Both experimental groups showed a decrease in anxiety. The younger children responded better to the peer modeling film, while the older ones responded positively to the preadmission visit. In both experimental groups there was a reduction of behavioral difficulties in the posthospitalization period. The different response according to age suggests that cognitive differences should be considered in the preparation of children for hospitalization. In a review of the literature on this subject, Eiser (1984) pointed out that most studies of preparation for hospitalization have been carried out in children undergoing minor surgical procedures. Further studies are needed to develop techniques suited for children with chronic illness.

Counseling and psychotherapy can help the medically ill child understand his difficulties. Cassell and Paul (1967) reported on the use of puppet play therapy for children hospitalized for cardiac catheterization. The puppets and miniature equipment were used to demonstrate the procedures to the children; they led to less disturbance and more cooperation during the procedure. However, this play did not reduce posthospital behavior difficulties in the prepared children. The use of puppets or toys can enable the child to communicate his distress and can help facilitate adaptive functioning; it can help the child cope with a traumatic experience.

CASE VIGNETTE

T.P., a 10-year-old boy, underwent an eye enucleation and was seen by the psychiatric consultant because of anxiety symptoms. During many therapy sessions, he spent time playing with a clay figure called "Mr. Bill," a television character who is mutilated in each episode. After several sessions the therapist pointed out that "in the hospital you must have felt like Mr. Bill; the doctors pulled you apart just like it happened to Mr. Bill." He nodded silently in agreement and after a few minutes said: "That is exactly how I felt." He continued playing "Mr. Bill" and several sessions later, spontaneously remarked: "In the hospital, people did things to me; but now it is better to be a 'doer' than a 'doee'." By changing passive into active, he was able to master this traumatic experience. In the next few sessions, his anxiety feelings decreased in intensity, he became engaged in other age-appropriate activities, and therapy was no longer necessary.

Family counseling and psychotherapy can help the families of physically ill children come to terms with the child's handicaps, to establish appropriate communication patterns, and to encourage autonomy and responsibility. For instance, Liebman et al. (1974) reported on the positive effects of long-term family psychotherapy in the overall management of asthmatic children. In a related study, Lask and Matthew (1979) reported on the positive effects of brief family therapy in children with asthma. They found a reduction of daily wheezing as well as improvements in ventilatory function after six hours of family psychotherapy in a four-month period.

Families of physically ill children can be very sensitive to the effects of social supports. Haggerty et al. (1975) reported on a therapeutic trial in which they asked mothers who had successfully raised a handicapped child to serve as counselors to an experimental group of families currently under the stress of bringing up a handicapped child. The control group received only high-quality medical care. The counselors and the mothers spent over half of their time talking about problems and receiving advice, information, or instruction. The rest of the time was spent providing concrete services: driving, transporting, and serving as advocate or as coordinator. In spite of the relatively small amount of time the counselors spent with the families, their efforts had a measurable effect on psychological well-being: 60 percent of the experimental children showed psychological improvement, compared to 42 percent of the controls. Conversely, 55 percent of the control children showed a deterioration in their psychological state, compared to 33 percent of the experimental children. In summary, family interventions can have very powerful positive effects on the psychological as well as the physical well-being of the children.

Behavioral approaches can be useful in treating the problems of physically ill children. LaGreca and Ottinger (1979) reported on the use of relaxation training to improve compliance with physical rehabilitation in a child with cerebral palsy. Magrab and Papadopoulou (1977) reported on the successful use of a token economy to increase compliance with dietary restrictions in a group of children on hemodialysis. Relaxation training or self-hypnosis can be used to help children control seizures, especially when a characteristic feeling state can be identified as a precursor of the seizure (Mostofsky and Balaschak 1977).

Pharmacological treatments may be helpful in reducing pathological behaviors in physically ill children. For instance, Pfefferbaum-Levine et al. (1983) reported on the use of tricyclic antidepressants to relieve symptoms of depression in leukemic children; Williams et al. (1982) reported on the beneficial effects of propranolol in brain-damaged children with rage attacks; and Kanner et al. (1983) reported on the effects of imipramine in separation-anxious children with intractable asthma. Most of the evidence on the effectiveness as well as the toxicity of psychotropic medications in medically ill children is anecdotal. Until further evidence accumulates, these medications should be used with caution in the medically ill child.

SUMMARY

The assessment of the psychological factors that influence medical conditions requires a high level of biopsychosocial sophistication. Although the notion that specific psychological conflicts can be expressed through specific physical symptoms has had a certain appeal in the past, a review of the recent literature suggests that this notion is incorrect. There are no specific personality patterns or psychological symptoms characteristic of "psychosomatic" disorders. A reading of currently available data suggests that psychological factors may precipitate, worsen, or modify the course of a wide variety of physical conditions through mechanisms that are complex and thus far only imperfectly understood. Similarly, physically ill children may exhibit the whole range of emotional and behavioral symptoms.

In the evaluation of physically ill children, the child psychiatrist's role varies from that of a consultant responding to a specific question about a child to that of a systems analyst guiding families and staff who are helping the child cope with an acute or a chronic illness. The child psychiatrist also functions as a teacher and a translator of psychiatric and medical concepts. He can function best when he becomes a member of the medical team.

Physically ill children have an increased vulnerability to environmental stresses, family disharmony, and toxicity from medications. The psychiatric consultant needs to evaluate many aspects of the child's life to arrive at a formulation of the child's difficulties that can be translated into effective treatment strategies. Psychotherapeutic and psychopharmacological techniques are available to help the child and his family cope with a medical disability.

REFERENCES

Anders, T. F. (1977). Child psychiatry and pediatrics: The state of the relationship. *Pediatrics* 60:616–20.

———, and Niehans, M. (1982). Promoting the alliance between pediatrics and child psychiatry. *Psychiatric Clinics N. Amer.* 5:241–58.

Apley, J. (1975). *The Child with Abdominal Pains.* 2d Ed. Oxford: Blackwell Scientific Publications.

———, and Hale, B. (1973). Children with recurrent abdominal pain. How do they grow up? *Brit. Med. J.* 3:7–9.

Baker, L., and Barcai, A. (1970). Psychosomatic aspects of diabetes mellitus. In O. U. Hill (Ed.). *Modern Trends in Psychosomatic Medicine.* London: Butterworths.

Birch, H. G., et al. (1970). *Mental Subnormality in the Community: A Clinical and Epidemiological Study.* Baltimore: Williams and Wilkins.

Bowlby, J. (1965). *Child Care and the Growth of Love.* 2d Ed. Baltimore: Penguin Books.

Breslau, N., Weitzman, M., and Messenger, K. (1981). Psychologic functioning of siblings of disabled children. *Pediatrics* 67:344–53.

Cantwell, D. P., Baker, L., and Mattison, R. E. (1980). Psychiatric disorders in children with speech and language retardation. *Arch. Gen. Psychiat.* 37:423–26.

Cassell, S., and Paul, M. (1967). The role of puppet therapy in the emotional responses of children hospitalized for cardiac catheterization. *J. Pediatrics* 71:233–39.

Christensen, M. F., and Mortensen, D. (1975). Long-term prognosis in children with recurrent abdominal pain. *Arch. Dis. Childhood* 50:110–14.

Coddington, R. D. (1972). The significance of life events as etiologic factors in the diseases of children. II. A study of a normal population. *J. Psychosom. Res.* 16:205–13.

Crowe, R. R. (1974). An adoption study of antisocial personality. *Arch. Gen. Psychiat.* 31:785–91.

Diamond, L. J., and Jaudes, P. K. (1983). Child abuse in a cerebral-palsied population. *Devel. Med. Child Neurol.* 25:169–74.

Dorner, S. (1975). The relationship of physical handicap to stress in families with an adolescent with spina bifida. *Devel. Med. Child Neurol.* 17:765–77.

Douglas, J. W. B. (1975). Early hospital admissions and later disturbances of behavior and learning. *Devel. Med. Child Neurol.* 17:456–80.

———, and Blomfield, J. M. (1958). *Children Under Five.* London: Allen and Unwin.

Dunbar, J. M., and Agras, W. S. (1980). Compliance with medical instructions. In J. M. Ferguson and C. B. Taylor (Eds.). *The Comprehensive Handbook of Behavioral Medicine Volume 3. Extended Applications and Issues.* New York: SP Medical and Scientific Books, p. 3.

Eiser, C. (1984). Communicating with sick and hospitalized children. *J. Child Psychol. Psychiat.* 25:181–89.

Ernst, A. R., Routh, D. K., and Harper, D. C. (1984). Abdominal pain in children and symptoms of somatization disorder. *J. Ped. Psychol.* 9:77–86.

Ferguson, B. F. (1979). Preparing young children for hospitalization: A comparison of two methods. *Pediatrics* 64:656–64.

Fishman, C. A., and Fishman, D. B. (1971). Maternal correlates of self-esteem and overall adjustment in children with birth defects. *Child Psychiatry Human Devel.* 1:255–65.

Frader, J. E. (1979). Difficulties in providing intensive care. *Pediatrics* 64:10–16.

Friedman, S. B., et al. (1963). Behavioral observations of parents anticipating the death of a child. *Pediatrics* 30:610–21.

Fritz, G. K., and Bergman, A. S. (1985). Child psychiatrists seen through pediatricians' eyes: Results of a national survey. *J. Amer. Acad. Child Psychiat.* 24:81–86.

Garrick, T. R., and Stotland, N. L. (1982). How to write a psychiatric consultation. *Amer. J. Psychiat.* 139:849–55.

Gath, A., and Gumley, D. (1984). Down's syndrome and the family: Follow-up of children first seen in infancy. *Devel. Med. Child Neurol.* 26:500–508.

Gath, A., Smith, A. M., and Baum, J. D. (1980). Emotional, behavioral and educational disorders in diabetic children. *Arch. Dis. Childhood* 55:371–75.

Gauthier, Y., et al. (1978). Follow-up study of 35 asthmatic pre-school children. *J. Amer. Acad. Child Psychiat.* 17:679–94.

Graham, P. (1985a). Psychology and the health of children. *J. Child Psychol. Psychiat.* 26:333–47.

———. (1985b). Psychosomatic relationships. In M. Rutter and L. Hersov (Eds.). *Child and Adolescent Psychiatry. Modern Approaches.* 2d Ed. Oxford: Blackwell Scientific Publications, pp. 599–613.

———, et al. (1967). Childhood asthma: A psychosomatic disorder? Some epidemiological considerations. *Brit. J. Preventive Soc. Med.* 21:78–85.

Greene, W. A., Jr., and Miller, G. (1958). Psychological factors and reticuloendothelial disease. IV. Observations on a group of children and adolescents with leukemia: An interpretation of disease development in terms of mother-child unit. *Psychosom. Med.* 10:124–44.

Hackett, T. (1985). The role of Liaison Psychiatry: Lecture to the Annual Meeting of the American College of Psychiatrists, Houston, Texas.

Haggerty, R. J. (1980). Life stress, illness and social support. *Devel. Med. Child Neurol.* 22:391–400.

————, Roghmann, K. J., and Pless, I. B. (1975). *Child Health and the Community.* New York: Wiley Interscience.

Heisel, J. S., et al. (1973). The significance of life events as contributory factors in the diseases of children. III. A study of pediatric patients. *J. Pediatrics* 83:119–23.

Hoare, P. (1984). Psychiatric disturbance in the families of epileptic children. *Devel. Med. Child Neurol.* 26:14–19.

Hodges, K., et al. (1985). Depressive symptoms in children with recurrent abdominal pain and in their families. *J. Pediatrics* 107:622–26.

Hovanitz, C. A., Gerwell, E. L., and Russo, D. C. (1984). Behavioral methods in pediatric chronic illness. In B. B. Lahey and A. E. Kazdin (Eds.). *Advances in Clinical Child Psychology.* New York: Plenum Press, pp. 253–93.

Hughes, M. C. (1984). Recurrent abdominal pain and childhood depression: Clinical observations of 23 children and their families. *Amer. J. Orthopsychiat.* 54:146–55.

Jacobs, T. J., and Charles, E. (1980). Life events and the occurrence of cancer in children. *Psychosom. Med.* 42:11–24.

Jellinek, M. S., Herzog, D. B., and Selter, L. F. (1981). A psychiatric consultation service for hospitalized children. *Psychosomatics* 22:29–33.

Kanner, A. M., et al. (1983). The use of imipramine in intractable asthmatic children: A preliminary report on its effect on the psychiatric and asthmatic disorders. Poster session presented at the annual meeting of the American Academy of Child Psychiatry; October 26–30, San Francisco, California.

Kaplan De-Nour, A. (1979). Adolescents' adjustment to chronic hemodialysis. *Amer. J. Psychiat.* 136:430–33.

Karasu, T. B., et al. (1977). What do physicians want from a psychiatric consultation service? *Comprehensive Psychiatry* 18:73–81.

Kashani, J. H., Venzke, R., and Millar, E. A. (1981). Depression in children admitted to hospital for orthopaedic procedures. *Brit. J. Psychiat.* 138:21–35.

Khan, A. U., Herndon, C. H., and Ahmadian, S. V. (1971). Social and emotional adaptations of children with transplanted kidneys and chronic hemodialysis. *Amer. J. Psychiat.* 127:1194–98.

Kim, P. S., Ferrara, A., and Chess, S. (1980). Temperament of asthmatic children. A preliminary study. *J. Pediatrics* 97:483–86.

Korsch, B. M., et al. (1971). Experiences with children and their families during extended hemodialysis and kidney transplantation. *Ped. Clinics N. Amer.* 18:625–37.

LaGreca, A. M., and Ottinger, D. R. (1979). Self monitoring and relaxation training in the treatment of medically ordered exercises in a 12-year-old female. *J. Ped. Psychol.* 4:49–54.

Lask, B., and Matthew, D. (1979). Childhood asthma: A controlled trial of family psychotherapy. *Arch. Dis. Childhood* 54:116–19.

Lewis, M. (1978). Child psychiatric consultation in pediatrics. *Pediatrics* 62:359–64.

————, and Coletti, R. B. (1973). Child psychiatry teaching in pediatric training: The use of a study group. *Pediatrics* 52:743–45.

Liebman, R., Minuchin, S. and Baker, L. (1974). The use of structural family therapy in the treatment of intractable asthma. *Amer. J. Psychiat.* 131:535–40.

Lilly, J. R., et al. (1971). Renal homotransplantation in pediatric patients. *Pediatrics* 47:548–57.

McNichol, K. N., et al. (1973). Spectrum of asthma in children. Psychological and social components. *Brit. Med. J.* 4:16–20.

Magrab, P. R., and Papadopoulou, Z. L. (1977). The effect of a token economy on dietary compliance for children on hemodialysis. *J. Applied Behav. Anal.* 10:573–78.

Mattson, A. (1976). Child psychiatric ward rounds on pediatrics. *J. Amer. Acad. Child Psychiat.* 15:357–65.

Meyer, R. J., and Haggerty, R. J. (1962). Streptococcal infections in families. *Pediatrics* 29:539–49.

Minde, K. K. (1978). Coping styles of 34 adolescents with cerebral palsy. *Amer. J. Psychiat.* 135:1344–49.

Monelly, E. P., Ianzito, B. M., and Stewart, M. A. (1973). Psychiatric consultations in a children's hospital. *Amer. J. Psychiat.* 130:789–90.

Morillo, E., and Gardner, L. A. (1979). Bereavement as an antecedent factor in thyrotoxicosis in children: Four case studies with survey of possible metabolic pathways. *Psychosom. Med.* 41:545–56.

Mostofsky, D. L., and Balaschak, B. A. (1977). Psychobiological control of seizures. *Psychol. Bull.* 84:723–50.

Mrazek, D. (1985). Child psychiatric consultation and liaison to pediatrics. In M. Rutter and L. Hersov (Eds.). *Child and Adolescent Psychiatry. Modern Approaches.* 2d Ed. Oxford: Blackwell Scientific Publications, pp. 888–99.

———, Anderson, I., and Strunk, R. (1985). Disturbed emotional development of severely asthmatic pre-school children. In J. E. Stevenson (Ed.). *Recent Research in Developmental Psychopathology.* New York: Pergamon Press, pp. 81–94.

Neuhaus, E. C. (1958). A personality study of asthmatic and cardiac children. *Psychosom. Med.* 20:181–94.

Oster, J. (1972). Recurrent abdominal pain, headache and limb pains in children and adolescents. *Pediatrics* 50:429–36.

Petrillo, M., and Sanger, S. (1980). *Emotional Care of Hospitalized Children. An Environmental Approach.* 2d Ed. Philadelphia: Lippincott.

Pfefferbaum-Levine, B., et al. (1983). Tricyclic antidepressants for children with cancer. *Amer. J. Psychiat.* 140:1074–76.

Pless, I. B., and Douglas, J. W. B. (1971). Chronic illness in childhood: Part I. Epidemiological and clinical characteristics. *Pediatrics* 47:405–14.

———, and Roghmann, K. S. (1971). Chronic illness and its consequences: Observations based on three epidemiological surveys. *J. Pediatrics* 79:351–59.

Purcell, K., et al. (1969). The effect on asthma in children following experimental separation from the family. *Psychosom. Med.* 31:144–64.

Quinton, D., and Rutter, M. (1976). Early hospital admissions and later disturbances of behavior: An attempted replication of Douglas' findings. *Devel. Med. Child Neurol.* 18:447–59.

Rasbury, W. C., and Fennell, R. S., and Morris, M. K. (1983). Cognitive functioning of children with end-stage renal disease before and after successful transplantation. *J. Pediatrics* 101:589–92.

Robertson, J. (1958). *Young Children in Hospitals.* London: Tavistock.

Rothenberg, M. (1968). Child psychiatry-pediatrics liaison: A history and commentary. *J. Amer. Acad. Child Psychiat.* 7:492–509.

Rothenberg, M. B. (1979). Child psychiatry-pediatrics consultation-liaison services in the hospital setting: A review. *Gen. Hospital Psychiat.* 1:281–86.

Routh, D. K., and Ernst, A. R. (1984). Somatization disorder in relatives of children and adolescents with functional abdominal pain. *J. Ped. Psychol.* 9:427–37.

Rutter, M., Tizard, J., and Whitmore, K. (1970). *Education, Health and Behavior*. New York: Wiley.

Shannon, F. T., Ferguson, D. M., and Dimond, M. E. (1984). Early hospital admissions and subsequent behavior problems in six year olds. *Arch. Dis. Childhood* 59:815–19.

Sherman, M. (1982). Communicating: A practical guide for the liaison psychiatrist. *Psychiatric Clin. N. Amer.* 5:271–81.

Skipper, J. K., and Leonard, R. C. (1968). Children, stress and hospitalization: A field experiment. *J. Health Human Behav.* 9:275–87.

Solnit, A. J., and Stark, M. H. (1961). Mourning and the birth of a defective child. *Psychoanal. Study Child* 16:523–37.

Sperling, E., et al. (1978). A survey of pediatric liaison programs-issues and implications. Paper presented at the annual meeting of the American Academy of Child Psychiatry, San Diego, California.

Strunk, R. C., et al. (1985). Physiologic and psychological characteristics associated with deaths due to asthma in childhood: A case-control study. *J. Med. Assoc.* 254:1193–98.

Wilkinson, D. J. (1981). Psychiatric aspects of diabetes mellitus. *Brit. J. Psychiat.* 138:1–9.

Williams, D., et al. (1982). The effect of propranolol on uncontrolled rage outbursts in children and adolescents with organic brain dysfunction. *J. Amer. Acad. Child Psychiat.* 21:129–35.

Wrate, R. M., and Kolvin, I. (1978). A child psychiatry consultation service to pediatricians. *Devel. Med. Child Neurol.* 20:347–56.

37

OPPOSITIONAL DISORDER AND ELECTIVE MUTISM

Patricio Paez and Michelle Hirsch

Listed among the other disorders of infancy, childhood, or adolescence in the current DSM-III classification are two clinical syndromes characterized by persistent noncooperation with authority figures: oppositional disorder and elective mutism. In oppositional disorder, defiance is expressed by overt negativistic behavior focused on the family. In elective mutism, the child is uncooperative in verbal communication with persons other than immediate family members.

OPPOSITIONAL DISORDER

Definition

Every parent knows what the "terrible two's" are really like: a child acts as if he knows that his behavior will create a desired chaos. This behavior is not significantly different from the attitude many teenagers display with parents, teachers, and to a lesser degree, with the rest of the adult world.

These two time periods are actually anticipated rites of passages in the developmental process of normal interpersonal relationships. The other stages of development normally demonstrate more cooperation and compliance. Working on the basis of a developmental framework, we could call the terrible two's and adolescence normal stages of oppositional behavior, as they are components of the maturational process.

Around the second year of life, the cluster of developmental phenomena that tend to appear have prompted different writers to conceptualize that period in different ways. The stubbornness, negativism, and provocative oppositional behavior that characterize this stage have received the names of anal sadistic stage; autonomy versus shame and doubt; the last two subphases of separation-individuation: rapprochement and consolidation; and so on.

The onset of oppositional behavior in adolescence is less clearly demarcated, although it has been traditionally associated with puberty. In our society, the lower limits of puberty are customarily set at the age of 12 years. This is called early adolescence; middle adolescence begins at 14 and late adolescence at the age of 17 years.

The rebelliousness, instability, arrogance, and discomfort that adolescents express are demonstrated by their anticomformist attitudes. The hormonal storm and the obvious physical growth they go through are probable biological contributants to these psychological changes.

During this stage, the process of emancipation from adult authorities is at its peak. The preadolescent pattern of interpersonal relationships and ways of dealing with environmental demands are now experienced as constricting, infantile, and inadequate. To take more control over one's life (Levy 1955) becomes the symbol of adolescents' struggle against a world ruled by adults. A partial identification with being "like an adult" offers an ego-syntonic sense of mastery that allows the adolescent to defend himself against the sense of internal chaos and disorganization.

Within these two periods in life clinicians have delineated the limits that separate the normal oppositional stages of the two's and adolescence from the psychopathology of a psychiatric disorder.

Classification

The currently used operational definition for oppositional disorder according to DSM-III is as follows:

DIAGNOSTIC CRITERIA FOR OPPOSITIONAL DISORDER

A. Onset after 3 years of age and before age 18;
B. A pattern, for at least six months, of disobedient, negativistic, and provocative opposition to authority figures, as manifested by at least two of the following symptoms:
  1. violations of minor rules
  2. temper tantrums
  3. argumentativeness
  4. provocative behavior
  5. stubbornness;
C. No violation of the basic rights of others or of major age-appropriate societal norms or rules (as in conduct disorder); and the disturbance is not due to another mental disorder, such as schizophrenia or a pervasive developmental disorder;
D. If 18 or older, does not meet the criteria for passive-aggressive personality disorder.

Under somewhat different and more severe circumstances, this syndrome could appear not as an oppositional disorder but as a conduct disorder. The main difference is a pattern of "violating the basic rights of others" that signals the definition of a conduct disorder. If this pattern of violation continues, the child may be identified by authorities, including the police, as a troublemaker and more than just an oppositional child.

CASE VIGNETTE

D.L. was a planned child who was born eight weeks premature. A series of medical problems (failure to thrive, high bilirubin, hyaline membrane disease) delayed his discharge for approximately five weeks. However, once at home, he was described as being an affectionate, happy and trouble-free baby who presented his developmental milestones on time.

D. was the only child; his parents were college-educated middle-class people with a joint income that permitted them to maintain an economically stable status. However, the boy's birth did not alleviate the parents' previous conjugal difficulties. The mother complained about the father's lack of involvement in family matters; the father complained that the mother was too independent and that she did not serve him enough. Family quarrels occurred daily and progressively got stronger, louder, and more physical.

D.'s behavioral problems were initially identified at the age of 1 year. He "would never listen," was prone to temper tantrums without any apparent reason, and could not be disciplined. The parents went through a series of baby-sitters who did not last long in the house because they felt they could not control D. The mother quit her job and stayed home to care for D. She was the disciplinarian, whereas the father was permissive and lax in his discipline.

D. was first seen by a child psychiatrist shortly after his fifth birthday. His nursery school had threatened to expel him because of his provocative, resistant behavior and "bad mouth." He was seen as moody, irritable, and aggressive and had angry outbursts that were clearly out of proportion with the environmental situation that preceded the incident. "If there is a new rule being implemented, he'll violate it."

Psychometrics done at that time classified him as functioning in the very superior range (WISC-R); his behavior during the intelligence testing showed that he had a remarkable ability to remain seated and attentive and to persevere at difficult tasks. During the projectives (Rorschach, drawings, and TAT), though, he became extremely restless and fidgety. These tests showed him as helpless and weak in terms of managing his own aggressive impulses, which, according to his parents, seemed often to occur when he found a situation confusing or ambiguous or when he was uncertain what was expected of him.

A very verbal and articulate boy, he started with weekly individual psychotherapy, where the main recurrent issue was his need to establish quickly his control over the situation. He would do this by expressing a preoccupation with his own physical strength and, during play therapy, with a most elaborate and ingenious array of fantastic creatures and deities with superpowers. On occasions, the therapist had to restrain him physically when he would insist that he had to show how strong he "really" was or when he insisted upon demonstrating his artistic abilities with magic markers on the walls of the office. He denied having any interest in talking treatment, and he insisted on loudly singing pop tunes while refusing to get engaged in the flow of conversation during therapy. This behavior was interpreted to him as an expression of his feelings of fears and anticipation of rejection.

His reality testing was good, and at no time throughout his five years of continuous therapy did he show any disorganized, bizarre, or psychotic thinking.

Slowly D. began to show improvement, first with a reduction of identified behavioral problems in school and, much later, at home. A temporary regression was evident at the time when his parents separated. As expected, the additional family strain created by the boy's behavioral difficulties had increased the quantity and quality of the discord and resentment between the parents.

The father's leaving home, however, resulted in D.'s projection of anger and hostility onto his mother, with whom he remained, and an idealization of the abandoning father. D. experienced no angry feelings directed toward the father. But the high levels of anger D. felt toward his mother at this point in his therapy resulted in a severe exacerbation in his oppositional disorder. The therapist used family meetings with the mother and child as a therapeutic adjunct.

At the present time, D. attends follow-up appointments every six months. According to his own account, corroborated by his mother and teachers, he is "like a different person." He attends a regular school program with enrichment courses, has several friends who have been approved as "good kids" by his mother, and is actively engaged in group sports. He says that he will not give up his wish to have his parents reunited, although he accepts that adults "can do and say very silly things." No medicines were used during the course of D.'s treatment. D.'s developing trust with his therapist allowed him to let go of his tough exterior at times and express his great sense of anger and hurt at his father's abandonment. As he slowly stopped idealizing his father, less rage was displaced from father to all other adults. Work with his mother also helped her to assert herself with the father, to see D. for the unique individual he was, and not to expect him to be just like father.

Assessment

This case history is consistent with the data generated by some researchers (Brehm 1977; Forehand and Scarboro 1975). Not only does it fit the diagnostic criteria for an oppositional disorder, but it also supports the experimental observation that oppositional behavior in children may at times have a facilitory or protective function (Levy 1955) in their developmental attempts to gain mastery over their dependency needs.

In D.'s case, severe parental conflict existed even before his birth. One can hypothesize that D. must have felt very frightened of losing his parents, particularly his father, who kept threatening to leave the house. Under these circumstances, D. had to protect himself from the anxiety generated by his dependency upon his parents, whom he feared were about to abandon him. His defense was to develop a tough, "macho" exterior, preoccupation with physical strength, and an arrogant, boisterous attitude toward authority figures, particularly his mother.

In addition, the rage that could not be expressed against the father was displaced onto his mother and other authority figures. This resulted in such behaviors as temper tantrums, fighting, and noncompliance.

Another approach to understanding oppositional behavior is through the principles of modeling. Children who are exposed to the pattern of dissension from their significant adults can learn the behavioral sequence of mutual discord and disagreement (Brehm 1977).

The oppositional disorder of childhood has common features with a variety of diagnostic entities. The theme of undermining authority and not bending to the demands and expectations of authority figures is seen in the passive aggressive personality disorder (PAPD). This syndrome formally has its onset after 18 years of age. In PAPD, the defiance is manifested in covert ways: procrastination, dawdling, and stubbornness, as opposed to the symptoms of oppositional disorder, which are presented in more overt ways: temper tantrums, argumentativeness, and violations of minor rules.

The behavioral cluster of temper outbursts, demandingness, disobedience, and a provocative, negative attitude is found in conditions as diverse as pervasive developmental disorders, schizophrenias, mental retardation, attention deficit disorders (with and without hyperactivity), and chronic organic mental disorder (DSM-III).

The currently available epidemiological data about oppositional disorder are scarce. There is no official information about its prevalence and incidence; the influence of genetic and congenital factors is also unknown as is the neurological, biochemical, and sexual profile of oppositional disorder.

As expected in a person who presents this diagnosis, there are many associated features that tend to appear together. These are children who show an absence of compliant and cooperative behavior, who habitually confront others in a position of authority, who are quick-tempered, and tend to get into trouble. Their disobedience becomes a constant issue at school and at home. They have problems in maintaining friends and membership in group-oriented activities such as sports and organized social and academic events. Peers will avoid their company. Some of these children, particularly those who do not receive prompt therapeutic attention, may be at risk for developing antisocial activities as they drift away from the range of what is culturally acceptable. The use of street drugs as well as other symbols of nonconformist behavior may be found. These are children who seem to understand at a preconceptual level the power of reverse psychology: the higher the request for a more socially desirable attitude, the lower the compliance (Forehand and Scarboro 1975).

Treatment

There are several different treatments available to children with oppositional disorder, which vary with the conceptualization of the treating therapist. A primarily dynamic treatment approach identifies and clarifies maladaptive defenses and transferences, which are changed through the working relationship with the therapist. An example of this has already been discussed.

The use of psychopharmacological agents is not recommended in most cases of oppositional disorder, as there are no documented therapeutic effects from them. Stimulants can be used in the cases associated with attention deficit disorder. Neuroleptics can be indicated in the instances when there is a diagnosable pervasive developmental disorder, schizophrenia, agitated organic mental disorder, or a substance-induced psychotic episode.

The choice of a behavioral therapeutic modality depends on several variables. The highest priority ought to be placed on an accurate assessment of the identified complaints, the circumstances that surround them, the quality of the parental supervision, and the mental status of the child. The evaluation of certain parental traits appears to provide useful information that separates parents who are successful in their efforts to educate their children from those who are not. Their attitudinal, conjugal, socioeducational, economic, and psychopathological profiles will yield a qualitative picture of their parental effectiveness. That material will help the clinician to formulate the appropriate diagnosis, which in turn will determine the hierarchy of treatment approaches that can be considered useful for that patient and his family (Griest and Wells 1983; Wahler and Graves 1983; Strain et al. 1981).

A variety of behavioral techniques has been designed to extinguish the unwanted, uncooperative behavior while reinforcing the acceptable, desirable one. The techniques can focus on the mother, the usual caretaker, with the combined use of modeling, role-playing, rehearsal, and feedback on her performance (Strain et al. 1982). If the focus is on the problem child, combined techniques using time-out and reinforcement have proven useful in controlling deviant behavior (Wahler and Graves 1983).

Because children with oppositional disorder often have a history of disturbed interpersonal interactions and a spotty academic achievement record, they are at risk for disturbance in their self-esteem and their perception of control over aggressive impulses. The mutual storytelling technique has also provided the clinician with an easy, gamelike approach to a resistive child without producing the high anxiety that more formal therapeutic settings tend to generate in the child (Gardner 1971). In this technique, the child first tells a story and then the therapist presents his, using the same characters in a similar context but within a healthier therapeutic design.

ELECTIVE MUTISM

Definition and Prevalence

Elective, selective, or partial mutism is a rare disorder with an estimated frequency of less than one percent of the referrals to treatment centers in this country (according to DSM-III classification). Although the condition of a persistent refusal to speak in certain social situations can occur at any time during the life cycle, the diagnostic label of elective mutism has been reserved for the pediatric population. The onset is usually before the age of 5 years, with a sex ratio that shows a slight prevalence of girls (DSM-III; Kolvin and Fundudis 1981).

The crucial diagnostic element in this condition is that the child has the ability to comprehend spoken language and speak it but will not do so outside the home. These children will show reasonably appropriate verbal and interactive skills when at home and in the presence of a few presumably safe relatives.

Many speech disturbances have been identified since ancient times (Black 1966), with one most interesting Danish legend about a young prince who was nicknamed The Submissive or the Quiet One (Goll 1979). The prince never said anything until his blind father's kingdom was threatened by the enemy; only then he spoke, stating that he and not the elderly monarch should go out to defend the country.

Classification

The term elective mutism separates total mutes from persons who demonstrate a selectivity in their reluctance to speak. The concept of "elective" can be misleading as it conveys the sense of a chosen attitude, an optional behavior that presumably is being controlled within the conscious apparatus of the mute child. This condition has also been labeled voluntary (Browne et al. 1963), selective (Rasbury 1974), partial or situational-specific mutism (Conrad et al. 1974), children with reluctant speech (Williamson et al. 1977), speech phobia (Halpern et al. 1971), and psychogenic mutism (Mack and Maslin 1981).

In spite of the relative scarcity of documented cases in the medical literature (Rutter 1977), this syndrome has captured the imagination of clinicians and researchers alike. For conceptualization purposes, we can identify two general presentations of elective mutism as a symptom: a persistent and a transient form (Wilkins 1985). The latter has also been called reactive mutism (Hayden 1980), as it is usually associated with an identifiable life circumstance acting as a stressor: starting school (Rutter 1977; Wilkins 1985); family immigration to a new environment, or a significant separation from family (Hesselman 1983); sexual or severe physical abuse (Hayden 1980); illness; and so on.

The persistent form of elective mutism has been estimated to be less common (Hayden 1980). A strong symbiosis with the caretaker, most often the mother, appears to be at the core of the conflict. The psychological profile of this mother is actually not specific for this entity: an overprotective and domineering mother who is "often jealous of the child's other relationships, especially outside the home" (Hayden 1980). She appears to be easily manipulated by the affected child, with whom she identifies as being vulnerable (Wilkins 1985).

The psychodynamic postulate that has been formulated in an attempt to explain this syndrome is based on a fixation or regression into the anal stage, with aggression and destructive impulses particularly directed against the mother (Hayden 1980). Because these impulses are unacceptable feelings, they are projected onto less significant people as well as turned against the self. The symptom formation will reduce the anxiety originated by the fears of separation, real or imagined, from the mother, who is the main target of the child's impulses.

Family Factors

Family structure and dynamics have received a great deal of attention, with a variety of material that indicates a possible pathogenic role. Parental shyness, aggression, and a personality type described as "markedly unusual" were found in 42 percent of the families with children with elective mutism studied at a clinic for children with speech, language, and behavioral problems (Kolvin and Fundudis 1981). More than half of their family cases (58 percent) presented "either a major personality or psychiatric problem or serious marital disharmony or combination of these." These families are conceptualized as vulnerable to a world that is perceived as menacing and hostile. To cut off the outside world is seen as the only way to protect oneself from it. This kind of family has received the name of ghetto family because of its insular life style and marginal position in society (Goll 1979).

These data provide additional support to the long-held belief that elective mutism is an expression of family conflict and anxiety about revealing family secrets (Goll 1979; Pustrom and Speers 1964; Bakwin and Bakwin 1972).

Assessment

The children who present elective mutism have been described as shy, tense, withdrawn, apathetic, manipulative, and clinging in their behavior away from home (Rutter 1977; Hayden 1980). At home, they tend to be demanding and verbal (Rutter 1977) but with detectable immaturities of speech when their spontaneous conversations with close relatives at home were taped and later analyzed (Kolvin and Fundudis 1981). The children's IQs have been difficult to assess in a formal manner but there is some evidence that, for the most part, they tend to function in the concrete level of the average range (Kolvin and Fundudis 1981; Rutter 1977). The physical and neurological evaluations are devoid of etiological significance, although clinical epilepsy, bedwetting, encopresis, a strange rolling gait, and an underlying speech and language handicap can be present (Kolvin and Fundudis 1981; Rutter 1977; Hayden 1980).

However, reliable epidemiological data about other variables (prevalence, incidence, perinatal complications, family size, developmental milestones, biological markers, social class, etc.) are not currently available (Kolvin and Fundudis 1981).

CASE VIGNETTE

V. was a 5-year-old who would not talk to any adults other than her parents. In school, she would talk to the other children, who then served as intermediaries with the teacher.

She had always shown good speech development as a toddler but would not speak with any adult other than her parents. She was a clinging child and reluctant to separate from her mother. Despite her shyness, other children seemed to like her and were willing to represent her to adults.

Her parents described themselves as quiet and controlled people who had great difficulty expressing feelings. They used their silence as a weapon in their marital conflicts. Both were in therapy prior to V.'s referral for mutism.

V. did not talk in therapy. In her doll play the mommy, daddy, and little girl were constantly falling from the roof of the house. They liked the violence and did not get hurt. These episodes began to take place in bed. At home, V. became expressive of angry feelings.

After a month of therapy, a baby evolved from the violent play. In fact, V. had a younger brother with whom she was frequently angry.

Eventually an interpretation made to V. based upon her play was that if she didn't talk, she could stay a little girl and hold on to her mother. As her dependent ties to her mother were interpreted, V. increased her verbal responsiveness. She was able to identify her worries and discuss them with her mother, thus becoming less scared of growing up, and then able to be more verbal with adults.

V. began to speak in the presence of her therapist when her mother was there. The only word ever said to the therapist alone was an accidental "O.K." on one occasion.

V.'s neurotic conflict was her fear that to speak was dangerous because she would lose her mother. She was temperamentally shy and was raised in a household where silence was used as a way of solving conflicts.

Both of V.'s parents were also in therapy, and work among all three therapists and family members sped up V.'s recovery. Sessions with different combinations of therapists and family members were helpful.

This case vignette (Bennett 1985) presents several of the previously identified factors in elective mutism: an absence of congenital and developmental issues; difficulty separating from the mother; the parents' discord, hostility, resentment, and difficulties in expressing themselves in clear, assertive ways; one parent identified as shy and reserved; the family use of silence as a manipulative tool; the child's temperamental features of tension, withdrawal, and affective ambivalence; and the significance of family involvement in the treatment.

Treatment

Elective mutism has a reputation for being either an intractable syndrome (Reed 1963) or a disorder particularly resistant to any therapeutic intervention (Halpern et al. 1971). The analytically oriented individual and family treatment of the case described illustrates one of the modalities reported to be successful.

Behavioral and family techniques are also helpful. Some of the behavioral approaches are: shaping of desired behavior through engagement of the child in behavior that approximates normal speech, such as whispering and mouthing words (Blake and Moss 1967); contingency management with a token economy that results in positive reinforcement of verbal behavior and nonreinforcement of nonverbal attempts to communicate (Williamson et al. 1977), with the tokens earned by producing the desired verbal behavior exchanged for items chosen by the patient; escape-avoidance (Van der Kooy and Webster 1975), in which the child is expected to produce a one-word response before being allowed to leave a particular setting; and positive reinforcement of the desired verbal behavior with extinction of the nonverbal communication (Brison 1966). The use of pharmacology is not indicated.

The prognosis appears to be a function of early detection and treatment. The inclusion of family members and school personnel in the treatment has been empirically beneficial (Hesselman 1983; Yates 1970).

CONCLUSION

Both elective mutism and oppositional disorder present particularly difficult treatment challenges to the therapist. Neither disorder is known to be ameliorated by a specific psychotropic drug. Children with these disorders resist forming a working relationship with the therapist. Oppositional children focus their overt negativistic behavior on the treating authority figures. Electively mute children refuse to communicate verbally with the therapist and often passively resist nonverbal communication as well. However, cumulated clinical experience of those who have worked with these patients suggests that psychotherapy with skill, persistence, and family treatment as an adjunct can in many instances lead to successful results.

REFERENCES

Bakwin, H., and Bakwin, R. (1972). *Behavioral Disorders in Children*. Philadelphia: Saunders.

Bennett, S. (1985). Personal communication.

Black, M. (1966). The origins and status of speech therapy in the schools. *Amer. Speech and Hearing Assoc.* 8:419–25.

Blake, P., and Moss, T. (1967). The development of socialization skills in an electively mute child. *Behav. Res. and Therapy* 5:349–56.

Brehm, S. (1977). The effects of adult influence on children's preferences: Compliance versus opposition. *J. Abnorm. Child. Psychol.* 5(1):31–41.

Brison, D. (1966). A non-talking child in kindergarten: An application of behavior therapy. *J. School Psychol.* 4:65–69.

Browne, E., et al. (1963). Diagnosis and treatment of elective mutism in children. *J. Amer. Acad. Child Psychol.* 2:605–17.

Conrad, R., Delk, J., and Williams, D. (1974). Use of stimulus fading procedures in the treatment of situation specific mutism: A case study. *J. Behav. Ther. Exp. Psychiat.* 5:99–100.

Forehand, R., and Scarboro, E. (1975). An analysis of children's oppositional behavior. *J. Abnorm. Child. Psychol.* 3(1):27–31.

Gardner, R. (1971). Mutual storytelling: A technique in child psychotherapy. *Acta Paedopsychiat.* 38(9):253–62.

Goll, K. (1979). Role structure and subculture in families of elective mutists. *Fam. Proc.* 18:55–68.

Griest, D., and Wells, K. (1983). Behavioral family therapy with conduct disorders in children. *Behav. Therapy* 14:37–53.

Halpern, W., et al. (1971). A therapeutic approach to speech phobia: Elective mutism re-examined. *J. Amer. Acad. Child Psychol.* 10(1):94–107.

Hayden, T. (1980). Classification of elective mutism. *J. Amer. Acad. Child Psychol.* 19:118–33.

Hesselman, S. (1983). Elective mutism in children, 1977–1981: A literary summary. *Acta Paedopsychiat.* 49:297–310.

Kolvin, I., and Fundudis, T. (1981). Elective mute children: Psychological development and background factors. *J. Child Psychol. Psychiat.* 22(3):219–32.

Levy, D. (1955). Oppositional syndromes and oppositional behavior. In P. Hoch and J. Zubin (Eds.). *Psychopathology of Childhood.* New York: Grune and Stratton, pp. 204–26.

Mack, J., and Maslin, B. (1981). The facilitating effect of claustral experience on the speech of psychologically mute children. *J. Amer. Acad. Child Psychol.* 20:65–70.

Pustrom, E., and Speers, R. (1964). Elective mutism in children. *J. Amer. Acad. Child Psychol.* 3:287–97.

Rasbury, W. (1974). Behavioral treatment of selective mutism: A case report. *J. Behav. Ther. Exp. Psychiat.* 5:103–4.

Reed, G. (1963). Elective mutism in children: A re-appraisal. *J. Child Psychol. Psychiat.* 4:99–107.

Rutter, M. (1977). *Child Psychiatry: Modern Approaches.* Oxford: Blackwell Scientific, pp. 688–716.

Sanok, R., and Ascione, F. (1979). Behavioral interventions for childhood elective mutism: An evaluation review. *Child Behav. Ther.* 1(1):49–68.

Strain, P., et al. (1982). Long-term effects of oppositional child treatment with mothers as therapists and therapists as trainers. *J. Applied Behav. Anal.* 15(1):163–69.

————, Young, C., and Horowitz, J. (1981). Generalized behavior change during oppositional child training. *Behav. Mod.* 5(1):15–26.

Van der Kooy, D., and Webster, C. (1975). A rapidly effective behavioral modification for an electively mute child. *J. Behav. Ther. Exp. Psychiat.* 6:149–52.

Wahler, R., and Fox, J. (1980). Solitary toy play and time-out: A family treatment package for children with aggressive and oppositional behavior. *J. Applied Behav. Anal.* 13(1):23–39.

————, and Graves, M. (1983). Setting events in social networks: Ally or enemy in child behavior therapy. *Behav. Ther.* 14:19–36.

Wilkins, R. (1985). A comparison of elective mutism and emotional disorders in children. *Brit. J. Psychiat.* 146:198–203.

Williamson, D., et al. (1977). The treatment of reluctant speech using contingency management procedures. *J. Behav. Ther. Exp. Psychiat.* 8:151–56.

Yates, A. (1970). *Behavior Therapy.* New York: Wiley.

38

ADJUSTMENT DISORDERS

Elliot M. Kranzler

DEFINITION

The adjustment disorders as described in DSM-III represent a series of conditions in which the presenting symptoms are thought to be in reaction to stressful life events and where they are of insufficient severity or duration to warrant another diagnosis. These disturbances in previous incarnations were referred to as situational, transient, or reactive disorders. The terms imply a lack of biological determination but rather a response to environmental or psychosocial factors, a temporary reaction to a recent, significant life stress. Given passage of time or improvement of circumstances they would be expected to remit. The prognosis, therefore, is expected to be good in most cases.

A comparison of DSM-II Transient Situational Disorder and DSM-III Adjustment Disorder reveals some important differences. The earlier version required that the disturbance be acute, transient, and in response to an overwhelming stress. Subsequent research by Andreasen and Wasek, describing a sample of four hundred and two adolescent and adult psychiatric patients who had received a diagnosis of adjustment disorders, found quite a different pattern. The precipitating stressors were found to be both acute and chronic. The kinds of stressors likely to precipitate symptoms resulting in this diagnosis were found to be "mundane" rather than overwhelming. For adolescents the most common precipitants were school problems, and for adults they were marital difficulties. Their disturbances were not necessarily time-limited. Half of the adults and three-quarters of the adolescents had a history of more than three months of symptoms, and half of the adolescents were symptomatic for more than a year.

The revisions in definition and criteria found in DSM-III reflect these findings as well as other classificatory decisions. In DSM-III, adjustment disorders can occur at any age. Therefore they are not considered separately in the section on childhood disorders. The diagnosis is given with a subcode that reflects the predominant symptoms, such as depressed or anxious mood or disturbance of conduct. Two other subcode categories reflect disturbances in specific areas of functioning, namely adjustment disorders with work or academic inhibition and adjustment disorder with withdrawal. These disorders, in which either work or social functioning is affected, exclude those where depressive or anxiety symptoms predominate.

The critical common features of the adjustment disorders are:

1. The symptoms must have developed within three months of the onset of an identifiable psychosocial stressor.
2. The reaction is maladaptive, as defined by an impairment in social or occupational functioning or symptoms in excess of what is expected in a normal reaction to the given stress.
3. The symptoms are not merely the result of an exacerbation of another psychiatric disorder and are not a part of a pattern of chronic overreaction to stress.

There is no requirement that the situation be acute in onset or transient in duration; however, there is an expectation that the symptoms will abate once the precipitating conditions have improved or when a new level of adaptation has been achieved.

Two other categories in DSM-III that also reflect direct symptomatic responses to life events are distinguished from the adjustment disorders: uncomplicated bereavement and posttraumatic stress disorder. Although bereavement is associated with many of the symptoms of a major depressive disorder, it is distinguished by the absence of worthless preoccupations, psychomotor retardation, and prolonged functional impairment. The grief response, which often includes depressed mood and anhedonia as well as vegetative symptoms such as decreased appetite and insomnia, is considered a "normal reaction" to loss and is therefore categorized in the V. codes. This means that although the symptoms may be quite severe, equal to those in some psychiatric disorders, uncomplicated bereavement is not considered a mental disorder. The definition of "normal" bereavement is difficult, given varied expectations for duration of symptoms in different cultures. No category for pathological grief reactions is offered in DSM-III. This approach requires that the criteria for another diagnosis such as those of major depressive disorder be met; it excludes the possibility that a grief reaction may be considered "abnormal" in either duration or intensity, as suggested by the work of Parkes and Weiss (1983) and Vachon et al. (1982).

Posttraumatic stress disorder (PTSD) is included in DSM-III, as a separate category from the adjustment disorders, and several distinctions are made. First, the precipitating event in PTSD is described as "outside the range of usual human experience" compared to those of the adjustment disorders, which are "within the range of common experience." Similarly, although as in bereavement, distress and even symptoms are expected in most people, PTSD excludes "uncomplicated bereavement" in that it is a common experience. The types of traumatic stressors associated with PTSD include natural and man-made disasters (e.g., floods or death camps), or assaults (e.g., rape or combat). They often result in physical damage to the victim, particularly to the central nervous system. Another major distinction between PTSD and the adjustment disorders is the presence of characteristic reexperiencing of the traumatic event in recurrent nightmares or intrusive recollections, autonomic arousal, and emotional anesthesia. This complex syndrome, which can include anxiety as well as obsessional, affective, and dissociative symptoms, is somewhat surprisingly included by DSM-III in the category of anxiety disorders and not as a variant of the adjustment disorders.

There are two revisions of the criteria for adjustment disorders in DSM-III-R. First, the disorder has to have lasted for less than six months. Those disturbances that last longer, even in response to an identified stressor, are felt to be inconsistent with the notion of a transient disturbance as implied in the term adjustment disorder. This change will force the diagnostician to consider another diagnosis once the time limit has been reached for the reaction to the identified stressor. The second change in DSM-III-R is the addition of a new subcategory, adjustment disorder with physical complaints, in which somatic symptoms predominate and criteria for a somatoform disorder are not met.

Perhaps because of the implied nonseriousness of these disorders, there is a relative paucity of research data on their description, causes, treatment, and outcome. Despite this lack of attention in the literature, the adjustment disorders are among the most commonly diagnosed disorders in both child and adult outpatient clinics. Weiner and DelGaudio (1976) reported that the diagnostic incidence of situational disorders was 27 percent in a group of 1,334 adolescent inpatients and outpatients. Jacobsen et al. (1980) found that transient situational disturbance was the most often used diagnosis in four different child psychiatry outpatient clinics. In these four different settings the proportion of children receiving this diagnosis varied from 24 to 66 percent. In a study of the validity of ICD-9 diagnostic categories, Gould et al. (in press) found that clinicians assigned the diagnosis of adjustment reactions to 17 percent of the outpatients in the study. This category was second only to disturbances of conduct (25 percent).

Clearly the diagnosis is frequently misapplied, at least as it is intended in DSM-III. In testing interrater reliabilities of DSM-III categories in children, Werry et al. (1983) found that the adjustment disorders were among the highly unreliable diagnoses, and that rather than consistently competing with one or two other diagnoses, the adjustment disorders generated noise throughout the diagnostic system.

The accurate use of this diagnosis suffers from at least three concerns, resulting in its overuse and misapplication by clinicians: 1) diagnostic hedging; 2) fear of stigmatizing patients by giving a "serious diagnosis"; 3) concern about confidentiality. Perhaps because DSM-III encourages its use when a patient does not meet criteria for other major diagnostic categories, and because it is almost always the case that a clinician can find some stress in the patient's life to which he might be reacting, the diagnosis is often applied when there is a wish to hedge and delay commitment to a more serious diagnosis. Some clinicians may prefer to place blame on the external circumstances or to use this neutral label to avoid stigmatizing the patient. The latter also becomes a problem with regard to confidentiality, particularly as applied to third-party reimbursement. With increasing demands for documentation and accountability and with clinicians' resistance because of fear of breaching the confidentiality of the client-therapist relationship, the diagnosis "Adjustment Disorder" becomes a safe, nonpejorative label to apply. It allows the therapist to comply with the patient's wish to be reimbursed without volunteering any meaningful information to third-party payers of whose intent and confidentiality both patient and therapist are cautious. The fear of applying a "loaded" label that will be frightening or misunderstood by the patient is another reason for therapists' overuse of more neutral labels, such as adjustment disorders.

In a five-year follow-up study of a subset of their original patients, Andreasen and Hoenk (1982) found reason to question some of the assumptions implied in the diagnostic definition of the adjustment disorders. Their report indicates that the disorder may not be the same in children and adults. In particular, the adolescents studied appeared to have a more malignant course than the adults. The positive prognostic prediction associated with adjustment disorders did not apply in half of the adolescents on five-year follow-up. Although 71 percent of the adults were well, more than half of the adolescents received treatment and another diagnosis in the intervening period between their first contact and the five-year follow-up. Only 44 percent of them were completely well at follow-up. There were few predictors associated with diagnostic outcome. The adolescents who received the longest outpatient treatment were most likely to be more disturbed at follow-up. Diagnostic outcome was predicted poorly by the type of presenting symptom. For example, no factors, including initial symptoms, predicted eventual major depressive diagnoses. Developing an antisocial personality disorder was associated with greater initial duration of symptoms and length of treatment but did not significantly correlate with initial assignment of the subtype of adjustment disorder with disturbance of conduct. This suggests that although useful for immediate descriptive purposes, the adjustment disorder subtypes do not have clear predictive validity.

CLINICAL VIGNETTES

The following are descriptions of two cases that will illustrate and introduce a discussion of the typical presentation, diagnostic, and treatment issues and course of the adjustment disorders in childhood.

Case #1

Peter (fictional name), an 11-year-old boy, was referred for a psychiatric evaluation by his pediatric endocrinologist after several months of complaints from his parents. Six months previously, with no prior medical history, he developed symptoms of fatigue, frequent urination, and unquenchable thirst. A diagnosis of juvenile onset diabetes mellitus was made by his pediatrician and he was referred to a pediatric endocrinologist for further work-up and management. Peter and his parents were informed that his condition required strict adherence to a diet as well as daily insulin injections. Peter was instructed in self-administration of these injections.

His doctor became concerned within a few months because Peter's blood sugars were in poor control and the family seemed to be having difficulties adhering to medical recommendations. He was informed by the parents that there had been a radical behavioral change in Peter since the diagnosis had been made. They reported that although previously Peter had required more attention than his younger siblings (he was the oldest of three), at this point Peter demanded almost all of his parents' time. His behavior at home had regressed in numerous areas. There were frequent physical fights with his sisters. He had tantrums, which usually focused on anger over his perception that his mother was being unfair to him and favoring his younger sisters. He complained that his mother was not providing him with sufficient assistance with his homework and refused to do it unless one of his parents sat with him. When they did help him, however, he argued constantly. Frequently verbal shouting matches and even physical fights with his parents ensued. Peter was not complying with his prescribed dietary schedule and restrictions. Many mornings his father would literally have to sit on top of Peter in order to administer the insulin injections, while he screamed and bit his father.

Upon evaluation, the parents reported that Peter had no prior psychiatric history or significant behavioral problems. He had functioned well at home and in school. His grades had been above average and he had several close friends. Although his parents felt that Peter's behavior stood in sharp contrast to his previous state, in fact the history revealed that several of his present symptoms actually reflected exaggerations of traits that had been part of his baseline personality. For example, prior to his illness his parents felt that he was not independent enough in completing his school assignments. Now he refused to try to do his work at all unless his parents aided him. Previously Peter had teased his sisters and fought with them over typical sibling issues. Now he teased them mercilessly and was exquisitely sensitive to the possibility that he might be "getting less" than they were.

Peter, although initially shy and suspicious about the reasons for seeing a child psychiatrist, was easily engaged. Soon, he revealed feelings of shame and anger about the changes in his behavior and his affliction with diabetes. He was aware that he was behaving irrationally at times and felt guilty about the extent to which he was verbally and physically abusive toward his parents and sisters. He felt justified, however, regarding the reasons for his anger. His anger was consciously focused on feelings of isolation. He compared himself to "everybody else," who did not have to deal with being a diabetic. He magnified his isolation by keeping his diabetes a secret. Peter did not want any of his peers to know about his condition, lest he be made to feel even more "different" than he did already. This sense of isolation persisted within the context of his family. Peter felt that he had been unfairly afflicted. He angrily complained that no one else in his family required the kinds of dietary restrictions, medical testing, and daily injections that he did. He felt entitled to all the attention from his parents as well as to particular consideration regarding his moods and abusive behavior.

The treatment model chosen reflected the need to combine a dynamic understanding of the acute stress reactions being experienced by the child and his family, while also recognizing the parents' and referring physician's need for concrete assistance in getting Peter to comply with the medical regimen and take an appropriately active role in his care. A treatment plan was formulated for a thirty-session focused brief therapy.

The plan included regular contact with the endocrinologist and weekly psychotherapy sessions with Peter and his parents, as well as individual psychotherapy with the child.

Specific problems around the implementation of the diet, urine testing, and insulin injections were discussed. A behavioral program was instituted, which determined the contingencies for Peter's noncompliance and approached them by positively reinforcing the desired behaviors. Rather than being allowed to gain the attention he sought negatively by acting out his anger in a way that was disruptive to the family and dangerous for Peter, he was now reinforced for taking an active role in his care. He was rewarded for compliance by having special time set aside for him to be together with his mother and father that was mutually rewarding and not abusive. This also satisfied Peter's extra needs for attention at this stressful point in his life, but with less anger and resistance from his parents over providing it.

It was clear during the evaluation that family members were all overwhelmed and underinformed regarding Peter's illness and that this was having an impact on the control of his diabetes as well. The endocrinologist had not satisfactorily explained to either Peter or his parents the dietary conditions and guidelines that needed to be met. Given the lack of information, Peter's mother, an anxious woman, responded by assuming the worst. As a reflection of her anxiety she made unnecessary demands of Peter, requiring him to eat such large meals and snacks that he was embarrassed to unpack his lunches in school, choosing rather not to eat at all. This only served to make him feel even more different from his peers. At home he felt once again singled out. Favorite snacks were provided to his sister while he was given "diabetes food." His mother placed such an anxious emphasis on his eating that Peter sensed this could be used as a powerful manipulative issue. Sure enough, he had been using the threat of not eating to gain all sorts of undeserved or inappropriate rewards. In the treatment these issues were addressed. The family was encouraged to seek more information regarding Peter's dietary requirements and to work more closely with the endocrinologist. Peter's mother was able to deal with her anxiety more appropriately in sessions and adopted a more relaxed but informed approach to his diet.

Peter and his parents had to grieve the multiple losses resulting from his serious medical illness. Their expectations of good health and a relatively carefree childhood existence for Peter were suddenly curtailed. The anger and fear associated with this loss were addressed in treatment. Efforts were made to help Peter and his parents readjust their expectations to realistic but not fatalistic goals, ones that took appropriate consideration of his illness but did not lose sight of the fact that appropriate management was possible.

By the end of the thirty sessions, there had been significant changes in the primary areas of initial concern. Peter's compliance with his medical regimen, for which he had assumed appropriate responsibility, had improved. As a result his blood levels were now in good control. His behavior at home returned to its previous level and he was less frightened of his peers' finding out that he had diabetes, which required medical attention and dietary restrictions. These restrictions were now more reasonable and he found it somewhat easier to live with them. Peter and his parents made progress in accepting and learning to live with and manage his illness. Although this remained an issue that required further work, each of them was doing so without the indirect, symptomatic expression that had characterized their immediate reaction to the stress of Peter's illness.

Although the stress of his illness would remain, Peter had achieved a measure of adaptation to his condition such that there was a reduction of symptoms and he was able to return to a level of improved psychological functioning.

Case #2

Susan, a 5-year-old girl, was referred by her pediatrician after several episodes of gastrointestinal complaints. She was brought by her mother, Mrs. R., a successful professional woman, who reported that Susan had developed recurrent stomachaches and vomiting just before and after her scheduled weekend visits with her father. The symptoms had recurred weekly for a month. The pediatrician investigated her GI complaints with an initial work-up, which proved negative. When the circumstances of the complaints were clarified he felt that they had a psychological rather than organic etiology.

Susan's parents were divorced two years before, and the father had regular weekend visitation rights. Their separation and divorce had been acrimonious and the relationship remained bitter. Susan had been in good health previously. She was doing well in kindergarten.

On initial consultation, the mother angrily described her ex-husband as dishonest and unwilling to help her deal with this problem, although she hoped he would participate in the sessions. In retrospect, she saw their marriage as disturbed from the start. She stated that he was very closely tied to his own mother and that this had been a major problem during their marriage. She reported that while she was pregnant with Susan, her husband had physically beaten her. Their breakup occurred several months after Susan's birth.

Although she had some reservations about some of his parenting practices, Mrs. R. still felt that her ex-husband had an acceptable relationship with Susan and that the child looked forward to spending time with her father. The mother stated that she had no interest in standing in the way of their ongoing contact. The weekend visitations with the father were of concern to Mrs. R. because Mr. R., who often had work to do over the weekend, relegated Susan to the care of his mother, her paternal grandmother. When she returned to Mrs. R. after the weekends, Susan would report that she and her grandmother had argued frequently. She said her grandmother called her "bad names" and sometimes spanked her. When Mr. R. was present, he was aware of the inappropriateness of his mother's manner of dealing with Susan but sided with his mother anyway and scolded Susan. He criticized his ex-wife's raising of Susan and held her responsible for the difficulties Susan was having with her grandmother. He felt that Susan was not compliant or respectful enough toward his mother and that perhaps she received some encouragement from her mother to misbehave during the weekend visitations.

Susan was an engageable, attractive, highly verbal 5-year-old. She showed no signs of disordered affect or thinking. Her physical and cognitive development was above average for her age. During the evaluation, she openly described the animosity she felt toward her grandmother, who would alternately buy Susan's affection by showering gifts on her and angrily berate her when she was imperfect or unappreciative. Susan was caught between her mother and grandmother in a tug for her loyalty. This was similar to the position her father was in while he was married. Given the options, Susan had chosen to ally herself with her mother, with whom she was closer and upon whom she depended for her daily care.

Susan had no insight into the relationship between her physical complaints and the difficulties with her visitations. The transitions between the care of her mother and father were fraught with their angry interactions over timing and conditions of the visits. Susan felt frightened by these arguments. Often she tried to divert the focus of attention from her parents' disagreements to her own stomachaches and vomiting. On several occasions this succeeded in causing her visitation with her father to be canceled, but neither parent wanted this to be the solution.

Based on these findings in the evaluation, a treatment plan was devised that would focus on the parents and the paternal grandmother. Susan was seen on several more occasions but it was felt that the symptoms would improve only if the environmental stress—the family feuding—could be modified. The concern was that Susan, a bright and perceptive child, was already too involved in a problem that was for the adults in her family to manage. In fact, because of their inability to do so, Susan was left with an inappropriate, powerful role as reporter to her mother and conveyer of the anger between her grandmother, mother, and father. The therapist felt that she had to be relieved of this responsibility. He therefore made the adults the focus of the treatment, deemphasizing the symptoms that brought the identified patient, Susan, in for consultation.

It was clear that Mrs. R. and her former mother-in-law were the prime players in this complicated family feud. Their relationship, troubled from the start, had deteriorated even further after the divorce. The hostility was mutual. Susan's role as a conduit for the expression of anger was confronted in sessions with her parents and the grandmother. The goal was not to resolve the differences between them, which were chronic and perhaps intractable, but to release Susan from her position in the center. Mother and grandmother were encouraged to have more regular telephone contact regarding the visitations and to have out their differences directly. Mr. R., who had previously felt it necessary to defend his mother against Susan and his ex-wife, was freed from this role and enlisted as an ally for Susan.

The issue of transition from her mother's to her father's care at visitation was addressed. The parents were encouraged to disengage Susan from their battles by not staging them when Susan was being picked up and returned to her mother. Concrete maneuvers such as this did not change many of the negative feelings between them. What was accomplished, however, was Susan's release from the center of their battleground. Susan's parents and grandmother, having confronted the effects of their destructive relationships on her, made efforts to work together on issues pertaining to Susan. The grandmother felt less threatened about her relationship with her granddaughter, which had been a concern of hers since the divorce agreement gave the mother custody. This change resulted from sessions with the grandmother and her former daughter-in-law, who conveyed her intent to maintain Susan's relationship with her father and his family. Because of this change and the opportunity for the parents to confront each other more directly, the grandmother was able to deal, on the whole, more appropriately with Susan, whose gastrointestinal symptoms abated. Her parents remained at odds on numerous issues, and although they recognized its usefulness, they chose not to continue with treatment as advocated by the therapist to enable them to manage these conflicts better. They had too much invested in their mutual anger to be motivated, at that point, to resolve matters between them, beyond the relief of Susan's presenting symptoms. They were, however, prepared to work in therapy as long as the focus was helping Susan with her problem, preventing it from recurring, and improving the parenting interactions required of them.

EVALUATION AND DIAGNOSTIC ISSUES

The evaluation of a child who presents with recent onset of symptoms that appear to be in response to an acute event or a set of ongoing stressful life circumstances must include several components. First, a thorough physical examination and appropriate laboratory tests must be done to rule out organic etiology for the presenting symptoms. In both case illustrations described it was necessary first to address the medical issues and possible causes for the symptoms. Peter's diagnosis of diabetes had already been made, but together with the presenting symptoms that were behavioral in nature, there was also the fact that his blood sugar levels were out of control as a result of his and his family's emotional reaction to the onset of his illness. The first step in evaluating this child was to communicate with his endocrinologist, determine what his medical condition and needs were, and establish a priority of improved control of his diabetes. For Susan, the presenting complaints were somatic. Before ascribing them to emotional causes it was necessary to rule out organic gastrointestinal etiologies such as viral illness, parasites, and so on. Having done so and having established the connection between the visitations and Susan's symptoms, the therapist was then justified in evaluating the psychosocial circumstances that appeared to have contributed to the onset of her symptoms.

After addressing the possible medical issues, it is then necessary to assess carefully the child's present symptoms to determine whether the reaction is in fact maladaptive, with an impairment in social or school functioning, and not an "expected reaction' to the stressor. Past history and baseline functioning will indicate whether the presenting symptoms do in fact reflect a change from previous level of adaptation and whether they began within three months of the onset of the stressor. According to DSM-III, preexisting conditions, such as personality or organic disorders, are thought to predispose one to the development of an adjustment disorder. Family history will provide potentially important predictive as well as diagnostic information. To date, however, there are no research data that clearly support the genetic transmission or even predisposition for adjustment disorders.

The presenting symptoms will determine the differential diagnosis and the particular subtype being considered. In the case of adjustment disorders with depressed mood or with anxious mood and disturbance of conduct, the primary diagnostic distinction to be made is with the respective primary disorders. In the adjustment disorders only a partial syndrome of the specific disorder is present. If, on the other hand, sufficient symptoms are present to make the diagnosis of a specific disorder, it should be made. For example, if a child presents with symptoms meeting criteria for a major depressive disorder, despite the fact that the onset was recent and appeared to be set off by a stressor, a diagnosis of major depression rather than adjustment disorder would be made. The same will be true if the child showed symptoms that meet the criteria for anxiety, conduct, or somatoform disorders.

The adjustment disorders, while occurring in response to identifiable psychosocial stressors, are a series of symptom complexes probably representing nonspecific, individual reactions that are determined by constitutional developmental as well as by environmental influences. Some children will respond to a given stress such as a serious medical illness or parental divorce by developing adjustment reactions in which depressive, anxiety, conduct, or somatic symptoms will predominate. Others will not show any evidence of an overt behavioral disturbance in response to the same events. Nor is there a specific set of symptoms associated with a given stress. The same circumstances will elicit varied symptom responses in different children. There is a lack of research data that might help clarify mechanisms and paths taken in particular children's symptomatic responses to given stressors.

It is possible that a child with no previous history of anxiety or affective disorder, but with a positive family history of these disorders, may be more likely to manifest symptoms of either depressed or anxious mood in response to a given stress. Since the child may present with evidence of only a partial syndrome, the specific disorder will not be diagnosed but rather a diagnosis of adjustment disorder will be made. Andreasen and Hoenk's (1982) five-year follow-up study showed that those adolescents who remained disturbed carried a series of diagnoses including affective and schizoaffective disorders, schizophrenia, antisocial personality, and substance abuse disorders. This belies the supposedly good prognosis associated with the adjustment disorders and also suggests that they are often in fact a preliminary or prodromal phase in the development of numerous psychiatric disorders. In their study Andreasen and Hoenk (1982) found that adolescent patients who had more behavioral symptoms at the time they were diagnosed with an adjustment disorder were more likely to develop an antisocial personality disorder. However, those adolescents who later developed major depressions did not differ significantly on predictor variables, including the presence of depressive symptoms at initial evaluation, from those who did not become depressed on follow-up. Although this issue has been insufficiently studied, as noted above, Andreasen and Hoenk's (1982) study shows that the presenting symptoms may not specifically predict eventual prognosis or diagnosis. Rather than the initial symptoms, a family history of specific disorders may more accurately predict the outcome of the adjustment disorders. This issue was not reported on in their study.

The developmental timing of stressful events may also affect the presentation of symptoms. Caplan (1974) described crises as times of high risk for children that could lead to either further growth or the onset of symptoms. It may be that there are certain points in a child's development, particularly at transitional phases, at which he may be more vulnerable to a pathological rather than a growth response to stress. For example, a recently toilet-trained child or one just entering puberty may be more likely to respond to a crisis with symptoms or regressive behaviors than the same child might be at another point when he is not in a state of developmental flux. The result can be a temporary setback in the rate or course of the child's development that will most likely be reversed once he or his environment have reequilibrated and a new level of adaptation is achieved.

The age and stage of development of a child may have impact on the particular manifestations of a child's reaction to stress as well. A 5-year-old child reacting to a recent move and beginning a new school might be more likely to react to this combination of stressors with an adjustment disorder with anxious mood. The difficulty he experiences in adjusting to the environmental changes may result in a regression to symptoms of separation anxiety, which he may have appropriately mastered the year before in the context of starting school in his old familiar setting. On the other hand, an adolescent who experiences the divorce of his parents may manifest a reaction with predominance of disturbance of conduct or depressed mood. Such responses to the loss would be more typically associated with the developmental challenges of adolescence. These might include a rebellious reaction to the increasing demands at school, expressed in "acting out" conduct disturbance, or the precipitation of a depressive episode in response to the loss of the "intact family" and the parent who is no longer living with the child.

PRECIPITANTS

The nature of the stressors that can precipitate a maladaptive response varies. There is debate in the literature regarding whether it is primarily the experience of life changes or the undesirability of the changes that causes the psychological stress reaction. Holmes and Rahe (1967) and Dohrenwend and Dohrenwend (1970) have posited that assessing change from prior circumstances and activities is the critical factor in the study of stress. Gersten et al. (1974) argued that the primary concern in measuring stress reactions is the degree of desirability versus undesirability of the changes experienced. They pointed out that anxiety is the first response to change and that this is what was primarily measured in those studies that found change to be more critical. They argued that other forms of pathological response, such as antisocial or withdrawn behavior and aggression, are more dependent on the quality of the change. They found that with children in particular, the undesirability rather than the amount of change was more predictive of psychological impairment. Vinokur and Selzer (1975) also concluded that it is the quality of events that is the crucial determinant of stress. Paykel (1974) found that psychiatric disorders, particularly suicide attempts and depressions, are associated with undesirable and not with desirable life changes. Depression was frequently preceded by exits from the person's life and suicide attempts were associated with both exits as well as entrances.

Sommer and Lasry (1984) and Canter et al. (1972) have suggested that personality is an important mediator of reaction to stress. Sommer and Lasry (1984) also pointed to the importance of duration of the stressor, cognitive factors, and the available coping skills. Magnusson and Ekehammar (1975) emphasized the importance of the individual's perception of stressful events as critical to an understanding of his reactions. A given event may be perceived as desirable by one individual and highly undesirable by another. They described a model of understanding actual behavior as a result of the interaction between the individual and the situation. In this sense individuals experience idiosyncratic or subjective reactions to a given stress.

Social environmental variables, for example being on welfare or the extent of social supports, have been implicated as important possible mediators of stress responses. Sandler and Block (1979) found that children whose families were on welfare were exhibiting disturbances at a lower level of stress exposure. Dohrenwend (1973) and Meyers et al. (1974) have shown that the negative effects of stressful events is greater among the lower than the upper classes. Meyers et al. (1974) found that lower-class individuals experience more undesirable events with a high readjustment or change impact. One would therefore expect that among children of the lower classes there might be higher rates of adjustment disorders. Additionally, one might hypothesize that lower-class children might have fewer personal, familial, and social coping strategies and supports available to them, and that a given stress might be more likely to precipitate a pathological rather than an adaptive response.

The kinds of stressful life events that have been associated with the adjustment disorders include those that are external to the child, such as loss experiences and catastrophes, as well as those that are internal to the child, including illness and developmental changes. Kaffman and Elizur (1983) and Van Eerdewegh et al. (1982) have described children's behavioral reactions to the death of a parent, as reported by the surviving parent. They have found significant behavioral disturbance, including dysphoria and impaired functioning in school. Neither of these studies gave diagnoses to the children, but it is likely that many showed symptoms beyond those of uncomplicated bereavement but would not have met criteria for other diagnoses and would have been diagnosed as adjustment disorders. In studying children's behavior after a natural disaster, Burke et al. (1982) found that parents were likely to deny their children's problems after the disaster. Unlike the posttraumatic distress disorders described by Terr (1981) and Adams and Adams (1984), it is likely that milder, transitory adjustment reactions following natural disasters (such as the severe storm reported on by Burke et al. [1982]) do not reach the attention of mental health professionals; or the parent may not report a connection between the event and the child's symptoms because of unawareness or denial.

Studies by Hetherington et al. (1982), Wallerstein (1983), and Dunn and Kendrick (1982) have described the reactions of children to parental divorce and the birth of a sibling. These represent, on face, contrasting undesirable and desirable life events that might be expected to have differing impacts on children. For the older child, however, the birth of a sibling is not necessarily a desirable event. The perspective of the displaced older sibling is colored by the reality that he will receive less overall and more negative attention from his parents after the arrival of a new sibling. This can lead to temporary shifts in the older sibling's behavior, including regressive, aggressive, or depressive reactions. From the child's point of view in most circumstances, parental divorce is seen as an undesirable loss and often results in their reacting with the onset of psychological and behavioral symptoms. In some circumstances, however, there can be a lack of obvious deleterious effect and even positive shifts in the child that will result from this stressful life event. This is particularly true where the level of overt conflict has been so great previously that the divorce results in a more stable and less persistently stressed environment.

Important developmental changes such as puberty can be stressful for vulnerable children, who may respond with transient symptoms that can meet criteria for the adjustment disorders. Previously it was thought that even "normal" adolescence was a time of such turmoil that clinical symptoms would be common (e.g., A. Freud [1958]). More recently Rutter et al. (1976) have challenged this notion, finding that the majority of adolescents do not experience major psychological or behavioral disruptions. It is true, however, that some of them may be more likely, based on prior personality, coping deficits, or lack of supports, to react to the multiple physiological, psychosocial, and educational changes inherent in adolescence with a variety of symptomatic responses. Frequently, these youngsters will be given a diagnosis of adjustment disorders, particularly when the onset is recent and the duration or severity of disturbance is insufficient to warrant a more serious diagnosis.

Stress reactions to the onset of a medical illness have been reported with numerous disorders. For example, Kovacs et al. (1985) described the reactions of children who developed insulin-dependent diabetes mellitus. They found that 36 percent of the children studied developed psychiatrically diagnosable reactions, most commonly depressive syndromes, that generally remitted within seven to nine months. Meichenbaum (1979), studying children who underwent surgery, found that a group of highly defensive children, who were less likely to engage in the "work of worrying" at the time of surgery, were more anxious following surgery. Ravenscroft (1983) described the phases of reaction frequently experienced by a child who has suffered an acute physical trauma. Kellerman and Siegel (1980) suggested that children who undergo serious medical procedures often develop symptoms of anxiety or depression.

A child with an impairment in educational or social functioning may develop low self-esteem of a chronic nature; at a given point of stress, such as when placed in a special educational setting, he could develop acute symptoms of an adjustment disorder. Faerstein (1981) described the stresses and coping patterns that children and their families often experience when a diagnosis of learning disability is made. In some ways the difficulties are special for the child with a hidden handicap, such as a learning disorder, and the expectations and family life can be as disrupted as much as when there is more obvious physical handicap or mental retardation.

TREATMENT

The modalities employed in the treatment of adjustment disorders will be determined by the particular symptoms and stressors. In the two cases described, interventions included individual, insight-oriented therapy, family therapy, and behavioral interventions, as well as environmental manipulations. Both treatment plans started with a plan for a time-limited, brief, focused intervention. Given that the definition of the adjustment disorders entails a temporary, reactive condition, a brief, rather than a long-term therapeutic intervention is generally indicated. It should be recognized that time and events unrelated to therapy, such as changes in the precipitating stressful circumstances, may be crucial factors leading to the child's readjustment. The therapist should keep this consideration in mind before deciding to recommend any therapeutic intervention at all. Given the nature of this disorder, one should at least consider the possibility that no treatment is certainly the most cost-effective and possibly the most effective approach. There are, however, no clear criteria for determining which cases will be most responsive to treatment, and therefore a clinical determination of the severity of the child's maladaptive response should guide the decision whether to treat or to wait. It is likely that many cases of adjustment disorders never reach clinical attention or improve while on clinic waiting lists.

When there is indication for clinical intervention, the choice of particular modalities is guided by the presenting symptoms, stressors, and capacity of the child and his family to participate in the therapeutic process. Particularly in children, the adjustment disorders often respond to family interventions, in that the stressors are often familial or the potential for effecting changes lies within the family. The family is often responding to the same stressor, as in the case of Peter's parents, whose reaction to his illness was contributing to his maladaptive response. Their participation in the treatment was necessary in order to help them understand their own reactions to the onset of Peter's diabetes and the effect this had on Peter. In the case of Susan, her symptoms were felt to be a direct response to stressors that were in the domain of the adults in the family. The intervention employed therefore focused on her family. Her parents and grandmother participated in sessions and to a great extent Susan was disengaged from the direct intervention. In this case the identified patient improved as a result of interventions that did not directly address her gastrointestinal symptoms but rather addressed the underlying family dynamics fueling them. In other cases, such as when the child is responding to a change in schools or a move, the family can be utilized to provide the support and consistency needed for him to return to his previous level of adaptation. Parental counseling will often help provide the parents with a developmental perspective necessary for understanding their child's stress reaction.

Individual therapeutic interventions are indicated when there is a need a) to help provide insight into the connection between the child's symptoms and precipitating stressors; b) to provide support that is not available in the family; and c) to help the child develop alternative, more adaptive responses to the experienced stress. The therapist, as a neutral participant, can help the child gain perspective and achieve a greater sense of control over his reactions, if not his circumstances. In most cases, the use of psychotropic medications will not be indicated. The use of antianxiety agents for temporary relief of anxiety symptoms is less common in children than in adults.

Environmental interventions, such as mobilizing and making use of available support systems in the family and community, are often important components of a treatment plan. Interactions between the therapist and other important individuals in the patient's life, such as teachers and physicians, are frequently indicated. In the case of Peter, improving communication between his parents and the endocrinologist resulted in more accurate knowledge about his illness, leading to better control of his blood sugar and decreased anxiety in Peter and his parents.

Research on the adjustment disorders, particularly in children, is sparse and the evidence that guides our clinical interventions is limited. The fact that this is one of the most commonly utilized diagnostic categories only emphasizes the need for additional information regarding individual vulnerability or resilience in the face of stress, familial patterns, diagnostic and prognostic predictors, treatment interventions, and outcome in the adjustment disorders. Clearly, some assumptions associated with adjustment disorders, such as the temporary duration of symptoms and good prognosis, are not necessarily valid, and further information is needed regarding the course and predictive validity of the diagnosis in children. It remains to be determined whether the subtypes of adjustment disorder represent variations of the same disorder or whether they are unrelated, nonspecific descriptive categories.

REFERENCES

Adams, P. R., and Adams, G. R. (1984). Mount Saint Helen's ashfall, evidence for a disaster stress reaction. *Amer. Psychol.* 39(3):252–60.

Andreasen, N. C., and Hoenk, P. R. (1982). The predictive value of adjustment disorders: A follow-up study. *Amer. J. Psychiat.* 139(5):584–90.

———, and Wasek, P. (1980). Adjustment disorders in adolescents and adults. *Arch. Gen. Psychiat.* 37:1166–70.

Burke, J. D., et al. (1982). Changes in children's behavior after a natural disaster. *Amer. J. Psychiat.* 139(8):1010–14.

Canter, A., Cluff, L. E., and Imboden, J. B. (1972). Hypersensitive reactions to immunization innoculations and antecedent psychological vulnerability. *J. Psychosom. Res.* 16:99–101.

Caplan, G. (1974). *Support Systems and Community Mental Health: Lectures on Concept Development.* New York: Behavioral Publications.

Dohrenwend, B. S. (1973). Social status and stressful life events. *J. Person. Soc. Psychol.* 28:225–35.

———, and Dohrenwend, B. P. (1970). Class and race as status related sources of stress. In S. Levine and N. A. Scotch (Eds.). *Social Stress.* Chicago: Aldine, pp. 111–40.

Dunn, J., and Kendrick, C. (1982). *Siblings: Love, Envy, and Understanding.* Cambridge: Harvard University Press.

Faerstein, L. M. (1981). Stress and coping in families of learning-disabled children: A literature review. *J. Learn. Disab.* 14(7):420–23.

Freud, A. (1958). Adolescence (Adolescence in psychoanalytic theory). *Psychoanal. Study Child* 13:255–78.

Gersten, J. C., et al. (1974). Child behavior and life events. In B. S. Dohrenwend and B. P. Dohrenwend (Eds.). *Stressful Life Events, Their Nature and Effects.* New York: Wiley, pp. 159–70.

Gould, M., et al. (In press). U.K.–WHO Study of ICD-9: Issues of Classification. In M. Rutter, H. Tuma, and I. Lann (Eds.). *Assessment, Diagnosis, and Classification in Child and Adolescent Psychopathology.* New York: Guilford Press.

Hetherington, E. M., Cox, M., and Cox, S. (1982). Effects of divorce on parents and children. In M. Lamb (Ed.). *Non-Traditional Families.* Hillsdale, N.J.: Lawrence Erlbaum.

Holmes, T. H., and Rahe, R. H. (1967). The social readjustment rating scale. *J. Psychosom. Res.* 11:213–18.

Jacobsen, A. M., et al. (1980). Diagnosed mental disorder in children and use of health services in four organized health care settings. *Amer. J. Psychiat.* 137(5):559–65.

Kaffman, M., and Elizur, E. (1983). Bereavement responses of kibbutz and nonkibbutz children following the death of the father. *J. Child Psychol. Psychiat.* 24(3):435–42.

Kellerman, J., and Siegel, S. (1980). Behavioral distress in children with cancer undergoing medical procedures: Developmental considerations. *J. Consul. Clin. Psychol.* 48(3):356–65.

Kovacs, M., et al. (1985). Initial coping responses and psychosocial characteristics of children with insulin-dependent diabetes mellitus. *J. Ped.* 106(5):827–34.

Magnusson, D., and Ekehammar, B. (1975). Perceptions of and reactions to stressful situations. *J. Person. Social Psychol.* 31(6):1147–54.

Meichenbaum, D. (1979). The work of worrying in children undergoing surgery. *J. Abnorm. Child Psychol.* 7(2):121–32.

Meyers, J. K., Lindenthal, J. J., and Pepper, M. P. (1974). Social class, life events and psychiatric symptoms: A longitudinal study. In B. S. Dohrenwend and B. P. Dohrenwend (Eds.). *Stressful Life Events.* New York: Wiley.

Parkes, C. M., and Weiss, R. S. (1983). *Recovery from Bereavement.* New York: Basic Books.

Paykel, E. S. (1974). Life stress and psychiatric disorder. In B. S. Dohrenwend and B. P. Dohrenwend (Eds.). *Stress Life Events, Their Nature and Effects.* New York: Wiley, pp. 135–49.

Ravenscroft, K. (1983). Psychiatric consultation to the child with acute physical trauma. *Annual Prog. Child Psychiat. Child Develop.* 448–61.

Rutter, M., et al. (1976). Adolescent turmoil: Fact or fiction? *J. Child Psychol. Psychiat.* 17:35–56.

Sandler, I. N., and Block, M. (1979). Life stress and maladaptation of children. *Amer. J. Comm. Psychol.* 7(4):425–40.

Sommer, D., and Lasry, J. C. (1984). Personality and reactions to stressful life events. *Canada's Mental Health* Sept., pp. 19–20.

Terr, L. C. (1981). Psychic trauma in children: Observations following the Chowchilla schoolbus kidnapping. *Amer. J. Psychiat.* 138(1):14–19.

Vachon, M., et al. (1982). Correlates of enduring stress patterns following bereavement: Social network, life situation and personality. *Psycholog. Med.* 12:783–88.

Van Eerdewegh, M., et al. (1982). The bereaved child. *Brit. J. Psychiat.* 140:23–29.

Vinokur, A., and Selzer, M. L. (1975). Desirable versus undesirable life events: Their relationship to stress and mental distress. *J. Person. Social Psychol.* 32(2):329–37.

Wallerstein, J. S. (1983). Children of divorce: Stress and developmental tasks. In N. Garnezy and M. Rutter (Eds.). *Stress, Coping and Development in Children.* New York: McGraw Hill, pp. 265–302.

Weiner, I. B., and DelGaudio, A. C. (1976). Psychopathology in adolescence. *Arch. Gen. Psychiat.* 33:187–93.

Werry, J. S., et al. (1983). The interrater reliability of DSM-III in children. *J. Abnorm. Child Psychol.* 11(3):341–54.

VIII

Assessment of Special Disorders and Situations

39

CLINICAL EVALUATION OF NONORGANIC FAILURE TO THRIVE

James Egan, Sharon S. Schaefer,
and Irene Chatoor

INTRODUCTION

Failure to thrive is a serious, complex disorder of multiple etiologies that afflicts infants and young children. It is a symptom complex, a syndrome rather than a specific disease entity. The failure to thrive disorder (FTT) is generally thought of as falling into two subgroups: failure to thrive secondary to chronic disease, or organic FTT; and functional failure to thrive, or nonorganic FTT.

Organic failure to thrive may be caused by almost any known pediatric disorder. Virtually all chronic diseases may result in FTT. Among these are metabolic, genetic, infectious, autoimmune and congenital disturbances that affect the gastrointestinal, nervous, respiratory, renal, hepatic, cardiac, or hematopoietic systems.

Nonorganic failure to thrive (NFTT) has been called hospitalism (Spitz 1945), anaclitic depression (Spitz 1946), psychosocial dwarfism (Caldwell 1971), or environmental failure to thrive (Rosenn et al. 1975). In DSM-III, nonorganic failure to thrive is called a "Reactive Attachment Disorder of Infancy" (313.89). Recent advances in our understanding of NFTT suggest that the reactive attachment disorder diagnostic label is not sufficiently precise (Egan et al. 1980). Specifically, some infants and children present with NFTT, not on the basis of an attachment disorder, but rather on the basis of a separation disorder occurring during the process of somatopsychological differentiation (Greenspan and Lieberman 1980).

The diagnosis of failure to thrive is established when one of two sets of conditions is met:

1) when there is an abrupt deceleration in the rate of growth, e.g., from the 35th to the 15th percentile, or
2) when weight is below the 3rd percentile.

INCIDENCE

The exact incidence of failure to thrive is difficult to determine, but Reinhart (1977) suggested that at least 1 percent of all children suffer from organic growth failure. Rosen (1978) found 8 percent of the children attending an inner-city ambulatory pediatric clinic to be below the 3rd percentile in weight. According to English (1978), between 1 percent and 5 percent of all admissions to a general pediatric hospital are for FTT and of these admissions, only 40 to 50 percent are discovered to have an organic cause.

A typical distribution (see Table 39.1) for children hospitalized with failure to thrive was reported by English (1978). Seventy-seven children were admitted to New York Hospital for FTT. Thirty-five were diagnosed as FTT nonorganic (including the "no determination" diagnosis), outnumbering any single organic diagnosis.

Our experience has confirmed that mixed etiologies exist in significant numbers. For example, we have found children with an original organic disorder (i.e., malrotation or metabolic disorders) who later developed a superimposed NFTT of either the attachment or separation disorder type (Chatoor et al. 1984b). A study done by Homer and Ludwig (1981) also suggests that organic and nonorganic etiologies may

TABLE 39.1   Final Diagnosis of 77 Children Admitted for Evaluation of Failure to Thrive

Final Diagnosis	Number of Children
Gastrointestinal disorder (physiologic) (Malabsorption, diarrhea)	11
Neurological disorder (Cerebral palsy, neurofibromatosis, microcephaly, asphyxia)	11
Cardiac disorder	5
Endocrine disorder (Panhypopituitarism, hypothyroidism, hypoglycemia)	3
Urinary disorder (Infection, reflux, congenital nephritis)	3
Cystic fibrosis	2
Syndrome	2
Multiple congenital anomalies	1
Myopathy (Nemaline)	1
Constitutional short stature	1
Gastrointestinal disorder (anatomical) (Pyloric stenosis, obstruction)	2
No determination	3
Nonorganic (Maternal child interaction, child abuse, maternal deprivation, feeding disorder	29

Source: *Pediatric Annals 7*, November 1978, p. 84 (including the "no determination" diagnosis), outnumbering any single organic diagnosis.

coexist for failure to thrive. Their study of a tertiary-care population of eighty-two hospitalized children found that 28 percent had primarily an organic contributant, while 46 percent had primarily nonorganic contributants. Twenty-six percent of the cases studied presented with a mixed etiology.

In psychiatry, as in medicine in general, a diagnosis is made on the basis of the history and physical examination (mental status examination). We agree with Accardo's (1982) statement:

> The overwhelming majority of organic etiologies for FTT are identified by the history and physical examination; nonorganic etiologies should be similarly identified. An overreliance on laboratory procedures to exhaustively "rule out" organic etiologies needs to be discouraged. . . . It is better to attribute incorrectly a small percentage of organic illness to functional causes than to condemn a large number of healthy patients to the fear of a nonexistent disease (Armstrong 1946).

To make a diagnosis of NFTT on the basis of inclusionary and exclusionary criteria (not just a diagnosis of last resort made because all laboratory studies are negative), the clinician must have full grasp of the various causes of organic and nonorganic FTT. As Pasteur said, "In the fields of observation, chance favors only the mind that is prepared" (Vallery-Radot 1923). Especially because mixed etiologies are common, the chance of making a proper diagnosis is increased when the clinician is educated to look simultaneously for multiple contributing factors.

THE FUNCTIONAL ASPECTS OF FAILURE TO THRIVE

NFTT is best understood in a developmental context. It can be thought of as comprising a disturbance primarily in either the attachment or the separation phase of development.

Disorder of Attachment

A disturbance in the early mother-child relationship (disorder of attachment) in which there is a lack of or inconsistency in maternal care and warmth can result in NFTT. Infants suffering from this disorder generally fail to thrive in the first six months of life. Frequently they are born to mothers who are overwhelmed by the emotional burdens of child-care. Typically, these mothers are needy themselves and are often young, unmarried, isolated, and without financial or social resources. Frequently they have experienced deprivation or abuse during their own childhoods.

The children who present with this type of NFTT are usually developmentally delayed, listless, apathetic, depressed, and are reminiscent of the hospitalism and anaclitic depression patients of Spitz (1945, 1946).

CASE VIGNETTE

Lisa was admitted to the hospital at 3 months weighing (at 7 lbs. 4 oz.) only 3 ounces above her birth weight. She was a passive, unhappy baby who stiffened when she was held, made poor eye contact, and lacked appropriate social development.

Her parents had arrived from out-of-state and had been ordered by Protective Services to bring the baby to a hospital as soon as they had arrived. The maternal grandmother and maternal aunt brought Lisa and her parents to the hospital's emergency room.

The parents were angry at Protective Services, their relatives, the hospital, and every helping professional connected with it. The mother was passive and unresponsive. Her affect was depressed, her hair was dirty, her complexion was grey. The father seemed belligerent and grandiose. He displaced onto everyone else the reasons for the baby's deteriorated physical condition and the family's total social upheaval. The parents and their five other children were living in an unwelcome atmosphere with the grandparents. After Lisa's admission, the parents left the hospital abruptly and did not visit for three weeks. Despite active efforts during this time, the staff was unable to locate and convince the family that Lisa was lonesome without them.

Work with Lisa was initiated by hospital staff on the day of admission. The goals were: (1) to increase her responsiveness to people; (2) to help her become more cognitively aware of her environment; (3) to encourage her to look to people and caretakers as sources of pleasure and satisfaction (instead of her singular lonely rumination); and most importantly, (4) to take increased amounts of food and calories. As Lisa gained weight and struggled toward health, it became critical to integrate her mother into the feeding process as soon as possible.

After repeated futile attempts, the mother came to stay with Lisa for a day. The staff rewarded this depressed and frightened mother with concrete examples of their concern. The mother accepted conversation, meal trays, and cups of tea from staff. A diagnostic videotape of mother and infant (feeding for twenty minutes and playing for ten minutes) revealed a depressed mother who made few attempts at engaging Lisa by talking and smiling. Lisa, an alert baby, actively sought to engage her mother by smiling and cooing at her. The social worker watched the tape with the mother and pointed out and interpreted all positive responses between mother and baby. After this experience, the mother found it easier to return and became increasingly confident in her ability to engage Lisa. Once she began to trust the social worker, the mother revealed her feelings of loss and depression after her grandmother's death, which had occurred shortly after Lisa was born. As the parents were helped by Protective Services in finding housing and school placement for their other children, the mother became more available to visit Lisa at the hospital.

Lisa, who had blossomed with the loving care of the nursing staff, rewarded her mother with smiles when she came to play with her. Lisa became instrumental in mobilizing her mother's depression. The parents received ongoing support services for themselves and their other children, and Lisa continued to thrive when she returned home.

Disorder of Separation

Beginning in the latter half of the first year of life and extending through the second year of life is another variety of NFTT—disorder of separation. Frequently this later onset NFTT begins with maternal concern about the infant's food intake (Egan et al. 1980; Chatoor and Egan 1983). Often a previous organic problem, such as mild milk intolerance or pyloric stenosis, has heightened the mother's concern and involvement. In some instances, although no organic antecedent exists, the mother seems overly involved in a need-satisfying relationship with her child. Generally, mothers of separation disordered NFTT children are from middle- or upper-middle-class families.

In later onset NFTT, the mother's involvement has allowed the infant to make an attachment. However, the child's thrusts for autonomy are met with ambivalence and inconsistent encouragement by the mother. For example, if a child's wish to feed himself is actively discouraged by his mother, a relatively benign "battle of spoons" (Levy 1955) can escalate into a clash of wills that may result in a severe eating disorder. Initially, the child may only refuse to eat for the mother, but if the condition persists, the oppositional food refusal will be generalized to other caretakers. This eating disorder is a severe exacerbation of the frequent developmental eating disturbances of the anal period described by Anna Freud (1946). Although these children do not exhibit the extensive developmental delays seen in children suffering from an attachment disorder, serious oppositional behaviors in other areas (bedtime, toilet training) frequently follow in this disorder of separation. If the food refusal persists, weight and sometimes height may be impaired due to chronic undernutrition.

CASE VIGNETTE

Karen, a 26-month-old white female, was referred by her pediatrician because of nonorganic failure to thrive, secondary to food refusal. At the time of referral, Karen's weight was far below the 3rd percentile and her height was in the 25th percentile for her chronological age. Her concerned parents reported that for the last few weeks she had been living almost entirely on apple juice and refused most solid food.

Karen was the only child of young parents, both of whom were professionals. She was born four weeks prematurely and had been a poor feeder from birth. Her mother had planned to give up her career and stay at home with her child, but felt frustrated and trapped when she spent hours and hours breastfeeding her infant, who had a very poor suck. After three months of struggle, the paternal grandmother supported the mother in switching to bottle feeding. Karen was thriving well until 9 months of age, when her mother introduced solid food. When Karen refused to eat certain foods, her mother became anxious and offered different types of food in the hope that Karen would eat better. The harder she tried, the more Karen refused to eat. The mother admitted that at this point she dreaded going in the kitchen and preparing any food. The mother also recalled her own childhood battles around food, which subsided at age 4 when her mother placed the maid in charge of her meals.

Karen turned out to be a charming little girl with precocious cognitive development, as evidenced in her speech and play. A diagnostic videotape of mother and child (during twenty minutes of feeding and ten minutes of play) revealed a maladaptive mother-child relationship during feeding. The mother tried to coax and distract Karen to get her to eat, but the harder she tried the more Karen seemed to enjoy her mother's attention and refused to open her mouth. When the mother became frustrated and tried to pry Karen's mouth open to get her to eat, Karen became furious and started to throw her spoon and food. The meal ended with Karen having eaten very little and mother and child being frustrated and angry. This feeding experience was in contrast to pleasurable give-and-take between mother and child during play.

Treatment started out with helping the mother see how well she had done in other areas of mothering. We then dealt with the feeding difficulties. The mother was helped to see that Karen's enjoyment of her mother's attention superceded her hunger for food, and that her oppositional refusal to eat was an expression of her need for autonomy. The parents were encouraged to separate meal times from play times and to set firm limits to the length of the meal times. Once the mother had convinced herself that Karen's food intake would be regulated by physiological feelings of hunger and satiation, she was able to follow through with the recommendations. On the first day, Karen refused two meals. Then she cried because her "tummy hurt." Her mother explained to her that she had hunger pains and that if she would eat, they would go away. Karen then proceeded to eat. This marked the turning point in her treatment. Mother and child did very well for a two-week period. Karen then engaged her father in the game-play around food. After a short period of regression, both parents were able to work together in helping Karen to separate her "emotional hunger" for her parents' attention from her physiological hunger for food.

Karen has done very well; she is thriving physically and emotionally. The mother was so excited about Karen's progress that she felt ready for another baby, whom she decided to bottle feed.

EVALUATION OF THE CHILD WITH NFTT

Infants and children whose growth failure may have identifiable organic pathogenesis require a simultaneous, systematic evaluation of any nonorganic factors that may compromise the child's growth and development. Just as organic FTT can be complicated by nonorganic variables, nonorganic FTT cases frequently present with a mixed clinical picture rather than with a pure disorder of attachment or a pure disorder of separation.

Factors to Be Evaluated

Evaluation of NFTT requires investigation and assessment of the following:

1. mother's personality structure, history of experience with her own parents, and current marital relationship (in this chapter "mother" is used in a generic sense to mean principal caretaker);
2. infant's behavioral characteristics and temperamental style;
3. mother-infant interaction and relationship;
4. social/environmental factors.

Mother's Personality Structure and Experience with Own Parents. Much has been written about mothers whose infants suffer from the early onset of NFTT. These mothers are frequently described as suffering from character pathology and affective illness. The mother's poor parenting, social isolation, and economic hardship are also evident. Although the description is valid, it is important during the NFTT evaluation to refine this generalized understanding by identifying particular factors that put the infant and mother at highest risk. Glaser et al. (1968) suggested that the highest risk exists when the mother's needs take precedence over the infant's. Fraiberg et al. (1975) emphasized that the need of mothers (and fathers) correlated to the "ghosts," the unmet needs, of their own growing years. However, Drotar and Malone (1982) suggested that the manner in which a traumatic or deprived childhood experience can influence the mother-infant relationship is affected by the current context of family life.

Our clinical experience has alerted us to the following particulars: the mother's feelings of isolation during pregnancy and birth, current marital distress or unavailability of the father, recent death or other loss, and the mother's perception that her infant is disappointedly less than average (Broussard 1979). Mothers of infants who have sustained organic insults and who consequently perceive their infants as damaged, disappointing, and burdensome also appear to be at higher risk.

The mothers of later onset NFTT (disorder of separation) appear to suffer less from chronic affective disorders. However, their ambivalence about motherhood must be evaluated. Like mothers of earlier onset NFTT, they experience anger and disappointment in their children; however, their defensive adaptation is generally at a higher level, that is, they develop reaction-formation defenses.

Some of the mothers whose children suffer from disorders of separation have an inordinate investment in their child to compensate for a paucity of relationship elsewhere, as with a husband. Therefore a careful marital history is needed. This may require that the father of the infant be interviewed separately, as well as conjointly with the mother.

Infant's Behavioral Characteristics and Temperamental Style. Observational research focused on infants in the last two decades has expanded our understanding of their innate attributes and capacities. In addition, such researchers as Pollitt and Eichler (1976) have studied behavioral qualities of infants with FTT. Our clinical work would concur that NFTT infants are often "difficult." Caretakers share the complaint that NFTT children send poor cues. Thus a NFTT evaluation must consider in what ways the infant may contribute to his own growth failure.

During the NFTT evaluation, an infant should be assessed for his state control—his ability to regulate his sensory and autonomic system and to control his motor movements. For example, is his homeostasis easily disrupted by internal as well as external stimuli? Does he have a low threshold for overstimulation? Can he organize to console himself? Does he thrash around and disorganize when uncovered or when exposed to loud noises?

The infant's response to the caretaker should be assessed: Does he alert and brighten to the human face? Will he sustain his gaze on the mother's face? Will he orient to the human voice? Does he vocalize in response to stimulation from the mother?

The infant's response to tactile stimulation should be evaluated: When held does he stiffen, arch, or fail to mold to caretaker's body? In the older infant or child, is there an anticipatory postural movement toward the mother when she reaches for him?

The infant's temperament should be assessed. How irritable is the child? Is he comforted and consoled relatively easily? Does he have difficulty establishing sleep rhythms? In the case of the older infant, is he moody, whining, and/or clinging?

Mother-Infant Interaction and Relationship. The range of mother-infant interaction in both the disorder of attachment and the disorder of separation is considerable. The experience of having observed relatively normal mother-infant dyads is important for the clinical evaluation of NFTT.

> The infant is a virtuoso performer in his attempts to regulate both the level of stimulation from the caregiver and the internal level of stimulation in himself. The mother is also a virtuoso in her moment-by-moment regulation of the interaction. Together they evolve some exquisitely intricate dyadic patterns (Stern 1977).

In the NFTT mother-infant interaction, the "exquisitely intricate dyadic patterns" are discordant. The task of the evaluation is to identify as specifically as possible what aspects of the interaction have gone awry, in order to rechoreograph the interaction. For example, it is not sufficient to say the mother and infant do not make eye contact. Does the mother initiate eye contact? Does the infant gaze and brighten to mother's face as the mother tries? Does the infant avert his gaze as an attempt at self-regulation of stimuli? Does the mother respect the gaze aversion in this instance, or does she rob the infant of self-regulation by heightened stimulation? Other aspects of the interaction to consider are: the amount of physical contact, the pleasurable quality of interactive behavior, consistency and predictability in the interaction, the mother's response to the infant's distress and the infant's response to the mother's attempts to soothe.

The evaluation of the mother-infant relationship must assess the appropriateness of the mother's expectations. Bithoney and Rathbun (1981) referred to several possible dyadic mismatches. Normal infant/inaccurate maternal expectations are included, with burdensome infant/poorly resilient mother and impossible infant/adequate mother.

When later onset NFTT is being evaluated, consideration must be given to the mother's capacity for empathic response to the child's developing ability to separate physiological needs (hunger) from needs for affectionate and stimulating interaction. Is the mother able to encourage her child's intentionally autonomous behavior, for example, his attempts to feed himself? The mother helps the infant in this differentiation by consistent and predictable responses. If the environmental responses are undifferentiated or inappropriate, the infant may then use physiological patterns to respond to situations where a social response would be more adaptive. For example, many parents respond to a fretful or bored infant by offering food, knowing that another response might be more appropriate. Although attentive to her child, the mother of the infant with a disorder of separation frequently misreads or responds inappropriately to her child's cues. When the mother is ambivalent, unpredictable, unwilling, or unable to read cues, the child's normal thrust for separation can be compromised.

Psychosocial Factors. In addition to assessing the personality structure of the mother, the personal history, and marital situation, the clinician must consider other environmental and social factors that can be stressful to a family and influence the family's response to their infant. These include: financial stress or chronic poverty, chronic illness, other children in the family who are exhibiting problems, isolation from extended family and neighborhood, and ineffective use of community and medical resources. Since any or all of these factors may exist within a family that does not have an FTT child, it is important to understand how these factors may exacerbate the problem without being the principal causative factor. Environmental variables need to be investigated carefully and not assumed on the basis of race, social class, or identified risk factors (Accardo 1982).

THE PROCEDURE FOR EVALUATION

To collect the data needed for a NFTT evaluation the following procedure is suggested:

1. a semistructured interview with the mother and father separately, and with both parents together;
2. a direct observation of the mother feeding the infant;
3. a direct observation of the mother playing with the infant.

Home visits can be beneficial but are more pertinent to monitoring treatment interventions than to the evaluation itself.

The reasons for interviewing parents are self-evident. The need for direct observation of the mother-infant dyad should also be clear, when it is understood as part of the physical examination. Direct observation of mothers feeding and playing with their children enables the diagnostic team to evaluate impoverished, indiscriminate, inconsistent, and dissonant interaction. In addition, the mother's report of the child's development and temperamental style can be confirmed.

We have found that videotaping our direct observations is particularly useful. The videotapes allow for careful repeated study of the mother-infant interaction. Specific behavioral feeding difficulties that may exist can be identified. Videotapes allow the clinician to use rating scales that can assess feeding and playing behavior. We have found the rating scales useful in diagnosing more precisely a particular type of NFTT (Chatoor et al. 1984a). In addition, videotapes of feeding and play sessions assist in the development and monitoring of a specific treatment plan.

SUMMARY

Failure to thrive is a condition that, without intervention, can lead to severe disturbances in physical, intellectual, social, and emotional development. Nonorganic variables that may compromise a child's growth should be an inclusionary part of the failure to thrive evaluation even when organic variables are present. The evaluation of nonorganic failure to thrive should be conducted within a developmental perspective. Nuances of separation as well as attachment must be understood. The mother, the child, and the mother-child interaction are all variables that need assessment in a nonorganic failure to thrive evaluation. Good treatment planning and therefore a more favorable outcome depends on careful and thorough assessment.

REFERENCES

Accardo, P. (1982). Growth and development: Interactional context. In P. Accardo (Ed.). *Failure to Thrive in Infancy and Childhood: A Multidisciplinary Team Approach.* Baltimore: University Park Press.

Armstrong, T. G. (1946). The use of reassurance. *Lancet* 2:480–82.

Bithoney, W., and Rathbun, J. (1981). Failure to thrive. In M. D. Levine, W. B. Carey, A. C. Crocker, and R. T. Gross (Eds.). *Developmental Behavioral Pediatrics.* Philadelphia: Saunders.

Broussard, E. (1979). Assessment of the adaptive potential of the mother-infant system: The neonatal perception inventories. *Seminars in Perinatology* 3(1)91–100.

Caldwell, B. (1971). The effects of psychosocial deprivation on human development in infancy. *Annual Progress in Child Psychiatry and Child Development.* New York: Brunner/Mazel, pp. 3–22.

Chatoor, I., and Egan, J. (1983). Nonorganic failure to thrive and dwarfism due to food refusal: A separation disorder. *J. Amer. Acad. Child Psychiat.* 22(3):294–301.

——, et al. (1984a). Pediatric assessment of nonorganic failure to thrive. *Ped. Annals* 13(11):844–50.

——, et al. (1984b). Nonorganic failure to thrive: A developmental perspective. *Ped. Annals* 13(11):829–43.

Drotar, D., and Malone, C. (1982). Family-oriented intervention in failure to thrive. In M. Klaus and M. Robertson (Eds.). *Birth, Interaction and Attachment.* (Pediatric Round Table, Vol 6). Skillman, N.J.: Johnson and Johnson.

Egan, J., Chatoor, I., and Rosen, G. (1980). Nonorganic failure to thrive: Pathogenesis and classification. *Clinical Proceedings* (Children's Hospital National Medical Center) 36:173–82.

English, P. C. (1978). Failure to thrive without organic reason. *Ped. Annals* 7:776–81.

Fraiberg, S., Adelson, E., and Shapiro, V. (1975). Ghosts in the nursery: A psychoanalytic approach to the problems of impaired infant-mother relationships. *J. Amer. Acad. Child Psychiat.* 14:387–421.

Freud, A. (1946). The psychoanalytic study of infantile feeding disturbances. *Psychoanal. Study Child* 2:119–32.

Glaser, H. H., et al. (1968). Physical and psychological development of children with early failure to thrive. *J. Ped.* 73:690–98.

Greenspan, S., and Lieberman, A. (1980). Infants, mothers and their interaction: A quantitative clinical approach to developmental assessment. In S. Greenspan and G. Pollock (Eds.). *The Course of Life: Psychoanalytic Contributions Toward Understanding Personality Development,* Vol. 1. Washington, D.C.: Department of Health and Human Services.

Homer, C., and Ludwig, S. (1981). Categorization of etiology of failure to thrive. *Amer. J. Dis. Child.* 135(9):848–51.

Levy, D. (1955). Oppositional syndromes and oppositional behavior. In P. Hoch and J. Zobin (Eds.). *Psychopathology of Childhood.* New York: Grune and Stratton.

Pollitt, E., and Eichler, A. (1976). Behavioral disturbances among failure to thrive children. *Amer. J. Dis. Child.* 130:24–29.

Reinhart, J. B. (1977). Syndromes of deficits in parenting: Abuse, neglect, and accidents. *Ped. Annals* 6:628–35.

Rosen, G. (1978). Reversible growth and developmental retardation in the first year of life. *Clinical Proceedings* (Children's Hospital National Medical Center) 33:193.

Rosenn, D., Stein, L., and Bates, M. (1975). The differentiation of organic from environmental failure to thrive. Read before the American Pediatric Society, Denver, Colo., April 19, 1975.

Spitz, R. (1945). Hospitalism, an inquiry into the psychiatric conditions of early childhood. *Psychoanal. Study Child* 1:53–74.

——. (1946). Anaclitic depression, an inquiry into the psychiatric conditions in early childhood. *Psychoanal. Study Child* 2:313–42.

Stern, D. (1977). *The First Relationship: Infant and Mother.* Cambridge: Harvard University Press.

Vallery-Radot, R. (1923). *The Life of Pasteur.* R. L. Devonshire (Trans.). Garden City, N.Y.: Doubleday, Page.

40

THE ABUSED CHILD AND ADOLESCENT

Arthur H. Green

INTRODUCTION

The concept of child-abuse has been broadened in recent years. In his seminal article (1962), Kempe and his colleagues described child-abuse as the infliction of serious injury upon young children by parents or caretakers. The injuries, which included fractures, subdural hematoma, and multiple soft-tissue injuries, often resulted in permanent disability and death. Fontana (1971) viewed child-abuse as one end of a spectrum of maltreatment that also included emotional deprivation, neglect, and malnutrition. These were all designated as components of the "Maltreatment Syndrome." Helfer (1975) stressed the prevalence of minor injuries resulting from abuse; he estimated that 10 percent of all childhood accidents treated in emergency rooms were consequences of physical abuse. Gil (1970) further expanded the concept of child-abuse to include any action that interferes with a child's achievement of his physical and psychological potential. Gil's definition appears to be too vague and overinclusive and would present enormous difficulties in reporting and investigation if it were to be legally enforced.

According to most state laws, child-abuse is defined as the infliction of injury on a person under 18 years of age by a parent or legally responsible caretaker. Abuse also includes the creation of a substantial risk of serious physical injury upon the child by the parent or caretaker and the committing of an act of sexual abuse against the child. Neglect refers to the failure of a parent or caretaker to supply the child with adequate food, clothing, shelter, education, medical care, and supervision. Abandonment of a child and caretaking failure associated with alcohol or drug abuse also constitute neglect.

This chapter will deal primarily with the physically and sexually abused child. Child-abuse is a complex phenomenon that cannot be ascribed to a single causal agent. Many early investigators sought to discover a specific personality trait or psychological abnormality in the abusive parent that could explain his or her violent behavior toward the child. Others looked exclusively toward environmental factors such as poverty and family disorganization as the major cause. These early studies failed to include control groups, which led to faulty conclusions and generalizations. More recent research has used appropriate control groups and is based on a theory of multiple causality. Three major etiological variables are now assumed to play a role in the genesis of child-abuse. These are: the "abuse-prone" personality traits of the parents; the special characteristics of the children that make them vulnerable to scapegoating and abuse; and adverse environmental factors that catalyze the violent interaction between the "abuse-prone" parent and vulnerable child.

CHARACTERISTICS OF ABUSING PARENTS

A large number of behavioral and personality traits have been attributed to abusing parents, such as dependency and passivity (Merrill 1962); impulsivity and aggression (Merrill 1962; Bryant 1963); criminality (Smith 1975; Oliver et al. 1974); low intelligence (Smith 1975); and marital friction (Green 1976). Demographic indices associated with child-abuse include low socioeconomic status (Gil 1970; Smith 1975; Lukianowicz 1972); younger age and social immaturity of abusing mothers (Simons et al. 1966; Smith 1975); premarital conception and illegitimacy (Smith 1975); social isolation with deficient support systems (Smith 1975; Wolock and Horowitz 1977; Starr and Ceresnie 1978); and nonwhite minority status (Gil 1970; Smith 1975).

In addition to their excessive reliance on physical punishment, typical child-rearing practices of abusing parents include "role-reversal," the tendency of the parent to seek emotional gratification from the child (Morris and Gould 1963); premature and inappropriate demands for performance from the child without regard for the child's helplessness (Gregg 1968; Johnson and Morse 1968; Green 1980); a lack of empathy for the child (Smith 1975; Green 1980); and a lack of knowledge about child development (Green 1980).

The childhood history and background of abusing parents include a high frequency of physical abuse and neglect, scapegoating, maternal deprivation, and exploitation (Green 1976; Steele and Pollock 1968; Wolock and Horowitz 1977). Child-abuse by fathers is often accompanied by spouse-abuse, frequent drinking, and vocational failure (Green 1979).

The wide variety of these behaviors and the fact that they frequently exist in nonabusive parents suggest that a specific "abusive personality" does not exist. However, individuals with these traits may be considered "abuse-prone." They will be more likely than others to strike their children, given other potentiating factors such as interpersonal and environmental stress and characteristics of the child that render him more difficult to care for.

More penetrating impressions of the parental psychopathology and psychodynamics associated with child-abuse have been derived from observations of the abusive interaction and the psychiatric treatment of abusing parents (Green 1976; Steele 1970). The key psychodynamic elements are role-reversal, excessive reliance on defenses of denial and projection, pathological identifications with the children and their own parents, and a displacement of aggression from frustrating relationships onto the child (scapegoating).

Role-reversal occurs when the unfulfilled, abusing parent seeks dependency gratification, unavailable from spouse and family, from the child. The child's inability to satisfy this inappropriate demand causes him to be unconsciously perceived as the original "rejecting parent." This intensifies the parent's feelings of rejection and worthlessness, threatening his fragile narcissistic equilibrium. These painful feelings are then denied and projected onto the child, who then symbolizes the parent's own "bad" self-image of childhood. The role-reversal is terminated when the parent identifies with his own abusive parent (identification with the aggressor) and redirects his self-directed aggression towards the child. By beating the child, the abuser assuages his punitive superego and attempts actively to master the traumatic experiences passively endured as a child. The scapegoating process continues as the child also becomes the target for aggression displaced from various despised and frustrating objects in the parent's current and past life—a rejecting spouse or lover, a hated sibling rival, or a depriving caretaker. These objects are unconsciously linked to the original "parent-aggression."

CASE VIGNETTE

Sonia, a 6-year-old Hispanic girl, suffered a fractured femur when she was 4 as a result of a severe beating by her mother. Sonia was the daughter by Mrs. G.'s first husband, who left her when Sonia was 1 year old, after frequent quarreling, drinking, and "running around."

Mrs. G. married in order to escape from her brutal godparents, who had raised her since the age of 18 months after her mother had abandoned her. They had been extremely punitive and restrictive: Mrs. G. remembered one occasion on which her stepfather had broken a flowerpot over her head. Mrs. G.'s marriage, which was arranged by the godparents, deteriorated rapidly. She went to work in a factory and was ignored by her husband. She soon became pregnant, but did not want the child, as her husband spent so little time with her. He deserted her when she was six weeks pregnant, and Mrs. G. moved in with her sister-in-law to have the baby. She hoped for a boy, stating, "I don't like girls, boys are more interesting."

In addition to displacing her rage toward her ex-husband and godparents onto Sonia, Mrs. G. identifies with her little girl and brutalizes her in the same fashion that she had experienced at the hands of her godparents. She described the following feelings about Sonia. "Since she was born, I let out all the anger and frustration that I had in myself on her. Whenever she came to me for something, I sent her away with a beating."

Mrs. G. subsequently entered into a common-law relationship with a man who fathered her two young boys. It is significant that she described them in warm and affectionate terms, and does not subject them to physical punishment.

An additional psychodynamic operates in abusing fathers (Green 1979). The father regards the child as a rival for the attention of his spouse, due to the lack of previous satisfaction of his own dependency longings. The competitive rivalry with the child for the mother's love is a repetition of the father's unresolved sibling rivalry during his own childhood. His jealousy of the child usually begins shortly after its birth, when it requires the greatest amount of nurturing and attention. The father frequently assaults his spouse as well as the child. In attacking his spouse and child the father unconsciously reenacts his anger at being excluded from the original mother-sibling relationship.

Child-abuse specialists have thus far been unable to identify a specific psychiatric diagnosis in abusing parents. Only a small percentage of the parents suffer from psychosis (Smith 1975; Steele and Pollock 1968; Green et al. 1980). The majority fall into the category of personality and character disorders. Smith (1975) described a high incidence of psychopathy and criminality in abusing fathers. Sex differences in psychopathology as measured by the MMPI have also been described by Paulson et al. (1974).

CHARACTERISTICS OF ABUSED CHILDREN

The child's role in the abuse process has become a subject of increasing interest. Usually only a single child in a family is selected for scapegoating and abuse, with the most likely candidate being the child who is perceived as the most difficult or burdensome. The majority of reported cases of child-abuse occur during the first two years of life. The infancy and toddler periods, during which the child is most helpless and dependent on caretakers, are particularly stressful times for most parents, especially for those who are "abuse-prone." Irritable, cranky infants who cry frequently, sleep poorly, and who are difficult to soothe may have a devastating effect upon the parent-child relationship. Infants who are relatively passive, lethargic, unresponsive, and slow in development may be equally frustrating to their mothers and provoke maltreatment. Both the irritable and the sluggish infants are readily scapegoated because their mothers perceive their unresponsiveness as a rejection reminiscent of similar experiences with their own parents. This will in turn reinforce their sense of inadequacy.

Physically or psychologically deviant children are also vulnerable to abuse. Children with prominent physical defects, congenital anomalies, mental retardation, or chronic physical illness are not only burdensome, but are readily viewed by narcissistic parents as symbols of their own defective self-image.

Low birth-weight and premature infants seem to be overrepresented in the child-abuse statistics (Klein and Stern 1971; Elmer and Gregg 1967; Simons et al. 1966). This might be explained in several ways: These infants might be perceived as difficult, "unattractive," and more irritable than their normal counterparts. They are also vulnerable to physical illness, feeding difficulties, and retarded development. Their delayed social responsiveness might be especially frustrating for "abuse-prone" parents with high expectations of their infants. The prolonged separation of the mother from her premature infant during the early postpartum period also interferes with normal attachment behavior or "bonding."

CASE VIGNETTE

Ira, an 8-year-old black youngster, was hospitalized at the age of 4 for multiple welts and bruises after a beating administered by his father. His mother complained about his provocative and disruptive behavior, which consisted of soiling, wetting, and failure to do what he was told. Ira has four younger siblings aged 6, 5, 4 years, and 9 months. His mother claims that he demands more attention than the infant. The father continued to beat Ira until he left home. Both the mother and her current boyfriend continue to hit the child when he becomes provocative, as they attribute his deviancy to willful disobedience.

Ira's developmental history indicated that he was born prematurely during the seventh month of gestation. He weighed two pounds at birth and exhibited a marked delay in his speech and motor development. Ira's speech was often incoherent during the interview, and at times he failed to comprehend what was said to him. His full-scale IQ on the WISC was 54, and the neurological examination yielded signs of unequivocal cerebral dysfunction. The impression was that Ira's receptive and expressive language impairment represented an aphasic disorder.

DETECTION OF CHILD-ABUSE

The possibility of child-abuse must be considered in every child who presents with an injury. A careful history and physical examination of the child should be obtained as soon as possible. The child should be hospitalized during the diagnostic evaluation.

A complete history regarding the nature and cause of the injury should be obtained from the parents or the person accompanying the child to the clinic or hospital. The physician or clinician should talk to the parents directly, as second-hand information is regarded as hearsay evidence in court. If he is old enough, the child should also be questioned about the injury. A good history may yield some of the following information, which is suggestive of an inflicted injury:

—unexplained delay in bringing the child for treatment following the injury;
—implausible or contradictory history;
—history incompatible with the nature of the injury;
—a history of repeated suspicious injuries;
—the parent blames the injury on a sibling or third party, or maintains that it was self-inflicted;
—the child has been taken to numerous hospitals for the treatment of injuries;
—the child accuses the parent or caretaker of injuring him.

A detailed history of the mother's own background; childhood; relationships with significant others, including family, spouse or boyfriend, and children; and the home environment can provide important information about parental "abuse-proneness" and current stress. A careful developmental history of the injured child, including a comparison to his siblings, will facilitate assessing the degree of caretaking difficulty posed by the child. The following findings are typical of child-abuse:

—the parent has a history of abuse as a child;
—the parent has unrealistic and premature expectations of the child;
—the child is regarded as "bad" and more difficult than his siblings;
—the parent is unsupported by spouse and/or family and is socially isolated;
—the family has experienced an unusual degree of stress prior to the injury, i.e., marital separation or divorce, death of a grandparent, loss of a job, or major problems with housing or finances.

The physical examination should include a routine X ray survey of all children under five and laboratory tests to rule out the possibility of a bleeding disorder. The child should be hospitalized during this diagnostic evaluation. The following "typical" injuries are frequently associated with child abuse:

—bruises on the buttocks and lower back;
—bruises in the genital area or inner thigh may be inflicted after a child wets or soils, or is resistant to toilet training;
—bruises and soft tissue injuries at different stages of healing—signs of repeated physical abuse;
—bruises of a special configuration such as hand marks, grab marks, pinch marks, and strap marks usually indicate abuse;
—certain types of burns are typically inflicted, for example, multiple cigarette burns, scalding of hands or feet, burns of perineum and buttocks;
—subdural hematoma with or without skull fracture;
—abdominal trauma leading to a ruptured liver or spleen;
—radiological signs, such as superiosteal hemorrhages, epiphyseal separations, mataphyseal fragmentation, periosteal shearing, and periosteal calcification.

Hospitalization of the child provides the staff with an opportunity for observing the daily behavior of the child and his parents, the parent-child interaction, and the visiting pattern of the family. The abused child is often hypervigilant and wary of adults in the hospital setting. He may appear anxious or frightened in the presence of the abusing parent. At times the abused child relates indiscriminately to staff members, making an apparently strong initial attachment to a caretaking figure, only to discard them at the slightest sign of rejection. The abused child is usually overcompliant and eager to please or hyperaggressive and destructive, often alternating between these extremes in behavior. Prior to discharge, he often appears anxious and may verbalize fears about returning home.

Parental visiting patterns are often quite revealing. Infrequent visits might reflect a disinterest in or a rejection of the child. Some parents may act in a harsh, punitive manner towards the child and may be verbally abusive and threatening to staff. They may accuse the nurses and doctors of improper care of the child—a projection of their own hostility. A rapid change in the child's behavior from spontaneous activity to a subdued hypervigilance in the presence of the parents suggests abuse.

The mental status examination of the abused child should be augmented by incorporating interview strategies designed to elicit information concerning the major sequelae and areas of psychopathology typically encountered in abused children, as they adapt to their abusive environment. One should specifically assess their capacity for impulse control, their ability to sustain attention, the damage to their self-esteem, and the extent of their depression, which can include self-destructive ideation and behavior. The presence and pervasiveness of primitive defenses such as denial, projection, and splitting should be documented. One should gauge the child's ability to separate from his parent or caretaker. The child should be provided with a variety of play materials such as dolls, puppets, crayons, and building materials so that his capacity to engage in symbolic play can be ascertained. The content of play may provide valuable information about the child's predominant fantasies, identifications, and the nature of his object ties. The "traumatic" impact of the abuse may be reflected by the intensity of the child's repetition or reenactment of the original abusive incidents with the play materials. The nature of the child's attachment and relatedness to the examiner might be predictive of his capacity to form object relationships. A pronounced avoidance of contact with the interviewer, accompanied by signs of marked anxiety, might represent the child's generalization of his fear of the battering parent. This type of reaction would be enhanced by a superficial physical resemblance of the interviewer with the parent. A marked difference in responsiveness to an interviewer of another sex or with a contrasting appearance would tend to confirm this phenomenon. The interview should also include questions regarding general information, vocabulary, comprehension, reading, and arithmetic calculations in order to assess the general intellectual and cognitive functioning of the child. The child's handwriting and ability to draw human figures should be assessed in order to yield information about body-image and perceptual-motor skills.

A full battery of psychological tests, including the WISC, Bender-Gestalt and human figure drawings, is useful for a mere definitive assessment of the cognitive and intellectual competence of abused children of school age. Projective tests such as the Rorschach and CAT may provide insight concerning the child's affective and fantasy life, the quality of his object relationships and identifications, and his impulses and defenses.

Infant tests such as the Bayley or the Gesell should be routinely administered to infants and preschool children. These measure their sensorimotor, intellectual, and social development. If psychological or developmental testing indicates marked impairment in speech or language, a more specialized evaluation of hearing and language should be administered.

School records of abused children should be routinely obtained, in light of their typical behavioral and academic difficulties. In cases of learning impairment, achievement test scores should be of benefit. Teacher reports regarding the child's classroom behavior might be augmented by completion of the Conners (1969) or Achenbach (1978) questionnaires.

The direct observation of the interaction between infants or preschool children and the abusing parent can yield valuable information about the contribution of each member of the dyad to their mutual frustration and lack of synchrony. These observations can take place in a variety of situations during caretaking activities such as feeding, bathing, or during play. Typical pathological features of these interactions include the mother's inability to engage the baby or to respond appropriately to its cues, a negative affective tone in both mother and baby, a paucity of verbalization directed towards the baby, and a lack of compliance by the baby to the mother's distractions (Wasserman et al. 1983). These types of observations are important in planning intervention. To be truly successful, any approach to treatment cannot be purely symptom-oriented, but must consider the totality of the relationship between parent and child. In abuse involving older children and more intact families, a family-systems approach may be useful in identifying and changing maladaptive patterns of behavior.

Since abused children commonly manifest neurological impairment, the standard pediatric neurological examination with EEG should be supplemented by a battery of perceptual motor tests, such as the Southern California Sensory Integration Tests (Ayers 1966) and the Sequential and Repetitive Finger Tapping Tests (Denckla 1973, 1974). The neurological evaluation should be geared towards the identification of "soft signs" of CNS dysfunction.

TYPICAL SEQUELAE OF PHYSICAL ABUSE

The abused child is traumatized not only by the repeated infliction of acute physical harm by the parent, but also by the ongoing pathological climate of childrearing upon which the abuse is superimposed. This includes harsh and punitive disciplinary methods, rough and inappropriate handling, scapegoating, gross under- or overstimulation, and insensitivity to the child's needs. Under conditions of poverty and neglect, deprivation and interruption of maternal care are frequently present. These have an adverse long-term cumulative impact on the child. The acute and cumulative aspects of the abusive environment combine with the pretraumatic vulnerability of the child to produce the following sequelae, which may be identified during a psychiatric assessment.

Abused children frequently exhibit cognitive and intellectual impairment associated with delayed development and CNS dysfunction when they are given standardized IQ or developmental tests. Significant numbers of these children fall into the retarded range and display deficits in speech and language (Elmer and Gregg 1967; Morse et al. 1970; Martin 1972; Sandgrund et al. 1974; Smith 1975). These children are often hyperactive and impulsive, with minimal frustration tolerance. Motor activity, rather than verbalization, is their preferred mode of expression. When abused children reach latency age, they fail to demonstrate the progressive ego growth and reorganization characteristic of this stage. They fail to develop the typical latency defenses that enable the normal child to bind anxiety from internal and external sources and cope with phase-specific stresses and conflicts.

Early and persistent exposure to parental rejections, assault, and deprivation impairs the child's capacity to form subsequent relationships. The abused child regards new objects with fear and apprehension. He anticipates similar frustration and maltreatment from others on the basis of previous experience. The earliest evidence of impaired object relationships may be observed in the avoidance and distancing behaviors of the abused infant and toddler. Robinson and Solomon (1978) described an avoidance of eye contact between abused toddlers and their mothers in a structured play situation. Ounstead et al. (1974) described a hypervigilant phenomenon in abused infants, who sit passively and immobile while gazing intensely around them. They called this behavior "frozen watchfulness." George and Main (1979) observed that abused toddlers tended to avoid their mothers, even when the mothers made friendly overtures. When they did respond, they approached their mothers to the side or to the rear, or by backstepping. These symptoms of visual avoidance and hypervigilance in the presence of a caretaker or individual perceived to be harmful might be a successor to gaze-aversion during infancy, a primordial defense against traumatic stimulation and a precursor of projective defenses and paranoid symptoms appearing later in childhood. Most abused children are unable to achieve Erikson's (1950) stage of basic trust. They learn to regard violence and rejection as the major ingredients of human encounters.

Abused children are forced to rely upon primitive defenses of denial, projection, and splitting in order to protect themselves from the terrifying perception that the very caretaker whom they depend upon for survival is confronting them with annihilation and rejection. Perceptions and internalized images of the "bad" parent are subjected to denial and projected onto others. Sometimes abused children assume the responsibility for their maltreatment by incorporating the "badness" of their battering parent. These defensive maneuvers permit the children to maintain the fantasy of having a "good" parent. Acknowledgement of the malevolence of the abusing primary caretaker would force the children to experience their painful affect, intense rage, and sense of vulnerability and helplessness. These defenses are reinforced by the typical patterns of denial, projection, and rationalization in their parents. When the splitting and projective mechanisms fail to obliterate the awareness of parental assault, abused children resort to denial and isolation of the accompanying painful affect.

Abused children of all ages have been cited for aggressive and destructive behavior. Gaensbauer and Sands (1979) observed that abused and neglected infants displayed more anger than their normal peers. This anger was more easily evoked, more intense, and less easily resolved than that anger observed in normal infants. In some cases, the infants hit the researchers. George and Main (1979) reported similar assaultive behavior in abused children from one to three years of age in a daycare setting. These children also frequently hit or threatened the daycare personnel. Galdston (1971) also described aimless, unprovoked assaultive behavior in abused preschool children in a special daycare program. Green (1978a) observed aggressive and destructive behavior in school age abused children involved in a child-abuse treatment program. These children engaged in bullying, fighting, and assaultive behavior with peers and siblings. The older children and adolescents were frequently involved in antisocial and delinquent behavior. There are numerous etiological factors associated with this hyperaggressive behavior. The abused children form a basic identification with their violent parents, which facilitates the use of "identification with the aggressor" as a major defense against feelings of anxiety and helplessness. The loss of impulse control is further enhanced by the presence of CNS dysfunction. These children also lack the usual superego restraints found in normal children during latency, due to inadequate superego models and faulty internalization.

Abused children are usually sad, dejected, and self-deprecatory. Their poor self-concept is the end result of chronic physical and emotional scarring, humiliation, and scapegoating, which is reinforced by each new abusive episode. When these children are repeatedly beaten and threatened with abandonment, they assume it is the result of their own "bad" behavior, regardless of their innocence. One may hypothesize that in cases of early maltreatment, the infant who is repeatedly assaulted and handled roughly and inappropriately will experience more frequent and intense periods of physical pain and generalized discomfort, which develop into painful affective states. These dysphoric affects and uncomfortable self-awareness are ultimately transformed into depressive states and low self-esteem during the rapid increase in cognitive development and ego differentiation in early childhood.

When abused children reach school age, their depression and low self-esteem are often transformed into various forms of self-destructive behavior, such as suicide attempts, gestures, threats, and other forms of self-injury. These are often accompanied by more subtle forms of pain-dependent activity in the form of provocative, limit-testing behavior that readily elicits beatings and punishment from parents, other adults, and peers. Forty percent of our research population of abused children manifested overt forms of self-destructive behavior (Green 1978b). This behavior was most often precipitated by parental beatings or by actual or threatened separation from parental figures. Since self-destructive behavior is relatively rare prior to adolescence, it would appear that the self-preservative functions normally operating during latency are interfered with in the abused child. One might regard self-destructive behavior as a means of submitting to the murderous wishes of the abusing parent; yet some adaptive and defensive motives might also be present. For example, the child's capacity to hurt himself or provoke abuse from the environment offers him a sensation of mastery and control over the more traumatic and terrifying parental beatings that occur spontaneously without warning. Many abused children ultimately adopt a pain-dependent lifestyle of successive relationships with sadistic or abusive love objects modeled after the abusing parent. This also represents an attempt by the child to repeat and master the traumatic impact of the original abuse.

Abused children often react to actual or threatened separations and object loss with intense anxiety, which is often attributable to early experiences of separation and abandonment, at times associated with placement in foster homes. Repeated physical abuse may increase the vulnerability of abused children to separation, because each beating implies the parent's withdrawal of love and a wish to be rid of the child. The children often manifest acute separation anxiety during their involvement in psychiatric treatment in response to their therapist's vacations and departures from the hospital.

Most abused children exhibit academic and behavioral problems in the school setting. Their cognitive impairment, particularly in the areas of speech and language, together with their limited attention span and hyperactivity contribute to their deficient academic performance. These children frequently demonstrate specific learning disabilities such as dyslexia, expressive and receptive language disorders, and perceptual-motor problems due to minimal brain dysfunction or developmental lags. Their poor impulse control contributes to behavior problems with peers and teachers. Their parents are often called to school because of their disruptive behavior and academic failure, which often leads to further abuse. These chronic school difficulties, often leading to placement in special classes for the intellectually and emotionally damaged, produce a further adverse impact on the abused child's previously damaged self-esteem.

Most retrospective studies of abused children demonstrate a significant amount of neurological dysfunction (Martin et al. 1974; Smith and Hanson 1974; Baron et al. 1970). However, the precise etiology of this impairment has been the subject of controversy. With the exception of obvious cases of massive head trauma resulting in skull fractures and subdural hematomas as originally described by Kempe et al. in their original paper on the "battered child syndrome" (1962), brain damage alone would not appear to be sufficient to account for the CNS impairment. Martin et al. (1974) demonstrated the uncertain impact of child-abuse on neurological functioning by showing that many abused children with skull fractures and subdural hematomas had apparently normal neurological examinations, while significant numbers of abused children without head injuries manifested neurological deficits.

Several explanations have been offered to account for neurological impairment in abused children without major head injuries. Caffey (1972) described how vigorous shaking of a child's head could result in petechial hemmorhages in the brain. Neglect (Coleman and Provence 1957), malnutrition (Scrimshaw and Gordon 1968; Birch 1972), and maternal deprivation (Bakwin 1949; Spitz 1945; Bowlby 1951) often accompanying child-abuse have all been implicated in impaired CNS development. Some observers (Sandgrund et al. 1974; Milowe and Lourie 1964) have theorized that this impairment may precede and even provoke abuse by rendering these children hyperactive and difficult to manage.

Green et al. (1981) carried out a study that explored the relationship between the abusive environment and CNS development. The neurological competence of sixty abused children without severe head trauma was compared with thirty neglected nonabused children and thirty normal controls. The children received physical and neurological evaluations, including an EEG and a battery of perceptual-motor tests. Fifty-two percent of the abused children were judged to be moderately or severely impaired, compared to 38 percent of the neglected children and only 14 percent of the controls. The CNS impairment indicated relatively subtle neurological dysfunction rather than structural damage, which would not have been detected by the usual neurological examination. Similarities in the nature and prevalence of impairment in the abused and neglected children in contrast to the relative intactness of the controls suggest that the adverse physical and psychological environment associated with maltreatment is probably of greater neurological consequence than the physical assault itself.

Many abused children perceive the severe episodes of battering as a danger to their physical and psychological integrity. They feel threatened with annihilation and/or abandonment. They become overwhelmed by the quantity and quality of the noxious stimulation, which paralyzes ego functions and results in severe panic. This situation resembles Freud's (1920) concept of traumatic neurosis and the breaching of the stimulus barrier. The children experience feelings of helplessness and humiliation, which are often accompanied by a loss of ego boundaries. These anxiety states occur during a beating or in the anticipation of an attack. Some children display psychotic behavior at this time, due to the severe ego regression with the temporary suspension of reality testing.

The failure of the abused child's defensive functioning is associated with a striking tendency to reenact the traumatic situation. The traumatic imagery derived from the beatings permeated the dreams, fantasies, play, and object relationships of abused children long after the cessation of physical abuse. Repetition of the trauma is incited by situations that resemble the original threats to the child's safety and self-esteem experienced during the abusive episodes.

Although repetition of the trauma may be regarded as a primitive defensive operation in which the traumatic elements are reenacted in a relatively unmodified form, it seems to have an adaptive value for abused children. It permits them to achieve active mastery of a passively experienced danger and allows them to re-create, master, and control painful affects and anxiety that might otherwise be initiated by the environment.

SEXUAL ABUSE

While sexual abuse of children is similar to physical abuse in that it generally involves the exploitation or misuse of a child by a parent or caretaker, major differences between them and their sequelae require separate consideration. Sexual abuse is more likely to escape detection because it usually does not result in physical injury; it arouses considerably more guilt and shame in both victim and perpetrator and often the entire family, so that a "conspiracy of silence" usually accompanies the event. This reaction is most typically encountered when a member of the family, usually a parent or stepparent, involves the child in a sexual act. Families are more cooperative when the child is victimized by a stranger or a nonrelative.

Child sexual abuse may be defined as contact between a child and an adult when the child is used as an object of gratification for adult sexual needs or desires. Sexual abuse varies in severity from gentle fondling to forcible rape resulting in physical injury. Sexually abused children can range in age from infancy to young adulthood. Girls are reported as victims of sexual abuse ten times more often than boys. The most common forms of sexual abuse encountered by girls are exhibitionism, fondling, genital contact, masturbation, and vaginal, oral, or anal intercourse by a male perpetrator. Boys are typically abused by a male offender, and are usually subjected to fondling, mutual masturbation, fellatio, and anal intercourse. About half of the child victims are involved in repeated incidents of sexual abuse; in some cases the sexual abuse may take place over a period of years.

Description of Families Involved in Sexual Abuse

The most typical patterns of familial sexual abuse involve father-daughter incest and sexual contact between stepfathers and stepdaughters. The latter is perhaps more common because the absence of biological paternity weakens the incest taboo. This inappropriate sexual exploitation of a daughter or stepdaughter is a sign of a pathological family structure, in which the mother usually plays a prominent role. The mothers often consciously or unconsciously encourage the sexual relationship between their husbands and daughters. These women have frequently experienced maternal deprivation or a deviant mother-daughter relationship during their own childhood. Their inadequate maternal role models and their unfulfilled dependency needs contribute to their casting their daughters in the maternal role. These daughters are often burdened with excessive household and child-care responsibilities and are ultimately placed in the role of a sexual partner for their father or stepfather.

Weinberg (1955) classified the fathers into three categories: psychopaths with indiscriminate promiscuity; socially immature and psychosexually retarded men with a pedophilic orientation; and introverts with an extreme intrafamilial orientation. Most of the men are in their thirties or early forties when the incestuous relationship begins. This age range often coincides with increased marital stress and the presence of a pubescent or prepubescent daughter in the home. Giarretto (1976) reported that the average age of the daughter when the sexual contact is initiated is ten years. Groth and Birnbaum (1978) subdivided male sexual offenders into two subtypes. Those men who established adult sexual relationships and turned to children for sexual gratification only where the adult relationships became stressful were classified as "regressed" offenders. A large majority of these individuals were married and they usually selected girls as victims. "Fixated" offenders, on the other hand, were attracted primarily or exclusively to children since adolescence. Their sexual contact with adults occurred only sporadically. Only a very small percentage of "fixated" offenders married, and this group continued to prefer children as sexual partners. They selected more boys than girls as their victims.

Incest between mother and son, mother and daughter, and father and son is more rarely encountered. The taboo against mother/son incest is very strong; when this type of incest occurs, it is usually accompanied by gross psychopathology in the mother.

Assessment and Diagnosis of Sexual Abuse

The sexual abuse of a child often precipitates a crisis in the child's family. This is especially true in cases where the perpetrator is a family member. Since taboos against intrafamilial sexual abuse are very strong, extreme feelings of shame, guilt, and rage often render the child, parents, and relatives highly resistant and defensive, requiring a most tactful, sensitive approach during the interview. The child and the parents should be interviewed separately so as to minimize the element of coercion. If the child's age or emotional state precludes the possibility of obtaining a verbal report of the incident, the child might be able to re-create the event through play. Therefore, it is advisable to provide the child with ample age-appropriate play materials, such as dolls, puppets, pencils, crayons, and paper, and so on. If the child is verbal, the interviewer should allay his anxiety by asking general questions about his home, family, school, and daily activities; some rapport and basic trust should be present prior to exploring the sensitive areas related to the sexual abuse. If the child is reluctant to describe the sexual encounter, he should not be forced. It is more productive to wait and try again after some of the resistance and anxiety is dissipated. A confrontational approach can be further damaging to the child. The child's unique vocabulary for sexual organs and excretory functions must be taken into consideration during the interview. This terminology may be elicited by having the child name the body parts of a doll.

One should be aware of the child's concerns about sharing his testimony with his parents and family. Children frequently experience shame and guilt about the incident and fear punishment for disclosure. They are often anxious and fearful in the presence of the perpetrator. When the offender is a parent or a close relative, a strong emotional reaction can be expected from the entire family. As a general rule, if a child is able to describe some details of the sexual molestation and identifies the perpetrator, it is quite likely that the sexual abuse has actually taken place. The child's denial of the incident, on the other hand, cannot be taken at face value, as it is frequently motivated by coercion and threats by the offender. Sometimes a child might be pressured by one parent to accuse the other falsely of sexual molestation, in order to secure leverage in a custody dispute. This type of "brain-washing" might also be a manifestation of a delusional system of a paranoid parent. The "accusations" of these children often have a "parrot-like" quality with a lack of genuine affect. The children do not appear to be uncomfortable in the presence of the "accused" parent.

A general physical examination should be performed to detect signs of physical injury or infection. Sexual assault might be accompanied by physical abuse. The mouth, anus, and external genitals should be inspected for signs of trauma. The genitourinary exam should be conducted with the utmost sensitivity; otherwise it may be perceived by the child as a repetition of the assault. The procedures should be explained to the child and parents prior to the examination. In female children, the use of instruments is usually not necessary. Most of the important information may be obtained through observation and simple inspection of the labia majora and minora, introitus, vaginal canal, hymen, and perineum. The presence of edema, erythema, hematomas, abrasions, or lacerations tends to confirm sexual contact. A stretched introitus and vaginal exudate are also suggestive of genital trauma. In a male child, the penis should be examined for evidence of injury. The urine should be examined for blood to detect urethral trauma. In both males and females, the anus should be inspected for bruises, fissures, tears, and bleeding in order to detect the possibility of anal intercourse.

Diagnostic tests for the presence of sperm are important for legal evidence of sexual assault. Cotton-tipped applicators or eyedroppers may be used to collect specimens from vagina, mouth, and anus. These specimens should also be cultured to detect the presence of gonorrhea. A blood test for syphilis should also be performed routinely. Clothing should also be examined for semen and pubic hair. One should consider the possibility of pregnancy in postpubertal females.

CASE VIGNETTE

Lydia R., a 5-year-old girl, was brought to the pediatric emergency room by her mother and stepfather with vaginal bleeding and fresh bruises on her face and neck. The parents claimed that Lydia had wandered away from them at a family picnic in the park. When they found her a short time later, Lydia told them that a man had taken her into the bushes and put his penis inside of her.

Physical examination revealed signs of vaginal irritation with slight bleeding. The hymen was intact, there was no evidence of major traumatic injury to the vagina, and no sperm was present. However, a throat culture was positive for gonorrhea, and the child was hospitalized.

Upon further questioning, the stepfather broke down and confessed to having subjected the child to vaginal penetration and fellatio over a period of months. He had recently beaten Lydia when she threatened to tell her mother. The mother, who was three months pregnant, filed criminal charges, and the stepfather was sent to jail.

Lydia was initially interviewed on the ward with her mother present. Mrs. R. appeared to be supportive, sympathetic, and appropriately concerned about Lydia, and their interaction was quite positive. When Mrs. R. attempted to leave the room at the male psychiatrist's suggestion, Lydia began to cry and clung to her. The child was able to engage with the interviewer only in the reassuring presence of a nurse. Lydia was initially taciturn and constricted, responding to innocuous questions with one-word answers. When finally asked why she came to the hospital, she responded "I don't know." Lydia became more spontaneous when hand puppets were introduced. While playing with the puppets, she had the male puppet jump up and down rhythmically on top of the little girl. When asked what was taking place, Lydia responded "The man is making pee-pee on the girl."

Lydia was temporarily placed in a foster home following her hospital discharge. She was accompanied by her foster mother during a follow-up interview. The child appeared cranky and ill-at-ease and refused to remain in the room without the foster mother. She spoke of missing her mother and having trouble falling asleep. When asked, she denied having nightmares, but the foster mother had heard her cry out in her sleep several times. The foster care caseworker reported that Lydia tended to avoid boys and male attendants at the agency's play group.

Sequelae of Sexual Abuse

There have been varying opinions about the impact of sexual abuse on the child victim. Some observers have asserted that incest and sexual abuse may be psychologically harmless (Bender and Blau 1937; Yorukoglu and Kemph 1966; Rascovsky and Rascovsky 1950). The majority of the clinicians in this area have reported a variety of physical, psychological, and psychosomatic symptoms associated with sexual abuse. The child's response depends on numerous factors, such as his age, level of pretraumatic psychological functioning, relationship to the perpetrator, and the family's reaction to the incident.

Generally speaking, one may differentiate immediate and long-term sequelae. The more acute symptoms are sleep disturbances including repetitive nightmares, loss of appetite, irritability, and crankiness; regressive symptoms including thumbsucking, nailbiting, and enuresis; a heightened fearfulness with phobic reactions towards men; and psychosomatic complaints such as headaches, stomachaches, dizziness, and so on. Some sexually abused children develop school avoidance. Older children and adolescents often run away from home and engage in delinquency and promiscuity. The acute impact of the sexual abuse is often compounded by the additional trauma of the family crisis following disclosure, hospitalization, and subsequent removal from the home, as depicted in the case vignette.

The long-term effects of sexual abuse and incest are difficult to document because of the absence of controlled longitudinal studies. However, case histories of adults who had been victims of incest and sexual abuse during childhood add a long-term perspective to this area of study. Giarretto (1976) noted that a high percentage of prostitutes, female drug addicts, and women with pronounced sexual difficulties were exposed to sexual abuse and incest during childhood. Rosenfeld et al. (1977) described frequent symptoms of frigidity, promiscuity, and depression in women who reported childhood sexual victimization. Sedney and Brooks (1981) reported a higher incidence of sleep disturbances, anxiety, depression, and self-destructive thoughts in female college students who had childhood sexual contact with a family member than in nonincestuous controls. The students who experienced incest were also more frequent victims of crimes and accidents. Meiselman (1978) found that many female victims of incest reported fears of sexual contact with men and sought homosexual relationships. Brooks (1982) discovered a high incidence of incest in the histories of psychiatric inpatients with a diagnosis of borderline personality disorder, suggesting that in some cases incest may be an etiological factor in the development of borderline psychopathology.

Brant and Tisza (1977) speculated that sexually abused children might be at risk for repeated sexual misuse. They maintained that these children provoked further sexual contact as a vehicle for obtaining pleasure and need satisfaction and as a means of mastering the original trauma. Katan's (1973) report on the psychoanalytic treatment of six women who had been raped during childhood also described their tendency to repeat the traumatic childhood experiences with adult partners or through their children. The study of Miller et al. (1978) corroborates the tendency of the victim to perpetuate the trauma. These investigators reported that recidivist adult rape victims had experienced a significantly higher incidence of incest than a nonrecidivist group.

On the other hand, many of the previously described symptoms are rooted in a phobic adaptation—fear of men, running away, homosexuality, school avoidance. Alexander (1980) reported on her experiences as a cotherapist in a group of adult women who had been victims of incest during their childhood. These women were unable to achieve fulfilling relationships with either men or women. Their marriages and sexual relationships were unhappy and they were unable to enjoy sex. Many of these women exhibited frigidity and tried to avoid intercourse.

These observations might suggest the existence of two contrasting adaptive styles in sexually abused children: one seeking mastery through active repetition of the trauma, and the other coping by the avoidance of sexual stimuli. The same set of contradictory responses was observed in victims of physical abuse, who were either fearful and hypervigilant or attempted actively to repeat the original trauma by masochistic provocativeness or by inflicting violence on others. Many victims of physical and sexual abuse deploy both types of defenses, either alternatively or simultaneously. While each of these defensive patterns initially served to protect the children from further traumatic physical and sexual assault, their persistent use in a normal environment must be considered pathological and maladaptive.

DIAGNOSTIC CONSIDERATIONS

About one-half of the abused children encountered in our treatment program satisfy the DSM-III diagnostic criteria for "Post-Traumatic Stress Disorder" in that 1) the acute and long-term traumatic components of the child-abuse syndrome constitute recognizable stressors; 2) reexperiencing of the trauma was evidenced by recurrent dreams and intrusive recollections of the parental violence and hostility; and 3) reduced involvement with the external world was manifested by signs of detachment and prominent constriction of affect. The following symptoms were often manifested as sequelae of the abuse: hypervigilance, sleep disturbance, avoidance of activities or situations that might result in retraumatization, and intensification of symptoms, for example, hyperaggressive, pain-dependent, or phobic behavior during exposure to events that symbolize or resemble the abusive situation.

The fear of retraumatization may produce an exacerbation of an acute posttraumatic stress disorder in a formerly abused child who previously appeared to be asymptomatic or afflicted with a chronic posttraumatic stress disorder.

Abused children display a wide variety of other psychiatric diagnoses that may or may not be related to their traumatization.

CONCLUSION

Any plan for the treatment of child-abuse must be designed to create a safe environment for the child and to modify the potentiating factors underlying the maltreatment. Therefore, an effective treatment program must deal specifically with the parental abuse-proneness, the characteristics of the child that make him vulnerable for abuse, and the environmental stress that triggers the abusive interaction. Protecting the children and preventing further abuse should receive immediate priority. One must immediately deal with the family crisis that usually follows the reporting of physical or sexual abuse. We try to keep the family intact, whenever possible, by providing appropriate psychological support and social services when required. If the abuser cannot be closely monitored or is uncooperative, he or she should be removed from the home. If this is not possible, the child should be referred for temporary placement.

The primary treatment objectives with the abusing parents are to help them improve their child-rearing techniques to encourage the use of nonabusive disciplinary methods instead of physical punishment. One tries to establish a supportive, gratifying relationship with the parent and to help him improve his chronically devalued self-image, so he will no longer need to depend on his children to bolster his self-esteem. One provides the parents with basic information about child rearing and child development. If necessary, the family receives concrete social services, homemaking assistance, medical care, and financial aid in order to strengthen its functioning. Outreach is provided in the form of home visiting and a hot-line for use in emergencies. Individual and group psychotherapy is available to treat psychiatric disorders of the parents. Sexually abusing parents are referred to specialized programs for sexual offenders.

Once the children are in a safe environment, every effort should be made to reverse the serious emotional and cognitive impairment associated with their traumatic experiences. Therapeutic intervention must deal with the psychopathological sequelae of maltreatment. Abused infants and preschool children usually benefit from a therapeutic nursery setting; this provides a means of observing the mother-child interaction, which can be used as a basis for corrective intervention. A crucial ingredient of the treatment process is the modification of the pathological identifications and inner world of the abused child.

REFERENCES

Achenbach, T. M. (1978). The child behavior profile in boys aged 6–17. *J. Consult. Clin. Psychol.* 46:759–76.

Alexander, H. (1980). The long-range impact of child and sexual abuse as examined in adult females. Workshop presented at the Tenth Annual Child Abuse and Neglect Symposium.

Ayers, J. J. (1966). *The Southern California Sensory Integration Test.* Los Angeles: Western Psychological Services.

Bakwin, H. (1949). Emotional deprivation in infants. *J. Ped.* 35:512–21.

Baron, M. A., Bejar, R. L., and Shaeff, P. J. (1970). Neurological manifestations of the battered child syndrome. *Ped.* 45:1003–7.

Bayley, N. (1968). Manual for the Bayley Scales of infant development. New York: Psychological Corporation.

Bender, L., and Blau, A. (1937). The reaction of children to sexual relations with adults. *Amer. J. Orthopsychiat.* 19:500–18.

Birch, H. G. (1972). Malnutrition, learning, and intelligence. *Amer. J. Public Health* 62:773–84.

Bowlby, J. (1951). Maternal care and mental health. *Bull. World Health Org.* 31:355–533.

Brant, R. S. T., and Tisza, V. B. (1977). The sexually misused child. *Amer. J. Orthopsychiat.* 47:80–90.

Brooks, B. (1982). Familial influences in father-daughter incest. *J. Psychiat. Treat. Eval.* 4(2):117–24.

Bryant, H. D. (1963). Physical abuse of children: An agency study. *Child Welfare* 42:125–30.

Caffey, J. (1972). On the theory and practice of shaking infants: Its potential residual effects of permanent brain damage and mental retardation. *Amer. J. Dis. Children* 124:161–69.

Coleman, R., and Provence, S. A. (1957). Developmental retardation (hospitalism) in infants living in families. *Ped.* 19:285–92.

Conners, C. K. (1969). A teacher rating scale for use in drug studies with children. *Amer. J. Psychiat.* 126:152–56.

Denckla, M. B. (1973). Development of speed in repetitive and successive finger movements in normal children. *Dev. Med. Child Neurol.* 15:635–45.

––––––. (1974). Development of motor coordination in normal children. *Dev. Med. Child Neurol.* 16:729–41.

Elmer, E., and Gregg, C. S. (1967). Developmental characteristics of abused children. *Ped.* 40:596–602.

Erikson, E. H. (1950). *Childhood and Society.* New York: Norton.

Fontana, V. (1971). *The Maltreated Child.* Springfield, Ill.: Charles C. Thomas.

Freud, S. (1920). Beyond the pleasure principle. In *Standard Edition*, Vol. 18. London: Hogarth Press, pp. 3–64.

Gaensbauer, T. J., and Sands, K. (1979). Distorted communications in abused/neglected children and their potential impact on caretakers. *J. Amer. Acad. Child Psychiat.* 18:236–50.

Galdston, R. (1971). Violence begins at home. *J. Amer. Acad. Child Psychiat.* 10:336–50.

George, C., and Main, M. (1979). Social interactions of young abused children: Approach, avoidance, and agression. *Child Develop.* 50:306–18.

Giarretto, H. (1976). Humanistic treatment of father-daughter incest in child-abuse and neglect. In R. E. Helfer and C. H. Kempe (Eds.). *The Family and the Community.* Cambridge, Mass.: Ballinger, pp. 143–58.

Gil, D. (1970). *Violence Against Children.* Cambridge: Harvard University Press.

Green, A. H. (1976). A psychodynamic approach to the study and treatment of child-abusing parents. *J. Amer. Acad. Child Psychiat.* 15:414–29.

––––––. (1978a). Psychopathology of abused children. *J. Amer. Acad. Child Psychiat.* 17:92–103.

––––––. (1978b). Self-destructive behavior in battered children. *Amer. J. Psychiat.* 135:579–82.

––––––. (1979). Child-abusing fathers. *J. Amer. Acad. Child Psychiat.* 18:270–82.

––––––.(1980). *Child Maltreatment.* New York: Jason Aronson.

––––––, et al. (1980). Psychopathological assessment of child-abusing, neglecting, and normal mothers. *J. Nerv. Ment. Disease* 168:356–60.

––––––, et al. (1981). Neurological impairment in maltreated children. *Child Abuse and Neglect* 5:129–34.

Gregg, G. (1968). Physician, child abuse reporting laws, and injured child (Psychosocial anatomy of childhood trauma). *Clin. Pediatrics* 7:720–25.

Groth, A. N., and Birnbaum, B. A. (1978). Adult sexual orientation and attraction to underage persons. *Arch. Sexual Beh.* 7:175–81.

Helfer, R. E. (1975). The diagnostic process and treatment programs (DHEW Publication No. [OHD] 75–69), Washington, D.C.: Department of Health, Education and Welfare, National Center for Child Abuse and Neglect.

Johnson, B., and Morse, H. (1968). Injured children and their parents. *Children* 15:147–52.

Kempe, C., et al. (1962). The battered child syndrome. *J. Amer. Med. Assn.* 181:17–24.

Katan, A. (1973). Children who were raped. *Psychoanal. Study Child* 28:208–24.

Klein, M., and Stern, L. (1971). Low birth weight and the battered child syndrome. *Amer. J. Diseases Child.* 122:15–18.

Landis, J. (1956). Experiences of 500 children with adult sexual deviants. *Psychiat. Quart.* (Suppl.) 30:91–109.

Lukianowicz, N. (1972). Incest. *Brit. J. Psychiat.* 120:301–13.

Martin, H. P. (1972). The child and his development. In C. H. Kempe and R. E. Helfer (Eds.). *Helping the Battered Child and His Family*. Philadelphia: Lippincott.

———, et al. (1974). The development of abused children. *Adv. Ped.* 21:25–73.

Meiselman, K. (1978). *Incest: A Psychological Study of Causes and Effects with Treatment Recommendations*. San Francisco: Jossey-Bass.

Merrill, E. (1962). Physical abuse of children: An agency study. In V. DeFrancis (Ed.). *Protecting the Battered Child*. Denver: American Humane Association.

Miller, J., et al. (1978). Recidivism among sex assault victims. *Amer. J. Psychiat.* 135:1103–4.

Milowe, I. D., and Lourie, R. S. (1964). The child's role in the battered child syndrome. *J. Ped.* 65:1079–81.

Morris, M., and Gould, R. (1963). Role reversal: A necessary concept in dealing with battered child syndrome. *Amer. J. Orthopsychiat.* 33:298–99.

Morse, W., Sahler, O. J., and Friedman, S. B. (1970). A three-year follow-up study of abused and neglected children. *Amer. J. Diseases Child.* 120:439–46.

Oliver, J. E., et al. (1974). Severely ill-treated young children in north-east Wiltshire (Research Report No. 4. Oxford Record Linkage Study). Oxford: Oxford Regional Health Authority.

Ounstead, C., Oppenheimer, R., and Lindsay, J. (1974). Aspects of bonding failure: The psychopathology and psychotherapeutic treatment of families of battered children. *Dev. Med. Child Neurol.* 16:446–56.

Paulson, M. J., et al. (1974). The MMPI: A descriptive measure of psychopathology in abusive parents. *J. Clin. Psychol.* 30:387–90.

Rascovsky, M., and Rascovsky, A. (1950). On consummated incest. *Int. J. Psychoanal.* 31:42–47.

Robinson, E., and Solomon, F. (1978). Some further findings on the treatment of the mother-child dyad in child-abuse. Presented at the Second International Congress on Child Abuse and Neglect, London, England.

Rosenfeld, A. A., et al. (1977). Incest and sexual abuse of children. *J. Amer. Acad. Child Psychiat.* 16:327–39.

Sandgrund, A., Gaines, R., and Green, A. H. (1974). Child abuse and mental retardation: A problem of cause and effect. *Amer. J. Ment. Def.* 79:327–30.

Scrimshaw, M. S., and Gordon, J. E. (1968). *Malnutrition, Learning and Behavior*. Cambridge: M.I.T. Press.

Sedney, M., and Brooks, B. (1981). Factors associated with childhood sexual abuse in a non-clinical population. Presented at the American Psychological Association, Los Angeles.

Simons, B., et al. (1966). Child abuse. *N.Y. State J. Med.* 66:2783–88.

Smith, S. M. (1975). *The Battered Child Syndrome.* London: Butterworths.

Smith, C. A., and Hanson, R. (1974). One hundred thirty-four children: A medical and psychological study. *Brit. Med. J.* 14:666–70.

Spitz, R. A. (1945). Hospitalism: An inquiry into the genesis of psychiatric conditions of early childhood. *Psychoanal. Study Child* 1:53–74.

Starr, R. H., and Ceresnie, S. J. (1978). Social and psychological characteristics of abusive mothers. Presented at the annual meeting of the Eastern Psychological Association, Washington, D.C., May.

Steele, B. (1970). Parental abuse of infants and small children. In E. Anthony and T. Benedek (Eds.). *Parenthood: Its Psychology and Psychopathology.* Boston: Little, Brown.

————, and Pollock, C. A. (1968). A psychiatric study of parents who abuse infants and small children. In R. E. Helfer and C. H. Kempe (Eds.). *The Battered Child.* Chicago: University of Chicago Press.

Wasserman, G., Green, A., and Allen, R. (1983). Going beyond abuse: Maladaptive patterns of interaction in abusing mother-infant pairs. *J. Amer. Acad. Child Psychiat.* 22:245–52.

Weinberg, S. (1955). *Incest Behavior.* New York: Citadel.

Wolock, I., and Horowitz, B. (1977). Factors relating to levels of childcare among families receiving public assistance in New Jersey. (First report. Grant No. 90-c-418.). Washington, D.C.: Department of Health, Education and Welfare, National Center on Child Abuse and Neglect, Office of Child Development.

Yorukoglu, A., and Kemph, J. (1966). Children not severely damaged by incest with a parent. *J. Amer. Acad. Child Psychiat.* 5:539–43.

41

THE BLIND CHILD AND ADOLESCENT

David A. Freedman, Carl Feinstein, and Karen Berger

INTRODUCTION

The psychiatric assessment of the blind child is a uniquely challenging task. The interraction of blindness with maturational, biological, temperamental, parental, and societal factors is an extraordinarily complex one, and the outcome is highly variable. At one pole of adaptation, we find blind individuals whose cognitive, social, and (eventually) vocational functioning is at the highest level. At the other, we find individuals who are so profoundly impaired as to appear autistic. The clinician must know thoroughly how the absence of vision may affect cognitive, social, and emotional functioning at each stage of development. However, there is no substitute for the capacity to empathize with the experience of being blind.

DEFINITION OF BLINDNESS, ETIOLOGY, INCIDENCE, AND PREVALENCE

The distinction between legal blindness and absolute blindness is an important one. In the United States, legal blindness is defined as a central visual acuity of 20/200 or less in the better eye with correction, or, if greater than 20/200, a field of vision no greater than twenty degrees in the widest diameter (National Society to Prevent Blindness 1980). Although children whose visual deficit falls close to the legal definition suffer from a serious disability, they are able to perceive, in some measure, the presence of objects and people in their immediate surroundings, and consequently are far less vulnerable to the most serious developmental arrests than is the child born lacking any useful vision.

The most recent useful statistics regarding etiology, prevalence, and degree of visual impairment were compiled in 1978, but they are based on extrapolations from data compiled in 1969–70, when the last systematic survey was undertaken (National Society to Prevent Blindness 1980). According to this information, in the United States in 1980 there were 6,450 children below age 5 and 34,750 between the ages of 5 and 19 who met the criteria for legal blindness. For children below age 5, 24.3 percent were totally blind and another 20.8 percent had light perception only. Thus, more than 40 percent of visually impaired infants and preschoolers had no useful vision. For children aged 5 to 19, 15.3 percent and 13.5 percent, respectively, had no vision or light perception only. The difference in figures for the younger versus the older age ranges is accounted for by the occurrence of later onset or progressive disorders impairing vision and by the fact that some preschool age visually impaired children with less than total blindness are not reported until they enter the educational system.

Congenital or hereditary etiologies account for over 50 percent of blindness in both younger and older children. Prenatal cataracts, optic nerve atrophy, retrolental fibroplasia, anopthalmos, micropthalmos, congenital glaucoma, and retinoblastoma are the most common known causes for the 0 to 5 age group, although for 45.7 percent of cases, no etiology is reported. For the age range 5 to 19, the above-cited causes of blindness are joined by trauma, later onset optic nerve atrophy, albinism, myopia, and nystagmus.

A significant but unknown percentage of blind children are multihandicapped. A 1964 study (Cruikshank) found 31 percent of blind children to have another physical disability, most commonly cerebral palsy and epilepsy. There are approximately 6,000 to 7,500 deaf-blind children in the United States (Dunham 1978). While this number may seem small, the developmental and adaptive problems these children face, lacking both distance sensory receptor systems and sight and hearing, are massive and complex.

It is critical that the diagnostician be aware of the different developmental implications for congenital versus later onset blindness. Although the congenitally blind child has been more extensively described in the psychiatric and developmental literature, there is a sizable group of children who become blind with increasing age as a result of physical trauma or the exacerbation of some preexisting pathological process. The child who becomes blind after developing a sense of self and of the world of objects suffers a psychological trauma and faces unique and stressful challenges to adaptation and emotional adjustment; however, he retains the basic psychological and cognitive structures from critical earlier stages of development. By contrast, the congenitally blind child has lost nothing. Here, the issue is developmental variations or deviations that derive from not being able to use vision to develop an inner representational world of objects or to perceive or use nonverbal social behavior, including "the language of the eyes" to interact socially with others.

CONGENITAL BLINDNESS

The situation of the congenitally blind child provides a particularly dramatic illustration of how deficits in timely and adequate input from the environment may profoundly alter development. The experiences of several independent workers (Blank 1957; Keeler 1958; Norris et al. 1958; Fraiberg and Freedman 1964) make it clear that congenital blindness carries with it a high risk for serious behavioral pathology. Without appropriate intervention, at least 25 percent of children born blind will develop a severe and pervasive developmental deviation that in many respects mimics infantile autism. This extraordinarily high incidence of an otherwise very rare condition lends an urgency to the study of the congenitally blind that goes well beyond the problems posed by the blind themselves. Investigation of the early life of the blind has added significantly to our understanding of the developmental process in all infants.

Congenital blindness may be considered as analogous to an inherited gene factor of limited penetrance. It is an element in the child's innate equipment that has both invariable consequences and other less rigidly determined effects, which are influenced greatly by the nature of the environment. From this second standpoint, the state of congenital blindness may be viewed as an experiment of nature that, by heightening susceptibility to autistic reactions, also clarifies how vision interracts with other aspects of the infantile experience in the processes of healthy psychological development.

The seminal research of Selma Fraiberg has been particularly significant with respect to our efforts to clarify these issues. In a series of studies of the first two to three years in the lives of congenitally blind infants, she elucidated many of the vicissitudes to which these children are exposed. Her own intervention results (Fraiberg 1977) (no autistic outcomes in a series of the ten cases) stand as testimony to the validity both of her analysis of the problems of blind infants and of the prophylactic measures she recommended.

During her early investigations of the development of the congenitally blind, carried out in collaboration with Freedman (1964), Fraiberg described a home visit to Lennie, a 9-month-old blind infant. This child, who had been kept in a darkened room since birth, had by family consensus been considered to be blind since his third month. However, when he was examined, it was apparent that he was capable of regarding their faces and tracking people's movements. Dr. Fraiberg was impressed by the difference in her reaction to this child in contrast to her response to Toni, a totally blind baby they were then studying intensively. Despite the fact that Toni was in many respects a more responsive, attractive, and endearing child than Lennie, she noticed that she engaged readily in a monologue with Lennie, while she rarely attempted to sustain a conversation with Toni, or, as her subsequent experience indicated, with other congenitally totally blind infants.

Fraiberg and Freedman were able to recognize that this response is an important general characteristic of the response of adults to blind infants. *Adults are not inclined to engage in social exchanges with blind infants and children.* This lack of response is not due solely to an antipathy to blindness, although this may be an element in the picture. Rather, the failure to attempt a social dialogue appears to be secondary to the infant's inability to make visual contact. The inability to achieve eye-to-eye contact leads to pervasive difficulties for the parents of blind infants in establishing appropriate parenting behavior.

Thus, even before the diagnosis of blindness is made, the mothers of these babies experience them as unresponsive and are likely to have withdrawn from the expectable level of social engagement. For example, infants suffering from retrolental fibrous dysplasia (RLF) show no external evidence of their blindness. Their mothers, however, consistently find them to be unusually quiet and unresponsive. As a consequence, they are handled and played with very little, even though the diagnosis of blindness has not been made. By the age of 6 months, however, their lack of responsiveness becomes so atypical that even the least experienced mothers consult their physicians.

This may be contrasted with reports of research with babies deformed by Thalidomide. Both Decarie (1965) and Roskies (1971) found that sighted Thalidomide babies whose mothers overcame their initial reaction to having deformed children and established dialogues with them experienced normal early psychological development. On the other hand, when the mother's emotional response to the defect was so strong that she could not engage the child in eye-to-eye dialogue, deviant emotional development similar to that observed in the blind was seen.

In summary, the absence of eye contact between blind babies and their mothers initiates a primary deficit in mother-infant interaction. A prolonged deficit of this early social engagement secondarily results in a characteristic developmental abnormality in social responsiveness. Bennett (1971) stated the situation most succinctly. In a study of the reactions of nursery attendants to babies who were being held for adoption he found that "of all the baby's cues, the most compelling were offered by his eyes. Wide, bright eyes, especially with search movements, were seen as signs of intelligence and curiosity" (p. 330).

The infant's vision and eye behavior as a powerful inducer of maternal response can be illustrated by a consideration of the emergence and development of smiling. The importance of smiling for the establishment and maintenance of attachment and object ties is well recognized.

The ability of the perioral muscles of the neonatal mouth to assume configurations that are "smile-like" is generally recognized. Thus, early "smiling" both occurs *before* the infant is capable of responding to visual stimuli and can be induced by other sensory modalities. This transient smile response appears to be predicated on the occurrence of patterns of neuronal excitation of uncertain origin. Emde, Gaensbauer, and Harmen (1976) found this smile to be associated with the REM state. There is no evidence to suggest that this earliest smile has any psychological significance. Neither does it appear to be related to specific environmental inducers. Nonetheless, its presence is, like early eye behavior, a powerful inducer of maternal response.

Sometime in the second or third month the neonatal smile either gives way to or is supplemented by a reflex smile. While this can be evoked by a variety of stimulus modalities, it is most characteristically associated with certain visual constellations resembling the face, although not necessarily the human face itself. Spitz (1965) and others (Freedman et al. 1969; Fraiberg 1974; Wolff 1963) have shown that it can also be evoked selectively by the mother's voice. This reflex smile is perhaps best conceptualized in ethological terms as the response of an "innate releasing mechanism" to a "sign-specific stimulus." It reflects the beginnings of the processes by which events occurring in the surrounding of the infant both excite reflexive responses and progressively modulate the functioning of its nervous system.

Sometime in the period between 5 and 9 months, the reflex smile is supplemented by the *recognitory* smile. The emergence of this response is made possible by repeated earlier encounters with some specific stimulus constellations. It is predicated on some form of recognition that links a stimulus from "out there" with a frame of reference already established within the nervous system. This combination of pleasurable affect and its reflective discriminatory application to particular individuals is a clear indicator that the infant at this age has attained the capacity to function at a psychological level. This conclusion is reinforced by the roughly simultaneous appearance of stranger and separation anxiety.

The recognitory smile, however, is not the end of this developmental sequence. The capacity to evoke mentally the image of the pleasure-giving parent, as opposed to immediate recognition, is not reliably established until the second or third year. Like the early endogenous smile, the *evocative* smile is not dependent on environmental stimulation. Unlike its earliest predecessor, however, it does reflect the functioning of the internalized residua of earlier encounters with the environment.

It is during the second and third phases of the evolution of the smile—the period between roughly 2 and 12 months—that the developing infant's vision plays a vital role. So dominant is the visual mode as a stimulus during this period that the tendency has been to confuse absence of a response to a visual stimulus (such as the presence but not immediate contact of the mother) with inability to respond at all. Blind infants require less well-recognized sensory pathways for gaining stimulation from the environment.

Fraiberg and Freedman (1964) were struck by the apparent seeking out of tactile stimulation by very young blind infants. Other observations indicated that as neonatal development proceeds there is a predictable shift in all infants' ability to respond to and utilize various sensory modalities. The following diagram (Fig. 41.1) (Freedman 1971) presents schematically the progressive change in relative responsivity to the indicated modalities. This sequence, which was deduced from clinical observation, has proven to be consistent with the sequence of the myelinization of tracts in the brain worked out by Yakovlev and LeCours (1971). It appears that the very young infant will be particularly receptive to somesthetic stimuli—those nonspecific modalities such as touch, vibration, position, equilibrium, and so on—which Freud and after him Spitz referred to as coenesthetic. In the average child, vision begins to take over as the "lead" sensory modality in the second or third month. By

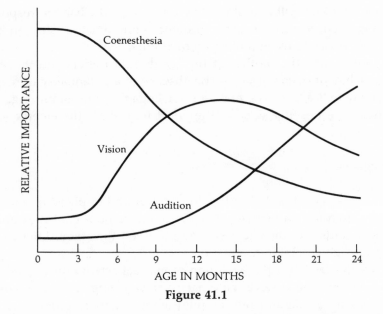

Figure 41.1

6 months, when according to Reinecke (1979) full adult visual capacity is achieved, it is the principal medium through which the infant apprehends the world around him.

The auditory system follows a slower maturational course. Despite the infant's very early response to the sound of the mother's voice, use of auditory stimuli for cognitive purposes in concert with the other sensory modalities is relatively less significant, and does not become manifest until roughly 11 months. Full development of auditory function may not occur until 4 years (Darwin 1877; Freedman et al. 1969; Piaget 1937; Yakovlev and LeCours 1971).

Fraiberg's recognition of the breakdown in the mother-infant dyad resulting from the absence of vision led her to search for other cues in the infant that, if recognized by the mother, could help her respond so as to promote psychological development. She identified three areas of infantile behavior that could be affected by appropriate adult intervention. Because the mother's intervention in these areas led to reciprocating responses on the infant's part, Fraiberg referred to them as languages. They are: the smile language, the hand language, and vocalization.

Smile Language

Mothers of blind infants, not surprisingly, tend to be put off by the infrequency with which their babies smile. Fraiberg dealt with this maternal reaction by emphasizing the use of stimulus modalities other than vision to induce smiling. This requires a great deal of effort on the part of the mother of the blind child. Repeated jiggling, bouncing, tickling, and nuzzling are necessary if one is to elicit even an approximation of the smile that comes so automatically to the face of the sighted baby. Whether a mother will redouble her efforts to get the baby to respond or give up in discouragement is a major factor in determining whether she can bypass the barrier blindness poses to her infant's potential inner life.

It is imperative that the mother of the blind child understand that her baby's unresponsive behavior does not imply the absence of a potentiality to respond. She must understand that alternative methods for engaging the infant (e.g., increased physical activity) are the first steps in the effort to prevent the emergence of deviance in the blind.

Hand Language

During her analysis of early barriers to communication posed by blindness and the correlated search for alternative pathways of interaction, Fraiberg came to study the way blind infants use their hands. She observed that they differ markedly in this regard from sighted children.

McGraw (1945) described the evolution of manual activity during the first three years. Beginning with the passive, automatic fist clenching and grasp reflex (analogous to the neonatal smile and reflex smile) manual activity progresses through a series of steps that culminate in the ability to engage in skilled manipulative behavior. It is an eloquent commentary on the problems of the blind that McGraw conceived of each step after the initial reflex stage from the standpoint of the child's response to a *visual* stimulus. Thus, she observed that at roughly 4 months the sighted baby, under the guidance of vision, brings his hands together in the midline and, very shortly thereafter, begins to reach for objects. The similarly aged blind baby does neither. Yet there are evidences that potentially exploitable development of manual function occurs. For example, the blind infant with light perception but no form perception will begin to engage in blindisms at roughly 5 months. These consist of repetitive passing of the hands before the eye. Presumably they are sustained by the resulting changes in the pattern of light. It is impressive that they begin at precisely the age at which sighted infants begin to reach for objects.

Two months later the congenitally blind child who is experiencing adequate mothering will, by touch, differentiate his mother's skin from that of a stranger and, just like a sighted baby, react with stranger anxiety. Some four months later both the blind and the sighted baby will give evidence of ability to utilize sound cues for cognitive purposes by seeking out and prehending sound-making objects. The use of sound for orientation in space and the prehension of objects is dependent on a complex, often misunderstood developmental progression. A complicating factor in understanding the development is the fact that the ability to react to a sound source anticipates the ability to use sound as the indicator of a sound-making object by roughly 6 months. Thus, the sighted 5-month-old infant will turn his head to a source of sound. If he then sees an attractive object, he will *under the guidance of vision* attempt to prehend. If, however, no exciting visual stimulus appears, he will not make a search for the sound source. The ability to make such a search will not emerge until approximately 11 months in both sighted and blind infants (Darwin 1877; Piaget 1937; Freedman et al. 1969).

At 5 months the blind baby, lacking visual guidance, is incapable of reaching out into space and prehending an object. The mother, ignorant of the process by which the nervous system matures, is inclined to interpret her baby's failure to use his hands as further evidence of his global defectiveness and apathy, or, perhaps even worse, as rejection of herself.

A major therapeutic objective of early intervention with the blind is to help the mother understand that the failure of her 4-month-old to reach out for objects does not necessarily portend a dire psychological future. Nor does it mean that the blind baby has failed to distinguish his mother as a special person. While there is a hiatus in behavioral evidence of progress because of the absence of age-appropriate visual stimulation, the maturation of the infant's brain is proceeding. The challenge of this period is how to provide input that can help organize neural function during this period, given that vision, the age-appropriate sensory modality, is unavailable. Once the auditory system "comes on line" as an apparatus for cognition, the blind young-ster, for whom stimulation in nonvisual modalities has been made available, will be able to show appropriate interest in sounds and their implications. It is the task of the parent of the blind child and his professional helper during the behavioral hiatus described here to continue stimulating the child by other means, in order to main-tain the child's readiness to continue development when the auditory system is mat-urationally ready.

Vocalization

Like the smile and the use of the hands, the ability to use the vocal/auditory apparatus as a medium for communication is the result of a lengthy process, involv-ing the synthesis of at least two separate lines of development. An understanding of this evolution will be useful in clarifying the problem posed by the blind child and in considering how the vocal/auditory system can be used by the blind child's parents.

Lenneberg (1965) has provided evidence that early vocalizing, like the early smile and hand activity, is endogenous in origin. It emerges and functions independently of hearing. He showed that during the first one hundred days of postpartum life, the sounds made both by deaf babies of hearing parents and by hearing babies of deaf parents reared in nonvocal environments were identical in amount and quality with those made by normal babies being reared in normal environments. Only at about 10 weeks does the *normally* hearing baby begin to give evidence that he ap-prehends that it is he who is producing the sound he hears. Obviously the ability to understand this is a necessary precursor of the later capacity to use sound to initiate and receive communications. Two well-recognized clinical phenomena estab-lish beyond reasonable doubt that aural/oral communication is the product of a syn-thetic process. In the first place, congenitally deaf individuals are able to utilize sign language with the same ease and fluency with which the rest of us use spoken language. On the other end of the spectrum, echolalia is seen very frequently in association with autism as well as the autistic syndrome that occurs so frequently among the blind.

A subgroup of congenitally blind children suffers a serious delay in or failure ever to develop usable language skills. This language deficit constitutes one of the more dramatic aspects of the autistic syndrome to which these children are prone. Another group of congenitally blind youngsters progresses more normally in the early stages of language development, but then lags in the ability to use pronouns. It is not unusual for congenitally blind children to continue to refer to themselves either in the third person or by their proper names until their third year. Among the more deviant groups the persistence of echolalia is often very striking. These youngsters may be able to repeat words and phrases or even long sentences and paragraphs without little or no understanding of what they are saying. These children show poor ability to use speech for even the simplest communication.

Locomotion

An analogous pattern of delay is seen in the development of locomotion. According to Fraiberg (1971) and her coworkers, independent walking is rarely seen before the blind child reaches the age of 2 and in some instances is delayed much longer. That such delays are not inevitable is indicated by the following previously unpublished observations. It will be apparent, however, that the pattern of emergence of locomotory functions was different from that seen in sighted infants.

CASE VIGNETTE

S.J., the product of a normal full-term pregnancy, was found at 6 weeks to have bilateral optic atrophy. He was in all other respects a healthy baby and his mother, from the beginning, was actively engaging and stimulating. When, at 6 to 7 months, he was placed on the floor, he would move forward by pushing with his legs, while keeping his ventral surface in contact with the floor. When he was stopped by an obstacle, he would change direction. He sat independently at 9 months and walked at 1 year. This child, whom I followed into his fifth year, also developed speech, including the first person pronoun, on schedule. He continued to be a mentally alert, physically vigorous, and socially engaging youngster despite his lack of vision.

Blind children who have managed successfully to negotiate the period during which vision is the critical sensory modality can go on to be well-coordinated and engage in a surprising variety of physical activities. Thus, a brief report in the proprietary publication *Roche Medical Images* (October 1962) describes and pictures a group of congenitally blind children engaged in gymnastics.

DEVELOPMENT OF "SELF" AND OBJECT REPRESENTATIONS

With respect to the emergence of both self and object representations as well as of drive organization, the severity of developmental complications varies significantly from child to child. It is important to keep in mind that several independent maturational processes are going on during the period of early development when the infant's "average expectable" interaction with the world is preponderantly mediated by vision. Absence of vision does not, therefore, imply absence of the *potentiality* to organize a conceptual world occupied by objects. Like visually defined object representations, the environmental sources of nonvisual representations are characterized by their ability to affect the available sensory end organs. Such representations, once established, can be libidinally invested and unequivocally defined and differentiated. Thus von Senden (1932), who reviewed the world's literature on treated cases of congenital cataracts, cited numerous instances in which individuals who were blind until early or middle childhood lived contentedly in a world of haptically and kinesthetically defined objects. For the most part, providing them with vision proved a mixed blessing. Many never could make use of visual stimuli. Others developed some degree of visual competence, albeit slowly and tortuously. For none did vision displace other modalities and assume the dominant role it has in the lives of those of us whose worlds were organized from the beginning on the basis of its use.

How significantly the critical early stages of development are affected by lack of vision is, then, a function of the circumstances under which the congenitally blind baby matures and develops. The outcome depends on how well the parents learn to recognize and promote nonvisual sensory modalities for social communication. During the blind child's early years, the clinician must work with the parents to bypass the enormous obstacles to development imposed by the deficit in input from the environment (nutriment, in Piaget's language) that blindness imposes.

THE OLDER CONGENITALLY BLIND CHILD

Although the first few years of life pose the greatest developmental hazard for the congenitally blind child, the nature of this disability continues to place considerable stress on personality formation at later stages as well. The young blind child never sees another person or object move, act, or interact; he is aware of this only by direct touch impingement, sound cues, or, occasionally, by verbal report. Consequently, there is a substantial delay in the formation of an inner representational world that includes the independent actions and behavior of others.

One result of this experiential deficit is a pronounced lag in the development of representational play. This type of play is further impeded by the fact that toys, which appear visually to the normal child as replicas of larger, real-life objects, may be uninterpretable as such by the child who lacks sight. Therefore, play in the preschool age blind child is largely concrete and manipulative. A delay in representational play is expectable, and should not be interpreted prognostically as it might be for the sighted child; however, its developmental vicissitudes should be closely followed. The eventual appearance of representational play is a critical indicator that a developmental barrier has been overcome.

In middle childhood, the blind child faces many difficulties in finding objects, orienting to unfamiliar surroundings, ambulating independently, and managing details of self-care, such as eating with utensils, dressing, and personal hygiene. One consequence is a greatly increased pull towards dependency. This creates problems for the parents, who must inevitably struggle with the dilemma of how to remain empathic on the one hand, while, on the other pushing their child to tolerate the inevitable high levels of frustration and failure involved in the process of mastering these skills. Parental overprotection is a relatively frequent response to this dilemma (Lairy and Harrison-Covello 1973).

Empathy and careful attention to detail, attributes that are not every parent's or teacher's strong suit, are required to devise creative ways to help the blind child master skills that normally require vision. How the parent interacts with the child in this arena will have major consequences for the child's later autonomous functioning, sense of efficacy, assertiveness, and self-esteem. Specialists in the education of the blind should be consulted. Listings of available facilities and programs for the blind throughout the United States can be obtained through the American Foundation for the Blind (1984).

As the blind child grows older, he becomes increasingly aware of the multiplicity of events surrounding him that he cannot directly observe. This ongoing deficit in visually mediated information, which is readily available to others, becomes a major practical and emotional impediment to effective functioning. Difficulty deciding how persistent to be in requesting verbal reports by others present and the worry that this is likely to be annoying are continuous sources of stress. The blind individual is frequently in a situation where the practical advantage of asking for or accepting the assistance of others conflicts with a sense of personal pride and with the wish not to be beholden. These everyday problems tend to force the developing personality towards either the pole of withdrawal, helplessness, or embitterment on the one hand, or overloquaciousness, denial, and an assumed insensitivity on the other. The middle path is sometimes difficult to find for the older child or adolescent, who, having overcome the early developmental challenges, is striving for social, educational, and recreational engagement.

Research suggests that social development is impeded by blindness (Van Hasselt 1983). The absence of vision affects social development in several ways. The social response set of the child's milieu, that is, the attitudes toward blindness and the relative willingness of adults and peers to develop friendships, must always be considered a significant factor. Communication without eye contact may also be a deterrent to extended or deeper social engagement on the part of sighted peers and adults. For the child, it is unquestionably true that he undertakes social interactions with significant disadvantages. The blind child is unable to gauge in advance the social appropriateness of his communications or to gain direct visual feedback about others' response to him, a source of considerable insecurity in most social situations.

The type of educational setting has been shown to play a significant role in the socialization of blind children (McGuinness 1970; Schindele 1974). It appears that younger children in special settings for the blind, isolated from significant sighted peer contact, seem more advanced socially than their counterparts in more mainstream programs. However, as blind children grow older this is reversed, and mainstreamed children are more advanced socially. This may be a consequence of the increased contact with sighted peers and with the social expectations placed on children in a mainstream setting.

The acquisition of sexual knowledge in congenitally blind children is a poorly understood area, although it is often acknowledged to be a topic of concern (Warren 1984). Deprived of visual sources of information, in a social context where exploration by touching is not acceptable, the older blind child or early adolescent is largely uninformed about adult bodies of either sex (Foulkes and Uhde 1974). The visual component of sexual stimulation and sexual behavior is also absent. Unfortunately, there is little information about how the psychosexual development of blind children and adolescents has been influenced by these considerations or whether there are different consequences for boys and girls.

LOSS OF VISION DURING CHILDHOOD

Despite the fact that a substantial number of children become blind after infancy, there has been relatively little written on this topic (Warren 1984). The experience of losing vision is in some ways similar to other disabilities in which there is loss or impairment of a body part. However, the loss, in this case, is complex and far-reaching. Since there are very few activities that do not rely at least in part on vision, many components of previously mastered cognitive, social, recreational, and self-care functioning are compromised. The amount of effort and organization involved in numerous routine tasks, such as maintaining a wardrobe, dressing, preparing a meal, finding objects, and so on, is forever increased. The performance of other functions, particularly those involving travel and written communication, will require special conditions or the partial assistance of others. In general, aside from the home, the familiar classroom, and the few other places where the older blind child or adolescent has spent enough time to memorize the physical/spatial surroundings, the degree of self-sufficiency previously attained cannot be entirely regained. In addition, the inability to participate fully in many peer activities and the resulting loss of friends may undermine the second separation/individuation process of adolescence and increase reliance on the parents. This new and extensive vulnerability in so many areas of functional and social autonomy following the onset of blindness undoes or weakens many of the developmental accomplishments of the child; it renders him more susceptible to regression, depression, and a wide variety of other symptoms. The problems are further compounded by aspects of the disability shared with the congenitally blind child, such as lack of visual feedback socially and adverse attitudes toward blindness on the part of children and adults alike.

CASE VIGNETTE

Frank, a 14-year-old boy with blindness of one year's duration following a long history of congenital, progressive retinal detachment, presented at the clinic with severe insomnia and depression. He had been born with partial retinal detachment and cataracts and had undergone several corrective surgical procedures while still a baby. Although the disorder he suffered from was known to be progressive in nature, the prognosis for retaining useful vision into adulthood had been considered good. Frank and his family were informed about the disorder, but no one in his family had anticipated total blindness. Prior to an accelerating loss of vision beginning at age 10, he had been a superior athlete and an above-average student.

At age 10, he first began waking up in the morning unable to see anything. These periods of blindness initially lasted only a few minutes, but over the next three years they increased in duration, until they lasted up to two hours each time. Frank kept these episodes a complete secret for many months. During this period, his visual acuity began to deteriorate during the intervals when sight was present. Although his academic work became increasingly difficult for him and he lacked sufficient vision to maintain his athletic competitiveness, he tried to conceal this with excuses, absences from school on the basis of made-up illnesses, and so on. A final effort at surgery was undertaken, which failed and resulted, according to his opthalmologist, in near total blindness. Following this, Frank still continued to insist for some time that he could safely perform activities such as riding his bicycle. Most of his friendships had been based on his participation in sports programs. When he was forced to withdraw from these, he lost contact with most of these peers. Although low-vision specialists were provided by his school in an effort to support his continued mainstream placement, his denial of vision loss and lack of cooperation greatly hindered this effort. He became extremely demanding and abusive of his parents, who attempted to placate him by responding to his every request and by failing to confront him about the reality of his blindness.

CONCLUSION

In this chapter, we have reviewed the principal psychosocial consequences of blindness in childhood. The emphasis has been on the distortions of and hazards to development posed by the absence of vision. Since blindness in childhood is relatively uncommon, it is likely that child psychiatrists without a great deal of clinical experience in this area may be called upon to evaluate or treat these children. Presented with unfamiliar clinical features, the following basic questions, modified from Warren (1984), may be a useful framework for organizing the developmental data:

1. In what ways is the blind child similar to other sighted or blind children of the same age, and in what ways different? How is the specific age of onset of blindness relevant to the child's current developmental status?
2. What are the biological, maturational, temperamental, parental, and societal factors that have led to this blind child's similarities to and differences from other blind children?
3. What special interventions are necessary to prevent this particular blind child's development from being derailed or distorted?
4. What special interventions are necessary to reengage this blind child in an optimal developmental progression or to provide alternative remedial pathways where disability is firmly established?

REFERENCES

American Foundation for the Blind (1984). *Directory of Agencies Serving the Visually Handicapped in the U.S.* New York.

Bennett, S. (1971). Infant caretaker interactions. *J. Amer. Acad. Child Psychiat.* 10:321–35.

Blank, J. R. (1957). Psychoanalysis and blindness. *Psychoanal.* 26:1–24.

Cruikshank, W. M. (1964). The Multiple-handicapped child and courageous action. *Intl. J. Ed. Blind* 14: 65–75.

Darwin, C. (1877). A biographical sketch of an infant. In M. Bates and P. S. Humphrey (Eds.). *Darwin Reader.* New York: Scribner, 1965, pp. 403–22.

Decarie, T. (1965). A study of the mental and emotional development of the Thalidomide child. In B. M. Foss (Ed.). *Determinants of Infant Behavior*, Vol. 4. London: Methuesen, pp. 167–87.

Deutsch, F. (1940). The sense of reality in persons born blind. *J. Psychol.* 10:121–40.

Dunham, J. (1978). The deaf-blind. In R. Goldenson, J. Dunham, and C. Dunham (Eds.). *Disability and Rehabilitation Handbook.* New York: McGraw-Hill, pp. 349–52.

Emde, R. N., Gaensbauer, T., and Harmen, R. J. (1976). Emotional expression in infancy. *Psycholog. Issues* No. 37. New York: International Universities Press.

Foulkes, E., and Uhde, T. (1974). Do blind children need sex education? *New Outlook for Blind* 68:193–200.

Fraiberg, S. H. (1971). Intervention in infancy: a program for blind infancy. *J. Amer. Acad. Child Psychiat.* 10:381–405.

———. (1974). Blind infants and their mothers: An examination of the sign system. In M. Lewis and L. Rosenbleuth (Eds.). *The Effect of the Infant on Its Caregiver.* New York: J. Whey, pp. 215–32.

————. (1977). *Insights from the Blind.* New York: Basic Books.

————, and Freedman, D. A. (1964). Studies in the ego development of the congenitally blind child. *Psychoanal. Study Child* 19:113–69.

Freedman, D. A. (1971). Congenital and perinatal sensory deprivation; some studies in early development. *Amer. J. Psychiat.* 127:115–21.

————, et al. (1969). The use of sound as a guide to affective and cognitive behavior—A two phase process. *Child Devel.* 40:1099–1105.

Keeler, W. R. (1958). Autistic patterns and defective communication in blind children and retrolental fibrodysplasia. In P. H. Hoch and J. Zubin (Eds.). *Psychopathology of Communication.* New York: Grune and Stratton, pp. 64–83.

Lairy, G. C., and Harrison-Covello, A. (1973). The blind child and his parents: Congenital visual defect and the repercussion of family attitudes on the early development of the blind child. *Amer. Found. Blind Res. Bull.* 25:1–24.

Lenneberg, E. H. (1965). The vocalization of infants born to deaf and hearing parents. *Human Devel.* 8:23–37.

McGraw, M. B. (1945). *The Neuro-Muscular Development of the Human Infant.* (Reprint Edition). New York: Hofner.

McGuinness, R. M. (1970). A descriptive study of blind children educated in the itinerant teacher, resource room, and special school setting. *Amer. Found. Blind Res. Bull.* 20: 1–56.

National Society to Prevent Blindness (1980). *Vision Problems in the U.S.* New York, pp. 3–18.

Norris, M., Spaulding, P., and Brodie, F. (1958). *Blindness in Children.* Chicago: University of Chicago Press.

Piaget, J. (1937). *The Construction of Reality in the Child.* New York: Basic Books.

Reinecke, R. D. (1979). Current concepts in ophthalmology—Strabismus. *New England J. Med.* 300:1139–1141.

Roche. (1962). *Medical Images.* A proprietary publication of Roche and Company.

Roskies, E. (1971). *Abnormality and Normality: The Mothering of the Thalidomide Child.* Ithaca: Cornell University Press.

Schindele, R. (1974). The social adjustment of visually handicapped children in different educational settings. *Amer. Found. Blind Res. Bull.* 28:125–44.

Spitz, R. (1965). *The First Year of Life.* New York: Basic Books.

Van Hasselt, V. B. (1983). Social adaptation in the blind. *Clin. Psychol. Review* 3:87–102.

von Senden, M. (1932). *Space and Sight.* P. Heath (Trans.). Glencoe, Ill.: Free Press.

Warren, D. (1984). *Blindness and Early Child Development.* New York: American Foundation for the Blind, p. 2.

Wolff, P. H. (1963). Observations on the early development of smiling. In B. M. Foss (Ed.). *Determinants of Infant Behavior,* Vol. 2. London: Methuen, pp. 113–138.

Yakovlev, P. I., and LeCours, A. (1971). The myelogenetic cycles of regional maturation of the brain. In A. Minkowski (Ed.). *Regional Development of the Brain in Early Life.* Oxford: Blackwell Scientific, pp. 3–70.

42

THE DEAF CHILD AND ADOLESCENT

M. Bruce Sarlin and John D. Rainer

Deafness has been called the invisible disability; at the same time it is the nation's most prevalent chronic health problem. There have been many definitions and classifications of hearing impairment; the size of the population and its adaptive problems vary according to the group under consideration. At recent estimate, the total hearing-impaired population of the United States was approximately 1.8 million. Of this number, about 450,000 people suffered severe hearing loss before 19 years of age (the prevocationally deaf population). About one-third of this latter group became deaf before the age of 5 (the prelingual deaf population). Most of this last group were deaf from birth (Schein 1987).

DEFINITION AND ETIOLOGY OF DEAFNESS

Deafness can be defined as a hearing disability that is present since birth or from the formative years of childhood, and that represents a loss of such severity as to preclude the ability to understand conversational speech even with the help of a hearing aid. This definition precludes hard-of-hearing persons who can understand speech with the use of a hearing aid and deafened persons who lose their hearing in later life.

Congenital and early deafness can be divided etiologically into hereditary deafness and adventitious deafness. About half of the congenitally deaf population are deaf for hereditary reasons. Eighty percent of this group have a recessive form of deafness. Some of these have deafness associated with other physical anomalies such as goiter, retinitis pigmentosa, or abnormal electrocardiogram. The rest are deaf by virtue of being homozygotes for one of a relatively large number of recessive genes, having inherited the same gene from each parent. The remaining 20 percent of hereditary deafness is due to dominant genes. A few of these are associated with such syndromes as Waardenburg syndrome with pigmentary anomalies; the others are the result of having inherited a dominant gene for deafness from one parent. Adventitious deafness is mostly acquired prenatally and perinatally, less often during the first few years of life. The causes of deafness include rubella, prematurity, postnatal infections such as meningitis and tuberculosis, or drugs such as streptomycin. A relatively small number of deaf children, about 2½ percent of the total prelingual deaf population, have deafness associated with congenital malformations of various types.

Deafness in children is often unnoticed until somewhere in the second half of the first year of life, when parents observe that the child is not as responsive as would be expected. Often the diagnosis is not made even when medical consultation is sought. (Deaf parents may be more sensitive to early signs; however, in most cases, their children will be hearing.) Important years may be lost unless early detection is accompanied by parent counseling and monitoring of parent-child interaction in the nursery.

Prekindergarten and primary education is conducted at residential or day schools for the deaf and in special classes at regular schools. Communication philosophy and methods vary, as discussed below.

RUBELLA SYNDROME

At the present time the large cohort of youngsters deaf as a result of maternal rubella during the epidemics of 1964–65 represent a multihandicapped group of older adolescents and young adults. About 50 percent of these are behaviorally disturbed, with symptoms either of cerebral dysfunction, reactive behavior disorder, autism, or mental retardation (Chess, Korn, and Fernandez 1971). Cerebral dysfunction is diagnosed on the basis of neurological disease coexisting with behavior disorder. Among the symptoms are hypo- or hyperactivity, attention abnormalities, and impulse disorders, existing together with neurological signs. Reactive behavior disorder is characterized by the development of stress under certain environmental circumstances. The implication is that improvement of the home or school situation may relieve the disorder. Autism, representing a childhood psychosis, includes the classical symptoms of inability to relate to people and situations from earliest days, repetitious utterances without meaning, inability to use language, limited spontaneous activity, avoiding outside stimuli, and relating best to inanimate objects. In addition to these classical symptoms, the rubella children with or without autism may show moderate to severe mental retardation. In many cases multiple psychiatric diagnoses are found, such as a combination of mental retardation and behavior disorder, autism, or cerebral dysfunction. Impulsivity has been found about three times as often in adolescents with such multiple handicaps as in those who are deaf alone (Chess and Fernandez 1980).

FAMILY STRESS AND PSYCHOLOGICAL DEVELOPMENT

To understand the basis of developmental stress in the deaf child, it is important to recognize that about 90 percent of deaf children have hearing parents. (By the same token, about 90 percent of the children of deaf parents are hearing.) Many of the subsequent psychological difficulties of deaf persons are certainly due to the lack of effective communication between the parent (usually hearing) and the deaf infant and child (Rainer 1976). The parents' feelings of panic, guilt, blame, and despair are often translated into denial of the child's defect, barriers in communication with the child, and the kind of hopelessness with which a mother may approach making contact with a child who does not respond to her voice.

At this point the parents are often confronted with the dispute over forms of communication. Mothers are told by some educators to avoid any gestural interplay and insist that the child learn to read lips; however, a number of studies seem to show that the deaf child who is exposed to a total communication environment develops more usable language than those in a totally oral one (Mindel and Vernon 1971, pp. 75–76). In any event the battles and conflicts that go on over speech in an oral setting may be akin to those that we usually associate with toilet training and other disciplinary problems.

Observations have revealed the relatively advanced and flexible development of object relations in the deaf child of deaf parents as compared with the average deaf child who has hearing parents; these suggest that it is the parent-child relationship that is important rather than the absence of auditory stimuli and the use of verbal speech as such. Developmental shortcomings related to object ties may in turn predispose deaf children to relatively shallow affective responses that are short-lived and impulsive, labile, and detached (Rainer 1976). Compounding the problem, of course, is the unknowing or unaccepting role of the hearing world toward the deaf minority.

It is apparent from the above data that assessment of the deaf child and adolescent must include an evaluation of the extent and cause of hearing loss, associated physical and neurological abnormalities, family milieu including adequacy of communication and parent-child attachment, performance and educational level, and symptomatic behavior in various settings. This chapter will provide some approaches and references to these procedures; more detailed information can be found in journals such as the *American Annals of the Deaf* and in various articles and books (Levine 1981; Altshuler 1974; Lesser and Easser 1972; Mindel and Vernon 1971).

REASONS FOR PSYCHIATRIC REFERRAL

The deaf child referred for psychiatric evaluation or psychological assessment may show a wide array of presenting problems. Vernon (1969) reported the largest evidence of organic brain damage in those children who were deaf due to Rh factor incompatability and prematurity. He found the least evidence for children with hereditary forms of deafness, with rubella and meningitis in the middle range. However, the lowest scores on psychological tests, reflected in poor school adjustment, were found in the rubella group. Gerber and Goldberg (1980) studied a group of multiply handicapped deaf children ranging in age from 4 to 14 years whose behavior and emotional difficulties precluded their attending regular classes for the deaf. Among the problems noted in a twenty-four-hour residential treatment center geared to this special group were hyperkinesis, distractibility, aggressiveness, self-abusive behavior, impulsivity, developmental delay, personal and social difficulties, and families in crisis.

Deaf adolescents and adults presenting with psychiatric problems have shown such personality traits as egocentricity, rigidity, impulsivity, a paucity of empathy, and a failure to realize the effects of their behavior on others (Altshuler 1971)—traits seen in those vulnerable to breaks in adaptation. Nevertheless the prevalence rate of schizophrenia in the adult deaf is no greater than that in the hearing population (Rainer and Kallmann 1959; Altshuler and Sarlin 1962). A few deaf children who present with impaired relationships, either symbiosis or autistic aloofness, self-mutilation, preoccupation with objects, echopraxia or echolalia, strange postures, or mannerisms resemble closely those hearing children with schizophrenic syndrome.

Although depressive symptoms associated with guilty self-recrimination have been reported to be less prevalent in the adult deaf (Altshuler 1971), there appears to be increasing evidence of depression in deaf children and adolescents. Two cases can be cited to illustrate the occurrence of suicidal ideation and gestures among deaf adolescents.

CASE VIGNETTES

A 16-year-old boy was referred because of "wishes to die" in order to join his sister, who had been killed in an auto accident. As the next oldest sibling in a large family, the boy's sister had learned to communicate with the patient in sign language. Figure drawings of the sister depicted a glorified blonde angel replete with halo and wings.

A 16-year-old girl was referred by her school guidance counselor because of the sudden onset of angry outbursts at home and school. A number of uncontrolled episodes with peers and teachers had resulted in suspension from school. An intelligent, likable student who was an excellent communicator in sign language as well as speech, she complained that her Spanish-speaking mother "never talked to her." Despite intervention with the student and her family, she jumped to her death from the roof of her building.

The latter case is typical of referrals of school age children for aggressive outbursts or truancy where there is usually a long history of neglect, rejection, or chaotic child-rearing practices in large or disorganized families.

DEVELOPMENTAL HISTORY

Obtaining a developmental history of the deaf child or adolescent requires, first of all, emphatic attention to the concerns and thoughts of the parent, teacher, or caretaking person responsible for the deaf youngster. Maternal rubella during pregnancy, prematurity, Rh incompatibility or neonatal infections, as well as hereditary factors, may generate massive feelings of parental guilt, often projected from one parent onto the other. Shock, dismay, and depression often accompany the initial diagnosis of deafness, while bitterness or demoralization may be the culmination of years of frustration and bewilderment over a variety of issues. When parent-child interactions are initially unfulfilling and disappointing, when effective communication requires months or years of training, and when inculcating values or administering punishment is ineffective, parents often throw up their hands in despair. A teacher may be the object of the hostile reproaches of a neglected, rejected youngster acting out against a parent who is too ill physically or mentally to provide an average expectable environment. Foster or adopting parents may blame the natural parents to assuage their own feelings of guilt or to justify removal of the child, attributing aberrant behavior solely to genetic or constitutional factors.

A developmental history can provide information as to the objective circumstances into which the baby was born as well as the etiology of the deafness. The length of the marriage, the number of previous pregnancies and live births, the parents' age, and family history of deafness are important background elements. Maternal health and drug ingestion during pregnancy, the length of the pregnancy and delivery, and the birth weight, as well as neonatal events such as resuscitation, exchange transfusions, or incubation can provide valuable information regarding the health of the baby. Patterns of feeding, sleeping, toilet training and other developmental milestones, and, with both hearing and deaf parents, how they recognize distress in their child, can shed much light on parental child-rearing practices as well as the infant's adaptation to them. Separation of mother and child for nursery school may uncover data on the child's level of social and emotional adaptation. Information pertaining to peer and teacher interaction on the first day of school may reveal patterns of stranger and separation anxiety. Some children may be slow to warm up, whereas others may find for the first time an environment where they are not different because of their handicap and quickly respond to the enriched program of communication, routinization, and socialization.

MEDICAL AND AUDIOLOGICAL ASSESSMENT

Medical history should include illnesses, hospitalizations, and the age at which the diagnosis of deafness was established. In those cases where deafness has occurred before the age of 2, speech acquisition by conventional means is usually not possible for children with a severe (90 decibel) or profound (70 to 90 decibel) hearing loss. If deafness occurs after age 2, some or all of the previous speech may be lost, or the clarity of speech may be markedly impaired. The quality of speech in the hearing-impaired child is the function of the age at which hearing is affected, the degree of hearing loss, and to whatever extent restoration through hearing aids is possible.

Since there is a critical period for language learning, the earliest possible detection of a hearing problem is imperative so that parents and educators may begin language training. Where clinical examination is inconclusive and standard audiometric techniques are not possible, an electrophysiological test using the EEG has proven useful in assessing hearing in infants and adults (Hecox and Galambos 1974). Recording has been reported effective in determining impaired hearing in infants as young as 3 weeks of age. This is of special importance in high-risk populations where early remediation may enhance residual hearing as well as early mother-child communication.

CURRENT FUNCTIONING IN SCHOOL

Evaluation of the current functioning of the child should include the level of adaptation as well as intellectual achievement. At schools for the deaf, IQ testing and achievement tests are routine, so that some estimate of the child's working to capacity at grade level can be assessed from the report card. Discrepancy between native ability and performance may give rise to reactive behavior or truancy and may require special educative efforts geared to the capability of the child, including supplementary training in communication.

Particular attention to communication ability is important. At many schools for the deaf, the dictates of their educational philosophy continue to proscribe the use of manual language. Where deaf children are forced to use speech and lip-reading exclusively, it is all too often noted that they emerge upon graduation with little or no effective means of communication, either speech or manual language. As Thomas and Chess (1980, p. 24) described it,

> . . . by the use of total communication, the deaf child's visual and motor abilities can be harnessed to compensate for his auditory deficit in learning language. It is the capacity of the brain for plasticity of development that makes possible this utilization of these alternative pathways to language mastery of the deaf child. He can argue, push limits, understand why and when safety rules are necessary, learn social necessities, express emotions early, explore ideas, and master abstraction and symbolization.

SYMPTOMS OF PSYCHOPATHOLOGY

Intellectual development and cognitive style are reflected in the vocabulary and syntax used in speech, sign language, and finger spelling by the deaf child and adolescent. Often rules of grammar are not adhered to, making it difficult to assess the degree of cognitive organization as thoughts proceed rapidly from one subject to another. This linguistic "deafism" may be observed in the "normal" deaf child and the hyperactive deaf child, as well as the deaf child with a thinking disorder. Disorganization of thought is frequently accompanied by behavioral aberrations, with overriding anxiety evident in a lack of ability to organize perceptions, impressions, and activities. In those children or adolescents with a thought disorder, evidence of echolalia, echopraxia, or markedly regressed behavior accompanies the irrelevancies or incoherence in language. Tests of common sense may reveal bizarre or inappropriate responses. Frank delusions and auditory hallucinations have been reported in deaf teenagers and adults (Rainer, Abdullah, and Altshuler 1970).

Evans and Elliott (1981) discussed screening criteria for the diagnosis of schizophrenia in deaf patients. They noted that deafness is a cultural phenomenon with its own language (American Sign Language), which is not readily translatable into syntactical and grammatical English, so that some characteristics of the communication of deaf persons may be mistaken for thought disorder. In studying a group of deaf patients, they distilled nine primary signs and symptoms of schizophrenia in deaf adults from Schneider's first-rank symptoms, the International Pilot Study of Schizophrenia, and DSM-III. These include loss of ego boundaries, delusional perception, illogicality, abnormal explanations, hallucinations, inappropriate affect, remoteness from reality, restricted affect, and ambivalence. Other symptoms—poor insight, lability of affect, poverty of content, poor rapport, vagueness, and inability to complete a course of action—were commonly found in nonpsychotic deaf persons as well and hence designated as "secondary symptoms" not pathognomonic of schizophrenia.

THE PSYCHIATRIC INTERVIEW

The interview with the deaf child or adolescent is designed to assess the level of communication skills and cognitive style and the role of precipitating environmental stressors, and to provide a descriptive mental status and a psychodynamic formulation. Examination of physical appearance and gross neurological status may shed light on the underlying genetic or neurological etiology of the deafness as well as its psychiatric sequelae as reflected in the presenting symptoms.

The interview may best be conducted initially in the presence of the parent or teacher who is familiar with the communication style and tempo of the child. Where the child has sufficient communication and a comfortable level of anxiety, the child may be asked to accompany the psychiatrist to the interview room. The interview will require a set of toys, which should include a house, a car, and family and pet figures; art supplies such as clay, crayons, paper, and scissors; a set of blocks; and a few games. Deaf children have been reported to enjoy and to be capable of engaging in fantasy play, where family themes, unconscious conflicts, and impulse control can be evaluated (Sarlin and Altshuler 1978). If the child does not voluntarily respond to questions or understand the need for the consultation, the psychiatrist should explain the reason for the referral in an easily understandable manner. Reassurance can be given that what material is elicited during the interview will be handled in the best interests of the child. This is crucial with adolescents, who may fear betrayal of their trust.

In addition to observing the child's size, nutrition, and evidence of trauma, the examiner should check for signs of a genetic disorder associated with deafness. A white forelock, heterochromia of the iris, lateral displacement of the medial canthi, and a wide bridge of the nose will establish a diagnosis of Waardenburg syndrome. An adolescent girl who presents with small stature, a webbed neck, and delayed menses may suggest chromosomal testing to confirm a diagnosis of Noonan syndrome. A child with evidence of poor or failing vision may show retinitis pigmentosa on ophthalmological examination, as seen in Usher syndrome.

Tics, mannerisms, facial expressions, and the way they change during the interview may provide clues to emotionally charged areas or indications of the child's mood swings. The level of motor activity may show fidgetiness, restlessness and impulsivity, or the child may be passive and unresponsive during the interview situation. Some children may exhibit normal activity in the interview, but when observed in a large waiting room or classroom, may behave like a buzz bomb. Such hyperactive children can be seen to run from one activity or toy to another, touching or breaking things in their path. Observations or reports of the child in different settings may be useful in differentiating an attention deficit disorder from anxiety.

The Metapsychological Profile (Freud 1965, p. 140–143), developed by Anna Freud and her coworkers at the Hampstead Child-Therapy Clinic, has been applied by Brinich (1981) to study the impact of deafness on personality development and to formulate a dynamic picture of the intrapsychic organization of the deaf child. In this framework, drive development may be affected by defects in early object relationships that are mediated by disturbances in communication. Aggression may be expressed more frequently in action, and often in the context of struggle with parents or authority figures. Ego development is assessed according to ego apparatus, ego functions, and defense organization; deafness may be associated with many limitations in ego function, including motor functions and of course those related to speech and communication (memory, reality testing, socialization). The roles of denial, externalization, and fantasy need to be assessed carefully to distinguish between their function as defenses or as signs of communicative isolation from the outside world. Superego controls may be rigid and stereotyped or absent and rejected, depending on communication problems and attitude toward the handicap.

Furthermore, according to the concept of developmental lines, there is a spectrum of evolving object relations and ego functions in such areas of transition as "from Dependency to Emotional Reliance," "from Egocentricity to Companionship," "from Irresponsibility to Responsibility in Body Management," "from Suckling to Rational Eating," "from Wetting and Soiling to Bladder and Bowel Control," "from the Body to the Toy," and "from Play to Work." The article by Brinich applies the profile and the concept of developmental lines to a deaf school age child and suggests the need for an additional line of development in the area of communication.

PSYCHOLOGICAL TESTS

The psychological test instruments employed in the evaluation of a deaf infant are the same as those for the hearing infant. However, when a deaf child or adolescent is to be evaluated the differences become increasingly complex. Considerable trial-and-error procedures accompany the choice of the instrument based on age, unique receptive and expressive ability in verbal, sign or written language, concept level, and scholastic standing. Other influencing variables can be motivation, the physical or emotional condition at the time of the testing, and test or interpersonal anxiety as well as the personality of the psychologist.

In a national survey, Levine (1981) reported that although there are a number of intelligence tests standardized on populations of deaf children, the most widely used instruments at schools, special classes, and agencies serving the deaf are the Wechsler Intelligence Scale for Children (performance part only) and the Leiter International Performance Scale. Of those tests standardized on hearing-impaired children, the Hiskey Nebraska Test of Learning Aptitudes (ages 4 to 10) was the most frequently used. The test includes such items as memory for colored objects; bead-stringing patterns; pictorial associations; block building; memory for digits; drawing completions; pictorial completions; pictorial identifications; paper folding; visual attention span; puzzle blocks and pictorial analogies. The Goodenough-Harris test, a paper and pencil test for ages 3 to 15 that involves drawing a man and woman, was the next most frequently used instrument. Neurologically impaired children may produce drawings of human figures that are not well-integrated, leading to an underestimation of their intellectual ability.

When questions or doubts arise as to the validity of the test results, Levine advised some generally accepted guide for assessing IQ in the deaf. In the older school age child, a fourth-grade reading level suggests an average mental capacity and a fifth-grade arithmetic achievement level suggests an above-average mental capacity. A fluent verbal expressive language, success in a mainstream program, leadership in recreational pursuits, and cognitive alertness in a preschooler or schoolager all suggest above-average mental capacity.

The most frequently used projective tests are the Draw-A-Person, House-Tree-Person, TAT, and the Rorschach. Because expressive language, either verbal or manual, is most useful in adolescent years and beyond, projective testing with children through young adolescence is best performed with play material. Sarlin and Altshuler (1978) noted that eliciting fantasy life in a group of 5-year-old middle- and lower-class deaf children revealed remarkable similarities to the verbal productions of a control group of lower-socioeconomic-class hearing children in a uniform play situation. This technique had been useful with older deaf children and adolescents in evoking wishes, fears, anxieties, and conflicts relevant to age-specific concerns.

The Vineland Social Maturity Scale may be useful in assessing the degree of social handicap and adaptational problems of deaf children, especially those with low intelligence and various physical defects. The findings on this test must be evaluated in light of parental expectations and the availability of a wide range of environmental cues and exposure. The items reflect such measures of social competence as self-help in dressing, eating, and general care; socialization; participation in games; ability to amuse self; and ability to be helpful to others. Another behavior-rating instrument standardized on the deaf is the Meadow-Kendall Social Emotional Inventory for Deaf Students (1980). Meadow (1983) revised this instrument for deaf preschoolers as well.

When the deaf child shows evidence of a lag in learning or behavior that seems unrelated to environmental cues or stress or otherwise suggests a cerebral dysfunction, tests of visual-motor perception are indicated. The most widely used instrument is the Bender Visual-Motor Gestalt Test. Examples of similar instruments are the Benton Revised Visual Retention Test, Frostig Developmental Test of Visual Perception, and the Lincoln-Oseretsky Motor Development Scale.

Proficiency in school subjects is measured by achievement tests, generally in terms of a grade score. Reading, arithmetic, social studies, and science are measured in upper grade levels. Special areas such as social insight, health knowledge, and sex knowledge are gaining attention in school curricula and related inventories, and achievement tests are currently available. Two of the best formulated and designed achievement tests in both subject coverage and flexibility are the Stanford Achievement Test (1983 edition) for grades 1.5 through 9.9, and the Metropolitan Achievement Test (1978 edition) for grades kindergarten through 12.9. The Test of Syntactic Abilities (Quigley et al. 1978) evaluates deaf schoolagers 10 to 18 years old, supplying valuable guides to teachers concerning remedial needs. The Peabody Picture Vocabulary Test (Dunn 1959) is generally used to assess lip reading and word knowledge with deaf children. Another test designed to evaluate the level of language development (6 months through 6 years) is the Houston Test for Language Development. The Illinois Test for Psycholinguistic Abilities (2 through 10 years) identifies specific language disabilities and serves as a teaching model for remedial language training.

Two instruments useful in assessing general vocational interests of deaf adolescents are the Geist Picture Interest Inventory, of which there is an adaptation for deaf and hard-of-hearing persons (Geist 1962), and the Wide Range Interest-Opinion Test (Jastak and Jastak 1979). Further vocational assessment has become the province of specially trained vocational rehabilitation counselors for deaf persons.

TREATMENT APPROACHES

Psychiatric treatment of deaf persons—children, adolescents, and adults alike—requires as much attention to the organization and staffing of services as to the therapeutic measures themselves. A number of comprehensive mental health centers are now functioning in the United States; these comprise outpatient, inpatient, aftercare, and community programs. For effective communication with deaf patients, skill in manual communication on the part of the staff is of prime importance. For a long time, there were few mental health professionals who also had manual communication skills, and interpreters were needed. The use of interpreters in a mental health setting, no matter how skilled and objective they are, has many disadvantages, often inhibiting frank discussion. By now, fortunately, more hearing professionals are acquiring the necessary skills and a group of deaf professionals has come upon the scene, adding an important new dimension to the mental health programs.

Besides having communication skills, those treating deaf persons need a thorough knowledge of the educational and social aspects of deafness and the deaf community. Deaf adolescent and adult patients needing special protective or intensive care with specially trained medical, nursing, and attendant staff now have access to special hospital services. These have functioned well to serve the needs of the deaf population in populated states or regions. After discharge, day hospital, halfway centers, and residential homes provide transitional environments for those unable to return immediately to family or independent living.

Psychiatric treatment centers for deaf persons also include outpatient clinics for diagnosis and treatment of nonhospitalized patients and aftercare for previously hospitalized patients, preventive services such as psychiatric consultation to schools for the deaf, and education of the deaf community to remove any stigma of emotional disorder. Any program requires the trust and cooperation of deaf persons in the community, so that it has been found useful to form an advisory committee of deaf leaders and grass-roots citizens. Such a committee can secure this understanding and cooperation and also prevail on legislatures and governing bodies to provide and support the specialized services.

Treatment methods in these settings are similar to those used in general psychiatric practice—pharmacological therapy combined with various forms of psychosocial treatment such as behavior therapy, supportive psychotherapy, and insight psychotherapy. Psychotherapy in particular, including insight and psychoanalytic methods and use of dreams, certainly requires excellent communication skills on the part of both patient and therapist.

Such psychotherapy has been found useful in treating deaf adolescents (Sarlin 1984). In selected cases, cognitive skills and abstract abilities were sufficiently developed to allow them to understand the symbols in their dreams and to connect them with current events. Through clarification and interpretation of the unconscious conflicts presented in the dreams, insight was derived into the motivation for their maladaptive behavior. A better integration of personality with greater autonomy and object constancy was achieved.

In other cases the therapist may act as a good provider, offering specific help and advice on difficult problems and decisions. Much effective therapy can be done in this context. Self-esteem and daily functioning can be improved by suggesting environmental changes and encouraging independence of action and breakthrough of isolation.

The social isolation and lack of empathy of many deaf adolescents, patterns of nonawareness of others, and noncooperation can be effectively attacked in group therapy (Sarlin and Altshuler 1968). By noting the behavior and reactions of others, the group members can achieve a greater degree of objectivity about themselves, learn concepts and techniques of cooperation, and achieve greater social maturity. The therapist can draw the group's attention to discrepancies between aims and actions, between actions and results, and between applications of the golden rule to oneself and to others. In group treatment, patients have been able to give up some of their distorted perceptions of social interaction and to achieve a sense of group identity.

CONCLUSIONS AND RECOMMENDATIONS

Careful assessment of the deaf child or adolescent should lead to diagnostic formulation in multiaxial terms and a program of treatment and/or environmental fashioning useful to parents, teachers, and clinical personnel. It should be clear that such evaluation is a specialized task, requiring on the part of the evaluator a knowledge of the many organic and developmental factors associated with deafness, a familiarity with deaf persons as a social group and with their education (Furth 1973) and community organization (Higgins 1980), and above all a facility in total communication, including American Sign Language and other manual modes (signed English, finger spelling). The task of evaluation as well as treatment can probably best be achieved in a specialized mental health unit staffed by psychiatrists, psychologists, social workers, rehabilitation counselors, and speech and hearing personnel. In practice, such groups can often make good use of the services of a sign language interpreter. A number of such units are functioning in various sections of the country and can be consulted for help in the evaluative process (Trybus and Edelstein 1981).

REFERENCES

Altshuler, K. Z. (1971). Studies of the deaf: Relevance to psychiatric theory. *Amer. J. Psychiat.* 127:1521–26.

———. (1974). The social and psychological development of the deaf child: Problems, their treatment and prevention. *Amer. Annals Deaf* 119:365–76.

———, and Sarlin, M. S. (1962). Deafness and schizophrenia: Interrelationships of communication stress, maturation lag, and schizophrenic risk. In F. J. Kallman (Ed.). *Expanding Goals of Genetics in Psychiatry.* New York: Grune and Stratton.

Brinich, P. M. (1981). Application of the metapsychological profile to the assessment of deaf children. *Psychoanal. Study Child* 36:3–32.

Chess, S., and Fernandez, P. B. (1980). Impulsivity in rubella deaf children. *Amer. Annals Deaf* 125:505–9.

———, Korn, S. J., and Fernandez, P. B. (1971). *Psychiatric Disorders of Children with Congenital Rubella.* New York: Brunner/Mazel.

Dunn, L. M. (1959). *Peabody Picture Vocabulary Test.* Circle Pines, Minn.: American Guidance Service.

Evans, J. W., and Elliott, H. (1981). Screening criteria for the diagnosis of schizophrenia in deaf patients. *Arch. Gen. Psychiat.* 38:787–90.

Freud, A. (1965). *Normality and Pathology in Childhood.* New York: International Universities Press, pp. 140–43.

Furth, H. G. (1973). *Deafness and Learning: A Psychosocial Approach.* Belmont, Calif.: Wadsworth.

Geist, H. (1962). Occupational interest profile of the deaf. *Personnel Guide J.* 51:50–55.

Gerber, B. M., and Goldberg, H. K. (1980). Psychiatric consultation in a school program for multi-handicapped deaf children. *Amer. Annals Deaf* 125:579–85.

Hecox, K. E., and Galambos, R. (1974). Brain stem auditory evoked responses in infants and adults. *Arch. Otolaryngol.* 99:30–33.

Higgins, P. C. (1980). *Outsiders in a Hearing World: A Sociology of Deafness.* Beverly Hills, Calif.: Sage.

Jastak, J. F., and Jastak, S. (1979). *Wide Range Interest-Opinion Test: Manual.* Wilmington, Del.: Jastak Associates.

Lesser, S. R., and Easser, B. R. (1972). Personality differences in the perceptually handicapped. *J. Amer. Acad. Child Psychiat.* 11:458–66.

Levine, E. S. (1981). *The Ecology of Early Deafness: Guides to Fashioning Environments and Psychological Assessments.* New York: Columbia University Press.

Meadow, K. P. (1980). An instrument for assessment of social-emotional adjustment in hearing-impaired preschoolers. *Amer. Anals of Deaf* 128:826–34.

———. (1983). Meadow-Kendall social-emotional assessment inventory for deaf and hearing-impaired students. In J. V. Mitchell, Jr. (Ed.). *Ninth Mental Measurement Yearbook.* Lincoln, Nebr.: Buros Institute.

Mindel, E. D., and Vernon, M. (1971). *They Grow in Silence.* Silver Spring, Md.: National Association of the Deaf, pp. 75–76.

Quigley, S. P., et al. (1978). *Test of Syntactic Abilities.* Beaverton, Oreg.: Dorimac.

Rainer, J. D. (1976). Some observations on affect induction and ego development in the deaf. *Int'l. Rev. Psychoanal.* 3:121–28.

———, and Kallmann, F. J. (1959). Genetic and demographic aspects of disordered behavior patterns in a deaf population. In B. Pasamanick (Ed.). *Epidemiology of Mental Disorder.* Washington, D.C.: American Association for the Advancement of Science.

———, Abdullah, S., and Altshuler, K. Z. (1970). Phenomenology of hallucinations in the deaf. In W. Keup (Ed.). *Origins and Mechanisms of Hallucinations.* New York: Plenum Press.

Sarlin, M. B. (1984.) The use of dreams in psychotherapy with deaf patients. *J. Amer. Acad. Psychoanal.* 12:75–88.

———, and Altshuler, K. Z. (1968). Group therapy with deaf adolescents in a school setting. *Int'l. J. Group Psychother.* 18:337–44.

———, and Altshuler, K. Z. (1978). On the interrelationship of cognition and affect: Fantasies of deaf children. *Child Psychiat. Human Devel.* 9:95–103.

Schein, J. (1987). Deaf population. In J. V. VanCleve (Ed.). *Gallaudet Encyclopedia of Deaf People and Deafness.* New York: McGraw-Hill, pp. 252–53.

Schlesinger, H., and Meadow, K. P. (1972) *Sound and Sign.* Berkeley: University of California Press.

Thomas, A., and Chess, S. (1980). *The Dynamics of Psychological Development.* New York: Brunner/Mazel, p. 24.

Trybus, R. J., and Edelstein, T. A. (1981). *Directory of Mental Health Programs and Resources for Hearing Impaired Persons.* Washington, D.C.: Gallaudet Research Institute.

Vernon, M. (1969). *Multiply Handicapped Deaf Children: Medical, Educational and Psychological Aspects.* Washington, D.C.: Council of Exceptional Children.

43

GENDER IDENTITY DISORDERS IN CHILDREN

Susan Coates and Kenneth J. Zucker

Clinical research on children who wish to be of the opposite sex began with reports by Green and Money in the early 1960s (Green and Money 1960). Since then a great deal has been written about these children, particularly in the past ten to fifteen years, from a variety of theoretical and clinical perspectives. In this chapter, we will consider a number of issues relevant for a comprehensive evaluation of the severely gender-disturbed child. The main points of emphasis will be a critical summary of current diagnostic issues, parameters required for an in-depth psychodynamic evaluation of the child and family, and reference to potential predisposing biological factors. The general perspective taken in this chapter is that familial psychopathology and intrapsychic factors in the child play central roles in the genesis and perpetuation of severe child gender identity disturbance.

The epidemiology of gender identity disorders in children is not known. Most authorities consider severe and chronic gender disturbance to be uncommon. Lesser forms of gender disturbance, however, are probably more common, and part of the clinician's task is to distinguish between those children whose behavior is likely to be chronic and those whose behavior is probably transient, perhaps in response to an isolated life stressor. The most reliable epidemiological data concern sex differences. More boys than girls are referred to psychiatric clinics for gender disturbance. In the first author's clinic, the male-to-female sex ratio has been 17:1, whereas in the second author's clinic, the ratio has been smaller, 6:1. Another research-clinician has reported a sex ratio of 30:1 (Rekers 1985). It is not really known whether the sex difference reflects a true difference in vulnerability to gender disorder or whether it is due to other factors, such as greater cultural tolerance for cross-gender behavior in girls than in boys. Whatever the reason, as a result of this strong gender gap in child referrals, very little material has been published on girls with severe gender identity disorder (Bradley 1980). Thus, this chapter's focus will emphasize what has been learned about severe gender disturbance in boys.

Before a case illustration is presented, a few terms that are commonly used in this area will be provided. Core gender identity refers to the self-designation of belonging to one sex or the other. It is the conviction that one is a male or a female. Gender role identity refers to one's self-evaluation of psychological masculinity and femininity. It is the belief that one is relatively masculine or feminine. Gender role behavior refers to culturally sex-typed interests and activities.

Children with gender identity disorder most often have a disturbed gender role identity. Invariably they know that they belong to their own sex, and therefore they do not have a disturbance in core gender identity. They can be said, however, to have a disturbance in gender role identity, since they feel they possess the qualities of the opposite sex. In gender role behavior, their interests and activities are typically associated with the opposite sex. Thus, gender-disturbed boys wish to be girls, prefer feminine interests and activities, and express a dislike of their male anatomy. Similarly, gender-disturbed girls wish to be boys, prefer masculine interests and activities, and express a dislike of their female anatomy.

The following vignette illustrates a case of a severe gender identity disorder in a 5-year-old boy who was referred to the Childhood Gender Identity Project at Roosevelt Hospital in New York City.

CASE VIGNETTE

Shawn R. was accompanied to the assessment by his parents, a white middle-class couple in their early thirties, and his 3-year-old sister, Deirdre. Mr. R. is a middle manager in a medium-sized business, and Mrs. R. is a housewife. Shawn's mother made the decision to seek professional advice after listening to a psychologist discuss gender development on a radio talk show. During this program, the psychologist remarked that severe cross-gender behavior was often a red flag for serious underlying psychological difficulties, which aroused great alarm in Shawn's mother.

Mrs. R. spoke of the first two years of Shawn's life as a period of considerable satisfaction. She described Shawn as a placid, amiable baby, easy to comfort and to care for. By age 2, however, he had sleep problems, either waking up frequently or wanting to sleep with his parents. He was afraid of the dark and always had to sleep with the light on. He endlessly followed his mother around the house and could not bear to have her out of his sight (when she went to the bathroom, the door had to remain open). He has occasionally been school-reluctant, but this has not been a serious problem.

Shawn's cross-gender behavior emerged at the age of two in the form of dressing-up in his mother's clothes. This occurred on the heels of his sister's birth. The cross-dressing lasted for a few months and then seemed to abate. At this time, the parents made no response to Shawn's cross-dressing. When his sister was 6 months old, she was in hospital for two weeks, during which time she had surgery for a physical problem. She had to wear a body cast for the next six months. During Deirdre's stay in hospital, Mrs. R. was with her at all times. When Mrs. R. returned home with Deirdre, she virtually abandoned all care of Shawn, turning his care over to her mother, who came to the family home during the day. Mrs. R. stated that for the next year she spent "100 percent" of her time devoted to Deirdre's recovery and that she stopped doing everything else. All she did was to hold Deirdre because she could not bear to hear her cry. This she did "day and night." Mrs. R. described herself as being constantly irritable, snappy, easily enraged, and often on the verge of collapse during this period: "It was the most depressing experience of my life. I just began to start coming out of it 6 months ago [when Shawn was 4½]." In retrospect, she feels that she exploited and took advantage of Shawn's good nature.

By the time Mrs. R. returned from the hospital with Deirdre, Shawn was intensely involved in cross-gender behavior. As time went on, he began to express the wish to be a girl, stating that women were more beautiful than men and that they got to wear prettier clothes. He displayed a marked interest in women's clothes, jewelry, and make-up. His imaginary play, which often took the form of doll play, focused entirely on female characters, such as Barbie dolls, Miss Piggy, and Wonder Woman. His favorite stories were Cinderella, Snow White, and Rapunzel. He often spent hours singing and dancing, during which he always portrayed women. He preferred girls as playmates as long as they would allow him to take female roles in play. He avoided rough-and-tumble play with boys.

Shawn's parents displayed a remarkable lack of concern about his cross-gender behavior other than worrying that in school he was often referred to as a "sissy" and was scapegoated. Instead of being concerned, Mrs. R. was proud of his civilized behavior, which she described as almost priestly. She stated that when Shawn was younger he was the most pleasant baby she had ever seen, just a nice person: "I'm happy I've met him."

Mrs. R. grew up in an intact family that included two older brothers. A year before she married, the brother closest to her in age committed suicide. Shawn was named after him. Mrs. R.'s mother had married a few months after having been raped. The rape had resulted in pregnancy and the man she married had agreed to raise the child, but then reneged, claiming that he would not care for a child who was not his own. The child was then given to the mother's sister, who raised him as her own. Mrs. R. described her mother as saintly, perfect, generous, "always there for you," and as one who could do no wrong. She also considered her mother to be willful and powerful. Mrs. R. described herself as having been unusually close to her mother as a child and as remaining unusually close to her. She recalled experiencing considerable anxiety whenever she was separated from her mother as a child and feels that this still continues today. She says that even when her mother is on vacation, she feels that there is a complete void in her life. Mrs. R. described her father as domineering, controlling, and prone to temper outbursts: "My father was the head of the house. Everything had to be quiet when he came home. We didn't eat until he picked up his fork." Mrs. R.'s maternal grandfather was an alcoholic, and her grandmother suffered from depressions. Her paternal grandfather abandoned his family, and the grandmother was violent and would often "go after him with a knife."

Mr. R. grew up in an intact family as the younger of two boys. He lived in a three-family house, the two other dwellings of which were occupied by maternal aunts and their husbands. All of the men worked in a family business that kept them away on weekends and holidays. Mr. R. remembers holidays as always being subdued because there were never any men around. He described his mother as a reclusive, family-oriented woman who felt that her sons were "God's gift to the world." He recalled that she constantly showered physical affection upon him, which he found embarrassing and often tried to get away from. During adolescence, he became closer to his father and began to stay away from home as much of the time as he could. He said that his older brother was overinvolved with his mother, unusually close to her, and remained so today. During Mr. R.'s adolescence, one of the cousins who lived in the house was hospitalized for schizophrenia and another for depression. Mr. R. stated that he had been the only child to make it safely out of the house. Upon his father's retirement, he became notably depressed but did not require hospitalization.

Mrs. R. presented as an attractive, overweight, intense, and engaging woman who was clearly the emotional center of the family's life. She was emotionally expressive, both verbally and physically, and she described herself as an energetic and powerful person who had "an iron fist in a velvet glove." She was pleased that her husband had been accepted into her family as one of its own and that he felt closer to her family than he did to his own. Although Mrs. R. valued her husband's reliability, stability, gentleness, and loyalty, she was very critical of his distance and passivity in family matters and in his dealings with Shawn. She held him responsible for Shawn's gender problems because of his lack of emotional involvement with him.

In both the interview and psychological testing, Shawn was engaging, verbal, and articulate. He easily established rapport with both interviewers. With intense feeling, he described himself as being lonely, claiming that no one really liked him. He said that he wanted to be a girl because a girl could wear dazzling dresses and be beautiful. When asked what were some good things about being a boy, he said "nothing, not one thing at all." He talked spontaneously about his mother, saying that she always looked fancy. He noticed that the female interviewer was wearing purple and commented on liking the color purple. He said that his grandmother always wore purple. When offered a choice between masculine and feminine toys, he chose to play exclusively with the Barbie dolls. When asked about what he wanted to be when he grew up, he said, "Get married, but my wife is going to go to work and I will stay home and take care of the kids."

On the Rorschach, Shawn displayed evidence of severe gender confusion and marked ego boundary disturbances. He saw male aggression as dangerous, violent, and easily beyond control; thus, he experienced contact with men as a threat to his intactness and self-cohesion. Another theme that emerged during psychological testing was marked separation anxiety in relation to his mother. He seemed to feel that he could be completely abandoned by her. From the psychological testing, it appeared that Shawn's gender disorder solved at least two major intrapsychic conflicts simultaneously:

(1) it protected him from having to be an aggressive, dangerous male who might destroy the very objects on which he depended; (2) by being a girl in fantasy, he could reclaim the psychological loss of his mother. Shawn confused having his mother with being his mother; thus, the operative psychological mechanism was a variation of an identification with a lost object.

DIAGNOSTIC ISSUES

In this section, we consider some of the major diagnostic issues involved in the assessment of child gender disturbance. The section includes an evaluation of the DSM-III diagnosis of Gender Identity Disorder of Childhood, a critique of Stoller's "etiological" diagnosis of "male childhood transsexualism," and a discussion of childhood transvestism. Emphasis is placed on data available to the clinician who relies primarily on interview material.

Gender Identity Disorder of Childhood

Table 43.1 presents the DSM-III diagnostic criteria for Gender Identity Disorder of Childhood. In our view, the criteria for boys appear to reflect accurately what one observes in clinical assessment. The most common diagnostic issue concerns the practical implication of separating Points A and B. This most often arises in cases in which a boy shows extreme cross-gender behavior yet does not verbalize the desire to be of the opposite sex. Technically speaking, a DSM-III diagnosis of gender disturbance cannot be given, since the child does not express cross-sex desires. One could, of course, employ the DSM-III residual diagnosis Atypical Gender Identity Disorder, but this does not really clarify the issue in any meaningful fashion. This particular pattern is most likely to be found in boys over the age of 7 (see Zucker et al. 1984). It is not at all clear whether the extremely cross-gendered boy who does not express overt wishes to be of the opposite sex differs from the boy who does, for example, with regard to later gender dysphoria, etiology, and response to treatment. This issue remains an important area for future research.

As argued elsewhere (Zucker 1982, 1985), the diagnostic criteria for girls are more problematic. In particular, this concerns the Point B criteria. One problem with these criteria is that they exclude feelings of aversion for one's sexual anatomy, which diverges from what the criteria permit for boys. Instead, the only evidence considered valid are statements that might be characterized as either delusional or immature, in the sense that they deny the reality, or the future reality, of the girl's anatomic status or biological capabilities. A second objection concerns the omission in Point B of a criterion dealing with a girl's extreme preference for culturally stereotypical masculine behavior (Rekers and Mead 1980). This omission appears to be based in part on a concern not to characterize "tomboys" as gender-disturbed, a differential diagnosis issue. By implication, the DSM-III criteria suggest that the tom-

TABLE 43.1   DSM-III Diagnostic Criteria for Gender Identity Disorder of Childhood

For males:

A. Strongly and persistently stated desire to be a girl, or insistence that he is a girl.

B. Either (1) or (2):

    (1) persistent repudiation of male anatomic structures, as manifested by at least one of the following repeated assertions:

        (a) that he will grow up to become a woman (not merely in role)

        (b) that his penis or testes are disgusting or will disappear

        (c) that it would be better not to have a penis or testes

    (2) preoccupation with female stereotypical activities as manifested by a preference for either cross-dressing or simulating female attire, or by a compelling desire to participate in the games and pastimes of girls

C. Onset of the disturbance before puberty.

For females:

A. Strongly and persistently stated desire to be a boy, or insistence that she is a boy (not merely a desire for any perceived cultural advantage from being a boy).

B. Persistent repudiation of female anatomic structures, as manifested by at least one of the following repeated assertions:

    (1) that she will grow up to become a man (not merely in role)

    (2) that she is biologically unable to become pregnant

    (3) that she will not develop breasts

    (4) that she has no vagina

    (5) that she has, or will grow, a penis

C. Onset of the disturbance before puberty.

Reprinted with permission of the American Psychiatric Association.

boy will not express frequent cross-sex desires or manifest anatomic dysphoria. As argued elsewhere (Zucker 1985), it is not clear whether these are the only, or even the crucial, behavioral signs that differentiate the tomboy from the gender-disturbed girl. For example, a strong aversion toward female clothing and cosmetics seems to be a meaningful characteristic of gender-disturbed girls seen clinically, yet it is not included in the formal DSM-III criteria. Because the revised version of DSM-III has taken these criticisms into account, it is hoped that their clinical validity will become known. In the revised version of DSM-III, the Point B criterion for girls reads as follows:

Either (1) or (2):

(1) Persistent marked aversion to normative feminine clothing and insistence on wearing stereotypical masculine clothing, e.g., boys' underwear and other accessories.

(2) Persistent repudiation of her female anatomic structures as evidenced by at least one of the following:

    (a) assertion that she has, or will grow, a penis;

    (b) rejection of urinating in a sitting position;

    (c) assertion that she does not want to grow breasts or menstruate.

In summary, the DSM-III criteria might best be viewed as representing an end point with regard to a spectrum of cross-gender identification. The clinician's main diagnostic task is to appraise the severity with which a child feels uneasy about his or her biological sex, as that severity is what will probably influence a variety of therapeutic decisions.

Male Childhood Transsexualism

Stoller (1968b, 1975, 1985) has made a number of theoretical and empirical contributions to our understanding of gender identity development. In this section, we limit ourselves to an analysis of his work on the diagnosis of gender disturbance in boys (he has not written about gender disturbance in girls). Stoller's work is important because of his claim that there is a subgroup of feminine boys who are qualitatively distinct from other feminine boys with regard to phenomenology and etiology. It is important for the clinician to know how valid this claim is.

With regard to phenomenology, Stoller has repeatedly noted that he was describing the most feminine of boys, whose behavior begins from age two or earlier and remains a "blatant and continuous, compelling preoccupation" (Stoller 1968a, p. 194). In Stoller's view, the aspect of the femininity of these boys that differentiates them from other feminine boys is the "fixed belief that one is a member of the opposite sex and will grow up and develop the anatomical characteristics of the opposite sex" (1968a, p. 195). As Stoller stated: "These boys do not only wish at times they were girls or fantasy themselves as girls. The latter is common, consciously and frequently in effeminate boys; less frequent or unconscious in more masculine boys; yet none of these effeminate or more normal boys *thinks he is a female*" (1968a, p. 200, emphasis added). Thus, Stoller seems to imply that male childhood transsexualism is a qualitatively distinct childhood gender disorder.

There are two main problems with Stoller's diagnostic criteria. Zucker (1982) has noted that Stoller is inconsistent on the defining feature of boyhood transsexualism; specifically, he does not always distinguish between "wishing" and "believing." For example, he has stated that "this condition is called childhood transsexualism because its most obvious manifestation is the boy's *feeling* he is a girl" (Stoller 1968b, p. 196, emphasis added). Given the difference between feeling and believing, one cannot be certain that the key diagnostic criterion is, in fact, the child's "fixed belief that [he] is a member of the opposite sex." The other problem with Stoller's criterion is a developmental one. All of Stoller's cases were quite young at assessment, and thus it is highly doubtful that the literal misclassification of their gender would persist over time, even in the most unusual of environments.

Despite these difficulties, the degree of cross-gender identification could still be utilized as a frame of reference in trying to decide whether a particular case might be similar to the ones observed by Stoller. A problem in this connection, however, is that Stoller (1975, Ch. 16) reported having evaluated a boy who was "as feminine as any seen," yet was not, in his view, a transsexual. Stoller's basis for this claim was etiological; that is, the variables that he felt had been associated with his other cases were not present. Thus, Stoller argues that an assessment of etiological factors is necessary in order to confirm the diagnosis of male childhood transsexualism, since the phenomenology on which the diagnosis is based may not, in fact, be as discriminating as originally thought. There is thus a conflation of descriptive and etiological criteria in his diagnostic scheme. Researchers are just beginning to evaluate Stoller's etiological variables, particularly the aspect of the mother-son relation that he refers to as a "blissful (conflict-free) symbiosis." Work that has been done has not supported this aspect of his etiological framework (Coates 1985; Coates and Person 1985; Marantz 1984).

Childhood Transvestism

The literal meaning of transvestism is to dress in the clothes of the opposite sex. Clinically, however, the term transvestism is now used to describe adolescent and adult males who cross-dress for the purpose of erotic arousal, particularly when the cross-dressing first occurs. A number of authors have pointed out that transvestism sometimes progresses to transsexualism. It has also been observed that cross-dressing serves an anxiety-reducing function in its own right, apart from its erotic function (Person and Ovesey 1978). Retrospective studies of transvestites indicate that cross-dressing without erotic arousal is common during childhood (Bradley et al. 1984; Buhrich and McConaghy 1977). This form of the cross-dressing differs sharply from that observed in children with gender identity disorder of childhood. Transvestitic cross-dressing typically involves the use of female underclothing, particularly that which is soft and silky. Gender-dysphoric children, in contrast, invariably employ outer clothing, whose primary function is to enhance cross-gender identification.

To the best of our knowledge, there are no published reports of childhood transvestism *in statu nascendi*. The second author has evaluated two prepubertal boys (ages 5 and 6) whose behavior was consistent with the diagnosis of childhood transvestism. The feminine clothes that these boys wore was maternal underclothing. These boys differed from gender-dysphoric boys in other ways as well— they did not profess the desire to be of the opposite sex, and their gender role behavior was typically masculine. This pattern of childhood gender identity and gender role converges with retrospective accounts from adolescent transvestites and their parents (Bradley et al. 1984). DSM-III does not have a specific diagnosis of this childhood behavioral pattern, although the residual diagnosis "Atypical Gender Identity Disorder" could be employed.

ASSESSMENT ISSUES

With any attempt to establish whether a disorder represents a meaningful behavioral syndrome, it is first necessary to show that the characteristics that define the putative disorder do, in fact, distinguish it from other types of disorders (Rutter

1978). The evidence for the discriminant validity of child gender disturbance appears to be reasonably well established, particularly for boys. Assessment of overt sex-typed play, fantasy play and aggression, human figure drawings, sex-typed motoric behavior, and parent report of sex-typed behavior indicates that gender-disturbed children differ from other groups of children, including sibling, psychiatric, and normal controls (summarized in Zucker 1985). Apart from the parent-report measures, these findings are based exclusively on testing in clinic settings. Little observational work has been done in naturalistic settings, although case reports (Rekers, Lovaas, and Low 1974) suggest similar differences in these environments as well.

These data represent the first step in determining whether child gender disturbance represents a meaningful syndrome of behavior. The data have been of special importance in the presence of critiques questioning whether such behavior is really different from the norm (Wolfe 1979). From an empirical standpoint, however, there seems to be no question that the sex-typed behavior of gender-referred children often departs dramatically from that of their same-sex peers.

Clinically, the assessment of the gender-disturbed child should focus on four factors: (1) identification of the behavioral syndrome; (2) evaluation of the family; (3) evaluation of the meaning of the gender symptoms; and (4) assessment of other psychiatric problems in the child.

Assessment of Gender Identity Disorder

Identification of the behavioral syndrome is usually first established in a parent interview. The focus of the interview is to determine whether the child expresses the wish to be of the opposite sex, shows a predominance of cross-gender interests, and expresses anatomic dysphoria. The questionnaire in Table 43.2 is a useful tool in making this evaluation. From this interview, a DSM-III diagnosis is made.

An interview with the child provides further information on gender role identification and behavior, including sex-typed preferences and interests. Gender-disturbed children usually have elaborate interests in opposite-sex characters in children's books and on TV. For example, gender-disturbed boys in early childhood are fascinated with female heroines such as Cinderella and Snow White; in middle childhood, TV characters such as Wonder Woman and the Bionic Woman are often favorites. By late childhood, female characters in soap operas and other TV serials are admired. One can often ask a child directly, particularly during the middle years of childhood, "What is better about being a boy or a girl?" Gender-disturbed boys often respond to this question by saying that there is nothing good about being a boy and that it's better to be a girl because a girl can wear dazzling clothes or because girls are nicer, stronger, or more powerful. Very young children often emphasize external attributes, whereas older children focus more on personality characteristics. In free play situations, gender-disturbed children often show a preference for cross-sex toys and dress-up apparel.

Evidence of gender identity disturbance can also be seen on psychological

TABLE 43.2 Gender Identity Questionnaire

Instructions

Please answer the following behavioral statements as they currently characterize your child's behavior. For each question, circle the response which most accurately describes your child.

01. His favorite playmates are:
    a. always boys
    b. usually boys
    c. boys and girls equally
    d. usually girls
    e. always girls
    f. does not play with other children
02. He plays with girl-type dolls, such as "Barbie"
    a. as a favorite toy
    b. frequently
    c. once in a while
    d. very rarely
    e. never
03. He plays with boy-type dolls such as "G.I. Joe" or "Ken"
    a. as a favorite toy
    b. frequently
    c. once in a while
    d. very rarely
    e. never
04. He experiments with cosmetics (make-up) and jewelry
    a. as a favorite activity
    b. frequently
    c. once in a while
    d. very rarely
    e. never
05. He imitates *female* characters seen on TV or in the movies
    a. as a favorite activity
    b. frequently
    c. once in a while
    d. very rarely
    e. never
06. He imitates *male* characters seen on TV or in the movies
    a. as a favorite activity
    b. frequently
    c. once in a while
    d. very rarely
    e. never
07. He plays sports with boys (but not girls)
    a. as a favorite activity
    b. frequently
    c. once in a while
    d. very rarely
    e. never
08. He plays sports with girls (but not boys)
    a. as a favorite activity
    b. frequently
    c. once in a while
    d. very rarely
    e. never
09. In playing "mother/father," "house," or "school" games, he takes the role of
    a. a girl or woman at all times
    b. usually a girl or woman

    c. half the time a girl or woman and half the time a boy or man

    d. usually a boy or man

    e. a boy or man at all times

    f. does not play these games

10. He plays "girl-type" games (as compared to "boy-type" games)

    a. as a favorite activity

    b. frequently

    c. once in a while

    d. very rarely

    e. never

11. He plays "boy-type" games (as compared to "girl-type" games)

    a. as a favorite activity

    b. frequently

    c. once in a while

    d. very rarely

    e. never

12. In dress-up games, he likes to dress up

    a. in girls' or women's clothes all the time

    b. usually in girls' or women's clothes

    c. half the time in girls' or women's clothes and half the time in boys' or men's clothes

    d. usually in boys' or men's clothes

    e. in boys' or men's clothes all the time

    f. does not dress up

13. He states the wish to be a girl or a woman

    a. every day

    b. frequently

    c. once in a while

    d. very rarely

    e. never

14. He states that he is a girl or a woman

    a. every day

    b. frequently

    c. once in a while

    d. very rarely

    e. never

15. He talks about *not* liking his sexual anatomy (private parts)

    a. every day

    b. frequently

    c. once in a while

    d. very rarely

    e. never

    If you circled a, b, c, or d, please describe what he says:

16. He talks about *liking* his sexual anatomy (private parts)

    a. every day

    b. frequently

    c. once in a while

    d. very rarely

    e. never

    If you circled a, b, c, or d, please describe what he says:

Note: Items 1 through 12 are derived from a questionnaire developed by Elizabeth and Green (1984). The questionnaire may also be used with girls with pronouns appropriately reversed.

testing. Gender-disturbed boys are likely to draw the opposite sex first on the Draw-A-Person test, whereas normal boys usually draw the same sex first. Gender-disturbed boys often draw the female larger than the male and with greater elaboration and detail. The drawings usually include stereotypical feminine attributes, such as long eyelashes, contoured lips, and various accessories, such as earrings, necklaces, bracelets, and ribbons (Coates 1985).

A similar pattern of stereotypical feminine percepts has been observed on the Rorschachs of gender-disturbed boys (Tuber and Coates 1985). Females are seen as ballerinas, belly dancers, cheerleaders, Miss Piggy, and superheroines such as Wonder Woman. Women's accessories such as dresses, high-heeled shoes, and bras are frequently described. The image of animals or people in the process of giving birth has also been noted.

Overt gender confusion also emerges in the Rorschach percepts of gender-disturbed boys. This is manifested in three ways. First, some responses combine male and female elements into a single response. Second, in single percepts of people, there are changes in the gender attributed to them. Third, in some responses the child is unable to decide whether a single percept is exclusively male or female. The following are examples of overt gender confusion:

(1) If it's a girl his (sic) hair goes up . . . or if it's a boy, it needs a haircut.
(2) This looks like a fat lady, no, looks like a fat man naked with lady's shoes.
(3) She's having a baby . . . could be a he, too, because he-monsters have babies sometimes.
(4) It looks like a lady, looks like a man turning into Superman.
(5) That's a butterfly. That's his (sic) tail where she has her babies through.

Although controlled studies have not yet been completed, the first author's clinical impression is that overt gender confusion on the Rorschach will be a highly specific indicator of childhood gender disturbance.

Assessment of the Family

The next step in the assessment is an evaluation of the family. Results from a number of studies have all found that disturbed family functioning plays a central role in the dynamics of the gender-disturbed boy (reviewed in Coates 1985). Several aspects of the family's functioning need to be evaluated: father absence, either physically or psychologically; maternal attitudes toward men; child-rearing attitudes; and maternal state.

A striking finding by a number of researchers has been the prevalence of father absence. Green (1974) reported that 34 percent of the feminine boys in his sample were physically separated from their fathers due to divorce, abandonment, or death. More recently, Green, Williams, and Goodman (1985) reported that the fathers of their feminine boys recalled spending less time with their sons during the first five years of life than did the fathers of masculine control boys.

In the first author's unit, father absence occurred with even greater frequency by the time the boys were 3 years old: 63 percent of the fathers were absent and by the time of referral this had increased to 85 percent. The prevalence of father absence held even for the white middle-class subsample that most closely corresponded to Green's (1974) sample. The few fathers who were present were either psychologically remote or explosive or violent. Thus, in the first author's cases, none of the gender-disturbed boys had a father who was appropriately involved (cf. Stoller 1979). None of the mothers either remarried or lived with a man on a long-term basis after the separation from the boy's father.

It is also particularly important to assess the attitudes that mothers of feminine boys have toward men. Bradley et al. (1980) and Coates (1985) have noted that such mothers often expressed overt or covert hostility toward men. They often devalued men and felt contemptuous of them; underlying these attitudes were often fears of male aggression.

These mothers often viewed their husbands either as violent and out of control or as inadequate, peripheral partners who were uninvolved in their lives or in the lives of their sons. Not surprisingly, these mothers usually chose as partners men who conformed to such expectations.

These mothers' fears of male aggression often led them to confuse normal boyhood assertiveness and rambunctiousness (rough-and-tumble play) with aggressive and destructive behavior. Many of them commented on how nice, gentle, or good their sons were ("priestly" in the case vignette) and how different their sons were from other boys, who were typically mean, aggressive bullies. These mothers were often proud of their sons' nonviolent qualities and saw their sons as special and better than the neighborhood boys, who they considered roughnecks.

There is a variety of evidence suggesting that the femininity of boys is either reinforced or tolerated as it emerges (Green 1974). It is rare, however, for a parent actively to feminize a boy, for example, by cross-dressing him. In assessment, it is important to try to understand the dynamics that underlie the reinforcement. The first author has observed that the boy is often encouraged to take an interest in the mother's femininity, such as her looks and recreational activities. For example, these mothers often encourage their sons to become mother's helper, so that they spend their time taking care of things in the kitchen and "fussing" in general with the house and helping mother at whatever she needs. Many of the boys become acutely attuned to their mothers' needs and mood fluctuations, particularly depression, and will often serve in the role of a child-parent. One of the mothers in the first author's unit even called her son "Ma."

Coates (1985) has noted that these mothers were overprotective in several ways. They often overreacted to minor physical illnesses. Many would prevent their sons from playing with others, using the rationale that this would expose them to germs and they would become ill. They would often discourage their sons from engaging in rough-and-tumble play or active sports lest they become hurt. These mothers had a phobic orientation to the world. Interestingly, these same mothers often used harsh, authoritarian, and punitive forms of discipline. They often responded to minor and age-typical transgressions with extreme forms of discipline such as withdrawal and with threats of abandonment or corporal punishment. In addition, they were very ineffective at setting limits. At some times they provided no limits or structure; at others they permitted the child to take over and control their lives. They alternated between remaining remote from the child and moving in on him with over-whelming, controlling force. This inconsistency occurred in most cases.

A maternal style of overprotection, harsh discipline, and ineffective limit-setting leads to an impaired development of autonomy in the child. Marantz (1984) system-atically evaluated the child-rearing practices of mothers of gender-disturbed boys. Compared to the mothers of normal boys, these mothers were more dependent on their sons; had more difficulty in separating from their sons; were less differentiated from their sons; were more intrusive and controlling; and were more disapproving of their sons' relationships with people other than themselves.

The first three years of life have been identified by researchers as a sensitive period in the development of normal gender identity; it is thus a time that is partic-ularly vulnerable to adverse psychological influences. Since gender disorders typi-cally emerge during this sensitive time period, it is crucial that the developmental history focus sharply on these years.

In the first author's research, much attention was paid to the evaluation of fam-ily stress, particularly evidence of severe stress on the mothers. Coates (1985) re-ported that in her sample 45 percent of the mothers experienced a trauma during the child's first year of life. This included serious physical injury, rape, death of a child, or abandonment by the father. In a majority of these cases, cross-gender symptoms emerged with great intensity for the first time. For example, one mother tried to break up a physical fight between two neighbors and in so doing had lye thrown on her. This resulted in an emergency hospitalization that lasted for a month. When the mother returned home, her son was compulsively cross-dressing in her clothes and saying that he wanted to be a girl. Coates (1985) reasoned that the traumas to the mother resulted in her precipitously withdrawing from the child in order to cope with her own stress. Such withdrawal can also occur with the birth of a sibling. This withdrawal produces separation anxiety in the child. In an attempt to handle that anxiety, the boy employs a variation of an identification with the lost object—he confuses having Mommy with being Mommy and in so doing takes on her femininity. This may be understood as a defensive fantasy solution to separation anxiety.

In those cases where cross-gender symptoms emerge for the first time on the heels of maternal withdrawal, we believe that the boys have already been primed by family dynamics to choose this solution. In most of these cases, cross-gender behaviors were evident before the mother's withdrawal; however, in the wake of her altered behavior, the behavior intensified to a degree that was marked and com-pulsive and appeared to take on the function of a symptom.

Assessment of the Meaning of the Symptom

Evaluating the meaning of the cross-gender behavior is complex and difficult and often must await the findings from long-term therapy before a definitive answer can be made. Nevertheless, one can gain clues and develop hypotheses about the meaning of the symptom to the child based on interview data, evaluation of the family, the developmental history, and especially through psychological testing.

It is crucial to evaluate the circumstances surrounding the onset of the symptoms. This is particularly important when there has been a rapid onset. In the first author's experience, rapid onset usually occurs on the heels of intense separation anxiety precipitated by the mother's withdrawal. In these cases, it is assumed that the symptom functions at least partially to allay separation anxiety. This connection is often echoed in psychotherapy, where one observes the content around which the symptom emerges. Frequently, cross-gender behavior intensifies at the end of sessions before the child has to leave the therapist or before holidays.

Projective psychological testing, particularly the Rorschach, can often be useful in identifying the underlying dynamics that are fueling the gender symptoms. Studies using the Rorschach have demonstrated that the major underlying fear for many gender-disturbed boys is separation-annihilation anxiety, which expresses itself in a fear for the very integrity of the self (Coates and Tuber, in press; Tuber and Coates 1985). In many protocols, the self is represented as in danger of total destruction and others are represented as devouring, exterminating, and annihilating.

The Rorschach is also useful in assessing how the boy experiences and handles his own internal aggression. In some protocols, one can clearly document the boy's attempt to protect his maternal representation from rage by using primitive idealization and by splitting off all aggression into male representations. In these protocols, females are seen as all good, beautiful, and giving, whereas males are seen as monstrous, dangerous, destructive, and devalued figures.

A simple and brief projective measure, the Revised Sex-Typed Animal Preference Test (Coates 1976), is often useful in further assessing a boy's ability to integrate assertion and aggression into his self-representation. The boy is asked to respond to the question "If you could be an animal, which would you rather be?"

1. A tiger or a rabbit?
2. A bird or a lion?
3. A gorilla or a deer?
4. A sheep or a bear?
5. A wolf or a puppy dog?
6. A duck or a dinosaur?

These animals are stereotypically sex-typed by size and aggressiveness so that each choice includes a large aggressive animal compared to a small nonaggressive animal. A score of 1 is given for each masculine response. Strong sex differences have been found between normal boys and girls aged 4 to 9, with boys preferring the large aggressive animals and girls preferring the small nonaggressive animals (Coates 1976).

Using the original version, Coates (unpublished data) found the mean masculine score of eighteen gender-disturbed boys to be 1.3, compared to a mean of 3.4 of eighteen matched normal control boys. Other unpublished data by Coates indicate that this test discriminates gender-disturbed boys from many other boys referred to a psychiatric clinic. It appears, therefore, that gender-disturbed boys perform more like girls on this test than do other groups of boys.

For most gender-disturbed boys, the cross-gender symptoms appear to handle both separation-annihilation anxiety and anxiety over their own aggression. For some boys, however, separation-annihilation anxiety may predominate, whereas in other cases the handling of aggression may be more central. Although the meaning of cross-gender symptoms is always complex and multiple, the two issues discussed here appear to emerge with the greatest regularity.

Evaluation of Other Psychiatric Problems

The assessment of other psychiatric problems includes disorders that may or may not be etiologically linked to the syndrome. Studies employing parent-report inventories of behavioral disturbance, such as the Child Behavior Checklist (Achenbach and Edelbrock 1981), have found that gender-disturbed boys are at least similar in the degree of their behavioral disturbance to other psychiatrically referred boys (Bradley et al. 1980; Coates and Person 1985; Zucker 1985). Coates and Person found that 84 percent of their sample were as behaviorally disturbed as other boys who were referred to child psychiatric clinics.

Coates and Person also found that 60 percent of their sample met the DSM-III criteria for separation anxiety disorder. As noted earlier, these authors have reasoned that separation anxiety is etiologically linked to the cross-gender symptoms in some boys and that these symptoms serve as a special defensive operation for handling such anxiety.

Coates and Person also observed a frequent occurrence of depressive symptoms in their sample, although none of the children met the DSM-III criteria for a major depressive episode. On the Child Behavior Checklist, 50 percent of the sample between the ages of 4 and 11 fell in the clinical range on the depression subscale. Many mothers reported that their sons expressed feelings of hating themselves, and such feelings were often expressed by the sons in therapy sessions. One mother quoted her son as saying, "I hate myself. I don't want to be me. I want to be someone else. I want to be a girl." The boys often referred to themselves as ugly, dumb, and stupid.

In terms of personality integration, none of the boys, either in interview or on psychological testing, appeared to be psychotic. On psychological tests, they functioned relatively well if the tests were structured. On unstructured tests, however, they displayed major ego impairments. In systematic studies of object relations, they produced primitive object representations and boundary disturbances that are typically symptoms of borderline psychopathology (Coates and Tuber, in press; Tuber and Coates 1985).

In summary, it appears that severe gender disturbance in boys is the end result of a sequence of complex psychological processes. It does not seem to be an isolated syndrome, but rather a pervasive psychological disorder (Coates 1985). In early childhood, intense dysphoria, including separation anxiety and depression, seems to be ameliorated by fantasies of fusion with the mother, and these fantasies appear to acquire rapidly unusual power in organizing subsequent psychological development. Part of the reason that this fantasy may become "locked in" is that it serves multiple functions. On the intrapsychic level, it solves conflicts involving separation anxiety and the management of aggression. In addition, aspects of the expression of femininity may become reinforced by the family, thus further strengthening the solution. It is not easy to modify because it occurs during a sensitive period of development vis-à-vis gender identity.

BIOLOGICAL ISSUES

Contemporary research on gender-disturbed children has not yet identified a biological marker or anomaly. There is, however, a variety of converging evidence from other subject populations that suggests possible biological influences on the sex-dimorphic behavior of gender-disturbed children. At present, these influences are best interpreted as lowering the threshold (Money 1980) for the child to behave in a particular fashion rather than as having fixed and unyielding effects. For the purpose of assessment, one need not refer a gender-disturbed child for an endocrinological evaluation unless there is an anatomical defect (e.g., hypospadias) or a history of maternal exposure to sex hormones during the pregnancy.

The most promising lead for a biological predisposition concerns variations in the prenatal hormonal milieu. Experimental manipulation of fetal sex hormones in lower animals has long shown influences on postnatal sex-dimorphic behavior. One particularly interesting strategy, employed so far only with rats, has been to stress the pregnant female with aversive exogenous stimuli. When this is done during a certain period of the pregnancy, an alteration occurs in fetal testicular enzyme activity, which, in turn, appears to have an anomalous effect on postnatal sex-dimorphic behavior. So far, such effects have been limited to male offspring (Ward 1984). This mode of influence has, of course, some potential for study with humans.

Apart from inherent limitations in using animal models for understanding human development, it should be noted that such models can never address directly certain aspects of psychosexual behavior, particularly the subjective, phenomenological experience of gender identity. Gender role and certain components of sexual behavior probably have more direct parallels in the behavior of lower animals. Accordingly, more compelling data come from the study of humans exposed to anomalies in the prenatal hormonal milieu. These anomalies can be divided into two types:

those that result from spontaneous endocrine abnormalities (e.g., congenital adrenal hyperplasia) and those that result from sex hormone treatment during pregnancy. Recent reviews of this growing body of literature may be found elsewhere (Ehrhardt and Meyer-Bahlburg 1981; Hines 1982; Meyer-Bahlburg 1984).

With regard to gender identity and gender role behavior, data from this literature have yielded rather consistent findings. When postnatal influences are found, gender role behavior appears to be more affected than gender identity. That is, the children may show an increase in cross-gender behavior (or a relative lack of same-gender behavior) but not a disturbance in gender identity. Girls with congenital adrenal hyperplasia (also known as the adrenogenital syndrome [AGS]) probably best illustrate this behavioral pattern (Ehrhardt and Baker 1974).

Most recently, three studies have documented a connection between putative anomalies in the prenatal hormonal milieu and adult sexual orientation. Money, Schwartz, and Lewis (1984) reported an increased incidence of bisexual and homosexual fantasy and behavior in a sample of AGS girls seen in young adulthood. All of the girls had been treated with cortisone at relatively young ages, so that continued production of high androgen levels postnatally would have been stopped (cf. Ehrhardt et al. 1968). Ehrhardt et al. (1985) have found that women whose mothers had taken diethylstilbestrol (a hormone that has masculinizing effects on the fetus) during pregnancy have a moderately increased incidence of bisexual or homosexual fantasy and behavior in adulthood. Money and Lewis (1982) have reported an increased incidence of homosexuality in adolescent boys with a diagnosis of idiopathic gynecomastia, which may be of prenatal origin.

Less direct evidence comes from hormone studies of adults, particularly research attempting to assess both sex and sexual orientation differences in neuroendocrinological responses in the hypothalamic-pituitary-gonadal axis (Dorner et al. 1975; Gladue, Green, and Helman 1984). The basis of such differences continues to be debated in the literature (Baum et al. 1985; Meyer-Bahlburg 1977, 1982, 1984).

In addition to hormonal influences, the study of temperament (e.g., in anxiety tolerance) may also prove fruitful in identifying a congenital disposition that might interact with family dynamics and intrapsychic factors during a sensitive developmental period to produce gender disturbance.

Taken together, the studies mentioned in this section should alert the clinician to the potential influence of biological factors on sex-dimorphic behavior. It should be noted, however, that only a small portion of the variance has been accounted for by these factors (which, one should realize, are still being measured imprecisely). In the studies by Money et al. (1984) and Ehrhardt et al. (1985), for example, only a minority of subjects reported an atypical sexual orientation, and of that minority, an even smaller number were "exclusively" homosexual.

TREATMENT ISSUES

The major focus of psychotherapy with the gender-disturbed boy is on working through the underlying issues of loss, separation anxiety, abandonment, and primitive rage—the core issues fueling the cross-gender symptoms. In all cases that have been treated and supervised by the first author, cross-gender symptoms decreased as these issues were worked through (for a more detailed account of these psychotherapeutic issues, see Schultz [1979] and Thacher [1985]).

Another major aspect of treatment involves the parents. In the first author's unit, the child is seen at least twice a week by a therapist who also sees the parents once a week. Often the parents need to be in psychotherapy of their own in order to work out their own issues of separation, loss, abandonment, and rage, which are being played out in their relationship with their son. Some parents need to be in couples therapy, where many of these same issues will become the focus. Empirical support for the role of parental involvement in therapy comes from a recent study by Zucker et al. (1985). They found that the number of treatment sessions attended by the parents correlated more strongly with reductions in the child's cross-gender behavior at a one-year follow-up than did the number of sessions attended by the child.

Many parents are unable to tolerate the child's relationship with the therapist unless they are seen regularly by the same therapist themselves. We believe that the child's treatment gains can be easily undermined if the parents are not helped to work through issues in themselves that are fostering the inappropriate gender solution in the child (see Newman 1976). In some very young children, anxiety on the part of both parents and child is so great that they will have to be seen simultaneously. Some common issues that often need to be addressed with the parents include helping them foster autonomy in their son, learning the distinction between aggressive and assertive behavior, finding appropriate male role models when a father is absent, or, when he is present, developing a closer tie with his son.

An issue that is often raised is whether the gender of the therapist is important in treating a gender-disturbed child. In our experience, and that of others (Gilpin et al. 1979), it is not. It is important, however, that the therapist be capable of staying connected to the child during deeply regressed, primitive states and during times when the child becomes overwhelmingly needy. The best therapists for gender-disturbed children are those who work well with children who have serious emotional disturbance. A more detailed summary of the psychotherapy literature on gender-disturbed children may be found elsewhere (Zucker 1985; Zucker and Green, in press).

When a female therapist is used, one must make an effort to ensure that there are appropriate male role models available in the child's life. When a male therapist is used, one should be aware of the danger the child may imitate the therapist and take on a new false self without working through the underlying conflicts that produce the symptoms. In the first author's unit, one strategy that has been successful is to have a boy begin therapy with a woman, and after major issues with the mother have been worked on, to shift him to a male therapist. With him, the underlying issues can continue to be worked on but in the presence of an appropriate identification figure.

Resolution of the gender dysphoria and its underlying problem usually takes several years to accomplish, although the overt expression of cross-gender behavior often decreases fairly rapidly once therapy has begun. The most notable outcome of therapy is that the boy no longer compulsively resorts to cross-gender behavior to handle anxiety elicited by loss, abandonment, or rage, but has developed many higher-level mechanisms for coping with these issues. Like any other extremely entrenched symptom of early childhood, however, the symptom may recur under extreme regressive pressures, even after years of therapy, though usually for a brief duration.

A final word about treating severely gender-disturbed children and their families. These children are among the most difficult cases in long-term (outpatient) psychotherapy, but they are also among the most gratifying once a treatment alliance has been established. The wish for repair on the part of the child and the parents is very profound, and when they can come to trust their therapist, both the child and the parents will make an enormous commitment and effort to bringing about a therapeutic change.

REFERENCES

Achenbach, T. M., and Edelbrock, C. S. (1981). Behavioral problems and competencies reported by parents of normal and disturbed children aged four through sixteen. *Monogr. Soc. Res. Child Dev.* 46(1), Serial No. 188.

Baum, M. J., et al. (1985). Neuroendocrine response to estrogen and sexual orientation. *Science* 230:960–61.

Bradley, S. J. (1980). Female transsexualism—A child and adolescent perspective. *Child Psychiat. Hum. Devel.* 11:12–18.

———, et al. (1980). Assessment of the gender-disturbed child: A comparison to sibling and psychiatric controls. In J. Samson (Ed.). *Childhood and Sexuality.* Montreal: Éditions Études Vivantes.

———, et al. (1984). *Gender Dysphoric Adolescents: Presenting and Developmental Characteristics.* Paper presented at the meetings of the American Academy of Child Psychiatry, Toronto.

Buhrich, N., and McConaghy, N. (1977). Clinical comparison of transvestism and transsexualism. *Aust. N. Z. J. Psychiat.* 11:83–86.

Coates, S. (1976). *Field Dependence-Independence, Sex-Role Stereotyping, and Sex-Typed Preferences in Children.* Doctoral dissertation, New York University.

———. (1985). Extreme boyhood femininity: Overview and new research findings. In Z. DeFries, R. C. Friedman, and R. Corn (Eds.). *Sexuality: New Perspectives.* Westport, Conn.: Greenwood.

————, and Person, E. (1985). Extreme boyhood femininity: Isolated behavior or pervasive disorder? *J. Amer. Acad. Child Psychiat.* 24:702–9.

————, and Tuber, S. (In press). Representations of object relations in the Rorschachs of feminine boys. In P. Lerner and H. Lerner (Eds.). *Primitive Mental States and the Rorschach.* New York: International Universities Press.

Dorner, G., et al. (1975). A neuroendocrine predisposition for homosexuality in men. *Arch. Sex. Behav.* 4:1–8.

Ehrhardt, A. A., and Baker, S. W. (1974). Fetal androgen, human CNS differentiation and behavior sex differences. In R. C. Friedman, R. M. Richart, and R. L. Vande Wiele (Eds.). *Sex Differences in Behavior.* New York: Wiley.

————, Evers, K., and Money, J. (1968). Influence of androgen and some aspects of sexually dimorphic behavior in women with the late-treated adrenogenital syndrome. *Johns Hopkins Med. J.* 123:115–22.

————, and Meyer-Bahlburg, H. F. L. (1981). Effects of prenatal hormones on gender-related behavior. *Science* 211:1312–18.

————, et al. (1985). Sexual orientation after prenatal exposure to exogenous estrogen. *Arch. Sex. Behav.* 14:57–77.

Elizabeth, P. H., and Green, R. (1984). Childhood sex-role behaviors: Similarities and differences in twins. *Acta Genet. Med. Gemellol.* 33:173–79.

Gilpin, D. C., Raza, S., and Gilpin, D. (1979). Transsexual symptoms in a male child treated by a female therapist. *Amer. J. Psychother.* 33:453–63.

Gladue, B. A., Green, R., and Hellman, R. E. (1984). Neuroendocrine response to estrogen and sexual orientation. *Science* 225:1496–99.

Green, R. (1974). *Sexual Identity Conflict in Children and Adults.* New York: Basic Books.

————, and Money, J. (1960). Incongruous gender role: Nongenital manifestations in prepubertal boys. *J. Nerv. Ment. Dis.* 130:160–68.

————, Williams, K., and Goodman, M. (1985). Masculine or feminine gender identity in boys: Developmental differences between two diverse family groups. *Sex Roles* 12:1155–62.

Hines, M. (1982). Prenatal gonadal hormones and sex differences in human behavior. *Psychol. Bull.* 92:56–80.

Marantz, S. A. (1984). *Mothers of Extremely Feminine Boys: Psychopathology and Child-rearing Patterns.* Doctoral dissertation, New York University.

Meyer-Bahlburg, H. F. L. (1977). Sex hormones and male homosexuality in comparative perspective. *Arch. Sex. Behav.* 6:297–325.

————. (1982). Hormones and psychosexual differentiation: Implications for the management of intersexuality, homosexuality and transsexuality. *Clin. Endocrinol. Metab.* 11:681–701.

————. (1984). Psychoendocrine research on sexual orientation: Current status and future options. In G. J. De Vries, et al. (Eds.). *Progress in Brain Research.* Vol. 61. Amsterdam: Elsevier.

Money, J. (1980). *Love and Love Sickness: The Science of Sex, Gender Difference, and Pair-bonding.* Baltimore: Johns Hopkins University Press.

————, and Lewis, V. (1982). Homosexual/heterosexual status in boys at puberty: Idiopathic adolescent gynecomastia and congenital virilizing adrenocorticism compared. *Psychoneuroendocrinol.* 7:339–46.

————, Schwartz, J., and Lewis, V. G. (1984). Adult erotosexual status and fetal hormonal masculinization and demasculinization: 46,XX congenital virilizing adrenal hyperplasia and 46,XY androgen-insensitivity syndrome compared. *Psychoneuroendocrinol*. 9:405–14.

Newman, L. E. (1976). Treatment for the parents of feminine boys. *Amer. J. Psychiat*. 133:683–87.

Person, E., and Ovesey, L. (1978). Transvestism: New perspectives. *J. Amer. Acad. Psychoanal*. 6:301–23.

Rekers, G. A. (1985). Gender identity problems. In P. A. Bornstein and A. E. Kazdin (Eds.). *Handbook of Clinical Behavior Therapy with Children*. Homewood, Ill.: Dorsey Press.

————, and Mead, S. (1980). Female sex-role deviance: Early identification and developmental intervention. *J. Clin. Child Psychol*. 9:199–203.

————, Lovaas, O. I., and Low, B. P. (1974). The behavioral treatment of a "transsexual" preadolescent boy. *J. Abnorm. Child Psychol*. 2:99–116.

Rutter, M. (1978). Diagnostic validity in child psychiatry. *Adv. Biol. Psychiat*. 2:2–22.

Schultz, N. M. (1979). *Severe Gender Identity Confusion in an Eight-Year-Old Boy*. Doctoral dissertation, Yeshiva University.

Stoller, R. J. (1968a). Male childhood transsexualism. *J. Amer. Acad. Child Psychiat*. 7:193–209.

————. (1968b). *Sex and Gender. Vol. 1. The Development of Masculinity and Femininity*. New York: Science House.

————. (1975). *Sex and Gender. Vol. 2. The Transsexual Experiment*. London: Hogarth Press.

————. (1979). Fathers of transsexual children. *J. Amer. Psychoanal. Assoc*. 27:837–66.

————. (1985). *Presentations of Gender*. New Haven: Yale University Press.

Thacher, B. (1985). *A Mother's Role in the Evolution of Gender Dysphoria: The Initial Phase of Joint Treatment in the Psychotherapy of a 4-Year-Old Boy Who Wanted to Be a Girl*. Paper presented at the meeting of the Division of Psychoanalysis, American Psychological Association, New York.

Tuber, S., and Coates, S. (1985). Interpersonal phenomena in the Rorschachs of extremely feminine boys. *Psychoanal. Psychol*. 2:251–65.

Ward, I. L. (1984). The prenatal stress syndrome: Current status. *Psychoneuroendocrinol*. 9:3–11.

Wolfe, B. E. (1979). Behavioral treatment of childhood gender disorders: A conceptual and empirical critique. *Behav. Mod*. 3:550–75.

Zucker, K. J. (1982). Childhood gender disturbance: Diagnostic issues. *J. Amer. Acad. Child Psychiat*. 21:274–80.

————. (1985). Cross-gender-identified children. In B. W. Steiner (Ed.). *Gender Dysphoria: Development, Research, Management*. New York: Plenum.

————, and Green, R. (In press). Treatment of the gender identity disorder of childhood. In T. B. Karasu (Ed.). *APA Task Force on the Treatment of Psychiatric Disorders*. Washington, D.C.: American Psychiatric Association.

————, et al. (1984). Two subgroups of gender-problem children. *Arch. Sex. Behav*. 13:27–39.

————, et al. (1985). Sex-typed behavior in cross-gender-identified children: Stability and change at a one-year follow-up. *J. Amer. Acad. Child Psychiat*. 24:710–19.

44

DRUG AND ALCOHOL ABUSE IN CHILDREN AND ADOLESCENTS

Robert Sbriglio, Neil Hartman,
Robert B. Millman, and Elizabeth T. Khuri

INTRODUCTION

Substance-abuse has become one of the leading causes of morbidity and mortality in youthful populations in Western society. Abuse patterns cross socioeconomic and cultural boundaries, and the drugs of abuse include alcohol and sedative-hypnotics, cannabis, the psychedelics, inhalants, narcotics, and stimulants, especially cocaine, alone or in sometimes bewildering combinations. Pediatricians, adolescent medicine and mental health specialists have been increasingly challenged to deal with these behaviors and many of the social, medical, and psychiatric complications that result from them. Until recently, substance-abuse disorders attracted little attention from medical and mental health specialists. This has been due to attitudinal barriers, misconceptions about the effectiveness of prevention and treatment, and inadequate professional training and education in this area (NIAAA 1983).

Our purpose is to enable professionals to recognize youngsters who are at risk or who have already progressed to a pattern of dangerous substance-abuse associated with possible physical or psychosocial deterioration. Since substance-abuse-related illnesses, accidents, suicides, and homicides are the leading causes of preventable death and disability in young people (Blum et al. 1979), competence in this area is essential. Patterns of substance-abuse established during adolescence increase the risk of medical, psychosocial, and occupational problems developing later in life.

A definition of the terms most frequently encountered in the substance-abuse literature and a presentation of general information relevant to the problem in the

This work was supported in part by the Adolescent Development Center Grant from the New York State Division of Substance Abuse Services.

juvenile population precedes discussion of its recognition and evaluation in the school, office practice, the emergency room, and in the medical inpatient setting.

DEFINITIONS

Psychoactive substance is one that alters perception, mood, thinking, or state of consciousness. A wide variety of over-the-counter, prescribed, naturally occurring and synthetic substances (legal and illicit) constitute this category. Drugs that are most subject to abuse are those that cause a rapid alteration in consciousness in almost any direction.

Substance-abuse refers to the use of a pharmacological agent, almost invariably psychoactive, in a way that deviates from the accepted social, medical, or legal patterns in a particular society. There is no sharp line that necessarily distinguishes use from abuse as, for example, in the situation with alcohol or in some segments of society, with cannabis. In operational terms, abuse should be defined as a pathological use pattern, greater than one month in duration and associated with impaired social or occupational functioning.

Substance-dependence is most strictly and usefully defined as the physiological and/ or psychological dependence on a psychoactive agent. "Addiction" is a widely used and misused term, often with pejorative connotations, which may refer to both behavioral and pharmacological events. It is more useful when restricted to a pattern of compulsive drug use and drug-seeking behavior that is associated with physical and/or psychological dependence (Millman 1985). Dependence is usually characterized by physiological tolerance and withdrawal symptomatology and is observed especially with alcohol, sedative-hypnotics, and opiates. There is controversy as to whether cocaine and cannabis are associated with withdrawal symptomatology. It is nevertheless clear, however, that people become compulsive abusers of both of these drugs.

Tolerance refers to the need for increasing amounts of a substance to achieve the desired effect, or diminishing effects with regular use of the same amount.

Withdrawal Syndrome (Abstinence Syndrome) refers to the development of characteristic physiological symptoms after cessation or reduction of sustained, regular substance use.

Cross-tolerance is the pharmacological capacity of one drug to induce tolerance to and dependence on another or to prevent withdrawal symptoms from another drug (Millman 1985). In this way, the sedative-hypnotics phenobarbital or chlordiazepoxide can be used to ameliorate symptoms in a detoxifying alcoholic. Similarly, methadone eliminates the narcotic craving of a heroin addict and prevents narcotic withdrawal.

Detoxification refers to the process whereby an individual who is physiologically dependent on a drug is taken off that drug. In certain cases of alcohol or sedative-hypnotic dependence, abrupt cessation of the drug may induce delirium and possibly a life-threatening withdrawal syndrome with seizures. Detoxification from alcohol, sedative-hypnotic, and opiate dependence requires substitution with an appropriate cross-tolerant drug followed by a gradual taper in a controlled medical setting. With other drug dependences such as cannabis or cocaine, the drugs can be abruptly withdrawn in a supervised setting. No specific pharmacological interventions are necessary, although the use of compounds such as tryptophan, desipramine and bromocriptine are currently being investigated for cocaine detoxification and treatment (Dackis and Gold 1985; Kleber and Gawin 1986).

MAJOR CATEGORIES OF ABUSED SUBSTANCES

Alcohol. Alcohol has long been used more than any other psychoactive drug. It is often difficult to distinguish between "social" and "problem" drinking in the young. The term alcoholism should be reserved for situations characterized by overwhelming involvement with the drug and physical dependence. Young people drink less often than adults but tend to consume greater amounts per drinking occasion. Relatively heavy drinking or intoxication may be the norm among certain adolescent groups at parties or other social occasions. Although this behavior has not changed significantly over the past thirty years, younger adolescents and more females are now involved (Blane and Hewitt 1977). Inner-city and other socially disadvantaged youngsters begin drinking at an earlier age, sometimes in their early teens. Suburban and middle-class adolescents begin drinking at a later age. Children of alcoholic parents, especially alcoholic fathers, appear to have a genetic and familial predisposition to become alcoholic (Goodwin 1984).

Late adolescence and early adulthood are the highest-risk periods for developing the negative consequences associated with the acute effects of alcohol. These effects include deterioration in school and work performance, violent behavior, suicides and homicides, and automobile accidents. Areas in which the minimum drinking age has been raised to 21 years have seen a significant reduction in traffic-related deaths among persons 18 to 20 years old (JAMA 1984).

Adolescents regard alcohol as a depressant and may use it in combination with a variety of other drugs. For example, alcohol may be used to counteract the tension and anxiety induced by marijuana or to prolong or potentiate the effects of opiates or other depressants. Some adolescents may use alcohol to self-medicate underlying psychopathology such as depression, anxiety, or psychotic symptomatology, which, when experienced with renewed force during periods of abstinence, reinforce the continuation of drinking patterns. A pattern of alcohol dependence usually leads to a general deterioration of functioning.

The psychoactive effects of alcohol are similar to those of the sedative-hypnotic tranquilizing agents. The alcohol content in a twelve-ounce glass of beer is approximately equivalent to a five-ounce glass of wine or approximately equivalent to 1.25

ounces of distilled liquor. There are also other sources of alcohol such as mouth washes, cough syrups, and various cold remedies, all of which can be subject to abuse. The degree of intoxication depends on the amount of alcohol consumed and the individual's degree of tolerance. In a nontolerant individual, a blood level of 100 mg% (100 mg/dl) produces mild to moderate intoxication, reducing anxiety and social inhibitions. At blood levels between 100 to 200 mg% (0.10 to 0.20), overt signs of intoxication occur, such as impairments in visual-motor coordination, attention, memory, judgment, and sexual performance. Blood levels above 200 mg% (0.20) are associated with severe intoxication and marked sedation. Individuals with patterns of regular alcohol consumption develop tolerance and become intoxicated only with much higher blood alcohol concentrations (i.e., individuals who can "hold their liquor"). Thus, chronic alcohol abusers may appear sober and are able to function effectively even at high blood levels (Watanabe et al. 1985). Potentiation of sedative effects occurs when sedative-hypnotics (depressants) or opiates (narcotics) are taken along with alcohol. Such combinations can be lethal as a result of these additive effects.

The alcohol-dependent adolescent should never be instructed to stop drinking without an assessment for medical detoxification. Physiological dependence requires detoxification in a supervised medical setting. Within several hours after abrupt discontinuation of alcohol in a chronically dependent individual, an acute withdrawal syndrome ensues characterized by tremulousness, agitation, diaphoresis, and elevation of blood pressure, pulse, and respiration. In general, this syndrome remits by the third day after alcohol cessation. However, in some cases delirium with auditory, visual, and tactile hallucinations (alcoholic hallucinosis) can accompany this syndrome. In severe cases, grand mal seizures may occur twelve to twenty-four hours after the last drink, followed by a syndrome marked by confusion, disorientation, agitation, delusions, hallucinations, and autonomic hyperactivity (delirium tremens). Although rare in adolescents and treated populations, this syndrome is potentially life-threatening. Hospitalization and intensive care are required.

Cannabis refers to the dried mixture of leaves, seeds, and stems of the hemp plant (Cannabis sativa, "marijuana," "pot," "weed," "grass," "reefer," "sin semilla"). The percentage of delta-9-tetrahydrocannabinol (THC), the major psychoactive component, varies from 1 percent to 15 percent depending on the preparation (Tennant 1986). Cannabis is rolled into a cigarette form ("joint") and smoked. Hashish (hash), the resin obtained from the tops of mature plants, is either smoked in pipes or eaten and is roughly five to eight times more potent than crude marijuana leaves. Hashish oil, manufactured by a refluxing method in clandestine laboratories, may contain up to 60 percent THC (Grinspoon and Bakalar 1981).

Many young people use marijuana on an intermittent basis limited to certain social occasions when it is smoked in a ritualistic fashion. A small number of adolescents may develop a compulsive use pattern in which they smoke throughout the day and develop a lifestyle centered around the use of the drug. The psychoactive effects of cannabis can vary markedly, depending on the dose, the social setting, the personality of the user, previous experiences with the drug, and personal expectations about its effects. Reported effects include enhanced perception of stimuli, sedation, hilarity, altered time perception, mood changes, a relaxed feeling of well-being and increased appetite. Adverse effects include occasional feelings of anxiety or panic (especially in naive users), impairment of short-term memory, impairment of motor performance and reaction time (experienced, for example, in driving an automobile), and in chronic users an "amotivational syndrome" characterized by apathy and lack of ambition—although this is controversial and has not been confirmed by extensive studies.

Stimulants are substances whose predominant psychoactive effect is central nervous system stimulation experienced as increased wakefulness and alertness and decreased sense of fatigue. Mood is elevated, accompanied by increased initiative and confidence. A variety of pharmacologically dissimilar compounds with vastly differing abuse potentials are stimulants. These include coffee, tea and other caffeine-containing compounds, methylphenidate (Ritalin), amphetamines and cocaine ("coke," "flake," "rock," "blow"), which may be the most powerfully reinforcing compound known. Cocaine is mistakenly thought by many young people to be relatively safe for recreational use or as a means of prolonging alertness in a variety of situations. Cocaine is used for its reported effects of euphoric mood, increased energy, increased confidence, and sexual arousal. Psychological dependence follows regular use, however, and the teenager then becomes dependent on the drug in order to function at what he perceives to be a satisfactory level. The drug is then taken in higher amounts at more frequent intervals. Insufflation ("sniffing") is the most frequent mode of use, but intravenous use also occurs and is fraught with greater danger. Most recently, an epidemic of smoking an alkaline extraction of cocaine ("crack," free-base) is occurring all over the country. This mode of administration rapidly produces high concentrations of the drug in the body, similar to intravenous use, and is associated with powerful reinforcement of continued, compulsive drug taking. Compulsive cocaine use is associated with psychiatric sequelae such as anxiety, paranoia, depression, and frank psychotic states. Visual and tactile hallucinations ("cocaine bugs") can also occur. Medical sequelae of intranasal use includes epistaxis, rhinitis, sinusitis, and perforated nasal septum. Medical complications also include stroke, cardiac arrhythmias, myocardial infarction, seizures, respiratory and pulmonary abnormalities (from free-base smoking "crack"), and in pregnant women, spontaneous abortion, miscarriage, and premature labor (Sbriglio and Millman, in press; Chasnoff et al. 1985). Complications related to intravenous use (IV) include skin abscesses, sepsis, hepatitis, and acquired immunodeficiency syndrome (AIDS). Although a withdrawal syndrome has been described (Kleber and Gawin 1986) and a few treatments are in a preliminary state of investigation, the syndrome is not severe and there are currently no specific medical treatments indicated for treating cocaine withdrawal.

Hallucinogens (psychedelics, psychotomimetics) are psychoactive substances that alter consciousness in a bizarre and unpredictable fashion. The term is inaccurate in that these agents rarely produce true hallucinations (Millman 1985). Rather, users experience a variety of perceptual, cognitive, and emotional distortions. These substances may be derived from natural sources (mescaline from the peyote cactus, psilocybin from mushrooms) or may be synthetically produced (lysergic acid diethylamide [LSD], phencyclidine [PCP], dimethyltryptamine [DMT]). The belladonna alkaloids (atropine, scopolomine), which are infrequently abused, can produce vivid visual hallucinations when ingested in large quantities.

Although dependence is rare, these drugs may precipitate severe psychiatric sequelae including panic attacks, paranoia, and frank psychotic episodes marked by auditory and visual hallucinations and loss of insight. The intermittent use of these drugs by adolescents may be associated with an antisocial stance and profound disruptions of performance in many phases of life.

Sedative-hypnotics are psychoactive agents that produce sedation and sleep as their main effects. They can be categorized as the barbiturates (Seconal, Amytal, etc.), the benzodiazepines or minor tranquilizers (Valium, Librium, Xanax, etc.), and others (chloral hydrate, paraldehyde, ethchlorvynol [Placidyl], methaqualone [Quaalude], etc.). This class of compounds is abused by teenagers largely because the immediate effect may be a relief of anxiety or inhibitions, experienced as a "high."

Sedative-hypnotics are associated with tolerance and physical dependence similar to that produced by alcohol. The time-course and breadth of these phenomena differ markedly from drug to drug. For example, cessation of short-acting barbiturates or methaqualone may result in withdrawal phenomena within twelve to twenty-four hours, whereas long-acting benzodiazepines (e.g., diazepam [Valium]) may be associated with a much delayed onset of these symptoms. In addition to the dependence, which may be profound and difficult to treat, sedative-hypnotics are associated with a large number of accidental and purposive pharmacological overdoses.

Opiates, or narcotics, are drugs derived from or cross-tolerant with opium (opiate agonists). Heroin and other illicit opiate preparations may be ingested, insufflated, smoked or injected alone or in combination with other substances. They produce a distinctive feeling of euphoria that has been described as a feeling of sensual pleasure, relief of anxiety, and a sense of completeness. Drugs in this class include heroin ("dope," "smack"), morphine, meperidine (Demerol), oxycodone (Percodan), hydromorphone (Dilaudid), codeine, and fentanyl (Sublimaze). They all induce a profound degree of tolerance and physical dependence. The depressed, anxiety-ridden, maladjusted, or environmentally deprived adolescent who is exposed to these agents is, therefore, at risk for developing an addictive pattern of use.

The long-acting opiate methadone warrants special consideration. Methadone maintenance is an effective modality for the treatment of narcotic addiction, and the supervised use of methadone in this setting does not produce euphoria, sedation, or impairment of functioning in stabilized patients (Kreek 1981; Lowinson 1981). In other settings and circumstances, however, methadone produces opiate effects and may be subject to abuse.

Complications of narcotic use include overdose with respiratory depression, the full range of infections associated with intravenous ("main-lining") and subcutaneous injection ("skin popping") use patterns, and the destructive cycle of dependence and drug-seeking behavior. Chronic opiate use is also associated with depressive states. Treatment includes detoxification procedures and long-term therapeutic modalities based either on pharmacotherapy with methadone or abstinence-oriented treatments, particularly therapeutic communities. Naltrexone is a recently introduced long-acting opiate antagonist, which blocks the effects of all narcotics, is not habit forming, and is useful as an adjunct to maintaining a narcotic-free lifestyle (Kleber 1985).

Inhalants abuse occurs with a wide range of organic solvents, particularly the toluene in glue (Millman 1985). Because these substances are readily available, inexpensive, and extremely easy to use, abuse may be encountered even in the elementary grades. When the substance's vapors are inhaled in a closed system such as a plastic bag wrapped around the head or nose, young people experience several seconds of light-headedness that resembles intoxication with alcohol. In addition to the occasional direct toxic effects of such behavior, including loss of consciousness and cardiac arrhythmias, heavy involvement with drugs, including glue sniffing during the early adolescent years, may have profound adverse effects on psychosocial development. Compulsive inhalant use suggests significant psychopathology, and there is a likelihood of progression to experimentation with other mind-altering drugs.

EPIDEMIOLOGY

The emergence of substance-abuse among young people as a major public health problem in the early 1960s occurred in the context of a counterculture that rebelled against parental authority and the value system of the larger society. The incidence and prevalence of juvenile substance-abuse can be expressed only as broad trends because of a variety of problems (Millman and Botvin 1983). These include biases introduced by the use of self-report data in large-scale surveys conducted in schools. Obviously, youngsters in attendance tend to deny or minimize their involvement in a disapproved activity, while those with the most advanced patterns of abuse might attend school irregularly if at all, and might not be included in surveys. On the other hand, data obtained from those who have come to medical (emergency room visits, hospital admissions, etc.) or legal (arrest records) attention would tend to measure only those who have been least successful in avoiding the consequences of their behavior. Moreover, combining data from several studies to obtain a more representative sample is hampered by the differing ways in which data is categorized or collected. Finally, rapid changes in drug-use patterns often renders survey information outdated even as it is published. Bearing in mind these limitations, it is possible to highlight the major periods in the evolution of juvenile substance abuse patterns in the United States and probably Canada and Western Europe over the past quarter-century.

During the past twenty years there has been a remarkable increase in the use of all drugs by adolescents. Several national surveys indicate that psychoactive drug-use by school age children and young adults continues to be widespread, though there may be some recent leveling off (NIDA 1985). Recent survey data from the National Institute on Drug Abuse (NIDA) indicate that the drugs most widely used and most socially accepted by adolescents are alcohol, marijuana, and nicotine (tobacco). Morbidity and mortality associated with the use of these three substances are greater than for all other substances combined.

In adolescence as in adulthood, alcohol is used and abused more than any other psychoactive drug (Blane and Hewitt 1977). The first two decades following World War II saw a significant increase in prevalence. In general, alcohol use has been increasing most rapidly in the younger age groups and in girls (Abelson et al. 1977; Johnston et al. 1979). Sixty-seven percent of high school seniors surveyed in 1984 reported having used alcohol in the past month, and 39 percent reported having had five or more drinks on at least one occasion in the two weeks prior to the survey (NIDA 1985).

Regarding marijuana, 5 percent of the high school seniors surveyed reported using the drug daily. It is estimated that daily marijuana smokers consume an average of 3.5 "joints" per day. At three-year follow-up, 50 percent of a cohort of daily marijuana users reported continuing use of the drug (NIDA 1980). Increasingly, nicotine is being recognized as an addictive drug with serious long-term health consequences. The 1984 high school senior survey found that nicotine (cigarette smoking) was used daily in 19 percent of respondents (NIDA 1985). Although nicotine was the most used drug class in that survey, there has since been a slight downward trend in the use of cigarettes by adolescents.

Cocaine abuse in all forms, especially the smoking of free-base in the form of "crack," has grown at an alarming rate. A recent survey (O'Malley et al. 1984) found that between 1976 and 1982 cocaine use among high school seniors increased from 6 percent to over 20 percent. With a dramatic 50 percent fall in the price of cocaine during 1983–84 and a concomitant increase in purity from 28 percent to over 40 percent, there has been an increase in teenage callers to the "cocaine hotline" (Washton et al. 1984). Of one hundred teenage callers, average age 16, thirty-eight were from middle-class or affluent families. The typical youngster was spending nearly one hundred dollars per week and most were also using marijuana, alcohol, and sedative-hypnotics in a polydrug-abuse pattern. The psychosocial consequences of abuse were severe, with half reporting disciplinary actions, including a third expelled from school, 44 percent dealing drugs, and 31 percent stealing from family, friends, or employers. Medical and psychiatric sequelae included seizures (19 percent), automobile accidents (13 percent), suicide attempts (14 percent), and violent behavior (27 percent).

The prevalence of other psychoactive drug use among adolescents varies markedly, depending on geographic region. For example, phencyclidine (PCP) use is higher in larger urban areas and low in rural areas. A recent phenomena has been the introduction of "designer drugs," which are illicitly manufactured drugs bearing a pharmacological resemblance to known parent compounds but having unpredictable and potentially dangerous effects (American Medical News 1985).

DETERMINANTS OF DRUG ABUSE

A variety of developmental, cognitive, behavioral, personality, social, and attitudinal factors are associated with tobacco, alcohol, and drug use. However, knowledge about the relative contribution and complex interaction of these variables is limited (Millman and Botvin 1983). Some studies have suggested common etiological patterns or causal pathways, but there are no tests or examinations that can predict the development of drug-abuse behavior or which people will use which drug.

Several unique or essential factors to the adolescent age group help account for their attraction to psychoactive substances.

Developmental and Cognitive Factors. As with other behavior patterns occurring in childhood and adolescence, substance use and misuse must be viewed in a developmental context. Changes in cognitive development bring about a transition from thinking that is rigid and concrete to thought that is more relative, abstract, and hypothetical. Consequently, the adolescent is able to consider a wider range of possibilities and alternatives, accept deviations from established rules and norms, and recognize the frequently inconsistent nature of adult behavior. For example, although younger children generally believe that cigarette smoking is bad and state that they will never smoke, as they approach adolescence they begin to view cigarette smoking from a more relative perspective and may consider arguments in favor of smoking (e.g., smoking will increase popularity, attractiveness, etc.). Similarly, this new cognitive orientation may lead the adolescent to discover inconsistencies in adult arguments concerning the risks of substance abuse. Citing adults who smoke or drink, young people may justify their own similar behavior.

Parental and Peer Influence. During early childhood, parents exert the most powerful influence on children. This influence gradually begins to decrease upon entry into the school environment, while the influence of peers and teachers becomes increasingly important. This developmental shift in the relative importance of parental and peer influence continues into adolescence, with parents maintaining some influence over educational choices and career, and peers influencing matters such as lifestyle, clothing, music, and social activities. Peer influence is predominant with regard to cigarette smoking and the use of alcohol or drugs and plays a central role in the initiation, development, and maintenance of substance-use (Freeland and Campbell 1973).

The developmental phenomenon of peer group pressure and responsiveness to conformity pressures may be important in the experimentation and early use of drugs. As dependence on the peer group increases, there is increasing pressure to conform to group patterns of behavior. Conformity behavior increases during preadolescence, then steadily declines from middle to late adolescence.

Adolescent substance-abuse may also be related to perceived supportive attitudes of peers and the perception that use of a particular substance is normative. Substance-abusers typically overestimate the prevalence of drug use among their peers, and the degree of their involvement with a particular substance is related to these estimates.

Family and Social Factors. Adolescent substance-abuse is influenced by factors related to both the family and the larger social environment (Millman and Botvin 1983). The earliest influence to smoke cigarettes, drink alcohol, or use drugs comes from the family. Adolescents growing up in families in which parents or older siblings are substance-abusers tend to become drug takers themselves. The predominant influence coming from the family is the modeling of substance-use behavior of parents or siblings, although other important family factors include perceived parental attitudes, family instability, parental rejection, parenting style, and divorce (Braucht et al. 1973).

Socioeconomic Factors. With regard to socioeconomic status, adolescents from lower socioeconomic groups are generally more likely to become substance-abusers than adolescents from higher socioeconomic groups (Millman and Khuri 1981). Educational variables are more important in substance abuse than income. Adolescents from families in which one or both parents went to college or who themselves plan to go to college and are enrolled in college preparatory courses are less likely to smoke cigarettes or get into trouble with drugs and alcohol (Millman and Botvin 1983).

Media and Culture. In general, the media tend to glamorize and support the use of alcohol and psychoactive substances. In advertising, drinking and smoking are often portrayed as mature, sophisticated, and glamorous. Although they are illegal and not advertised, use of marijuana, cocaine, and other drugs is often portrayed in popular music, movies, and television as socially acceptable behavior.

Psychological Factors. Despite a great deal of research data, controversy persists as to whether drug-abuse or dependence results from certain personality patterns and psychodynamics or whether particular drug-use patterns are associated with certain personality types (Millman and Khuri 1981). No research studies have identified specific psychodynamic patterns or psychopathology as predictive of substance-abuse, and there is no evidence for the existence of an "addictive" or "alcoholic personality" type (Millman 1978; Zinberg 1975). Youthful drug-abusers have been described as having lower self-esteem, a higher degree of dissatisfaction and pessimism, a greater need for social approval, and less social confidence (Braucht et al. 1973; Coan 1973). They have also been characterized as more anxious, less assertive, more impulsive and rebellious, and more impatient to assume adult roles than nonusers (Williams 1973; Jarvik et al. 1977). These characteristics have limited diagnostic or predictive value, since they do not occur exclusively in substance-users and are not absent in nonusers.

Adolescent substance-abusers vary markedly in their range of personality patterns and psychopathology. Some may function within a normal range and others may be significantly disabled. It is necessary to identify and define the meaning of the alcohol or drug use in each individual. In some youngsters, substance-use may represent attempts to self-medicate painful affects resulting from shame, rage, loneliness, and depression (Khantzian et al. 1974) or to satisfy or control unacceptable and overwhelming sexual or aggressive drives. It has been suggested that some drug-use may be symptomatic of masked depression and that boredom, restlessness, apathy, and sexual promiscuity may represent depressive states (Carlson and Cantwell 1980; Gallenmore and Wilson 1972). Adolescents with severe narcissistic or borderline personality disorders and overtly psychotic adolescents may also use alcohol and drugs to self-treat their serious symptomatology.

The choice of drug may reflect certain personality patterns or psychiatric symptomatology. Borderline or psychotic adolescents may preferentially use opiates, depressants, or alcohol to control their symptoms (Khantzian et al. 1974). Opiates have been shown to have significant antipsychotic properties (Brizer et al. 1985). Stimulants such as amphetamine or cocaine may be used as self-medication for some young people with attentional deficits. Alcohol or sedative-hypnotic depressants may be used to suppress anxiety, panic attacks, or anger. Some psychotic adolescents may avoid drugs such as marijuana, hallucinogens, or cocaine because these drugs exacerbate anxiety and paranoia. Other severely disabled youngsters may prefer these drugs perhaps because the intense and unpleasant psychoactive effects isolate them from their own inner psychotic turmoil or perhaps assist in rationalizing their "craziness" ("I am crazy because I'm on drugs.") (Millman and Khuri 1981).

Sex. Initial and early sexual experiences are always a stressful rite of passage, which low doses of sedatives, opiates, or alcohol may make easier. Lack of experience and anxiety can make adolescent sexual performance difficult, awkward, and even unpleasant. For example, young men may complain of an inability to sustain an erection unless "stoned" on an anxiety-reducing sedative. With frequent use, tolerance and dependence develop. Withdrawal symptoms add to the anxiety and more drug is taken. Often the new focus on the drug supplants other interests and drives, including sex, resulting in a temporary "solution" to this conflict. Cannabis and stimulants may also be used by some to increase sexual desire and performance, although their effects vary greatly from user to user and eventually, as with all compulsive drug-use, desire and performance decrease (Millman 1978).

DRUG-USE PATTERNS

The youth of today has access to an unprecedented variety of psychotropic agents both natural and synthetic, and in many instances has learned to use these agents to produce reliable and reproducible alterations in perception, mood, and thinking. This phenomenon parallels our rapidly expanding knowledge and utilization in medical practice of psychoactive substances intended specifically to alter and improve dysphoric moods, disordered thinking, and problematic behavior.

In part, this teenage interest in the use of chemicals to alter moods or states of consciousness can be viewed as analogous to the younger child's more primitive efforts at altering consciousness and perception by hyperventilation, breath holding, spinning in place, or hanging upside down (Weil 1972). To be sure, the majority of teenagers who experiment with alcohol or marijuana in order to gain acceptance in their peer group do so without significant adverse consequences, either because they do not repeat the experience or because they continue to use these more easily obtainable substances intermittently or in a controlled fashion.

The use of psychoactive substances by adolescents can be classified into four different patterns:

> *Occasional recreational use* during which drug-use is controlled and confined to a particular setting, such as the use of marijuana or a hallucinogen prior to attending a rock concert. In a minority of cases, there is progression to experimental use.
>
> *Experimental use* in which numerous compounds from various drug classes may be taken as a form of entertainment or to cope with intolerable feelings as described above.
>
> *Regular use* may then ensue such that the drugs become an integral part of living and there may be deterioration in function in academic, home, and social settings.
>
> *Compulsive use* in which there is overwhelming involvement with the acquisition and use of various substances (addiction). Intermittent or rare use of any drug is not necessarily associated with psychopathological disorders, while compulsive use patterns more often are (Khantzian et al. 1974). The more aberrant an individual's drug-abuse pattern is for his or her social or cultural setting, the more likely that there will be a significant degree of psychopathology.

Patterns of substance use and misuse are extremely nonuniform across cultural groups and locations. Frequently, one drug is used to counteract the unpleasant aftereffects of another, so that dual dependences are common (alcohol and cocaine; heroin and cocaine). Abuse patterns may reflect personality structure and psychopathological disturbance (Zinberg 1975). Poorly compensated, disorganized psychotic or borderline teenagers often chaotically abuse a wide variety of substances, suffering frequent severe adverse reactions and overdoses. Such youngsters, who often call themselves "garbage heads," may pride themselves on the risk taking inherent in their behavior and may depend upon a "negative identity" (Erikson 1963) as a means of achieving self-definition and esteem.

Regular and compulsive psychoactive drug-use in adolescents is rarely confined to a single substance. Unlike their adult counterparts, who more often concentrate on one or two favored substances, youngsters frequently practice polypharmacy, either in a chaotic risk-taking fashion, or with drugs taken simultaneously or sequentially for their specific desired effects. Common examples include the augmentation of a narcotic high by simultaneous use of the tricyclic antidepressant amitriptylne (Elavil), or other drugs with sedative properties. Alcohol, which potentiates the sedative properties of the opiates, is frequently abused by addicted teenagers when only small amounts of narcotic are obtainable. The clinician must be alert to the possibility of toxic drug to drug interactions occurring from the depressant effects of some of these combinations.

OBSTACLES TO EVALUATION AND TREATMENT

Resistance. Adolescent substance-abusers referred for evaluation or treatment are often reluctant or unwilling participants, and it may be difficult to engage them adequately enough for diagnostic assessment or therapy. Initially, it may be more useful to conduct short, informal sessions that are practically oriented towards the adolescent's legal, financial, and social problems. Discussions about music, sports, and clothing may be very helpful in fostering a therapeutic alliance.

Attitudes. Adolescent substance-abusers are frequently more knowledgeable than their physicians and therapists about drugs, drug subculture, and drug-related behavior. This may be quite threatening for those specialists more accustomed to dealing with patients who are relatively naive about their own physical or psychological problems and who look to "specialists" for expertise and guidance. Similarly, substance-abusing adolescents can quickly sense a clinician's naiveté or lack of knowledge regarding drugs and may devalue or manipulate the clinician and interview process. Thus, both clinician and patient attitudes can hinder adequate assessment and treatment.

Therapeutic Stance. Adolescents frequently test limits and attempt to provoke punitive rejection. In general, therapists should avoid assuming a critical parent role involving lectures, exhortations, and threats. This stance precludes the development of a working therapeutic alliance and delays effective intervention. The clinician should strive to develop a supportive relationship with the adolescent, characterized by respect, dignity, and acceptance. Confrontation and coercion should be viewed as last resorts to be used only in the most compelling circumstances. In serious or life-threatening situations, strong actions may be necessary, such as emergency hospitalization or psychiatric commitment.

Misinformation. It is not unusual for adolescents either to minimize or to exaggerate the extent of their substance-use. Adolescents may give much misinformation, deliberately distorting historical data and even lying about current behavior. Accurate assessment may be difficult in a single session with the adolescent. With permission, it is helpful to obtain collateral or corroborating information from family, school, court records, hospitals, and healthcare personnel. Urine toxicology can provide important additional information regarding current and recent drug-use.

Culture and Environment. Chronic drug-users may be involved with a subculture that rejects conventional values and mores. It is very difficult to dissuade an adolescent from continued use of substances if he or she continues to live and work in an environment that is conducive to continued substance-abuse. Removal to a hospital, residential drug treatment program, or specialized school may be the only options to effect change.

RECOGNITION AND EVALUATION

The School

School personnel at the junior high school level and beyond should be aware of telltale signs of substance use and abuse in students. Deterioration in the quality of school performance, patterns of tardiness and absenteeism, and an unusually di-shevelled and unclean physical appearance may be early indications of substance-abuse. Signs of drug intoxication include changes in appearance, manner, thinking, mood, and behavior such as: reddened eyes, constricted or dilated pupils, slurred speech, unsteady gait, slowed or hyperactive movements and behavior, poor concentration, difficulty in attending to classroom tasks, drowsiness or hyperalertness, and irritability and belligerence toward peers and/or authority figures. Unexplained changes such as these are causes for concern and warrant further investigation.

The classroom teacher is often the first child-care professional to be aware of a problem. However, administrative, guidance, and school nursing personnel, in the course of their interaction with students, can play critical roles in the identification of substance-abuse problems. Since aberrant behavioral changes may be evident in any area of the school, personnel assigned to halls, gyms, playgrounds, lunch-rooms, and auditoriums should also be knowledgeable and watchful.

Office Practice

Significant substance-abuse usually comes to the attention of the clinician either after a critical incident involving family, school, or legal authorities or as an incidental finding in an assessment, either routine or for another, seemingly unrelated illness. Rarely does the adolescent reveal to a physician a drug-abuse problem per se as a chief complaint. There are several reasons for this delay in seeking treatment.

Despite warnings from parents, teachers, and the media, most adolescents have the illusion that their drug-taking behavior is under their control. This illusion, related in part to inexperience but more to unconscious denial, results in a remarkable lack of concern about the degree to which they have become dependent, and to an overestimation of their ability to avoid self-destructive use patterns. Denial may persist despite repeated failures to cease drug and alcohol use, and even after adverse sequelae have occurred.

Teenagers who have begun to recognize a drug-abuse problem may be reluctant to seek help from adult authority figures whom they view as hostile or because of concern over confidentiality. Moreover, primary-care physicians who have had previous contact with the patient may have omitted or avoided the consideration of substance-abuse in their history taking and examination. Often, their lack of interest is reflective of society's pejorative attitude toward patients whose illnesses are viewed as self-inflicted. On previous contacts the patient may have been experienced as uncooperative and hostile, even intimidating to the inexperienced professional because of a strange vocabulary or a seemingly superior knowledge about street drugs. Direct and insensitive confrontations or demands for "the truth" may have paradoxically hardened the youngster's adversarial position.

Providers of health care for teenagers must always include inquiries about the use of drugs as an integral part of the assessment of behavioral and psychosocial functioning. Assessment may also include urine for toxicology screening. Obtaining reliable information upon which to base diagnosis and treatment is dependent on the examiner's skill and attitude, and on the appropriateness of the therapeutic setting. Accurate assessment is a key element in the formulation of a diagnosis and an appropriate treatment plan.

It is necessary to clarify with the patient and the parents the circumstances that led to the referral. The patient should be interviewed privately and should be informed further that his or her participation in the evaluation and acceptance of recommendations is voluntary. It may also help set the tone of the interview to encourage the teenager to verbalize what he or she expects to gain from the interaction. It would be unreasonable to expect honest answers given freely without some explicit statement about confidentiality. The youngster should be gently but firmly advised, however, that if the assessment reveals imminent danger, parents will be advised of this.

The issue of the teenager's personal involvement with psychoactive substances can be approached in a nonthreatening way by placing questions in the context of the patient's environment. Most teens will readily enter into such a discussion, sometimes exaggerating the degree to which drug-use has permeated their milieu, since popular media have already made such information common knowledge. The patient may also be offering guardedly predictable responses to test their effect. An interviewer who is condescending or whose verbal or nonverbal reaction connotes disgust, dismay, or disapproval is unlikely to get candid information when the questioning turns to the youngster's own drug-use behavior. Rather, the interviewer should strive to build a dignified and supportive relationship in which he or she is experienced as an accepting, caring, and knowledgeable adult. Early in the process of assessment it may be necessary to remain neutral while listening to questionable statements. These should be noted and returned to for clarification when a stronger alliance has been established.

As rapport develops, the interviewer should inquire about the details and circumstances in which the patient participates, with and without his or her peer group, in the use of psychoactive substances. Questioning should focus on which drugs are being taken (quantity and cost), route of administration (oral, smoking, intranasal, or intravenous), and for what reasons. Typical phrases and areas of questioning might include the following:

—Has the youngster ever used drugs when alone, at school, or at work?

—Is use infrequent and recreational, restricted to parties and rock concerts?

—Is use confined to the more easily obtainable alcohol and marijuana?

—Do friends drink at parties or use marijuana at rock concerts?

—Is marijuana obtainable at school?

—Has the patient ever taken "acid" or "tripped" (hallucinogens), experimented with "uppers" (stimulants), "downers" (sedative-hypnotics), "coke" (cocaine), "crack" (cocaine free-base smoking), or "dope" (heroin)?

—Has the patient ever been "stoned" or "bombed" (intoxicated) to the extent that accidents, injuries, or "near misses" have resulted?

—Has he or she ever passed out, had a seizure, "ODed" (overdosed), developed skin infections (from needle use), or lost time from school or work from drug-related illness?

—Has he or she ever tried to cut down or discontinue completely, felt sick, or found that the craving was overpowering?

—Have there been any perceived changes in the nature of the patient's relationships with parents, other family members and peers, or in academic or occupational accomplishments and goals?

—Has the patient ever been "busted" or nearly "busted" and has there been previous contact with social agencies or healthcare professionals related to drug-use?

—On the average, how much money does the patient spend on drugs and where does the money come from (regular income, savings, allowance, stealing, prostitution, drug dealing)?

—Finally, what is the teenager's own appraisal of his or her needs regarding treatment?

Often, the evaluation serves as a first opportunity for the patient to come to terms with a problem previously denied or minimized. It is also an opportune time to convince the youngster to seek and accept help.

Not infrequently, youngsters are brought for evaluation by overanxious parents who have exaggerated the dangerousness of their child's drug-abuse behavior. Sometimes, however, parents are underinvolved, indifferent, or may even be facilitating a youngster's substance-abuse problem. It is often useful to engage the immediate family in therapeutic encounters with the patient, particularly when intervention in family dynamics might be expected to lead to improvement in the patient's behavior.

As the initial contact with the teenager draws to a close, the clinician must decide what if any further intervention is needed. If thorough history taking indicates convincingly that the abuse is rare, remains appropriate to the youngster's social and cultural group, and has not caused nor is likely to cause medical or functional disability, the parents should be reassured and the child followed, to monitor and reduce the extent of the behavior. It is extremely important to avoid overdiagnosing problems in need of treatment since some treatment modalities (therapeutic communities or special schools) can be very disrupting to the youngster's life and because the child's erroneous perception that he is "sick" may be more disabling than his occasional and recreational drug-use.

In other cases, with extremely guarded youngsters, the information obtained may be sufficient only to raise the possibility of self-destructive substance-abuse. A follow-up session should be scheduled soon after to attempt to enhance the relationship and the motivation to accept treatment. The time between contacts could be used, with the patient's permission, to arrange an interview with the parents or guardians and to contact school or other agencies that have been involved with the teenager and his family. Motivation and treatment efforts begin with the first contact and evolve as additional information emerges.

Occasionally the physician may be called upon to assess a troubled youngster who adamantly refuses to participate or even to present himself or herself at the office. In certain instances, especially when the physician is a primary-care provider with a longstanding relationship with the family, a home visit may permit a preliminary assessment while allowing the patient to "save face."

TREATMENT AND REFERRAL

Adolescent substance-abusers may require intensive and comprehensive care, including educational, vocational, legal, medical, and psychological services. Pediatricians, family practitioners, and psychiatrists are often unable to provide this range of services, and an interdisciplinary effort may be necessary. When intervention is urgently needed and all attempts to gain the patient's participation have failed, the physician should assist the parents in arranging involuntary hospitalization in a closed setting. For youngsters who are completely resistant to parental authority, it may prove necessary to assist in obtaining a "Person in Need of Supervision" (PINS) petition, in which case the courts can authorize professional intervention on an involuntary basis.

There are a variety of inpatient and outpatient substance-abuse treatment programs available, differing in both quality and effectiveness. Types of programs include psychiatric and nonpsychiatric inpatient detoxification units, medical and nonmedical rehabilitation programs (inpatient and outpatient), outpatient clinics (hospital-based and free-standing), school and community-based programs, residential treatment facilities (drug-free therapeutic communities), and twelve-step self-help programs such as Alcoholics Anonymous (AA), Ala-teen, Drugs Anonymous (DA), Cocaine Anonymous (CA), and Narcotics Anonymous (NA). Some programs employ chemotherapeutic techniques (such as methadone maintenance and Antabuse), while others strongly emphasize an abstinent, drug-free approach. Most programs utilize counseling or psychotherapeutic techniques. Given this array of services, significant skill and knowledge are required in order to effect an appropriate referral.

Comprehensive treatment programs designed specifically for adolescent populations appear to be the most efficient and most effective means of providing care and preventive services. Many of these programs are run by graduates of similar programs, who themselves are former drug-users. In addition to providing a broad range of services, these programs help to reduce the sense of isolation that many youngsters feel, and the staff provides the patients with positive role models. Unfortunately, some of these programs lack the appropriate professional staff to handle adolescents with severe medical or psychiatric disorders.

A youngster might enter treatment as an inpatient, progress to an intensive day program, and eventually enter a more limited outpatient setting. Early stages of treatment are more intensive. As the patient develops a healthier level of functioning in psychological, social, educational, and vocational areas, the need for specialized services and support decreases. Some long-term follow-up and monitoring are necessary to promote and prevent relapses. In fact, patients and staff members might be encouraged to recognize that these behaviors are often chronic, and relapse is an ever-present possibility.

The physician should attempt to maintain contact with individual patients whether or not they are referred for treatment. The following criteria may be used to guide treatment planning and referral (Millman 1983):

1) Continued follow-up by primary clinical provider if:
   a) Provider knowledgeable in these areas;
   b) Substance use intermittent, experimental, and appropriate for age and sociocultural group;
   c) No significant psychopathology;
   d) Function in educational, social, and vocational spheres unimpaired;
   e) Reasonable progress in developmental tasks;
   f) No antisocial behavior.
2) Referral to specialized practitioner or treatment program if:
   a) Uncertainty or lack of experience on the part of the primary physician;
   b) Frequent, regular, or compulsive drug abuse;
   c) Psychopathology requiring evaluation and treatment;
   d) Impaired function in educational, social, legal, or occupational spheres;
   e) In certain circumstances (e.g., when a specialized unit is available), evaluation on an inpatient basis.
3) Referral to inpatient drug-treatment program or specialized hospital if:
   a) Compulsive or addictive drug use (e.g., youngster brought for evaluation intoxicated or actively abusing drug);
   b) Impaired function in educational, social, legal, or occupational spheres;
   c) Imminent danger to physical or mental health of the patient;
   d) Persistent antisocial behavior (e.g., stealing or dealing);
   e) Failure at prior outpatient treatment;
   f) Psychopathology requiring behavioral and/or pharmacological management;
   g) Behavior presenting danger to self or others requiring containment or physical restraint.

EMERGENCY ROOM

Sedative-hypnotic, narcotic, hallucinogenic, and stimulant drug overdose can produce extreme emergencies in which, without prompt evaluation and treatment, the patient can die (Millman 1985; Sbriglio and Millman, in press). The teenage emergency room (ER) arrival, brought in because of bizarre behavior, acute psychosis, coma, or respiratory or circulatory collapse, is more frequently suffering from a drug overdose than from any of the more traditionally presumed diagnoses such as encephalitis, epilepsy, schizophrenia, diabetes, or head trauma. Even when head trauma has occurred, intoxication may well be implicated. Since tolerance to narcotics and sedative-hypnotics develops, reaction to similar doses may vary widely. In addition, mixing drugs with each other and especially with alcohol enhances their potential toxicity.

Emergency personnel should be knowledgeable about common drugs of abuse and should be skilled in the recognition and initial management of poisonings involving the agents most commonly abused by teenagers. Opiates (heroin and other narcotics) and sedative-hypnotics (most commonly benzodiazepines [Valium] and barbiturates [Tuinal]), often in combination with alcohol, cause the overwhelming majority of coma-inducing poisonings. The tricyclic antidepressant amitriptyline (Elavil), abused often in combination with narcotics, is relatively easily obtainable in large amounts and should always be considered in obtunded or comatose known narcotic addicts. Since specific toxicology tests are often unavailable and always impractically slow, emergency management must rely solely on history and neurological examination. Nevertheless, drug screens of urine, blood, and stomach contents should always be obtained, for these can be valuable guides to future definitive treatment. When a patient is unconscious, or for any other reason unable to provide information, the history should be obtained from those who brought in the patient. Unfortunately, comatose youngsters are not infrequently brought to the ER by terrified companions (often co-users) who, in order to avoid further involvement, leave before they can be questioned. Although this information can be crucially important, it is generally an unreliable guide to the potential depth of coma or risk of medical complications.

Physical signs that should alert the physician to substance-abuse include needle tracks, cellulitis or skin abscesses from repeated injections, or injury to the nasal mucosa and septum (edema, inflammation, ulceration or perforation) from concomitant intranasal use (snorting). There is a specific antidote (naloxone [Narcan]) for pure narcotic overdoses. However, for mixed drug overdoses there are no specific antidotes, and emergency treatment is largely supportive (nasogastric suctioning, maintenance of airway and respiration, hydration, etc.). Such patients should never be left alone or with unskilled attendants, since they can sink rapidly and unexpectedly into deeper levels of unconsciousness. They should be transported as soon as possible to an inpatient intensive care unit where specific therapy can be administered.

Overdose with a stimulant (usually cocaine or amphetamines) or hallucinogen (usually phencyclidine [PCP] or LSD) commonly presents as a toxic psychosis with agitation, confusion, paranoid delusions, perceptual distortions, and hallucinations. The emergency room assessment of such patients should be conducted in a quiet, calm, and supportive atmosphere, while the acute management consists of verbal reassurance ("talking down") and low-dose diazepam (Valium) for severe agitation. Following resolution of acute symptoms, the patient should be admitted or referred for further evaluation, treatment, and follow-up.

INPATIENT MEDICAL SETTING

The medical complications of drug-abuse account for a significant proportion of adolescent medical admissions and are probably even more common as a primary reason for receiving outpatient medical attention. Essentially every organ and organ system can be adversely affected by abuse of psychoactive substances, so that it is not unusual for a drug problem to be detected first on the basis of physical and neurological examination (Millman 1985).

Accidents and injuries (head trauma, fractured bones, burns, penetrating wounds, etc.) are often the result of trauma sustained during periods of intoxication, impaired judgment and motor coordination, and loss of consciousness from drug or alcohol use. The general appearance and behavior of the youngster may suggest either an intoxicated state (lethargy, slurred speech, ataxia, poor coordination) or a state of withdrawal (tremor, diaphoresis, intense anxiety, restlessness, hyperreflexia). As described earlier, erosions of the nasal mucosa and septum are suggestive of intranasal drug-use. Evidence of liver disease (jaundice, hepatitis) may be present as a complication of alcohol abuse or IV drug-use. The presence of needle "tracks," cellulitis, or abscesses at common skin sites strongly suggests IV or subcutaneous needle use under unsterile conditions. Other complications of IV drug-abuse that may be encountered include septicemia, endocarditis, hepatitis, and osteomyelitis. More recently, AIDS has been recognized as a serious complication of IV drug-use and needle sharing. The population of IV users of illicit drugs now represents the second largest AIDS risk group (Marmor et al. 1984). Diseases referable to the genitourinary system, related to the substance-abuser's sexual practices and lifestyle, may be diagnosed incidently. Menstrual irregularities and secondary amenorrhea in an adolescent girl can be related to the effects of narcotics on endocrine function. Various obstetrical complications can be a result of cocaine abuse.

In the course of evaluating and treating an adolescent for a medical complication of suspected drug or alcohol use, the primary clinician should thoroughly explore the underlying substance-abuse problem and, with the assistance of specialists, make appropriate recommendations for further assessment, treatment, and follow-up.

CONCLUSION

Drug and alcohol-abuse behaviors are at once a rite of passage for many young people and a significant cause of death and disability. Those who care for this population should be prepared to provide a skilled assessment and secure appropriate treatments for these disorders. They are disorders of the mind and body and as such are fascinating to study and treat. There are few areas of disease and disability where such dramatic change can be effected in the lives of young people.

REFERENCES

Abelson, H. I., Fishburne, P. M., and Cisin, I. (1977). National Survey on Drug Abuse: 1977. Rockville, Md.: National Institute on Drug Abuse.

American Medical News. (1985). MDs wary of increase in "designer drug" abuse. *American Medical Association.* August 2, p. 18.

Blane, H. T., and Hewitt, L. E. (1977). Alcohol and youth: An analysis of the literature, 1960–1975. Final report prepared for National Institute on Alcohol Abuse and Alcoholism.

Blum, R., et al. (1979). Youthful drug use. In R. I. Dupont, A. Goldstein, and J. O'Donnel (Eds.). *Handbook on Drug Abuse.* Washington, D.C.: Department of Health, Education, and Welfare and Office of Drug Abuse Policy, pp. 257–67.

Braucht, G., et al. (1973). Deviant drug use in adolescence: A review of psychosocial correlates. *Psychol. Bull.* 79:92–106.

Brizer, D. A., et al. (1985). Effects of methadone plus neuroleptics on treatment-resistant chronic paranoid schizophrenia. *Amer. J. Psychiat.* 142(9):1106.

Carlson, G. A., and Cantwell, D. P. (1980). Unmasking masked depression in children and adolescents. *Amer. J. Psychiat.* 137:445–49.

Chasnoff, I. J., et al. (1985). Cocaine use in pregnancy. *New Eng. J. Med.* 313(11):666–69.

Coan, R. W. (1973). Personality variables associated with cigarette smoking. *J. Person. Soc. Psychol.* 26:86–104.

Dackis, C. A., and Gold, M. S. (1985). Bromocriptine as treatment of cocaine abuse. *Lancet* 1:1151–52.

Erikson, E. H. (1963). *Childhood and Society.* 2d ed. New York: Norton.

Freeland, J. B., and Campbell, R. S. (1973). The social context of first marijuana use. *Int'l. J. Addict.* 8:317–24.

Gallenmore, J. L., and Wilson, W. P. (1972). Adolescent maladjustment or affective disorder? *Amer. J. Psychiat.* 129:608–12.

Goodwin, D. W. (1984). Studies of familial alcoholism: A review. *J. Clin. Psychiat.* 45 (12, sec. 2):14–17.

Grinspoon, L., and Bakalar, J. B. (1981). Marihuana. In J. H. Lowinson and P. Ruiz (Eds.). *Substance Abuse: Clinical Problems and Perspectives.* Baltimore: Williams and Wilkins, pp. 140–47.

JAMA: Medical News. (1984). *J. Amer. Med. Assoc.* 251(13):1647.

Jarvik, M. E., et al. (1977). *Research on Smoking Behavior.* (National Institute on Drug

Abuse Research Monograph 17, DHEW Pub. No. (ADM) 78–581). Washington, D.C.: United States Government Printing Office, p. 383.

Johnston, L. D., Bachman, J. G., and O'Malley, P. M. (1979). *1979 Highlights: Drugs and the Nation's High School Students, Five-Year National Trends.* Washington, D.C.: Department of Health, Education and Welfare, Public Health Service; ADAMHA.

Khantzian, E. J., Mack, J. E., and Schatzberg, A. F. (1974). Heroin use as an attempt to cope: Clinical observations. *Amer. J. Psychiat.* 131:160–64.

Kleber, H., and Gawin, F. (1986). Cocaine. In A. J. Frances and R. G. Hales (Eds.). *Psychiatry Update Annual Review,* Vol. 5. Washington, D.C.: American Psychiatric Press, pp. 160–85.

Kleber, H. D., (1985). Naltrexone. *J. Substance Abuse Treat.* 2:117–22.

Kreek, M. J. (1981). Medical management of methadone-maintained patients. In J. W. Lowinson and P. Ruiz (Eds.). *Substance Abuse: Clinical Problems and Perspectives.* Baltimore: Williams and Wilkins, pp. 660–73.

Lowinson, J. H. (1981). Methadone maintenance in perspective. In J. H. Lowinson and P. Ruiz (Eds.). *Substance Abuse: Clinical Problems and Perspectives.* Baltimore: Williams and Wilkins, pp. 344–54.

Marmor, M. M., et al. (1984). The epidemic of acquired immunodeficiency syndrome (AIDS) and suggestions for its control in drug abusers. *J. Substance Abuse Treat.* 1:237–47.

Millman, R. B. (1978). Drug and alcohol abuse. In B. B. Wollman, J. Eagan, and A. C. Ross (Eds.). *Handbook of Mental Disorders in Childhood and Adolescence.* Englewood Cliffs, N.J.: Prentice-Hall, pp. 238–67.

————. (1983). Treatment and modalities. In I. F. L. H. (Ed.). *Adolescent Substance Abuse.* (Report of the Fourteenth Ross Roundtable). Columbus, Ohio: Ross Laboratories, pp. 57–67.

————. (1985). Drug abuse and dependence. In J. B. Wyngaarden and L. H. Smith (Eds.). *Cecil Textbook of Medicine,* 17th ed. Philadelphia: Saunders, pp. 2015–24.

————, and Botvin, G. J. (1983). Substance use, abuse, and dependence. In M. D. Levine, et al. (Eds.). *Developmental Behavioral Pediatrics.* Philadelphia: Saunders, pp. 683–708.

————, and Khuri, E. T. (1981). Adolescence and substance abuse. In J. W. Lowinson and P. Ruiz (Eds.). *Substance Abuse: Clinical Problems and Perspectives.* Baltimore: Williams and Wilkins, pp. 739–51.

National Institute on Alcohol Abuse and Alcoholism. (1983). Health professions education. *Alcohol Health Res. World* 8(1).

National Institute on Drug Abuse. (1980). *Marijuana and Health.* Rockville, Md.: National Institute on Drug Abuse.

————. (1985). *Use of Licit and Illicit Drugs by America's High School Students, 1975–1984.* Rockville, Md.: National Institute on Drug Abuse.

O'Malley, P. M., Bachman, J. G., and Johnston, L. D. (1984). Peroid, age and cohort effects on substance use among American youth, 1976–1982. *Amer. J. Pub. Health* 74:682–88.

Sbriglio, R., and Millman, R. (In press). Emergency treatment of acute cocaine reactions. In A. M. Washton and M. S. Gold (Eds.). *Cocaine Abuse: Recent Trends and Clinical Perspectives.* New York: Guilford Press.

Tennant, F. S. (1986). The clinical syndrome of marijuana dependence. *Psychiat. Annals* 16(4):225–34.

Washton, A. M., et al. (1984). Adolescent cocaine abusers [letter]. *Lancet* 2:746.

Watanabe, A., et al. (1985). A report of unusually high blood ethanol and acetaldehyde levels in two surviving patients. *Alcoholism: Clin. Exper. Res.* 9(1):14–16.

Weil, A. (1972). *The Natural Mind.* Boston: Houghton Mifflin, p. 19.

Williams, A. F. (1973). Personality and other characteristics associated with cigarette smoking among young teenagers. *J. Health Soc. Behav.* 14:374–80.

Zinberg, N. E. (1975). Addiction and ego function. In R. S. Eissler et al. (Eds.). *The Psychoanalytic Study of the Child.* New Haven: Yale University Press.

45

EATING DISORDERS IN CHILDREN AND ADOLESCENTS

Stephen L. Bennett, Richard Pleak, and Joseph A. Silverman

This chapter will examine three aspects of the assessment of the eating disorders in children. The first section will review the physical findings in anorexia; the second will offer one psychiatrist's view of evaluation; and the third will consider the assessment of obesity in children.

DSM-III defines anorexia with the following criteria:
A. Intense fear of becoming obese, which does not diminish as weight loss progresses;
B. Disturbance of body image, e.g., claiming to "feel fat" even when emaciated;
C. Weight loss of at least 25 percent of original body weight or, if under 18 years of age, weight loss from original body weight plus projected weight gain expected from growth charts may be combined to make the 25 percent;
D. Refusal to maintain body weight over a minimal normal weight for age and height;
E. No known physical illness that would account for the weight loss.

Diagnostic criteria for bulimia are:
A. Recurrent episodes of binge eating (rapid consumption of a large amount of food in a discrete period of time, usually less than two hours);
B. At least three of the following:
    (1) consumption of high-caloric, easily ingested food during a binge;
    (2) inconspicuous eating during a binge;
    (3) termination of such eating episodes by abdominal pain, sleep, social interruption, or self-induced vomiting;
    (4) repeated attempts to lose weight by severely restrictive diets, self-induced vomiting, or use of cathartics and/or diuretics;
    (5) frequent weight fluctuations greater than ten pounds due to alternating binges and fasts.

C. Awareness that the eating pattern is abnormal and fear of not being able to stop eating voluntarily;

D. Depressed mood and self-deprecating thoughts following eating binges;

E. The bulimic episodes not due to anorexia nervosa or any known physical disorder.

Anorexia is found predominately in females. Halmi noted that the percentage of males in an anorectic population varies between 4 and 6 percent. Onset is usually between the ages of 10 and 30, with 85 percent of all anorectic patients developing the illness between the ages of 13 and 20 (Halmi 1974). Mortality rates range from 5 to 21 percent (Morgan and Russell 1975).

THE PEDIATRIC ASSESSMENT OF ANOREXIA NERVOSA

Almost three hundred years ago, Dr. Richard Morton stated that anorexia nervosa "does almost always proceed from sadness and anxious cares." However, it is not the psychopathology but the emaciation with its metabolic changes that propels the patient—usually a female—and her family to the doctor's office. The typical history, physical and laboratory findings that will be described are based on one hundred cases of anorexia admitted to Babies Hospital, the pediatric wing of the Columbia-Presbyterian Medical Center. By definition, these are all patients whose precarious nutritional state or out-of-control symptoms required inpatient treatment.

The typical pattern observed by family members begins as follows. Generally, there was a period of teasing about the patient's weight, which was followed by a systematic program of strict food avoidance and marked weight loss. This was followed by bizarre behavior, cachexia and metabolic changes. In addition, all patients complained of perpetual chilliness, severe constipation, and, in those girls who had reached menarche, amenorrhea.

Frequently, early weight loss was either not noticed or ignored by the family. The few parents who were worried and reported weight losses to their physicians were often reassured and occasionally scolded for being so concerned. Only after the onset of frank anorexia and markedly aberrant behavior were the complaints taken seriously.

Physicians who study this disease are amazed by the body's ability to withstand the many sequelae of starvation. Furthermore, it is clear that each patient's body tolerates malnutrition in different ways, depending on such variables as weight and condition at onset; speed of weight loss; use of cathartics; and self-induced vomiting. The duration of the period of starvation must be ascertained quickly, because the body seems to tolerate chronic weight loss more efficiently than it does the acute variety. It is often useless to compare idealized and actual weights to determine the degree of physical risks. A 5'4", eighty-pound female who has lost sixty pounds over a period of five years is probably much sturdier than one who sustained a similar loss in only three months. To complicate matters, two individuals with similar acute, sudden major weight loss may react quite differently. For these reasons, a speedy and thorough physical examination is necessary.

Physical Findings

All of the abnormalities found on physical examination of the patient with anorexia nervosa are caused by malnutrition and are essentially identical to those found in victims of other types of deliberate starvation. The following physical findings are most common:

1. The skin is almost always affected in patients with anorexia nervosa. It appears dark and dirty, with roughened texture resembling a fine sandpaper. Desquamation is common, as is the presence of a coat of silken hairs resembling lanugo on the trunk, extremities, and face. In addition, very severely malnourished patients often present with petechiae and ecchymoses (usually not due to thrombocytopenia).
2. Hypothermia is the second most common finding. It is well known that patients with anorexia nervosa complain of chilliness. Eighty of the one hundred patients were found to have rectal temperatures of 96.6°F or below.
3. Bradycardia (with rates below sixty beats per minute, and occasionally dropping to a low of twenty-nine beats per minute in the sleeping state) was detected in seventy-seven of our patients. This was accompanied by bradypnea in sixty-one patients. A total of fifty-three patients had hypotension with systolic blood pressure of 70 mm hg. or below.
4. The presence of frank cachexia was variable and is related to the speed with which the patient first presents herself to the physician and the diagnostic acumen of the physician. Doctors attuned to thinking about nervosa often have fewer cachectic patients.
5. Transitory, unexplained systolic heart murmurs were detected in twenty-eight patients.
6. Pericardial effusions were detected in four of the patients. In each case, there had been a loss of 30 to 53 percent of so-called ideal body weight.
7. Falling weights are associated with falling vital signs, and these in turn (particularly hypotension and bradycardia) can be followed by light-headedness, syncope, orthostatic hypotension, circulatory collapse, and death.
8. The presence of abdominal distention associated with chronic regurgitation of small amounts of fluid in a severely cachectic, weakened patient suggests the possibility of an intestinal obstruction, a life-threatening emergency. In severe starvation, abnormalities of peristalsis can occur.
9. Petechiae and ecchymoses are frequently seen in severely emaciated patients and are probably due to increased capillary permeability, rather than thrombocytopenia or hypoprothrombinemia.
10. The presence of edema is troublesome but rarely life-threatening. It is not as a rule due to cardiac, renal, hepatic, or serum protein abnormalities. It may be caused by protracted standing and increased capillary permeability.

In the past, it was said that infection was a common cause of death. This is not the case today. There are, however, pitfalls concerning infection in emaciated anorectics, which are related not to the patient's defense mechanisms, but rather to the physician's diagnostic acuity. For example, anorexic patients respond somewhat differently to infection, specifically in the area of fever production. One should regard a sick anorectic with a temperature of 101°F as having a high fever (if her basal body reading is usually 94°F). Infection should be considered at once, and appropriate diagnostic and therapeutic steps taken.

Laboratory Abnormalities

Laboratory workup was performed in order to provide appropriate baseline studies, to evaluate the degree of starvation, and to rule out other causes of wasting and inanition. Seventy-four percent of our patients had electrocardiographic changes. The principal abnormalities were sinus bradycardia, extremely low voltage, and low or inverted T waves. The greater the degree of wasting and cachexia, the more pronounced were the electrocardiographic changes.

Chest X rays of cachectic patients with anorexia nervosa generally show a heart that appears relatively small in size. Despite this, echocardiograms revealed the presence of pericardial effusions in four patients who had lost 38 to 53 percent of ideal body weight. The cause of these effusions is unknown.

Elevation of blood urea nitrogen (BUN) probably reflects contributions of prerenal azotemia (secondary to poor fluid intake and/or catabolism of endogenous or exogenous protein (Sustagen, Sustacal, etc.).

Decreases in serum thyroxine (T4) and triiodothyronine (T3) were found in some of our patients. These decreases actually represent normal physiological levels for the starved patient. According to Vagenakis (1977), these changes in association with previously mentioned hypothermia and bradycardia in essence turn down the body's thermostat so that it can function optimally when proper nutrition does not exist. Other findings can be hypovitaminosis A and hypercarotenemia. There can also be an absence of the usual diurnal variation of plasma glucocorticoids. Bone marrow hypoplasia can occur. Anemia almost never occurs in anorexia nervosa.

Virtually all of the abnormal laboratory tests are a direct result of starvation and can be experimentally produced. The aberrations quickly revert to normal as nutrition is restored. An exception to this statement concerns the problems of amenorrhea, which is a universal finding of the postmenarchic patient with anorexia nervosa.

There is a decrease in luteinizing hormone (LH) and follicle-stimulating hormone (FSH) as a result of hypothalmic influences; ovarian stimulation does not take place and menses cease. At least one-half of the patients described here who had reached menarche developed amenorrhea long before significant weight loss had occurred, indeed in a few, before any noticeable weight loss had taken place. (After physical recovery, many patients must wait for several months before LH and FSH levels return to normal. In some cases, twelve to eighteen months may pass, after return of physiological levels of LH and FSH, before menses resume.)

Despite the severe semistarvation present in most patients, certain organ systems function very well, as revealed by laboratory tests. They include plasma levels of electrolytes (Na+, K+,C−), proteins, immunoglobulins, and total calcium, as well as serum levels of vitamin B_{12}, folate, and iron. Although one might expect a starved individual to be afflicted with hypoproteinemia, this is usually not the case. It appears that anorexic patients eat just enough to sustain serum protein levels.

Electrolyte imbalance rarely occurs in anorexia nervosa, but when it does, it presents in the form of hypokalemic, hypochloremic alkalosis. Deceased serum K+ and C1− are almost always a result of chronic self-induced vomiting.

THE PSYCHIATRIC EVALUATION OF THE ANOREXIC PATIENT

A combined treatment approach—medical and psychological—is most suited for the assessment and treatment of anorexia nervosa. The diagnosis can often be difficult to make. Now that anorexia is considered commonplace and drastic weight loss less significant a feature, the diagnosis is likely to be made all too glibly. Nevertheless this diagnosis can still be missed or established only after a long and extensive work-up in a situation similar to that found in infants with failure to thrive. What becomes most important in assessment are those special fantasies and ideas that occur with an intensity and torment the patient.

Barbara, age 17, was referred for inpatient treatment by a psychiatrist near her community. Evaluation confirmed the diagnosis of anorexia nervosa but what was of major interest was the length of time it had taken to arrive at this diagnosis. Her symptom of stomach pains and with it progressive weight loss had begun 1½ years before and had led to extensive work-ups in local hospitals. Findings were negative; the patient was referred to a major medical center in a large city. There, gastrointestinal investigations were carried out. A psychiatrist had seen her once but did not feel that psychological issues contributed to her stomach pains. Finally, her parents brought her to a local psychiatrist who did a full evaluation and made the diagnosis.

On first meeting, Barbara appeared solidly competent and boyishly proud of her championship athleticism. Only after two or three sessions did the flavor of her fear of gaining weight appear. The first understanding was that moving on with adolescence meant a threat to her tie to her parents. Only much later on did the confusion over her gender role come out. A month into regular therapy, however, her stomach pains decreased markedly and appeared only at discrete times. They appeared to be similar to abdominal fantasies described so well by Rollins and Piazza (1978).

There is a special character to anorexia, a complex weave of traits, dynamics, and fantasies that are as important for a diagnosis as the objective signs. This is illustrated by the curious use by clinicians of long novelistic case histories. Anorexia is so entwined within personality and culture that clinicians such as Sours (1980) have felt the need to turn their hands to writing stories. This "feel" of anorexia is important not only in the initial diagnosis but also in prediction about outcome. The method of presentation will be to take the material in the sequence it would appear in listening to a patient.

Pursuit of Thinness/Fear of Fatness

In general, the first meeting with a young teenager who has been dragged in by her parents will be characterized by sullen noncommunication or an eloquent statement that she has no problems. The wish for thinness is a prominent idea, at first described merely as a desire to lose a little weight. It can thus be difficult to distinguish the early stages of anorexia nervosa from an adjustment reaction of adolescence or the simple decision to diet. Some sadness, anxiety, and weight loss are a common part of a teenager's reaction to stress. The idea that things will be better with a few pounds less is universal in our culture. In the early stages of anorexia the most frequent warning signals are social withdrawal from peers and family and amenorrhea. Also prominent are mood swings, depression, feelings of inadequacy, a great surge of activity, and an intensification of whatever have been the previous food idiosyncracies.

At a particular point in anorexia, the diet takes on a momentum of its own and the weight loss itself becomes a powerful pleasure. A troubled teenager with a minimal sense of worth will describe feeling a purpose and well-being for the first time in months. She may express disdain and a feeling of grandiosity toward other individuals whom she considers overweight and weak-willed. Her depression can be relieved by the "high" of abstinence and a sense of emptiness filled by a sense of dietary purpose.

For the anorexic, each drop of weight can create the sense of a task completed, and this feeling of accomplishment becomes very important. Food is avoided so as to "store up" a reserve for when she is forced to eat. Much of the time there is no definite goal other than to be less, so that if left alone the adolescent would continue on until collapse.

Fear of fatness becomes a central theme as the illness progresses. With the challenge to weight loss posed by the family or through therapeutic intervention, it becomes the reason not to change and is expressed in a repetitious litany of fears. DSM-III and III-R make this one of the cardinal diagnostic criteria. The fat feeling becomes a defense against almost everything.

The degree to which this fear of being fat takes over the mind and thereupon dominates food intake becomes a good indicator of progress. The more insightful patients will understand that these feelings and thoughts are not random events but shorthand statements about body image and ultimately the sense of self. Starting with the fear of fatness, the trail leads to an awareness of an internal dialogue, conscience, body image, fantasies about an abdominal mass, separation-individuation, and a view of the representational world.

The clinician must explore deeply the patient's fears of fatness to make contact with the patient's experience and to reveal the patient's "interior dialogue." Many patients seem to experience an inner voice that will take on a unique personality. The voices are different from someone just talking to herself, and on first hearing it one can wonder whether the patient is experiencing auditory hallucinations. These occur especially around food temptations and pressures. Most often a battle is described with a frail and corruptible sense of self becoming the target of righteous scorn. This idea of an interior war becomes most vivid during the process of recovery, when there is an attempt by the healthy aspects of the personality to challenge the anorexic self. This voice of opposition is often silent and always weak in the beginning. Somewhere the teenager will have found her own arguments against the shrill demands of the anorexic conscience, but she will need help in giving it a voice.

One girl personified the harsh voice that warned her against becoming fat like her mother. Only as therapy progressed did the full dimensions of this internal object emerge. Resembling an imaginary companion, but in a 17-year-old, this voice, named Sylvia, was shrewd and willful, even mean like the mother, but by her nasty strength showed the way through starvation to establish a position of high visibility within the family. Only later on was Sylvia perceived as a bad companion who had to be resisted.

One consequence of these battles is asceticism (Mogul 1980). This is a typical adolescent defense that appears frequently in anorexia and becomes an end itself. These ideas can take on spiritual or moral tones. Frequently the adolescent's first experience with anorexia is similar to a religious conversion. The child psychiatrist should assess the meaning of this to the patient. It is important to help the teenager describe her feelings of purpose, purity, and spirituality.

The experience is often put in moral tones. There is pleasure and pride that she has "accomplished something." There is a moral superiority that comes from being able to succeed in the weight loss and hold off the jealous people who have tried to stop her.

The anorexic's presentation of her exercise and diet rituals leads to two therapeutic stances. The first reaction by parents and physicians is to comment on the harm done to the body. This is like interdicting prayer: Warnings are seen as confirmation that she is succeeding. Certainly, limits are crucial for any treatment program, but the therapist needs to be aware that high ideals can be the most precious thing a teenager in turmoil possesses. Acknowledgement of this at the beginning of treatment can help create an emotional connection (Mogul 1980).

Beyond the search for slimness and the terror of obesity there is the anorexic's implacable conviction that her body looks fat. It is a fascinating manifestation of body image disturbance that is as dramatic as the phantom limb. This fixed idea, in spite of the reality of emaciation, has been used as one of the cardinal diagnostic features of anorexia. Bruch (1973) considered it a "disturbance of delusional proportions" and related it to the more basic misperception of internal states.

The degree of body image disturbance provides an indication of progress after the acute stage of illness is over. Bruch described a realistic body image as a precondition for recovery. We can use this as one moderately reliable indicator of progress. Body image disturbance will improve as nutrition improves and as there is as well some resolution of personal and family conflicts. It will change from an idea that is so charged with feeling that eating is impossible to a less frequent and weaker event, so that the anorectic can eat in spite of it.

Often a patient is told only that her sense of her body is false and that she must ignore these misleading perceptions. Although this is true, it is distressing to the patient not to be able to trust herself. It can nonetheless be demonstrated that this distorted image of the body is a sensitive indicator of self-esteem. These internal cues can be used rather than ignored. "You get the fat feeling whenever you feel crummy about yourself." That it is a flashing red light signaling the state of esteem or the sense of self will then allow for exploration of the real trouble. Often, painful events that were not fully in awareness can then be picked up.

Sours (1980) pointed out correctly that a distortion of body image is seen not only in the eating disorders, but is present in all adolescents, especially girls, because of their changing body contours. In addition, many groups such as runners and dancers have quite special views about their bodies.

One aspect of the body often singled out is secondary sexual characteristics. This has led to the idea that anorexia is a defense, an escape, from adult sexuality. Fantasies about the abdomen are of particular interest. There can be diffuse complaints that the stomach is too fat, but more than that there will be insinuations that there is something growing inside. It can be expressed by elaborations of the common fantasy that food can "turn to fat" and "become solid and stick." Often there will be discomfort and pains. Sometimes the sensation of having a thing inside suggests a pregnancy fantasy. Rollins and Piazza (1978) saw this as a conscious expression of covert body image distortions and the fantasy that there is something inside. Although linked with sexual worries, they stem more basically from the most early tie to the parents and the intense fear that this tie will change.

Body image preoccupation can be linked directly to the sense of self; put the other way, concerns about the self are displaced onto the body. It requires the material obtained from psychoanalysis, whether it be object relations (Selvini-Palazzoli 1974; Masterson 1978) or self-psychology (Goodsitt 1985) language, which allows further exploration.

The ability of the anorexic to deny the body's importance is illustrated by a late adolescent seen early on by this writer before these issues were well understood [S.B.]. She was devoted to literature and very appealing intellectually. In spite of weighing only seventy pounds, she would walk miles a day and supported herself by running a catering service. On the surface she seemed to have resolved her social problems by being nice and caring for others. It finally became clear that she was "getting better" in every way but in her body. After one of her long hikes she finally collapsed, forcing her admission to a hospital. It was as if she had become pure spirit. This is a frequent trap. Improvements—even those that are genuine—can be used to draw attention from the body.

Garner et al. (1983a) have described the role of sociocultural factors in the development of the eating disorders. The role of these issues in treatment from a feminist perspective is discussed by Orbach (1985). The question "why do you put everything off on your body" will be answered (if at all) by some version of "doesn't everybody?"

Many of the symptoms we have examined have a direct line to the sense of self-worth and esteem. Hidden often behind a mask of competence regarding the anorectic's "success" at weight loss is a failure to master the basic tasks of adolescence. As one girl of 18, who had been in and out of hospitals for several years, put it, "Not eating is the only way I have to make people pay attention to me. It is my craft." She, indeed, was a "hunger artist."

Lapses in self-esteem are only one part of ego deficits. Bruch (1973) has described a "paralyzing sense of ineffectiveness." This may not be recognized easily because often these patients, when in a fair state of nutrition, are at the top of their class and engaged in many activities. Many are energetic participants in sports and appear successful and tough. When caught in their illness there can be negativism and considerable resistance to attempts at intervention.

Linked together by Bruch (1973) as one of three cardinal features of anorexia—along with body image disturbance and sense of ineffectiveness—is the more basic misperception of inner experience. The most apparent aspect of this is the difficulty in recognizing hunger and satiation. As has been described frequently, the term anorexia is a misnomer because hunger is often present. Such a lack of clarity on when to stop eating can become the persistent terror of being unable to stop. There are also magical ideas about food—that small portions will cause immediate and immense weight gains.

There is as well difficulty in distinguishing hunger from other body states and emotions. For Bruch this all arises from the fundamental issue in the pathogenesis of the eating disorders, including obesity. There is a distortion of family communication around not only the feeding experience but emotional experience as well. There is a mislabeling within the family of all feeding states. "Thus a child comes to mistrust the legitimacy of his own feelings and experience" (Bruch 1973).

We can begin now to make some assumptions about what occurred in the early life of the anorexic patient. There can be typical developmental and family histories, just as there can be a stereotypical full-blown picture of anorexia; there can also be an unfortunate tendency to assume that the story is known and thereby to miss the variations and richness of detail. In obtaining personal and family history, one should recall Bruch's warning not to assume anything until one is told in detail. This is what she called "the constructive use of ignorance."

Parents of these children often give neutral or sparse accounts of development or tell a story that may have little to do with the facts. If you listen you can sometimes hear about the child admired for her niceness and conformity, possessing traits of rigidity and perfectionism, a child who responds to external cues. Others will reveal different histories. Needless to say, it is important to explore all aspects of the child's development to gain a coherent sense of the family life.

Chapter 39 in this volume, "Clinical Evaluation of Nonorganic Failure to Thrive," tries to put this early eating disorder in a developmental context. It acknowledges that the DSM-III diagnosis "Reactive Attachment Disorder" does describe one category of FTT where the failure of attachment is due to sparsity or inconsistency of maternal care. This is often in the setting of poverty. This is the type of FTT referred to when the assertion is made that there is little relationship with the later eating disorders. However, there is another variety of FTT that is a disorder of separation; this occurs in the last half of the first year and throughout the second year. Here, an attachment has been made but the child's moves toward autonomy have been met with inconsistency and ambivalence. It is possible that a link can be found between the eating disorders at this time and those of later onset.

The theme of separation difficulties runs through the childhood of these patients. This is obscured for two reasons: Often, these girls demonstrate considerable academic success and school becomes a temporary safe haven. Also, these families have a way of covering insecurities. This all breaks down somewhere in adolescence, when the girl feels that the world has turned against her. Often, one of the precipitating events is summer camp or going away to school for the first time.

Two 10-year-old girls seen in recent years developed their symptoms during periods of family turmoil. Anorexia at this young age could only be considered an oddity by someone unaware of the demands—internal and external—that occur at this time. Each showed a fierce determination that Sours (1980) aptly described as a "caricature of will." This urgent attempt at autonomy led to a relentless pursuit of thinness.

A common view of anorexia is that the adolescent girl is unable to cope with the stresses of puberty and regresses in all areas. Crisp (1980) saw anorexia as a maladaptive method of coping with pubertal weight and body changes. While this may not be satisfactory as the ultimate cause, it does help us clinically. Much of the material the patient offers will concern how the world around her has changed from little-girl security to a nightmare of sex, drugs, and new relationships. Also important are the changing ties to the parents. Self-object differentiation can be vague and separation anxiety can be intense. This can be most apparent in the hospital, which may be her first separation from home. She will describe an almost mind-reading relationship with her mother as part of this explosion when her needs are not intuitively met. We need to know not only the underpinnings of the personality, but also where the adolescent stands in what Blos (1967) called the second individuation process of adolescence.

The various developmental patterns in anorexia have been described by Sours

(1980). The groups who have onset early in adolescence were felt to have a better prognosis than the larger group whose onset is in middle to late adolescence. The latter are more likely to have a borderline organization. It is important to note the psychopathology behind these groups and to obtain a careful psychodynamic assessment that includes an idea of self-object differentiation. We can assume that a major determinant of outcome is the degree of sturdiness or fragility.

Striking overactivity is part of most cases; its degree and form is a good indicator of what is going on. For one girl who was a superb athlete it was not enough that she was state champion but that she had managed to be the first girl able to push her way into the high school weight room. For her, pumping iron meant changing her body into a male shape and relieving her depression. The teenager who said that starvation was her craft would hide in the hospital bathroom and do a hundred jumping jacks every hour. She described this as the only way besides starvation to relieve her sense of emptiness.

Epling et al. (1983) described an activity-based anorexia that they felt is a subgroup of anorexia nervosa. Here, activity and starvation interact. Yates et al. (1983) described a group of male athletes they called "obligatory runners," who in class and personality characteristics resembled individuals with anorexia nervosa. Allegiance to either diet or exercise creates a purpose and identity. Both articles emphasize the delicate balance between intake and output.

There has been an evolution and spreading of anorexia, with vomiting rather than starvation as the way of controlling intake. A parallel change is the use of exercise to control output. This new form does not seem to have reached its limits.

SUBGROUPS OF ANOREXIA NERVOSA

Our diagnostic skills are put to the test when we move from the inpatient hospital setting of severe cases of anorexia to the larger population. There one can see a wide range of individuals with body weight preoccupations, not only within special groups such as dancers, models, and athletes among whom such concerns are adaptive, but also in an even larger group of middle-class college girls or physical fitness devotees.

Garner et al. (1983b) questioned whether anorexia occurs on a continuum, with the classic picture on the severe end of the spectrum of eating concerns. However, there can be a tendency to link this with the consummatory and weight problems that occur throughout the population, and hence to overdiagnose severe psychopathology. Weight and diet concerns are hardly synonomous with anorexia. Garner et al. attempted to differentiate weight-preoccupied women with poor psychological adjustment from those who do not have severe personality disturbance. In other words, how does one tell a weight-preoccupied teenager who takes ballet lessons from a real anorectic? They emphasize going beyond the behavior because "the meaning and motivation behind the anorexic's diet may be different in essential ways from that of the extreme dieter."

It has been only within the past decade that bulimia has been considered as a distinct subgroup of anorexia nervosa. Attention was paid to bulimia because its presence was felt to indicate a poor prognosis. Besides the overt symptoms of gorging and vomiting, there are several characteristics that distinguish it from anorexia nervosa, including family history. There is more likely to be a family background of alcoholism and depression than in anorexia nervosa. Also, one-half of the mothers are obese, and the girl herself is more likely to have been obese. The bulimic personality is organized differently. The bulimic has difficulty controlling not only appetite but drives and emotions as well. The overall personality organization is impulsive, and there is likely to be lying, stealing, sexual acting out, and a propensity to use alcohol and drugs. The bulimic personality can be considered hysterical and impulse-ridden and stands in contrast to the rigid and obsessive structure of the restricting anorexic.

Casper et al. (1980) and Garfinkel et al. (1980) have shown that half of anorexics use food restriction exclusively to control weight and half use occasional vomiting. Numerous studies have shown that bulimia is common within a population of middle-class young women. Most writers feel there has been an upsurge in bulimia symptoms over the past decade, and in fact it appears to be endemic.

Binging and purging can occur not only in the anorexic but in individuals of normal weight and in the obese. Attempts have been made to distinguish groups based on weight history. Are girls of normal weight who gorge much different from emaciated girls who do the same thing? DSM-III uses the term bulimia only for those who do not fit the diagnosis of anorexia nervosa. DSM-III-R does not use this exclusion. Garner et al. (1985) felt that differences cannot be distinguished on the basis of weight history. They pointed out also that there are changing referral patterns. Ten years ago most patients with bulimia had anorexia nervosa. However, there are now increasing numbers of patients with equally severe symptoms who are of normal weight and without a history of anorexia. The psychological underpinnings seem to have remained constant; the diagnosis based on psychological make-up rather than on weight is most useful.

The terms bulimic and restricting anorexic can be used to describe anorexia with or without bulimia (Wilson and Mintz 1982). This describes behavior but also suggests the personality structure of the rigidly defended versus the impulse-ridden personality. The core anorexic symptomatology is shared, but it is bulimia that often shows the more striking difficulties with behavioral and affective controls.

Developmental research has demonstrated conclusively the infant's ability for self-regulation and the mother-child dyad's capacity for mutual regulation. Both the restricting and bulimic types of anorexia represent a pathology of arousal and can be considered as a radical departure from the dyadic and interactive matrix, wherein self-regulation is exaggerated with the reward of predictability and control at the cost of interpersonal relations and body physiology. By starving, binging, and vomiting, the bulimic exerts control over her inner state but not over her interpersonal world. Symptoms can be interpreted in these terms. Also, these ideas justify placing order and limits on dietary behavior, whether it be through firm controls in the hospital or whatever structure regular psychotherapy provides.

The full sweep of the sequence of binge eating then purging needs to be examined. Assessment can be difficult because the details are kept secret. Often the patient will admit to occasional episodes and lie about the real frequency. One of the first tasks of therapy is to help the girl identify feeling states, then to try to understand the affects and conflicts that the gorging relieves. The first attempt at this finds hunger as the explanation, but in time acknowledges the state of panic, rage, emptiness, or disorganization that is relieved by food. The struggle over food—the battle of internal objects—is the same as in the restricting anorexic, but this time the child loses. One girl would tie herself up to prevent the binging. The temporary relief and pleasure the food provides is followed by self-recrimination and guilt. The purging relieves this; it is literally a catharsis, a sense of cleansing that can be even more powerful than the gorging. Often the description has a strong erotic flavor. Food can be ingested just to provoke vomiting, and the disgust that follows the vomiting sets the bulimic up for the next cycle. Assessment must also include history of diuretic, laxative, and enema abuse as additional means of purging.

Depressed mood and often overt depression are a frequent part of the clinical picture of anorexia and bulimia. It can be difficult to tell one from the other. Similar themes exist in both: crumbling self-esteem, a profound sense of loss, despair leading to thoughts of suicide, and a merciless conscience. Also, starvation itself leads to irritability and depression. Quite often those patients referred for inpatient treatment, especially those who have gone through a number of clinicians, have been tried on one or some combination of antidepressants. It has been our practice to withdraw all such medication at the time of admission. Experience has shown that most of the depressive symptoms diminish as treatment progresses and good nutrition is restored. If a depressive picture still remains when the patient has regained a healthy weight, then there should be a trial of antidepressants.

This relationship between eating disorders and depression has become a major research theme. Cantwell et al. (1977) have shown not only that a large number of patients evince symptoms of depression before the onset of anorexia, but that on follow-up there are major symptoms of a depression. Winokur et al. (1980) found an increased incidence of affective disorders in families of patients with anorexia. They wondered if anorexia represents an end point that can be reached by various paths. Bulimia would appear to have the stronger relationship with depression. When restricting anorexics were compared with bulimics, depressive symptoms were found more often in the latter (Garfinkel et al. 1980; Casper et al. 1980). Walsh et al. (1985) found a high frequency of affective disorder—90 percent met DSM-III criteria for some affective disorder—among patients with bulimia. There was a heterogeneous picture of depression. Major depression was frequent; however, bulimic patients exhibited a variety of depressive features rather than one fixed syndrome. Starvation effects may pass as depression. Moreover, there may be a variety of depressive themes that require treatment in their own right, whether by psychotherapy or the use of antidepressants.

Many of the symptoms of anorexia are not specific to the illness but are effects of starvation. The classic and often quoted study by Keys et al. (1950) demonstrated that volunteers who were starved took on symptoms similar to anorexia nervosa. An interesting phenomenon was searching the environment for food-related items. This included a sensitivity to any food items found in magazines and movies; it could explain the anorexic's sensitivity to the media.

When there has been serious malnutrition—especially an acute and relentlessly downhill course—nutritional repair becomes the primary task. There is disagreement over whether psychotherapy is possible during starvation. Many feel that it is fruitless at this time when not to hospitalize the patient places her in danger. Others feel that there are some motivated patients who can participate in a frequent and intensive treatment.

This writer's experience has been with teenagers who are referred because they are in a psychological and nutritional crisis. Office psychotherapy has not often been successful at that time. It should be given a quick try, however. It is at this point that the clinician must take seriously the danger of body collapse and death. It is here, also, that the patient must be under the care of a pediatrician who understands these dangers. With the stability and surety that hospitalization offers, a therapeutic relationship can form and treatment can begin. The hospital facilitates rather than prohibits a relationship with the psychiatrist.

In the stable environment of the hospital there are issues that appear immediately. The usual themes are fury with being in the hospital, struggles with the parents, and fears about being forced to gain weight. Even during starvation or out-of-control bulimia, this material can be engaged. Therapy begins the minute you start seeing the patient.

Often many of the symptoms, especially the apathy, irritability, and the obsessive preoccupations, will lessen as nutrition improves. The internal dialogue tends to diminish also. This can be described to the patient, and it becomes a motivation for weight gain beyond an arbitrary authority demanding an increase in pounds.

THE FAMILY

Assessment of the family should follow two parallel themes. First is the awareness that stereotypical family patterns have been described (Bruch 1973; Selvini-Palazzoli 1974; Minuchin et al. 1978; Wilson 1983). Five characteristics of family interaction with an anorexic member are described by Minuchin et al.: enmeshment, overprotectiveness, rigidity, lack of conflict resolution, and involvement of the sick child in unresolved parental conflict. To spend time with these families is to be impressed not only by the textbook pictures but also by the varieties of family structure. Garner et al. (1983a) compared the characteristics of families with an anorexic child with normal controls and found little difference, which challenges the generalization that all these families are the same. In each situation we need to ascertain the weight of the families' contribution to the pathology or their potential contribution to resolution of the problems.

Each clinician will bring his own particular bias and experience to the treatment of a child within a family. Individual therapy can help the child understand and cope with her family. Formal family therapy can concentrate on interactions. Wilson (1983) has involved the other family members in therapy in their own right. Within child psychiatry the mainstream trend in treating adolescents appears to be a flexible combination of individual and family work. To see a teenager exclusively or to work only with the family is to lose one or the other.

TREATMENT

The question must be asked: Where in development has the adolescent been stopped? The stages of adolescence look easy to identify in textbooks, but in reality, being able to discern them from the teenager's internal world is a different matter. Treatment then means a freeing of any area of stasis and conflict so that development can continue. Seeing problems when they first arise rather than when they are fixed and chronic offers an opportunity for their resolution. Anyone who has enjoyed a therapeutic triumph has probably seen an adolescent at a time when the individual and family conflicts could be engaged and reconciled.

This presentation has argued that weight gain is essential but by itself does not count for much unless there has been an exploration of the basic issues. At the same time, alleged progress without nutritional improvement is a dead end. In fact, the anorexic is good at self-improvement that draws attention from weight. Structured programs that stress weight gain in the main would seem most helpful for older patients, for those who are not able to respond to psychotherapy, and for those whose symptoms are entrenched long-term. Halmi (1985) has over the years been the most eloquent exponent of the behavior modification approach. A knowledge of these principles is important for a comprehensive inpatient approach.

An intensive and full-range treatment is often necessary. A unique treatment approach can be fashioned for each adolescent and her family out of individual and family therapy. At any particular time the focus shifts back and forth from the teenager's interior world to family interaction. These ideas are similar to the multidimensional psychotherapy that is advocated by Garfinkel and Garner (1982).

The use of medication in the eating disorders has been tested by only a limited number of controlled studies so that at present it has only a small role, if any, in a total treatment strategy. Antipsychotic medication has little use in anorexia, especially in view of the side-effects; it should be used only for patients who are outstandingly agitated or compulsive. Antidepressant use in anorexia has been of limited benefit and has the hazardous side-effects of orthostatic hypotension and cardiac conduction disturbances. Antidepressant medications have been shown to be effective with some patients with bulimia. However, the presence or absence of depression in bulimics does not indicate which patients will respond to antidepressant medication (Walsh 1986).

Hospitalization is often required. Silverman (1983a,b) has described the themes of hospital management. Teenagers in an urgent nutritional situation do not require a special eating disorders ward; most of them can be handled on a small and stable pediatric unit with one or more senior nurses who are experienced with anorexia. The other necessity is easy cooperation between pediatrician and psychiatrist. Such a hospital approach, combined with frequent work with patient and family, is powerful. It also contains many of the basics of behavior modification. Halmi (1985) has described the behavior elements that exist in many therapies not seen as behavioral. There is structure and limited visits with parents, and increased privileges depend on progress. The most powerful force in this is the intense separation anxiety. The desire to make contact with the parents and to go home becomes a major motivation for change.

The acute phase in an adolescent, with or without hospitalization, usually brings good short-term results. In a few there can be a resolution of their troubles, almost in the nature of a reorganization after a crisis. The great majority, however, will return to their families, friends, and schools to face the problems that led to the illness in the first place. It is here that long-term treatment to prevent the chronic course seen so often in adults becomes crucial. As with other problems, when there is any period of peace, both teenager and family will often lose interest. The renewal of the frantic food battles of the acute phase can bring a family back into treatment. Family sessions are then useful, especially if the teenager is recalcitrant. Some teenagers are quite unable to deal with one-to-one treatment but are able to participate if another family member is present. An eclectic approach is effective with a difficult teenager and family, but it must be utilized with flexibility and dogged perseverance. Therapy will need to swing between the individual and family approach and to be responsive to issues of different developmental levels.

Some adolescents have the capacity to handle a more intensive treatment and have families who are sympathetic to the recommendation of psychoanalysis. Mintz (1983a) described the analysis of an 18-year-old whose anorexia was severe. He felt that many such cases can be treated with minimal hospitalization. His views are thoughtful, and he supported them with a discussion of the analytic aspects of hospitalization (1983b). Much of the writing about intensive psychotherapy comes from analysts familiar with borderline pathology. Masterson (1978) and Sours (1980) used a developmental/Mahlerian and object relations theory approach. Self-psychology is well described by Rizzuto et al. (1981) and especially Goodsitt (1985). Its theory and treatment approach emphasizes repairing the damaged sense of self, avoidance interpretation, the awareness of subtle transference issues, and an emphatic commitment to understanding the patient's internal world. However, this approach should be done only by those fully trained in its use.

OBESITY

The "fear of being fat" or desire to avoid obesity is rampant not only in anorexia nervosa and bulimia, but in most of the population. Despite this, obesity continues to be a major health problem. Conventionally, obesity is defined as weighing 20 percent or more over standard weight (that weight given in height-weight tables) (Stunkard 1985). Practically, however, most clinicians go by appearance rather than weight or fat-fold measurements.

Estimates of the prevalence of obesity in children vary widely, due to differences in definition, measurement, and populations. A frequently quoted estimate is that 25 percent of American children are overweight (Forbes 1975). Estimates of childhood obesity have ranged from 10 to 40 percent in the U.S., 5 to 15 percent in Britain, 8 percent in West Germany, and 5 percent in Yugoslavia (LeBow 1984). The prevalence varies among ethnic groups and social classes, and in some populations obesity is considered a desirable status symbol. Goldblatt, Moore, and Stunkard (1965) found obesity to be six times more common in women of low rather than high socioeconomic status and a similar but less strong correlation in men. This correlation is also seen in children, although the very poorest tend to be the thinnest, while the poor have a high prevalence of obesity (LeBow 1984). However, this is only a tendency, and there is no accurate method of predicting which children from which families will be obese (LeBow 1984).

The etiology of obesity is still inadequately understood; many consider it to be multifactorially determined. The concept of a "set point" for weight has gained much support, with the theory that obesity results from a disruption of the caloric intake versus calories expended regulatory process (Stunkard 1985). Why this disturbance of regulation exists is the crucial question. Various models have been proposed, including an inherited tendency to obesity, "altered hedonism," increased fat cell size and number (see Hirsch and Leibel 1984), and faulty gastric perception (Coddington and Bruch 1970). Studies on the genetics of obesity have shown widely differing results, from heredity being much less important than environment (Hartz et al. 1977) to the opposite (Borjeson 1976 and Annest et al. 1983). A recent large-scale study of adoptees and their biological and adoptive parents done by Stunkard et al. (1986) has shown that genetic influences have the major role in determining obesity, and that the family environment alone has no apparent effect.

Environmental factors do influence the expression of this genetic vulnerability to obesity. These were once seen as being of primary etiological importance, but now may be seen as contributants. Assessment of the obese child should include a history of early feeding practices (reaction to baby's cries, over- or underfeeding), levels of activity (persistent physical inactivity), and food intake (type and amount—

notoriously underreported by obese children and their parents). Bruch (1973) found no psychiatric diagnoses nor psychodynamics specific to obese children or adolescents.

Endocrinological disturbances were, and to some extent still are, thought to be of primary importance in the etiology of obesity. In the 1930s, most obese children were evaluated for Frohlich syndrome (hypogonadotropic hypogonadism, diabetes insipidus, mental retardation) (Bruch 1973). However, actual primary endocrine disorders are rarely found in obesity; as most obese children are of normal height or even advanced in growth (tall, accelerated skeletal maturation, sometimes early puberty) (Bruch 1973), those children whose obesity is secondary to endocrine, metabolic, or chromosomal disorders are readily recognized by their below-average height, as well as the other manifestations of the particular disease. Charting a youngster's height and weight on a standard growth chart is clearly helpful to the clinician in making this assessment more precisely. Short obese children should be evaluated for hypothyroidism, Cushing syndrome, and pseudohypoparathyroidism, and for rarer syndromes such as those of Frohlich, Laurence-Moon-Biedl (retinitis pigmentosa, hypogenitalism, mental retardation, skull deformities, poly- and syndactyly) and Alstrom (retinitis pigmentosa, nerve deafness, diabetes mellitus).

The need for effective prevention and treatment of obesity seems obvious, but it has been questioned (see Wooley and Wooley 1984). 80 percent of obese children become obese adults, 36 percent of infants exceeding the ninetieth percentile of weight become overweight adults, and 30 percent of obese adults become obese during childhood and adolescence (Brownell 1984; Charney et al. 1976; Collipp 1980). The sequelae of obesity are numerous. Obesity is a risk for coronary artery disease, cerebrovascular disease, and hypertension; it results in hyperinsulinemia, hyperlipidemia, carbohydrate intolerance, and decreased growth hormone response. The more severely obese may develop Pickwickian syndrome, characterized by alveolar hypoventilation and hypoxic somnolence. Severe obesity is also characterized by adipocyte hypertrophy and hyperplasia (increase in both size and number of fat cells), whereas mild or moderate obesity has only adipocyte hypertrophy. Reduction of weight is associated with decrease in size, not number, of adipocytes, and there is some indication that weight loss is much more difficult if adipocyte hyperplasia is present, as the fat cells must then be reduced to below-normal size. Early intervention may curtail adipocyte hyperplasia (Brownell 1984), which may make later weight reduction more effective. Social sequelae are also prominent. Obese children suffer from discrimination and peer disapproval even from peers as young as 6 years, and they show poor self-image and body image disparagement (Brownell, 1984).

The results of the adaptive study by Stunkard et al. (1986) indicate that prevention and treatment may be more efficiently directed towards those with vulnerability to obesity. A multitude of treatment approaches to obese children has been attempted. Starvation, appetite suppressants (stimulants), nutritional counseling, and exercise regimens are conventional treatments, which result in limited weight loss (if any), high attrition, high relapse, and negative emotional effects (Brownell 1984;

Coates and Thoresen 1978). Programs for children and adolescents have been offered by such organizations as Weight Watchers and Overeaters Anonymous, but there is little in the literature about them or their effectiveness. Positive treatment results have been reported for intensive behavior modification programs, especially those that include parental involvement and treatment in schools. Such programs have been detailed by Brownell (1984) and LeBow (1984).

CONCLUSION

The assessment of the eating disorders in adolescence involves not just the relatively easy task of diagnosis but also touching the teenager's interior world so that therapeutic contact can be made and plans formed for redirection of the developmental flow. Although there can be fixed pictures and familiar refrains on first look, the diversity and complexity soon become apparent. The eating disorders are influenced by culture, family, individual personality, psychopathology, developmental experience, and biology, especially the effects of starvation. Accordingly, treatment recommendations need to be flexible and can include psychotherapy or psychoanalysis, behavior modification, family therapy, medication, and hospital treatment. This versatility is within the mainstream of child psychiatry assessment and treatment.

REFERENCES

Annest, J. L., et al. (1983). Familial aggregation of blood pressure and weight in adoptive families III. *Amer. J. Epidemiol.* 117(4):492–506.

Blos, D. (1967). The second individuation process of adolescence. *Psychoanal. Study Child* 22:162–86.

Borjeson, M. (1976). The etiology of obesity in children: A study of 101 twin pairs. *Acta Paediatr. Scan.* 65:279–87.

Brownell, K. D. (1984). New developments in the treatment of obese children and adolescents. In A. J. Stunkard and E. Stellar (Eds.). *Eating and Its Disorders.* New York: Raven Press.

Bruch, H. (1973). *Eating Disorders: Obesity, Anorexia Nervosa and the Person Within.* New York: Basic Books.

Cantwell, D. P., et al. (1977). Anorexia Nervosa: An affective disorder? *Arch. Gen. Psychiat.* 34:1087–93.

Casper, R. C., et al. (1980). Bulimia: Its incidence and clinical importance in patients with anorexia nervosa. *Arch. Gen. Psychiat.* 37:1030–35.

Charney, E., et al. (1976). Childhood antecedents of adult obesity: Do chubby infants become obese adults? *New Eng. J. Med.* 295(1):6–9.

Coates, T. J., and Thoresen, C. E. (1978). Treating obesity in children and adolescents: A review. *Amer. J. Public Health* 68(2):143–51.

Coddington, R. D., and Bruch, H. (1970). Gastric perceptivity in normal, obese, and schizophrenic subjects. *Psychosomatics* 11:571–79.

Collipp, P. (1980). Obesity in childhood. In A. J. Stunkard (Ed.). *Obesity*. Philadelphia: Saunders.

Crisp, A. H. (1980). *Anorexia Nervosa—Let Me Be Me*. New York: Plenum.

Epling, W. F., Pierce, W. D., and Stefan, L. (1983). A theory of activity-based anorexia. *Intl. J. Eating Disorders* 3:27–46.

Forbes, G. B. (1975). Prevalence of obesity in childhood. In G. H. Bray (Ed.). *Obesity in Perspective*, Vol. 2. (DHEW Publ. No. (NIH) 75–708). Washington, D.C.: U.S. Government Printing Office.

Garfinkel, P. E., and Garner, D. M. (1982). *Anorexia Nervosa: A Multi-dimensional Perspective*. New York: Brunner/Mazel.

———, Moldofsky, H., and Garner, D. (1980). The heterogeneity of anorexia nervosa: Bulimia subgroup. *Arch. Gen. Psychiat.* 37:1035–40.

Garner, D. M., and Bemis, K. M. (1982). A cognitive-behavioral approach to anorexia nervosa. *Cog. Ther. Res.* 6:123–50.

———, Garfinkel, P., and Olmstead, M. P. (1983a). An overview of sociocultural factors in the development of anorexia nervosa. In P. Darby et al. (Eds.). *Anorexia Nervosa: Recent Developments in Research*. New York: Alan R. Liss, pp. 65–82.

———, Olmstead, M. P., and Garfinkel, P. (1983b). Does anorexia nervosa occur on a continuum? *Int. J. Eating Disorders* 2:11–19.

———, Olmstead, M. P., and Garfinkel, P. (1985). Similarities among bulimic groups selected by different weight and weight histories. *J. Psychiat. Res.* 19:129–34.

Goodsitt, A. (1985). Self-psychology and the treatment of anorexia nervosa. In D. M. Garner and P. E. Garfinkel (Eds.). *Handbook of Psychotherapy for Anorexia Nervosa and Bulimia*. New York: The Guilford Press.

Goldblatt, P. B., Moore, M. E., and Stunkard, A. J. (1965). Social factors in obesity. *J. Amer. Med. Assoc.* 192(12):97–102.

Halmi, K. A. (1974). Anorexia nervosa: Demographic and clinical features in 94 cases. *Psychosom. Med.* 36:18–24.

———. (1985). Behavioral management for anorexia nervosa. In D. M. Garner and P. E. Garfinkel (Eds.). *Handbook of Psychotherapy for Anorexia Nervosa and Bulimia*. New York: The Guilford Press.

Hartz, A., Geifer, E., and Rimm, A. A. (1977). Relative importance of the effect of family environment and heredity on obesity. *Ann. Hum. Genet.* 41:185–93.

Hirsch, J., and Liebel, R. L. (1984). What constitutes a sufficient psychobiologic explanation for obesity? In A. J. Stunkard and E. Stellar (Eds.). *Eating and Its Disorders*. New York: Raven Press.

Keys, A., et al. (1950). *The Biology of Human Starvation*. Minneapolis: University of Minnesota Press.

LeBow, M. D. (1984). *Child Obesity: A New Frontier of Behavior Therapy*. New York: Springer.

Masterson, J. F. (1978). The borderline adolescent: An object relations view. In S. C. Feinstein and P. L. Giovacchini (Eds.). *Adolescent Psychiatry*, VI.

Mintz, I. L. (1983a). An analytic approach to hospital and nursing care. In C. P. Wilson, C. C. Hogan, and I. L. Mintz (Eds.). *The Fear of Being Fat*. New York: Aronson.

———, (1983b). Psychoanalytic therapy of severe anorexia: The case of Jeanette. In C. P. Wilson, C. C. Hogan, and I. L. Mintz (Eds.). *The Fear of Being Fat*. New York: Aronson.

Minuchin, S., Rosman, B., and Baler, L. (1978). *Psychosomatic Families: Anorexia Nervosa in Context*. Cambridge: Harvard University Press.

Mogul, S. L. (1980). Asceticism in adolescence and anorexia nervosa. *The Psychoanalytic Study of the Child*, Vol. 35. New Haven: Yale University Press, pp. 155–75.

Morgan, H. E., and Russell, G. F. (1975). Value of family background in clinical features as predictors of long-term outcome in anorexia nervosa: Four-year follow-up study of 41 patients. *Psychol. Med.* 5:355–71.

Orbach, S. (1985). Accepting the symptom: A feminist psychoanalytic treatment of anorexia nervosa. In D. M. Garner and P. E. Garfinkel (Eds.). *Handbook of Psychotherapy for Anorexia Nervosa and Bulimia*. New York: The Guilford Press.

Rizzuto, A., Peterson, R. K., and Reed, M. (1981). The pathological sense of self in anorexia nervosa. *Psychiat. Clin. N. Amer.* 4(3).

Rollins, N., and Piazza, E. (1978). Diagnosis of anorexia nervosa: A critical reappraisal. *J. Amer. Acad. Child Psychiat.* 17:126–37.

Selvini-Palazzoli, M. (1974). *Self-Starvation*. New York: Aronson.

Silverman, J. A. (1983a). Anorexia nervosa: Clinical and metabolic observations. *Int'l. J. Eating Disorders* 2:159–66.

———. (1983b). Medical consequences of starvation: The malnutrition of anorexia nervosa: Caveat medicus. In P. Darby et al. (Eds.). *Anorexia Nervosa: Recent Developments in Research*. New York: Alan R. Liss, pp. 239–99.

Sours, J. A. (1980). *Starving to Death in a Sea of Objects*. New York: Aronson.

Stunkard, A. J. (1985). Obesity. In H. I. Kaplan and B. J. Sadock (Eds.). *Comprehensive Textbook of Psychiatry*, Vol. 2. Baltimore: Williams and Wilkins.

———, et al. (1986). An adoption study of human obesity. *New Eng. J. Med.* 314(4):193–98.

Vagenakis, A. G. (1977). Thyroid hormone metabolism in prolonged experimental starvation in man. In R. A. Vigersky (Ed.). *Anorexia Nervosa*. New York: Raven Press, pp. 243–53.

Walsh, B. T., et al. (1985). Bulimia and depression. *Psychosom. Med.* 47:123–30.

———. (1986). Pharmacotherapy of eating disorders. In B. F. Blinde (Ed.). *Modern Concepts of the Eating Disorders*.

Wilson, C. P. (1983). The family psychological profile and its therapeutic implications. In C. P. Wilson, C. C. Hogan, and I. L. Mintz (Eds.). *The Fear of Being Fat*. New York: Aronson.

———, and Mintz, I. (1982). Abstaining and bulemic anorexics. *Primary Care* 9:517–30.

Winokur, A., March, V., and Mendels, J. (1980). Primary affective disorder in relatives of patients with anorexia nervosa. *Amer. J. Psychiat.* 137:695–98.

Wooley, S. C., and Wooley, O. W. (1984). Should obesity be treated at all? In A. J. Stunkard and E. Stellar (Eds.). *Eating and Its Disorders*. New York: Raven Press.

Yates, A., Leehey, K., and Shisslak, C. M. (1983). Running: An analog of anorexia? *New Engl. J. Med.* 308:251–55.

46

DIVORCE-SPECIFIC ASSESSMENT OF FAMILIES

Julia M. Lewis and Judith S. Wallerstein

OVERVIEW OF DIVORCE

The dramatic increase of divorce in this country within the last quarter-century has been well documented and widely recognized as a phenomenon of critical social importance. United States Census reports indicate that divorce rates have tripled since 1960 and doubled from 1970 levels (U.S. Bureau of Census 1982). Glick and Norton (1970) projected that at the current divorce levels 40 percent of existing marriages will end in divorce. Hetherington (1979) predicted that 40 to 50 percent of children born in the 1970s will experience divorce, and of these, 25 percent will experience a second divorce before they are eighteen (Guidubaldi et al. 1983). One result of these changes in family structure is that a generation of children have or will have experienced not only the disruptions or losses of significant parenting figures, but also will have spent some portion of their growing years in households characterized by the continual change and instability that divorce often brings in its wake (Wallerstein 1983a).

At issue is not only the psychological status of the children at the time of the marital breakup, but also the long-term psychological and social consequences of growing up in these environments. At the very least, these children may develop conceptions of what is expectable from human relationships that are different from those of their counterparts who are raised in intact families.

In contrast to the widespread community concern and media interest in divorce, recognition of the ramifying clinical implications of these changes within the family has been a slow process. Knowledge of the effects of divorce has rarely been included in professional training programs, despite the fact that child psychiatrists and psychotherapists face caseloads in hospitals, clinics, and private offices that are made up of 50 to 75 percent children of divorce—numbers disproportionate to the incidence of divorce in the general population (Kalter 1977). The number of adult patients who have experienced parental divorce in their childhoods is probably high, although this has not been systematically documented.

There are many indications that the divorce experience occupies a central, significant emotional place in the psyche of those individuals who have experienced the divorce of their parents during childhood or adolescence. Kulka and Weingarten (1979) suggested that experiencing parental divorce may serve as an organizing psychological framework that can influence an individual's stance, expectations, and manner of responding to adult life roles. In a long-term study of children and adolescents, Wallerstein (1984) described their vivid, detailed memories of events surrounding parental separation, and the endurance of the acute suffering in young adults ten years after the divorce of their parents. She suggested that the experience of parental divorce in childhood may lead to the formation of a lasting identity as a "child of divorce," which colors mood and attitude and has an enduring influence on subsequent relationships and social roles.

COMMON CLINICAL CONSEQUENCES OF DIVORCE

Although divorce resembles other psychological trauma in its disequilibrating impact on children and adults, it presents very particular challenges that differ from other stressful or crisis situations.

As the pressures associated with divorce are often likened to the more familiar stresses associated with the death of a parent, an examination of some of the common divorce stressors in comparison to the processes involved in death and mourning may highlight the child's experience during and after the marital breakdown. Wallerstein has distinguished the psychological consequences of divorce from those of bereavement along several dimensions (1983b).

Loss by death is final; loss by divorce is inconclusive. While children who have experienced the death of a parent often deny their loss and create elaborate fantasies to bolster their denial, the absolute nature of the event, reinforced by the behavior of the other people involved, usually induces a mourning process that culminates in acceptance and resolution. In divorce, the departing parent is usually partially lost and partially mourned, then returns to be reunited with the child, only to be lost again. Whether this process takes place within a regular visiting relationship or is kept alive through sporadic contact, or whether it is prolonged by an ambivalent emotional attachment of the other parent, the divorced child continually faces loss without the comfort of resolution. The intermittent nature of contact, often accompanied by a sense of longing and need, creates fertile ground for the development of long-lasting and unrealistic fantasies of reunification haunted by the apprehension of disappointment and the sense that relationships are fleeting. The child's perception of himself as unsatisfactory or unworthy of love and commitment is not an unusual outcome.

Although it is common "divorce lore" that children assume responsibility for the divorce, we have not found that children generally believe that divorce is their fault.

Actually, because divorce, unlike death, is a voluntary decision on the part of one or both parents, the responsibility for the divorce (and for the suffering involved) can be pinpointed (Wallerstein 1983b). Children are often acutely aware of the facts and events leading to the marital rupture. In many instances they have witnessed, or overheard, or have been party to marital difficulties; in the instance of death, they are more likely to have been shielded. In bereavement, the child is united with other family members in experiencing hurt and sorrow at the loss. In divorce, adults and siblings are likely to take contradictory stands, and children are subjected to highly conflicting demands on their feelings and loyalties. Younger children often ascribe blame for the divorce to the parent who retains physical possession of the household. This parent, most often the mother, is perceived as very powerful and dangerous, because she is seen by the child as having ousted the father.

Regardless of how children perceive the situation, whether complexly or concretely, they are aware that their pain has been caused by those very parents who are responsible for their protection and care. This sets up an almost intolerable singular psychological paradox, as the same parent who becomes the object of anger and anguish, of fear, anxiety, and uncertainty, is often the sole source of comfort for the child. Thus the child faces the rupture of the family without the help of the parents, further burdened by the knowledge that he cannot expect relief or comfort from the parents because they indeed are the source of the distress.

THE COURSE OF DIVORCE

Divorce is no longer conceptualized as a single event in which one parent leaves and sets up a separate household. Rather, divorce involves a complex process in which multiple and overlapping changes and events occur. An extraordinary number of life changes involving children follow the marital rupture. A child facing divorce must often live through a series of stressful experiences, each of which, together with their cumulative effect, may require profound cognitive and psychological reorganization.

Divorce involves a long-lasting period of disequilibrium, characterized by successive but overlapping stages. During the initial acute phase of divorce, adults and children experience inner crisis and external instability. This acute period has been observed to last, on an average, from six months to over one year from the decisive separation (Wallerstein and Kelly 1980). Hetherington et al. (1976) found the highest level of disorganization in the homes of both mothers and fathers at one year after separation. The next phase, which Wallerstein labeled the "transitional" phase, is characterized by less acute emotional upheaval, as parents attempt to begin restructuring their lives. Hetherington similarly described such coping efforts of the parents as characteristic of this second phase (Hetherington et al. 1982). For the child, this second phase may involve new stresses as parents begin dating, return or start to work, move the household, or demand new responsibilities and roles from the children. Wallerstein and Kelly (1980) found that it took women an average of three to three and one-half years and men two to two and one-half years after separation to reestablish a relatively stable postdivorce living situation. For a preschool child, well over one-half of his lifetime may be lived in such an environment.

Furthermore, the relatively stable plateau may be only one more phase in a continuing pattern of dissolving and reorganizing relationships and households. Hunter and Schuman (1980) described the lifestyle of such "chronically reconstituting" families as involving a series of recombined households interspersed with periods of single parenting.

Many researchers emphasize the individual range of response to the same event (Caplan 1981; Rutter 1971; Hetherington and Camara 1984). The degree of felt stress experienced from an event or situation depends on the individual's perception of the level of threat involved. Since it is well known that the perception of an event as threatening depends on many factors, including the individual's past history and, for a child, his developmental level and capabilities, a child's reaction to an event or situation may not coincide with that of an adult. Many of the practical stresses associated with divorce, such as moving and disruption in household routine, may be mildly stressful to the parent, but may be viewed by a child, particularly a young child, with terror. Assessing the degree of practical or concrete changes in the household is crucial in attempting to understand a child's experience. The child's response to change and instability may be mediated but not governed by the parent's response and emotional reaction to the same changes (Wallerstein and Kelly 1980).

Stolberg and Anker (1983) examined children's perceptions and evaluations of consequences of increased environmental change. Increased change in homes of divorced children was associated with more childhood pathology, while increased change in the homes of children of intact families was associated with lower levels of childhood behavioral pathology, especially in younger children (ages 5 to 9). There is ample evidence to support their hypothesis that change in divorced families reflects more chaos and decreased economic and emotional stability, while change in intact families is associated with improved family conditions. While older children may cognitively understand such distinctions, the difference in young children's reactions may be understood largely through the reactions of their parents.

The downward economic mobility of divorced families, particularly those headed by mothers, is widely recognized (Wallerstein and Kelly 1980; Hetherington et al. 1982; Guidubaldi et al. 1983; Weitzman 1985). The practical consequences of a sudden decrease in income are obvious and can be extremely threatening for children: mother returning or starting to work, and the family perhaps moving to another home with the consequent loss of familiar neighborhood friends and the necessary adjustments to new schools, new caregivers, new furniture, new routines, and so on. An abrupt economic decline is also associated with feelings of deprivation, which for many families may be quite real. Preliminary reports from the ten-year follow-up of Wallerstein's Children of Divorce study indicate that these feelings may last into adulthood, particularly in the surprisingly high number of divorced families were children of affluent fathers are not supported educationally beyond 18 years of age (Wallerstein and Corbin 1984), and in families where a parent's stepchildren or the children born into the parent's second or current marriage enjoy a higher standard of living than do the children from the original marriage.

Guidubaldi et al. (1983) found that single parenthood, rather than socioeconomic status, was most highly predictive of lower academic, personal, and social competence in divorced children. Hetherington et al. (1978) and Wallerstein and Kelly (1980) painted vivid pictures of the ambiance of homes in which one parent abruptly assumes the economic, disciplinary, and psychological responsibilities formerly shared by two parents. These responsibilities are often assumed at a time when the parent is emotionally depleted and faced with severely restricted social and economic support. For all children, but particularly for young children, the juggling of their daily routines by overburdened, overwrought parents is extremely frightening.

CHANGES IN THE PARENTS

During the early postdivorce years, the greatest disruption in children's lives is caused as much by the abrupt changes in emotional state, behaviors, and attitudes of the parents as by the marital separation (Wallerstein and Kelly 1980). Faced with psychological loss and disappointment, with the absence of structure of the marriage, and with the often unanticipated hardships and demands of being single, formerly stable adults react in ways that could not be predicted from their predivorce behavior. Explosions of rage, decreased reality testing, depression, and sexual acting out are not uncommon. Increased alcohol and drug intake, sleep disruption, and weight fluctuations are prevalent. Associated with these abrupt and, for children, frighteningly incomprehensible changes, is a diminution in the quality of parenting. Physical caregiving becomes more erratic and less conscientious. Disciplinary attitudes and practices change and are often widely discrepant between parents.

The place and status of children in the family and in the psychological orbit of the parents often shifts. Pleasure in their children sometimes decreases when the locus of the children's existence and care—the marital partnership—disintegrates. Instead of being a validation and mutual accomplishment of the marriage, the presence of the children often becomes a burden, a source of guilt, and a painful reminder of the failed marriage (Wallerstein 1985). At the same time, children become needed and valued sources of comfort and support to depleted parents. Children willingly try, often far beyond their emotional capabilities, to shore up and care for their parents. They share the same bed with the troubled parent. They are the recipients of sorrows, angers, and confidences, as they try to assume new and advanced household responsibilities. In his article entitled "Growing Up a Little Faster" (1979), Weiss acknowledged that this shouldering of responsibility on the part of the child may be valuable for the parent and for the functioning of the household, but he questioned the toll on the child. Younger children, whose need for parental control and nurturance is profound, may adapt superficially while continuing to experience strong underlying needs, and they may erect powerful defenses against the expression of these needs.

In assessing the family environment, it is critical to consider the time span of the divorce process. The turmoil may endure for long periods of time. Hetherington et al. (1982) found the most marked changes in parental mood, self-esteem, and sexual and dating behavior at one year postdivorce. Wallerstein and Kelly (1980) found unrelenting anger toward the ex-spouse and continuing stressful parent-child relationships in significant numbers of families in their sample at five years postdivorce. Preliminary findings from the ten-year follow-up of the same sample indicate that for many parents, anger, bitterness, guilt, and loneliness persist. Their children, by now nearly adults, are still acutely aware of these feelings in themselves and in their parents.

Changes in the Father-Child Relationship

Although father custody and shared custody have received considerable publicity recently, the incidence of children who live primarily with their fathers or in joint physical custody remains relatively low (Glick and Norton 1979). Fathers are often lost to their children or visit them erratically. One of the most striking and clinically relevant findings of the Wallerstein and Kelly (1980) study was that the quality of the postdivorce father-child relationship could not be predicted from the predivorce relationship. Children who had had loving and involved fathers suffered when these fathers became distant and uninvolved after the separation. Conversely, father-child contact actually increased and became closer after the divorce in some families where the father had previously been a relatively unavailable parent. Although many factors can be seen to influence these patterns, such as the psychological health of each parent, the degree of conflict surrounding visiting, the psychological and economic circumstances of the separation and divorce, and the age and attitude of the child, the postdivorce relationship between father and child is rarely continuous with the preseparation relationship. With some exceptions, both children and fathers feel the loss of everyday contact and are aware of a psychological and physical void that each had previously filled for the other.

Wallerstein and Kelly (1980) argued that the visiting relationship is inherently unsatisfying and artificial as compared with the prior richness, structure, and meaning of the father-child bond within the intact family. After the separation, children are often bewildered and unsatisfied with their contact as well as unsettled and upset in the new residence. Fathers may feel incompetent to care for their children and at loose ends as to how to engage and entertain them. Hetherington et al. (1976) delineated significant changes in the habits and attitudes of fathers with their children in the two years following divorce. The entire psychological and physical context of the relationship with the father is transformed within the postdivorce family. This presents a serious and puzzling set of issues to the child.

The lasting psychological importance of the father, the emotional intensity of feelings associated with him, is one of the early striking impressions from the ten-year follow-up of Wallerstein's families. Regardless of the amount of actual contact—and even in families where children had no contact with their fathers for years—there existed a vivid, ongoing, often highly ambivalent, cathected bond with the father. Often these psychological relationships were largely built on fantasy and colored by disappointment and feelings of rejection. But they were still very alive at ten years postdivorce, exercising important influences on the children.

Diminished Social Support

There are social rituals and supports for people experiencing a death in the family; there are few if any for divorce. The ceremonies attendant upon death emphasize the universal nature of this experience, and by providing historical, cultural, social, and spiritual contexts, they offer comfort. Death is usually characterized by a coming together of family and an increase in social supports. The bereaved are nurtured with compassion. Children who have sustained a loss receive sympathetic attention from adults and sometimes achieve special status among their peers for having passed through such a tremendous and uncommon experience.

Divorce is attended by no ceremonies. Families going through divorce often experience a falling away of supports as the nuclear family is dissolved. The extended family may in fact retreat. Certainly, social acquaintances back away from an embarrassing and highly charged situation. Although divorced adults can and do talk with friends who have gone through the experience, the divorced child's isolation is striking. School aged children and adolescents are keenly aware that, although it is common, divorce is neither universal nor socially desirable. Thus, they rarely talk to other children or adults about their experience (Wallerstein and Kelly 1980). The people usually available for comfort and reassurance are, as we have already noted, the very parents who are perceived to have caused the child's present suffering. In sum, children in a divorcing situation are likely to have less available support than do children who are undergoing other life crises.

CHILDREN'S INITIAL REACTIONS TO DIVORCE

We turn next to a consideration of expectable responses of children in general, and as manifested at each developmental level.

Universal Responses to Divorce

The overwhelming majority of children do not welcome divorce and react negatively to it. Although Hetherington et al. (1982) have shown that children may be better off in a stable single parent household than in a family with a sustained but conflicted marriage, children clearly do not think so (Wallerstein and Kelly 1980). A marriage that may be damaging to the adults involved can still provide a framework for children that fulfills their psychological and physical needs. Wallerstein and Kelly (1980) pointed out that the parenting system that includes a structure for caregiving and appropriate close parent-child relationships can remain relatively free from conflict even within extremely deprived, violent marriages. Children's reactions at nearly all ages to the breakup of this system are most succinctly conceptualized as being egocentric. The loss of the intact family for the child involves loss of a host of familiar and psychologically necessary elements, including bonds and attachments, figures for identification, stable routines, a predictable environment, an identity involving "mother," "father," "home," and "family," as well as comfortable future expectations. Children of divorce face these losses in the present along with a future that is unknown and terrifying.

Children of all ages commonly react to divorce with fear and anger, which leads to a highly aroused, anxious state. How these feelings are manifested, defended, and later mastered involves factors that include age at the marital rupture, sex of the child, the preexisting psychological functioning of child and parents, and the support available within and outside the family.

Preschool Children

Divorce can threaten each of the developmental achievements that a young child has so rapidly and tenuously accomplished in the early years. The divorce environment is perceived as unreliable and disordered. The very relationships that nurtured physical growth and psychological and social development are suddenly rendered untrustworthy, and in some cases they disappear entirely. The young child has not developed the capacity to comprehend cognitively marital rupture and has neither the psychological resources to cope nor the social skills to seek help. When asked how they prepared their young children for the separation or divorce, parents commonly respond that they did not prepare them, that the children were too young to understand. Thus, the very young children with the most limited intellectual and emotional capacity are often plunged into a frightening and confusing divorce situation with little or no warning, preparation, or help.

Marital breakdown creates fear, confusion, and high anxiety for the young child. We commonly see in their play overwhelming and vivid fantasies of being abandoned in a dangerous world inhabited by hungry, sharp-toothed monsters and angry, assaultive adults. The intense anxiety often results in massive ego regression. Recent achievements such as toilet training, reciprocal play, or feeding oneself are forgotten as the anxiety forces a retreat into babylike, insecure, and frightened forms of behavior. Out of their anxiety, young children become clinging, irritable, and fearful of separation. Often the most regressed behaviors occur when the overburdened parent returns from work, or when the child is put to bed, for the child has been overwhelmed with relief at the "lost" parent's reappearance and then filled with anxiety at the prospect of losing her, again, at bedtime.

The much more complicated and unpredictable conditions in the child's new life, now often containing two households, new schedules, new caregivers, and longer distances, may be an overwhelming burden on young children already reeling from multiple changes, and may force further regression. When faced with the normal demands of a postseparation environment, there are very few children in this age range who are not at some point symptomatic. Children may exhibit acute regression in toilet training, in feeding habits, and in reversion to babyish forms of language. Increased irritability, whining, crying, and sleep problems usually accompany general fearfulness, separation anxiety, and cognitive confusion. An escalation in aggressive behaviors and tantrums is also quite common (Wallerstein and Kelly 1975).

Although regression can offer temporary relief to the suffering child, a relevant assessment issue is the determination of the pervasiveness and time span of the regression. In some children the regression may consolidate. Thus, rather than a temporary sanctuary, the regression may be associated with long-standing developmental disturbance.

Latency Children

Divorce threatens the latency age child's outward strivings toward independence and cathexis of the worlds of school and play, because the child's attention becomes riveted on the events happening within the family. The family structure no longer forms a secure base from which the child forays into the world. Their somewhat greater ability to understand is both an asset and a liability to children in latency years. While intellectually and socially more sophisticated than preschool children, latency children are still too young to obtain for themselves sustained support outside the family circle. Latency children are more liable to be enlisted as an ally by one parent against the other.

Wallerstein and Kelly (1980) differentiated responses of latency children aged 6 to 8 from those in the 9- to 12-year-old group. The predominant response of the younger children was open and pervasive sadness (Kelly and Wallerstein 1976). Their feelings of grief were overwhelming, and ordinary defenses seemed temporarily ineffective in allaying anxiety and providing comfort. Their sadness was consciously connected to their longing for the father; it seemed as well a reaction to the loss of the parental unit at a time when drives and identifications were solidifying. High anxiety and sorrow over the loss of the father, together with anger and feelings of fear towards the mother, were especially characteristic of boys at this age. Powerful fantasies of reconciliation were common in this age group.

Older latency children showed less open sorrow and more anger. Wallerstein wrote of a "layering of response" as characteristic of this age group. While more superficially controlled and less obviously overwhelmed by their feelings, they felt intense underlying anger and were the most vulnerable of any age group to having this anger channelled into vendettas by equally angry parents.

A striking incidence of depressive fantasies, thoughts, and ideation appears in this age group, particularly among the boys. Obsessive thoughts, preoccupation with symbols of death, and feelings of emptiness are not uncommonly encountered in the child's play or in response to gentle inquiry. The overwhelming sadness, the guilt produced by anger towards the parents, and the limited ability to use outside resources defensively often induce feelings of despair together with suicidal ideation that are rarely expressed openly without encouragement by the adult. These reactions may appear in children who had no previous history of depression or psychopathology.

Adolescents

The divorce experience intersects with the developmental process and tasks of adolescence. Although the adolescent is capable cognitively and emotionally of more sophisticated understanding and is able to use outside supports, he is also more vulnerable to temporary or permanent psychological derailment. Like their younger counterparts, adolescents view the divorce as an unwelcome event and react with anxiety, sorrow, and anger, and intense feelings of betrayal, shame, and outrage. The erratic, often regressed behavior of the parents can precipitate a panic as the adolescent's own tenuous sexual maturity and early adult social experimentation are severely threatened. Adolescents typically respond with rage, embarrassment, and moral outrage to the actions of their parents. The emergence of the parents as sexual beings often evokes sexual fantasies in their children, who are in the process of decathecting their intense libidinal attachments to the parents. The loosening of external limits and rules that occurs in many postdivorce households makes containment and control more difficult and may even promote a tendency to act out, especially in adolescents who have shaky internal controls.

The studies of Hetherington et al. (1982) and Wallerstein and Kelly (1974) cite radical changes in the perceptions of parents as one of the unique hazards that divorce poses for adolescents. Rather than a gradual process of disengagement and disillusionment, the divorce provokes rapid shifts in the parent-child relationship. The abruptness of these changes can leave the adolescent with a sense of not having the supportive environment that he needs.

Adolescents are especially worried about their future. The termination of their parents' long marriage precipitates anxiety about commitment and changes in expectations regarding relationships and their own future marriage prospects. Although as likely as their younger counterparts to suffer loyalty conflicts and to be recruited as allies by parents, adolescents typically show more ability to cope emotionally with these issues by disengaging and withdrawing into activities outside the arena of their parents' conflict.

Those adolescents who are not able to maintain distance from the parental conflict seem to be at particular risk, for remaining embroiled in the divorce battles causes them to avoid the normal activities with peers necessary for the formation of early adult social skills and attitudes. Among our recent findings was a subgroup of young adolescents, several of whom not only failed to disengage from the parental battles, but who became physically violent towards one parent (Springer and Wallerstein 1983). These young adolescents had parents who had been physically abusive to each other. After the separation, the youngster appeared to move into the role of the abusive parent who had left the home. Some of these children engaged in direct attacks on their parent and seemed dangerously out of control.

CRITICAL FACTORS IN LONG-TERM PROGNOSIS

We turn next to a consideration of some factors which research has shown to be directly associated with longer-term outcome. Wallerstein and Kelly's five-year follow-up of their Children of Divorce sample and preliminary findings from the Wallerstein ten-year follow-up of the same sample constitute the primary source for this information.

Sex of the Child

Findings from divorce research and from research on reactions to stress in general are that boys are more vulnerable to stress. Searching for the mechanism through which sex differences to stress may operate, Rutter (1970) tentatively concluded that the data indicate that males are more susceptible to physical and biological stress, and this vulnerability may lead to less resistance to psychological stress. Hetherington et al. (1982) tracked a possible source of divorced boys' difficulties to escalating cycles of coercion and poor control between custodial mothers and their sons, which lead in turn to ineffective aggressive behavior, peer problems, and poor social skills in boys at two years postdivorce.

Santrock et al. (1982) also examined the hazards involved in custodial mother-son relationships. Like Hetherington, they found custodial mothers were more ineffective than custodial fathers in controlling boys, who showed more demanding and aggressive behavior than did girls. Their general findings revealed that the boys in father custody had higher levels of social competence than those in mother custody. Although these tentative findings may have merit, the social reality is that most children from divorced families remain in the primary care of their mothers postdivorce.

While Wallerstein and Kelly (1980) found few sex differences in acute reactions to the separation, they concluded, like Hetherington, that by eighteen months postdivorce, boys appeared significantly worse off. For boys, the mediating effects of the quality of the mother-son relationships and the degree of felt loss of the father were important. By five years postdivorce, sex differences had diminished as critical to outcome; relationship to the father still emerged as important to both sexes, but particularly to boys.

Factors in the Constitution and History of Children

Children with constitutional vulnerabilities and/or histories of multiple stresses tended to be less resistant and less able to effectively cope with stresses associated with divorce (Rutter 1971). Children with more difficult temperaments—those who from infancy were harder to soothe, made transitions slowly, adjusted to change with suspicion—were found to be more susceptible to stress. Likewise, children whose lives had contained multiple previous stressful situations, such as the long illness of a parent, prolonged separations, or chronic instability, were less able to master successfully divorce-related stresses. Rutter (1971) as well as Wallerstein and Kelly (1980) emphasized that for children most environmental stress acts through the mediating influence of parent-child interactions. These relationships and interactions are in turn affected by the sex, temperament, and coping ability of the child.

In interviewing children, the single most distressing component of the dissolving family and of the postdivorce family situation referred to is the degree of conflict between the parents. The extent of conflict is directly related to the ability of the parents to resolve their feelings for each other. Much to the continuing anguish of children, to the astonishment of divorcing adults, and to the surprise of divorce researchers, this is a formidable task. Although divorce is seen as a solution—a way out of an unhappy marriage—we found at five years postdivorce, and now at ten years, that anger lasts. At ten years postdivorce, 40 percent of the mothers and 30 percent of the fathers maintained high degrees of anger and bitterness towards each other, which were rooted in apparently still festering feelings of having been rejected and wronged. More significantly, from the children's standpoint, these intense angers were often not kept private but intruded upon the lives of the children through ongoing competition for loyalty and difficulties over contact with the other parent.

This persistence of anger and lack of resolution resulted in the maintenance of highly conflicted, ambivalent emotional ties to the ex-spouse. This is especially troubling given the considerable body of research findings linking poor child outcome with disturbed, conflicted parent relationships. In his studies of delinquency and family factors, Rutter (1970, 1971) concluded that the long-term effects of parent-child separation must be examined through the nature of the separation experience. He found separation per se was not predictive of delinquency or neurosis. Only when separation was accompanied by discord and disturbance and especially when this lasted over time was the outcome of children adversely affected. At five years postdivorce in Wallerstein and Kelly's sample, a central factor related to outcome in the children was the "failure of the divorce." When the parents maintained ongoing bitterness and were unable to decrease or to cease fighting, the children experienced a chronic state of stress and distress and were unable to master the divorce.

Quality of Postdivorce Environment

The reliability and predictability of the custodial home, the degree (or child's perceived degree mediated through the parent's attitude) of economic stability, and the level of parenting are all components of the quality of the child's life. Overall, those families who were able most quickly to restabilize their households, including the patterns of parenting and the general structure of their caregiving, were more likely to contain children who were able to cope most successfully with divorce. It is important in the assessment of these factors to determine the capacity of the adults to recover or at least to reorganize in the face of their own psychological distress, in order to stabilize caregiving functions for the children. Parents who developed or maintained a chronically embittered outlook toward the other parent and toward the unfairness of the world in general, communicated their sense of deprivation and hopelessness to their children directly, as well as through their continued inability to build and maintain a relatively stable household.

Of central importance in the long-term outcome of all children was the quality of their relationships with their parents. The appropriateness, closeness, and dependability of the child's relationship with the custodial parent was the single most important ingredient in the determination of outcome at five years postdivorce. Distortion in parent-child relationships under severe stress in the short-term were not necessarily predictive of the ability of the parent eventually to resume more appropriate behavior and stance toward the children over time. Both Hetherington et al. (1982) and Wallerstein and Kelly (1980) noted the deterioration and increasing inappropriateness of parent-child bonds in the acute phase of divorce. Both also noted the improvement in these relationships over time. When parents, particularly custodial parents, were not able to recover their equilibrium and maintained inappropriate and severely demanding relationships with their children, the children deteriorated over time. The degree to which parents were able to keep their children outside of and separate from the parents' ego orbits appears to be the key element to resumption of adequate parenting and parent-child relationships. Parents who were able to maintain appropriate generational boundaries, to make distinctions between their needs and their children's needs, to recognize and empathize with a child's point of view, and to keep the child from becoming enmeshed in adult conflicts, were successful with their children over time.

Although the presence of these elements was critical in the custodial mother-child relationship, the importance of a good father-child relationship was also predictive of good outcome for all children, especially for boys. The assessment of the value and desirability of contact with the noncustodial parent is complicated, however. Frequency of contact alone is not necessarily indicative of a quality relationship that benefits the child. Just as for the custodial parent, the visiting parent's psychological status and ability to maintain an appropriate interaction with the child influences the overall quality of their relationship. Frequent contact with a psychologically ill parent, which exposes the child to repeated upsetting incidents and unhealthy conditions, may result in more longer-term damage, even though the child may not feel rejected by or deprived of the presence of the parent. Contact that frequently exposes the child to painful arguments between the parents, to interrogations that induce guilt, and to chronic confusion due to inconsistent attitudes and loyalty conflicts, is more likely to result in poorer adjustment (Hetherington et al. 1976). Thus, the assessment of the relationship with both parents as it changes under severe stress, and for its potential for longer-term functioning, involves examining multiple and interacting elements rather than a single relationship at a single point in time.

THE METHOD OF ASSESSMENT

In assessing children of divorce, we have encountered specific problems different from those found in other clinical groups. Assessment of children during the process of divorce occurs when the family is in crisis and when far-reaching decisions must be made quickly. The clinician often does not have the requisite time with each family member or with the various combinations of family members in order to make a thoughtful diagnosis. Moreover, the data to be observed are often clouded. The lability of ego organization in childhood makes assessment of status during an acute crisis difficult. Additionally, Wallerstein and Kelly (1980) have found that a child's long-term outcome could not be predicted by the child's initial reactions to the divorce crisis. Children with severe psychological distress and notable behavioral reactions at the time of the separation were just as likely to cope well eventually as those who displayed few initial symptoms. Thus, the severity of a child's initial response to the divorce crisis is probably not indicative of the child's overall stability or level of functioning. A child's symptomatic behavior in a divorce situation is more appropriately viewed as stemming from the child's felt perception of the level of threat to his integrity presented by the family crisis, rather than as reflecting customary psychological functioning.

The presence of preexisting psychopathology in children is likely to create a condition of special vulnerability during the divorce crisis. Such children are more likely to be overwhelmed by anxiety. Psychoticlike symptoms or even transient psychotic experiences and acute severe depressions have been observed by us repeatedly in children with preexisting neurotic or borderline illness. Diagnosis is further clouded at this time by the unreliability of parents as observers and reporters of their children's behaviors and histories. Although variable as accurate sources of information at any time, parents' perceptions of their children become especially skewed at the time of divorce. Reflections on their children's histories and reactions are often selective and contradictory. The parents' own often unstable psychological status, their own regressions, their projective identification with their children, their guilt-driven worries as well as their genuine concerns for their children, make accurate memories and objective observations unreliable for use by the clinician.

The necessity to move quickly, to understand individuals and family systems in a state of instability or chaos, to formulate a diagnostic picture of the whole, and to develop appropriate interventions underscores the usefulness of an intensive, multimethod assessment approach that is specific to divorce.

At the Center for the Family in Transition, we have used a multimethod approach employing an interdisciplinary team in the assessment of divorcing families. Huntington (1985) has described the underlying theoretical concepts and the complete test battery used at the center. A divorce-specific diagnostic picture involving evaluation of individual family members, of the dyadic or relational systems within the family, and of the overall functioning of the family environment is formulated, which is then used to formulate intervention strategy. This approach entails the assessment of individuals by a convergence of methods, which taps several levels of functioning. Adults and children are first assessed separately in direct semistructured interviews with a clinician. This provides a beginning clinical impression of the individual's status, his conscious attitudes and feelings, and information regarding his perception or version of the parents' history, of the courtship and marriage, and of the circumstances surrounding the failing marriage.

A variety of structured paper-and-pencil assessment instruments and history questionnaires are used to supplement the interview. Socioeconomic information, details of history, marriage and divorce, and self-reported moods, attitudes, and perceptions of level locus, type of conflict, and family supports or other stressful events are elicited via these supplemental methods. One interesting and important finding is that children and adolescents are more willing to admit to suicidal ideation via a questionnaire, rather than in a direct, initial clinical interview.

Less structured and more projective techniques, such as traditional TAT-like stimulus pictures and play procedures, are designed to elicit conscious and unconscious fantasies, preoccupations, anxieties, and special fragilities, as well as potential or available psychological resources.

Issues inherent in the assessment include distinguishing chronic or ongoing functioning from acute stress-related reactions, and evaluating the patterning, rigidity, and fragility of the defensive system; the intensity of the distress and cognitive confusion; the intensity and pervasiveness of anxiety, conflict and guilt, immobilization, depression, and suicide. It is especially important at this time to assess the efficacy of the defenses in alleviating distress, in controlling the aggressive impulses and the ever-present potential for a breakthrough of violence.

Finally, it is important to know the areas of strength and intact functioning in the parents, especially the capacity to relate to the children and to respond to their needs.

Additional divorce-related diagnostic issues in children include responses that are mediated by sex and developmental status; the degree of felt anxiety; the perceived and actual threat to integrity the divorce crisis poses; the manner in which the child copes, including defensive and regressive moves and the way in which coping facilitates or interferes with achievement of psychological mastery and resumption of developmental tasks; and the way in which divorce-induced changes in parent-child relationships interact with the child's psychological status and developmental needs.

The following case presentation and discussion illustrates some of the issues and methods used in the assessment process we have presented in this chapter. The data related to each level of functioning, from clinical interviews, structured paper-and-pencil methods, and projective techniques, are discussed separately, to illustrate how information from each method contributes to the formulation of the overall functioning of the divorcing family.

CASE VIGNETTE

This case illustrates several divorce-specific aspects of assessment. The family contains members who had suffered chronic psychological problems and who were enmeshed in severe pathological relationships within the family long before the separation. While clearly not universal, the presence of preexisting psychopathology in individuals and systems is not uncommon in marriages that fail. The way these conditions and relationships were activated and affected by the separation, both in terms of actual behavior and in the burgeoning of dramatic, anxiety-ridden fantasies, can be vividly seen. The reactions of the children represent typical—and in the case of one child, unusually clear—issues and anxieties of preschool and latency boys regarding the separation of their parents.

The family consists of four members: Mrs. B., age 35; Mr. B., age 38; and two sons; Sean, age 9, and David, age 4. Mr. and Mrs. B. had been married for eleven years and separated for the past four months. Mr. B. had filed for divorce three months earlier. The family was referred to the center by Sean's school. His teacher reported that although he was always somewhat aggressive, inattentive, and given to daydreaming, during the months since his parents' separation Sean had become increasingly belligerent and was well on his way to becoming the school bully.

Assessment of Individuals

MOTHER

Mrs. B., 35 years old, was a very pleasant, engaging woman who spoke with pride of her competence and independence as an executive secretary, referring several times to her husband's poor employment history and to her role as the major breadwinner in the family. She was reluctant to participate in counseling, expressing her concern that the counseling would be "therapy" and more "high pressure" than her children needed. She noted with confidence that her children were not having problems in response to the divorce.

Mrs. B. related her history easily, stressing a happy childhood with strong family ties and heavy religious emphasis. Before marrying Mr. B. at age 23, she had dated extensively but had formed no serious relationships.

On the paper-and-pencil, self-report measures, Mrs. B. presented as nondepressed with low felt anxiety, essentially matching her presentation during the clinical interview.

In marked contradiction to the clinical interview, Mrs. B.'s performance on the projective tests contained strong themes of rejection. Connected to such percepts were sadness and despair. Of particular note was a marked increase in distortion, confusion, and regressive references to Mrs. B.'s own teenage years when she responded to card situations involving male adults and female teenage children.

As a result of the grave findings from the projective tests, during the second interview the clinician probed into areas of Mrs. B.'s history indicated by the projective test performance. With considerable hesitancy, Mrs. B. gradually revealed repeated instances of sexual stimulation, many of which bordered on incest, between herself and her father during her entire adolescence. Mrs. B. had dealt with this by taking the position that such practices between parent and child were healthy, desirable, and loving.

FATHER

Mr. B. was a 37-year-old insurance salesman. He was a plump, morose man who stared solemnly at the clinician throughout the interview. Unlike his wife, Mr. B. was in great distress, appeared acutely depressed, and at some risk for suicide. He reported one previous serious suicide attempt at age 25 after the failure of a romantic relationship. He seemed minimally connected to either his wife or his children. Some strengths were noted, including Mr. B.'s starting to work regularly, his joining a singles group, and his efforts to control his alcoholic intake and to lose weight after the separation.

Mr. B. reported a family and childhood history replete with depressions, physical illnesses, and early deaths.

Mr. B. admitted to moderate to high levels of depression and anxiety on the self-report measures. Significantly, he left blank the item referring to the possibility of inflicting harm to himself. His degree of locus of control was strikingly external, indicating a person who feels quite ineffectual and at the mercy of outside events.

The projectives added to this grave formulation, revealing repeated themes of sadness, anger, and ineffectual attempts at assertion, along with pervasive feelings of rejection and worthlessness. Of major concern was a story he told, in which, in a flash of anger and despair, a father and his child are killed together. As in the clinical interview, however, some indications of strength were noted. He appeared to be intelligent, with some capacity for observation and self-evaluation.

SEAN

Sean, a pale, markedly overweight, anxious 9-year-old, stared fixedly at the clinician's breasts throughout the interview. Speaking in a pressured manner, he offered an analytic, pseudosophisticated explanation of the family situation that reflected overinvolvement in the parental relationship. He reported feeling relieved since the separation and happy that there was less fighting in the home. When asked to draw his family, Sean drew very tiny stick figures, putting a knife in his father's hand, and depicted himself standing between his mother and his brother, sticking his tongue out at his father.

The psychological tests elicited a completely different picture from the defiant stick figure of Sean's drawing.

In his dollhouse play and draw-a-person task, an anxiety-ridden, oedipal victory related to the divorce emerged with unusual clarity. For the draw-a-person, Sean drew a figure of Hitler, holding a gun. Sean explained that "it is Hitler at the moment before killing himself." He said, "Hitler killed himself because he lost one war and knew he was insane." Asked to draw a female, he drew a faceless figure clothed in a bikini, holding a lasso. The figure's genital area was decorated with spiderwebs and butterflies.

Sean presented an unusually clear illustration of the far-reaching anxieties and intense affects that are often stimulated and reactivated by divorce in a latency boy with preexisting psychological difficulties.

DAVID

David, aged 4½, was a chubby, serious child who appeared moderately anxious, somewhat constricted, with good control of affect, functioning, and impulses during the first clinical interview. He spent most of the interview asking, in a pressured manner, what various toys were, how they worked, and especially, where they were kept. David avoided responding to divorce-related questions and exhibited anxiety each time the topic was broached. When asked to draw a picture of a family, David drew a large figure, which he identified as his father, and then said that was all he wanted to draw.

Unlike his brother's session, where the psychological test data was markedly revealing of underlying conflict, David's testing session elicited much the same information as was gathered during the clinical interview.

Assessment of Relationships

RELATIONSHIP BETWEEN MOTHER AND FATHER

In contrast to many divorce situations, it was notable how much Mr. and Mrs. B.'s accounts of their courtship, marriage, and separation coincided. Both described a relatively quick courtship and marriage. Both also admitted to having had doubts about the marriage from the beginning. The marriage was characterized by Mr. B.'s "domineering" and Mrs. B.'s "submission"—terms used by both. Each parent reported the severe problems in their eleven-year marriage as being eight or nine years before the separation, around the time of the birth of their first child, and at the time of the death of Mrs. B.'s father, although neither parent made these connections in their interviews. As with many divorcing couples, it was unclear why their marriage broke up at the particular point that it did. Mr. B. left the family home in a rage when his wife requested a separation and, characteristically, hurried to be the first to file for dissolution, even though he did not want a divorce and, at the time of his interview, stated that he still hoped for a reconciliation.

One of the major contributions of the projective testing was to highlight the discrepancy in attitudes and future outlooks between Mr. and Mrs. B. at the time of the separation. This clearly had important implications for planning intervention strategy, since each denied, in different ways, that the marital rupture was stressful to the children. On the projective tests, Mrs. B. avoided stimuli evocative of marital or divorce-related themes, and she repeatedly minimized the possibility that children and adults, particularly males, might be distressed by divorce. Mr. B. also avoided recognizing divorce-related material, preferring to view adult figures as being married and repeating the sadistic/aggressive theme of the marital relationship. He revealed much more anger at his wife on the projectives than he did in the clinical interview.

RELATIONSHIP BETWEEN MOTHER AND SEAN

Sean reported to the clinician that his mother had become more powerful since Mr. B. had left. Sean professed to be happy now that his mother was strong and happier and had become "queen of the house."

In contrast to the attitude toward his mother expressed during his clinical interview, Sean revealed many more frightened, angry, and quite disturbing feelings about her during the testing session. In response to some items on the paper-and-pencil measures, Sean said it was his mother who bothered him, and he told long stories of his mother chasing him, of fleeing from her, trying to hide from her under his bed and getting trapped.

Sean's polite, cooperative attitude, which he maintained with both the clinician and the tester, changed radically when Mrs. B. entered the room to do their joint drawing. Sean immediately adopted a bossy, provocative, hovering manner; Mrs. B. became girlish and coy. She allowed Sean to direct the interaction and encouraged his escalating references, both verbal and pictorial, to sexual, aggressive, and scatological themes. Mrs. B. drew Sean as a large figure in combat boots holding an American flag that covered the genital area of Mr. B., her second figure. Sean was severely critical of Mrs. B.'s drawing and retaliated by drawing a small, undefined figure of Mrs. B., showing her engaged in sexual and scatological activities. Mrs. B.'s strongest criticism was to remark that Sean wasn't showing the interviewer what a good artist he was.

RELATIONSHIP BETWEEN FATHER AND SEAN

Sean seemed frightened of his father, as he described Mr. B.'s knife collection and several incidents when Mr. B. pushed and yelled at Mrs. B., incidents when Sean felt he had to intervene by trying to divert Mr. B.'s attention.

As with the material regarding his mother, Sean's feelings towards his father emerged quite differently during the testing as feelings of identification, affiliation, and concern appeared. The figure of Hitler, described earlier, represented a synthesis of Sean's confused and conflicted feelings about his father and himself, as they contain admiring, omnipotent, dictatorial, despairing, and threatening elements. In the projective stories, there were striking themes of boys needing their fathers for comfort and for protection, and of the father acting as buffer between a boy and "trouble."

Sean's combined drawing with his father was more appropriate and less laden with aggressive, sexual themes than was the drawing with his mother. Their interaction was brief, with occasional discussions about technical details.

RELATIONSHIP BETWEEN MOTHER AND DAVID

In discussing the family members, Mrs. B. spoke the least about David. She said that David had stated vehemently to her several times his wish that his parents would reunite. David did not mention Mrs. B. at all during the initial clinical interview.

The joint drawing between David and Mrs. B. illustrated a much different relationship from that between Mrs. B. and Sean. With David, Mrs. B. was initially intrusive. David did not respond to her questions, but focused soberly and intently on the figure of his father that he was drawing. Mrs. B. soon desisted, and they spent the majority of time absorbed in their own drawing.

RELATIONSHIP BETWEEN FATHER AND DAVID

Although stating he was mostly concerned about Sean, Mr. B. in fact described in some detail the history of David's nightmares, which had begun since the separation. His description of David as being "lovable, easy, loving and extroverted" clearly indicated a more positive relationship than what he had with Sean.

For his part, David talked almost exclusively of his father. He described his father's apartment and talked about the good times he had when he and Sean visited there. During the testing session, David's mood brightened visibly when Mr. B. entered the room to do their joint drawing. Mr. B., though quiet and somewhat withdrawn, would occasionally smile and appeared genuinely amused by one of David's comments and by his picture. David clearly enjoyed having his father instruct him and seemed quite eager to prolong their interaction, asking many questions and wanting to add elements to the drawing.

Formulation of Some of the Family Dynamics

THE MARRIAGE AND BREAKUP OF THE MARRIAGE

The clinical material from both parents was consistent in their reports that this was a quick courtship and marriage characterized by a particular and mutually agreed upon allocation of roles. Although never a happy relationship, the marriage had clearly satisfied each person's needs. The birth of the first child, together with the death of her father, appeared to have been a turning point for Mrs. B. Her intensely cathected relationship with Sean appeared to replicate her eroticized attachment to her father as well as her identification with her father in the aggressor role. The development of her bond with Sean may have reflected as well some of the deficiencies of the marital relationship.

Formulation of Central Issues and Strategy

The divorce had significantly altered the psychological matrix for each child in this troubled family. Although Mr. B. was limited in the degree of emotional nurturance that he had offered his children, within the intact family his presence had provided a buffer between his wife and his sons. Especially for Sean, who had few effective defenses against his mother's seductive approaches, Mr. B. had provided a physical and psychological barrier, as well as a significant presence, that helped to mitigate the impact of her behavior on the boy.

Thus, although both children were seriously at risk in the intact, unhappy marriage, they were more gravely at risk following the separation. Divorce in this instance threatened to solidify the pathological mother-child relationship. It threatened as well to trigger the flight—or the exclusion—of the father, who, despite his serious neurotic conflicts, had some capacity to love and to parent his children.

The assessment governed the intervention strategy. Briefly noted, the goals of the intervention at the time of the marital rupture were fivefold:

1) The strengthening of the father-child relationship. Efforts were directed at maintaining the father's role as buffer and as presence in the intensely troubled relationship between mother and sons, which placed the children, especially Sean, at greater risk within the single-parent family than they had been in the failing marriage. Efforts were also directed toward reinforcing and broadening the father's parenting role, increasing his sensitivity to and understanding of his sons and their needs, and at teaching father and children how to spend time together without the structure of an intact family to support their togetherness.

2) Psychotherapy for the father. This was directed in the immediate present at his acute depression and his need to reorganize his life, and more lastingly directed at long-standing issues such as chronic depression, and especially at his troubled relationships with his employers and with women.

3) Educational guidance and supportive treatment for the mother in a group of other adults, and supplemented by individual interviews. Although the mother's need for help emerged clearly in the assessment, her resistance to treatment—even counseling for herself or her children—and her massive denial, combined with her underlying fragility, dictated a careful circumventing of issues that would arouse anxiety, especially at this stressful time in her life, and that might lead her to take flight and refuse to provide help for Sean.

4) Intensive psychotherapy for Sean. His preexisting severe psychological disturbance was rapidly consolidating, and his intense suffering needed to be given priority. Both parents were enlisted, separately and together, to support extended individual psychotherapy for this boy.

5) Finally, David needed help immediately in clarifying the many changes within the family, to undo his sense of confusion and to address his concern about being abandoned "without a place." David also needed the establishment of an orderly program of frequent contact with his father, as well as good school, after school, and play programs that would provide him with the distance from the parental quarrel that he so desperately sought, as well as providing him with an alternative holding environment during the period of maximum turmoil within his family.

SUMMARY

Children and adults who have experienced divorce represent a substantial portion of the clinical population. This group presents particular problems and issues for diagnosis and treatment, because divorce brings a long-lasting chain of unique psychological stresses and hazards in its wake. Some of these hazards are the incomplete nature of the loss, the difficulty in ascription of blame, the long course during which parents change and the quality of parent-child relationships deteriorates, and the economic and social deprivation.

A divorce-specific assessment requires careful examination of the multiple factors in the family's social and psychological environment, in the changing patterns of the relationships, and in the individual status and developmental levels of each member of the family as they bear on the adults and on the children in the present and in the immediate future. Interventions that derive from these formulations include special psychological strategies, as well as more customary approaches.

REFERENCES

This research has been supported by the San Francisco Foundation, the Zellerbach Family Fund, and the Marion E. Kenworthy–Sarah H. Swift Foundation at the Center for the Family in Transition in Corte Madera, California.

Caplan, G. (1981). Mastery of stress: Psychosocial aspects. *Amer. J. Psychiatry* 138 (4):413–20.

Glick, P. C., and Norton, A. J. (1970) (updated 1979). Marrying, divorcing and living together in the U.S. today. *Population Bulletin*, 32, 5. Washington, D.C.: Population Reference Bureau.

Guidubaldi, J., et al. (1983). The impact of parental divorce on children: Report of the nationwide NASP study. *School Psychol. Rev.* 12(3):300–23.

Hetherington, E. M. (1979). Divorce, a child's perspective. *Amer. Psychologist* 34(10):851–58.

———, and Camara, K. A. (1984). Families in transition: The processes of dissolution and reconstitution. In R. D. Parke (Ed.). *Review of Child Development Research. Vol. 7, The Family*. Chicago: University of Chicago Press.

———, Cox, M., and Cox, R. (1976). Divorced fathers. *Family Coordinator* 25:417–28.

———, ———, and ———. (1978). The aftermath of divorce. In J. H. Stevens, Jr., and M. Matthews (Eds.). *Mother-Child, Father-Child Relations*. Washington, D.C.: National Association for the Education of Young Children.

———, ———, and ———. (1982). Effects of divorce on parents and children. In M. E. Lamb (Ed.). *Nontraditional Families: Parenting and Child Development*. Hillsdale, N.J.: Erlbaum.

Hunter, J. E., and Schuman, N. (1980). Chronic reconstitution as a family style. *Social Work* 6:446–51.

Huntington, D. S. (1985). Theory and method: The use of psychological tests in research on divorce. *J. Amer. Acad. Child Psychiat.*

Kalter, N. (1977). Children of divorce in an outpatient psychiatric population. *Amer. J. Orthopsychiatry* 46:20–32.

Kelly, J. B., and Wallerstein, J. S. (1976). The effects of parental divorce: Experiences of the child in early latency. *Amer. J. Orthopsychiatry* 46(1):20–32.

Kulka, R. A., and Weingarten, H. (1979). The long-term effects of parental divorce in childhood on adult adjustment. *J. Soc. Issues* 35:50–78.

Rutter, M. (1970). Sex differences in children's responses to family stress. In E. J. Anthony and C. Koupernik (Eds.). *The Child in His Family*, Vol. 1. New York: Wiley.

———. (1971). Parent-child separation: Psychological effects on the children. *J. Child Psychol. Psychiat.* 12:233–60.

Santrock, J. W., Warshak, R. A., and Eliot, G. L. (1982). Social development and parent-child interaction in father-custody and stepmother families. In N. E. Lamb (Ed.). *Nontraditional Families: Parenting and Child Development*. Hillsdale, N.J.: Erlbaum.

Springer, C., and Wallerstein, J. S. (1983). Young adolescents' responses to their parents' divorces. In L. A. Kurdek (Ed.). *Children and Divorce*. (New Directions for Child Development, No. 19). San Francisco: Jossey-Bass.

Stolberg, A. L., and Anker, J. M. (1983). Cognitive and behavioral changes in children resulting from parental divorce and consequent environmental changes. *J. Divorce* 7:23–41.

U.S. Bureau of the Census, Current Population Reports (1982). (Series P-20, No. 371). *Household and Family Characteristics: March, 1981.* Washington, D.C.: U.S. Government Printing Office.

Wallerstein, J. S. (1983a). Children of divorce: The psychological tasks of the child. *Amer. J. Orthopsychiatry* 53(2):230–43.

————. (1983b). Children of divorce: Stress and developmental tasks. In N. Garmezy and M. Rutter (Eds.). *Stress, Coping and Development in Children.* New York: McGraw-Hill.

————. (1984). Children of divorce: Preliminary report of a ten-year follow-up of young children. *Amer. J. Orthopsychiatry* 54(3):444–58.

————. (1985). Changes in parent-child relationships during and after divorce. In E. Anthony and G. Pollock (Eds.). *Parental Influences in Health and Disease.* Boston: Little Brown.

————. (1986). Women after divorce: Preliminary report from a 10-year follow-up. *Amer. J. Orthopsychiatry* 56(1):65–77.

————, and Corbin, S. (1984). Educational opportunity following divorce. Paper presented at the National Council on Family Relations, San Francisco.

————, and Kelly, J. B. (1974). The effects of parental divorce: The adolescent experience. In E. J. Anthony and C. Koupernik (Eds.). *The Child in His Family,* Vol. 3. New York: Wiley.

————, and ————. (1975). The effects of parental divorce: Experiences of the preschool child. *J. Amer. Acad. Child Psychiat.* 14(4):600–16.

————, and ————. (1980). *Surviving the Breakup: How Children and Parents Cope with Divorce.* New York: Basic Books.

Weiss, R. (1979). Growing up a little faster. *J. Soc. Issues* 35(4):97–111.

Weitzman, L. J. (1985). *The Divorce Revolution: The Unexpected Social and Economic Consequences for Women and Children in America.* New York: Free Press.

47

CHILD CUSTODY

Alan M. Levy

INTRODUCTION

Many attorneys, judges, and behavioral scientists have questioned whether it is indeed possible to make an objective determination in child custody cases. Some have claimed that these cases are indeterminate (Mnookin 1975) and that a flip of a coin is as good a way to decide as any. Judges have long said that child custody cases are the most difficult cases of all to decide (Botein 1952). While "the best interest of the child" is held to be the pivotal factor in the determination of child custody, no agreement exists among attorneys, judges, or behavioral scientists as to the exact meaning of this phrase. As the divorce rate increases, so do contested cases of child custody. The divorce rate has unquestionably been growing at a rapid pace in recent years. In 1950, there were 2.6 divorces for every one thousand Americans; by 1975 that figure had nearly doubled to 4.8 but recently stabilized at about 5.0 per 1,000 population. There are now more than one million divorces in this country every year, of which 60 to 75 percent involve children (National Center for Health Statistics 1984).

The number of children involved in divorce is also increasing. Over one million children annually now experience the divorce of their parents (Miller 1979). The total number of children living with a divorced parent in 1981 was about five million, or 9 percent of all children under the age of 18 in the United States (National Center for Health Statistics 1984). The changing role of women in society has increased the number of women working and correspondingly increased the number of men involved directly with child-care. These factors have had an impact on child-care patterns and consequently on the nature and frequency of child custody disputes. Accordingly, pressure is building for a better system of resolution.

At present there are many approaches to custody resolution. They vary from locale to locale and state to state. More often than not the court makes a custody determination without any mental health input: Either there is no mental health assistance available or this contribution, not being valued or trusted, is not even sought. In some locales, if available, the court's own mental health service is called upon to assist the judge, or the litigants are referred by the court to private mental health practitioners for an evaluation. In these cases the belief in the value of a mental health perspective and the financial resources available play an important role in the process.

In some instances marital and custody disputes are initially dealt with by counseling or mediation arrangements that have been voluntarily selected by the parents. Increasingly throughout the country the idea of court-mandated pretrial mediation is gaining favor. Only when these above steps fail do the parties proceed to the courtroom. It is at this point that a mental health evaluation and assessment may be sought. Neither attorneys, courts, mental health professionals, nor society as a whole can agree on the best method for this evaluation and assessment of child custody cases. The mental health professions themselves are just now beginning to address the serious questions involved. No uniform or agreed upon process currently exists. However, some initial steps have already been taken to clarify and structure the mental health professional's evaluation in child custody cases (American Psychiatric Association 1982; Group for the Advancement of Psychiatry 1980; Levy 1984b). Still, the very basis of the evaluation itself is being questioned. Outsiders can readily point to areas of child psychiatry, psychology, and child development in which theories differ and are in flux. Many commonly held axioms and past assumptions are being challenged. Crucial questions in the child's developmental process are being raised. In this atmosphere it is easy to understand the reluctance of the legal profession and the public to accept a mental health evaluation as binding and final, or even helpful. Finally, some have even wondered if the same "fault finding" attitude in the law that dominated divorce litigation has not now subtly shifted to the adjudication of child custody cases. As "no fault" divorce laws have emerged, custody disputes may represent the next repository for the "need to find fault" in the resolution of family matters.

Finally, how good is our ability to evaluate the crucial questions raised in custody litigation when we have so little follow-up or research data available to guide and correct our methods? There is a growing literature on follow-up studies of children of divorce (Chess et al. 1983; Hetherington, Cox, and Cox 1979; Kulka and Weingarten 1979; Levitin 1983; Luepnitz 1982; Wallerstein 1983; Wallerstein and Kelly 1980). There is even now some follow-up data on families where joint custody has been tried (Ahrons 1981; Abarbandel 1979; Atwell et al. 1984; Galper 1978; Grief 1979; Irving et al. 1984; Luepnitz 1982; Steinman 1981), but there is extremely little information available regarding how custody determinations are made by the court (Lowery 1981). No studies have been made following the court determination in regard to how well or badly the recommendations worked, though Phear et al. (1983) did an empirical study of custody agreements.

GENERAL PRINCIPLES

Evaluations in child custody are never simple uncomplicated matters, nor are they solely of the child alone. The evaluation process is a serious matter and must be viewed accordingly and not undertaken lightly. Adequate time and thought must be allocated to this process. All members of the family must be seen alone and in various combinations in order for an evaluation to be considered complete. In addition, significant others, such as teachers, grandparents, new or intended spouses, and so on, should be seen or contacted.

A request for an evaluation can come about in a number of ways (American Psychiatric Association 1982): by a parent before he has consulted an attorney, by a parent's attorney, or by the court itself. The evaluator's first goal is to achieve a complete evaluation—to see all parties and to have access to all available data. Short of this, the evaluation is incomplete, but not necessarily without value. Court-appointed status affords the best chance to do a complete assessment. Unilateral invitations limit the clinician's knowledge and accordingly his ability to evaluate. Everyone concerned should understand this. Sometimes one can achieve full parental participation by requesting the parent or his attorney to invite the other parent to join in the evaluation. Even if this does not occur the partial evaluation can be of some value. This partial evaluation may cause the other parent to seek his evaluation from a second psychiatrist.

The evaluator's second goal is to strive toward a therapeutic resolution of the family's problem. This means that every effort should be made to get the family to resolve the custody problem in the consultation room and not in the courtroom. This will involve getting the cooperation and permission of the attorneys, parents, and even the judge for an open feedback type of evaluation that uses the evolving information about family and individual psychodynamics. This information, as well as principles of child mental health and development, is combined with legal principles to aid the family in self-understanding and to urge that they find their own solution rather than submit to one that is court imposed (Levy 1978b).

There may be pressures to limit time or money spent on the evaluation process. These must be resisted as far as possible, and one must exert every effort to explain to all concerned the importance and value of a carefully conducted process.

Evaluation in child custody differs in some significant ways from the evaluation done in everyday clinical practice. If these differences are overlooked, one may make serious errors (Levy 1984a). The parents involved in the evaluation are seeking a specific outcome; therefore, they must be viewed as self-serving. This does not mean that they never have mental health principles in mind or that they are not concerned with the best interests of the child or that they are consciously falsifying the accounts of the events. It does mean, however, that they are more subject than other parents to retrospective falsification and distortion. These parents have not come with a specific symptom or a generalized personal complaint; they have generally come with a point of view and hope to convince the examiner of it. In addition, there are times when the temptation to lie consciously is too great, as the stakes are so high.

Not all the problems of evaluation are on the side of the parents and the children; some are present from the perspective of the evaluator. Involvement with a parent and his attorney may, despite the wish not to do so, foster identification with that side and cause a loss of objectivity (Schuman 1981). Unwittingly, subtle pressures from the parent's attorney may influence the evaluator. Even in cases when evaluation is court-ordered and both parents and both attorneys are equally involved, innocent attempts may be made to influence the examiner one way or the other. There is no such thing as an impartial expert (Diamond 1959). In short, the potential for countertransference problems may even be greater in custody evaluations, as there are more individuals involved—parents, children, attorneys, judges, and "significant others." In addition, the type of relationship the examiner has with all the individuals in the case is not as circumscribed as that of the clinician and parent focusing on specific emotional problems.

There is another significant difference between custody and other clinical evaluation. This is the presence of the legal process and the adversarial system, which creates pressures to complete the evaluation quickly, to meet court dates, and to arrive at a definite, usable conclusion or decision. Pressure builds toward disposition of the matter and the creation of a "winner or loser." All of these factors run counter to the clinician's usual method of operation, which tends to encourage the gradual unfolding of the relationships and emotions of those involved—stressing the fact that much of the easily obtainable conscious material that appears on the surface may, over time, change measurably as underlying or unconscious material emerges. Thus, there may be too much reliance by the examiner on quickly obtained impressions, emerging emotions, and direct answers to questions, which may prove misleading. Clinicians are oriented by training toward healing and a therapeutic approach—not toward polarization and division. Accordingly, it should be remembered that the court dates can usually be postponed if additional time is required to do a thorough evaluation. The evaluator's conclusions and preferences regarding custodial parents can be stated in balanced ways. If no preference is possible, that too can be said. Some may unrealistically expect certainty in mental health findings and conclusions; this can be dispelled by giving a balanced elucidation of the findings, stating the pros and cons of the various options open to the court.

The evaluation process presents still other hazards that may seduce the evaluator out of his clinical role into that of a judge or detective. Many statements will be made during the evaluation by each parent and/or attorney. The truth or falsity of these should not be the focus of attention. In the usual clinical situation when patients voluntarily come seeking relief from problems, their statements can generally be taken to be true in the conventional sense; this is not always the case in custody evaluations. However, the evaluator should never become a detective and try to find out the "truth." That is a job of the court. Mental health clinicians are not very effective at determining who is telling the truth and who is lying. The courts and the attorneys are best at this task. Instead, the clinician does what he does best—direct observations and examinations of parents and children, both as individuals and as they relate to each other.

Caution should be observed when the evaluator reads hospital and other records. Often, he reads them uncritically and accepts their validity. The law will not allow one to assume this, since records represent material gathered by others outside the evaluators' direct first-hand observation and is therefore regarded as hearsay. The evaluator brings a clinical focus to bear for a relatively brief period on the situation, like taking a snapshot of the family. Consequently, the margin for error is substantial. One must not overestimate the capability to understand fully and know the "true" situation. The evaluator is often put in an omnipotent position by the family or the court and it is easy to be seduced. One must retain clinical soundness and balance and not force conclusions or answers, anymore than one would do in the course of regular evaluation and therapeutic work. The mental health evaluation will be only one of the factors bearing on the deliberations of the judge.

Finally, one should think through carefully one's own theoretical perspective and bias regarding child-care principles and practices, individual psychodynamics, family relationships, and principles of child development, since these views will be called upon when the clinician answers a variety of questions regarding such issues as single-parent custody versus shared or joint custody, custody with same-sex parent or opposite-sex parent, custody by homosexual parents, splitting the custody of siblings, the special prerogatives of either motherhood or fatherhood, length, duration, and frequency of visitations of infants, factors involved in the creation and maintenance of psychological parenthood, and finally, the role of constancy and reliability in child development. Child custody determinations today severely test some of the old assumptions, theories, and practices of psychoanalysis, developmental psychology, and child psychiatry. New questions are now being asked. New research is underway and a reformulation of some basic thoughts in these areas is being offered (Thomas 1982; Lewis 1982). For example, recent research has demonstrated that children raised primarily by men can be vigorous, competent, and thriving (Pruett 1983). Few things seem as certain as they once appeared to be.

THE EVALUATION

However imperfect a psychiatric custody evaluation may be by virtue of the constraints noted above, the realistic need for it persists. There are three principal goals of a good evaluation.

1. To gather the maximum data available and to have clinical interviews and sessions with all concerned parties, both alone and in various combinations together.
2. To work toward or maximize the therapeutic potential inherent in every evaluation.

3. To form an opinion that is both informative and useful to the family and/or the court.

The best and most thorough evaluation is when all parties can be seen individually and together and when all pertinent data, records, and so on, can be made available to the examiner. There will be times, however, when not all of this will be possible, making the evaluation partial and incomplete. A child psychiatrist need not shrink from this evaluation, as something useful can still be done. It is important, however, that all participants and each attorney realize from the start that the evaluation will be only a partial one, and, therefore, the opinion qualified. No matter how one gets involved in the custody case, whether approached by one or the other parent or by an attorney, one must resist being drawn into an adversarial position. The examiner should at all times convey by attitude, conduct, direct expression, and explanation to all parties, his impartiality vis-à-vis the two parents, with a primary focus on trying to ascertain and advocate what is in the child's best interest and to balance that with the family dynamics. One should insist on a fair and full evaluation, with its findings made available to all parties. This needs to be known clearly from the beginning by both parents, the child or children, and the attorneys. The potential for reaching a therapeutic solution of the family problems (a consultation room approach rather than a courtroom approach) will be enhanced if one so acts, as will one's availability for follow-up treatment to the parents and child after the evaluation is finished.

CONTENT AND PROCESS

The evaluation should shed light on: (1) the individual personalities of the parents and children; (2) the parent-child relationship, including psychological parenthood and bonding; and (3) the family dynamics.

Specifically, for the children, we should want to accomplish an overall assessment of each child's resources, including the degree to which each is dealing with age-appropriate developmental issues, his emotional stability, and identity formations. The assessment of the child or children should also include the emotional needs of each child, the nature, depth, and quality of the relationship with each parent and stepparent, and the potential harm or benefit to each from separating from the other. The assessment should include the parents' personal resources—intellectual, emotional, interpersonal—as they bear upon the relationship with the child. One should look for insight and potential for adaptation to the emerging needs of the children. These are the areas that mental health practitioners are trained to examine and evaluate. Data in these areas are best attained by direct clinical examination (direct evidence in legal terms) and secondarily obtained by history taking, record gathering, and talking to "significant others." This latter material is subject to the bias of the reporter (self-interest of parents, and so on) and considered indirect evidence by the law and therefore not as reliable.

In addition to interviewing parents and children, one should obtain pertinent school or hospital records, legal documents, and other reports that bear directly on the matter. Consideration should be given to interviewing "significant others," such as the new or intended spouse of either or both parents, housekeeper, teachers, and others who could shed light on the situation and may become (or are already) important people in the life of the child. Discussions with the attorney or even the judge may enhance the evaluator's knowledge of the case—especially in regard to whether a mental health or an adversarial solution is being sought. Upon occasion, a psychological test of the child may be requested to illuminate the child's unconscious perception of either or both parents—especially as it may reflect a positive or negative relationship and a sense of having been well or poorly nurtured.

As in any other clinical evaluation process, one starts with a history. Insofar as the parental history is concerned, the caveat of having "a vested interest" must be recalled. Otherwise one would want to develop a sufficient history to understand each parent's personality—its development and present status. To this end childhood history, premarital history, history of the courtship, marriage, birth and development of the children, and present circumstances need to be known. At the end of the history taking, one should know what kind of children these parents were, how they themselves related to *their* parents, proceeded through school, emerged through adolescence and young adulthood, and how and why they picked their spouses, as well as how their marital relationship unfolded. Then one would inquire into that aspect of their life that reveals their relationship to their children—what kind of parents are they, how involved with the children are they, what is the quality of their relationship, how do they perceive a child's developmental needs, what in fact do they wish to achieve in a custody suit, and, finally, how they see events and relationships proceeding after a custody decision has been made. One would want to know also how these parents related to their friends and families. Additionally, their medical, psychological, and psychiatric histories have special bearing on their fitness to become a custodial parent. At all times one must distinguish between factors and features that pertain to the parent as a marital partner or as a parent. This distinction is crucial, since our concern is largely how an adult will function as a parent, not a marital partner. The bitterness of the struggle or the ease with which a mental health solution is sought will be dictated by the parental personalities. Angry, bitter, depressed, dependent, unfulfilled, competitive, and immature parents may view gaining custody of the child as "winning" or as proof of their competence and self-worth and confirmation of being a good parent. They may fight more for themselves and their own survival than for the child's best interest. Stronger, more independent and empathetic parents can more readily separate their needs from the child's. They do not need to "win." They recognize the value to the child of having two parents. In short, conscious and unconscious forces operate together to determine the predivorce parental problems and the emotional environment for the children, as well as the motivation for divorce and subsequent custody struggle.

The psychodynamics of marriage and custody loss have been elucidated in the literature (Schuman 1981; Sager et al. 1971). Obviously, frequent marital and personal problems interfere with a parent's ability to be a parent. However, it is possible to be a good parent while being a bad spouse.

In the course of obtaining a parental history the clinician has already obtained much of the child's history. This can be completed by focusing directly on the child's birth and the developmental history. One should inquire about signs and symptoms of psychological and psychiatric disorders, especially as they may be related to pre-divorce family life as opposed to the child's life after the separation or divorce. As the parent talks about the child one can gauge his degree of understanding and empathy for children—and thus the nature and quality of the parenting. One goal of history taking is to develop a picture of the child both as an individual and in relationship to each parent.

While taking a history from the parent the clinician makes observations and conducts a psychiatric evaluation of sorts, remembering that parents are not in his office with a personal complaint, but with a point of view regarding custody. At the end of the evaluation stage the clinician hopes to be able to state if there is or is not a psychological disorder or significant emotional problem, and if so, if it significantly interferes with that person's capacity to parent, thus making him "unfit" in a legal sense. A crucial and indispensable part of the examination is the joint parent-child interview. It should be a gold mine of information and observations about parent-child interaction and relationship. We can observe directly the parent's handling of the child as well as empathy, sensitivities and flexibility, respect, and concern (or lack of it). In addition, the child's sense of comfort, trust, reliance, dependence, and affection (or lack thereof) can be observed. These observations can sometimes be based on body language, without the necessity for words. Questions can be directed to each about life together, the divorce, and subsequent plans for the family, including individual preferences regarding custody. The joint interview can have therapeutic value, as it provides an opportunity under professional supervision for clarification, confrontation, and guidance regarding many questions they may have feared to ask. Of course, one needs to see the child alone and together with each parent. Without doing so, no adequate conclusions can be reached regarding custody. In addition, one will have a chance to compare the child's statements made while alone with the examiner and then together with each parent. A variation in response may signify a wish to be on the good side of either or both parents, or it may reflect the pressure and influence brought to bear on the child by one parent against the other (Levy 1978a). At the end of the interview, one should be able to evaluate the parent-child relationship and the amount of psychological parenthood present.

The clinical interview with the child alone is a cornerstone of the evaluation process. Here one gains direct information regarding the child's mental status in general as well as his attitude toward the custody issues at hand. The evaluator should always explain his role to the child—that of being on neither parent's side and of ensuring that the child's views find their way to both parents and if necessary to the court, in order to help the judge decide the issue of custody. In addition, one assures the child that he does not and will not make the decision—therefore relieving a sense of guilt that he may have about feeling omnipotent. The age of the child in question dictates not only the form of the interview but some of the content: the younger the child, the more play and picture drawing and less direct probing for custody preference; the older the child (late latency and adolescence), the more direct conversation and open discussion regarding custodial preference or lack of it. Controversy exists about asking children directly their preference as to custodial parent (Levy 1980). This author believes that there is more to be gained than lost by doing so. Given the relatively brief period of time allocated to the evaluation process and given the fact that the productions and expressions of the children have a conscious and unconscious level of meaning, we are faced with great uncertainty in understanding their true feelings and attitudes. However, direct discussions with the children both alone and together with the parents, while potentially painful, can also relieve anxiety and suffering and add a dimension to our understanding. Almost always children have been asked their custodial preference by one or both parents. If we fail to recognize this and do not address this problem ourselves, the child will feel that we are joining in a conspiracy of silence.

DECISION MAKING

The same factors that make the evaluation process risky also create risk in the decision-making process (Levy 1984a). These factors include the usually brief exposure the evaluator has to the participants and the fact that much information regarding the family and its situation never reaches him. In addition, there is always present the high risk of countertransference and subtle pressure from the families and attorneys. Finally, one is dealing with evaluator bias and with conflicting theories and beliefs in psychiatry, psychology, and child development. It should be remembered that any decision reached might be a good one short-term but not necessarily long-term. Our clinical tools are meant principally for diagnosis and therapy and not for intrusion into family life in the form of crucial decision making.

The concept of psychological parent is central to custody evaluation and decision formation. It should be remembered that children of divorce more often than not have two psychological parents, even if each may not be "good enough" in all respects. Any decision-making process must take this into account. Frequently decisions are made based on the mistaken concept that the child can have but one true psychological parent. There will of course be times when the evaluation reveals only one "good enough" psychological parent—more rarely none will be found. The psychological parent relationship has been described in various ways (Goldstein, Freud, and Solnit 1973; American Psychiatric Association 1982). Musetto (1978) gave a very complete description.

No exact description of the decision-making process is possible. Only a few papers even address the issue (McDermott et al. 1978; Levy 1984b). Each case is, however, truly unique and different in the ages, sex, and numbers of the children, family situation, time of assessment, degree of emotional or mental illness in one or both parents, and so on. Nonetheless, some general guidelines for decision making can be suggested.

1. Joint custody is preferable to single-parent custody, when certain specific conditions prevail (to be detailed later).
2. When single-parent custody seems the likely alternative, then ask:
   a. With whom has psychological parenthood been established—with one or both parents?
   b. Is one parent "unfit" by virtue of a significant physical or emotional illness?
   c. When both parents are essentially "fit" and psychological parenthood has been equally established, then examine the current major developmental needs of the specific child or children as they may relate to the child's age and/or sex, developmental stage, and so forth.
   d. Are both parents "fit" and apparently of equal psychological parenthood, but one inflexibly unwilling to share the child, considering himself the superior parent by virtue of sex, morality, or finances?
   e. Are both parents equally "fit," but one parent is "brainwashing" the child or children by exerting undue pressure or influence?
3. If both parents appear either "unfit" or give no evidence of the establishment of psychological parenthood, then explore other options such as biological relations and/or placement facilities.
4. No hard or fast rule exists regarding whether or not siblings should remain together.

THE OPTIONS

Joint Custody

The terminology in this area is sometimes confusing. One hears the terms joint custody, split custody, and divided custody. Split custody refers to a situation in which the custody of two siblings has been divided between the parents, with each parent having full and complete custody of at least one child.

Divided custody refers to a situation in which the parent and child live together for part of the year with reciprocal visitations with the other parent. The parent with whom the child lives has complete control during that period of time.

Joint custody has two aspects: There is legal joint custody, in which two parents share the decision-making process regarding such issues as schooling, religious education, medical care, and so on. The other aspect of joint custody is residential, in which any variation of residential arrangement may occur; that is to say, the child may live with each parent 50 percent of the time, alternating households on a weekly, monthly, or yearly basis. Or the residential arrangement may be one in which the child lives with one or the other parent most of the time, with visits to the other parent. In other words, the residential aspect of joint custody can be anything that is appropriate to the specific case involved and still may be called joint custody. Shared parenting may be a better term to use.

For years, single-parent custody decisions were scarcely challenged in practice or in theory. In the late seventies the concept of joint custody emerged—first the idea and then the reality (Abarbandel 1979; Galper 1978; Grief 1979; Roman and Haddad 1978). Ideas and attitudes change slowly; experience and research accumulate gradually. There has been a steady if slow movement toward joint or shared custody, away from the automatic single-parent custody. Today thirty states have some statutory language about joint custody. Not all the answers are in as yet. Strong resistance to change is still present in many quarters. Some evidence to support these newer ideas is just emerging. Serious questions remain, however—such as whether to order joint custody over the objection of a parent or even both parents, and, if it is ordered, what mechanism should be in place to monitor its progress or lack of progress. Finally, does it work better than single-parent custody?

Factors favoring joint custody determination are: (1) the child or children have established such a relationship with each parent that they would benefit from joint custody. This can be viewed as the establishment of adequate psychological parenthood by each parent and the child's recognition of both parents as a source of security and love and his wish to continue to relate to both of them. (2) At a minimum, both parents must be fit, physically and psychologically, must be capable of fulfilling the role of parent, and must in addition be willing to accept custody, although their opposition to joint custody does not preclude it. Although a positive relationship is preferable successful joint custody requires only that the parents be able to isolate their personal conflicts from their role as parent. In addition, certain practical aspects need to be considered, such as financial status of parents, proximity of the respective homes, demands of parental employment, and ages and number of the children. The proximity of home is especially important, as it impinges on school arrangements, children's access to relatives and friends, and ease of travel between two houses. If joint custody is feasible except for one or more of these practical considerations, legal joint custody could go to each parent with physical custody to one parent and liberal visitation to the other. When joint custody seems the best solution and one parent insists that cooperation is impossible and refuses to do so, that parent may be viewed as not acting in the child's best interest by depriving him of a relationship with the other parent. Custody could be removed from the uncooperative parent (*Beck v. Beck* 1981; Miller 1979).

Arguments in Favor of Joint Custody. Single-parent custody has been viewed as unsatisfactory and dysfunctional—leading to a great deal of disagreement and litigation. In an era of increasing social change in the roles of men and women, notions of actively sharing the children make more and more sense. In addition, joint custody is a more flexible arrangement and can better adapt to the changing needs of the family. Parents and not the court should regulate the living schedule. Children derive benefits from both parents, and with joint custody they retain a parent of each sex. In joint custody arrangements the relationships are more natural, since each parent spends routine time as well as leisure time with the child. This would include school time, wake-up time, bedtime, and so on, and would be divided between both parents. With joint custody, each parent has not only more time with the children but also more time for himself and his own personal life, which parents often find will improve. Frequently parents find that joint custody arrangements improve the relationship they have with each other, as their need for cooperation becomes a continuing one. Each parent can thus feel worthy and meaningful as a parent. Each child will feel less or no loyalty conflict between parents and have more contact with each than in a single-parent custody arrangement.

Arguments Against Joint Custody. Some feel that a child needs a consistent and stable environment (Goldstein et al. 1973). They point out that a child may get confused about discipline and authority when he shifts from home to home; they cite the need for consistency and continuity in care as well as sameness of environment. This argument was firmly refuted by Schuman (1981) as follows:

> "Continuity" as applied to child custody cases also has its roots in attachment theory, in a child's developmental need for stable relationships in order to obtain stable, benevolent object introjects that in turn ease passage into a generative adult life. In the regressed, heated atmosphere of adversary litigation, "continuity" has often been used synonymously with "sameness" or "consistency" and in that rush to judgment the presumption of benevolent, flexible structure which is inherent in the psychiatric concept of "continuity" has often been lost. Maintaining the "same" circumstances is not necessarily useful for a child's growth. What requires "continuity" is an environment which is firm but responsive to a growing child's changing developmental needs. Thus, the concept of continuity is neutral with respect to the distinction between biological and psychological parent; it can be asserted by biological parents against each other, or by any presumptive custodian versus a biological parent (p. 69).

The same opponents point out that there are needless tensions caused by the increased demands of logistical and administrative difficulties, such as clothing and books left at the wrong residence. Opponents also point out that joint custody is a way out or an evasive action for judges or parents who wish to avoid hurting someone's feelings. Finally, the opponents of joint custody state that the requirements of joint custody are inherently contrary to facts of divorce—which are absolute parental incompatibility.

If joint custody is tried and problems ensue, there are a variety of follow-up mechanisms proposed in order to prevent the parties from returning to court. Mediation may be tried or agreed upon in advance. Mental health professionals may be consulted for advice and opinions—with the preagreement that this advice will be followed. Some follow-up studies of joint custody are beginning to appear in the literature (Abarbandel 1979; Ahrons 1981; Atwell et al. 1984; Galper 1978; Grief 1979; Ilefeld et al. 1982; Irving et al. 1984; Luepnitz 1982; Roman and Haddad 1979; Steinman 1981). Some feel it is too early to tell the results of this new direction (Derdeyn and Scott 1984). Is it a solution or an illusion? (Benedek and Benedek 1979). Ilefeld et al. (1982) felt it reduces parental conflicts, increases support payments, and lessens the amount of relitigation. Luepnitz (1982) believed that at its best it is better than sole custody, but it is not a panacea. Atwell (1984) stated that in favorable circumstances where desire, commitment, and cooperation are present, it benefits the children. Steinman (1981) felt that joint custody is not a simple solution to the problem of postdivorce parenting. She found the reactions of the children highly individualized. Abarbandel (1979) found that joint custody arrangements work well under certain circumstances. It has advantages and disadvantages but is at least as good as any other arrangement. Significantly she found that the children maintain strong relationships with both parents and did not suffer a profound loss, characteristic of many children of divorce. Grief (1979) found that fathers with joint custody continue to have a high degree of involvement in and influence on their children's growth and development. Irving et al. (1984) divided 201 parents into three groups. In the first, joint custody had instant success. In the second there were difficulties but ultimately the results were satisfying. The third (and smallest group) found it difficult and were dissatisfied.

It can be said that children today are more likely to have mothers who have substantial employment outside of the home and fathers who play more active nurturing roles in their lives than ever before. It is more likely that the children today will be required to deal with their parents' divorce as another growth event in their lives than were children in the past. Despite these changes in society and within the home, a child's need for warm intimate relationships with both parents remains constant.

Joint custody is not appropriate for all divorcing parents nor is it a cure for all those who choose to adopt it. Today the statutes in many states provide for either preferred or mandated joint custody. It can even be imposed on reluctant parents—after all, single-parent custody is. This, however, is a subject of much judicial skepticism as well as criticism from mental health professionals. The real goal is to promote the child's emotional stability by facilitating the maintenance of the parent-child relationship. This may not be synonymous with the assumptions of mother–nurturer, father–breadwinner or the assumption that having one home is more beneficial than having separate homes with two active concerned parents (Bratt 1978).

It has been suggested that the very words "custody" and "visitation" create problems. In ordinary situations parents parent their children—they do not own them or have custody of them. Visiting is what you do with neighbors or friends in the hospital. How do you visit your own children? Accordingly, the words "coparenting" or "shared parenting" are suggested, since they preserve the involvement, rights, and responsibility of each parent—regardless of the exact details of the time-sharing process.

Recently, Kelly (1985) summarized some of the important findings from the research on children and parents of divorce as follows:

1. The children desired more contact with the noncustodial parent than they were getting.
2. The frequency of contact with the noncustodial parent correlated with positive postdivorce adjustment, especially for boys.
3. Anger and depression relate to the loss of the noncustodial parent.
4. Infrequent and erratic visits contribute to lowering of self-esteem and to depression and anger in children after divorce.
5. Every other weekend is still the most common visitation arrangement in the country. It actually turns out to be even less time than that. This arrangement is not sufficiently emotionally nourishing to sustain the parent-child relationship, as the parent loses touch with the child's development.
6. The language of sole custody creates its own negative psychology.
7. Feeling legally shut out adds to the father's postdivorce depression.
8. There is a decreased sense of parental responsibility for the noncustodial parent in sole custody.
9. There is a common but untrue assumption that divorcing parents cannot cooperate regarding their children. Parents divorce due to poor communication between themselves, but their communication about the children can remain good. Attorneys especially foster this myth.
10. The worst time for parental anger and lack of communication is at the time of separation. In six to eighteen months it improves significantly for 85 percent of the parents; thus it is not appropriate to judge their ability to communicate too early.

Kelly went on to comment that the resistance to joint custody has preceded the development of data about it, and it follows a time when data about single-parent custody pointed out how bad this was.

The sources of resistance to joint custody are:

1. Older attitudes about mothering;
2. The attorneys promoting the adversarial system, even telling parents *not* to talk to each other;
3. Mental health professionals viewing joint custody as a repository of unsuccessful divorce by allowing the pathological attachment between the parents to continue and not to end in an emotional divorce and effective separation;
4. Old concepts of stability and continuity that need reexamination in the context of the children of divorce. Competition of developmental needs was not there before the divorce but often is afterwards. For example, a preschool child needs stability yet has a competing need for continuity of relationship with both parents. There must be a balance struck between competing needs to see that the relationship with both parents remains;
5. The lawyers' or mental health experts' unconscious and conscious attitudes about parents—countertransference.

Single-Parent Custody

When joint custody has been ruled out because factors favoring it (as referred to previously) are absent, single-parent custody must be selected (unless for some unusual reason neither parent is fit for custody). The question then is which of the two parents should be selected. Some general guidelines can be set forth.

1. When all the criteria for joint custody are present in that each parent is fit, a good enough psychological parent, and desirous of having custody of the child, and yet one parent remains steadfastly inflexible with regard to sharing the child, even when the evaluation indicates that the reasons offered to substantiate the inflexible parent's position ("I am a better parent" or "he/she is a bad parent") lack confirmation, then the inflexible parental position, in effect, represents a "must win" attitude. Accordingly, the one who refuses to share and preserve the child's two-parent relationship and puts his own insistence ahead of the child's best interest should be made the *noncustodial* parent, and the flexible parent, who would guarantee the child adequate time and involvement with each parent, should be given custody.

2. The situation of the inflexible parent may, however, be compounded not just by unwillingness to share and cooperate with joint custody, but by an inflexibility that extends to "brainwashing" the child against the other parent. Such a situation is pathological and also requires custody assignment to the other parent (Levy 1978a).

(Both of the above situations could be viewed as instances of such significant weakness in psychological parenting that the custodial decision must reflect this.)

3. When both parents are emotionally and physically fit, are good enough psychological parents, and are desirous of having the children, and when the children have a good psychological and emotional relationship with both parents, but joint custody will not work because of such practical considerations as school, distance between jobs, houses, and so on, then how can one choose *who* should be the custodial parent? In this situation one would look at the developmental needs of each specific child at that time, assuming all else was equal. Developmental needs have to do with the age, sex, and the specific developmental phase of a given child. Role model and identification may be paramount for latency age of children, whereas training and nurturing needs may be more prominent for a preschool child. In this situation one would determine which parent could meet which child's needs at that given time. However, one must remember that the child's needs change with growth and the parent's ability to meet these needs may become less (Lewis 1974). This may necessitate another change in the future.

4. On occasion one or the other parent is not emotionally or physically "fit." Such illness as major affective disorders, schizophrenia or severe personality disorders, alcoholism, drug addiction, and so on, would usually give rise to this kind of situation. Psychiatric illness itself, of course, does not automatically make the parent unfit. The effect of the illness on the parent and his ability to relate to and care for the child, and the child's ability to relate to that parent, are the critical factors, along with the severity of the illness and its amenability to successful treatment. Physical illnesses that would seriously compromise a parent's abilities to parent, such as progressive neurological disorders, malignancies, and debilitating chronic illnesses, must also be considered in formulating assessment of parental fitness.

5. Finally, there are situations in which one parent has either a very weak or

even nonexistent psychological relationship with the child or children, even if he can be considered "fit" emotionally and physically. Such situations arise when a parent has been absent from the child's life for long periods of time, especially during the crucial early years, or when a parent, while not demonstrably emotionally ill, has been distant and uninvolved with the child or children even while living in the home. Some parents unfortunately fail to form substantial bonds with children, lacking in empathy, understanding, and sense of responsibility.

The likelihood of these various situations is listed in order:

1. Joint custody suitability;
2. Single-parent custody—with custody decided by the developmental needs of the child (same-sex parent, child's choice, etc.);
3. Single-parent custody—decided because one parent is inflexible, brainwashing, or has little or no psychological bonding;
4. Single-parent custody decided by the unfitness of one parent, who has an emotional illness or physical disease;
5. Custody to neither parent.

With the exception of the few studies previously mentioned, the outcome of child custody decisions in general has seldom been followed up or studied systematically. Consequently, it has been difficult to identify and correct the deficiencies in the decision-making process.

CASE VIGNETTE

By mutual agreement between their attorneys, I was asked to see Reverend B. and Mrs. B. (also a reverend) and their two children, Sally, age seven, and Fred, age five, in order to give an opinion about custody and visitation.

I saw each parent alone for two forty-five-minute sessions and once together with the children for forty-five minutes. Each child was seen once alone for forty-five minutes and together with the sibling for thirty minutes.

The history of the parents and children was negative for any significant emotional or psychiatric problems. Fred had a mild learning disability that had already been evaluated, and remedial efforts had begun. Both parents were eager to parent and had a history of sharing the childrearing. The history of each parent's own childhood and family of origin revealed normal childhood development and family relationships. According to the history obtained, each parent related well and meaningfully to the children. Direct observations made during the evaluation confirmed this. On direct examination of the children it was noted that they were essentially normal children whose development had gone well. They showed some "expected" reactions to the parental separation—mild anxiety and sadness—but so far these reactions had not reached a level of significant psychopathology that would interfere with their normal developmental process. The children clearly loved each parent and talked in an animated fashion about what they did with each of them. They expressed a wish to see each parent "a lot." When the children were seen with each parent separately they demonstrated a close, easy, comfortable relationship to each of the parents. The parents and the children talked openly and freely about the parental separation and about now living in two houses.

When the parents separated the children moved with their mother to another parsonage house in an adjoining town only a fifteen-minute drive away. They could have stayed in their former school, but their mother chose to enroll them in one in their new town. Both parents, by virtue of their religious work, were busy on the weekends, having a more flexible weekday schedule. The mother wanted custody of the children as "I am their mother" and "he is too domineering and overbearing to allow for joint custody." The father wanted shared or joint custody, as he had always been involved with the children and their care. He wanted to continue his extensive involvement on a regular basis, not as a visitor. He could adjust his schedule with ease and found the fifteen-minute drive between homes no problem logistically. He observed that the proximity of the two homes allowed the children to retain their old school friends as well as to make new ones. The father said that if joint custody were awarded he would submit any and all problems about schedules of shared time or about decisions in regard to school and doctor selection to a mental health arbitrator, whose decision would be binding. He also agreed that if the time-sharing plan that was finally agreed upon resulted in any obvious stress or emotional problems for the children, he would seek and agree to an appropriate modification in order to relieve the stress.

The mother refused to discuss any sharing of the children beyond the usual every other weekend and Wednesday night arrangement. "Maybe in two or three years if all goes well, I'll consider some change," she said.

It was the opinion of the evaluator that both parents were excellent parents—desirous and capable of parenting their children. The mother did not have confidence that the father would treat her fairly in any way and felt somewhat helpless in the face of his self-assurance and assertiveness. She wanted the children to spend a lot of time with their father and saw him as a good parent but clearly let the children know that she wanted to be the boss. The father was an articulate, outgoing person who was clear and definite about how he saw his life and his relationship to the children. He was soft but firm in his rebuttal of his wife's allegations.

Given a situation in which one has two good, effective, loving parents who both want to and are able to care for their children; and where both children show a closeness and warmth to both parents as well as an overt desire to be with each as much as possible; and where logistically the parents live only minutes from each other, allowing for the children to go to the same school and have the same friends no matter which house they are in on any given day; and where each parent has a flexible schedule, it makes sense to propose a shared or joint physical and legal custody arrangement.

Such an arrangement would continue each parent as coequal in responsibility and preserve for each his parenthood status. The argument and disagreement between the parents is about their spousal role and not about their parenting role. Each child would receive effective and substantial parenting from each parent, and in all likelihood this would permit a reduction in any loyalty conflict that might follow the separation.

There are two problems associated with this recommendation—neither, I believe, weighty enough to countermand it. Firstly, the mother doesn't trust her husband and feels she has a greater right to the children. Secondly, a sharing of the children would entail some movement back and forth (any schedule would, however) and could create problems for the children if it were too complicated or too frequent. If the above recommendation is tried with the availability of a counselor–arbitrator, the mother could be helped to share the children and simultaneously be protected against the father should he indeed turn out to be as she described. An ongoing assessment could be made about how the sharing program was working from the children's viewpoint. Any changes or flexibility in the schedule could be implemented almost immediately before trouble began.

Custody Evaluations When the Child Is in Treatment

Some important questions arise when a child in psychiatric treatment becomes simultaneously involved in a contested child custody situation. Should the therapist become involved? If so, to what extent and in what fashion? How should the therapist deal with the child? How does the therapist deal with the attorneys and the legal process? Should he go to court or supply any information in writing? There are no easy answers to these questions. Bernet (1983) saw both advantages and disadvantages to becoming actively involved in custody disputes, and he offered some suggestions for those therapists. Miller (1976) described an actual therapy case in which she planned her intervention into the custody litigation and worked successfully with parents, lawyers, and the court to modify the custodial arrangements in the child's best interest. She also explained the effect of her involvement in the therapeutic relationship and her own countertransference. Each case and each situation will be different. Even the law in respect to the therapist's obligations may vary depending on the locale. Factors that relate to the way these questions are answered would be (1) the type of therapy in progress, (2) the therapist's attitude toward and understanding of the legal process, and (3) the specifics of the case at hand.

If the therapy is psychoanalysis or intensive psychotherapy where objectivity or strict neutrality are indispensible to the therapist's ability to help the patient, then the therapist should state this to the parents, attorneys, and the child and suggest that someone else undertake the evaluation and give an opinion on custody. The therapist could then restrict his role solely to the preparation of the patient for this evaluation by another person and should not even talk with that individual. In a rare situation, the therapist may be in possession of persuasive information that granting custody to one or the other parent would be clearly detrimental to the child; some modification of an absolutely neutral stance would then have to be sought.

Most of the cases probably involve children who are in less intensive treatment, where psychodynamic principles are used alongside principles of guidance, pharmacological therapy, and case management. Even so, the therapist would be best advised not to do the custody evaluation even if asked, but to limit his participation to cooperative efforts with the attorneys, parents, child, and the person doing the evaluation—provided that all legal clearances have been obtained. In those cases where there is an interaction between the therapist and others, problems can still arise. Competent attorneys involved in the custody case are usually trying to get the parties to settle the case out of court and to do so with as little harm or stress as possible to the family. When they or the parent they represent seek information from the treating person or request that person's cooperation with an outside evaluator, these requests need not be viewed as interference with treatment or pressure on the therapist, but rather as a way to shed more light on difficult issues. Too often therapists are frightened by the mention of attorney or courts and see this as an intrusion into the treatment process. This resentment brings on anger and defensive maneuvers, often leading to a breakdown in communication with one or both parents and the attorney. Subsequently, the temptation is great to side with one or another parent; this only hurts the patient. When the therapist views the custody struggle as an expression of individual and family dynamics mixed with reality, he can deal with it productively. The legal realities involved should be discussed with the child as well as the possibility that he will be able to speak out on his own behalf. The therapist will emphasize his neutrality in regard to the parents and his willingness to point out to either parent any excess or unfairnesses. In rare cases (mental illness of the parents) the therapist may have to discuss with the child which parent is realistically better able to care for him. Discussion may also be held with parents and their attorneys without fear; the therapist can explain the nature of the treatment relationship so that his delicate position can be respected as far as possible. The realities of the legal process, including a court determination, will greatly affect the parents and the child and the therapist should include them in his discussion. The therapist may even be in a position to move the parents and attorneys toward seeking a voluntary solution to their problems rather than a court-imposed one.

More often than not the clinician in child custody cases will have to submit a written report of the assessment. In addition, the clinician may be called to court to testify about his findings and recommendations. The literature in this area is growing (American Psychiatric Association 1982; Levy 1984b; Benedek and Schetky 1980).

THE COURTROOM

When the psychiatric assessment in child custody is made the subject of courtroom testimony, this is simply the legal way of making the findings open and available to all parties. This is done through both the direct examination of the child psychiatrist and cross-examination by the other side.

The purpose of direct examination is to bring out by questioning a full and complete picture of the assessment and evaluation, along with the conclusions reached and opinions formed. On direct examination you will be asked to state your name, address, your educational background, and professional experience. Having a curriculum vitae available will be helpful. You will be asked how you came to be involved in the case (who contacted you and when) and what you were asked to do (treat, evaluate, etc.). You will be asked with whom you met, when, how often, and how long the sessions were. You will be asked to describe your examination procedures and to relate your observations; whether or not you read any documents about the case; what your opinions are, and why and how you reached them. You may be asked to respond to hypothetical questions. (A hypothetical question is one that permits you to assume that certain statements given to you by the attorney are factual and then to give your opinion as derived from this set of assumed facts.) This mechanism allows the witness to provide general information to the court to assist in its understanding of psychological and psychiatric matters.

The purpose of cross-examination is to weaken, destroy, or undermine your testimony and/or your credibility. It is not a personal attack on you or your honesty; it is a normal adversarial process designed to elicit all the facts and possible viewpoints in the case and to bring out any weaknesses or errors in the direct testimony. To that end, attempts will be made to shake your testimony or to cast doubt about your motives for participating in the evaluation and your assessment. You will be asked if you were paid for your assessment and your testimony, how much, and by whom. You may be asked how often you testify and for whom (fathers or mothers). You may be asked if you kept notes of your work and if you brought them with you, and if so, a request to see them may be made. From this examination further questions could be asked about the details of your evaluation process in an effort to pick out contradictions in your prior testimony, unwarranted assumptions you may have made, biases you have shown, omissions you may have made in spending enough time in the evaluation, seeing all parties available to you alone and together with each other, and reading all available records. If you have written articles in the field you may be questioned about them and how your testimony now differs from what you said in the article. You will be asked upon what exactly you based your opinion and how much weight you gave to the various elements—records, telephone calls with others, other parents' statements and observations, and so on. You may be given certain additional hypothetical facts and asked if your opinion would now be different. You may be asked if you could be wrong in your opinion.

Cross-examination provides us an impetus to do careful, thorough, objective, and fair assessments. It challenges us to be open, direct, honest, nonjudgmental, nonominiscient, nonomnipotent, and unbiased.

As for the other questions—just "tell it as it is." Your usual office procedures regarding note taking, your usual careful clinical examination and attention to the special requirements of the assessment process, and your calm, nonpartisan, consistent, jargon-free explanation of your findings will guarantee your usefulness as a witness.

SUMMARY

Large numbers of children and families find themselves involved in custody or visitation struggles. They automatically are at high risk for the development of emotional problems. Their inability to solve their own family problems thrusts the resolution into the legal process.

This process in turn seeks help from the child psychiatrist to evaluate the family members as individuals and to elucidate the family dynamics. It asks for an exploration of all possible custody and visitation options, with recommendations as to which seem the best—and why.

Assessment in child custody is a special but stimulating challenge for child psychiatrists. It calls upon all the usual interviewing and diagnostic skills of the practitioner, but asks that the resultant evaluation be brought into the unfamiliar world of lawyers, judges, and courtrooms. The exposure of psychiatric clinical skills to the adversarial process requires special attention to some common pitfalls lying in wait.

Special skills and knowledge will be required of those participating in the evaluations. Much has already been learned about children and families of divorce, useful methods of assessment in child custody, and the pros and cons of various options for disposition. This information can help develop the required new skills. However, not all the answers are in as yet; the need for additional clinical experience and subsequent research remains. This adds to the challenge of assessment in child custody.

REFERENCES

Abarbandel, A. (1979). Shared parenting after separation and divorce: A study of joint custody. *Amer. J. Orthopsychiatry* 49:330–39.

Ahrons, C. (1981). Joint custody arrangements in the postdivorce family. *J. Divorce* 3:189–205.

American Psychiatric Association. (1982). *Child Custody Consultation: A Report of the Task Force on Clinical Assessment in Child Custody.*

Atwell, A., et al. (1984). Effects of joint custody on children. *Bull. Amer. Acad. Psychiat. Law* 12(2):149–57.

Beck v. Beck. (1981). 86 New Jersey 480.

Benedek, E., and Benedek, R. (1979). Joint custody: Solution or illusion? *Amer. J. Psychiat.* 136(12):1540–44.

———, and Schetky, D. (1980). *Child Psychiatry and the Law.* New York: Brunner/ Mazel.

Bernet, W. (1983). The therapist's role in child custody disputes. *J. Amer. Acad. Child Psychiat.* 22(2):180–83.

Bratt, C. (1978–79). Joint custody. *Kentucky Law J.* 67(2):271–308.

Botein, B. (1952). *Trial Judge.* New York: Simon and Schuster.

Chess, S., et al. (1983). Early parental attitudes, divorce and separation and young adult outcome: Findings of a longitudinal study. *J. Amer. Acad. Child Psychiat.* 22:47–51.

Derdeyn, A., and Scott, E. (1984). Joint custody: A critical analysis and appraisal. *Amer. J. Orthopsychiatry* 54(2):199–209.

Diamond, B. (1959). The fallacy of the impartial expert. *Arch. Crim. Psychodyn.* 3(2):221–36.

Galper, M. (1978). *Co-Parenting.* Philadelphia: Runncar Press.

Goldstein, J., Freud, A., and Solnit, A. (1973). *Beyond the Best Interests of the Child.* New York: Free Press.

Grief, J. (1979). Fathers, children, and joint custody. *Amer. J. Orthopsychiatry* 49(2):311–15.

Group for the Advancement of Psychiatry. (1980). *Divorce, Child Custody and the Family.*

Hetherington, E. M., Cox, M., and Cox, R. (1979). Play and social interaction in children following divorce. *J. Soc. Issues* 35(4):26–49.

Ilefeld, F., Ilefeld, H., and Alexander, J. (1982). Does joint custody work? A first look at outcome data of relitigation. *Amer. J. Psychiat.* 139(1):62–66.

Irving, H., Benjamin, M., and Trocme, N. (1984). Shared parenting: An empirical analysis utilizing a large data base. *Family Process* 23(4):561–69.

Joint Custody: A Handbook for Judges, Lawyers and Counselors. (1979). Portland, Oreg: The Association of Family Conciliation Courts.

Kelly, J. (1985). Symposium on Shared Parenting After Divorce. Annual Meeting of American Orthopsychiatric Association, April, New York. Available on tape.

Kulka, R., and Weingarten, H. (1979). Long-term effects of parental divorce in childhood on adult adjustment. *J. Soc. Issues* 35(4):50–78.

Levitin, J. (1983). An overview of research on the effect of divorce on children: Problems, questions, and perspectives. *Psychiat. Hospital* 14(3):145–51.

Levy, A. M. (1978a). Child custody determination—A proposed psychiatric methodology and its resultant case typology. *J. Psychiat. Law* Summer, 189–214.

———. (1978b). The resolution of child custody cases—The courtroom or the consultation room. *J. Psychiat. Law* 499–517.

———. (1980). The meaning of the child's preference in child custody determination. *J. Psychiat. Law* 8(2).

———. (1982). Disorders of visitation and child custody cases. *J. Psychiat. Law* 10(4):471–89.

———. (1984a). Major pitfalls in child custody evaluations. *Psychiatry Letter,* April, 8(4). Summit, N.J.: Fair Oaks Hospital.

———. (1984b). The divorcing family: Its evaluation and treatment. In D. Shaffer,

L. Greenhill, and A. Ehrhardt (Eds.). *Clinical Guide to Child Psychiatry.* New York: Free Press.

Lewis, M. (1974). The latency child in a custody conflict. *J. Amer. Acad. Child Psychiat.* 13:635–47.

————. (1982). Child development research and child analysis. *Annual Prog. Child Psychiat. Child Devel.* New York: Brunner/Mazel.

Lowery, C. (1981). Child custody decisions in divorce proceedings. *Profess. Psychol.* 12(4).

Luepnitz, D. (1982). *Child Custody: A Study of Families After Divorce.* Lexington, Mass.: Lexington Books.

McDermott, J. F., et al. (1978). Child custody decision making. *J. Amer. Acad. Child Psychiat.* 17:104–16.

Miller, D. (1979). Joint custody. *Family Law Quart.* 13(3).

Miller, E. (1976). Psychotherapy of a child in a custody dispute. *J. Amer. Acad. Child Psychiat.* 15:441–52.

Mnookin, R. (1975). Address on termination of parental rights. Presented at the Conference on Child Advocacy, University of Wisconsin, September.

Musetto, A. P. (1978). Evaluating families with custody or visitation problems. *J. Marriage Family Counsel.* 4(4):59–65.

National Center for Health Statistics, Bureau of the Census. *Advance Report of Final Divorce Statistics 1981 and 32 Monthly Vital Statistics.* Report, January 17, 1984. Washington, D.C.: Human Resources Administration.

Phear, W., et al. (1983). An empirical study of custody agreements: Joint versus sole legal custody. *J. Psychiat. Law* 11(3):419–41.

Pruett, K. D. (1983). Infants of primary nurturing fathers. *Psychoanal. Study Child* 38.

Roman, M., and Haddad, W. (1978). *The Disposable Parent.* New York: Holt, Rinehart and Winston.

Sager, C., et al. (1971). The marriage contract. *Family Process* 10(3):311–26.

Schuman, D. (1981). The psychiatric aspects of custody loss. In J. Stuart and L. Abt (Eds.). *Children of Separation and Divorce.* New York: Van Nostrand Reinhold.

Steinman, S. (1981). The experience of children in a joint-custody arrangement: A report of a study. *Amer. J. Orthopsychiatry* 51(3):403–14.

Thomas, A. (1982). Current trends in developmental theory. *Annual Prog. Child Psychiat. Child Devel.* New York: Brunner/Mazel.

Wallerstein, J. (1983). Children of divorce: The psychological tasks of the child. *Amer. J. Orthopsychiatry* 53:230–43.

Wallerstein, J. S., and Kelly, J. B. (1980). *Surviving the Breakup: How Children and Parents Cope with Divorce.* New York: Basic Books.

48

THE COURT-REFERRED AGGRESSIVE CHILD AND ADOLESCENT

Jerome D. Goodman

INTRODUCTION

The development of child and adolescent psychiatry in the United States has closely paralleled that of the juvenile court. Both developed during the latter part of the nineteenth century. Later, the American Orthopsychiatric Association was founded with the express purpose of meeting the needs for a central organization to deal with the "psychiatric aspects of delinquency." Throughout much of the twentieth century, the court of juvenile and domestic relations basically adopted a "paternalistic" approach. In 1967, the Gault Decision totally changed the direction of the juvenile justice system. It supplanted the "in place of parents" standard with the concept of due process and equal protection of juveniles under the law. This appellate decision, heard by the United States Supreme Court, gave the juvenile the same rights as an adult before the law: to have notice of the charge or charges against him; representation by counsel; the privilege against self-incrimination; and other rights concerning confrontation and cross-examination of witnesses, transcripts of proceedings, and review in appellate courts. This decision led to concerned discussions between child psychiatrists and the judiciary regarding its effects on the usual relationship between mental health professionals and the court. As a result, the juvenile court has shed some of its image as social agency and has formalized its approach, especially in serious and violent offenses.

Since 1970, considerable effort has been made to separate juveniles whose offenses represent nonviolent status problems (incorrigibility, running away, truancy, etc.) from violent offenders. A recent development in many states has been the lowering of the age at which children can be tried in the adult court. This has deprived the court of juvenile and domestic relations of whatever remained of their umbrella of protection. This court was increasingly called upon to deal with nonstatus offenders as protector of the law rather than as a form of social agency for the child. In the matter of juveniles in need of supervision, it was the courtroom as usual, but in regard to violent offenses, the juvenile court more closely approximated adult courts or sent the offender to the adult court for trial. In addition, there were a number of other developments, including the publishing of the juvenile's identity if the violent crime warranted it, a move toward standardization of sentencing, and an increased utilization of the suspended sentence in tandem with probation and psychotherapy (Goodman 1977).

INCIDENCE AND PREDICTABILITY OF VIOLENT BEHAVIOR

Another recent development has been the trend toward increasing accountability of therapists in terms of their duty to warn of potential violence committed by their patients. As Beck (1985) has outlined, the Tarasoff Decision in 1976 set into motion a standard of practice wherein it became necessary for a therapist, by virtue of accumulated knowledge derived from therapy, to use reasonable care to protect intended victims against danger. By extension, a juvenile correlate was added in 1979 that required therapists to protect not only potential victims, but society in general. Evaluating juveniles who have been referred by the court has begun to reflect the expectation that future violence is in some measure predictable.

Changes in the legal approach to juveniles may be related to the increase of violent crime committed by juveniles. Between 1960 and 1971 serious crimes by juveniles doubled. Rates of delinquency among girls rose much faster than boys, and the ratio of boys to girls arrested dropped from 4:1 to 3:1. Even more startling, violent crimes by girls increased over 300 percent between 1960 and 1971. The *New York Times* (1981) stated that juveniles committed 23 percent of the violent crimes against individuals in the United States from 1973 through 1977. This finding was contained in a comprehensive analysis of juvenile crime produced by the Justice Department's Office of Juvenile Justice and Delinquency Prevention. In those five years, juveniles made up 14.6 percent of the population, had higher offense rates for personal crimes than adults, and were more likely than adults to commit crimes in groups or gangs.

The potential for violent acts exists in younger as well as older children. There seems to be an innate resistance or denial on the part of adults that such violent behavior can exist. Lewis and coworkers (1983) found that a high proportion of children admitted to a psychiatric inpatient service were homicidally aggressive. In addition to the finding that these aggressive children were often raised in the context of violence, there was a very strong correlation with central nervous system dysfunction—particularly seizure states—and a vulnerability to psychotic disorganization.

A number of studies have tried to develop criteria by which to evaluate potentially dangerous juveniles. However, analyses of the data have resulted in conflicting theories of the development of violence in juveniles. In the restrospective studies of Glueck and Glueck (1952), three factors were found to be most predictive of delinquency: 1) high incidence of paternal physical punishment; 2) maternal laxity or neglect; and 3) poor family cohesiveness. However, use of the Glueck Social Predictions Tables in prospective studies has yielded contradictory results and a tendency to overpredict delinquency.

In a review of retrospective studies begun in 1960, Samenow and Yochelson (1976) focused on the nature and development rather than the etiology of criminal thoughts. The results were unexpected. It was determined that no particular sets of childhood experiences, either familial or societal, would predict criminality. Potentially criminal children might be good-looking, precocious, talented, healthy, and energetic. However, they were likely to be restless with a short attention span. Talents and energies generally moved from socially accepted activities to those that produced excitement. Interests in the subjects of crime and sexuality were expressed at an early age. These young children, later to become criminals, were often dependent upon parents, particularly mothers. Although they had many fears, they developed a thought mechanism that Yochelson and Samenow labeled "The Cut-Off." The "Cut-Off" enabled such children to suppress their fears, as well as other emotions such as guilt or compassion. The developmental history of these children also included social unreliability and lying, with withdrawal of affection. Unacceptable activities and behavior patterns became justifiable to dangerous children. The motivations for many crimes became an assertion of control and superiority, as they came to regard both people and possessions as part of their rightful ownership.

An earlier anterospective study by Thomas, Chess, and Birch (1968) utilized nine categories of observation as a template of the child's temperamental characteristics. In assessing the interaction of temperament and environment in the development of behavioral disturbance, Thomas and his associates identified such difficult children, noting: "The intense reactions of these children are not necessarily an accurate index of the importance to them of the activity which invokes them or toward which they are expressed. Their reactions tend to have an all or nothing quality, with little modulation, so that most negative responses are intensely negative and most positive responses are expressed in great enthusiasm; difficult children seldom express merely mild enthusiasm." Although juveniles with the cluster of temperamental characteristics identified as difficult children comprised only 4 percent of the nonclinical sample for this group, they made up 23 percent of the behavior problem group. The authors further stated: "It is of interest that approximately 70 percent of the temperamentally difficult children developed behavior problems, and only 30 percent did not." They further stated: "Examination of the characteristics of the parents who had difficult children reveal that they did not differ from those of the parent group as a whole with regard to their approach to child care." It is important to note that this study moves away from a sociological approach, which places emphasis on environment, and implicates factors of temperament as an essential consideration in prediction of behavioral disorders.

In a review of the literature, Allison and Hartman (1979) referred to an older theory that dangerousness in children may be predicted by the childhood triad of pyromania, enuresis, and cruelty to animals. However, the reliability of predictions can be enhanced greatly by consideration of the following:

1. A record of fighting; anger, hostility, or resentment toward authority; explosiveness; enjoyment in fantasizing, witnessing, or inflicting suffering;
2. Thought disorders; paranoid psychosis; habitual blame onto others; distortions of reality in accordance with wishes;
3. Selfish concern with personal pleasures; impulsiveness; low frustration tolerance; temper tantrums; frequent truancy from school;
4. Severe depression; suicidal thoughts; aloneness; doubts about manhood or feminity; victimization by others; alcohol or drug-abuse;
5. Violence or alcoholism in siblings or father;
6. Failure to learn from experience and a lack of compassion and concern for others (perhaps the most frequently cited).

Although such studies provide useful guidelines by which to evaluate potential criminal behavior, the results have led to the conclusion that dangerousness is indeed difficult to predict. In fact, it had generally been considered that psychiatrists were unable to predict future violence in their evaluations. First-generation studies found such predictions to be highly inaccurate. As Monahan (1984) has noted, a second generation of research and theory concerning violence has accumulated evidence pointing toward improvement in predictive technology. Psychiatrists polled in the early 1980s generally believed they could predict dangerousness, at least to a limited extent.

FACTORS IN DIFFERENTIAL DIAGNOSIS

In a recent comparative examination of violent delinquents and less aggressive male juvenile offenders, Lewis et al. (1979) found that the most striking difference between the two groups was that a significantly higher proportion of very violent children presented clear histories of paranoid symptomatology and were significantly more likely to be loose, rambling, and illogical in their thought processes during interview. Other significant findings in this study were that violent delinquents had problems in concentration and at least one or more signs of neurological impairment. They were also more likely to have suffered from classic child-abuse. Comparable results were earlier expressed by the neurologists Pincus and Tucker (1978) in their study of violence in children and adults. As they reported, those individuals displaying violent behavior provoked by minimal stimuli were largely "young men from disruptive families, who show some evidence of neurological dysfunction and often have an unusual susceptibility to alcohol." Thus, the cluster of predictive factors, as outlined in this study, includes neurological damage, paranoid ideation, and disruptive family life.

In exploring the etiology of explosive rage, the most concentrated form of dangerous-aggressive behavior, Elliott (1977) noted that explosive rage was part of the syndrome of minimal brain dysfunction or attention deficit disorder in children. Some children continued to exhibit more serious explosive behavior in adolescence and adult life. As Elliott stated,

> There is no record of explosive rage being produced by damage to the neocortex, either in man or in animals. Some—but not all—of the children reared in an atmosphere of unrestrained temper, parental dissension and separation, or emotional deprivation, become violent themselves. Hence it is not always easy to decide whether the effect is due to emotional trauma, bad example, heredity, or a mixture of all three. Uncontrollable temper can run in families, involving about half of siblings in each generation.

However, the possibility of organic etiology of explosive rage and the potential for effective medical intervention should be evaluated in each case.

Another approach to understanding the possible causes for juvenile aggression includes learning theory and social exposure. Nordlicht (1980) emphasized that violence witnessed on a screen does not provide any catharsis of fantasy: "Witnessed violence increases the probability that the observer will behave more aggressively. Also, stimuli that have frequently been associated with a certain type of action will be capable of evoking similar and stronger responses on later occasions. Ultimately it will be recognized that violence does lead to further violence."

In summary, the accumulated body of data tends to favor the association of delinquency and violence with temperament, attitude, neurological substrate impairment, and the history of parental violence. There is considerably less emphasis placed on sociological variables such as social class, economic opportunity, and family cohesion.

The highlights of the social and developmental record help set the stage for the assessment. Those areas within the social developmental history particularly germane to the total evaluation include the following:

1. Developmental history: relative health of pregnancy, birth weight, relative normality of delivery, achievement of developmental milestones;
2. Neurological history of any head trauma, history of any important febrile illnesses, seizures, tantrums, and rages;
3. Educational history including evidence of any primary or secondary learning disabilities, school attendance record, retention in grade, intervention of special education;
4. Family data: history of divorce or separation of parents, history of any child-abuse, history of important major family psychiatric illness or sibling problems in delinquency.

The exact nature of the infractions that have precipitated the examination must be known in advance. It is part of every diagnostic work-up to ask for the juvenile's version of the offense, comparing that version with official records. The evaluator should not rely on historical data to reach conclusions, but should refer to such data to refine the focus of the examination.

Predicting potential for dangerousness—difficult as it may be—is one of the tasks that confronts the child psychiatrist routinely. Decisions need to be made for recommendations, including periods of civil commitment to hospitals and length of probation, decisions about pretrial detention, and possible waiver of juveniles into adult courts.

With the accumulation of experience, the assessment of dangerous juveniles becomes a systematized refinement of various diagnostic possibilities. One of the best predictors for dangerous violence is the continuation of offenses in the face of "controls" or authority. Thus, if the parents are present yet ineffective in setting limits, the capacity for dangerousness in the juvenile is increased. The adolescent who can continually "put one over" on the parents, the school, the law, and therefore any authority figure, is potentially if not already a dangerous individual. It is therefore important to have access to either arrest records and/or a probation department review before examining the juvenile offender. The presence or absence of a control or authority figure is a critical statistic.

SOME LEGAL ISSUES

There are a number of legal implications pertinent to the examination of juveniles who have been arrested. The examination may take place in an institution, or on an outpatient basis. Usually the psychiatrist is court-appointed. There are other occasions where the psychiatrist may be retained by the attorney for the defense or the prosecutor's office. In the latter circumstances, pretrail conferences are essential. In all instances, introductory comments by the psychiatrist must be a standard part of the examination. As Roberts (1975) pointed out: "Introductory comments by the psychiatrist to the client should state the reason for the examination and the relationship of the psychiatrist to the client. The absence of confidentiality in this relationship should be revealed at the outset." The report of the psychiatrist to the court remains a privileged document, generally regarded as the property of the court. No copies or excerpts from this report can be shared with other professionals without the direct authorization of the court. The final diagnostic statement, reduced to DSM-III terminology with its multiaxial approach, allows considerable latitude for courtroom direct and cross-examination. Ancillary supporting documents for the court include other tests and data, where applicable, such as EEG, skull films and computed axial tomography (CAT Scan), drug screens, and graphics drawn during the interview.

Psychological testing is useful in the realm of psychometry and testing for organicity or primary learning disabilities. With regard to projective testing, such data should only serve to confirm possible clinical suspicions; it rarely finds—with reliability—that which is not available in clinical examination. In general, the evaluation of a potentially dangerous child should not rely heavily on data and interpretations from projective testing. The harvest of false-positive findings in this area appears to be higher than warranted, since projective testing too often finds what it sets out to explore in terms of a pathology, especially among adolescents.

SPECIAL SKILLS OF THE EXAMINER

There is no substitute for experience, and it is therefore fortunate that training in the evaluation and testimony for juvenile courts is an integral part of training in the preparation of child psychiatrists. Since the majority of the children who require evaluation with reference to aggression and dangerousness are adolescents, it is necessary for the examiner to speak their language, know their jargon. For example, many adolescents use the common words or phrases "later," "really," "getting over," "I might." Each has a covert, usually ironic, meaning. "Getting over" does not mean recovery, but rather getting the best of someone: "I got over on him." "I might" as voiced by a surly adolescent usually means he never would. An extreme example of jargon is the following: "I got me some legs—gave it flower—put it in check—and then it was Hawaii Hyena." The literal translation of that statement (I asked for it to be translated by the user) was: "I got a hold of this girl, gave her a lot of sweet talk, she then came under my influence, and now I have an ongoing sexual relationship with her." These examples emphasize that familiarity with jargon is required of the psychiatrist not so much for usage as for understanding. There are times, however, when jargon can be used by the psychiatrist to pointed effect. Therefore, unfamiliarity with current jargon is a serious handicap probably precluding the effective evaluation of wayward adolescents.

Another special skill is the ability to make rapid assessments of the possible influence of drugs. The "burnt-out" adolescent who has been smoking marijuana incessantly has lost the ability for retention and immediate recall. Such incessant smokers also have a peculiar, often laissez-faire affect. Four chosen words should be given to such an individual early in the interview and asked for in recall later in the examination. Digits forward and, more critically, reversed can also be utilized for assessment of recent recall. The adolescent who has been involved with more potent hallucinogenic agents should be assessed in terms of hallucinations in all of the senses. The presence of "trails" (persistent visual hallucinatory phenomena) should be evoked in the examination for individuals where the index of suspicion remains high. Similarly, the use of amphetamines should be suspected where paranoia and emotional lability—particularly irritability—persist. If still in clinical evidence, amphetamines produce dilated pupils, rapid pulse, and cold extremities. The examiner should look for such easily determined clinical signs. Similarly, nasal sniffles may lead to questions about "snorting" either cocaine, amphetamines or heroin. Any alteration in level of alertness or conscious awareness—in fact, any variation from the usual sensorium—should be questioned and examined. In general, one of the special skills of the examiner is a familiarity with the commonly abused drug substances and their readily identifiable clinical sequelae.

The next special skill has to do with a flexibility in activity levels and intrusiveness in the interview itself. The psychiatrist should be able to move from one role to another in terms of assertiveness. At times his role assumption should remain neutral and deliberately naive, as disagreeing via an attempt at understanding: "I don't know why you would say that, because it says in this report that . . ." At other times the approach can be direct and confrontational, as: "Why are you telling me that when I have a written record of your saying the opposite?" At times a role is supportive, and certainly it should remain responsive to changes in the feeling tone of the child. The key is flexibility and improvisation.

Another special skill is the circumlocutory approach. This approaches one of the major problems in the interviews of the aggressive and potentially violent juvenile: the recalcitrance of the interviewee. Initial statements should be made following introductions that the psychiatrist recognizes the juvenile is not voluntarily presenting himself for interview. (On those rare occasions when an aggressive child is seeking help—and when such examinations are not court-ordered—an entirely different direction is called for.) The psychiatrist should acknowledge that neither he nor the juvenile is present voluntarily, and that therefore both should make it as easy as possible for the other. The interview should progress from pleasant topics (identifying areas that are neither threatening nor conflictual) to neutral areas, ultimately homing in on well-guarded or defended areas. As in every interview of a child or adolescent, the psychiatrist should then attempt to repair the negative interaction of conflictual areas, leaving the examination with the juvenile in as close to recovery toward the primary state as possible. On those rare occasions when the juvenile has chosen to remain mute, the psychiatrist becomes increasingly active and uses a number of ploys to evoke responses. Among these ploys are his voiced comments on referral data, increased activity levels including walking about, voiced monologues about any written material the juvenile may produce, and at times deliberate distortion for effect.

Another special skill is embodied in the recording of the interview itself. Plain paper should be visible to the juvenile, and note taking should be as demonstrable as possible. In addition to providing a nexus of the accomplished task, the written material is a permanent document and record of the examination. It further serves to evoke comment from the recalcitrant child. A formerly mute or uncooperative subject may ask, "What are you writing?" The chosen reply could open up the entire interview. Handwritten notes also become the source from which the report is prepared and are ultimately available for incorporation into trial procedures.

The last special skill requires the psychiatrist to walk the fine line between lack of confidentiality yet goal-oriented task and the need to provide something in the way of support and understanding for the child. Almost all juveniles will ask questions about their chances in court, or in other contexts query the examiner about the immediate future. As an example, some examinations with relevance to danger take place in school settings wherein the psychiatrist is called upon to evaluate whether the child can be reinstated (from suspension) or banned via medical suspension because of violent behavior. Although examining psychiatrists should promise nothing, they are able to support the child by merely recounting the possibility of the options. It is axiomatic that the examiner who is familiar with the processes of the court, school, or other agency of authority achieves a fuller and more comprehensive evaluation than the examiner who is inexpert in these matters.

THE EXAMINATION

The examination should take place in a neutral setting. Such settings occur in juvenile detention centers, reformatories, hospitals, and in child study team facilities in school districts. If at all possible, the psychiatrist should examine more juveniles in settings other than in his office. Recalling that many juveniles are seen via authoritarian direction and would not ordinarily be seen under other circumstances, there is an expected attitudinal set. The juvenile is ordinarily unmotivated about the interview, may be recalcitrant and distrustful, and is expected to be generally negativistic. The interview itself is therefore regarded as intrusive, unwanted, and intimidating by the juveniles who often reveal their sentiments about society and moral issues via their choice of responses.

Every interview has certain predicted interactions; deviations from such predictions are the essence of important findings. As in the psychiatric examination of all children, the clinician attempts to narrow the range of diagnostic abilities (Goodman 1972). The early part of the interview is relatively nondirective and samples rather than probes. It seeks neutrality, bases itself on less sensitive topics, and remains pleasant. Midway during the interview, the examiner takes his hunches drawn from myriad sources (appearance and behavior, the presenting symptomatology—in brief, a mental status examination) and applies them. Once the gist of the adolescent's problem has been surmised, the pathway toward appropriate and more special investigating procedures has been established. The interview is thus divided into thirds, of which only the first is standardized. The first third is a roving scan of possibilities. The second third of the interview is the pursuit of different possibilities. The last third remains the most artful and demanding part, because the psychiatrist attempts to implement clinical judgment by moving still closer to the juvenile and interacting, yet sealing over the experience with sensitivity and closure.

The behavior of the juvenile during the interview can tell the skilled psychiatrist about one of the most important facets of personality—attitudes toward limit setting. The juvenile's manner of relating to the psychiatrist and vice versa should show some movement during the interview. As previously noted, the choice of topics and activity level are altered during the course of the interview. If the psychiatrist starts out as neutral, the juvenile may be friendly, and then the psychiatrist can become more authoritarian. If the juvenile starts out as openly aggressive, the psychiatrist becomes increasingly supportive, and then perhaps the roles can reverse. There should be some imposed accommodation between the extreme of attitudes. If no effective degree of accommodation about attitude can be reached between the examiner and the juvenile, either the juvenile is seriously disturbed or his potential for recidivism and dangerousness remains high.

Another determinant for predicting dangerousness is the motor response of the juvenile concerning the offense. Nonverbal behavior is worthy of scrupulous attention. For example, if the adolescent cracks knuckles during the early part of the examination, he is thought to be anxious. If he cracks them in exact consonance with the first questions about the offense he may be anxious, angry, or particularly defensive. The examiner, having noted this response, should attempt to reproduce it via return to the stimulus. In other words, salient nonverbal communication can be clearly understood when it can be evoked anew as a signal response to subject matter. Yawning, stretching, nervous tapping and knuckle cracking usually are nonverbal correlates to pertinent attitudes. Such behavior provides important information about those who remain wary. It is worthwhile to emphasize that skills in the observation of nonverbal behavior and ambiguous communication, particularly with regard to affected interviewees, are as important as clinical acumen. Those juveniles most revelatory through nonverbal expression are unable to dissimulate attitudes and basic feeling while intent on denial.

An additional clue to temperament and possible dangerousness is the adolescent's use of bragging or exaggerated claims. Almost all adolescents distort their activities, emphasizing prowess, skills, and strength. They also prefer to portray themselves as sophisticated and independent. Yet it is the adolescent whose distortion is most persistent and profound, reaching counterphobic levels, who has a need to prove himself (and increasingly herself) immune to the usual concerns and fears of the age group, who may resort to violent behavior precisely to divert attention from felt inadequacy. The same is true for the potential for self-directed violence. The interview should include some inquiry into these areas of counterphobic display, especially if the bragging and exaggerated claims are offered spontaneously. Material may often emerge about earlier teasing and rejection by peers. At times the juvenile can recall cruel and abusive treatment from parents or older siblings. Therefore, some of the illegal and possibly dangerous behavior may have issued from a need for pure acceptance and/or a ritual proof of identification and credentials. It is the degree to which such dynamics are either repressed or denied that has bearing on possible future behavior. Generally speaking, adolescents who can recognize that they can perform certain acts as ritual demonstrations have a better prognosis for reform. Those who persist in denying their felt inadequacy, those who cannot recognize at all that they have attempted to buy acceptance through illegal behavior, are potentially more at risk for repeating and escalating such behaviors. As a corollary, the examiner usually has several opportunities to comment on the juvenile's history and behavior on more than an observational level. If such comments are briefly considered or discarded out-of-hand by the adolescent, or if they are violently rejected, such interactions provide further insight into whether the adolescent is potentially open or closed for therapeutic intervention.

Adolescents rationalize freely; they often attempt to explain after the fact, particularly about their offenses. The skilled interviewer begins to assess attitudes by these modes of rationalization as well as by his interaction with the juvenile. The choice of words becomes increasingly important during the examination. As an illustration of word choice, a series of phrases will be presented in four groups. These groups (derived from actual examinations) represent responses to the question of how the juvenile got into the particular difficulty that led to the examination. The first group is the least noxious and contains a veiled sentiment of contrition.

> "I just went along . . ."
> "I didn't mean to do it . . ."
> "It was an accident . . ."
> "I don't know what got into me . . ."
> "It wasn't even my idea . . ."

Bravado and false courage, which is either counterphobic or represents slightly less acceptable and possibly early psychopathic thinking, is represented in the next set of responses:

> "I have the right to choose my friends . . ."
> "It's my life . . ."
> "I'd rather not say anything about that . . ."
> "Why didn't anybody else ask what I wanted, first?"
> "I can't remember . . ."

The next group represents passive-defiance, obstructionism, and even less reality testing and contrition.

> "I don't care about it anymore . . ."
> "Leave me alone . . ."
> "It's none of your business . . ."
> "I don't need to say anything . . ."
> "You have all the answers, so why are you asking me the questions?"
> "Speak to me like a human being!"

The last group is the most ominous and represents active defiance embodying the most serious prognosis for dangerous behavior.

> "I'm not saying anything as long as you're writing it down . . ."
> "I don't have to put up with this!"
> "Keep it up and I'll remember it."
> "You'll pay for this someday . . ."
> "You want to mess me up . . . screw my dome."
> "You're the one who's crazy . . . there's nothing wrong with me."

The mix and match of these responses, the attitudinal movement during the interview, and of course other clinical aspects are some of the basis for the prediction of dangerousness. Basically, the capacity for recidivism is a function of the child's development of conscience and the structure of the group mores (family and community) from which the child issues. The child who considers that his chief offense was his bad luck to be caught—that is, apprehended, suspended, or incarcerated—and who will cite antisocial behavior occurring all around him, perpetrated by those fortunate enough not to be apprehended, is the one most likely to repeat the offense.

It is important that the psychiatrist be able to see some evidence of anger (by extension, potential for violence) directly. Therefore, it is part of the technique of this examination to have at least one or two interchanges with the juvenile that are evocative of the angry response. These exchanges must take place toward the latter part of the interview. Not only is the intensity of the anger therefore gauged against the template of the psychiatrist's expectation, but its duration in time and mollifying requirements in terms of recovery and restitution are also noted. At times the psychiatrist has to devise a face-saving maneuver in order to limit the angry display that had been evoked. Just as in play therapy with children, where interpretations are later observed in play activity for confirmation or denial, statements that are provocative during the psychiatric interview of aggressive juveniles can result in a panoply of responses. The juvenile may respond to the evocative statements through various denial mechanisms, or he can rise to the challenge directly or display other emotional responses that are judged to be overreactive. Above all, the examiner needs to know where he is going and how to recover *before* such anger is called forth.

There are other ways to assess anger. In general the degree of cooperation during the interview is inversely correlated with anger. Anger can also be seen in figure drawings. A most characteristic angry response is the quickly drawn stick figure for the human figure requested. Such a perfunctory response usually means that the subject is loathe to reveal anything and complies grudgingly. The child who exhibits poor frustration tolerance is not necessarily angry. Therefore, some distinction has to be made between impulsivity and poor frustration tolerance as opposed to active and direct manifestations of hostility. True anger may boil up suddenly, but it also takes more time and effort to subside.

It is also important to estimate the moral development of aggressive children. As Simmons (1969) noted: "We can observe or examine only the conscious part of the superego. We are interested in the child's ideals and his value system. Naturally, it is important to know the child's intellectual concept of right and wrong." Simmons further wrote:

> Frank, nonjudgmental discussion of the child's delinquent actions can disarm him and help him to confide to you his concepts of the outer limits of right or wrong. No matter how far he is from the social average, each individual has some line or point beyond which he considers behavior to be wrong. Some homely examples are the common belief that it is all right to steal small amounts, but not large ones, or that it is not particularly reprehensible to pilfer from the government or large corporation, but it is serious to appropriate a neighbor's possessions.

Moral development in the child, like other cognitive development, proceeds through a sequence of stages. The child develops morally through concrete terms of punishment and obedience, later concepts of social systems, role expectations, and authority, and still later in terms of abstract moral principles (Kohlberg 1964). Piaget (1932) studied moral development and found it to parallel the development of rational morality via the assimilation of schemata. Therefore the examiner should have some notion of the developmental level of conscience in the juvenile with reference to age-level expectancy. The notion of moral development includes the juvenile's concept of what constitutes fair and adequate punishment. It also deals with the varieties of prevarication and how lying is utilized as a primary or secondary defense mechanism.

Most workers in the field acknowledge that compassion and empathy portend better prognoses in terms of moral development and capacity for recidivism. Therefore, human compassion is always assessed in terms of the child's discussion of the events in question whether they be disciplinary infractions, arrest records, or other material dealing directly with violence or aggression. In terms of prognosis, empathy and compassion always carry a better outlook than mere contrition. When neither empathy, compassion, nor contrition is present—but rather only open defiance, the outlook for further violence mounts.

The younger the child, in general, the less the ability to disguise affect, and therefore the more directly observable is the aggressive potential. Kanner (1957) considered cruelty as: "the most serious and educationally most serious form of destructiveness. It makes a difference whether the harm is done under the influence of a strong emotion or whether the act is performed in 'cold-blood,' with apparent enjoyment of the deed itself as well as of its result." Kanner also stated: "The spiteful, jealous, or angry child at least reacts to some definite situation. The cruel child needs no specific provocation. He derives pleasure from seeing others suffer. He lacks any trace of sympathy."

The experienced examiner tries to untangle the distortion of bragging for effect. Statements such as: "I stomped all over him"; "I put him in the hospital"; "I took her down, and she won't mess with me again" should be explored to factor out the exaggeration. In addition, the feeling tone while such material is recited provides a gauge of the dangerousness. The less the feeling tone, the more ominous the allegation.

Meyerhoff (1984) developed a screening device for "sociopathy" within the mental status examination. He classified answers to a standardized set of questions in a continuum for nonsociopathic (n) through concrete (c) to sociopathic (s) with intermediary measures. The set of questions is asked in the middle of the psychiatric examination after an introductory statement: "Now I would like to understand how you think about some things, maybe understand values . . . so try to give me a simple answer to these questions, maybe even the first idea that comes to you." The seven questions are all varieties of: "Why would it be wrong for a person to . . . ?" The various questions relate to aggressive, furtive, and disloyal activities. Meyerhoff considered that a preponderance of s responses is characteristic of continued failure to profit from experiences (thus, also the basic inutility of psychotherapy). He also emphasized that the initial response is the most illustrative and predictive.

PREPARING THE REPORT

The most effective and far-reaching psychiatric examination has little value unless that report is committed to paper. Rather than a lengthy and prolix speculation, the report should be concise and standardized. It should identify the child and the purpose of the examination, emphasizing highlights of important background and pertinent history. The report should then describe the child, his general attitude and behavior, and certainly direct quotes about the offense or deeds in question. It should note observations about the child's mental apparatus and emotional responses and identify any psychopathology. The more directly quoted material to illustrate the child's thought processes, the better. It should contain statements about the child's titre of anger, as well as estimates about his potential for violence and ultimately the capacity for recidivism. Similarly, the juvenile's moral development and quality of judgment should be described. In addition, mention should be made of the quality and extent of the child's relating capabilities—as gauged during the interview proper. A brief diagnostic formulation mentioning certain differential possibilities follows, concluding with the diagnosis itself. Following this, the examiner should commit himself to a statement of prognosis—particularly whether the juvenile represents high- or low-risk potential for both violence and recidivism. Finally, recommendations can then be made appropriate to the evaluation context, whether legal, educational or other. These recommendations consider the malleability of the child's personality, that is, whether he is a candidate for therapy, counseling, probationary supervision ranging downward to suspension, expulsion, or frank incarceration.

The present state of diagnostic categories as offered in DSM-III tends to lure the examiner into overusage of the five varieties of conduct disorder. As Lewis and colleagues pointed out (1984), the DSM-III definition of conduct disorder is a direct descendent of attempts to classify behavior disorder via the manifest behavior itself—an older sociological classification scheme. If the violent behaviors were themselves excluded from the criteria, such diagnostic categories would become meaningless. There is also little provision in the DMS-III categories for the often found neuropsychiatric accompaniments of aggressive behavior. The examiner should search for primary diagnostic entities via the usual criteria and resort less to the varieties of conduct disorder, unless they are all that remain to describe the adolescent who has manifest behavior without evidence of other prevailing psychiatric or neurological presentation. Unfortunately, the varieties of conduct disorder remain a diagnosis of convenience rather than illumination.

A FEW CAUTIONARY NOTES AND CONCLUSION

Until more recent experience, it was assumed highly unusual for any juvenile under the age of eighteen to be capable of homicide, in particular within the family. Since a large percentage of homicides are intrafamilial, and since it is now known that more than a handful of juveniles have carried out this heinous act, psychiatrists must be prepared to evaluate juveniles who have been charged with the most violent crimes, including rape, atrocious assault, and homicide. Juvenile murderers can present themselves as calm, reasonable, and even arrogant in their pursuit of ajudicated innocence. Juveniles are also capable of manufacturing elaborate alibis and portraying extenuating factors for themselves. The point worthy of emphasis here is that adolescents do have the capacity to dissimulate and willfully pose. They can also mislead the examiner intentionally.

The psychiatrist therefore has a responsibility not only to the mandating authority for the examination, but also to the society that comes in contact with such offenders. If the adolescent is a high-risk offender, and if the capacity for recidivism and violence remains high, it is the obligation of the psychiatrist to convey such impressions in his written report. To do any less is to misrepresent the state of our capability to predict or forecast any future behavior. For those who hold to the contrary—that is, that psychiatrists have limited expertise for making legally related prognostications—the counterbalance of other expert opinions and courtroom procedure of cross-examination remains their safeguard. Even within the educational system, an appeals mechanism is ordinarily available. Therefore, the clinical examination of every juvenile who is charged with serious infractions includes the obligation of a searching and thorough investigation of personality, interaction, range of affect, capacity for violence, and moral development—all gauged during the interview itself.

The fledgling professional regards the initial challenge of assessing even normal children as somehow mysterious and remote from ordinary office procedures. With special training in the techniques of child interviewing, however, that which initially appeared formidable becomes natural and reproducible. Another challenge confronts the examiner of special children who are handicapped in the ability to communicate freely—the mute child, psychotic child, or the organically impaired child. Here again, knowledge of special techniques and benefit of experience enable the psychiatrist to evoke data that is comparable to interviews with less impaired children. A third order of challenge presents itself in the assessment of the recalcitrant juvenile—recalcitrant either because of wayward behavior or deliberate efforts to withhold or distort information. The same basic skills of child-interviewing technique nevertheless underlie the assessment of recalcitrance in children, with only minor modifications. In general these modifications include a circumlocutory approach, increased activity levels, and various special skills in intrusion, improvisation, and role assumptions. In those areas where the examination becomes a part of a legal process, clear identification of the lack of confidentiality and purpose of the examination further complicate the procedure.

An especially challenging aspect in interviewing delinquent juveniles is the task of gathering information from an unwilling and perhaps dissimulating subject. The examiner needs to know the details of the offense in question, pertinent historical data, and medical and family background of the juvenile. Further, the examiner must adopt a flexible approach, evoking and tapping the extent of anger and moral development. While doing all this visibly, he should be taking notes and observing the nonverbal material as well as utilizing quotations from the juvenile. The essential familiarity of the examiner with the language of the juvenile will provide the necessary sensitivity to nuances of behavior that can indicate—when considered in conjunction with other aspects of the interview—the potential for violence and recidivism. Finally, the examiner, having created a possibly emotionally charged interchange, must be sufficiently skilled to give closure to the interview while not promising an unrealistic outcome.

A BRIEF GUIDE TO THERAPY WITH COURT-REFERRED AGGRESSIVE YOUTH

Motivational problems ranging to frank resistance and rejection of therapy constitute the most difficult hurdles in working with court-referred aggressive youth. The entire range of the court apparatus and network therefore must be utilized in concert with individual or group psychotherapy. The therapist is well-advised to get visible court orders for therapy, maintain contact with probation officers, send periodic reports to the court, and to share in advance such communications with the juvenile.

It is preferable that no time limit be set for therapy, so that cooperation and improved behavior can be rewarded with reports to the court that document progress and forecast conclusion of the treatment. All reports can be read aloud and shared with the juvenile, so that he can know his status as well as have some input into the reality of the situation.

Since a great deal of aggressiveness is merely the presenting symptom for a variety of disorders, some attempt should be made to treat those that are readily responsive to medication—if there is such a possibility provided in the diagnostic differential. Among the readily treated problems are endogenous depression, attention deficit disorder, latent or manifest psychotic reactions, varieties of seizure disorders, and the residua of hallucinogenic substances. With a positive history of substance-abuse, random urine sampling for drug detection can be incorporated into probation department scheduled visits. Drug checks should not take place in the psychiatrist's office, except for the usual clinical examination of content and appearance.

The aggressive behaviors as presenting symptoms should be understood in the context of psychodynamics, once organic or drug-usage factors are ruled out. Therapy therefore becomes a collaborative search for the origin of the aggression. Is it a derivative of more profound problems with trust, socialization, and self-image? Is it a manifestation of identification with the aggressor, particularly if there has been a history of child-abuse? Is it part of a long history of rebellious attitude, conflict with authority, and a generalized neurotic constellation? Or is this aggressive behavior a camouflage of inadequacies, particularly in the academic areas? Many children and adolescents prefer to be known as anything other than intellectually slow—even if it requires an early label of uncooperative or disruptive. More "class clowns" gravitate toward detention centers than do primarily emotionally disturbed children. They need to realize that their behavior is the result of their inadequate feelings and accomplishments.

It is usually difficult to establish trust and a working therapeutic alliance with aggressive and delinquent children. If the early therapeutic work goes easily one should suspect the depth of the understanding and intentions for change. It is common for delinquent youth to attempt manipulations, distort, and lie for effect, and generally to seek short-range goals of escaping from surveillance. For those who are particularly refractory to individual therapy, group therapy provides the collective reflection of similar peers who recognize maneuvers and are usually adept at seeing the ploys of others rather than their own.

Finally, it is generally agreed that improvement via psychotherapy is rarely substantial unless there is some ongoing control of the environment. For the less seriously aggressive offenders such control includes the cooperation of parents and the court network. Concurrent counseling of parents is often helpful. For more seriously aggressive offenders, particularly older and recidivistic adolescents, sufficient control may require incarceration, be it in residential treatment settings or detention centers.

REFERENCES

Allison, J., and Hartman, K. (1979). Predicting dangerousness. *Med. Trial Technique Q.* 131–36.

Beck, J. D. (1985). *The Potentially Violent Patient and the Tarasoff Decision in Psychiatric Practice.* Washington, D.C.: American Psychiatric Press.

Blackman, N., and Hellman, D. (1966). Enuresis, firesetting, and cruelty to animals, A triad predictive of adult crime. *J. Psychiatry* 122:1431–35.

Elliott, F. A. (1977). The neurology of explosive rage. *The Carrier Clinic Letter,* No. 38. Belle Mead, N.J.: The Carrier Clinic.

Gault. US 187 Supreme Court 1428. (1967).

Glueck, E., and Glueck, S. (1952). *Delinquents in the Making.* New York: Harper and Row.

Goodman, J. D. (1970). New directions for child psychiatry in the juvenile court. *Juv. Court Judges J.* 2:2.

————. (1972). The psychiatric interview. In B. B. Wolman (Ed.). *Manual of Child Psychopathology.* New York: McGraw-Hill.

————. (1977). Juvenile crimes of violence: A psychiatrist's view of the court's responsibility for sentencing and publication of identity. Address delivered January 12, 1977, to the State Council of Juvenile Court Judges of New Jersey.

Halleck, S. (1965). American psychiatry and the criminal: A historical review. *Amer. J. Psychiat.* (Sup): i-xxi.

Johnson, A. M., and Szurek, S. S. (1969). The genesis of anti-socially acting out in children and adults. In D. Robinson (Ed.). *Experience, Affect and Behavior.* Chicago: University of Chicago Press, pp. 145–54.

Kanner, L. (1957). *Child Psychiatry.* Springfield, Ill.: Charles C. Thomas, pp. 710–16.

Kohlberg, L. (1964). Development of moral character and ideology. In M. L. Hoffman (Ed.). *Review of Child Developmental Research.* New York: Sage Foundation.

Lewis, D. O., et al. (1979). Violent juvenile delinquents, psychiatric, neurological, psychological and abuse factors. *J. Amer. Acad. Child Psychiatry* 18:307–19.

————, et al. (1983). Homicidally aggressive young children: Neuropsychiatric and experiential correlates. *Amer. J. Psychiat.* 140(2):148–53.

————, et al. (1984). Conduct disorder and its synonyms: Diagnoses of dubious validity and usefulness. *Amer. J. Psychiat.* 141(4):514–19.

Meyerhoff, G. (1984). Personal communication.

Monahan, J. (1984). The prediction of violent behavior: Toward a second generation of theory and policy. *Amer. J. Psychiat.* 141(1):10–15.

New York Times. Monday, August 17, 1981.

Nordlicht, S. (1980). Dynamics of juvenile violence. *N.Y. State J. Med.* 80:926–28.

Piaget, J. (1932). *The Moral Judgment of the Child.* London: Kegan, Paul.

Pincus, J. H., and Tucker, G. J. (1978). Violence in children and adults—Neurological view. *J. Amer. Acad. Child Psychiatry* 17:227–28.

Roberts, L. M. (1975). Some observations on the problems of the forensic psychiatrist. *Wis. Law Rev.* Spring: 240–67.

Samenow, S. E., and Yochelson, S. (1976). *The Criminal Personality, Volume I: A Profile for Change.* New York: Jason Aronson.

Scott, P. (1977). Assessing dangerousness in criminals. *Brit. J. Psychiatry* 131:127–42.

Simmons, J. E. (1969). *Psychiatric Examination of Children.* Philadelphia: Lea and Febinger.

Thomas, A., Chess, S., and Birch, H. G. (1968). *Temperament and Behavior Disorders in Children.* New York: New York University Press.

49

THE TRANSCULTURAL CHILD

Ian A. Canino

INTRODUCTION

In an attempt to widen the already large spectrum of variables in the psychiatric evaluation and treatment of children, this chapter will focus on some basic issues that a clinician should consider when confronted with a child of another culture. The assumption will be made that individual temperamental styles, neurological substrates, life experiences, and family particularities interact with sociocultural nuances and determine the relative strengths or vulnerabilities in the individual child. As clinicians, we acknowledge that children are in the process of acquiring physical, cognitive, emotional, and social skills within their particular environments and are thus in a dynamic state of growth and readjustment. Only within this framework can the complexity of assessing one dimension of the child's external world—his culture—be understood.

This chapter will underline the issues relevant to those children of other cultural styles seen mainly in this country. In view of the wide variety of children seen in this pluralistic society, an extensive overview will be impossible and many cultural styles will not be reviewed. The concept of what is cultural, ethnic, racial, or socio-economically determined cannot be easily defined. This chapter will consist of an overview of some relevant general principles of transcultural psychiatry and a description of some of the questions and suggestions in the research and clinical literature that can guide the clinician in his assessment of those children culturally different from himself. Guidelines will be followed that will transcend particular cultural subgroups and increase the awareness of the clinician to the nature of the complicated, interacting questions he should consider in performing his evaluation of these children.

GENERAL PRINCIPLES

In general, the field of transcultural psychiatry has consisted of the study of the effects of culture on the patterns, attitudes, frequency, and management of psychiatric disorders (Wittkower and Prince 1974). Terms such as comparative or crosscultural psychiatry or ethnopsychiatry have been used interchangeably in the literature. Leighton (1982) reminded us that a culture has not yet emerged that can avoid placing some of its members in psychological jeopardy as well as strengthening some of its other members. Singer et al. (1978) spoke of cultural influences serving to ameliorate psychiatric disorders as well as altering or at times determining the choice of symptoms. They discussed the impact of culture on symptom identification, referral patterns, and assessment.

When we refer to the complexities of our pluralistic society, many factors have to be considered. The impact of migration, urbanization, rapid social and economic change, levels of acculturation, language barriers, and the exposure and interactions of many cultural and ethnic groups in our urban areas are some of the variables that interplay with the cultural nuances of each subgroup.

A particularly important aspect in this country is the migratory status of many families of other cultures that come to our large cities. In many cases they have to adapt not only to their own rapidly changing culture but also to the rapidly changing culture of their host society. In general, it has been assumed that those cultural features showing the greatest degree of contrast between the society of origin and the host society will demand the greatest amount of relearning and adaptation by the migrant. If there are few supportive institutions on arrival, greater social and psychological vulnerabilities can be expected (Danna 1980). Leighton (1982) advised clinicians not to mistake for cultural patterns what are really complicated expressions of rapid social change, loss of culture or class position, and minority or racial membership. In terms of the impact of urbanization alone, Weisner (1981) recommended some caution in implying that urbanization may be stress-enhancing. He described the importance of the context, educational and occupational status, acculturation levels, language proficiency, socioeconomic status, and family size of the sample being studied. In order to assess the impact of some of the stressing variables met by members of other cultures on their arrival to this country, Rabkin and Struening (1976) underlined the importance of assessing the magnitude of the stressor, the length of exposure, the intensity and the rate of change, the prior preparedness, and the absence of prior experience with the stressing factors.

Within this framework we have to consider the specific principles related to transcultural child psychiatry. Singer et al. (1978) described the importance of the cultural milieu on the adaptive development of the child. They also described the importance of understanding the parental cultural attitudes about mental illness in their children.

In the particular case of the child patient, assessment issues become more difficult. The interaction between child-rearing styles and social circumstances and the child's own physical and psychological malleability creates further factors to consider.

The physical state of the child is crucial. Quinton (1980) discussed variations that may seem cultural, but are influenced by the nutritional status of the child. Mussen et al. (1974) suggested that there are marked health differences between whites and blacks of the same socioeconomic status in terms of the quantity and quality of nutrition and prenatal and postnatal medical care. In New York City, for example, Puerto Rican and black babies are more likely to be premature than those born to non-Hispanic, white parents (Canino et al. 1980). Furthermore, black and Puerto Rican children of New York City are disproportionately at risk to contract lead poisoning (Guinee 1972). The interaction of these physical vulnerabilities with cultural nuances and behavioral manifestations is a relevant dimension.

The child's particular developmental state and personality structure as well as his special social circumstances are added factors. To offer some examples, De Vos (1974) suggested that issues of social deviancy and delinquency as they relate to culture and as they interact with structural personality still need to be assessed. Quinton (1980) mentioned the possibility that a wide range of cultural patterns may be equally effective in achieving the same developmental tasks and states. He stated that it is not conclusive that particular child-rearing practices have long-term consequences. He finally suggested that within broadly similar cultural circumstances, nuances in particular cultural values may affect the outcome of the same event. The type of social familial circumstances in which the child is reared also interacts with the particular cultural style. Simple societies have been described as more responsible and nurturant of children than more complex societies, which elicit more attention-seeking and competitive behavior in their children (Quinton 1980). In an excellent study of children in Kauai, Werner and Smith (1982) utilized a model indicating the interrelationship between the protective factors within the child's environment that increase stress resistance, and the risk factors and stressful life events that increase their vulnerability. If the children are also part of a migrant population, the impact of a new sociocultural setting has to be assessed. Danna (1980) discussed the impact of the new environment on the child's socialization patterns, sex role behavior, discipline, cognitive style, and field dependence versus field independence training. Quinton (1980) concluded that family patterns that relate to satisfactory development in one cultural context may be indicative of developmental difficulties in other cultural settings.

Furthermore, there have been ethnic differences suggested in parents' attitudes toward symptomatology and treatment. Warren et al. (1973), in a study of twenty white families versus twenty black families, concluded that black parents saw therapy as less beneficial than white parents, in spite of the fact that 80 percent would return for help. In terms of parental attitudes and social class differences, Lurie (1974) found that upper social class parents reported more problems with peers and concerns about issues of self-esteem and capacity to cope in their children than did lower social class parents. They found that concerns about school performance were more often reported by upper and lower social classes than by middle socioeconomic groups. Dohrenwend and Dohrenwend (1969) found that Puerto Ricans reported significantly greater numbers of psychiatric symptoms than their social class counterparts in other ethnic groups, and they stated that the observed differences may have been due to methodological factors such as cultural differences in response styles, language used to express psychological distress, and concepts of socially desirable behavior.

Culture-Specific Disorders

There are numerous articles describing focused areas of behavioral expression in different ethnic and cultural groups. Some of them offer cross-cultural comparisons, others do not. The studies that will be reviewed are examples of some of the issues a clinician should explore. The expression of aggression and guilt, sexual role differences, affective styles, and the impact of particular school experiences or multiple dislocations are crucial. The tolerance or intolerance of certain behavioral patterns, as well as the definition of what is considered symptomatic in their cultural subgroup, should be part of the evaluation of these children.

Many syndromes have been described as culturally expressed. Amok in the Malayan and Philippine population, Ufufuyana in the Bantu women of South Africa, Pibloktoqu, or Arctic hysteria, and Koro in Chinese men are syndromes familiar to many. De Vos (1974) stated that these syndromes seem to have some features in common, such as the dissociative or altered state of consciousness and the high degree of panic and/or anxiety. He stated that the strong correlation to cultural beliefs is evident. Yap (1969) described culture-bound syndromes as unusual forms of psychopathology occurring in special areas and proposed a tentative classification. He described Koro as a state of depersonalization, and Latah, Amok, and Hsieh-ping as syndromes of disordered consciousness. Lin (1953) described Hsieh-ping in Taiwan; he reported it as a possession syndrome in which a person, while in a trance state, identifies with a deceased from the afterlife world. He explained that these spiritual trances are culturally understood to be possessions by ghosts, or Kwei. The Wu priests, possessed by Shen, or good spirits, can draw these evil spirits away through their exorcisms.

In terms of syndromes that may be more applicable in this country, Wilkeson (1982), in discussing the Mexican population, stated that they do not dichotomize or separate emotional illness from somatic diseases. She gave as examples of this the "caida de mollera," or fallen fonatelle (affecting only infants), "mal de ojo" or evil eye, "empacho" or surfeit, and "susto" or fright. The fallen fontanelle is culturally believed to be the consequence of an infant falling, or of the nipple abruptly being pulled away from him. The result is "caving in" of the anterior fontanelle. The baby then develops symptoms characterized by inability to grasp the nipple, crying, diarrhea, vomiting, and sunken eyes. Gomez (1982) described the "dolor de cerebro," or brain ache, in the Puerto Rican population. This is characterized by headaches in the occipital and upper cervical areas and usually has a psychosomatic origin. He further described the "ataque" or attack, as a syndrome characterized by histrionics or released aggression that culminates occasionally in stupor or a full hysterical seizure. Marsella (1980) reviewed three other syndromes and correlated them to depressive equivalent disorders. He mentioned the "Tawatl ye sni" or totally discouraged syndrome among the Sioux Indians, the "Hiwa: Itck" or heartbreak syndrome among the Mohave Indians, and the "susto" or soul loss seen in Central and South American populations. He described how they are similar to the Western societies' expressions of grief reactions, agitated depressions, and feelings of helplessness.

The whole area of culture-specific disorders, nevertheless, continues to be controversial. Some researchers feel that these disorders are unique to some cultures, while others feel that they are variants of disorders seen around the world. This issue becomes more complicated in this country because the expressions of these disorders may be correlated to the levels of acculturation of the particular cultural subgroup. Of more interest, though, is that nothing has been written on the effect of these disorders on children. The clinician, aware of the existence and name of these syndromes, may nevertheless use this knowledge to assess what impact, if any, the adult expression of the disease has on the child. His familiarity with the disorders may facilitate a more reliable family history of mental illness and offer better assessment of cultural syntonicity or dystonicity of the child's presenting symptomatology.

Assessment and Treatment Considerations

In many studies clinicians have attempted to look at symptomatic profiles and treatment issues and have concluded that there are a variety of explanations for their findings.

Schechtman (1971), utilizing the Achenbach clinical research inventory, studied a normal versus a clinical sample of black boys aged 5 to 14. The results indicated the clinic children to have loaded profiles in the externalizing factors of disruptive problems, fighting and aggressive behavior, and poor schoolwork. He questioned if these behaviors would cause more referrals and be identified as more problematic than nervous habits and somatic complaints, which may have been seen as more acceptable outlets in their ethnic group. In attempting to compare a population of child guidance patients, Stokes and Meadow (1974) studied a sample of Mexican-American children and Anglo-American children matched for social class. In giving a seventy-four-item symptom list, they found Mexican-American boys to be higher in disturbance of affect, while their Anglo-American counterparts scored higher in nail biting, enuresis, nervousness, anxiety, and poor social relations.

Canino (1985), in a study of 149 Hispanic and black children attending a psychiatric outpatient clinic, found that both groups of children belonged to highly dysfunctional families experiencing many psychosocial stressors. He found both groups to have high rates of sadness, anxiety, restlessness, and sleeping disturbances.

In general, a clinician approaching a culturally different patient must be aware of the particularities of body language, eye contact, tone of voice, loudness and manner of speech, and the importance of the timing and appropriateness of verbalizations on culturally acceptable topics. He must be particularly sensitive to affective nuances, issues of biculturality, cooperation versus competition, verbalness, punctuality, assertiveness, and family values (Sue 1981). For example, Arce (1982) described that Puerto Ricans as a group have difficulties dealing with aggressive feelings and anger. If those feelings are expressed, they are usually followed by intense feelings of guilt. Underlining the importance of the extended family for Puerto Rican migrants, Canino and Canino (1982) suggested a family therapy approach. Spurlock (1982), discussing the black patient, urged clinicians to reconsider the diversity of experiences that black patients have and reminded us that there is no one response of black people to the stresses generated by racism. Spurlock (1985) described a patient in her practice whose mother negatively incorporated an Afro-American stereotype. She felt that in part that could explain her patient's self-effacing behavior. In the same article she described the following case:

> A sixteen-year-old black girl of an interracial union was seen in consultation following an attempted suicide. . . . In addition to the overt depressive picture, a prominent feature of this adolescent's turmoil was her conflict about her racial identity. This identity conflict and her parents' handling of the matters of race . . . prompted the therapist to focus on this early in treatment. The therapist, a black woman, elected to be quite direct (in contrast to the patient's mother) about the issue. At the same time, the therapist remained alert to the possibility that the conflict about racial identity might have served to conceal or mask other roots of the patient's sense of low self-esteem.

Comer (1985a) reminded us of the importance of the black church and the black family in serving protective functions for the child during the history of black powerlessness and abuse, and furthermore, of the relationship of the mental health of black children to the sociopolitical environment in which they have been raised.

In describing some of the values of the Chinese community, Gaw (1982) stated that their filial piety, need for order, and interdependence and reciprocity are typical cultural sentiments. He also mentioned the variety of languages and subgroups within the Chinese-American group; he believed it important to include the family as part of the treatment of an Oriental patient in any therapeutic regimen of either tranquilizers or antidepressants. He suggested that more research is needed to assess any differential ethnic responses to drugs. He mentioned that in Tokyo psychiatrists often see their patients with a relative. In terms of children and adolescents, Singer et al. (1978) described how the yin-yang ideology plays an important function in ideas of health and disease in the Chinese population. They described the folk belief that masturbation and nocturnal emissions represent an unbalanced loss of yang, which can cause exhaustion, a variety of ailments, and possibly even death. Mc-Michael and Grinder (1966) looked at guilt after transgression issues in three groups: Japanese, Hawaiian, and white American children. They used projective story completion tests and concluded that the more guilt-oriented the standards, the more acculturated the group was; the Japanese subgroup least exposed to American standards were found to be more shame-oriented.

Saslow (1968) found that the school experiences of many Native-American children particularly accentuate their identity problems. He mentioned the devalued ethnic self-image and the tendency towards hostility of Western society in these children. Krush et al. (1966) mentioned the constant needs of these children to adjust to shifting settings and standards and called it "psychosocial nomadism." They mentioned that these children eventually "back off" and avoid further stressful situations. Allen (1973) underlined the impact on the Native-American adolescent of the lack of his traditional mourning rituals. He described this group as quieter, not offering direct eye contact, and delaying verbal responses before they reply. He discussed the problems of alcoholism and the impact of boarding school on these children. In terms of the relevance of cultural nuances in the Native-American population, Clevenger (1982) stated:

> . . . it was not unusual for an Anglo physician to recommend hospitalization or perhaps surgery for a youngster, only to have the parents turn to the child and say, in very soft Navajo terms, some communications. The parents would then turn back to the physician and say, "No, we won't do that. He won't stay." The physician would almost invariably be perplexed and say, "But why?" And the parents would say, "Because he doesn't want to." . . . As an Indian, she would not presume to speak on behalf of anyone else.

Prince (1980) suggested a link between cultural features and psychotherapeutic interventions. He described Morita therapy in Japan as emphasizing the culturally accepted value of acceptance of mental suffering rather than its alleviation, the autogenic training in Germany with its culturally syntonic drill-like procedures, and the success of individual therapies in the United States, which parallels its cultural style of individualism. Gluckman (1959) and Beaglehole (1937) described other cultures in which its healing rituals seem to aim at the preservation of emotional equilibrium. They described these rituals as allowing temporary reversals of sexual and social status roles as well as permitting temporary expression of suppressed sexual and aggressive feelings. Kiev (1964) implied that the therapy of functional disorders is more effective if it utilizes the symbolic representation and beliefs of the individuals treated. In a review of therapeutic approaches, Murphy (1964) described the psychotherapeutic aspects of shamanism in Eskimos, and Prince (1964) offered a description of indigenous Yoruba psychiatry in Nigeria.

There are many healing practices relevant to population subgroups in this country. La Barre (1964) described the therapeutic effect of confession as a social therapy in some Native-American tribes. Gaw (1982) described a dual system of care in the Chinese-American community: Western medicine (hsi-i) and Chinese medicine (chung-i). Chinese medicine consists of many healing practices and practitioners, from herbalists and shamans to acupuncturists. Their treatment may consist of extensive use of herbs, exorcism, and fortune telling. Since this dual medical system exists, a clinician should inquire what medications the patient may be taking from the Western doctor, and which may have been recommended by his belief in folk medicine. Stewart (1971), discussing Afro-American healers, listed the use of biblical phrases from an "old folk medical book," observations, and entering the spirit of the client as diagnostic techniques utilized by these practitioners. Ruiz (1982) mentioned the use of "santeria" in the Cuban population. He stated that while symptoms of mental illness are usually seen as indications of psychopathology by clinicians, the santeria practices may view some of these symptoms as signs of strengths in the process of development. In her observations of spiritualist practices in the Puerto Rican population, Garrison (1971) noted that the mediums interpreted the symbolic significance of visions, frequently based their comments on postural cues or visible evidence of tension, and gave direct attention to and support of mood and feeling states. She found that the mediums asked multiple questions regarding interpersonal relationships and that their revelations covered physical as well as emotional symptomatology. The prevalence of some of these practices among migrants to this country or in more acculturated groups was offered by Creson et al. (1969). He found that 48 percent of a general hospital outpatient clinic population (twelve cases out of twenty-five) of Mexican-American adults had sought services of a curandero. On the other hand, Padilla (1976), studying a sample of 666 subjects in three southern California communities, found that only 2 percent of them had sought curandero assistance. Lubchansky et al. (1970) studied the prevalence of spiritualism in a random sample of fifty-two Puerto Ricans living in New York City; they found that 31 percent had visited a spiritualist at least once.

As a clinician from another culture, it is thus imperative to ask if the child has been involved in any of these healing practices. The investigation of such material may elucidate what the family and belief system understand to be the precipitating cause, what treatment modalities have already been instituted, and what impact on the child's emotional and cognitive development some of those experiences have had. For example, in one of the very few studies of the prevalence of spiritualism on the Hispanic child population, Bird and Canino (1980) found that 29 percent of Hispanic parents had consulted spiritualists regarding their child. Unknown to the clinicians treating these children, the children had been told that their problems originated secondary to undeveloped spirits within them that had to be exorcised by a series of visits to the mediums. As a case vignette, Bird and Canino (1980) described the following.

> Maria, age 10, was referred to a Hispanic mental health center with a presumptive diagnosis of childhood-onset schizophrenia. The diagnosis was

based on visual and auditory hallucinations and social withdrawal. Careful inquiry revealed that two years prior to consultation the child had been taken to a spiritualist because of a sleep disturbance. In the child's presence, the spiritist informed the family that an evil spirit was disturbing the child at night and recommended that two pans of clear water be kept under the child's bed to cleanse the room of spirits. Nine months prior to the psychiatric consultation, the child's grandmother, with whom she had been very close, died. The so-called hallucinations consisted of hypnagogic phenomena in which the child saw and heard the grandmother's spirit, who visited her at night. Clinical assessment revealed no evidence of psychotic illness, but, rather, a prolonged grief reaction.

Finally, there remain many complex questions. As was described before, the influence of sociocultural variables in mental health and disease, and the correlation of these variables with the temperament and the physical status of the child still need to be explored.

Social Class Variables

The fact that our large urban population consists of different ethnic, social, and cultural classes further complicates some of these issues. Some of the research studies, for example, look at cultural style but not at social class, or vice versa. Others do not include normal controls, issues of migration, cross-generational styles (Sauna 1981), levels of acculturation, language proficiency, adaptive and maladaptive styles within their culture and social class, and the impact of poor pediatric health-care. Many children of other cultural styles concentrate in large urban centers and their largest groups are in the lower social class; it is imperative to consider the variables impinged upon by their inner-city living in their assessment and treatment. What follows is a sampling of some questions relevant to the assessment and treatment of these children.

Cobb (1972) described some of the problems in the literature in studying the lower socioeconomic groups: the absence of a common definition of socioeconomic status; difficulties in specifying and evaluating treatment programs for these populations; the absence of sufficient studies comparing treatment approaches effectiveness with specific subgroups of lower socioeconomic patients; and finally, the absence of multivariate research approaches. Langner et al. (1974b) studied a large sample of welfare children and compared them to a nonwelfare group in Manhattan. They found that referral rates increased as the mother's education increased. They also found that a greater number of welfare children were seriously impaired, but that the referral rate and long-term treatment rate of the children in two samples were similar. It was surprising to find, though, that less than 50 percent of the seriously impaired children were actually referred, and only one in five received treatment for six months or longer.

In a study looking at the impact of social class on choice of treatment, Harrison et al. (1965) used a questionnaire filled out at the time of evaluation and correlated it to treatment recommendations and occupational status of the parents. They found that a child of professional or executive parents had twice as great a chance of being offered one of the individual psychotherapies as did a child from a blue-collar background. In studying the questionnaires, they found that the lower-class children were more frequently described in terms of psychosis and character disorder, while the middle-class children were described more as neurotic and normal. In another study, Langner et al. (1974a) measured the sources and levels of stress to which children of different ethnicity (white, black, and Spanish-speaking) were exposed and the relationship between impairment levels and exposure to stress. Measurement of both impairment and stress was based upon interviews collected from over one thousand mothers. The results of the research indicated that the major sources of stress to which Spanish-speaking children were exposed were in the marital/parental sphere, as well as high levels of stress associated with frequent changes in residence. Black children were more exposed to stress emanating from the parent-child relationship, and white children showed the least impairment based upon exposure to stress. In a study that collected city-wide intake data, Canino et al. (1980) reviewed a large sample of children under the age of 13 who had visited outpatient mental health facilities in New York City. In terms of presenting symptoms, they found that Puerto Rican and black children demonstrated a higher frequency of articulation problems, physical problems, intellectual development difficulties, anxiety, fears, and hyperactivity than the white sample. Puerto Rican children had higher reported rates of sleep problems and anxiety fears and phobias than black children. Nevertheless, they described the limitations of the intake forms and discussed these data within the framework of a systems approach. Physical, psychological, and sociocultural variables were understood as potential areas of stress, and their interplay more than any one specific factor is postulated as the explanation of the behavioral manifestations in these children. Lustman (1970) focused on the impulsivity of inner-city, culturally deprived children and observed that in comparison to middle-class children, these children seem more immature, less directed, less communicative, and more unfocused in their behavior.

Some studies have concentrated on specific clinical issues. For example, La Vietes (1979) observed that crowded housing exposed children to difficult contingencies such as bed sharing, limited areas of play, lack of privacy, and a potentially excessive degree of body contact and sexual stimulation. Meers (1973) expressed well the difficulties in distinguishing what is psychopathology from what is culturally, socially, or ethnically normal or deviant. Working within a psychoanalytic model, he described how the sociocultural milieu of inner-city children exposes them to early and chronic distress, contributing in some cases to the impairment of ego functions. He admitted to the added complications of intrauterine damage as well as postnatal nutritional deficits in some of the members of these groups. Particularly relevant is the difficulty in differentiating the symptoms and coping behaviors that are reactive to external distress from those derived from internalized conflicts. His observations led him to conclude that many of the children he saw discharged anxiety or tension by actions and utilized the defenses of identification with the aggressor and isolation of affect. He admitted to the particular difficulties in the analysis of these children where drive discharge was either supported or encouraged by their environment. In another paper, Meers and Gordon (1972) discussed the propensity of some of the children to turn aggression against themselves, to somatize their distress, and to be vulnerable to accidents and seductions. Continuing on the theme of aggression, Heacock (1976) postulated that the aggression seen in inner-city children may at times be an attempt at mastery of the life-threatening aspects of the inner-city and may not always be a desire to cause pain and destruction. He underlined the importance of considering the decreased living space, unsupervised television viewing, and the violence in the streets and the school. Montare and Boone (1980) attempted to study aggression and paternal absence among a racially mixed inner-city population of boys. They compared levels of aggression in this group to that in father-present homes. They found their white sample to be more aggressive, Puerto Ricans equally aggressive, and blacks less aggressive. Nevertheless, they questioned cultural values, migratory status, and the particular majority black population of the community they studied as variables that could have explained the findings.

In a review of the literature on disadvantaged adolescents, De Blassie (1978) stated that some authors (Crow et al. 1966; Riessman 1962; Eisenberg 1967) have described this population as aggressive, having a poor self-concept and poor attention span, more inductive than deductive, symbolically deprived, and unaccustomed to insight building. Cota-Roble (1971), discussing the alienated Hispanic adolescent, described him as denying his ethnic group membership, withdrawing, passive, obsessively concerned with the negative implications of ethnicity, and aggressive against his own group. Paton and Kandel (1978) conducted research suggestive of sociocultural factors involved in adolescent drug-use. They found that depressive mood was negatively related to multiple drug-use for black and Puerto Rican adolescent boys, but black and especially Puerto Rican adolescent girls were more likely to use drugs when depressed.

Many of the minority children and adolescents seen in large urban areas are immigrants or children of immigrants from other countries or from rural areas of this country; there have been many studies assessing the degree of acculturation of these children. In a paper describing the degree of acculturation of second- and third-generation Mexican-American children, Knight (1978) concluded that acculturation may take different forms for a subcultural group, depending on the ecological setting. He clarified the issue further by stating that acculturation is either behavior-specific (i.e., different cultural patterns for different behaviors) or sample-specific (i.e., characteristic of a special population subgroup like "el Barrio" or Spanish Harlem). These children usually speak another language on arrival and acquire the language of their host society faster than their parents. They may speak their language of origin at home, and thus may be able to express their family life best in that language. Other aspects of their world, such as school and peer group activities, may be expressed best in the language of their host society. In terms of therapy, Marcos (1979) pointed out that a patient's bilingualism can interfere with his ability to understand the meaning of a therapist's vocal or paralingual cues, such as emotionality, intonation, and pauses. The therapist, on the other hand, may encounter difficulties in distinguishing clinically relevant verbal cues of his patient.

If these children enter a school system that helps them in their process of cognitive and social development and facilitates their adaptation to their new environment, many other stressors may be met adequately. If, on the other hand, as is the case in many inner-city areas, the schools are burdened with too many children, underpaid teachers, understaffing, and unresponsive political institutions, the child may be further exposed to a detrimental situation. In a study of elementary school children, Rutter et al. (1975) observed that the children's behavior varied according to the elementary school they attended. They found that behavioral difficulties were more frequent in children attending schools with higher rates of teacher and pupil turnover. They described the conflict created by the child's values and those of the school, and the impact of particular styles of teaching.

We must not forget that in spite of all these stressors many children seem to manage and not to require mental health interventions. In terms of particular family variables, Sandler (1980) studied a sample of kindergarten to third-grade inner-city children. He found that in those children with older siblings and two parents, the negative effects of stress were reduced. This extended network many times served to moderate the stress situations. Malone (1963) and Pavenstedt (1965) expressed striking cognitive and personality differences between older preschool children from stable poor families, and those from poor and in addition socially disorganized families. Whereas the former were able to benefit from preschool enrichment programs, the latter, even those of average or even superior intelligence, demonstrated serious learning problems by the time they entered nursery school at three years of age. Eisenberg (1967) stated that some of the inner-city children's strengths consist of accuracy of perception, belief in group values, good coping abilities, and freedom from self-blame.

Powell (1983) reminded us that Afro-American children have survived a history of repression and racism, and although there have been some casualties, there have been many more survivors.

Murphy and Moriarty (1978), talking about inner-city children, stated that some of the children in their study developed self-protective preventive devices such as timing rest, an ability to limit or fend off excessive stimulation, an ability to control the impact of the environment through strategic withdrawal, delay, and caution, and ability to select and restructure their environment.

These are thus added dimensions the clinician must consider. During his assessment he must evaluate the impact of migration, the degree of acculturation, and the particular community and family structure, with its concomitant ability to offer support or to cause stress. Canino (1985) stated that the clinician should first ask

TABLE 49.1 Sociocultural History

A. Sociocultural Family Attitudes	1. Family Religion (describe frequency of involvement)

	2. Family Belief System (describe frequency of involvement and for what purpose)
	  a. Spiritualism
	  b. Santerismo
	  c. Curanderismo
	  d. Root work
	  e. Shamanism
	  f. Other (specify)

	3. Family Festivities, meals, and special celebrations. Family feelings and identification with their own race or ethnic group.

	4. Family attitude towards:
	  a. Physical/mental health services
	    1. Overutilization
	    2. Underutilization
	  b. Schools/Education System
	  c. Children and adolescents
	  d. Child-rearing practices
	    1. dependency vs. autonomy
	    2. respect/discipline
	    3. familism
	    4. fatalism
	    5. sexual role expectations
	    6. expressions of aggression
	    7. socialization skills
	  e. Death and illness

	5. History of Culturally Expressed Syndromes
	  a. "Ataque"
	  b. Fallen fontanelle
	  c. Hiwa-Itck
	  d. Other (specify)

	6. Family Strengths and Coping Styles
B. Level of Acculturation of the Family to Their Community as Assessed by Diet, Language, Manner of Dress, Identification with the Larger Culture	1. absent 2. mild 3. moderate 4. complete

C. Migratory History (from another country or from the same country but a different city or state)	1. Reason for migration (describe briefly)
	  a. economic
	  b. illness-related
	  c. religious/political
	  d. other

	2. Area of origin
	  a. Description of area
	    1. rural
	    2. urban
	    3. other

     b. Ethnic or racial distribution and language spoken in area of origin
     c. Brief history of migrant's social standing in his society of origin
       1. level of employment
       2. level of education
       3. involvement in religious or social networks
     d. Language
  3. Back and forth migration to area of origin
     a. Level of extended family in area of origin
     b. Frequency of visits—ask specifically if child related
     c. Family members visiting area of origin
     d. Impact on child's:
       1. schooling and peer interaction
       2. family functioning
  4. "Migration" within host society
     a. Level of extended family in host society
     b. Frequency of moves
     c. Reasons for moves (specifically ask for child-related reasons)
     d. Family members involved
     e. Impact on child's school, peer interactions, family functioning, and health services

D. Sociocultural Environment

  1. Present or Host Society/Community
     a. Area:
       1. Urban
       2. Rural
     b. Describe present social network of the family and child
       1. ask for participation in social, religious, or educational organizations
     c. Hollingshead-Redlich level of S.E.S. of the family
     d. Living quarters
       1. home, apartment
       2. room allocation and distribution specifically as it relates to the child
     e. Language spoken by:
       1. the parents
       2. the children
      Describe what language is spoken at home and what language is spoken outside the household.
     f. Discriminatory stressors in the community or larger society
     g. Racial/ethnic and social class composition and stressors of the neighborhood and its schools

about dietary habits, major holidays, musical and religious interests, and community activities, and then should inquire about child-rearing practices and cultural attitudes toward teaching, disciplining, and playing with other children. Table 49.1 describes a series of variables that need to be considered in a family assessment of a culturally different child.

The neurological substrate of the child, coupled with his adaptive style and ego strengths, will be as important to assess as his areas of impairment. The child's ability to play and learn must be balanced by the capacity of his environment to offer adequate playgrounds and schools. The clinician working with these groups must thus try to maintain a wider tolerance of differences and unknowns and must attempt to integrate the larger variety of factors impinging on this population.

Spurlock (1985) stated that clinicians should "educate" their black patients about the process of therapy, be sensitive to the transference/countertransference issues that may evolve in working with a patient of a different race, consider the use of parameters, and be aware of any racial stereotyping.

In an article describing psychotherapy for these children, Graffagnino et al. (1970) strongly supported therapy concurrent with special school and environmental intervention; they cautioned therapists about their own countertransferential feelings of inadequacy and of being overwhelmed by the chaotic background of some of these children. Langner et al. (1974b) added that multifaceted preventive programs will be effective for these children. They recommended total medical care, increasing social levels, promoting minority group acceptance, and educating the parents in appropriate behavioral responses to their children.

CONCLUSION

This chapter has offered a multifaceted profile of children of other cultural subgroups in this country, primarily those in our large urban areas. General issues such as the impact of culture on symptom identification, referral patterns, assessment, and treatment modalities are mentioned. The complexities created by migration, education, urbanization, acculturation, social class, physical and psychological development, and language do not allow for a clear differentiation of what is cultural and what is not in children of our pluralistic society.

The clinician is formidably challenged to achieve adequate assessment; and it is advisable to be cautious in making generalizations. A sample of clinical and research articles is reviewed to emphasize the multidimensional aspects that have to be considered. Parental attitudes towards treatment, the nuances of proxemics, and the subtle interactions between social class and culture and between physical and psychological developmental stages are issues that become crucial during the evaluation and treatment of these children.

Finally, more research needs to be done on the effectiveness of particular treatment approaches for particular groups, on the assessment and evaluation tools that include a wider spectrum of relevant variables, and in assessing the strengths of those children who are able to cope and survive well under the impact of constant change.

REFERENCES

Allen, J. R. (1973). The Indian adolescent: Psychosocial tasks of the Plains Indian of western Oklahoma. *Amer. J. Orthopsychiat.* 43(3): 368–75.

Arce, A. (1982). Discussion: Cultural aspects of mental health care for Hispanic Americans. In A. Gaw (Ed.). *Cross Cultural Psychiatry.* Bristol: John Wright, pp. 137–48.

Beaglehole, E. (1937). Emotional release in a Polynesian community. *J. Soc. Abnorm. Psychol.* 32:319–38.

Bird, H., and Canino, I. (1980). The sociopsychiatry of Espiritismo: Findings of a study in psychiatric populations of Puerto Rican and other Hispanic children. *J. Amer. Acad. Child Psychiatry* 20(4):725–40.

Canino, G., and Canino, I. (1982). Culturally syntonic family therapy for migrant Puerto Ricans. *Hospital Comm. Psychiatry* April 299–303.

Canino, I. (1985). Taking a history. In D. Shaffer, A. Ehrhardt, and L. Greenhill (Eds.). *The Clinical Guide to Child Psychiatry.* New York: The Free Press, pp. 393–408.

———, Early, B., and Rogler, L. (1980). The Puerto Rican child in New York City: Stress and mental health. (Hispanic Research Center Monograph No. 4). New York: Fordham University.

———, et al. (1985). A comparison of symptoms and diagnoses in Hispanic and black children in an outpatient mental health clinic. *J. Amer. Acad. Child Psychiatry.* 25(2):254–59.

Clevenger, J. (1982) Native Americans. In A. Gaw (Ed.). *Cross Cultural Psychiatry.* Bristol: John Wright, pp. 149–58.

Cobb, C. (1972). Community mental health services in the lower socioeconomic classes: A summary of research literature on outpatient treatment (1963–1969). *Amer. J. Orthopsychiat.* 42(3):404–14.

Comer, J. (1985a). Black children and child psychiatry. *Amer. J. Child Psychiatry* 24:(2):129–33.

———. (1985b). Social policy and the mental health of black children. *Amer. J. Child Psychiatry* 24(2):175–81.

Cota-Roble de Suarez, C. (1971). Skin color as a factor of racial identifications and preferences of young Chicano children. *Aztlan* 2:107–50.

Creson, D. L., McKinley, C., and Evans, R. (1969). Folk medicine in the Mexican American subculture. *Dis. Nerv. System* 30(4):264–66.

Crow, L. D., Murray, W. I., and Sruythe, H. H. (1966). *Educating the Culturally Disadvantaged Child.* New York: David McKay.

Danna, J. J. (1980). Migration and mental illness: What role do traditional childhood socialization practices play? *Cult. Med. Psychiatry* 4(1):25–42.

De Blassie, R. R. (1978). Counseling with culturally disadvantaged adolescents. *Adolescence* 13(50):221–30.

De Vos, G. A. (1974). Cross-cultural studies of mental disorder: An anthropological Perspective. In S. Arieti (Ed.). *American Handbook of Psychiatry*, Vol. 2. 2d ed. New York: Basic Books, pp. 551–67.

Dohrenwend, B., and Dohrenwend B. (1969). *Social Status and Psychological Disorder: A Causal Inquiry.* New York: Wiley.

Eisenberg, L. (1967). Strengths of the inner city child. In A. Passow, H. Goldberg, M. and A. J. Tannenbaum (Eds.). *Education of the Disadvantaged.* New York: Holt, Rinehart and Winston, pp. 78–88.

Garrison, V. (1971). Supporting Structure in a Disorganized Puerto Rican Migrant Community. Paper presented at 70th Annual Meeting of the American Anthropolitical Association, New York, N.Y.

Gaw, A. (1982). Chinese Americans. In A. Gaw (Ed.). *Cross Cultural Psychiatry.* Bristol: John Wright, pp. 1–29.

Gluckman, M. (1959). *Custom and Conflict in Africa.* Oxford: Blackwell Press.

Gomez, A. G. (1982). Puerto Rican Americans. In A. Gaw (Ed.). *Cross Cultural Psychiatry.* Bristol: John Wright, pp. 109–36.

Graffagnino, P. N., et al. (1970). Psychotherapy for latency-age children in an inner-city therapeutic school. *Amer. J. Psychiatry* 127(5):626–34.

Guinee, V. (1972). Lead poisoning. *Amer. J. Med.* 53(3):283–88.

Harrison, S. I., et al. (1965). Social class and mental illness in children: Choice of treatment. *Arch. Gen. Psychiatry* 13:411–17.

Heacock, D. R. (1976). The black slum child and the problem of aggression. *Amer. J. Psychoanal.* 36:219–26.

Kiev, A. (Ed.). (1964). *Magic, Faith, and Healing.* New York: The Free Press.

Knight, G. P. (1978). Acculturation of second and third generation Mexican American children. *J. Cross-Cult. Psychol.* 9(1):87–97.

Krush, T. P., Sindell, P. S., and Nelle, J. (1966). Some thoughts on the formation of personality disorder: Study of an Indian boarding school population. *Amer. J. Psychiatry* 122:868–75.

La Barre, W. (1964). Confession as cathartic therapy in American Indian tribes. In A. Kiev (Ed.). *Magic, Faith, and Healing.* New York: The Free Press, pp. 36–49.

Langner, T., Gersten, J., and Eisenberg, J. (1974a). Approaches to measurement and definition in the epidemiology of behavior disorders: Ethnic background and child behavior. *Int'l. J. Health Serv.* 4:483–501.

———, et al. (1974b). Treatment of psychological disorders among urban children. *J. Consul. Clin. Psychol.* 42:170–80.

La Vietes, R. (1979). The Puerto Rican child. In J. Noshpitz (Ed.). *Basic Handbook of Child Psychiatry*, Vol. 1. New York: Basic Books, pp. 264–71.

Leighton, A. (1982). Relevant generic issues. In A. Gaw (Ed.). *Cross Cultural Psychiatry.* Bristol: John Wright, pp. 199–236.

Lin, T. (1953). A study of the incidence of mental disorder in Chinese and other cultures. *Psychiatry* 26:313–36.

Lubchansky, I., Egri, G., and Stokes, J. (1970). Puerto Rican spiritualists view mental illness. *Amer. J. Psychiatry* 127:312–21.

Lurie, O. R. (1974). Parents' attitudes toward children's problems and toward use of mental health services: Socioeconomic differences. *Amer. J. Orthopsychiatry* 44(1):109–20.

Lustman, S. L. (1970). Cultural deprivation: A clinical dimension of education. *Psychoanal. Study Child* 25:483–502.

McMichael, R. E., and Grinder, R. E. (1966). Children's guilt after transgression: Combined effect of exposure to American culture and ethnic background. *Child Devel.* 37(2):425–31.

Malone, C. A. (1963). Some observations on children of disorganized families and problems of acting out. *J. Amer. Acad. Child Psychiatry* 2:22–49.

Marcos, L. (1979). Effects of interpreters on the evaluation of psychopathology in non-English-speaking patients. *Amer. J. Psychiat.* 136(2):171–74.

Marsella, A. J. (1980). Depressive experience and disorder across cultures. In H. Triandis and J. Draguns (Eds.). *Handbook of Cross Cultural Psychopathology*, Vol. 6. Boston: Allyn and Bacon, pp. 291–349.

Meers, D. R. (1973). Psychoanalytic research and intellectual functioning of ghetto-reared black children. *Psychoanal. Study Child* 28:395–417.

———, and Gordon, G. (1972). Aggression and ghetto-reared American Negro children: Structural aspects of the theory of fusion-defusion. *Psychoanal. Quart.* 41(4):585–607.

Montare, A., and Boone, S. L. (1980). Aggression and paternal absence: Racial-ethnic differences among inner-city boys. *J. Genet. Psychol.* 137(2):223–32.

Murphy, J. M. (1964). Psychotherapeutic aspects of Shamanism on St. Lawrence Island, Alaska. In A. Kiev (Ed.). *Magic, Faith, and Healing.* New York: The Free Press, pp. 53–83.

Murphy, L. B., and Moriarty, A. E. (1978). *Vulnerability, Coping, and Growth: From Infancy to Adolescence.* 2d ed. New Haven: Yale University Press.

Mussen, P. H., Conger, J., and Kagan, J. (1974). *Child Development and Personality.* New York: Harper and Row.

Padilla, A. M., Carlos, M. L., and Keefe, S. E. (1976). Psychotherapy with the Spanish speaking: Issues in research and service delivery. (Spanish Speaking Mental Health Research Center Monograph 3). Los Angeles: UCLA.

Paton, S. M., and Kandel, D. B. (1978). Psychological factors and adolescent illicit drug use: Ethnicity and sex differences. *Adolescence* 13(50):187–200.

Pavenstedt, E. (1965). A comparison of the child-rearing environment of the upper, lower, and very lower class families. *Amer. J. Orthopsychiatry* 35:89–98.

Powell, J. (1983). Coping with adversity: The psychosocial development of Afro-American children. In J. Powell (Ed.). *The Psychosocial Development of Minority Group Children.* New York: Brunner/Mazel, pp. 49–76.

Prince, R. (1964). Indigenous Yoruba psychiatry. In A. Kiev (Ed.). *Magic, Faith and Healing.* New York: The Free Press, pp. 84–120.

———, (1980). Variations in psychotherapeutic procedures. In H. Triandis and J. Draguns (Eds.). *Handbook of Cross-Cultural Psychology-Psychopathology*, Vol. 6. Boston: Allyn and Bacon, pp. 291–349.

Quinton, D. (1980). Cultural and community influences. In M. Rutter (Ed.). *Scientific Foundations of Developmental Psychiatry.* London: Heinemann Medical Books, pp. 77–91.

Rabkin, J. G., and Struening, E. L. (1976). Life events, stress, and illness. *Science* 194:1013–20.

Riessman, F. (1962). *The Culturally Deprived Child.* New York: Harper and Row.

Ruiz, Pedro (1982). Cuban Americans. In A. Gaw (Ed.). *Cross Cultural Psychiatry.* Bristol: John Wright, pp. 75–86.

Rutter, M., et al. (1975). Attainment and adjustment in two geographical areas: Some factors accounting for area differences. *Brit. J. Psychiat.* 126:520–33.

Sandler, I. N. (1980). Social support resources, stress and maladjustment of poor children. *Amer. J. Comm. Psychol.* 8(1):41–52.

Saslow, H. L. (1968). Research on psychosocial adjustment of Indian youth. *Amer. J. Psychiatry* 125(2):224–31.

Sauna, V. D. (1981). Familial and sociocultural antecedents in psychopathology. In H. Triandis and J. Draguns (Eds.). *Handbook of Cross-Cultural Psychology-Pathology.* Vol. 6. Boston: Allyn and Bacon, pp. 175–236.

Schechtman, A. (1971). Psychiatric symptoms observed in normal and disturbed black children. *J. Clin. Psychol.* 27(4):445–47.

Singer, K., Ney, P. G., and Lieh-Mak, F. (1978). A cultural perspective on child psychiatric disorders. *Comprehen. Psychiatry* 19(6):533–40.

Spurlock, J. (1982). Black Americans. In A. Gaw (Ed.). *Cross Cultural Psychiatry.* Bristol: John Wright, pp. 163–78.

———. (1985). Assessment and therapeutic intervention of black children. *Amer. J. Child Psychiatry* 24(2):168–74.

Stewart, H. (1971). Kindling of hope in the disadvantaged: A study of the Afro-American healer. *Mental Hygiene* 55:96–100.

Stokes, D. H., and Meadow, A. (1974). Cultural differences in child guidance clinic patients. *Int'l. J. Soc. Psychiatry* 20(34):186–202.

Sue, D. W. (1981). *Counselling the Culturally Different: Theory and Practice.* New York: John Wiley.

Warren, R. C., et al. (1973). Differential attitudes of black and white patients toward treatment in a child guidance clinic. *Amer. J. Orthopsychiatry* 43(3):384–93.

Weisner, T. (1981). Cities, stress, and children: A review of some cross-cultural questions. In R. Munroe, R. Munroe, and B. Whiting (Eds.). *Handbook of Cross-Cultural Human Development.* New York: Garland, pp. 783–808.

Werner, E. E., and Smith, R. S. (1982). *Vulnerable But Invincible: A Study of Resilient Children.* New York: McGraw-Hill.

Wilkeson, A. G. (1982). Mexican Americans. In A. Gaw (Ed.). *Cross Cultural Psychiatry.* Bristol: John Wright.

Wittkower, E., and Prince, R. (1974). A review of transcultural psychiatry. In S. Arieti (Ed.). *American Handbook of Psychiatry.* Vol. 2. 2d ed. New York: Basic Books, pp. 535–50.

Yamamoto, J., et al. (1979). Psychopharmacology for Asian Americans and Pacific islanders. *Psychopharmacol. Bull.* 15:29–31.

Yap, P. M. (1969). The culture-bound reactive syndrome. In W. Candell and T. Y. Lin (Eds.). *Mental Health Research in Asia and the Pacific.* Honolulu: East-West Center Press, pp. 33–53.

IX

Approaches to Treatment

50

PSYCHODYNAMIC PSYCHOTHERAPIES

Jerome H. Liebowitz and Paulina F. Kernberg

Theories of human development and of the mind, when viewed through the everyday experiences of the child analyst, are alive, exciting, and applicable to clinical experiences and phenomena. In understanding that theory does not precede clinical fact, the child analyst is able to closely study techniques and tactical maneuvers in all child treatments. Child analytic concepts help the child psychotherapist map his course and explore the rugged terrain of therapeutic intervention. Through the child analytic experience, the therapist obtains a fuller appreciation of actual childhood events, adultomorphized memories of childhood, the family romance, screen memories, and the highly personalized myths of childhood.

John A. Sours, M.D. (1978)

Writing about the application of child analytic principles to forms of child psychotherapy, Sours (1978) observed that "child psychotherapy has been comparatively neglected over the years." At the turn of the century, the only childhood disorders that psychiatrists paid attention to were mental retardation, epilepsy, cerebral palsy, and juvenile delinquency, in which:

> . . . neurological defects and organic symptoms were emphasized to the exclusion of "psychological" factors. Behaving disorders did not seem to attract the attention of the psychiatrists; . . . [they were] looked at from the angle of misbehavior, of learning difficulties and poor social adjustment, and were thought to require "remedial teaching" or disciplining rather than psychological methods of treatment.
>
> Smirnoff (1971, p. 148)

The responsibility for helping children with emotional problems was thus initially invested in educators whose efforts "were to foster controls and facilitate mastery and achievement" (Sours 1978). As psychoanalysts became interested in childhood itself, and Freud indicated with the case of "Little Hans" how analytic concepts could inform the indirect treatment of children, psychoanalytic concepts were made available to educators. Child analysis itself, however, as a direct treatment of the child, had a slow, protracted birth. Around 1915, Hermine von Hug-Hellmuth modified analysis to make it applicable for children by introducing techniques like drawing and playing to facilitate the child's expression of fantasies. Child analysis emerged as a specialized discipline a decade or so later, with the publication of Anna Freud's first works and Melanie Klein's early papers in 1926–27.

In America, strongly influenced by child analytic concepts, the child-guidance clinic movement brought the focus of psychiatry "to problems which had hitherto been frankly regarded as 'minor' incidents in the development of the child, or as manifestations of some physical disorder" (Smirnoff 1971). With this development, however, the number and variety of child psychotherapies increased—ranging from the so-called "supportive" techniques to child psychoanalysis proper. Most of the therapies, however, were time-limited and focused play therapies with an emphasis on casework with the parents. The expectation, Sours (1978) noted, was that "education of parents would eventually be therapeutic and prophylactic for children."

But the problem-solving orientation of casework was disappointing. Child analysis became increasingly accepted as a treatment modality rather than just a body of knowledge of human behavior, as more disturbances of childhood were understood as manifestations of pathological intrapsychic processes or structures, requiring a psychodynamic treatment aimed at intrapsychic change.

With the increase of knowledge about the earliest stages of development came the "widening scope" of analysis and attempts at applying it to a wider variety of disorders. Modifications and parameters were introduced, resulting in several varieties of psychoanalytically oriented child psychotherapy for the treatment of more disturbed children. Social and environmental constraints also contributed to this development, through attempts at treating those children for whom analysis was indicated but unavailable because of limited time or money or lack of parental support. But little attention was paid to distinctions among the various types of psychotherapy, and there has been very little study and refinement of techniques comparable to those of adult psychotherapy. Buxbaum's (1954) call for research in this area over thirty years ago is still applicable: "When we know *which technique is best suited for which particular disturbance*, we will be able to make optimum use of the constructive ideas of child therapy produced under the influence of psychoanalysis" (p. 297).

This chapter follows Offenkrantz et al. (1982) in their use of the broadest definition of the term "psychodynamic," referring to all the propositions that derived from the application of the psychoanalytic point of view and not only to the specific psychoanalytic hypothesis of intrapsychic conflict. Defining individual psychodynamic psychotherapies largely in terms of the therapist's actions and goals, this chapter will consider four paradigmatic types of therapy—child psychoanalysis proper, expressive (or exploratory) child psychotherapy, supportive psychotherapy, and expressive-supportive child psychotherapy—focusing on similarities and differences among them. Such distinctions are important for effective and efficient treatment planning, as well as a necessary prerequisite for research.

DISTINCTIONS

The need to distinguish psychodynamic psychotherapy from child analysis has been debated by child analysts and child psychotherapists for decades. On one level, of course, all psychological interventions share certain goals: relief of psychic pain, improvement in human relationships, development of a clearer self-definition, better overall adaptive functioning, and increased learning and coping skills (McDermott and Harrison 1977). Beyond this, a psychodynamic orientation is distinguished by a focus on intrapsychic change as the central pathway to psychological improvement. The so-called "supportive" psychotherapies may also be understood as psychodynamic to the degree that they focus on intrapsychic processes, such as supporting appropriate "defenses." Pine's (1985) distinction of supportive versus interpretive therapies is helpful. In his discussion of "the interpretive moment," he showed how to develop variations on psychoanalytic technique "to bring a psychoanalytic orientation to bear on the realities of therapeutic work with . . . seriously disturbed patients" (p. 138). He distinguished "interpretations given in the context of support" from "interpretations given in the context of abstinence" (as in classical psychoanalysis). Maintaining "an underlying belief that insight is one of the best forms of support" (p. 157), he elucidated how support can be used to advance interpretation to work toward insight.

With this in mind, one may more clearly distinguish the kinds of "support" utilized in the four paradigmatic therapies mentioned above, as well as the differences in focus and goal in their use of interpretation and other verbal interventions. Such clear differentiation should allow the clinician to undertake a treatment, whether child analysis or one of the child psychotherapies, with more consistency in setting goals, choosing interventions, and responding empathically to the child.

Consistency and predictability are far more important with children than in adult work because of the child's need to anticipate and to trust as a prerequisite for optimal development. Thus, establishing a consistent technique permits the clinician to provide a clear model for the therapist's role. In turn the child will feel more confident and secure in the therapeutic relationship, which will enable him to concentrate optimally on therapeutic issues without the interference of such changing frameworks as educational interventions, seeing the child with the parents, varying frequencies of sessions, and gift giving.

With a clear scheme in mind, the analyst or therapist can avoid the pitfalls of either wild child analysis or wild child psychotherapy. Child analysis and psychodynamic child psychotherapy require specific training in technique and theory. Expressive-supportive psychotherapy, probably the most common treatment in our clinics and private practices, is not a lesser form of child analysis and cannot be improvised. Although its theory is still evolving, it will in time become as rigorous as child analysis.

Comparisons among the various therapies based on psychoanalytic theory, ranging from child analysis on one end of the spectrum to psychoanalytically oriented supportive psychotherapy on the other, must begin with an examination of the goals and technical considerations, including the nature of transference and countertransference. Interventions also vary, including the handling of dreams, play, and the nature of contact with the parents.

Child Analysis

Others have written in great detail about the theory and practice of child analysis and how it is the most intensive (with sessions four to five times a week) and ambitious of the psychotherapies, achieving its goals by promoting fundamental intrapsychic changes (A. Freud 1948; Glenn 1978; Pearson 1968; Sandler et al. 1980; Smirnoff 1971). The aim of child analysis is the resolution of conflicts and resistances stemming from the various psychosexual levels and the full resumption of development. To be achieved are the resolution of symptoms and character change with adaptive compromise, including sublimatory activities. Central to this is the child's acquisition of insight so that symptoms and pathological character traits become ego-dystonic and can then be resolved. As Sours (1978) summarized:

> Child analysis relies principally on interpretation for its effectiveness. . . . It offers the person of the analyst as a transference object for the revival and interpretation of unconscious fantasies and attitudes. . . . Relief of tension doesn't come from catharsis, but from lifting material from primary thought process to secondary thought process. Like adult analysis, child analysis turns id into ego content (p. 618).

Insight also facilitates the child's self-awareness and perceptions of ways of coping with anxiety and depression. Although the expression of insight may differ in children and adolescents compared with adults, this achievement can still be expected. Heinicke et al. (1965), for instance, cited the case of Steven, an 11-year-old who clearly indicated his awareness of his own motivations and potentially self-defeating behavior. Child patients may interpret their own behavior by attributing their understanding to the analyst (Kennedy 1979) or by applying their insight to situations outside analysis. One 10-year-old explained, "If I am afraid of you, I can see how easy it is for me to be afraid of my teacher!"

Nevertheless, although the general goal of structural change is the same for adult and child analysis, it is important to recognize the child's immature and developing personality. Structural change therefore has to be redefined in accordance with this process of development and further growth (Bernstein and Sax 1978).

Expressive Child Psychotherapy

This category of therapy, often called long-term psychoanalytically oriented or exploratory psychotherapy, is a form of analytic work conducted under less than optimal circumstances. It is less intensive than analysis (with frequency of sessions usually twice weekly instead of four to five times per week) and has somewhat more limited goals. Regressive transference experiences are less intense. The therapist is less likely to use transference interpretation as a major technical tool and is as likely to employ extratransference-related interpretations to work on unconscious interactions. Interpretation is still the predominant intervention, with clarification and confrontation as preliminary steps. Reconstructive and genetic interpretations may be used, but character change is not necessarily a goal. Resolution of conflicts from relevant developmental levels is sought, but not from all developmental levels as in child analysis.

From another vantage point, symptom resolution and the resumption of development are goals, but with a focus on only those areas in which an interference with development prevails. Compared to supportive psychotherapy, which provides or enhances the repertoire of defenses and coping mechanisms, expressive child psychotherapy uses uncovering techniques to confront defenses and decrease the need for using defenses excessively or rigidly. Likewise, the emergence of anxiety-provoking fantasies and feelings is encouraged rather than suppressed. The providing of generalized reassurance or advice is generally avoided.

Supportive Psychotherapy

Although there are many forms of "supportive" psychotherapy, this chapter addresses only that in which the use of psychodynamic principles is primary. To be sure, no such therapy is purely and totally supportive, "in that elements of support and uncovering are intermixed inextricably in any form of psychodynamic psychotherapy" (Offenkrantz et al. 1982). But looking at supportive psychotherapy as if it existed in a pure state, one can distinguish certain characteristics for the purpose of further discussion. As Offenkrantz et al. (1982) defined it, "The goal of supportive psychotherapy is to help maintain or restore the individual to the highest previous level of functioning while attempting to alleviate symptoms and improve self-esteem. The goals do not include character change, increased self-awareness, or the confrontation of defenses" (p. 9).

Supportive techniques, to the contrary, have as their goal the strengthening of appropriate adaptive defenses to deal with conflict; as Pine (1985) put it, "to keep the patient's defenses functioning at their best" (p. 157). In pursuit of this goal, pathological defenses may indeed need to be confronted, but such confrontation is not itself a goal.

The therapist's psychodynamic understanding and insight will be used to plan appropriate interventions (and the therapist's verbal activity will often be greater here than in other forms of psychodynamic psychotherapy), but insight is not itself a goal and, when applied, it is more toward the child's impact on others and social awareness rather than self-awareness or awareness of motivational antecedents stemming from the child's past.

Symptom relief rather than symptom resolution is a goal, as is reintegration of character rather than character change. In this way, supportive psychotherapy is structure-maintaining and growth-producing. Instead of interpreting behavior and feelings, the therapist might use suggestion, instruction, and advice to help the child solve specific problems or to find alternative courses of action. As Offenkrantz et al. (1982) pointed out, "It may be useful for the psychotherapist to communicate feelings and personal information in order to provide the patient with a model and to avoid the development of transference distortions" (p. 9). By maintaining the patient's ties to human objects in the context of the patient-therapist relationship, all psychotherapies, according to Pine (1985), provide a "holding" object-relational environment that provides a nonspecific form of support. This relationship itself, however, is often a specific therapeutic element in the long-term supportive psychotherapy of extremely disturbed children. Referring to it as "the therapeutic context of safety," Pine noted how it "permits not only exploration and the risks of change but also the emergence of more benign, healthy, adaptive modes at each developmental step" (p. 134). Such treatment may be short-term or long-term, with sessions varying in frequency from one to three sessions per week to only once or twice a month.

Expressive-Supportive Child Psychotherapy

With the above distinctions in mind, a fourth type of therapy can be defined that uses both expressive and supportive techniques in a deliberate manner to treat the many children who do not have indications for child analysis or expressive psychotherapy (see below) or for whom a more focused treatment is indicated. The theory for this form of treatment is still being explicated, although it is probably the most widely used form of individual child psychotherapy and is what most writers and clinicians are referring to when they speak of child psychotherapy. For the remainder of this chapter, unless specifically noted otherwise, we shall be referring to this form of treatment when writing about "child psychotherapy."

Insight is less central to expressive-supportive child psychotherapy, where the goals are partial or more focal, than to analysis or expressive psychotherapy. Here, the acquisition of insight refers mainly to increased self-awareness, including awareness of one's own behavioral characteristics, impact on others, and awareness of others, rather than insight about the causes and repetitions from the past into the present.

Moreover, we can draw certain inferences about goals from the reasons a child is referred for psychotherapy. In a child population there are mainly three types of reasons for referral: (1) specific symptoms; (2) persistent interpersonal conflicts with family members, teachers, or peers; and (3) delay, arrest, or regression in adaptive and emotional development. Therefore, the individual therapist attempts to act in such a way as to: (1) relieve symptoms; (2) improve interpersonal functioning; and (3) facilitate the resumption of social and emotional development.

These objectives can be implemented through the therapeutic setting, the therapist's attitudes, the use of play, and specific verbal interventions, among which clarification, confrontation, and such supportive interventions as suggestion, manipulation, and education play a significant role. Interpretations are more frequently extratransference interpretations addressed to the child's relation to important persons or transference interpretations referring to the therapist in the "here and now" situation. Nonverbal interventions are present throughout the treatment and may even become more important than the verbal interventions. Relief from symptoms and increased ego strength are achieved through the strengthening or facilitation of adaptive defenses, the resolution of primitive defenses as they express themselves in current interactions, and environmental manipulation or restructuring more than insight. Sessions range in frequency from one to three times per week. Length of treatment is more definite and may be determined in advance by the therapist, parents, and child, with specific behaviors or symptoms targeted for improvement.

The therapeutic alliance—which in analysis and expressive psychotherapy is established as a background for interpreting resistances and transferences with maximum collaboration of the child's observing ego—may be an end in itself, providing a corrective object relationship (Curtis 1979). Through the actual relationship with the therapist and his providing a holding function, identifications occur more with the therapist as a person than, as in analysis and expressive psychotherapy, with the therapist's function as therapist.

Compared to analysis and expressive psychotherapy, where the unfolding process is left largely to the child with great autonomy regarding subject matter and timing, here the therapist focuses actively on specific areas and is more involved with parents and school. There may be conjoint parent-child work at different points in the treatment.

The therapist may follow a specific path aimed at reaching the targeted goals and may choose topics for discussion that take into account the outside reality. To an 8-year-old suffering from encopresis, the therapist might say, "You have not mentioned to me your soiling, yet your parents told me you have been worried about it."

Being a combination of insight-oriented and supportive techniques, this form of treatment may lead to interpretation and insight in some patients and to treatment via the therapeutic alliance of the holding environment in others. Along these lines, Anna Freud (1948) emphasized that the treatment situation is like a smorgasbord from which the child may take what he needs to get better. Not infrequently, a consistently well carried out supportive psychotherapy may evolve into expressive psychotherapy.

TREATMENT PLANNING: INDICATIONS AND CONTRAINDICATIONS

Other chapters in this book cover the varieties of assessment and gathering of data used in understanding the nature of the individual child patient's disorder from biological, psychological, and social perspectives. All of this is necessary for the development of the full psychodynamic formulation that will be more than a descriptive diagnosis or listing of symptoms. It will also include a developmental perspective, focusing on continuities and discontinuities in development, as well as the level of development of the structural components of the personality—reflected in the degree of object constancy, frustration tolerance, impulse control, reality testing and such intrapsychic factors as the degree of internalized conflict, predominant defense mechanisms, the quality of object relations, and the nature of the self-system. It will also include an assessment of such factors as intellectual endowment, psychological mindedness, character traits, and coping styles. And all of this will be understood as well in the context of the child's family—including family characteristics that encourage clear ego boundaries and autonomy, as well as the possible role of the child's symptoms in maintaining a precarious family equilibrium or the possible role of family members as participants in the child's psychopathology. Especially when psychodynamic treatment is considered, this should also include an assessment of the parents' emotional capacity to facilitate treatment, to recognize their child's suffering, and to want him to be well, independent of their own psychopathology (Bernstein 1958).

Once a psychodynamic formulation has been derived from the clinical data, the task is to match the available treatment modalities to the needs of the child. Choosing the best method of treatment in the least restrictive and most cost-effective manner would be an easier task than it is if we already had more definitive answers to this research question. For the time being, we must rely on clinical experience to guide us in our choice of treatment modality, recognizing that different therapies may have different effects as well as goals.

Indications

With the different goals discussed above in mind, we can explore the indications for child analysis/expressive psychotherapy, expressive-support child psychotherapy, and psychodynamic-supportive psychotherapy. For individual psychodynamic psychotherapy, an essential indication is an internalized problem or conflict. Pearson (1968) listed four criteria that "show that the child's symptoms are the result of an inner attempt to *change himself* and only secondarily to make a change in his environment":

1) the nature of the symptoms (e.g., phobias, etc.);
2) the child's environment, particularly the parents' attitudes, seems to be reasonably helpful to his development, despite the persisting problem;
3) the child's symptomatic reactions "do not seem to be triggered by outstanding events in his personal life but rather by the minor daily events or even without any noticeable event taking place" (p. 52);
4) change of environment seems to make little difference to the course of the symptom picture.

A second essential indication is an interference with development that is not adequately dealt with by the child's ego assisted by parental support (A. Freud 1948). When this is present, psychodynamic therapy may help to reduce anxiety, resolve pathological defensive structures, and open up appropriate outlets for the drives so that development can progress.

With either of these two indications present, more specific indications for each of the psychodynamic treatments may be considered. In general, severe chronic neurosis can be treated best with child analysis (A. Freud 1948). In this category we would include symptomatic neuroses that interfere with developmental processes, such as hysterical, depressive, phobic, and obsessive-compulsive neuroses, as well as neurotic sexual perversions and character neuroses. Children suffering from psychosomatic disorders such as anorexia nervosa or with narcissistic personalities may also benefit from analysis if motivated for treatment and if there are general signs of ego strength, such as a degree of tolerance for anxiety, frustration, and depression. Along similar lines, we should consider analysis for high-functioning borderline patients with similar ego strengths as well as the capacity for sublimation and some degree of superego integration. Child analysis may also be indicated for behavior disorders due to character neurotic problems or antisocial behavior caused by an unconscious need for punishment as a result of a strong sense of guilt, but not for the so-called unsocialized conduct disorders. Finally, certain psychosomatic disorders, such as asthma, constipation, and some cases of enuresis, should be included as indications for child analysis if they are also interfering with development.

For children in those groups in which analysis is indicated but treatment is not feasible due to lack of parents' motivation, a lack of psychoanalysts, financial factors, or other circumstances, expressive child psychotherapy can approximate child analysis. Although done under less than optimal circumstances, it has definite, if more limited, effects.

Heinicke et al. (1965) followed up children seen four times a week versus once a week by the same child analysts. At follow-up, children seen four times a week were generally more advanced in their libidinal development, showed greater growth in their overall self-esteem, and more frequently demonstrated the capacity to form interpersonal relations characterized by a gratifying libidinal exchange with a realistic give-and-take. They could express a greater variety of affects and were less dependent on others, showing considerable autonomy with a positive balance between effective assertion and defensive passivity. In other words, these children had made greater progress in terms of ego integration, differentiation, and adaptation. Although they might have shown evidence of fixation, the regressive forces were less intense, and they showed more neutralized and adaptive forms of functioning. Character traits could be traced to fixation points, but they were adequately integrated into the child's functioning. Their defensive organization was more balanced, and they revealed capacities for sublimation and creativity. Even in reading and spelling, they improved more than children seen only once a week. Last but not least, they showed a greater insight in their ability to observe their own behavior and the motives underlying it.

Because of this, it is recommended that expressive psychotherapy be conducted twice weekly, to maximize the expected therapeutic gains.

Child analysis is a powerful treatment modality when well indicated and is the method that most respects the child's individuality. But for children with internalized problems who do not have indications for child analysis, expressive-supportive child psychotherapy is the treatment of choice. It is recommended for children with severe forms of character pathology, such as lower functioning borderline patients with ego weaknesses and narcissistic personalities with borderline features. Children with separation anxiety or conduct disorders with contraindications for analysis, some forms of psychosis, minimal brain dysfunction, or mild mental retardation can also be treated with expessive-supportive psychotherapy with particular variations for each of these syndromes.

A specific form of expressive-supportive psychotherapy, focal or brief psychodynamic psychotherapy, should also be considered for children functioning at a neurotic level with strong motivation, psychological mindedness, and a clearly delineated problem understood as a manifestation of an intrapsychic conflict. Acute neurotic symptom formation, adolescent crises, and acute grief reactions are also indications for focal psychodynamic psychotherapy with a goal of symptom relief. With sessions scheduled once or twice weekly for twelve to forty sessions, the therapist maintains a high level of activity, planning, and data selection. The work is limited to the exploration and resolution of a specific area in intrapsychic conflict felt to be central to the symptom picture and amenable to insight. The goal is for the child to learn new and more adaptive coping and problem-solving skills through increased understanding of his contribution to what had previously been experienced as mostly external problems. Such treatment should not begin during a life crisis that may require immediate action or support, such as acute bereavement or traumatic accident, for which a crisis-intervention form of supportive psychotherapy is indicated.

Children with chronic, characterological forms of pathology, when circumstances preclude longer term analytic therapy, may also benefit from a more supportive, focal, symptom-relief form of treatment.

Other indications for psychodynamically supportive psychotherapy may include children suffering from the effects of mild mental retardation, physical handicap, terminal illness, or psychosis, where a strengthening or enhancement of their adaptive defenses and coping mechanisms would help them deal better with issues of low self-esteem and competence, conflicts with the environment and within themselves, and developmental fixations or arrests.

When considering any form of psychodynamic therapy, the clinician must also evaluate the possible usefulness of other therapeutic modalities such as medication, behavior modification, family therapy, group therapy, and environmental manipulation and modification. For optimal treatment, however, there must always be an understanding of the relevant psychodynamic factors, whichever treatment modality is primary.

Contraindications

These are more relative than absolute. For child analysis or expressive psychotherapy, psychoses and pervasive developmental disorders are contraindications. Regressive symptomatology that is only an expression of a temporary developmental disturbance requiring no therapeutic intervention other than parent counseling is a contraindication for any form of individual psychotherapy. An unstable life situation that requires immediate or repeated emergency interventions is also a contraindication for psychodynamic psychotherapy. The presence of "unstable parents who provide a threatening or excessively stimulating or depriving environment" (Bernstein and Sax 1978) constitutes a contraindication to analysis, expressive psychotherapy, or expressive-supportive psychotherapy without prior environmental manipulation. Likewise, long-term individual psychotherapy cannot be conducted in the context of an unstable life situation that requires immediate or repeated emergency interventions.

BASIC PRINCIPLES AND TECHNICAL CONSIDERATIONS

The basic principles of the psychodynamic point of view have been summarized by Offenkrantz et al. (1982). They include:

1) The concept of *psychic determinism*—that psychological behavior can be understood in terms of psychological causes;
2) The *pleasure-unpleasure principle* as a motivational basis for behavior;
3) The concept of a *dynamic unconscious* with repression of intrapsychic conflict;
4) The *genetic point of view* that early life experiences and the vicissitudes of maturation and development have a lasting effect on behavior;
5) The concept of *symptoms* as attempts at adaptation through unconscious compromise formation;
6) The concept of *transference*, referring to the "perceptions, needs, and quality of interactions that the individual tends to create in relationship with the therapist and other significant persons" (p. 5), reflecting past experiences and ongoing needs imposed upon current relationships;
7) The concept of *intrapsychic structures* (id, ego, superego, and self) and the view that "psychopathology may occur either as a result of failure of adequate structure formation due to developmental vicissitudes or as a result of conflict between or within structures" (p. 5).

Child psychotherapies based on these principles are by necessity different from adult psychotherapies because of important developmental factors. Because of the child's position of real dependency on his parents, we must reckon with the actual presence and ongoing influence of the parents in the child's daily life. Even if the relationship with the parents is not itself a pathogenic factor, therapeutic work with the parents becomes essential. The child's ongoing development is itself another significant factor, since developing defense mechanisms and character traits are less structured and more fluctuating.

Taking these factors into account, certain technical considerations and distinctions become important: the nature of transference and countertransference, the functions of the therapist, the use of play, the use of dreams, the nature of verbal interventions, and the inclusion of the parents in the treatment process.

The Nature of Transference and Countertransference

Because the child's immature superego is still very dependent on the outer world and often makes excessive demands on the child's ego, the therapist may have to guide the child, much as a parent, thereby lessening the technical neutrality of not taking sides with the child's wishes or prohibitions. The therapist may have to take sides. As Anna Freud (1948) suggested, the therapist "must succeed in putting himself in the place of the child's ego ideal," exerting an "educational" influence to enable the superego to be less tyrannical and approximate social reality. To enhance the treatment process, other parameters are frequently used in child psychotherapy, with a further lessening of the therapist's technical neutrality. Gift giving or eating during sessions, for instance, may be used if indicated.

In our opinion, a variety of transference reactions develops in child psychotherapy. Partial aspects of the transference are actively selected by the therapist according to external reality, the level of transference reactions, and the goals of the treatment. For the most part, it is the negative transference that is explored, whereas the positive transference, including idealization, is left untouched. In child analysis, on the other hand, the movement is more toward the development of a transference neurosis, with as many past object relations relived in the transference as possible, given the personalities of both the child and the analyst. Positive as well as negative transferences are systematically explored.

One reason for the different handling of the transference, in addition to the more focused nature of psychotherapy, lies in what is often the different nature of the transference. Children with indications for analysis can usually maintain the separation of self and object representations. The mechanisms of defense they most generally employ are repression, reaction formation, isolation, withdrawal into fantasy, projection, introjection, suppression, and higher forms of denial.

With children in psychotherapy, however, especially those with borderline structure, the transference is often characterized by the activation of preoedipal object relations and encompasses issues of self-integration. The child may project self images while enacting internal and partial object images. In some cases of psychotic regression there are instances of outright fusion. Also problematic are the shifting ego states and primitive defense mechanisms such as denial, splitting, primitive forms of projection, devaluation, and idealization. Deanimation of people or animation of inanimate objects may occur in instances of psychosis.

These differences affect the nature of the therapist's reaction in the different modes of treatment. In child analysis, when the patient's object representations are projected onto the analyst, the analyst reacts to these projections with the preservation of distance in time and space. In other words, the analyst has already experienced in the past what the patient is experiencing and can at all times maintain the delineation between himself and the patient. The tripartite structures of ego, id, and superego are evident, and one can distinguish superego or id projections vis-à-vis the patient's ego.

A contrasting situation can emerge in expressive-supportive psychotherapy, where the therapist loses perspective with the child's severe psychopathology. The therapist may at times identify with the child's projections, losing transitorily the distance between self and patient. Or because the projections are so intense and accompanied by primitive affects, the therapist may lose true empathy and instead "relive" in unison the experiences of the patient, again lessening the differentiation between patient and therapist. Moreover, because the tripartite structures are less delineated in the patient and self or object representations are projected in an oscillating manner, the therapist may assume a partial aspect of the patient's self while the patient becomes an object, or vice versa. For instance, the therapist may be in the position of the defenseless frightened child, while the child adopts the role of the overcontrolling, strict, and sadistic teacher.

Functions of the Therapist

As discussed above, the therapist provides a "holding function" as well as being an object for transference. In child psychotherapy the therapist may also function as a "new object" for repetition and mastery and perhaps a "corrective emotional experience" (Alexander 1956), since the therapist *is* different from the parent. In this way, many of the child's attitudes to the therapist are not really transferred, since the child uses him as a "new object" (Smirnoff 1971).

Anna Freud (1965) pointed to yet another function when she noted that many relations between the therapist and child are due to externalization—"a process in which the person of the analyst is used to represent one or the other part of the patient's personality structure"; representing the child's *id*, by tolerating freedom of thought, fantasy, and, to a certain extent, action; becoming an auxiliary *ego* for help and protection against anxiety; and acting as an external *superego* in his role as an adult.

In addition, the "educational" influences of the therapist must not be overlooked. These include the guidance the therapist provides to the child's immature superego, the inevitable identifications with the therapist, and some degree of positive conditioning as well as direct education and information giving.

Play

We have come a long way from Ferenczi's (1913) complaint that he was unsuccessful in his attempts to analyze a child because the child wanted only to play! Play for the child often is a form of "talking," an expression of his feelings, impulses, attitudes, fantasies, and concerns, since verbal expression requires a language of considerable abstraction and complexity not available to most children. Developmentally we may also understand the child's propensity for play as reflecting his tendency to motor activity rather than thinking or remembering. By permitting some distance from the self and others through displacement, play and drawings, which are "midway" between motoric play and verbalizations (Cooper and Wanerman 1977), also allow the child safe expression of feelings and thoughts and a means for attempting resolution of conflict and compromise formation. Tactful inquiry can usually elicit further elaboration of fantasies and concerns.

Thus play can serve as a substitute for free association and the basis for verbal interpretation. In child psychotherapy, play also takes place for its own sake, capitalizing on its intrinsic healing qualities for externalizing conflict, for mastering anxiety, for serving as a respite from internal pressure, and for exercising new solutions. In this way, play itself may fulfill the therapeutic goals.

Caution is necessary with some children, however, when instead of liberating fantasies, play ends in play disruption, with the child discharging aggressive drives directly rather than playing them out. This makes for technical problems, requiring some degree of limit setting as well as understanding.

With older children, the functions of play are more limited, although play may still be used for relationship building ("playing while we talk"), for the inherent fun, and for necessary periodic retreats from anxiety-laden discussions.

Dreams

Different focuses of intervention can be seen in the therapist's use of and response to dreams in the different therapeutic modes. Although children do not free associate, they are sometimes able to say "what pops up" in their minds about their dreams. In child analysis or expressive therapy, dream interpretation may be possible. In expressive-support child psychotherapy, only the manifest content of the dream is looked at, as it relates to general issues in the treatment and the life situation. Integration of psychic life can be promoted by retranslating the dream into secondary process—the opposite of child analysis, where the latent content of the dream is explored.

Verbal Interventions

Emphasis on verbalization of unconscious fantasies is a key element in the therapeutic efforts of psychodynamic child psychotherapy. Indeed, verbal interventions assume a progressively more important role relative to nonverbal interventions as the treatment proceeds. Clarification and confrontation are used as therapeutic interventions themselves as well as preliminary steps for interpretation. They may take the form of invitations to continue (e.g., "Does that make you think of anything?"; "What do you think about_____?"; "What pops into your thoughts when you picture that?") or "see the pattern . . ." statements (P. Kernberg et al. in preparation) that show connecting shapes or patterns in events, affects, behaviors, or ideas, focusing on the relationships among them and implying that certain observed material is dynamically connected, significant, and therapeutically relevant (e.g., "Every time we talk about your sister you change the subject to something else"; "Have you noticed that your stomachaches almost never happen on weekends or holidays?"). These interventions may also be made indirectly, by the therapist's use of play, fantasy, or the child's imagined responses to other people or things (e.g., "How did that make rabbit feel?"; "No matter how many gifts the Dolly gets, she's always unhappy").

Interpretations are inferences about the significance of the child's experience. Usually they connect in meaningful ways conscious experiences to unconscious material such as wishes, fears, distortion, and defenses. These inferences, made directly or indirectly, may be: about defenses (e.g., "The horse tries to scare the other horses so that they won't guess he's scared of them"; "You expect me to yell at you because actually you're mad at me and feel like yelling at me"); about motives (e.g., "The little calf wished her mother would take a trip so she and her daddy could stay home together, just the two of them"; "When you get scared you'll never have enough, that's when you eat up all the cookies"); and about past experiences, i.e. reconstructive-genetic ("When the mommy and daddy doll had that new baby, the girl doll thought that she wasn't enough for them, and now she had the same idea whenever she thinks she's disappointed them; it started back then"; "When you keep playing the 'falling off the table' game, I think you're playing what you think happened to Mommy when she got hurt").

WORK WITH PARENTS

The child's parents must be included in the field of treatment at least to maintain a collaborative alliance. Of course, the parents might be referred for therapy quite independent of the child's problems. But, as parents, and not only if there is an impaired relationship with the child, there is therapeutic work to be done, since the child's treatment must deal with the total family situation and not isolated elements. Parents may feel guilty, defensive, or jealous—and their feelings must not be neglected. With children up to midlatency age, it is both therapeutic and prophylactic to see the parents regularly to increase their understanding of their child and his behavior and pathology. As Buxbaum (1954) pointed out, "The specific nature of the relationship between child and parent should, in each individual case, determine the recommendation for the extent of contact to be maintained, and for the therapeutic method to be used with the parents" (p. 313).

Parents need to be seen to ensure that they provide the continuing emotional and practical support that the child must have to continue in therapy. This includes not only providing the financial resources and transportation necessary, but also a tolerance for change. With younger or emotionally immature children, there may also be a "need to have mother's approval and permission for their feelings and thoughts" (Buxbaum 1954). In fact, the child may not be able to be seen without mother in the room.

In each form of psychodynamic psychotherapy, the collaborative alliance with the parents entails discussing the overall maintenance of the treatment and the parents' fantasies about the treatment process and the therapist's role, as well as clarifying the child's developmental needs—all without interfering with the confidentiality of the process. The goals of working with the parents include increasing parental empathy, obtaining general information about the child, clarifying the child's developmental needs, and resolving any fantasies about the treatment or the analyst which may threaten the continuation of treatment.

In expressive-supportive or supportive psychotherapy, in addition, the therapist may undertake dynamic counseling with the parents, giving information, advice, and practical suggestions. E. Sperling (1979) has reviewed and explicated these techniques in detail. Such counseling remains focused around the child's difficulties and the parent's reactions to the child and the therapy. In this setting, the nature of contact with the parent(s) is determined by the needs arising from the child's psychopathology and problems in external adjustment and by the parent's reaction to the child's treatment. Buxbaum (1954) noted, "Whenever the parent reacts to the treatment of the child with such apprehension, jealousy, and guilt feelings that his own disturbance affects the child, the amount of time spent with the parent must be increased" (p. 304). The goal would be to reduce frustration, guilt feelings, and the tension arising from the child's treatment to effect a change of attitude in the parent, thereby permitting the child's therapy to proceed without interference.

Such counseling could, of course, go beyond this and begin to help the parent to face his own problems and accept a referral for his own psychotherapy.

A specialized form of therapeutic work, called tripartite therapeutic design by Margaret Mahler (1968), was first described by Paula Elkish (1953), who treated simultaneously a 2½-year-old boy and his mother. This treatment is indicated for separation anxiety in preschool age children (or older children developmentally still at this stage), especially when the mother shows greater difficulties in separating than the child and the mother-child relationship needs to be the focus of therapy.

In such cases, mother and child represent a pathological unit that cannot and should not be broken. The role of the therapist is to make the interplay the subject and the patient of the therapy—the dyad of mother and child is respected. In terms of the child, the therapist's role is to play an auxiliary ego, especially in mastering in doses the various aspects of the separation-individuation process. In terms of the mother, the therapist's role is to be a model. But to be accepted as a model and to build a collaborative alliance with the mother, the therapist must empathize with her anxiety as well as the child's, and verbalize how difficult it is for her to let go of the child. It is important to support the mother's own autonomy by encouraging her to have her own dependency needs acknowledged and by encouraging her to socialize and have other experiences in addition to taking care of her child.

The therapist must be careful not to play with the child and exclude mother, nor to talk with mother and exclude the child. Clarifications and interpretations must be made so that both child and mother can understand them. Role playing may be useful, with the therapist, mother, and child interchanging roles to actualize concretely projections and introjections so that the child can experience what it is like to be grown up, and vice versa.

NATURE OF CHANGE AND CRITERIA FOR TERMINATION

The changes we hope to effect in any child with psychodynamic psychotherapy may be attributed to a combination of factors, including those specific to the therapy, such as the development of insight into and resolution of intrapsychic conflict, as well as those nonspecific factors that Pine (1985) described as "all things that the ordinary sensitive parent provides for the growing child" (p. 167). These include the opportunity for growth and further development, identifications with the therapist, corrective emotional experiences (Alexander 1956), and positive conditioning.

Although it remains a research question which of these factors is more important in bringing about which changes, the changes themselves can be assessed reliably to know when treatment should end—that is, when the psychodynamically derived goals have been attained and normal development has resumed.

Smirnoff (1971) has outlined criteria for termination: symptomatic improvement (including the disappearance of symptoms, improved family relations, resumption of schoolwork, adjustment into a social group, and the disappearance of openly aggressive behavior or the lifting of interfering inhibitions); the development of a fantasy life (with a gradual lessening of inhibitions and increasing variety and freedom of expression in play and word); and structural criteria, especially flexible defenses and ego mastery, sublimatory activities, autonomy from fantasy, and improved adaptation.

Current trends continue to press the psychotherapist towards a more efficient use of time and of the family's economic resources. It becomes especially important to know when therapy has advanced sufficiently so that termination may begin to be considered. In addition to extratherapeutic sources of information that indicate symptomatic improvement as well as better adaptation to family, school and peers, and the resumption of development, we can look at changes within the therapy sessions themselves as a guide to an independent assessment of change and improvement, with the child as his or her own comparison.

Kernberg (in press) has gathered a number of such criteria from looking at behaviors within the sessions that suggest improved psychological functioning and hence a justification for considering termination. These criteria have been grouped under:

1. Statements about the therapist that reflect the emergence from transference distortion, the capacity to test reality, and the existence of an observing ego. The child may begin to acknowledge the therapist's role directly, commenting, for example, on a sense of being listened to or helped to find connections. A sense of individuation within the context of a trusting relationship may be illustrated by the child's capacity to talk about the therapist's traits and to use his observing ego. The child may begin to anticipate comments by the therapist or to make statements reflecting an identification with the therapist or the therapist's role. A child may describe thinking about the therapist "in my head" or may imagine that the therapist, had he been present at a particular moment, would have asked, "What could be the connection between how you are feeling and what you are doing?"

2. Changes in the child's perception of the treatment that represent trends toward the resolution of transference paradigms as the child's interests expand in the outside world. A clear sign of this shift is the child's bringing in more material from current reality. An important change in the child's perception of the treatment is a beginning sense of the passage of time within the treatment situation. Statements about the history of the treatment portray the child's sense of continuity of himself throughout time and his ability to synthesize different aspects of the self in a cohesive self-representation. This sense of time may also be projected into the future indicating a continuity of oneself in the future without the therapist and signifying a capacity for autonomy and age-appropriate independence.

3. Changes in the quality of communications that reflect the child's greater capacity to put needs into words rather than action. The quantity of verbalization may increase, and reflectiveness in general may be more apparent, signifying the capacity to delay, to contemplate alternatives through thinking, and thereby to master conflicts more efficiently. Towards the end of treatment, although conflicts may remain, their resolution proceeds at a faster pace, with less interpretive work required.

4. Changes in affects that indicate the capacity for tolerating frustration and anxiety, for integrating superego functions, and for the integration of ambivalence. The modulation of affects should be increased, and there should be an appropriate range, intensity, and content in the affects. Shifts in affects should fit the situation, and the child should talk spontaneously about what he is experiencing on a feeling level. High-level affects, such as gratitude and concern, reflect high-level object relations and the resolution of greed and envy into a sense of trust and empathy.

5. Sublimatory behaviors that reflect the opening of new expressive channels for drives. Within the sessions, sublimatory behavior can be seen in the child's bringing in and sharing new interests, whether this involves new toys or games or reports about achievements in sports or the arts.

6. Signs of insight, indicating the capacity for self-monitoring and for assessing

oneself in changing circumstances. Such insight may be revealed in the child's capacity to express humor about himself, to laugh about "silly" mistakes without denying them. It may also be seen in remarks like that of the grinning 8-year-old girl who said, "I got my mother to leave me at home from school by pretending to have a stomachache." Another sign of insight is the ability to reflect on the possible meaning of an event, such as a 12-year-old boy's saying, "I had this accident on the bike because I really wanted to get at my father." Empathy with peers can be an indirect expression of insight, as seen in the comment, "Johnny is in trouble at school—maybe he should see somebody like you," revealing an attempt to understand others through an understanding of oneself.

7. The quality of flexible and adaptive defense mechanisms. Although not so easy to evaluate, the predominant defenses used can be identified, and the therapist can assess their flexibility and adaptiveness. The ability to assume responsibility for oneself and one's actions is observed in such comments as "I think I provoked that reaction from my brother by teasing him." Related to this is the absence of externalization. Another sign of growth in this area is the application of the therapist's interpretations to other areas of the child's life.

8. Behavior during sessions pointing to a decrease in acting out and a decrease in symptoms or pathological character traits. Age-appropriate behavior should predominate, indicating an age-appropriate sense of identity. Body posture and manner of dress may provide further clues to an objective self-image and positive self-esteem.

When psychodynamic psychotherapy brings about the changes listed above, the child, functioning more adaptively within himself, is in a position to avoid endless repetitions of maladaptive behaviors. With a concomitant lessening of secondary social complications, the child can enter peer interactions more advantageously and proceed with development. Therapy will then have done its job and no longer will be needed. The parents may need support in their anxieties about resuming full responsibility for their child, but if they have been included successfully in the field of treatment, they will also be ready for termination.

Child psychotherapy, with its primary overriding goal being the promotion of optimal development, is in certain obvious ways similar to parenting. As Cooper and Wanerman (1984) pointed out:

> Therapists and parents alike strive to promote growth, to create the best possible circumstances in which growth can occur, and offer themselves as models to the child for identification and internalization. . . . There are, of course, important distinctions between therapy and parenting. Parents are typically continuous figures in the child's life, while therapists are invariably temporary figures. Ideally therapists relate to the child in a planned, conscious, deliberate fashion, whereas parents usually simply live with their children without thinking out every interaction. Parents are real objects to the child while therapists serve both as real people and as transference representatives (p. 14).

It is important for the therapist to know when his work is done and the work of the child and his parents can continue unaided by professional interventions. Humility is important here. Psychotherapy is not intended to reconstruct the child so that he becomes invulnerable to any emotional stress and will remain symptom-free for the rest of his life (Carek 1979). But the goals and effects of psychodynamic psychotherapy are intended to liberate the child from cumbersome symptoms, intrapsychic restraints, and interferences with development, so that he can continue to develop in as rich and full a way as possible.

REFERENCES

Alexander, F. (1956). *Psychoanalysis and Psychotherapy.* New York: Norton.

Bernstein, I. (1958). The importance of characteristics of the parents in deciding on child analysis. *J. Amer. Psychoanal. Assoc.* 6:71–78.

———, and Sax, A. M. (1978). Indications and contraindications for child analysis. In J. Glenn (Ed.). *Child Analysis and Therapy.* New York: Jason Aronson, pp. 67–109.

Buxbaum, E. (1954). Technique of child therapy: A critical evaluation. *Psychoanal. Study Child* 9:297–333.

Carek, D. J. (1979). Individual psychodynamically oriented therapy. In S. I. Harrison (Ed.). *Basic Handbook of Child Psychiatry, Volume Three: Therapeutic Interventions.* New York: Basic Books, pp. 35–57.

Cooper, S., and Wanerman, L. (1977). *Children in Treatment.* New York: Brunner/Mazel.

———. (1984). *A Casebook of Child Psychotherapy.* New York: Brunner/Mazel.

Curtis, H. C. (1979). The concept of therapeutic alliance: Implications for the "widening scope." *J. Amer. Psychoanal. Assoc.* 27 (Suppl.): 151–92.

Elkish, P. (1953). Simultaneous treatment of a child and his mother. *Amer. J. Psychother.* 7:105–30.

Ferenczi, S. (1913). A little chanticleer. In *Sex in Psychoanalysis: The Selected Papers of Sandor Ferenczi,* Vol. 1. New York: International Universities Press, 1950, pp. 240–52.

Freud, A. (1948). *The Psychoanalytical Treatment of Children.* New York: International Universities Press.

———. (1965). *Normality and Pathology in Childhood.* New York: International Universities Press.

Glenn, J. (Ed.) (1978). *Child Analysis and Therapy.* New York: Jason Aronson.

Heinicke, C. M., et al. (1965). Frequency of psychotherapeutic session as a factor affecting the child's developmental status. *Psychoanal. Study Child* 20:42–98.

Kennedy, H. (1979). The role of insight in child analysis: A developmental viewpoint. *J. Amer. Psychoanal. Assoc.* 27 (Suppl.): 9–29.

Kernberg, P. (In press). Termination in child psychoanalysis: Criteria from within the sessions. *Studien zur Kinderpsychoanalyse 1986.* Vienna: Verband der Wissenschaftlichen Gessellschaften.

———, et al. (In preparation). Inventory of Therapist Verbal Interventions with Children. Child psychotherapy research project.

McDermott, J. F., and Harrison, S. I. (Eds.). (1977). *Psychiatric Treatment of the Child.* New York: Jason Aronson.

Mahler, M. S. (1968). *On Human Symbiosis and the Vicissitudes of Individualism.* New York: International Universities Press.

Offenkrantz, W., et al. (1982). Treatment planning and psychodynamic psychiatry. In J. M. Lewis and G. Usdin (Eds.). *Treatment Planning in Psychiatry.* Washington, D.C.: American Psychiatric Association, pp. 3–41.

Pearson, G. (Ed.) (1968). *A Handbook of Child Psychoanalysis.* New York: Basic Books.

Pine, F. (1985). *Developmental Theory and Clinical Practice.* New Haven: Yale University Press.

Sandler, J., Kennedy, N., and Tyson, R. (1980). *The Technique of Child Analysis: Discussions with Anna Freud.* Cambridge: Harvard University Press.

Smirnoff, V. (1971). *The Scope of Child Analysis.* New York: International Universities Press.

Sours, J. A. (1978). The application of child analytic principles to forms of child psychotherapy. In J. Glenn (Ed.). *Child Analysis and Therapy.* New York: Jason Aronson, pp. 615–46.

Sperling, E. (1979). Parent counseling and therapy. In S. I. Harrison (Ed.). *Basic Handbook of Child Psychiatry, Volume Three: Therapeutic Interventions.* New York: Basic Books, pp. 136–48.

Sperling, M. (1950). Children's interpretation and reaction to the unconscious of their mothers. *Int'l. J. Psa.* 31.

51

CHILD-CENTERED FAMILY THERAPY

Richard C. Evans

INTRODUCTION

Child and family therapy have each arrived at a stage of development such that their models and methods may be integrated for purposes of evaluation and treatment. This integration is based both upon an appreciation of the constant interplay between context and internal dynamic forces and upon the premise that reciprocal influences between developing child and family are the matrix in which dysfunction may occur. The chapter will review antecedents of this child-family therapy integration and show how it has developed into an approach that provides guidelines and techniques for the engagement of family subsystems and individuals in treatment.

It is worth briefly considering the sociohistorical context in which this development has occurred. The profound social upheaval that followed World War II has clearly been reflected in the American family. The civil rights movement, women's movement, the Vietnam War and the peace movement all served to challenge the established order and called into question those values that were considered the basis of our stability and security. It is small wonder, then, that the most crucial transmitter of these cultural values, the family, has undergone such severe trials and transitions during this period. The therapist working with children and their families will be increasingly confronted by patients experiencing the immediate effects of these painful transitions in the form of divorcing, single-parent, and stepfamilies. It may not be coincidental that a family systems perspective has assumed clinical relevance during just this period when the traditional two-parent family can no longer be taken for granted.

As we look back to the origins of family therapy (Broderick and Schrader 1981) in the early '50s, we find many of its pioneers were therapists working with and sensitive to the needs of children (Ackerman 1970; Satir 1964; Bell 1967). In addition, we find scattered throughout the literature descriptions of child therapists who had decided to include the family in their work. Bruch (1966), reviewing her early work with obese children and their families, stated, "The idea of studying whole families from a psychological point of view forced itself upon me while observing a group of obese children." She went on to say further, "We consider the influence of the family as something that stood in dynamic interaction with the child's constitution and responses and not as something that would cause the abnormality through its toxic or traumatic effects on a passive subject." Mittelman (1958), an analyst, reported the simultaneous treatment of a child with his parents and described the advantages to the child of this approach. He also pointed out that in the sessions he was able to observe "circular reactions between both parents and the child."

We now seem to be well into a period of integration (Malone 1983), in spite of what has been called the "undeclared war between family therapy and child psychiatry" (McDermott and Chan 1974). While rarely made explicit, there seems to have occurred a cross-fertilization of ideas between practitioners in both fields. Enactment, such as sculpting or role-play in a family session, has its direct counterpart in the enactment within the playroom (Bloch and LaPerriere 1973), while play sessions have been used within family treatment (Keith and Whitaker 1981). Therapeutic metaphor, recognized as having central importance in play therapy, is used by a number of family therapists, particularly those influenced by the work of Milton Erickson (Haley 1973; Watzlawick et al. 1974). The positive forces of growth and development have always been recognized and used by child therapists; this recognition finds its counterpart in the positive intention that family therapists regularly attempt to discern within presenting symptoms.

Integration was somewhat slowed down by a concern that the child's special relationship with the therapist would somehow be compromised by including parents within treatment. The so-called "Holy Trinity" arrangement within child guidance clinics, in which psychologists performed testing, child psychiatrists saw the child and social workers saw the mother (and, rarely the father), was presumably used in order to avoid this. Nonetheless, parents came to be involved in the treatment of their children in a number of ways, such as direct counseling and filial therapy, during the period of time that the family systems perspective was evolving. It is to this systems model that we now turn our attention in order to examine the specific ways in which it can be useful for the child therapist.

THE SYSTEMS MODEL

Originally devised as an explanation of the way in which biological and communications systems phenomena are regulated, systems thinking was picked up by those who had begun working with the families of schizophrenics in the early '50s (Bateson et al. 1956; Lidz et al. 1957; Weakland et al. 1974). The approach seemed to provide a new way of understanding the patterns of interaction and reciprocal influence, described first in families with schizophrenic offspring and subsequently in normal families. The thinking was first elaborated in the clinical setting by Jackson (1957) and others who came to believe that context, as well as character, played a determining role in human behavior. Since families include children and adolescents, it was inevitable that child therapy would be influenced by and react to systems thinking. As noted above, however, reluctance to take on this point of view was expressed by those who felt that the approach would somehow leave children out and ignore their needs for a special therapeutic relationship. In a seminal paper directly addressing this concern, Boszormenyi-Nagy proposed the idea that children seen without their families were placed in a loyalty conflict that could subvert the purpose of therapy and compound their problems (1972). In his later work, he elaborated this theme, maintaining that families function within a network of loyalties made up of debts and obligations spanning the generations. The struggle to develop personal autonomy within this network created the tension that brought families to treatment (Boszormenyi-Nagy and Sparks 1973). Montalvo and Haley (1973), in a humorous but trenchant analysis of the problem, said that child therapists were unwittingly doing family therapy by acting as a communication go-between, thus pulling the child out of his triangulated position. They then went on to ask why therapists did not do this explicitly to reap the full benefits of the systems approach.

Specific aspects of systems thinking that have shown most value to child therapists are related to:

1. Circularity and reciprocal influence;
2. Balance between stability and change;
3. A theory about the nature of change;
4. An analysis of structure that elicits the relationship between symptom and system (Tomm and Wright 1979).

Significant events, or behaviors, are viewed as occurring in a number of positive and negative feedback loops. Behaviors within a positive loop will be amplified while those in a negative loop will be diminished. Since within these loops events are both "caused and causative" (Goldner 1985), it follows that the search for an originating cause or linear sequence of causes is not meaningful. Thus, giving Ritalin to a child with attention deficit disorder may be viewed as treatment not only for the child but also as an intervention that will have feedback effects within the entire family.

This model, which views behaviors as part of a continuing cycle, presents both opportunity and dilemma. Since in a cycle there are many possible points of intervention, the question becomes: Which point would be most responsive? Can a move at point A affect something at point B where change is most needed? A reasonable response to these questions is suggested by Hoffman (1981), who stated, "It is possible that one can remain faithful to the systemic vision, even if one sees only an individual or a fragment of the family. It is up to the therapist to decide whether working with this fragment provides enough leverage to bring about change" (p. 336).

Since families maintain stability yet undergo change across time, both tendencies must be taken into account. Stability is conferred by regulators such as family rules, limits, myths, expectations, standards, and values (Ferreira 1963). Change occurs as the inevitable consequence both of growth and development of family members and of those unforeseen external events and crises that occur in most families (Carter and McGoldrick 1980). In a pure systems model, all dysfunction is conceptualized as the reflection of imbalance among these forces. When functioning well, a given family has both enough stability and capacity for change to maintain healthy equilibrium. Symptoms in an individual become manifest when one of these two processes has gone too far and a compensatory reaction sets in. For example, an adolescent girl's so-called promiscuity, her parents' severe reaction in order to correct this, or a combination of both, may bring a family for treatment. One family may be caught in its inability to change if, for example, adolescent children are not being granted age-appropriate autonomy, while another may be disorganized by too much pressure for a change, as when adjusting to a mother's return to work as the family moves to a new home.

The distinction between first- and second-order change (Watzlawick et al. 1974) is an important corollary to the idea that stability is maintained by both repeated patterns and a superordinate set of values, rules, or limits. First-order refers to patterns of behavior, while second-order refers to the rules (implicit or explicit) that govern the behavior. For example, first-order change would occur if a couple were simply taught to stop trading insults whenever they disagreed. This attempt at change could, however, break down in the heat of argument. The form of their disagreement might be more permanently altered if their shared value, such as "respect for one another as the basis for a relationship," was mutually endorsed. At this higher or second-order level a powerful regulator of many behaviors, involving disagreements or shared decisions, could be activated. This important distinction does not necessarily indicate which kind of change needs initially to occur in a system. It does, however, suggest to the therapist that if his efforts to produce change at one level are unsuccessful he should shift to the other.

While much of what is observed in a family interview may be unique or idiosyncratic to that situation, repeated patterns of interaction occur and can reveal information about structure in the family. Although there is no single structure for a given family, regularities occur in areas such as the exercise of authority, communication modes, maintenance of gender and generational boundaries, alliances, and the maintenance of affective distance between individuals (Minuchin 1974). The initial impression of a family might indicate that the mother maintained authority while revealing closeness with the eldest daughter, with both of them set against a distant father who acted like a chum with his unruly 8-year-old son. While only a bare outline needing to be filled in and modified, this information could provide the therapist with a beginning model of the system he is engaging. Current structures are, however, only one part of the picture of the family's life. To develop a fuller appreciation, we would next want to consider what has been called "the family life cycle." It is to this time dimension that we next turn our attention.

FAMILY GENERATIONS

The family life cycle (Carter and McGoldrick 1980) is divided into stages with the starting point arbitrarily defined. For our discussion, the time when children are introduced into the family, grow, develop, and as young adults, take their initial leave, is of most interest. Including grandparents provides us with a three-generational perspective, which many family therapists believe is essential (Bowen 1978). The family genogram is used to elaborate upon this perspective. Consideration of a family moving through time alerts us to anniversary reactions, entrances and exits brought about by normal developmental crises, and extraordinary interruptions, such as severe illness, premature death, or divorce. As noted above, we are increasingly confronted by divorced, single, three-generation, and stepfamilies. According to Wallerstein (1984), "It is now estimated that 45 percent of all children born in 1983 will experience their parents' divorce, 35 percent will experience a remarriage, and 20 percent will experience a second divorce. In 1981, approximately 22.5 million young people, or 36 percent of all children under 18, were living in a family other than the traditional two-parent family" (p. 144). These difficult, painful family transitions occur in several stages, each presenting new challenges for the therapist interested in the well-being of both children and their caretakers (Beal 1980). With both the systems and life-cycle perspectives in mind (Wen Shing and McDermott 1979), the family can be considered as an organism with discernible structures in the present, a powerful heritage from the past and an equally compelling obligation to the future. Family dysfunction should be viewed from all of these perspectives.

Families may fail to carry out their tasks, become dysfunctional, and present one or more symptomatic members. Symptomatic individuals or interactions result from the intersection of several patterns having both remote and proximate aspects. On a more concrete level, a symptom is a repeated, unwanted event (feeling, behavior, thought or interaction), that one or several members of the family have decided exceeds an acceptable limit. In some cases, it may be difficult to determine whether the exceeded limit has to do with a legitimate expectation or is based on distorted projection, bias, or irrelevant social value. In the latter case, the distorted expectation, not the presenting symptom, would become the initial focus of intervention.

Approach to symptoms is determined by the particular theory of symptom genesis and maintenance held by a therapist. An interesting approach to this is advocated by the Mental Research Institute Group (Weakland et al. 1982), who held that most symptoms result from energetic, but misdirected, attempts at solving problems. They maintained that behind a symptom there is a self-perpetuating pattern of failed attempts at problem solving. The therapist works to deactivate these attempts, thereby permitting new alternatives to emerge that are consonant with the family's value system.

CASE VIGNETTE

The divorced mother of three was deeply concerned about her youngest, a 16-year-old boy who showed no initiative to obtain a job, stayed out late, and was experimenting with drugs. She saw him becoming like his unreliable father, who had deserted her after what she considered to have been a loyal marriage. Her attempts to get the boy to work were of no avail and she finally came to therapy after a violent argument in which he threatened to leave home. The boy refused to come to sessions, so the therapist had only the mother to work with at the outset. After reviewing the failed attempts, she advised the mother to pull back and stop admonishing her son. The mother said that she would try this but was unable to, declaring that pulling back made her feel that she was abandoning her child and not providing him with the leadership that she knew he needed. She revealed in this statement a strong commitment to being a conscientious mother. In consultation, the therapist decided to utilize these values in order to help the mother shift tactics with her son. She advised the mother that her son needed "understanding" even more than "leadership."

Further information from the mother confirmed the idea that her son felt caught between a desire to keep a relationship with his father and remain loyal to a mother with whom he actually sided after the divorce. He also had said that he felt uncomfortable because he had many girlfriends, whereas she was still alone. These conflicts were described to the mother as a "very hard emotional job that your boy now has for which he needs your understanding." The therapist stated her faith that the mother, as a conscientious person, would be able to make the shift from "leadership" to "understanding," and the new approach was rehearsed in sessions. It proved to lessen tensions at home, open new avenues of communication, and eventually resulted in a positive change in the boy's attitude towards obtaining a job.

The idea that within a symptom or dysfunctional pattern there lies a failed attempt at problem solving or adaptation has assumed central importance in the thinking of many family therapists. This differs from the psychodynamic idea that symptoms reflect the best possible compromise solution between conflicting impulses in its emphasis upon symptoms as a potential stepping-stone into what is adaptive within an individual or family. It is buttressed by the corollary idea that families are imbued with positive values, standards, loyalties, and points of pride; when these are made explicit in the course of treatment, a positive connotation around the symptoms is made all the more credible and useful (Hoffman 1981). While family therapists advise focusing upon current factors that sustain symptoms, they seem frequently to ignore important sustaining factors within the individual. It is clear that children often make a substantial contribution to their own as well as their family's difficulties. Since there seems to be no reasonable way to ignore this interplay, an approach that fully acknowledges both aspects has the most chance for success. This position is well articulated by Malone (1983):

> The issue is not and should not be whether individual treatment or family therapy is indicated. The issue is how to combine family, subsystem, and individual interviewing in order to explore effectively the interplay between levels within the family system and to determine whether the family, subsystem, and individual treatment are indicated separately or in combination, one at a time or in stages over time.

INDICATIONS FOR FAMILY ASSESSMENT AND TREATMENT

It is difficult to imagine a clinical situation in which family assessment is not indicated when a child or an adolescent is the presenting symptomatic individual. The question of indications and contraindications for family therapy somewhat distorts the picture in terms of a single yes-no decision, rather than a continuing process of evaluation about which aspects of the system to deal with at any point in treatment. The controversy often described between adherents of family and child therapy is usefully replaced by a series of questions that will be answered only by examination of our own clinical experience, longitudinal studies that focus upon the influence of families and children upon each other, and outcome evaluations of family therapy with children. Longitudinal studies (Chess et al. 1983; Rutter 1985) indicate strong links between some kinds of family dysfunction and certain child and adolescent problems. Often, however, the links are not clear and do not in themselves provide a simple or direct guide to clinical intervention. In terms of outcome, various forms of family involvement have been used in most child and adolescent syndromes and have frequently been found valuable. From school refusal (Hersov 1985), a disorder believed to be primarily of psychological origin (though a primary anxiety disorder may be nested within the syndrome), through anorexia nervosa, a syndrome recognized as having social, psychological, family, and biological determinants (Garfinkel and Garner 1982), family therapy has been used with positive outcome. Behavior disorders have yielded to an approach that uses the family structure in order to develop programs such as contracting, reward systems and shaping (Alexander and Parsons 1973; Eisler and Hersen 1973). One may still wonder even when family therapy is not contraindicated, if there are situations in which it has relatively little value. What about intrapsychic self-perpetuating problems, unworkable parents, a totally disorganized family, or an intensely mistrustful adolescent? Questions phrased in this manner are built upon presuppositions that most family therapists would dispute, and they tend to perpetuate the controversy. If, however, one considers the possibility of shifting focus as a case proceeds, there is an opening for alternatives. Parents initially believed to be "unworkable" may begin to respond after their child is seen alone for several sessions, evaluated, and described to them within a new frame. Conversely, a suspicious adolescent may become receptive for individual sessions after he has "sized up" the therapist in family meetings where he has been guarded and silent. The process of starting at one point and then shifting as indicated begins at the initial family assessment.

FAMILY ASSESSMENT AND TREATMENT: SHIFTING SYSTEMS

The rationale for family assessment can be stated by asking the question: What relevant information can be obtained by seeing two or more family members together that would not be elicited by seeing any one of them alone, and conversely, what relevant information may be elicited from individual meetings that might not be forthcoming in a family meeting? With this in mind, we can consider four relevant areas for a family assessment: the presenting problem, the desired outcome of therapy, family values and structure.

Presenting Problem. Although focus is often on an individual, one finds more and more families who come to treatment declaring that they know their child is a problem but, "We know that the family has a problem, too." Rather than help the family-oriented child therapist, this opening may simply mean that parental guilt and demoralization have begun to take over. While an initial goal is to connect symptom and system in a positive manner, one needs first to obtain details concerning context, duration, frequency, and so on, and ask for various members' ideas about why the problem has developed and how they have attempted to solve it. We often find parents disagreeing about their child, with one being more involved or concerned, angry or discouraged than the other. Sometimes this reflects disguised marital rift and, sometimes, the polarization that occurs when parents share an unsolved nagging dilemma about their child. In any event, the therapist may need to gradually shift from the presenting focus to one that permits an entry point for intervention.

Outcome. Closely related to a description of the problem is an idea of the outcome that therapy is supposed to accomplish. While this cannot easily be formed at the outset, it is well to consider it so that divergent views and unrealistic expectations can be elicited. Somewhere between a democratic concensus and therapeutic authoritarianism an initial outcome should be defined, taking into account feasibility, possible unwanted consequences, and the particular context in which the request change can be of value.

Family Values. Family meetings present an opportunity to elicit those values, standards, hopes, beliefs, points of pride, and treasured heritage that families possess. This valuable information does not automatically appear and may actually be pushed into the background by the family sense of demoralization when first encountered. In order to bring out the information as soon as possible, the clinician may ask, while preparing a genogram, "What did you learn from your own family that you want to transmit to your children" or, "How do you want to do things differently from your parents?" Children and adolescents can be asked about areas of interest, skill, and what they believe to be special about their family. Ethnicity can provide a clue to general value systems in such areas as seeking help from outsiders, expression of emotion, and the payment of respect, but specific questions about this should be asked in order to avoid prejudgment based on ethnic stereotype (McDermott et al. 1983; McGoldrick et al. 1982). This information is essential to develop a three-dimensional view of the family, establish rapport, and begin the process of reframing, whereby individual symptoms become an entry point.

Current Structures. The structure of a family refers to the organization of various systems and is inferred from observations of repeated patterns. For assessment purposes, the important systems to consider are as follows.

Communication Modes. These are observed as family members talk and either achieve satisfactory communication or become entangled in misunderstanding, frustration, anger, and sometimes despair. The unsatisfactory patterns can be understood in terms of faulty sending and receiving of messages in what has been referred to as a "calibrated communications cycle" (Bandler et al. 1976). For example, a wife may complain that her husband "always" leaves child-rearing problems to her when, in fact, this happens only in a certain context. He may not challenge her generalization but take it as confirmation that he is "never appreciated" and withdraw from further communication. His withdrawal then reconfirms her belief, reinforcing the cycle. Or, a father may praise his son's good school grades by saying, "It's about time. I hope it will continue." The son, hearing this as evidence of his inability to obtain his father's ungrudging approval, wonders if school effort is worth the trouble and begins to do poorly again. Family sessions produce many examples such as this and provide direct information about the way in which problems are being perpetuated as family members attempt to solve them.

Boundaries, Coalitions and Triads. In a well-ordered family, boundaries are maintained between generations and gender. Parents possess authority and are entitled to their privacy; children are entitled to receive goods but also maintain their own subsystem that may include within it an age-determined hierarchy among siblings.

Any group of three or more people provides the opportunity for either an alliance of two against one or triangulation in which one member is caught between two others in conflict. While these appear as shifting patterns in healthy families, in those that are dysfunctional we find fixed alliances and triads. For example, paternal authority may be compromised by an alliance between a mother and her children that excludes the father from decision making. Often these patterns endure after a family break-up has occurred; thus, the child of a divorced couple may continue as a messenger between two noncommunicating parents. Structural family therapists regard making changes in triads and coalitions as the most powerful way of affecting a family (McDermott et al. 1983) and elaborate upon this within the concept of the "triangulated child." Described on a structural level, this concept suggests that the child of an unsatisfactory marriage in which there is no direct conflict resolution becomes caught in a manner harmful to his development and productive of symptoms. This child has been variously described as a scapegoat, detour route, or go-between (Vogel and Bell 1960).

One does find children either in alliance with one parent or another, serving as spouse substitute, acting like a messenger, or working as a peace maker. Although this situation is phrased in the language of systems thinking, which attempts to avoid simple linear cause-and-effect explanations, it often sounds close to simply calling both parents (instead of only the mother) the villains. While an unhealthy marital *quid pro quo* is often maintained at the expense of children's development and suboptimal parenting can be the result, it is equally true that difficult children can play havoc with a reasonably sound marriage (Evans 1974). Although there are cases on the extremes, most clinical situations seem to present an unfortunate combination of an unstable or unsatisfactory marriage, poor child-rearing coalition, and a "difficult" child. A careful past history of both the child's development and history of symptoms is helpful in order to tease out the balance of factors. With the principle of reciprocity in mind, the triangulated child is thus seen as a crystallization, not the cause or result, of family difficulty.

Child-Rearing Functions. Adequacy of child rearing may be taken as a reflection of how well communication and coalitions are working. Caretaker provision of an authority structure, age-appropriate expectations that are relatively free from distortion and projection, and models for effective bonding and social interaction are some of the complex tasks required of families raising children.

In a traditional two-parent family, marital stability and satisfaction is a critical dimension. Though there is a relationship between marriage and parenting, it is not always simple or easy to determine. At best, both are working well. While poor marital interaction frequently interferes with adequate child rearing, it is possible to cope with marital dysfunction in adaptive ways that do not necessarily compromise child rearing. Conversely, the presence of a symptomatic or problem child does not automatically indicate a hidden marital rift. This is important to stress, since making a quick inference from a child's symptoms to problems in a marriage may be misleading and result in the loss of parental involvement in treatment.

Background Information. How is one to take a history from three or more people? Obtaining a history of the family is facilitated by the use of such techniques as the genogram and family album, both of which breathe life into a large amount of information by providing a picture of the three-generational life line and current connections with relatives. In cases with a symptomatic child or adolescent, there is clearly need for developmental history in order to determine whether or not significant individual dysfunction is present. An attention deficit disorder in a 9-year-old boy, or for that matter severe depression in a 35-year-old mother or alcoholism in a 42-year-old father cannot be ignored within the family therapy frame. Here one can use family and individual sessions concurrently to sort out relative importance of internal individual and systems factors. If the purpose of these individual meetings is made clear from the outset, there should be no concern about either scapegoating an individual family member or losing the family frame. In those cases where special treatment is warranted for one family member, either in the form of psychotherapy, medication, or both, the family frame can be maintained.

Shifting Systems

With information about problem focus, outcome, family values and strengths, communication system and other aspects of structure in mind, the therapist is in a position to decide upon a point of entry. A family orientation can be maintained, even though not all members are present at every meeting. Many family therapists insist on having all the members at the first meeting, thereby establishing both a family frame and their authority at the outset. Others tend to use whomever is present with the belief that the entire structure will be revealed in the course of the first few meetings. One may thus begin with the entire family when the total structure appears involved, with parents alone, or with parents and child when triangulation appears to be in center stage. Several initial meetings with parents may be needed when their polarization about a child is predominant, or individual meetings may be needed with one member when the focus cannot initially be shifted.

CASE VIGNETTE

The L. family, consisting of mother, father, and two daughters, Mary, 12, and Barbara, 15, came to treatment because of concern about Barbara, who was "having thoughts that are ruining my life." There was no concern about Mary, who did not appear at the first session though this had been requested. A family frame was described to which the parents gave verbal agreement while retaining focus on their daughter. Barbara sat silently between her parents, who poured out their concerns, continually interrupting each other and showing little regard or respect for each other's opinions. When asked about herself, Barbara shrugged her shoulders and leaned against her mother. She was asked to rise and accompany the therapist to another room, where she spoke easily and shared her many obsessions about dirt, pregnancy, and her school work. Having thus enacted a removal from the triangulated position, treatment began with the girl alone and her parents seen concurrently. The first stage consisted of dealing with her obsessions, which yielded easily to reassurance, and her parents' unresolved marital struggle, which took the form of mother's depression and father's withdrawal. Although significant marital work could not be done, enough headway was made to bring the girls and their parents together at the seventh session in order to focus upon the connections among mother's depression, father's withdrawal, and Barbara's "worries." As they achieved recognition of a connection between their daughter's symptoms and the family, the parents agreed to work on their own difficulties for "the sake of our daughter." Positive outcome was achieved in terms of Barbara's presenting symptoms, while the marriage remained stable but relatively unsatisfactory. The mother, however, became activated in her own behalf, developing a long-deferred interest in opening a small business.

Therapeutic movement in this type of case may be unpredictable at the outset but can be guided by certain principles related both to starting and to shifting configurations as treatment proceeds. In the family described above, subsystem work was necessary before the family could usefully be brought together. As described in the next case vignette, reframing is valuable for this kind of shifting, for it both contains acknowledgement of positive intent and facilitates entry into family interactions. It is not done in one step and needs to be accompanied by acknowledgement of the family's values.

CASE VIGNETTE

A 9-year-old boy was brought for treatment by his parents because of increasing reluctance to attend school. An only child and conscientious student who presented no other areas of difficulty, he declared that he was "afraid of becoming sick and vomiting in class," something he knew had happened to another student recently. At a first family meeting, it was noted that his parents communicated well as a couple and were supportive of him but felt stymied in their attempts at encouraging school attendance. They had tried to help him for several months before coming for treatment, explaining that they wanted to be "self-reliant" and did not usually ask for outside professional help. It was found that the boy was skilled at both downhill and water skiing, and he was encouraged to describe how he had mastered his physical fears when learning these sports. At first, a direct approach using anxiety-reduction techniques, which had been effective in these areas, was attempted but was not successful. The therapist then formulated the following "reframe," which he presented to the family at the sixth session.

> Your son is at a stage of development when he wants to develop his own self-reliance and control anxiety without your support. Thus, he is having anxiety at school where he knows you cannot help him, in order to learn new ways of dealing with it. I believe this will continue until he begins to learn ways of feeling better using the help of people other than his parents.

The "symptom" was thus described as an attempt at adaptation being made in terms of a legitimate family value, namely "self-reliance." Reactions were mixed; the boy became angry and later said he would "show the doctor that I can go to school without being scared." Both parents slowly nodded understanding of what was said and encouraged their son to speak with his guidance counselor (who had announced his availability for this) if he became anxious in school. The boy began to attend school and made frequent contact with his guidance counselor for several weeks until he began to feel comfortable handling things on his own. A one-year follow-up revealed no recurrence of the symptom.

After a number of sessions with the beginning configuration, there may be need for a change, either because progress is blocked or because a task has been accomplished. The therapist may then need to shift from a parental pair to the entire family in order to learn about new sources of resistance, untapped strengths such as sibling bonds, or unexpected effects of change. Although it is often stated that the development of new problems is evidence of the necessity of a symptom in order to maintain family homeostasis, it is equally often the case that new problems present a "back burner effect"; namely, that as one problem improves in treatment, others previously considered less pressing can move to the foreground. It may be then necessary to shift focus, explaining this to the family as a new stage in treatment.

FAMILY THERAPY SKILLS

Since the "how to" of family therapy arises from several different models, there is no single set of techniques to be described (Beels and Ferber 1972). There are, however, several sources of information that can serve as an overview of the skills useful in carrying out family treatment. Interviewing techniques were well described by Satir (1964) and Grunebaum and Glick (1983). While some of these skills are not unique to the repertoire of those doing family therapy, several are worth special consideration. Establishing rapport with family members so that they all become sufficiently engaged in treatment demands a wide range of sensitivities. Along with this responsiveness there needs to be enough "directing" so that information can be gathered and important transactions permitted to occur without interruption. Directing is also useful for conducting enactments, such as sculpting (Papp et al. 1973), in which family members assume postures that describe their experience of the family problem and how they want it to change. This is a powerful emotional experience, at times more memorable than many hours of talking. As treatment proceeds the therapist may need to assign tasks, redefine focus, and decide who should attend sessions. All of these skills are based upon a posture in which the therapist needs to be both receptive and active at the same time.

The special problem of children under age 8 in family sessions deserves mention here. Since several of the pioneers in family therapy came from child treatment backgrounds, their work deals with this issue (Ackerman 1970; Satir 1964). Play techniques in family sessions have been described (Zilbach et al. 1972) and parallels drawn between enactment in the playroom and family sessions. It is worth noting how children are the same and how they are different from adolescents and adults in the session. Like their elders, children wish to make sense of the treatment situation, reduce anxiety, ward off humiliation, and maintain family loyalty, at the same time letting the therapist know of their distress. The child's construction of reality and therefore of the family session will determine how he sends and receives messages. Concrete, centered on himself in time and space, and relatively unable to hold more than one perspective in mind at a time, he will sometimes see things very clearly and at other times be in a state of confusion. His unguarded emotional and body expression may reveal the complex state of his relationships with parents and siblings; though he speaks fiercely of anger at his elder sister, he may quietly play "footsie" with her across the space that separates them when he thinks no one is looking. Age-appropriate levels of play can be used; coloring, block or puppet play within family sessions may reveal a capacity for enjoyment that would otherwise go unnoticed.

CASE VIGNETTE

A 4½-year-old boy was brought by his parents because of adamant refusal to become bowel-trained. In a family session, the father assumed the disciplinarian role, often engaging in bitter struggles with his son, while the mother pulled back in despair. His 9-year-old sister enjoyed the proceedings but did not participate. In a playroom session, the boy appeared bright, energetic, imaginative, and skilled at frustrating what he perceived to be adult expectations. In addition, fear about bodily damage or loss related to the toilet appeared in doll play. With both parents alone, the mother revealed that she had worked as a writer and director of theater programs for children, though now she was home full-time. Her ambivalence about returning to this work was greeted by her husband's belief that, "You decide one way or another and that's it."

A family "game" was developed in order to address the boy's conflicts about obedience and fears about the toilet while stimulating pleasurable family interaction. The mother's talents were enlisted to construct a board game, containing a family of frogs who hopped and swam all day in their lilypad-covered pond. With coaching, both parents were quick to see isomorphism between their son's life dilemma and the reluctance that one "little boy frog" had about hopping from one pad to another. The game was played first in family sessions and then repeatedly at home with various family members. The affect at family sessions lightened considerably. During this time, the boy and his father made an agreement that he would decide to use the toilet at his fifth birthday when he was a "big boy." This prediction was fulfilled, to no one's surprise.

Paradoxically, many family therapists have come to the belief that intervention directly aimed at changing a symptom or problem can be the least effective strategy. In this, they have been most heavily influenced by the work of Milton Erickson, the Mental Research Institute Group, the Milan Group, and the Ackerman Short Term Therapy Project (Hoffman 1981). While it is beyond the scope of this chapter to describe the intricacies involved in these approaches, it is worth mentioning that all make use of the central presupposition of reframing: that behind or within a symptom lies a positive or adaptive intent that can, if properly activated, ultimately lead to a resolution of the problem. Having acknowledged this positive intent and connected it to values and beliefs held by the family, the therapist can slow down the family's attempts at problem solving while helping them search for better alternatives.

Going a step beyond this, the therapist may engage in what has come to be known as "paradoxical therapy" (Weakland et al. 1974). This frequently misunderstood term describes a therapist who seems to be operating in a way opposite to that expected, when, for example, he tells an unruly adolescent that he should redouble his efforts to "keep his mother busy." Paradoxical instructions such as this are based upon the hope that a healthy rebound creating more desirable behavior will occur, and they should be attempted only in a situation where this is a strong possibility.

OUTCOME OF FAMILY THERAPY WITH CHILDREN AND ADOLESCENTS

Outcome studies of family and marital therapy have been well described elsewhere (Gurman and Kniksern 1981). None has conclusively demonstrated which treatment approach is better for which child or adolescent disorder. Individual studies have reported good results with juvenile offenders (Alexander and Parsons 1973) and behavior disorders in children under 12 (Mittelman 1958). Although these are reports of behavior therapy, they indicate having taken into account a family systems model, especially in their consideration of the authority structure within the family. Effective work has been done with anorectics and their families (Minuchin 1974). Impressive results have been described using a psychoeducational approach in families with a schizophrenic member living at home (Leff et al. 1983). This is noteworthy because it establishes the effectiveness of a systemic intervention upon the frequency of relapse in a disorder that has powerful biological determinants. It should not be difficult to extrapolate from this to see the value of a family-based psychoeducational approach for children with attention deficit disorder. The outcome of several psychotherapy studies reported by Shaffer (1984) indicates that inclusion of both parents and the child provides the best results, even in such direct approaches as parent management training. Taken together, the family therapy and child psychiatry literature suggest a distinct value for the planned and direct inclusion of parents in the treatment of their children.

SUMMARY

Using family therapy to help children and adolescents inevitably plunges one into the challenging task of balancing "inner and outer space" (Rabkin 1970). The question that confronts us now is not whether or not we should do this, but how it can be best done. This chapter has attempted to respond to the question by describing a model that combines individual and family work using ideas that derive from both child therapy and the family systems approach. Others are involved in this effort (McPherson et al. 1974). A recent, stimulating attempt in this direction (Ritterman 1983) is based upon a synthesis of the work of Minuchin and Erickson. Observing that powerful family interactions can induce symptoms in its members much like hypnosis, Ritterman (1983) proposed that a therapist be able to "shift quite naturally and at any moment, from observing family members interacting to using formal or informal trance-deepening techniques with one or more family members to obtain another, more private level of communication about the symptom." Shifting within a single session (which may be done without the use of trance techniques) has its analog in the shifting between systems described in this chapter and moves in the direction of consolidating an integrated model. We should expect to see similar models proposed by those who share the belief that combining the resources of children and their families in treatment is beneficial for both.

REFERENCES

Ackerman, N. (1970). Child participation in family therapy. *Family Process* 9:403–10.

Alexander, J., and Parsons, B. (1973). Short-term intervention with delinquent families. *J. Abnor. Psychol.* 81:219–25.

Bandler, R., Grinder, J., and Satir, V. (1976). *Changing with Families*. Palo Alto: Science and Behavior Books.

Bateson, G., et al. (1956). Toward a theory of schizophrenia. *Behav. Sci.* 1:251–64.

Beal, E. (1980). Separation, divorce and single parent families. In E. Carter and M. McGoldrick (Eds.). *The Family Life Cycle*. New York: Gardner Press.

Beels, C., and Ferber, A. (1972). What family therapists do. In A. Ferber, M. Mendelsohn, and A. Napier (Eds.). *The Book of Family Therapy*. New York: Aronson.

Bell, J. (1967). Family group therapy; A new treatment method for children. *Family Process* 6:254–63.

Bloch, D., and LaPerriere, K. (1973). Techniques of family therapy: A conceptual frame. In D. Bloch (Ed.). *Techniques of Family Therapy*. New York: Grune and Stratton.

Boszormenyi-Nagy, I. (1972). Loyalty implications of the transference model in psychotherapy. *Arch. Gen. Psychiatry* 27:374–80.

———, and Sparks, M. (1973). *Invisible Loyalties*. Hagerstown, Md.: Harper and Row.

Bowen, M. (1978). *Family Therapy in Clinical Practice*. New York: Aronson.

Broderick, C., and Schrader, S. (1981). The history of professional marriage and family therapy. In A. S. Gurman and D. P. Kniksern (Eds.). *Handbook of Family Therapy*. New York: Brunner/Mazel.

Bruch, H. (1966). Changing approaches to the study of the family. In I. Cohen (Ed.). *Family Structure, Dynamics and Therapy*. Psychiatric Research Report No. 20. Washington, D.C.: American Psychiatric Association.

Carter, E., and McGoldrick, M. (Eds.). (1980). *The Family Life Cycle: A Framework for Family Therapy*. New York: Gardner Press.

Chess, S., et al. (1983). Early parental attitudes, divorce and separation: Findings of a longitudinal study. *J. Amer. Acad. Child Psychiatry* 22:47–51.

Clarkin, J., Frances, A., and Moodie, J. (1979). Selection criteria for family therapy. *Family Process* 18:391–403.

Eisler, R., and Hersen, M. (1973). Behavioral techniques in family oriented crisis intervention. *Arch. Gen. Psychiatry* 28:11–116.

Evans, R. (1974). Family and hospital: The disturbed child within a system. *J. Bronx State Hosp.* 2:189–97.

Ferreira, A. (1963). Family myth and homeostasis. *Arch. Gen. Psychiatry* 8:213–34.

Garfinkel, P., and Garner, D. (1982). *Anorexia Nervosa: A Multidimensional Perspective.* New York: Brunner/Mazel.

Goldner, V. (1985). Family therapy. In D. Shaffer and L. Greenhill (Eds.). *The Clinical Guide to Child Psychiatry.* New York: Free Press.

Grunebaum, H., and Glick, I. (1983). The basics of family treatment. In L. Grinspoon (Ed.). *Psychiatric Update*, Vol. 2. Washington, D.C.: American Psychiatric Association.

Gurman, A., and Kniksern, D. (1981). Family therapy outcome research. In A. Gurman and D. Kniksern (Eds.). *Handbook of Family Therapy.* New York: Brunner/Mazel.

Haley, J. (1973). *Uncommon Therapy: The Psychiatric Techniques of Milton Erickson, M.D.* New York: Norton.

———. (1978). *Problem Solving Therapy.* San Francisco: Jossey-Bass.

Hersov, L. (1985). School refusal. In L. Hersov and M. Rutter (Eds.). *Child and Adolescent Psychiatry.* Oxford: Blackwell Scientific.

Hetherington, E., and Marten, B. (1972). Family interaction and psychopathology in children. In H. Quay and J. Werry (Eds.). *Psychopathological Disorders of Childhood.* New York: Wiley.

Hoffman, L. (1981). *Foundations of Family Therapy.* New York: Basic Books.

Jackson, D. (1957). The question of family homeostasis. *Psychiat. Q. (Supplement)* 31:79:90.

Keith, D., and Whitaker, C. (1981). Play therapy: A paradigm for work with families. *J. Marital Fam. Ther.* 6:243–54.

Leff, J., Berkowitz, R., and Kupers, L. (1983). Intervention in families of schizophrenics and its effect upon relapse rates. In W. McFarlane (Ed.). *Family Therapy in Schizophrenia.* New York: Guilford Press.

Lidz, T., et al. (1957). The intra-familial environment of schizophrenic patients. *Amer. J. Psychiatry* 114:241–48.

McDermott, J., and Chan, W. (1974). The undeclared war between child and family therapy. *J. Amer. Acad. Child. Psychiatry* 13:422–36.

———, et al. (1983). Cultural variations in family attitudes and their implications for therapy. *J. Amer. Acad. Child Psychiatry* 22:454–58.

McGoldrick, M., Pearce, J., and Giordano, J. (1982). *Ethnicity and Family Therapy.* New York: Guilford Press.

McPherson, S., Brackelmans, W., and Newman, L. (1974). Stages in the family therapy of adolescents. *Family Process* 13:77–94.

Malone, C. (1983). Family therapy and childhood disorder. In L. Grinspoon (Ed.). *Psychiatric Update*, Vol. 2. Washington, D.C.: American Psychiatric Association.

Minuchin, S. (1974). *Families and Family Therapy.* Cambridge: Harvard University Press.

Mittelman, B. (1958). Simultaneous treatment of both parents and their child. In G. Bychowski and J. L. Despert (Eds.). *Specialized Techniques in Psychotherapy.* New York: Grove Press.

Montalvo, B., and Haley, J. (1973). In defense of child therapy. *Family Process* 12:227–44.

Papp, P., Silverstein, O., and Carter, B. (1973). Family sculpting in preventive work with well families. *Family Process* 12:197–212.

Patterson, G. (1973). Intervention for boys with conduct problems. *J. Consult. Clin. Psychol.* 42:471–81.

Rabkin, R. (1970). *Inner and Outer Space.* New York: Norton.

Ritterman, M. (1983). *Hypnosis in Family Therapy.* San Francisco: Jossey-Bass.

Rutter, M. (1985). Family and school influences: Meanings, mechanisms and implications. In A. R. Nicol (Ed.). *Longitudinal Studies in Child Psychology and Psychiatry.* New York: Wiley.

Satir, V. (1964). *Conjoint Family Therapy.* Palo Alto, Calif.: Science and Behavior Books.

Shaffer, D. (1984). Notes on psychotherapy research among children and adolescents. *J. Amer. Acad. Child Psychiatry* 23:552–61.

Tomm, K., and Wright, L. (1979). Training in family therapy: Perceptual, conceptual and executive skills. *Family Process* 18:227–50.

Vogel, E., and Bell, N. (1960). The emotionally disturbed child as family scapegoat. In N. Bell and E. Vogel (Eds.). *The Family.* Glencoe, Ill.: Free Press.

Wallerstein, J. (1984). Children of divorce: The dilemma of a decade. In L. Grinspoon (Ed.). *Psychiatry Update,* Vol. 3. Washington, D.C.: American Psychiatric Association.

Watzlawick, P., Weakland, J. H., and Fisch, R. (1974). *Change: Principles of Problem Formation and Problem Resolution.* New York: Norton.

Weakland, J., et al. (1974). Brief therapy. *Family Process* 13:141–68.

———, Fisch, R., and Segal, L. (1982). *The Tactics of Change.* San Francisco: Jossey-Bass.

Wen Shing, T., and McDermott, J. (1979). Tri-axial family classification. *J. Amer. Acad. Child Psychiatry* 18:22–43.

Zilbach, J., et al. (1972). The role of the young child in family therapy. In C. Sager and H. Kaplan (Eds.). *Progress in Group and Family Therapy.* New York: Brunner/Mazel.

52

PSYCHOPHARMACOLOGICAL TREATMENT

Harold S. Koplewicz and Daniel T. Williams

The use of psychopharmacological agents in adult psychiatric patients has revolutionized American psychiatry. Shorter stays in hospitals for psychotic patients and the successful treatment of anxiety and depressive disorders have been some of the major advances. The use of medication for childhood psychiatric disorders has usually followed the use in the adult population. However, starting with Bradley (1937), who introduced the use of amphetamine for behavior-disordered youngsters, innovative psychopharmacological treatment for childhood psychiatric disorders has offered both great promise and many disappointments. Today, demands from the public and the media for child practitioners to find easy, quick answers to complicated problems creates a temptation to use the psychopharmacological agent as a "magic pill." The unsophisticated clinician can be easily infected by the contagious passion of the public, the enthusiasm of those working on a new medication, and the general hope for a cure of chronic, painful disorders. Hence, the contemporary child psychiatrist has to be up-to-date with the latest psychopharmacological research, judicious enough to know when a medication should be tried, and knowledgeable about the risks and benefits. In multidisciplinary settings, psychopharmacological evaluation and treatment have become the unique and sometimes the most important role for a child psychiatrist.

The clinician should have a clear understanding of the diagnosis of the child before medication is prescribed. Purely symptom-based prescription is often shortsighted and sometimes dangerous, since a symptom can be associated with more than one syndrome. For example, school refusal can be part of the classic picture of separation anxiety disorder, or a symptom of conduct disorder, a depressive disorder, or even schizophrenia. The treatment approach to these four different disorders would be very different, and therefore there is no one medication that can be used to treat the symptom of school refusal. The use of DSM-III and more recently DSM-III-R, though limited in many ways, does help to clarify the diagnostic procedure, which is the essential first step in the assessment of pediatric psychopharmacological treatment.

This chapter outlines some general considerations in approaching child or adolescent patients and their parents when psychopharmacological treatment appears indicated. Several representative diagnostic categories will then be discussed individually. Some entities, such as enuresis, tics, and Tourette syndrome, whose pharmacological management has been discussed elsewhere in the volume, will not be reviewed here. The reader wishing more detailed consideration of psychopharmacological issues regarding children and adolescents is referred to the recent volume edited by Wiener (1985) on the subject.

ADDRESSING COMMON PARENTAL AND PATIENT CONCERNS

The use of medication for childhood psychiatric conditions carries a stigma in the minds of many parents of children requiring treatment. The education of parents and the general public in this regard remains an important task for child psychiatrists. Explaining to parents the rationale for the use of an indicated medication, the potential benefits, potential side-effects, and projected length of treatment is essential. This approach can achieve improved compliance and less alarm when side-effects occur. An informed parent, in the long term, will assist in the therapeutic trial of the medication. It is not unusual to have parents enter one's office with many misconceptions, fears, and misguided hopes for a treatment for their child. Discussing the child's diagnosis and prognosis and the range of possible treatment approaches is necessary. This discussion should include an explanation of the usual efficacy of the treatment modalities proposed as well as how they would be integrated in the treatment plan for the individual patient. Outlining this plan as coherently as possible at the outset is important, as one hopes to recruit the parents as part of the child's treatment "team."

Many parents worry about the addictive nature of psychotropic medication. Some parents state that giving their child medication offers a model of taking a pill to deal with problems. The evidence does not support this idea. For example, among adolescents being treated for attention deficit disorder, compliance is often problematic with psychostimulants, which have the most immediate and best-documented therapeutic effect. Moreover, there is no higher incidence of drug-abuse in the population of children treated with the psychostimulant methylphenidate (Ritalin) than in their untreated counterparts (Henker et al. 1981). It is helpful to explain that the medications utilized by child psychiatrists generally have no addictive propensity (one exception being minor tranquilizers). Furthermore, these are not "pleasurable" medications to take. An explanation of the biomedical model and current understanding of specific drug action can help parents understand that a patient may need the medication because of a biochemical predisposition, not as an unwarranted "crutch" to get through life. Finally, since drug treatment is most appropriately employed as an adjunctive component of an overall treatment plan, supportive reality testing on this issue with reference to other clearly formulated aspects of the treatment plan should also be helpful.

Another common complaint is that the medication is not a cure and will have to be taken indefinitely. It is important to be candid with parents in projecting the anticipated course of treatment and the uncertainties involved. In many cases, such as in acute depressive and anxiety disorders, a time-limited medication trial of several weeks or months may be all that is needed. However, some disorders require pharmacotherapy for years, and in the case of major tranquilizers, they run a risk of potential long-term side-effects. This has to be explained to parents in a clear, rational manner, describing the benefits and risks of taking the medication as well as the risks of *not* taking the medication.

All of the issues noted thus far regarding parents' concerns, queries, and misconceptions apply with equal importance to the primary patient in question. Adolescents especially, but some older children as well, may marshal more articulate expressions of resistance to medication than their parents. In general, all children and adolescents merit a supportive, realistic, and age-appropriate explanation of the rationale for the use of any psychotropic medication.

It is worth noting that in most of medicine (with rare exceptions like bacterial infections) we have few pharmacological cures, but many successful treatments that allow patients to live more comfortable lives. In child psychiatry, adding medication as part of treatment can in many instances increase the effectiveness of other non-medication approaches. For example, the use of stimulants in the treatment of a child with attention deficit hyperactivity disorder (ADHD) is often the most effective way of diminishing the primary presenting symptoms. It is most advisable, however, to include other adjunctive treatments as well, such as behavioral therapy, parent counseling, and/or tutoring, to address problems not ameliorated by stimulant treatment alone. The increased attentiveness and reduced impulsivity associated with psychostimulant, however, may maximize the benefits obtained from behavioral treatments (Gittelman et al. 1980) and tutoring (Gittelman 1983) and may contribute as well to improved mother/child interaction (Barkley 1981), thereby making parent counseling more effective.

GUIDELINES FOR PSYCHOPHARMACOLOGICAL EVALUATION

The pediatric psychopharmacological evaluation may originate from two general sources: a medical or nonmedical colleague refers a patient for evaluation for psychotropic medication; or the patient is self-referred. In either case, a complete evaluation is necessary. This includes a history of the present illness; review of the developmental history, including pregnancy, delivery, and developmental milestones; school history (including report cards and any psychological educational testing); medical and psychiatric history, with associated treatments and outcome;

and any relevant medication history, with dosage and side-effects. In addition, summary reports from previous therapists should be requested, as well as any hospital records. Finally, a family history can be very helpful in clarifying significant psychopathology that puts the patient at risk either genetically and/or environmentally and consequently may be most informative diagnostically.

A questionnaire assessing present and past history, completed by the parents (and the child when applicable) before their appointment, can be very helpful (Gardner 1986). Such a questionnaire not only provides the child psychiatrist with necessary information, but also helps the parents formulate the child's presenting problems and their onset. It may also refresh the parents' memories of important past events. The questionnaire format can be modified and developed by the individual psychiatrist to obtain the information he finds most useful. Parent rating skills are also potentially helpful. These can be tapped by including relevant forms in the packet of materials sent to the parents before the appointment. The most popular scale in this regard is the Conners Parent Questionnaire (Goyette et al. 1978). This instrument can be a particularly useful addition to the diagnostic evaluation of attention deficit disorder with hyperactivity and later, if psychostimulants are prescribed, in evaluating their effectiveness. Other parent rating scales useful in psychopharmacological evaluation are the Werry Weiss Peters Activity Rating Scale and the Child Behavior Check List (Routh et al. 1974; Achenbach 1978). If possible, each parent should fill out the scales individually. Their separate ratings can be useful in evaluating interrater reliability of the parents, and consistency and severity of the symptoms. When these materials (scales, questionnaire, previous records) are reviewed before the appointment, the psychiatrist has a clinical picture of the child before he enters the office. This provides a more focused direction of the interview, as well as an opportunity to clarify any discrepancies in the parents' reports, the clinician's interview, patient mental status, and the history. After a diagnosis has been made and a treatment plan formulated, the parents should be informed of these, including all the relevant treatment options.

Preadolescent children should not be given treatment recommendations until the parents have been consulted. If medication is indicated, it is helpful to supplement one's verbal explanation to the parents by giving them some written material about the specific medication or even a reference to a general sourcebook about psychopharmacology (Wender and Klein 1981). A return appointment should be offered to discuss any questions the family may have after giving the treatment recommendations some thought. Unless one is dealing with an emergency situation, it is most often preferable not to prescribe medication at the first session. An interval of follow-up is often helpful to both the psychiatrist and family in further clarifying impressions, questions, and decisions regarding the appropriateness of medication.

When medication treatment has been recommended by a psychiatrist and agreed upon by the parents, the next step is to explain this decision to the adolescent or child patient. In the case of adolescents, their cooperation is particularly important, since they usually participate in the administration of the medication. However, parental supervision is still essential in monitoring the medication. In explaining the use of medicine to a child, it may be helpful to refer to a medical model. Children can be told that they will be receiving medication for their emotional problems much as they might for a physical complaint. The clinician should specify whether it is a thinking, feeling, or behavior disorder. It is important to explain the potential benefits and side-effects to the child without generating magical expectations. Before the prescription is written, the following should be completed: a physical examination (in the past six months), blood pressure, pulse, height and weight taken that day, and in some cases, an electrocardiogram (if antidepressants are to be prescribed). Finally, prior to the initiation of the treatment regimen, a review of general physical symptoms (preferably including a side-effect checklist) should be completed. This sensitizes the clinician to any of the patient's hypochondriacal concerns and helps him evaluate any subsequent complaints of "side-effects" by the youngster. While psychotropic medications are being titrated, patients should generally be seen weekly, with side-effects, blood pressure, and pulse ratings taken routinely at each visit.

Obtaining blood levels for psychotropic medications is most often not necessary on a routine basis to achieve therapeutic results. Monitoring the blood levels may be useful, though, when there is a question of noncompliance or when therapeutic results have not been achieved on what one would have expected to be a therapeutic dose. This applies, of course, only to those medications where a therapeutic range in terms of blood level has been established. Even in the case of tricyclic antidepressant medication, where such levels are rather clearly established for adults, their relevance for children and adolescents is as yet unclear.

Once a therapeutic response has been achieved, based on clinical reports from the patient, parent, and teacher(s), it is often unnecessary for a psychiatrist to see the patient weekly if the psychiatrist is not the primary therapist. Monthly visits for maintenance monitoring, or even visits every two to four months may be all that is needed, depending on the individual patient. The psychiatrist's ongoing contact with the primary therapist is necessary, however, as is the primary therapist's awareness of potential side-effects and of when to notify the psychiatrist of problems that may arise. A reevaluation of the need for continuing medication is essential every six months, and a drug holiday should be considered to aid in this reassessment.

Contact with the school is important. The child spends more time at school than at any other location besides his home. Teachers are therefore an essential source of information. Telephone contact with the teacher, either via the parents or directly by the psychiatrist with the parents' consent, should be arranged at the earliest possible opportunity. Teachers should be asked about the child's behavior in class, in group activities, in one-to-one interactions with the teacher, and in relations with classmates. In the case of children with multiple teachers (junior or senior high school students) the guidance counselor is usually the best person to coordinate this inquiry. A school visit with classroom observation and a conference with all of the patient's teachers and guidance counselor is optimal, but not always practical. Teacher ratings obtained from standard teacher rating scales often supply sufficient information. In general, teacher ratings of the child's behavior are more reliable and sensitive than parent ratings, since teachers usually have a clearer sense of age-appropriate norms of behavior and have a clearer basis therefore of assessing deviations from these norms. Consequently, teachers' assessments are often a vital part of the diagnostic evaluation. The most widely used teachers' scale is the Conners Teacher Rating Scale (Goyette et al. 1978). The scale has twenty-eight items and has been analyzed to five general areas. The scale can be completed easily and quickly and can also be used on a repeated basis to rate medication efficacy in hyperactive youngsters. Another widely used teacher rating scale is the Behavior Rating Scale (Kendall and Wilcox 1979).

PSYCHOPHARMACOLOGICAL TREATMENT ISSUES

Pharmacokinetics. This term refers to the mode by which a drug is absorbed, distributed throughout the body, metabolized into an inactive compound, and eventually excreted from the body (Gittelman and Kanner 1986). It is clearly important for the prescribing physician to be cognizant of these issues as they pertain to the clinical effects of particular medications. Relevant examples would include the knowledge of the general time of onset of a medication's clinical effects as determined by its rate of absorption and distribution, as well as the general time of "wearing off" of clinical effects, as determined by the medication's rate of metabolism and excretion. Knowledge of the characteristics of specific medications in this regard enables the clinician to be most effective in timing the administration of medication. Similarly, the physician's awareness of the general range of individual differences in rates of absorption, distribution, metabolism, and excretion of different medications allows for maximal individualization of medication dose as clinically indicated by a particular patient's needs. Sensitivity to this issue can avoid the common errors of iatrogenic overdosing or underdosing of a patient based on overly rigid adherence to a narrow, fixed-dose format of medication administration.

In light of the above, it is advisable to begin any new medication at a low and most often subtherapeutic dose. This minimizes the potentially distressing extent of initial side-effects that may be encountered, since most side-effects are dose-dependent. Furthermore, many side-effects are more marked at the beginning of treatment and diminish over time as the patient accommodates to the medication. Consequently, if one can establish a patient's tolerance to an initially low dose of medication, one is then in a stronger position gradually to titrate the dose upward with less likelihood that the sudden, frightening appearance of a severe side-effect will discourage the patient and/or family from any continued use of the medication. Nevertheless, there is enormous individual variation of susceptibility to untoward medication effects, so that the same dose may be well tolerated by some patients and totally intolerable for others.

Balancing Benefits Versus Side-Effects

The psychiatrist should be familiar with the clinical pharmacological profile of different medications within a particular group of psychopharmacological agents; a given patient may be very sensitive to a side-effect (e.g., sedation) of one medication within the group, but be quite accepting of another medication that is less prone to cause that side-effect. Since all medications have side-effects and there is no currently available method of predicting which patient will be more sensitive to the side-effects of any given medication, one must engage in what amounts to an empirical clinical trial. The physician may be aided by a reasoned clinical estimate of which side-effects would be most acceptable to a patient; thus a patient with insomnia as a secondary symptom of depression or anxiety may welcome the sedative side-effect of an antidepressant or anxiolytic medication that is prescribed for treatment of the primary psychiatric condition. (Clearly, most or all of such a medication should preferably be administered at bedtime to maximize the desired benefit of the sedative side-effect.) In light of the large and unpredictable variation in individual tolerance to side-effects, it is best to share this uncertainty with the patient and family at the outset, noting that a change of dose or of medication may be needed, depending on the patient's pattern of response. This diminishes the disillusionment of the patient and family when a medication change is in fact needed, which is relatively frequently the case.

ANXIETY DISORDERS

Separation anxiety disorder, avoidant disorder, and overanxious disorder are the three anxiety disorders listed in the childhood section of DMS-III-R. In addition, some of the adult anxiety disorders, specifically simple phobia and obsessive-compulsive disorders, are applicable to children. The treatment literature pertaining to childhood anxiety disorders antedates the current diagnostic nomenclature. Therefore, describing the efficacy of certain medications for the current diagnoses is problematic. The review of pharmacological agents here will be limited to those that have been evaluated specifically using the diagnostic criteria described in DMS-III. Some degree of anxiety is an inevitable and natural, albeit dysphoric, part of child and adolescent development. Consequently, the mere presence of anxiety would not by itself justify pharmacotherapy until and unless the anxiety is diagnostically defined and judged by the psychiatrist to be of sufficient clinical significance to warrant medication (see Chapter 34).

Separation Anxiety Disorder

The essential feature in this disorder is that the child experiences excessive anxiety upon separation from the parent, home, or significant attachment figure. These children are worried whenever separation occurs. Their worries are centered on a threat to the integrity of their family; they may worry that some harm may befall their parent or themselves during the separation. These children also experience extreme distress upon separation, so that attending school or having their parents go out for the evening creates excessive stress for the child. The third symptom that these children consistently complain of is homesickness. They describe being at school, on an overnight date or at sleep-away camp as painful and difficult. It is at these times that the longing for home and for mother or father is most intense. The age of onset may begin as early as the preschool period and seems to have peaks at 11, 14, and sometimes at 18 years of age. These time periods are usually associated with a change of school setting from elementary to junior to senior high school or during the application process to college. Both boys and girls suffer from this disorder with equal frequency. Separation anxiety disorder is more common in family members of patients with separation anxiety disorder than in the general population. Adult researchers have reported that as many as 50 percent of their adult patients diagnosed with panic disorder had experienced separation anxiety disorder during childhood (Klein 1964). Prospective longitudinal studies are needed before one can definitely conclude the long-term outcome for the separation-anxious child or adolescent.

Differential Diagnosis. The differential diagnosis of separation anxiety disorder includes school truancy, usually associated with conduct disorder. Typically, the child with separation anxiety disorder will avoid school, but will prefer staying at home and keeping in touch with his parents. The school truant, by contrast, is often hanging around outside the school or some other location besides his home. The truant child does not express concern about himself or his family as would the separation-anxious child.

The more difficult differential is between the separation-anxious child and the one meeting diagnostic criteria for major depressive disorder. Children and adolescents with severe anxiety symptoms are inevitably in pain and unhappy. However, while the child with separation anxiety disorder may meet diagnostic criteria for depression while away from home or his parents, in the presence of the "major attachment figure," the patient will become more relaxed, may demonstrate a sense of humor, and his mood will lift. The classic vegetative signs of depression, if they exist, are often fluctuating in the separation-anxious child. There may be disturbance in appetite that is limited to breakfast and lunch on school days; however, during dinner and meals on weekends the appetite will be normal. Concentration, sleep disturbance, and somatic complaints are generally limited to the weekdays versus the weekends.

Medication. The drug of choice for separation anxiety disorder at the present time is imipramine (Tofranil). The previously reported effective use of imipramine in adults suffering from agoraphobia led to trials of tricyclic antidepressants in children with separation anxiety disorder. Klein (1964) hypothesized that agoraphobic patients with panic attacks suffered from a disruption of the biological processes that regulate anxiety triggered by separation. Since imipramine relieved adult panic anxiety, it was thought possibly to be useful in children with separation anxiety. An initial open clinical trial with imipramine was conducted in children with school phobia, and 85 percent of the children returned to school (Rabiner and Klein 1969). This study was followed with a placebo-controlled six-week study of imipramine in 7- to 15-year-olds who were unable to attend school regularly (Gittelman-Klein and Klein 1971, 1980). Imipramine was significantly superior to placebo both in inducing school return, and in reducing anxiety symptomatology, physical symptoms before school, and separation difficulties. Clomipramine has been found ineffective in treatment of school phobia (Berney et al. 1981), though it should be noted that the clomipramine dosage used was lower than the imipramine dose used by Gittelman-Klein. The low dose of clomipramine may explain the discrepancy in results. A benzodiazepine, alprazolam (Xanax), has been reported to be effective in adults with panic disorders (Sheehan et al. 1984). In our clinical experience, limited to only ten youngsters with separation anxiety disorder refractory to psychotherapy, alprazolam was very effective in nine patients over a six-week period in daily doses of 0.5 to 6 mgms. a day. One patient suffered severe sedation and medication was discontinued. It is necessary for placebo-controlled and double-blind studies to evaluate the efficacy of alprazolam in separation-anxious children.

Side-Effects. There has been a low frequency of reported side-effects in imipramine and other tricyclic antidepressants in children (Gualtieri 1977). The most common side-effects reported are drowsiness and dry mouth. Disinhibition, consisting of poor frustration tolerance and temper outbursts, has been reported less frequently but is a more clinically troubling side-effect in the management of anxious children. Cardiac toxicity is the most serious and therefore the side-effect that causes the greatest concern for the clinician. Arrhythmias, ventricular fibrillation, and congestive heart failure have been reported with imipramine acute overdoses. Rapid increases of imipramine dose are to be avoided at all times. Baseline electrocardiograms should be obtained, as changes in the EKG have been reported in children receiving long-term treatment. Cardiac side-effects have included conduction changes without clinical evidence of heart block, increases in systolic and diastolic blood pressure, and increased pulse (Greenberg and Yellin 1975).

The convulsive threshold of seizure patients may be lowered with imipramine use, and simultaneous barbiturate use may lower the serum level of the imipramine. Conversely, simultaneous use of stimulants will raise serum imipramine levels. Therefore, careful monitoring of imipramine levels is essential if there is combined use of other medications.

Dosage. The Food and Drug Administration (FDA) has recommended the maximum dose of 5 mgms/kgm per day, because of the potential cardiac side-effects of imipramine. A recommended starting dose is 25 mgms at bedtime for three days to rule out any idiosyncratic reaction, raising the dose by 25 mgms each four to seven days. Parents and patients should be informed that most side-effects from imipramine are usually transient and that with time patients may develop a tolerance to the adverse effects. As is the case with the use of tricyclics in depression, it is recommended that the patients and family be informed that four to six weeks of medication is necessary before a full therapeutic effect will be demonstrated. Electrocardiograms should be taken with each increase of 75 mgms. Once the patient has reached the maximum dose, EKG need only be taken every year. Blood levels should be taken eight to twelve hours after the last dose of imipramine in children who are nonresponders. It should be noted, however, that blood levels do not necessarily correlate to clinical response in childhood and adolescent depression as they do in the adult population. Data regarding this correlation in childhood and adolescent separation anxiety are not yet available. After a twelve-week symptom-free trial of medication, the patient should have a medication-free period. The decrease in dose should be done slowly (25 mgms a week) and medication reinstituted if symptoms occur. Symptom recurrence would indicate the advisability of a longer period on medication at a therapeutic dose before tapering is reattempted.

Avoidant Disorder

This disorder refers to children who are shy and severely inhibited in a variety of social situations. Shyness can be a temperamental variant; in the avoidant-disordered child it assumes pathological proportions. Differential distinction should be made from children with schizoid disorder whose presentation may be similar to the avoidant disorder. The schizoid child generally has no social interest, awareness, or activity, whereas the avoidant child is acutely aware and anxious about his social deficits. At the present time there are no controlled psychopharmacological studies in the treatment of avoidant disorder. In the adult population, social phobia, which may be viewed as a developmental variant of avoidant disorder, has been treated with group therapy, psychotherapy, and social skills training. Phenelzine, an MAO inhibitor, has been successful in open clinical trial in an adult population with social phobia (Liebowitz et al. 1986). Systematic trials with children and adolescents are wanting.

Overanxious Disorder

This is a mixed condition in that it includes children who are overly concerned about the quality of their performance, worry obsessively about their grades, and have excessive fears of many new situations. The overanxious child worries before taking the examination, during the examination, and even after the examination before test results are returned. The overanxious child often suffers from somatic complaints that are present after school and on weekends as well as during school days. This distinction differentiates a child with separation anxiety versus overanxious disorder. Up to the present, many different pharmacological agents have been utilized for the overanxious disorder, including major and minor tranquilizers and antihistamines. For empirical use in clinical situations, minor tranquilizers are preferred if pharmacological treatment is warranted, because of a less dangerous profile of side-effects. To date, there are no controlled studies demonstrating efficacy of any of these agents in children with anxiety disorder. Benzodiazepines are used extensively as preanesthetic compounds in children, and this suggests that they may reduce situational and anticipatory anxiety. Placebo-controlled studies are essential, however, before general guidelines can be delineated.

Obsessive-Compulsive Disorder

Obsessive-compulsive disorder, included in the adult section of the DSM-III-R, frequently has an onset in childhood or adolescence. The essential features consist of persistent, intrusive, unwanted ideas and ego-dystonic repetitive impulses to perform acts that are regarded as unreasonable even by the children performing them. These children experience severe anxiety if they are prevented from carrying out these rituals. The most common obsessions are repetitive thoughts of violence, contamination, and doubt. The most common compulsions involve handwashing, counting, checking, and touching. The children will report a "crazy idea" in their heads and an inability to remove the thought. They perform the compulsive behavior in an effort to rid themselves of this obsession. Quite often, the compulsive behavior is not done in the absolute correct manner and therefore needs to be repeated. During this procedure, the child is aware of what he is doing and realizes that it is purposeless. The anxiety generated by not being able to perform these behaviors is nevertheless extremely severe. This is a rare disorder occurring in approximately .2 percent in child inpatient and outpatient psychiatric observations (Hollingsworth et al. 1980).

Differential Diagnosis. Patients with obsessive-compulsive disorder often demonstrate depressive symptomatology. The distinction between the affective illness and this disorder is important. Thus, some children may be demoralized secondary to the obsessive-compulsive disorder, but their mood disorder does not precede the onset of the obsessions and compulsions. Some children with separation anxiety disorder may develop obsessive-compulsive behaviors. The obsessions in this case have separation content and focus on threats to the integrity of the patient's family; once treatment for the separation anxiety has been effective, the obsessive-compulsive behaviors are eliminated.

Medication. Clomipramine (Anfaril), a tricyclic antidepressant, has been found to be efficacious in adult patients with obsessive-compulsive disorder (Thoren et al. 1980). Rapoport has reported clomipramine efficacy superior to placebo in children with obsessive-compulsive disorder (Flament et al. 1985). At the present time, clomipramine is being compared to other tricyclic antidepressants for efficacy in obsessive-compulsive disorder (Rapoport, personal communication 1986). Clomipramine has not yet been approved by the Food and Drug Administration, and therefore the pharmacotherapy in obsessive-compulsive disorder in children and adolescents is quite limited. Other tricyclics such as desimipramine, imipramine, and amytriptyline may be useful.

AFFECTIVE DISORDERS

The diagnosis of depression in children and adolescents has gained acceptance during the past ten years (see Chapter 29). Systematic diagnosis, utilizing structured interviews and adaptations from the adult diagnostic criteria to a child and adolescent model along with placebo-controlled drug studies, adds support to the acceptance of affective disorders as a recognized psychiatric condition in children and adolescents (Puig-Antich et al. 1978; Carlson and Cantwell 1980; Puig-Antich 1982b). According to DSM-III-R, the essential feature of the major depressive episode is either dysphoric mood, or loss of interest or pleasure in all or almost all usual activities and pastimes. Symptoms also include appetite disturbance, sleep disturbance, decreased energy, decreased concentration, and suicidal thoughts. These symptoms are not sensitive to the environment and therefore are consistent in all areas of the patient's life. The children are sad, unhappy, have weight loss, and have difficulty with school work. Although clear epidemiological data are lacking, this appears to be a relatively rare disorder in prepubertal children and is encountered more commonly among adolescents.

Atypical depression may have a more fluctuating clinical picture (Klein et al. 1980). These patients, though intensely depressed and even suicidal at moments, may enjoy some activities in a changed environment. Even though they have disturbances of sleep, appetite, and concentration, they very often will oversleep, overeat, and be attentive at times. Nevertheless, these depressions can be disabling and these patients may have a significant suicide potential.

The K-SADS, a structured diagnostic interview, has documented reliability and validity for affective disorders in children (Chambers et al. 1985). This instrument systematically obtains information from both the child and the parent as to the child's current psychiatric state, with a particular focus on affective symptomatology. Even though this instrument requires training for use, the detailed material covered in the interview and the principal of obtaining information directly from both child and parent(s) are two premises that should be put into practice by the clinician. The BDI (Beck Depression Inventory) has normative data in the child and adolescent population and can be utilized for baseline and for treatment evaluations once medication has been instituted.

There have been open clinical trials of antidepressants in children with affective disorders, suggesting a positive response to treatment (Puig-Antich et al. 1978). Yet three double-blind placebo-controlled studies in prepubertal children have failed to demonstrate that an antidepressant medication is better than placebo in treating major depressive disorder (Puig-Antich et al. 1985). Complicating factors in these studies included an unexpectedly high placebo response rate and the relatively low imipramine dosages used. When the data are examined pharmacokinetically, the results of plasma level clinical response studies of imipramine do suggest its effectiveness in this age group. The data suggest that antidepressant response to imipramine in prepubertal children can be optimized by titrating the dose of imipramine to achieve a plasma level above 150 mg/ml. Further double-blind studies that take into account these pharmacokinetic considerations are clearly needed.

The treatment of adolescent depression with tricyclic antidepressants has been assessed with one placebo-controlled study. Kramer and Feigurne (1983) studied amitriptyline and placebo in adolescents hospitalized for major depression; the study demonstrated no significant difference between the medicated and placebo groups. Thus, the efficacy of tricyclic antidepressant medication in adolescent depression remains to be demonstrated.

In our own clinical experience, phenelzine, a mono-amine oxidase inhibitor (MAOI), in dosage between 30 mgms to 90 mgms, has appeared to be effective in adolescents with major depressive episodes. Compliance to the dietary restrictions associated with all MAOI antidepressants is necessary, as well as an understanding of the potential adverse side-effects when combined with other medications. The reduction of the dose of phenelzine and/or the institution of lithium as a prophylaxis to hypomania secondary to phenelzine may be necessary at the first sign of manic symptomatology, for example, sleep disturbance or sustained hypomanic mood. MAOI antidepressants require a tyramine-free diet. This is particularly difficult for impulsive adolescents, who will often consume proscribed alcoholic beverages and foods. Patients must not use any illicit drugs while on MAOI antidepressants, and even prescription medication must be cleared with the treating psychiatrist.

Further studies are necessary in evaluating tricyclic antidepressants and MAOIs in the adolescent population.

Bipolar Affective Disorders in Childhood and Adolescence

Although bipolar affective disorder is rarely encountered in children and infrequently reported among adolescents, systematic surveys note that such cases do occur and are often responsive to treatment with lithium carbonate (Youngerman and Canino 1978). Therefore, despite a lack of controlled trials, a course of treatment with lithium may well be advisable if a diagnosis of mania is substantiated. Because of potentially adverse thyroid, renal, and other effects of long-term lithium use, it should be discontinued after three to six months, while monitoring for the possible recurrence of manic symptoms.

Before starting lithium, a physical assessment should be done, including thyroid function tests, urinalysis, serum creatinine and EKG. Lithium should be started at 150 to 300 mg/day and increased by 150 or 300 mg every five to seven days, depending on the age and size of the youngster (Puig-Antich et al. 1985). Blood levels of lithium should be obtained in the morning before the first dose of lithium and the dose titrated until either clinical improvement is observed, side-effects are encountered, or a blood level of 0.8–1.2 mEq/1. is obtained. Common side-effects include nausea, diarrhea, weakness, and excessive thirst. Whenever any of these is reported, a plasma lithium level should be obtained promptly to avoid potentially dangerous toxicity, which may include cardiac arrhythmias.

ATTENTION DEFICIT-HYPERACTIVITY DISORDER

In the DSM-III classification, there are three attention deficit disorder (ADD) subtypes: ADD with hyperactivity, ADD without hyperactivity, and ADD residual type. In DSM-III-R, these are combined into the attention deficit-hyperactivity disorder (ADHD), reflecting the intervening clinical experience and observations in field trials that a continuum, rather than discrete subtypes, more accurately characterizes this psychopathological entity.

The essential features of this disorder are developmentally inappropriate inattention, impulsivity and hyperactivity (see Chapter 25). These symptoms are usually present in both the school and home settings. Teachers report that in the classroom these children are disorganized, somewhat unfocused, often do not complete their work and are off-task. At home, parents describe the child as always on the go and unable to sit still. Certain activities such as dinner, religious services, and group activities may be particularly problematic. The onset of this disorder is before the age of 7 but most frequently during toddlerhood. Parents will state that the toddler is difficult to control, that babysitters do not want to be with the child, and that any kind of play group is problematic. Identification of these children has become more systematic and at an earlier age (S. B. Campbell 1985). Boys outnumber girls approximately 10:1 and the disorder is relatively common, with approximately 3 to 5 percent of prepubertal children in the United States meeting the diagnostic criteria. The course of this disorder may take three general forms: The patient continues to maintain all the symptomatology throughout his life; the patient becomes asymptomatic at puberty; the patient continues to remain impulsive with a short attention span but does not remain hyperactive into adolescence and adult life (Gittelman et al. 1985).

Medication. The drugs of choice for attention deficit disorder with hyperactivity are the psychostimulants. Methylphenidate (Ritalin) has been studied most extensively and has proven efficacy in improving attention, as well as diminishing hyperactive and impulsive behaviors (Klein et al. 1980; Conners and Werry 1979). Methylphenidate engenders improvement in global readings on both parent and teacher scales (Werry and Aman 1975; Gittelman-Klein et al. 1976). Methylphenidate has also yielded demonstrated improvement in the mother/child interaction (Cunningham and Barkley 1978; Humphries et al. 1978). Dextroamphetamine (Dexedrine) and magnesium pemoline (Cylert) have also demonstrated clinical efficacy (Dykman et al. 1976).

Pharmacotherapy for the treatment of attention deficit hyperactivity disorder should be instituted only in cases where the severity of the child's difficulties are refractory to nonpharmacological treatments such as family-based psychotherapy and/ or behavioral therapy. The age of the patient is not necessarily a primary factor in the consideration to begin treatment. In the past, school age children were the only population that usually received psychostimulants. Even though the *Physician's Desk Reference* states that methylphenidate should be utilized only in 6-year-old and older children, several studies have shown efficacy in the preschool population (Conners 1975; Schleifler et al. 1975; Koplewicz and Gittelman 1983). The preschool child may benefit from medication because of the potential effectiveness in relieving many of the key symptoms of the disorder. Poor self-esteem, peer interaction difficulties, and a disturbed mother/child relationship may be lessened by this earlier intervention.

Varley (1983) has conducted a placebo-controlled study of the use of methylphenidate in adolescents with attention deficit disorder with hyperactivity, with positive results. Compliance with the adolescent population is usually problematic and necessitates closer monitoring. There is a need for more placebo-controlled studies in this particular age group.

Since dexoamphetamine has been shown to have more short-term and long-term side-effects than methylphenidate, the latter is the drug of first choice for this disorder (Greenhill 1984). Patients should be started on methylphenidate, 5 mgms p.o.a.m. for four to seven days. The medication should then be titrated upward, with regular monitoring of clinical response after each dose increment. Five mgm increments should be added, with the dose divided between breakfast and lunch times. The maximum recommended dosage of methylphenidate is 60 mgms a day, with most youngsters being maintained at a dose of between 10 and 40 mg/day. Some patients require a third dose upon return from school, since the usual effective clinical duration of the medication is three to four hours, though some individuals may experience effects for up to twelve hours. There have been reports of decrements in cognitive functioning at higher dosages of methylphenidate, but these reports are controversial and necessitate further research (Sprague and Sleator 1977). Several studies have reported improvement in cognitive functions of children with ADDH treated with methylphenidate (Cohen et al. 1971; Conners 1971; Gittelman-Klein and Klein 1975).

Recently, a sustained-release preparation of methylphenidate has been marketed in the United States. Greenhill's systematic preliminary studies on the efficacy of this preparation suggest that it is less effective than the standard preparation (personal communication 1986). This sustained-release preparation may be helpful nevertheless in those patients whose compliance is problematic. In such cases, the combination of sustained-release methylphenidate and short-acting methylphenidate may help the child get through a school day with only one dose in the morning.

Dextroamphetamine can be given to children under the age of 6 (PDR). The recommended starting dose for preschoolers aged 3 to 5 is 2.5 mgms a day, with increments of 2.5 mgms every four to seven days based on clinical response. In the older child, the starting dose is 5 mgms per day with a recommended maximum dose of 40 mgms. Dextroamphetamine should be given before meals, and height and weight should be monitored carefully. In the adolescent population, this medication should be used with caution since it has potential for abuse as a recreational drug.

The initial dose of magnesium pemoline (Cylert) is 37.5 mgms per day with a maximum dose of 112.5 mgms. A three-week period is usually required before therapeutic results are demonstrated. Its main advantage is that it is relatively long-acting, and therefore may be sufficiently effective if given just once a day, in the morning. However, it is often not as effective as methylphenidate or dextroamphetamine.

Delayed onset of sleep and decrease in appetite are the two most common side-effects of psychostimulants. Administration before meals and before 1 P.M. may reduce these side-effects. In the adolescent population sleep is not as disturbed as in the preschool and school aged groups. Baseline CBC and yearly monitoring are recommended by the *PDR* because of the rare blood dyscrasia that may occur secondary to psychostimulant administration. Long-term effects on height and weight have been reported with dextroamphetamine, and temporary delays in growth have been reported with methylphenidate (Safer et al. 1972; Mattes and Gittelman 1983). Consequently, regular monitoring of height and weight is advisable for all patients on these medications. In this regard, many youngsters whose symptoms cause them adjustment difficulty primarily in the school setting are able to be off the medication on weekends and vacation periods. Other patients whose severity of symptoms interferes markedly with functioning outside of school in interactions with family and peers may require the medication on a daily basis.

For all patients on psychostimulants, periodic reassessment of the patient off medication is advisable. When benefits of the medication are dubious or the patient is resistant to taking it, an earlier trial off medication should be encouraged and feedback sought from both teachers and parents regarding the results. Even when dramatic benefit from the medication has been observed, reassessment off the medication every six months is warranted. Many patients are eventually able to integrate the improved behavioral mode engendered by the medication into their "repertoire" and to sustain it even without the medication. When the patient and family sense that the psychiatrist is invested in the medication only as a means to the goal of improved adjustment and only for as long as it is demonstrably needed, this diminishes the frequently encountered resistance to taking the medication.

The presence of tics or an anxiety disorder requires careful consideration before the initiation of psychostimulants. A history of Tourette syndrome in the patient or a first-degree relative of the patient is a contraindication for psychostimulants. This is because the use of stimulants has been reported to increase the propensity to tics and other Tourette symptoms in vulnerable patients. Such a patient may benefit from a trial of antidepressants for the treatment of the attention deficit hyperactivity disorder. Studies of tricyclic antidepressants have demonstrated efficacy in the treatment of ADDH (Klein et al. 1980).

Anxiety-disordered children have been reported to have exacerbation of symptomatology while on psychostimulants. A preschool hyperactive child with mild anxiety symptomatology became separation-anxious while on 20 mgms of Ritalin.

Once the psychostimulant was discontinued, the separation-anxious symptomatology was eliminated (Gittleman, personal communication 1981).

Neuroleptics have been used in clinical practice for many years for treating the symptoms of ADDH. Systematic studies confirmed the clinical efficacy of neuroleptics in ameliorating symptoms involving motor activity, disruptive behavior, concentration, and social behavior (Gittelman-Klein et al. 1976). However, the beneficial effects achieved with neuroleptics are generally not nearly as great as those achieved with stimulants. Furthermore, neuroleptics carry with them the potential for significant short-term side-effects, including sedation and possible impairment of cognitive performance, as well as the potential for serious long-term side-effects, in the form of tardive dyskinesia (see below). Consequently, appropriate clinical management would dictate that an adequate clinical trial of treatment on each of the three commonly used psychostimulants as well as imipramine be attempted (including adequate dose titration for each) before a clinical trial on neuroleptics is considered.

PERVASIVE DEVELOPMENTAL DISORDERS

As indicated in the DSM-III-R classification, pervasive developmental disorders (PDD) are characterized by: a qualitative impairment in reciprocal social interaction; a qualitative impairment in communication; a markedly restricted repertoire of activities, interests, and emotional development; and onset during infancy or childhood. (These diagnostic characteristics and the diverse formats of their appropriate assessment are outlined in detail in Chapter 23.) The empirical basis of a specific diagnostic designation for autistic disorder is very well documented, while this has not been so for the separate category in DSM-III of childhood onset pervasive developmental disorder. This has been addressed in DSM-III-R by subsuming both under the rubric of autistic disorder and subcategorizing: infantile onset (before 36 months of age), childhood onset (after 36 months of age), and age of onset unknown or unspecified. Nonpharmacological treatment of the pervasive developmental disorder is discussed briefly in Chapter 23.

Medications

Pharmacotherapy of the pervasive developmental disorders has for some time involved primarily the neuroleptics. Only recently, however, have systematic studies included diagnostically homogeneous patient samples and sound methodology (M. Campbell 1985). Currently, haloperidol (Haldol) is the psychoactive drug about which there is most systematic knowledge in terms of efficacy and safety. This derives from the earlier experience that the less potent phenothiazines, such as chlorpromazine, frequently caused significant sedation in autistic children at doses sufficient to diminish symptoms. Typically, autistic children who have normal activity levels or are hyperactive, disruptive, or aggressive respond better to haloperidol, while those who are hypoactive are less likely to benefit. Benefits observed in patients who respond favorably include significant decreases in sterotypies, hyperactivity, withdrawal, abnormal object relationships, fidgetiness, negativism, angry affect, and labile affect. In preschool age children, a reasonable starting dose is 0.25 to 0.5 mg/day, with gradual titration in increments of 0.25 to 0.5 mg at intervals of three to four days in order to reduce the incidence of acute dystonic reactions. Dosage should be regulated individually for each child and, as with all psychopharmacological assessment, input from parents, teachers, and any other reliable observers should be integrated in formulating the decision regarding dosage titration. Because of concern about both short- and long-term side-effects, it is advisable to maintain patients at the lowest dose compatible with maximum clinical benefit. This will usually be in the range of 0.5 to 4.0 mg/day. If improvement is observed, periodic tapering and possible discontinuation of the medication is advisable after an interval of three to six months to clarify whether maintenance on the medication at a given dose is warranted.

In Campbell's carefully monitored studies of young autistic children, there were no adverse effects of haloperidol on cognition or learning at doses that were effective in reducing behavioral symptoms (Anderson et al. 1984). Above these optimal doses, excessive sedation was the most common adverse effect, and it is reasonable to assume that this would have negative impact on cognitive functioning. It should be noted that in the series of forty patients studied, the mean optimal dose was relatively low (slightly above 1 mg/day).

It is sometimes overlooked that a worsening of preexisting symptoms or the emergence of new symptoms may be the first adverse effect observed in the course of neuroleptic titration. Such symptoms may include irritability, apathy, tantrums, and hyper- or hypoactivity. Indeed, our own clinical experience and that of others (Schulz et al. 1984) prompts consideration of a possible "therapeutic window" effect with neuroleptics. This indicates that if one exceeds the designated therapeutic range (which may vary among patients, but would be easier to miss by overly rapid titration), one can iatrogenically engender a worsening of the patient's condition. Other side-effects involving the central nervous system include dizziness, confusion, headache, insomnia, depersonalization, ataxia, seizures, and extrapynamidal effects. Seizures occur with a relatively high frequency in youngsters with pervasive developmental disorder independent of the use of neuroleptics. Chlorpromazine (Thorazine) is reported particularly likely to increase the frequency of seizures in such patients, whereas molindone hydrochloride (Moban) is reportedly the neuroleptic least likely to have this effect (Trimble 1985).

Commonly encountered extrapyramidal side-effects include acute dystonic reactions, dyskinesias, Parkinsonian reactions, and akathisia. Acute dystonic reactions include tonic contractions of muscles manifested as oculogyric crisis, torticollis, opisthotonus, and spasms of the tongue and torso. These are most often encountered within the first few days of neuroleptic administration and are best relieved by an intramuscular or oral dose of 25 mg of diphenhydramine (Benadryl). Acute dyskinesias also tend to be encountered early in the course of neuroleptic treatment. They consist of chronic muscle spasms, such as blinking, facial tics, lip smacking, tongue movements, and movements of the extremities. Parkinsonian reactions include muscular rigidity (cogwheel phenomenon), finger and hand tremor, drooling, masklike faces, and akinesia. These tend to occur within the first few weeks of treatment and generally respond to dosage reduction. Akathisia denotes agitation, constant pacing, and inability to sit still; it also tends to occur within the first few weeks of treatment.

There are divided opinions on the use of prophylactic and maintenance antiparkinsonian medication together with neuroleptics as a way of minimizing extrapyramidal side-effects and consequently enhancing compliance (S. B. Campbell 1985; Siamek et al. 1986). Patients taking low-potency neuroleptics, particularly thioridazine (Mellaril), are much less likely to experience extrapyramidal side-effects than those taking high-potency neuroleptics, such as haloperidol (Haldol). It seems best to individualize the decision regarding antiparkinsonian medication in terms of particular patients' needs. The recently available anti-Parkinsonian amantadine (Symmetril) does not cause much in the way of anticholinergic effects and may be useful when needed.

Tardive dyskinesia has recently come into increasingly justified prominence as a potentially severe, long-term, and sometimes irreversible side-effect of neuroleptics. These abnormal movements usually involve the muscles of the face, tongue, and mouth and may extend to the eyelids, extremities, torso, and neck. The movements may be rhythmic or irregular, repetitive, transient, or persistent. A recent review (Campbell et al. 1983) indicates that 8 to 51 percent of children and adolescents who receive neuroleptics over an extended period will develop either tardive dyskinesia or its variant, withdrawal dyskinesia. In the latter, dyskinetic symptoms are encountered on withdrawal of neuroleptic medication, but tend to subside within six months. Because of the potentially serious and long-lasting nature of these symptoms, it is advisable clinically, ethically, and medicolegally to obtain informed consent from a child's parents before instituting neuroleptic medication.

The rationale for using fenfluramine for autistic patients derived from its ability to lower levels of serotonin, since a substantial minority of autistic patients have elevated serotonin levels (Ritvo et al. 1984). In a double-blind cross-over study using fenfluramine, 1.5 mg/kg, Ritvo et al. found a decrease in hyperactivity and sensorimotor symptoms, increased social awareness, and improved communication when patients were on fenfluramine, as compared to placebo. Preliminary results from a multicenter, collaborative project on fenfluramine have tended to support the impression of a predominance of clinical benefits, with a paucity of side-effects (August et al. 1984). Patients with relatively higher IQ tended to respond best in both studies. The possibility that fenfluramine may represent a new treatment option for patients with autism remains to be clarified by further research.

CHILDHOOD PSYCHOSIS: SCHIZOPHRENIA, CHILDHOOD AND ADOLESCENT ONSET

Prior to the advent of DSM-III, the distinction between autistic disorder (pervasive developmental disorder) and prepubertal schizophrenic disorder was not always made. In many pre-DSM-III clinical and research reports, for example, autistic children were often diagnosed as "schizophrenic, with autistic features." Labels such as childhood schizophrenia (Bender 1942); schizophrenic reaction, childhood type (DSM-I); and schizophrenia, childhood type (DSM-II) have been deleted in DSM-III and DSM-III-R. In terms of current nosology of schizophrenic disorder, a child has to meet the criteria listed for adults in order to qualify for the diagnosis of schizophrenia: loosening of associations or incoherence, hallucinations, delusions, continuous signs of disease for at least six months, and deterioration of functioning. While schizophrenia rarely if ever starts before the age of 5 years and is very infrequent before puberty, the onset of autism occurs by definition during the first thirty months of life. Further discussion regarding differential diagnosis of the two disorders and assessment of childhood psychosis is contained in Chapters 23 and 27.

The literature documenting the efficacy of neuroleptics in schizophrenia is substantial (Klein 1980). The data extending these observations to children and adolescents with schizophrenia, however, are quite sparse (M. Campbell 1985). There is evidence that neuroleptics can ameliorate the principal psychotic symptoms of schizophrenia in adolescents, including hallucinations, thought disorder, and delusions (Pool et al. 1976). This is in contrast to the fact that neuroleptics affect only the secondary symptoms of autistic disorder—hyperactivity, irritability, and aggressiveness. Preliminary impressions suggest that prepubertal children with schizophrenia respond to neuroleptics to a much lesser extent than their adolescent or adult counterparts (Green et al. 1984).

Clinical guidelines regarding neuroleptic titration with childhood and adolescent psychosis are essentially the same as those outlined above for pervasive developmental disorder. This also applies to consideration of side-effects and to the merits of maintaining patients at the lowest dose of neuroleptics consonant with optimal symptom alleviation. It has been amply documented in adult schizophrenic patients that concomitant psychosocial therapies serve as a powerful ingredient in improving the functional level of these patients, independent of the role of neuroleptics (McGlashan 1986). There is good reason to believe, both by analogy with the above and based on clinical experience, that similar considerations would apply with children and adolescents as well.

CONDUCT DISORDERS

As outlined in chapters 25 and 26, conduct disorders are complex conditions, with apparently multiple etiological contributants and without any uniformly effective treatments. Research in this area has been hampered by diagnostic heterogeneity that has varied among different study samples. Difficulty in controlling multiple variables has similarly hampered attempts to evaluate effects of treatment.

The psychopharmacological standpoint views the behavioral spectrum constituting conduct disorders as the final common pathway of a variety of other disorders, each of which, in turn, may require a somewhat different psychopharmacological strategy. The fact that there has been no single documented effective strategy for conduct disorder, together with the fact that conduct disorder has been linked clinically with a number of other psychiatric disorders, lends support to this hypothesis. An operational imperative deriving from this hypothesis is the requirement that every youngster presenting with conduct disorder should be carefully assessed for associated psychiatric disorder. An associated corollary, as observed with other disorders, is that pharmacological treatment should be only a part of the overall strategy. No psychosocial treatment approach has been demonstrated to be uniformly effective with the broad spectrum of conduct disorders. Yet individually tailored psychosocial treatment planning, with emphasis on strengthening parental and other social milieu, enlightened limit-setting capacities, as well as clarifying special educational needs, appears warranted.

Attention deficit hyperactivity disorders are a common concurrent condition with conduct disorders and this merits prime consideration, since, as noted above, relatively effective medications exist for ADHD. Yet few studies have directly assessed the use of stimulants in conduct disorders. Eisenberg et al. (1963) found that dextroamphetamine improved the behavior of aggressive institutionalized delinquents. A subsequent study (Conners et al. 1971) comparing methylphenidate (Ritalin) and diphenylhydantoin (Dilantin) in the treatment of young delinquent boys found no effect for either medication, though the active treatment time was quite short. Werry et al. (1975) compared methylphenidate and haloperidol in a combined ADHD-conduct-disordered group of children and found that either group was superior to placebo. Yet the data here did not clarify whether conduct-disordered behavior improves with such treatment only if it is associated with hyperactivity, or even when it is not. It certainly appears reasonable to consider a trial of stimulant medication when encountering a youngster who has symptoms of both conduct disorder and ADHD.

Gittelman and Abikoff are currently conducting a double-blind study of the efficacy of methylphenidate in conduct-disordered youngsters with and without ADDH. When completed, this investigation should shed light on the behavioral specificity of methylphenidate. Study outcome measures include teacher and parent ratings, as well as blind observations of children's classroom comportment and interpersonal interactions in less structured, physical education settings. (Abikoff, personal communication 1986).

As noted in Chapter 26, substantial numbers of delinquent children also appear to have affective disorders, and the prominence of conduct disorder symptoms may easily lead one to overlook depression (Carlson and Cantwell 1980). In this regard,

Puig-Antich (1982a) reported substantial improvement in the conduct problems of children who had both conduct disorder and preexisting major depressive disorder. Further, prospective controlled studies are needed in this area.

Neuroleptics are commonly used in the treatment of aggressive children (O'Donnell 1985). However, while neuroleptics have an appropriate place in reducing aggressive behavior in psychotically disturbed children, the recent growing awareness of potential long-term side-effects of neuroleptics calls this practice into question in the case of conduct disorder uncomplicated by psychosis. The presence of alternate pharmacological agents with comparable effectiveness and fewer side-effects dictates that the agents with less prospect for long-range toxicity be tried first.

Campbell et al. (1984) have reported the outcome of the only double-blind, placebo-controlled study of the effects of lithium in sixty-one clearly diagnosed undersocialized aggressive conduct disorder children. The results indicated that both haloperidol and lithium were clearly superior to placebo in reducing aggressive behavior. The children receiving haloperidol, however, had significantly greater interference with daily functioning from side-effects than those receiving lithium or placebo. It is of note that the patients in this study did not have documented histories of affective disorder. It is certainly cogent to maintain that a youngster presenting with conduct disorder who has a clear personal or family history of affective disorder merits a clinical treatment trial with lithium. If the results of the Campbell study noted above are replicated, patients with conduct disorder even without personal or family history of bipolar affective disorder would merit treatment with lithium prior to consideration of neuroleptics.

The issue of aggressive behavior in patients with epilepsy has been addressed in Chapter 21. As noted, there has been some controversy in this area, owing in part to occasional difficulty in establishing a clear-cut diagnosis of epilepsy and an etiological link between the epilepsy and a propensity for aggressive behavior. In a patient with a documented seizure disorder and coexisting conduct disorder, pharmacological considerations would center initially on optimizing the existing anticonvulsant dosage, as reflected by serum anticonvulsant levels, drawn at an appropriate interval (generally ten to twelve hours) after the last (usually bedtime) oral dose. In the absence of clinical improvement once this has been achieved, consideration of a change of anticonvulsant would be warranted. By virtue of carbamazepine's demonstrated mood-stabilizing properties (Post and Uhde 1983), its lesser propensity to engender cognitive impairment, irritability, somnolence, and other serious side-effects than other anticonvulsants, it will frequently merit use in this context. The possibility that carbamazepine by itself may actually decrease the frequency and severity of rage outbursts and aggressiveness in patients with or without documented seizure disorders remains to be further investigated. The clinician must be alert to the sometimes subtle indications of a complex partial seizure disorder, which may be easily overlooked if one focuses too narrowly on presenting aggressive symptoms of a seemingly straightforward conduct disorder. A thorough history and targeted review of symptoms, supplemented, if indicated, by a routine or sleep-deprived EEG, will help to minimize diagnostic oversight in this regard.

Many patients with uncontrolled aggressive outbursts and associated seizure disorder or other forms of organic brain impairment have not responded adequately to sustained clinical trials on the currently established spectrum of psychotropic medications reviewed above. Serendipitous events led to observations of apparent antiaggressive properties of propranolol (Inderal), a B-adrenergic blocking agent widely used as an antihypertensive, when given to uncontrollably aggressive adult patients who had sustained acute brain damage (Elliot 1977). An open clinical trial of propranolol for treatment of rage and aggressive behavior in children and adolescents with organic brain dysfunction yielded a predominance of positive results (Williams et al. 1982). All of these patients had previously failed to respond to clinical trials on anticonvulsants, stimulants and/or neuroleptics. The majority of these patients were diagnosed as having conduct disorder, unsocialized aggressive type, with a minority carrying the DSM-III diagnosis of intermittent explosive disorder. Further investigation is needed to substantiate this finding with double-blind controlled studies. It would also be important to delineate further the particular type of patient by the nature of organic brain injury who is most likely to respond to this as opposed to other psychopharmacological treatments.

CONCLUSION

This brief overview emphasizes the importance of basing any psychopharmacological treatment intervention on a thorough preexisting diagnostic assessment of the patient. Such an assessment enhances the probability that the intervention will be effective, as it allows the clinician to draw upon the growing body of systematic clinical research trials that can inform the clinician's treatment decisions. There is a need to integrate psychopharmacological treatment with other psychosocial modalities and with cognizance of the important attitude-shaping role of the therapist-patient relationship. It is important to determine the benefit-risk ratio of given medications and to monitor these parameters in ongoing treatment. Finally, some sophistication in pharmacokinetics is clearly needed to enable appropriate dose titration of clinically indicated medications so that patients have the benefit of an adequate trial of treatment. Psychopharmacological knowledgeability is essential as part of the armamentarium of the well-trained child and adolescent psychiatrist.

REFERENCES

Achenbach, T. M. (1978). The child behavior profile. Boys aged 6–11. *J. Consult. Clin. Psychol.* 46:478–88.

Anderson, L., et al. (1984). Haloperidol in infantile autism: Effects on learning and behavioral symptoms. *Amer. J. Psychiat.* 141:1195–202.

August, G., et al. (1984). Fenfluramine treatment in infantile autism: Neurochemical, electrophysiological, and behavioral effects. *J. Nerv. Ment. Disorders* 172:604–12.

Barkley, R. A. (1981). *Hyperactive Children: A Handbook for Diagnosis and Treatment.* New York: Guilford Press.

Bender, L. (1942). Schizophrenia in childhood. *Nerv. Child* 1:138–40.

Berney, T., et al. (1981). School phobia: A therapeutic trial with clomipramine and short-term outcome. *Brit. J. Psychiat.* 138:110–18.

Bradley, C. (1937). The behavior of children receiving benzedrine. *Amer. J. Psychiat.* 94:577–85.

Campbell, M., et al. (1983). Neuroleptic-induced dyskinesias in children. *Clin. Neuropharmacol.* 6:207–22.

———, et al. (1984). Behavioral efficacy of haloperidol and lithium carbonate: A comparison in hospitalized aggressive children with conduct disorder. *Arch. Gen. Psychiat.* 120:650–56.

———. (1985). Schizophrenic disorders and pervasive developmental disorders/infantile autism. In J. M. Wiener (Ed.). *Diagnosis and Psychopharmacology of Childhood and Adolescent Disorders.* New York: Wiley.

Campbell, S. B. (1985). Hyperactivity in preschoolers: Correlates and prognostic implications. *Clin. Psychol. Rev.* 5:405–28.

Carlson, G., and Cantwell, D. (1980). Unmasking masked depression in children and adolescents. *Amer. J. Psychiat.* 137:445–49.

Chambers, W., et al. (1985). Assessment of children and adolescent psychopathology by semi-structured interview: Test, re-test reliability K-SADS-P. *Arch. Gen. Psychiat.* 42:696–702.

Cohen, N. J., et al. (1971). The effect of methylphenidate on attentive behavior and autonomic activity in hyperactive children. *Psychopharmacologia* 22:282–94.

Conners, C. K. (1971). The effect of stimulant drugs on human figure drawings in children with minimal brain dysfunction. *Psychopharmacologia* 19:329–33.

———. (1975). Controlled trial of methylphenidate in preschool children with minimal brain dysfunction. In R. Gittelman-Klein (Ed.). *Recent Advances in Child Psychopharmacology.* New York: Human Sciences Press.

Conners, C. K., and Werry, J. S. (1979). Pharmacotherapy. In H. C. Quay and J. S. Werry (Eds.). *Psychopathological Disorders of Children.* 2d ed. New York: Wiley, pp. 336–86.

———, et al. (1971). Treatment of young delinquent boys with diphenylhydantoin sodium and methylphenidate. *Arch. Gen. Psychiat.* 24:156–60.

Cox, W. H., Jr. (1982). An indication for youth of imipramine in attention deficit disorder. *Amer. J. Psychiat.* 139:1059.

Cunningham, C. E., and Barkley, R. A. (1978). The interactions of hyperactive and normal children with their mothers in free play and structured task. *Child Devel.* 50:217–24.

Dykman, R. A., et al. (1976). Two blinded studies of the effects of stimulant drugs on children: Pemoline, methylphenidate, and placebo. In R. P. Anderson and C. G. Haliamb (Eds.). *Learning Disability/Minimal Brain Dysfunction Syndrome.* Springfield, Ill.: Charles C. Thomas.

Eisenberg, L., et al. (1963). A psychopharmacological experiment in a training school for delinquent boys. *Amer. J. Orthopsychiat.* 33:431–47.

Elliot, F. (1977). Propranolol for control of belligerant behavior following acute brain damage. *Annals Neurol.* 1:489–91.

Flament, M. F., et al. (1985). Clomipramine treatment of childhood obsessive compulsive disorder: A double-blind controlled study. *Arch. Gen. Psychiat.* 42:977–83.

Gardner, R. (1986). *The Psychotherapeutic Techniques of R. A. Gardner.* M.D. Cresshill, N.J.: Creative Therapeutics, pp. 165–95.

Gittelman, R. (1983). Hyperkinetic syndrome: Treatment issues and principles. In M. Rutter (Ed.). *Developmental Neuropsychiatry.* New York: Guilford Press.

Gittelman, R., and Kanner, A. (1986). Psychopharmacotherapy. In H. Quay and J. Werry (Eds.). *Psychopathological Disorders of Childhood.* 3d ed. New York: Wiley, pp. 455–95.

———, et al. (1980). A controlled trial of behavior modification and methylphenidate in hyperactive children. In C. K. Whalen and B. Henker (Eds.). *Hyperactive Children: The Social Ecology of Identification and Treatment.* New York: Academic Press, pp. 221–43.

———, et al. (1985). Hyperactive boys almost grown-up; I: Psychiatric status. *Arch. Gen. Psychiat.* 42:937–47.

Gittelman-Klein, R., and Klein, D. F. (1971). Controlled imipramine treatment of school phobia. *Arch. Gen. Psychiat.* 25:204–7.

———, and ———. (1975). Are behavioral and psychometric changes related in methylphenidate treated, hyperactive children? *Intl. J. Ment. Health* 4:182–98.

———, and ———. (1980). Treatment methods in school refusal: Drug therapy. In L. Hersov (Ed.). *School Refusal.* New York: Wiley.

———, et al. (1976). Comparative effects of methylphenidate and thioridazine in hyperactive children. *Arch. Gen. Psychiat.* 33:1217–31.

Goyette, C. H., et al. (1978). Normative data on revised Conners Parent and Teacher Rating Scales. *J. Abnor. Child Psychol.* 6:221–36.

Green, W., et al. (1984). A comparison of schizophrenic and autistic children. *J. Amer. Acad. Child Psychiat.* 23:299–309.

Greenberg, L. M., and Yellin, A. M. (1975). Blood pressure and pulse changes of hyperactive children treated with imipramine and methylphenidate. *Amer. J. Psychiat.* 132:1325–26.

Greenhill, L., et al. (1984). Prolactin, growth hormone, and growth responses in boys with attention deficit disorder. *J. Amer. Acad. Child Psychiat.* 23:58–67.

Gualteri, C. T. (1977). Imipramine and children: A review and some speculation about the mechanism of drug action. *Dis. Nerv. System* 38:368–74.

Henker, B., et al. (1981). Licit and illicit drug use patterns in stimulant treated children and their peers. In K. D. Gadon and J. Loney (Eds.). *Psychosocial Aspects of Drug Treatment for Hyperactivity.* Boulder, Colo: Westview Press, pp. 443–62.

Hollingsworth, C. E., et al. (1980). Long-term outcome of obsessive-compulsive disorder in childhood. *J. Amer. Acad. Child Psychiat.* 19:134–44.

Humphries, T., Kinsbourne, M., and Swanson, J. (1978). Stimulant effects on cooperation and social interaction between hyperactive children and their mothers. *J. Child Psychol. Psychiat.* 19:13–22.

Kendall, P. C., and Wilcox, L. E. (1979). Self-control in children: Development of a rating scale. *J. Consult. Clin. Psychol.* 47:1020–29.

Klein, D. F. (1964). Delineation of two drug-responsive anxiety syndromes. *Psychopharmacologia* 5:397–408.

———, et al. (1980). Diagnosis and drug treatment of childhood disorders. In *Diagnosis and Drug Treatment of Psychiatric Disorders: Adults and Children.* 2d ed. Baltimore: Williams and Wilkins.

Koplewicz, H., and Gittelman, R. (1983). Efficacy of methylphenidate in preschoolers with ADDH. Presented at the American Academy of Child Psychiatry, San Francisco, Oct.

Kramer, E., and Feigurne, R. (1983). Clinical effects of amitryptiline in adolescent depression. *J. Amer. Acad. Child Psychiat.* 20:636–44.

Liebowitz, M., et al. (1986). Phenelzine and social phobia. *J. Clin. Psychopharmacol.* 6:93–98.

Lucas, A. R., Locket, H. J., and Grimm, F. (1965). Amitryptiline in childhood depression. *Dis. Nerv. System* 26:105–10.

McGlashan, T. (1986). Schizophrenia: Psychosocial treatments and the role of psychosocial factors in its etiology and pathogenesis. In A. J. Frances and R. E. Hales (Eds.). *Psychiatry Update: American Psychiatric Association: Annual Review,* Vol. 5. Washington, D.C.: American Psychiatric Press, pp. 96–111.

Mattes, J., and Gittelman, R. (1983). Growth of hyperactive children on a maintenance regimen of methylphenidate. *Arch. Gen. Psychiat.* 40:317–21.

O'Donnell, D. (1985). Conduct disorders. In J. Wiener (Ed.). *Diagnosis and Psychopharmacology of Childhood and Adolescent Disorders.* New York: Wiley, pp. 249–88.

Pool, D., et al. (1976). A controlled evaluation of loxitane in seventy-five adolescent schizophrenic patients. *Current Therapeut. Res.* 19:99–104.

Post, R., and Uhde, T. (1983). Treatment of mood disorders with antiepileptic medications. Clinical and theoretical implications. *Epilepsia* 24 (Suppl. 2):97–108.

Puig-Antich, J. (1982a). Major depression and conduct disorder in prepuberty. *J. Amer. Acad. Child Psychiat.* 21:118–28.

———. (1982b). The use of RD criteria for major depressive disorder for children and adolescents (editorial). *J. Amer. Acad. Child Psychiat.* 21:291–93.

———, et al. (1978). Prepubertal major depressive disorder: A pilot study. *J. Amer. Acad. Child Psychiat.* 17:659–707.

———, Ryan, N., and Rabinovich, H. (1985). Affective disorders in childhood and adolescence. In J. M. Wiener (Ed.). *Diagnosis and Psychopharmacology of Childhood and Adolescent Disorders.* New York: Wiley, pp. 151–77.

Rabiner, C. J., and Klein, D. F. (1969). Imipramine treatment of school phobia. *Compr. Psychiatry* 10:387–90.

Ritvo, E., et al. (1984). Study of fenfluramine in outpatients with the syndrome of autism. *J. Pediat.* 105:823–28.

Routh, D. K., Schroeder, C. S., and O'Tuama, L. (1974). Development of activity level in children. *Devel. Psychol.* 10:163–68.

Safer, D., et al. (1972). Depression of growth in hyperactive children on stimulant drugs. *New Eng. J. Med.* 287:217–20.

Schleifer, M., et al. (1975). Hyperactivity in preschoolers and the effect of methylphenidate. *Amer. J. Orthopsychiat.* 45:38–50.

Schulz, S., et al. (1984). Beyond the therapeutic window: A case presentation. *J. Clin. Psychiatry* 45:223–25.

Sheehan, D. V., et al. (1984). Some biochemical correlates of panic attack with agoraphobia and their response to a new treatment. *J. Clin. Psychopharmacol.* 4:66–75.

Siamek, J., et al. (1986). Anticholinergic agents for prophylaxis of neuroleptic-induced dystonic reactions: A prospective study. *J. Clin. Psychiat.* 47:305–9.

Sprague, R., and Sleator, E. (1977). Methylphenidate in hyperactive children: Differences in dose effects on learning and social behavior. *Science* 198:1274–76.

Thoren, P., et al. (1980). Clomipramine treatment of obsessive compulsive disorder. I. A controlled clinical trial. *Arch. Gen. Psychiat.* 37:1281–85.

Trimble, M. (1985). The psychoses of epilepsy and their treatment. In M. Trimble (Ed.). *The Psychopharmacology of Epilepsy.* Chinchester, England: Wiley, pp. 83–94.

Varley, C. (1983). Effects of methylphenidate in adolescents with attention deficit disorder. *J. Amer. Acad. Child Psychiat.* 22:351–54.

Wender, P., and Klein, D. (1981). *Mind, Mood and Medicine.* New York: Farrar, Strauss, and Giroux.

Werry, J. S., and Aman, M. (1975). Methylphenidate and haloperidol in children: Effects on attention, memory and activity. *Arch. Gen. Psychiat.* 32:790–95.

———, Aman, M., and Lampen, E. (1975). Haloperidol and methylphenidate in hyperactive children. *Acta Paedopsychiat.* 42:26–40.

Wiener, J. (Ed.) (1985). *Diagnosis and Psychopharmacology of Childhood and Adolescent Disorders.* New York: Wiley.

Williams, D., et al. (1982). The effect of propranolol on uncontrolled rage outbursts in children and adolescents with organic brain dysfunction. *J. Amer. Acad. Child Psychiat.* 21:129–35.

Youngerman, J., and Canino, I. (1978). Lithium carbonate use in children and adolescents: A survey of the literature. *Arch. Gen. Psychiat.* 35:216–24.

53

BEHAVIOR THERAPY

Richard S. Feldman

Behavior therapy with children, as a systematically gathered and broadly applied body of knowledge, is barely twenty years old. *Child Behavior Therapy*, the journal devoted exclusively to the area, was first published in 1979. This modern enterprise is not without its precursors, of course, some of them famous. Jones (1924) and Watson and Rayner (1920) applied principles of respondent conditioning to children's fears, the former to alleviate a specific fear in a child named Peter and the latter to enstate one in the unfortunate Albert, who thereby became, next to Freud's Hans (1909), the best-known child in the clinical literature. Witmer (1907), generally acknowledged as the founder of clinical psychology, emphasized observed behavior rather than inferred internal phenomena in his approach to diagnosis and treatment, thus anticipating the spirit of much of current behavior therapy. However, his work in this regard is rarely cited in the behavior therapy literature (for exceptions, see texts by Ross 1981, and Graziano and Mooney 1984). The powerful role of Freudian theory in both psychological treatment and views of child development effectively overshadowed the reports that appeared from time to time from the 1920s through the 1950s of the application of laboratory-derived principles, particularly those relating to conditioning, to the treatment of a variety of problems (e.g., enuresis; Mowrer and Mowrer 1938). However, the growing influence of Skinner's work and the technology it provided for functional analysis and alteration of behavior, the application of operant conditioning to the behavior of autistic and schizophrenic children by Ferster and DeMyer (1961) and Lovaas (e.g., Lovaas et al. 1965), and the work of Bandura on social learning and the role of observation and modeling (Bandura and Walters 1963; Bandura 1977), all combined by the late 1960s to produce an enormous expansion in the range of clinical problems to which behavioral methods were applied. This development was also fueled in part by reports of a lack of evidence for the effectiveness of the traditional psychotherapeutic approaches with children (Levitt 1957); the controversy thereby sparked is still very much with us, but at the very least it can be said to have stimulated the search for alternative treatment approaches.

WHAT IS BEHAVIOR THERAPY?

If it was ever possible to formulate a definition of behavior therapy acceptable to all its adherents, that time is certainly not now. "The boundaries of behavioral therapy," Phillips and Ray (1980, p. 7) noted in their review, "are becoming increasingly permeable." Some features remain clear enough: the key role accorded to principles derived from learning theories, operational definitions of procedures, an emphasis on current behavior and circumstances, and a statement of treatment goals in terms that allow objective ongoing monitoring of the course of treatment and evaluation of the degree of treatment effectiveness. Beyond these considerations, child behavior therapy has become highly diverse in its theory and practice, so much so that even the word "behavior," which might have been thought unassailable, not to say indispensable, has been challenged as "a somewhat unfortunate relic of earlier days," appropriate "only if the definition of that term is stretched to cover cognitive processes" (Ross 1981, p. 7).

Such a stretch as Ross referred to has been widely but not universally welcomed. The earlier days he spoke of, characterized by an insistence on dealing with overt behavior only, without postulating psychodynamic, cognitive, or any other inferred mediating processes, still seem preferable to some. For example, in arguing for the more radical behaviorist position of accounting for behavior change by specifying the relationships between events that are at least in principle directly observable, Rachlin called such mediating concepts "crypto-mythological models of events inside the head" (Rachlin 1977, p. 373), a phrase that neatly conveys the flavor of this sometimes very heated debate. Extended consideration of the matter would be inappropriate here; the point is that the role of cognition in social learning theory, and especially the emergence of cognitive behavior therapy (about which more below), have made it increasingly difficult to define the theoretical basis of behavior therapy as a whole. Of course, it is still quite possible to describe child behavior therapy in terms of the procedures therapists employ, even as the arguments continue over the concepts that must be invoked to account for the effects of those procedures. That will be the main business of the remainder of the present chapter.

BEHAVIORAL ASSESSMENT

Closely tied to the development of behavioral interventions has been the enormous expansion of assessment techniques and instruments (e.g., Mash and Terdal 1981a, b). Behavioral assessment necessarily overlaps with clinical assessment more generally; after all, the territory is much the same even if the theoretical framework or the focus is different. There are, however, some distinctive features of both substance and emphasis.

First, it should be noted that behaviors (deviant or otherwise) seen during the assessment process are viewed as samples of the child's repertoire, not as signs of underlying intrapsychic processes or personality characteristics. One consequence of this is the heavy emphasis on careful description of the child's behavior as a prerequisite for identifying problems and strengths and designing interventions, and the lack of reliance on personality tests and many other familiar psychometric instruments. The principal aim of behavioral assessment is to give objective definition to the behaviors of interest, to specify the environmental characteristics (both immediate events and broader ecological factors) related to the occurrence or severity of those behaviors and perhaps serving to maintain them, and to determine the most relevant strategies for changing the behaviors—in other words, to arrive at a "behavioral diagnosis" (Kanfer and Saslow 1969) rather than a diagnosis in the more usual clinical sense.

Where individual behaviors are grouped into larger response classes, this is done not according to psychiatric diagnostic categories, but rather as much as possible in terms of their functional equivalence—for example, at least as a first approximation, all the behaviors a child engages in on weekday mornings that have as their consequence staying home from school. Psychiatric diagnostic categories are often constellations of behaviors that are functionally very different. A child diagnosed hyperactive might display high rates of motor activity, excessive time off task, frequent violations of classroom rules, disturbances of the peace through any number of disruptive behaviors, failure to do homework, and poor social skills with peers. The extent to which these things tend to co-occur in the same children is a purely descriptive issue, but from the standpoint of behavioral assessment with a view toward possible behavioral intervention, each component would initially have to be separately defined and measured and related to its own contextual antecedents and consequences. The extent to which the contexts (and not simply the topographies) of the child's various behaviors were found to overlap would play a significant role in grouping those behaviors and in determining the intervention strategies. Even in a case like hyperactivity, where the existence of a significant biological substrate is widely accepted (if poorly understood), the behaviors' situational variability and impact on the child's social interactions are of important clinical relevance and merit careful behavioral assessment, as Barkley (1985), for one, has discussed.

Furthermore, while such a summary characterization as "fails to do homework" or "poor social skills" has an apparent coherence, each referring as it does to a rather distinct behavioral domain, assessment will certainly have to be more refined than this if the most appropriate behavioral intervention is to be designed. From the teacher's point of view, a homework assignment is either handed in or it is not, but the therapist had better know also whether, for example, the child fails to write down what the assignment is, whether the materials somehow get lost between home and school, whether an inadequately supervised sibling in a chaotic household regularly vandalizes the child's belongings (an instance from the writer's recent experience), or whether the child requires homework assistance not currently available. These circumstances suggest a range of possible interventions, from a simple monitoring and reward system to better organization of household routines and child-care arrangements to parental or professional tutoring; in the instance just cited, the intervention is focusing in part on the *sibling's* behavior and related parent training. An analogous assessment in any of the other problem areas might turn up the need for similar or quite different interventions for other behavior, but, as in the case of homework, the therapeutic decisions depend on knowledge of specific behaviors and their contexts, and on recognition that the assessment must address at least the major components of a whole chain of contingencies leading to the end point or target behavior.

One additional general comment on behavioral assessment: If we take seriously the notion that a child's behavior is to a significant degree a function of its social context, then the behavior we need to describe in our analysis is not only the child's but also the parent's, the teacher's, or that of anyone whose interactions with the child are of relevance to the problem at hand. Patterson's (1982) detailed observations of the behavior of the parents of aggressive children—for example, their irritability, empty threats, and ineffective punishment procedures—have taught us a great deal about where to look for some of the ways the child's behavior is maintained, although proper clinical practice will still require an individualized assessment. White's (1975) data on the kinds of behavior teachers are most likely to reinforce at various grade levels tell us in a general way what we might be up against when we try to change classroom contingencies or when we hope that "natural" classroom contingencies will take over where the therapist's efforts leave off. These issues become critical in behavior therapy with children because of the central role often given to parents or other individuals as mediators (Tharp and Wetzel 1969) or agents of behavior change in the child. Behavior therapists can hardly be credited with being the first to discover that the adults and peers in the child's world matter when it comes to the child's current behavior and clinical course. However, by stating the therapist's task squarely in many cases to be one of changing the behavior of these other persons as a primary means of changing the behavior of the child, we emphasize the importance of assessing an area sometimes described in much too general or circumscribed a manner. As many therapists learn the hard way, correct identification of at least some of the determinants of parents' or others' behavior is often as crucial to a successful therapeutic outcome as thorough assessment of the child's behavior itself; indeed, it is often a vital aspect of that assessment. We should note that the journal mentioned at the beginning of this chapter soon changed its name to *Child and Family Behavior Therapy*.

Techniques of Behavioral Assessment

The techniques of behavioral assessment emphasize those that generate data directly relevant to treatment design and implementation. Priority is given to procedures, such as direct observation or some relatively objective reporting or sampling, that permit repeated measurement at frequent intervals, so that assessment continues throughout the entire therapeutic course. This is again in contrast to many psychometric instruments included in traditional clinical assessment batteries, which are part of initial (and occasionally follow-up) evaluation but which are not designed for repeated administration.

Behavioral assessment characteristically employs a great variety of interviews, inventories, rating scales, standardized tests, clinic or laboratory observations, and role-playing or other analogue situations, as well as the kinds of structured observations in the child's natural habitats, so to speak, which have been so heavily emphasized in the behavioral literature that their use, as Mash and Terdal (1981a) remarked, has sometimes been taken to be the virtual equivalent of behavioral assessment. All of these assessment modalities have both assets and liabilities that have been discussed at length (e.g., Mash and Terdal 1981a) and in brief (e.g., Feldman 1985) in the context of child behavior therapy. Role-playing provides a convenient way to sample complex social behavior, but does not necessarily provide a valid measure of the child's actual social functioning (Van Hasselt et al. 1981). Rating scales and behavior checklists are economical and sensitive to clinical change, but do not provide the contextual information needed to design behavioral interventions. Direct observation allows for sampling of current behavior and contingencies but requires trained observers, entails considerable time and expense, and is of little value for low-frequency or secretive behaviors; the use of parents or other persons in the child's environment to provide observational data is a frequent and sometimes essential adjunct to treatment, but the necessary degree of cooperation is not always easily achieved. Sociometric data, which are receiving increased attention in the developmental and clinical literature, are of great value because of the significance of peer status, but while they can be collected quite easily in the child's classroom, as Stewart (1985) noted in the context of the assessment of behavior problems in school, it is hard to imagine their use any time soon except in very special circumstances. Similar comments could be made regarding other instruments and procedures.

In practice, behavioral assessment is defined not so much by the particular classes of techniques it employs but rather by its strong methodological concern with issues of reliability and validity, its preference for low levels of inference, its emphasis on observable behavior, and its view of assessment as an ongoing activity and an essential guide to the course of treatment. As Mash and Terdal's (1981a) and Achenbach's (1985) remarks suggest, behavioral assessment may have broadened to a degree that the early behavior modifiers would scarcely countenance (Achenbach called recent developments "counterrevolutionary"), but the earlier ideal served as an effective and much needed stimulus for more objective assessment than had previously been practiced.

BEHAVIORAL INTERVENTIONS

Texts and overviews of child behavior therapy are sometimes organized according to the various clinical categories being treated: conduct problems, hyperactivity, fear, and so on. This has the virtue of familiarity to clinicians and it implicitly acknowledges that different behaviors present different strategic and tactical challenges; however, it suggests—incorrectly from the behavioral perspective—that the diagnosis determines the choice of behavioral techniques to be employed. Organization of the area according to the site of intervention (or, rather, the site of the behavior's characteristic occurrence)—primarily home and school—properly emphasizes the critical role of the physical and social environment in shaping the nature of the behavior, in defining its appropriateness or inappropriateness, and in determining to a significant degree the resources available to deal with it. More in keeping with a behavioral approach is the categorization of target areas outlined, for example, by Kanfer and Grimm (1977): behavior deficiencies, behavior excesses, inappropriate external stimulus control, inappropriate self-generated stimulus control, and problematic reinforcement contingencies. This comes closer to suggesting how intervention techniques are to be matched to the functional characteristics of the behaviors to be changed.

The interventions themselves have been applied in an ingenious array of variations as wide as the range of behaviors addressed. However, it is possible to organize the bulk of them according to relatively few principles (or sets of principles). For purposes of the presentation here, these will be: (1) techniques based on respondent (or classical or Pavlovian) conditioning; (2) techniques based on operant (or instrumental or Skinnerian) conditioning; (3) techniques based on social learning theory; and (4) techniques based on cognitive formulations.

Respondent Conditioning

Near the start of this chapter, reference was made to the famous (or notorious) report by Watson and Rayner (1920) in which they claimed a fear was experimentally induced in a young child. The paradigm they employed is a classic example of respondent conditioning. Albert initially displayed signs of fear (unconditioned response) to a loud noise (unconditioned stimulus) but not to a white rat. After several pairings of the noise and the rat, the latter (now a conditioned stimulus) came to elicit signs of fear (now a conditioned response). Furthermore, furry objects sharing certain salient characteristics with the rat also became capable of eliciting fearful behavior: that is, the response generalized so that it was elicited by stimuli not part of the original training.

The course, effectiveness, and durability of respondent conditioning depend on many factors—for example, the intensity of the unconditioned stimulus, how often it has been paired with the conditioned stimulus in the initial conditioning, and then how often the conditioned stimulus is presented alone—which are the subject of a large and technical literature. It has not been established that clinically significant fears typically come about in this way. An attempt to replicate the Watson and Rayner experiment failed (English 1929). Nevertheless, the basic paradigm figures prominently in accounts of how fears and other emotions may be acquired, maintained, and altered in relation to stimuli that did not initially evoke them. For example, it may explain some of the untoward emotional consequences that can arise through the use of operant punishment procedures.

Albert's example, while it clearly illustrates the paradigm, can hardly be said to illustrate therapy. The study by Jones (1924) is another story and an early example of the kind of extension of Pavlovian principles later given wide currency by Wolpe (1958). Jones's child was afraid of rabbits. Jones paired the child's eating (eliciting in this case presumably positive or pleasurable unconditioned responses) with the presence of a rabbit gradually moved closer to the child but always kept at sufficient distance so that if it did not exactly function as a neutral stimulus, it elicited a negative response much weaker in absolute strength than the positive responses elicited by food and eating. The fearful response to the rabbit was thereby eliminated. It should be noted that, in principle, Jones's paradigm could have been used to condition the fear elicited by the rabbit to the food, the eating utensils, the room, or to Jones herself. The child's behavior in such circumstances must be carefully observed, and where this procedure is employed to treat children's fears (see, e.g., Morris and Kratochwill 1983), food, favorite toys, trusted adults, or anything likely to elicit behavior strongly incompatible with the responses to be neutralized or eliminated are used to assure that conditioning occurs in the desired direction.

The terms *systematic desensitization* and *reciprocal inhibition* (Wolpe 1958) are more familiar from the literature on behavior therapy with adults, but they represent extensions of respondent conditioning in the manner just described above. With adults, muscle relaxation (Jacobson 1938) is perhaps the most frequently used response established to counter fear or anxiety; and imagining, in contrast to actual exposure to, a hierarchy of fear-eliciting stimulus situations is more common than with children, but both of these procedures have in fact been used with children with some success and are reviewed in detail by Morris and Kratochwill (1983).

Operant Conditioning

In 1980, when Phillips and Ray published their review of the child behavior therapy literature, they noted that the volume of work based on the operant model was far greater than that based on any other approach. While the balance may have shifted somewhat, it remains true that an enormous portion of the work reported in the literature derives from operant-conditioning principles.

The essential features here are the objective definition and measurement of the behavior targeted for change, specification of the antecedents (*discriminative stimuli*) associated with the occurrence of that behavior, and specification of the social or other consequences (*reinforcing stimuli*) of the behavior. These three factors—antecedents, behavior, consequences—together constitute the *reinforcement contingency*, the basic unit of functional behavior analysis. *Contingency management* is a general term referring to the therapeutic rearrangement of the relationships among these factors, which constitutes a good deal of operantly based behavioral treatment.

Effective consequences come in two varieties: those that make it *more* probable that the same or a similar behavior will be repeated (*reinforcers*) and those that make it *less* probable (*punishers*). Reinforcers are popularly called rewards and indeed often appear to be so (candy, money, praise, privileges), but this is one case where a bit of jargon serves a real purpose. Reprimands, to cite a frequent example, certainly not rewards in anyone's vocabulary, may function as reinforcers because of the attention they necessarily bring to the child's behavior. Praise, a quintessential social reinforcer, may not function as such for all behaviors we seek to strengthen; for some children, it may hardly function at all, and one therapeutic goal may be to establish its effectiveness by pairing it with an already functional reinforcer such as candy or privileges. For some children praise might even function as a punisher if, for instance, it is given publicly for a behavior ridiculed by the child's peers (as in one variant of the "teacher's pet" phenomenon). The point of these comments is to underscore the empirical nature of the design and implementation of behavioral programs. As with all other aspects of behavioral interventions, reinforcers are defined by their actual effects on behavior, not by the judgment or intent of the person prescribing or delivering them. Numerous inventories of possible reinforcers are available (see, e.g., Cautela et al. 1983), which may be used as self-report instruments or as interview guides, but the therapist must still establish the functional status of any items considered significant for behavioral programming.

The consequences briefly described above are *positive reinforcers*, that is, reinforcers that strengthen behavior when they are presented contingently. There are *negative reinforcers* as well, sometimes terminologically confused with punishers but opposite in effect (all reinforcers, by definition, strengthen behavior). Here, the consequence strengthens the behavior through the termination or removal of something unpleasant or aversive. The reprimands just mentioned may function as positive reinforcers for the child, but their use may be negatively reinforced in the parent because their immediate result is to attenuate or terminate, however briefly, the child's nagging, fighting, or other objectionable behavior. Many ineffective or counterproductive behavior management tactics are maintained in just this way—because the person using them is negatively reinforced in the short run. Of course, negative reinforcement can be used constructively also, as when a child is relieved of the responsibility of performing an odious chore as a consequence of achieving some behavioral goal.

While social reinforcers are often available on a more or less continuous basis, they are not always sufficient to the task, as already mentioned. Other kinds of reinforcers—privileges, toys, special events, and so on—may be more effective but cannot routinely be made immediately available in all situations or with the requisite frequency, due to their intrinsic nature or to inconvenience or expense. Being allowed to stay up later than regular bedtime or out past curfew is a privilege that can be exercised no more than once in twenty-four hours. Being taken to a movie is, for most children, reserved for weekends and holidays. Earning expensive new sports equipment implies some major behavioral accomplishment, shaped over a considerable time by lesser reinforcers for steps along the way. Parents are sometimes in a much better position than teachers to provide effective reinforcers for behavior that is being shaped in school (e.g., Schumaker et al. 1977). In all such circumstances, the use of *tokens* (see Kazdin 1977) is a valuable resource. A token—which can be a star or checkmark on a chart, a "good behavior card" sent home by the child's teacher, a poker chip, or even play money—is essentially an I.O.U. signifying that the agreed-upon reinforcer will be dispensed as soon as the requisite number of tokens has been earned. If parents and children (particularly older children and teenagers) are in conflict over exactly what behavioral requirement must be met and what the pay-off will be, the therapist should help the family negotiate a *behavioral contract* (DeRisi and Butz 1975), which is a written agreement spelling out the parties' mutual obligations.

It is frequently the case that the behavior we would like to reinforce is not yet actually present in the child's repertoire, or is present but in an inadequate or otherwise problematic form, as in the case of a child who typically speaks in nearly a whisper, with all the adverse social consequences that implies, even though there is no physiological impairment related to speech production. In such cases, reinforcement is employed in the process of *shaping*—that is, reinforcers are initially given for the closest behavior the child currently has to the goal behavior, and then gradually the criterion is shifted so that reinforcers are given only for behavior that approximates the goal more closely than the initial behavior, and so on, until the goal is achieved. While the criterion is gradually raised, it must always remain within the range of the child's actual behavior at each stage of the shaping process, or else reinforcement cannot be delivered often enough to be effective. It is important, and sometimes difficult, to get parents or others to accept the notion that the behavior to be reinforced at intermediate stages of shaping will not necessarily be very different from the behavior that constituted the problem in the first place. Nevertheless, successful shaping, like successful teaching of all kinds, requires reinforcement for improvement, even if there is still a long way to go.

Punishers are defined as consequences that weaken the behavior on which they are contingent. While the terms positive punishment and negative punishment are seldom used (to no one's great regret), punishment procedures may be implemented in ways analogous to positive and negative reinforcement. Physical punishment and penalties of various kinds (e.g., imposition of a chore) are examples of positive punishers, while loss of a privilege and a monetary fine subtracted from the child's allowance would be negative punishers. Other common and easily implemented examples of the latter are turning off the television set or terminating a game in progress.

One of the simplest and in some ways the most benign procedures for directly weakening behavior consists of withholding a consequence previously shown or hypothesized to be reinforcing for that behavior—a procedure known as *extinction*. In keeping with the well-known axiom that no procedure is so simple as to be trouble-free or immune to misuse, extinction provides a convenient opportunity to stress again the importance of careful assessment and ongoing monitoring. Parents who remain resolute in the face of tantrums at home may quickly abandon an extinction program at the child's first sign of a tantrum in a public place such as the super-market. In addition, it should be noted that behavior under extinction frequently gets worse before it gets better. Emotional behavior of various kinds often appears when reinforcement is no longer forthcoming for a previously successful behavior (e.g., tantrums get louder and longer before they get weaker and shorter). There-fore, parents attempting to wait for the behavior to subside, in accordance with the therapist's instructions to ignore it until some behavior more deserving of reinforce-ment comes along, may give in at precisely the wrong time and wind up reinforcing a behavior even worse than what they started with. Technically speaking, this is shaping, a process already described. Invaluable as the procedure is for establishing healthier behaviors, it can unwittingly accomplish the opposite result if the therapist fails to anticipate how things might go wrong.

Just as bad as shaping the behavior in the wrong direction is giving in to it only some of the time. When a new behavior is to be established, it is best to reinforce its every occurrence—a process known as *continuous reinforcement;* this applies par-ticularly to behaviors that cannot be expected to occur many times in the course of a day, as in the case of toilet training, being on time for meals, or walking past a toy store without making a scene. However, once the desired behavior is occurring with reasonable strength, it is best to begin reinforcing it only some of the time—a process known as *intermittent reinforcement,* which is the way the real world is most likely to respond when formal treatment ends. Intermittent reinforcement makes behavior more resistant to extinction, since unreinforced occurrences are already part of the contingency. Therefore, when the therapist gets a report that extinction did not work in spite of the fact that the behavior was diligently ignored "most of the time," what this probably means is that the behavior was put on a schedule of intermittent reinforcement, thereby maximizing the chances that it will persist in-definitely.

There are yet more pitfalls here. Parents who pay little attention to their children except for behaviors, like tantrums, that are in fact very hard to ignore, are best taught how to attend to desirable behaviors before (or at least at the same time as) they are taught to ignore undesirable ones. Interventions for children who are al-ready receiving too little attention should not result in their receiving even less. It cannot be assumed that all parents (or teachers, or nurses, or anyone else) will recognize good or improved behavior, will agree that they should acknowledge it rather than simply take it for granted when it occurs, or know how to express ap-proval for it to the child even if they agree in principle to do so.

And finally, while extinction has proved to be an effective component in pro-grams to deal with tantrums and related behavior at least since Williams's (1959) classic report, such behavior may actually be reinforced if the so-called extinction procedure involves removal of the demands (academic demands in the classroom, for instance) that precipitated the behavior in the first place (e.g., Carr and Newsom 1985). This example demonstrates as clearly as any why interventions must take into account the context as well as the topography of the behavior to be changed, and why it is in general irresponsible for a therapist to attempt to implement ready-made programs without carrying out an individualized assessment.

Time out is another familiar, frequently effective, essentially simple, and sometimes misunderstood procedure for decreasing undesirable behavior. For some very brief period of time and immediately contingent on the occurrence of the behavior to be decreased, the child is deprived of the opportunity to receive any reinforcement, typically by being removed to another location that is, ideally, very safe (to eliminate the reinforcement that close supervision inevitably introduces) and utterly boring. The child is then welcomed back when the time-out period has elapsed, or when the problematic behavior (including protests about the consequence) has ended and not recurred for an interval equal to the duration of the original penalty.

It is unfortunately true that, especially in institutional settings but at home as well, the actual functional significance of moving the offending child from the setting in which the offense is committed is sometimes forgotten: The teacher or ward staff or parent is negatively reinforced by the temporary absence of the disruptive child, the activity in progress can continue with the remainder of the participants, and no one cares much about the psychologist's data showing that no decrease in problem behavior is occurring for the case in question. "Time out" is short for "time out from reinforcement," and if the setting *from* which the child is removed has not been providing considerably more reinforcement than is available in the setting *to* which the child is removed, the desired result may well not be forthcoming.

Happily enough, most children (especially young ones, for whom the procedure is in any case most appropriate) prefer not to be banished from their parents' or peers' presence, and most would rather remain in their classrooms than sit on a bench alone in the hall or receive a reprimand in the principal's office. Not always, however. For a child who, whatever the reason, is overwhelmed by the academic or social demands of the classroom, boredom or brief embarrassment is likely to prove less aversive than prolonged distress; behavior accomplishing escape from such circumstances will thereby be reinforced, not punished, irrespective of the justification given for imposing the consequence.

As part of the decision to employ time out, there must be an assessment of whether in fact the child has the skills to survive in the situation from which his or her removal is being contemplated (if not, the behavior needs to be taught), and whether the situation is properly reinforcing to begin with (in its general aspect and in its responsiveness specifically to the child's more appropriate behavior). This admonition applies in fact to all punishment procedures. The goal of any child therapy must be to establish, to the greatest extent possible, developmentally appropriate levels of healthy adaptive behavior where it is shown to be deficient. The use of punishment to reduce or eliminate maladaptive behavior is often a useful component of treatment, and when this goal is met, it may well open up new opportunities for the child. Very likely, it will result in a reduction of complaints about the child. Even so, the therapist's job may be at most half done, for it cannot be assumed without evidence that desirable behavior has replaced undesirable behavior. On both ethical and methodological grounds, that is why—with the exception of such extraordinary behaviors as serious self-injury or physical aggression whose immediate suppression to preserve life or limb may justify the immediate imposition of some harsh punishment procedure—behavioral interventions should begin and, wherever empirical data show it to be possible, end with the use of positive reinforcement.

Social Learning

Social learning has a variety of referents. Patterson, for example, uses the term social learning to refer particularly to the social context of family interactions where aggressive and other seriously deviant behavior is developed and maintained (Patterson et al. 1975). Here, however, it is Bandura's work on modeling and observational learning (Bandura and Walters 1963; Bandura 1977) that is the focus of interest.

Observational learning as a therapeutic modality has been of particular, although certainly not exclusive, interest in the treatment of fears and avoidance behaviors generally. Fearful or avoidant or incompetent behavior has been shown to decrease, and nonfearful or approach or competent behavior to increase, in children who have been systematically exposed to others displaying the behaviors to be acquired. In general, the procedure is more likely to be successful when the model is similar to the observer (another child, for example, rather than the therapist), when the model is high-status or in some way particularly admirable in the child's eyes, when the model is seen to be reinforced for the behavior the observer is to acquire, and perhaps also when the model initially behaves much like the observer (behavioral similarity) and then gradually demonstrates performance of the new behavior (i.e., shows the process of learning to cope or the acquisition of mastery) rather than models the goal behaviors (i.e., shows only mastery) from the outset (see Meichenbaum 1977).

The models themselves may be shown on film or videotape or present live demonstrations, and the observing child may either watch passively or participate with the model in graduated performance of the behavior to be acquired, often with guidance, encouragement, and reinforcement by the therapist. The latter case begins to look like a combination of modeling, desensitization, and shaping, a not uncommon amalgam of ingredients that is frequently difficult to avoid in therapy but that also makes it difficult to determine precisely what is responsible for a successful outcome.

For all the empirical support and intuitive reasonableness of modeling procedures, it is well to be reminded that children who are fearful, or socially incompetent, or whatever, are constantly surrounded by fearless and competent models, but to no avail. Children with mortal fear of dogs can be seen clinging frantically to their mothers even as their friends are playing happily nearby with their poodles and spaniels. Socially withdrawn or incompetent children are surrounded daily by countless examples of their classmates' or siblings' social successes, and can even be observed on occasion to watch them intently, but their own behavior does not change. The point here, as with other behavioral interventions, is that while the therapy may consist in large measure of arranging or rearranging elements already familiar and present in the child's environment, success is achieved through systematic application of the principles involved according to knowledge of how they operate.

It should perhaps be added here that one of the skills involved in observational learning is, of course, imitation. It appears so naturally in the normal course of development that it is taken for granted unless it fails in the most conspicuous way. Nevertheless, if observational learning is being considered for therapeutic use, especially in the case of very young children, it might be wise to ascertain that the child has the attentional and performance skills necessary to acquire behavior of the general level of difficulty of that being modeled.

Cognitive Behavior Therapy

The juxtaposition of "cognitive" and "behavior" to describe a therapeutic approach is well established and at the same time something of an oddity with several possible interpretations. As mentioned earlier, the definition of what constitutes behavior might be broadened to include such things as cognitions. Or, cognitions might be defined as private behaviors, different from other behaviors only in being unobservable; of course, this difference is much more than a minor methodological embarrassment if one wishes to show that it is these behaviors whose change is critical to therapeutic success. Or, cognitions and behaviors might each retain their accustomed identities, the former, still invisible, being taken as mediators between the activities of the therapist and changes in the behavior of the child. As if to emphasize the hybrid nature of the approach, Meichenbaum (1977), whose work is primarily responsible for initiating a substantial and growing body of applied research in this area, employs a hyphen, as in "cognitive-behavior modification."

Baer (1985) has given a particularly clear statement of the fundamental issue here:

> Only two things can be done with unobservable processes. One is to make inferences about them. . . . [The other is to] *teach* some mediating events that are likely to become private shortly after their acquisition. If we teach them, we know what their attributes are at the time; they may become unobservable later, and so we will not know, later, what they are like then—but we still shall know what we taught. The primal experiment here is to describe behavior as a set of interactions between observable stimuli and observable response[s], and then to teach in an observable way some currently observable potential mediators, and watch to see what difference that makes (p. 33).

Baer's "primal experiment" is in fact characteristic. Using the familiar mix of modeling, prompting, reinforcement, or any of the elements of teaching or behavioral training, the cognitive-behavior therapist shapes in the child (1) systematic verbalizations concerning the specific requirements and appropriate plan of attack for some academic, social, or other task; (2) a correspondence between those verbalizations and the child's subsequent performance of each step, so that they will come to function as self-instructions guiding the child's proper performance; and (3) systematic verbalizations that the child uses to evaluate how well the actual performance has matched the task requirements and to assess what corrections or adjustments might be necessary. These verbalizations are ultimately supposed to become covert; they are rehearsed as self-talk and continue to foster improved cognitive strategies for coping, problem solving, and self-control.

Reasonably enough, such an approach has been of particular interest in teaching impulsive children a more structured, reflective, and successful behavioral style. For example, in applying cognitive training to the behavior of hyperactive children, Douglas modeled the following verbalizations for children engaged in a paper-and-pencil task: "I must stop and think before I begin." "What plans could I try?" "How would it work out if I did that?" "What shall I try next?" "Have I got it right so far?" "Gee, I made a mistake there—I'll just erase it." "Now, let's see, have I tried everything I can think of?" "I've done a pretty good job!" (Douglas et al. 1976, p. 394). (Note the self-reinforcement as the last component of the verbalization sequence.) For cognitive training in relation to peer interaction skills, these verbalizations might include statements describing the peer's behavior, anticipating how the peer would respond (overt behavior and perhaps feelings also) if the child being trained were to behave in a given way, and so on. If the usual operant shaping is not sufficient to get the inattentive, impulsive, or hyperactive child to engage in this learning process in the first place, a bit of straightforward behavioral engineering can help; Douglas reports having some of the children literally sit on their hands initially, to delay their plunging unproductively into the task before at least a few elementary strategies were organized and verbalized.

Overall, work in this area remains vigorous, and success is reported often enough to assure continued use and refinement of the techniques, regardless of how the debate over the status of cognitions plays itself out. However, for the two areas—generalization of treatment effects and persistence of therapeutic gains—in which the provision of cognitive strategies was hoped to do significantly better than the earlier behavioral therapies, the results have not always lived up to expectations. In a detailed review substantiating this state of affairs in the case of ADDH children, Abikoff (1985, p. 507) concluded that "To increase generalization [of training effects on behavior] to school and home, the significant others in these settings must be actively involved in cognitive training. Their involvement should include exposure to training rationale and procedures, as well as support, encouragement, and reinforcement of the youngsters' attempts at self-control." We have heard that sort of thing before. It appears that at our present state of knowledge and technical skill, we must still live with a fact long since recognized by behavior therapists: that the children's environments must by some means or other be made to respond differently to their behavior as an integral part of the job of therapy if that job is to be properly and fully accomplished.

CONCLUSION

The widespread acceptance and application of behavioral techniques to therapy with children is more than justified by evidence of effectiveness. Nevertheless, two important sets of issues must not be overlooked.

First, a little knowledge can indeed be a dangerous thing. Stein (1975), for example, commenting on the proliferation of brief workshops and seminars (he might have referred also to training manuals of various kinds and to packaged programs), pointed out the potential ethical problems in directing such material to persons who are otherwise without behavioral training and who may attempt to apply what they have learned without further consultation or supervision. We have already discussed briefly how even the most elementary behavioral interventions can be carried out incorrectly, to the child's detriment. However uncomplicated a program appears on the face of it, it is necessarily carried out in social or ecological contexts that may work their effects without regard for the child's welfare and certainly without regard for the therapist's goals or convenience. The therapist, therefore, if not always in a position to do all of what needs to be done, must at least be aware of the range of possible factors bearing on the choice of techniques and the way they are employed.

Second, we should be aware of the areas that bear directly on the way treatment is conducted but in which many significant basic questions remain unanswered. The problem of achieving generalization of treatment effects has already been mentioned. The selection of target behaviors remains problematic (see the special miniseries on target behavior selection in *Behavioral Assessment*, 1985, 7:1–78.); serious questions of technique and values are involved here, and we do not have very clear decision rules, even if in clinical practice the choices often seem to get made rather easily. Considering how active are the fields of both behavior modification and pharmacotherapy, we still know very little about their interactions; this is not simply a matter of which works better, or even of state-dependent learning, but of the way particular contingencies interact with particular drugs in particular circumstances, of the influence of prior conditioning histories, and so on. This is a set of issues reviewed in detail by Schroeder, Lewis, and Lipton (1983). Developmental issues, such as the appropriateness of a given intervention technique to a child's developmental level, have been inadequately attended to (Phillips and Ray 1980; Harris and Ferrari 1983).

And finally, although this hardly exhausts the possibilities, we return to the training of parents and other agents in the child's environment (for a review, see Bernstein 1984), as much relevant to issues of prevention as to treatment. O'Dell (1985, p. 93) observed, "Parent-training researchers are increasingly investigating the factors associated with unsuccessful cases and, in doing so, discovering the hard lessons of producing behavior change in the diverse types of adults in our society." Of course, the point applies not only to parents. Probably few professionals still believe, if they ever did, that therapy should begin and end at the office door or that the therapist alone can usually accomplish the entire therapeutic task. Behavioral techniques appear to be an essential component of any effort to extend effective treatment into the child's actual world.

REFERENCES

Abikoff, H. (1985). Efficacy of cognitive training interventions in hyperactive children. *Clin. Psychol. Rev.* 5:479–512.

Achenbach, T. M. (1985). Behavior disorders of childhood: Diagnosis and assessment, taxonomy and taxometry. In R. J. McMahon and R. DeV. Peters (Eds.). *Childhood Disorders: Behavioral-Developmental Approaches.* New York: Brunner/Mazel.

Baer, D. M. (1985). Applied behavior analysis as a conceptually conservative view of childhood disorders. In R. J. McMahon and R. DeV. Peters (Eds.). *Childhood Disorders: Behavioral-Developmental Approaches.* New York: Brunner/Mazel.

Bandura, A. (1977). *Social Learning Theory.* Englewood Cliffs, N.J.: Prentice-Hall.

———, and Walters, R. H. (1963). *Social Learning and Personality Development.* New York: Holt, Rinehart, and Winston.

Barkley, R. A. (1985). The social behavior of hyperactive children: Developmental changes, drug effects, and situational variation. In R. J. McMahon and R. DeV. Peters (Eds.). *Childhood Disorders: Behavioral-Developmental Approaches.* New York: Brunner/Mazel.

Bernstein, G. S. (1984). Training behavior change agents. In M. Hersen, R. M. Eisler, and P. M. Miller (Eds.). *Progress in Behavior Modification,* Vol. 17. New York: Academic Press.

Carr, E. G., and Newsom, C. (1985). Demand-related tantrums: Conceptualization and treatment. *Behav. Mod.* 9:403–26.

Cautela, J. R., Cautela, J., and Esonis, S. (1983). *Forms for Behavior Analysis with Children.* Champaign, Ill.: Research Press.

DeRisi, W. J., and Butz, G. (1975). *Writing Behavioral Contracts.* Champaign, Ill.: Research Press.

Douglas, V. I., et al. (1976). Assessment of a cognitive training program for hyperactive children. *J. Abnorm. Child Psychol.* 4:389–410.

English, H. B. (1929). Three cases of "conditioned fear response." *J. Abnorm. Soc. Psychol.* 24:221–25.

Feldman, R. S. (1985). Functional analysis of children's behavior. In D. Shaffer, A. A. Ehrhardt, and L. L. Greenhill (Eds.). *The Clinical Guide to Child Psychiatry.* New York: Free Press.

Ferster, C. B., and DeMeyer, M. K. (1961). The development of performances in autistic children in an automatically controlled environment. *J. Chron. Dis.* 13:312–45.

Freud, S. (1909). The analysis of a phobia in a five-year-old boy. *Standard Edition of the Complete Psychological Works of Sigmund Freud*, Vol. 10. London: Hogarth Press, 1963.

Graziano, A. M., and Mooney, K. C. (1984). *Children and Behavior Therapy*. New York: Aldine.

Harris, S. L., and Ferrari, M. (1983). Developmental factors in child behavior therapy. *Behav. Ther.* 14:54–72.

Jacobson, E. (1938). *Progressive Relaxation*. Chicago: University of Chicago Press.

Jones, M. C. (1924). A laboratory study of fear: The case of Peter. *J. Gen. Psychol.* 31:308–15.

Kanfer, F. H., and Grimm, L. G. (1977). Behavioral analysis: Selecting target behaviors in the interview. *Behav. Mod.* 1:7–28.

———, and Saslow, G. (1969). Behavioral diagnosis. In C. M. Franks (Ed.). *Behavior Therapy: Appraisal and Status*. New York: McGraw-Hill.

Kazdin, A. E. (1977). *The Token Economy: A Review and Evaluation*. New York: Plenum Press.

Levitt, E. E. (1957). The results of psychotherapy with children: An evaluation. *J. Consult. Psychol.* 21:189–96.

Lovaas, O. I., et al. (1965). Experimental studies in childhood schizophrenia: Analysis of self-destructive behavior. *J. Experimental Child Psychol.* 2:67–84.

Mash, E. J., and Terdal, L. G. (1981a). Behavioral assessment of childhood disturbance. In E. J. Mash and L. G. Terdal (Eds.). *Behavioral Assessment of Childhood Disorders*. New York: Guilford Press.

———, and ———. (Eds.). (1981b). *Behavioral Assessment of Childhood Disorders*. New York: Guilford Press.

Meichenbaum, D. (1977). *Cognitive-Behavior Modification: An Integrative Approach*. New York: Plenum Press.

Morris, R. J., and Kratochwill, T. R. (1983). *Treating Children's Fears and Phobias: A Behavioral Approach*. New York: Pergamon Press.

Mowrer, O. H., and Mowrer, W. M. (1938). Enuresis—A method for its study and treatment. *Amer. J. Orthopsychiat.* 8:436–59.

O'Dell, S. L. (1985). Progress in parent training. In M. Hersen, R. M. Eisler, and P. M. Miller (Eds.). *Progress in Behavior Modification*, Vol. 19. New York: Academic Press.

Patterson, G. R. (1982). *A Social Learning Approach to Family Intervention: Coercive Family Processes*, Vol. 3. Eugene, Oreg.: Castalia.

———, et al. (1975). *A Social Learning Approach to Family Intervention: Families with Aggressive Children*, Vol. 1. Eugene, Oreg.: Castalia.

Phillips, J. S., and Ray, R. S. (1980). Behavioral approaches to childhood disorders: Review and critique. *Behav. Mod.* 4:3–34.

Rachlin, H. (1977). A review of M. J. Mahoney's *Cognition and Behavior Modification*. *J. Applied Behav. Anal.* 10:369–74.

Ross, A. O. (1981). *Child Behavior Therapy*. New York: Wiley.

Schroeder, S. R., Lewis, M. H., and Lipton, M. A. (1983). Interactions of pharmacotherapy and behavior therapy among children with learning and behavioral disorders. In K. D. Gadow and I. Bialer (Eds.). *Advances in Learning and Behavioral Disabilities*, Vol. 2. Greenwich, Conn.: JAI Press.

Schumaker, J. B., Hovel, M. F., and Sherman, J. A. (1977). An analysis of daily report cards and parent-managed privileges in the improvement of adolescents' classroom performance. *J. Applied Behav. Anal.* 10:449–69.

Stein, T. J. (1975). Some ethical considerations of short-term workshops in the principles and methods of behavior modification. *J. Applied Behav. Anal.* 8:113–15.

Stewart, M. A. (1985). Disturbance in school. In D. Shaffer, A. A. Ehrhardt, and L. L. Greenhill (Eds.). *The Clinical Guide to Child Psychiatry.* New York: Free Press.

Tharp, R. G., and Wetzel, R. J. (1969). *Behavior Modification in the Natural Environment.* New York: Academic Press.

Van Hasselt, V. B., Hersen, M., and Bellack, A. S. (1981). The validity of role-play tests for assessing social skills in children. *Behav. Ther.* 12:202–16.

Watson, J. B., and Rayner, R. (1920). Conditioned emotional reactions. *J. Experimental Psychol.* 3:1–14.

White, M. A. (1975). Natural rates of teacher approval and disapproval in the classroom. *J. Applied Behav. Anal.* 8:367–72.

Williams, C. (1959). The elimination of tantrum behavior by extinction procedures. *J. Abnorm. Soc. Psychol.* 59:269.

Witmer, L. (1907). Clinical psychology. *The Psychol. Clin.* 1:1–9.

Wolpe, J. (1958). *Psychotherapy by Reciprocal Inhibition.* Stanford: Stanford University Press.

54

HYPNOSIS

Daniel T. Williams

Assessment of the child and adolescent for treatment with hypnosis requires a basic understanding of the nature of hypnosis. The long-standing underuse of hypnosis with youngsters appears to be due to a tradition whereby hypnosis, having been initially oversold as a panacea in its heyday in the nineteenth century, has been ignored or disparaged subsequently by the mainstream of psychiatrists and other therapists in an overcompensatory reaction. Further, some latter-day proponents of hypnosis have continued to be overzealous in its advocacy, thus reinforcing the prevailing uninformed skepticism about its validity and efficacy as a treatment modality. Over the past twenty years, however, the scientific contributions of both psychologists (Hilgard 1965) and psychiatrists (Frankel 1976; Spiegel and Spiegel 1985) have established a firmer data-based understanding of the nature of hypnosis and its clinical applications. As a result, the capacity of hypnosis to accelerate and augment the impact of psychotherapeutic intervention has been more widely appreciated and the use of hypnosis with children and adolescents has been given more systematic consideration (Williams 1979; Gardner and Olness 1981).

It has become evident that in terms of final clinical outcome, gains achieved in psychotherapy with hypnosis can also be achieved without it. Nevertheless, the enhanced therapeutic leverage afforded by hypnosis can often aid the conversion of insight into action as well as facilitate the more rapid relief of disabling symptoms. Once its limitations and its range of clinical usefulness are appreciated, hypnosis can be a valuable addition to the psychotherapist's armamentarium.

DEFINING HYPNOSIS

Two basic components of hypnosis are dissociation and transference. Dissociation refers to the human capacity for variability in focus of attention regarding various aspects of the external and internal environment. This phenomenon occurs spontaneously in the form of transient daydreams and reveries that most individuals can readily recognize in themselves upon reflection. Being engrossed or "entranced" by a dramatic presentation or gripping life experience represents another common example in which one spontaneously tunes out less significant features of one's external or internal environment. In clinical uses of hypnosis, this commonly observed capacity is first identified and then purposely channeled for defined therapeutic purposes.

Transference, referring to the tendency of the patient to develop subjective elaborations of the therapy relationship based on prior life experiences, plays an equally important role in clinical hypnosis. In contrast to the psychoanalytic approach, where the transference is gradually fostered nondirectively and then analyzed, hypnosis actively and directively exploits the therapeutic leverage inherent in the transference with a view to expediting therapeutic change.

An integration of these two concepts leads to a definition of hypnosis as a state of aroused, attentive, receptive, focal concentration with a corresponding diminution in peripheral awareness (Spiegel and Spiegel 1978). When used clinically, this state is actively initiated and enhanced by the hypnotist for therapeutic purposes. The therapist provides cues geared to shifting the patient's attention to specified areas. The goal of this process is to engender shifts in the emotional and cognitive perspective of the patient and hence achieve behavioral change as well.

This definition dispels the common misconception that hypnosis is a form of sleep. There is a superficial similarity: In both states peripheral awareness contracts, but for different reasons. In sleep, peripheral awareness contracts as part of a general withdrawal of attention from the environment. In hypnosis, peripheral awareness contracts as it enhances a heightened level of focal concentration.

Efforts of neurophysiologists to understand cognitive and affective processes have been strongly influenced by experimental studies of the role of the reticular formation (Kelly 1985). Accumulated data points to the role of the reticular formation as an active, selective information modulator in the brain that appears to filter out incoming stimuli of less interest or value to the organism, thus accentuating the organism's attention and response to those that are of more significance. These developments provide a plausible conceptual model for understanding the neurophysiological basis of focal attention and altered states of consciousness, including hypnosis (Putnam 1984; Spiegel and Spiegel 1984).

A major contribution of both experimental psychologists (Hilgard and Lauer 1965) and clinicians (Spiegel and Spiegel 1985) in recent years has been the establishment of objective reproducible measures of hypnotizability. While several different scales have been employed, there is reassuring general agreement among independent researchers, surveying large samples of volunteer subjects and patients, regarding certain basic features of hypnotizability. It is clear that hypnotizability is a psychological capacity of an individual, similar to intellectual capacity or musical ability; it is not something "projected" onto the subject by the hypnotist. As such, there is a broad range of hypnotizability within the population. The consensus of different large sample surveys is that standardized testing disclosed a typical bell-shaped curve, reflecting a normal distribution of hypnotizability within the population. Thus, a minority of subjects will be not at all hypnotizable, another minority at the other end of the scale will be very highly hypnotizable, and the rest of the population will fall somewhere in between.

This finding helps to engender modesty in the informed hypnotherapist, who can now forego the sometimes tempting illusion that a patient's dramatic response to hypnosis is a testament to the therapist's charismatic or otherwise uniquely gifted personality. At the same time, a patient's lack of response no longer should engender the type of narcissistic injury in the therapist, who might have otherwise seen the patient's lack of response as necessarily reflecting a failure in the therapist.

From a psychodynamic frame of reference, it is noteworthy that Freud's early experiences with hypnosis played a central role in his elaboration of the concepts of repression and associated unconscious processes (Freud 1925). As Freud developed the psychoanalytic method, he initially abandoned the use of hypnosis because of what amounted to an incomplete understanding of the nature of hypnosis and its transference implications. In subsequent years, however, he foresaw that public health needs would reactivate a role for hypnosis to allow more widespread therapeutic applications of psychoanalytic insights than the protracted and expensive method of psychoanalysis could permit (Freud 1919).

Reactivated interest in hypnosis by some contemporary psychoanalysts has led to a reformulated theory of hypnosis in ego-psychological terms, with a special emphasis on transference factors (Gill and Brenman 1959; Spiegel and Spiegel 1984). Such a reformulation views hypnosis as a circumscribed, guided regression in the service of the ego; it indicates how hypnosis can be structured effectively for therapeutic purposes, using a psychodynamic frame of reference.

Special Considerations with Children and Adolescents

Based on the sampling surveys noted above, it has been established that roughly 70 percent of the adult population is hypnotizable to a clinically significant degree (Spiegel and Spiegel 1985). Similar surveys with children and adolescents, using adaptations of adult scales, indicate that children and adolescents are generally more hypnotizable than adults. Such studies find increases in hypnotic responsivity between the ages of 5 and 10, a peak in the preadolescent years (11 to 12), and a gradual decline thereafter, which continues through adulthood (Morgan and Hilgard 1973). As in adulthood, there are no overall differences between the sexes in hypnotizability during childhood and adolescence.

Morgan (1973) explored genetic and environmental influences of hypnotic responsiveness by studying 140 twin pairs, ranging in age from 5 to 22 years, together with their parents and siblings. Both members of each twin pair were hypnotized simultaneously, in separate rooms, so as to avoid experimental bias. The parents also completed a questionnaire, rating each of their children for similarity to each parent on eleven personality and temperamental variables. The correlations of hypnotizability for monozygotic twins were statistically significant for both males ($r = 0.54$) and for females ($r = 0.49$). In contrast, correlations for dizygotic twins and for sibling nontwin pairs were not significantly different from zero ($r = 0.08; -0.25$). These data were consistent with the interpretation of a genetic contribution of hypnotizability. Morgan also found, however, that personality resemblance as rated by the parents on a standardized questionnaire was positively related to hypnotizability scores for either sexed child and the like-sexed parent. Morgan interpreted these results as suggesting an environmental contribution to hypnotizability, based primarily on the child's identification with the like-sexed parent and emulation of the parent's behavioral pattern. She thus concluded that hypnotizability appears to be the result of both a genetic predisposition and subsequent environmental influence, as well as of their interaction.

From a cognitive standpoint, children focus more on the immediate present than adults. Piaget's description of the child's natural tendency toward concrete, literal thinking helps to explain the child's more ready acceptance of the ceremony of hypnosis (Gardner 1974). As in the case of religious ceremony, children give much less consideration than adults to theoretical questions and logical complexities if the underlying message of the ceremony is plausible and emotionally acceptable. The greater ease with which children intertwine fantasy and reality also tends to facilitate their acceptance of hypnosis. To the extent that adolescents develop more sophisticated cognitive operations, some of them begin to demonstrate the more critical and skeptical thought styles that often constitute a potential source of resistance to hypnosis among adults. As with adults, however, a therapist's preparedness to respond clearly and effectively to questions raised in that spirit may often overcome such potential resistance.

Emotional factors contributing to the greater hypnotizability of children include their general openness to new experience, their emotional malleability, their intrinsic orientation to learning new skills, and the greater ease with which they can accept regressive phenomena. In this respect, the hypnotic relationship more closely approximates the ways in which children relate to adults, rather than the ways in which adults usually relate to each other. The child's propensity for trusting responsiveness to suggestions, as well as his readiness to accept help from a respected adult authority, are both part of a natural developmental progress toward achieving mastery and autonomy. The therapist's choice of language and metaphor is important in meeting the individual youngster's cognitive level, range of experiences, and emotional needs. As in any psychotherapeutic transaction, it is important in adapting a hypnosis format to avoid talking "over the head" of a younger child, or, conversely, to avoid oversimplification to the point of condescension with an adolescent.

A key task is that of enlisting parental understanding, cooperation, and support for the use of hypnosis as a basis of enhancing the prospects for its acceptance by the patient. Because of continued common misconceptions about hypnosis as shamanistic or dangerous, the therapist should explain to the parents as well as to the patient, before using hypnosis, how this modality can play a safe and useful part in the overall treatment strategy. In order to elicit this vital parental consensual validation and patient acceptance, the therapist does best, as in any family-based intervention, to tread the fine line of avoiding excessive judgmental criticism of either the parents or the patient. In the setting of a therapeutic rapport with both the patient and the parents, based on the premise of a shared desire to change the status quo, the ceremony of hypnosis can serve as a catalyst for emotional and behavioral change. Although this change is usually sought primarily in the patient, it often requires concomitant adjustments by the parents as well.

The physical setting for hypnosis should preferably foster a sense of comfort, privacy, and freedom from distracting stimuli. In the hospital setting, other important consensual validators besides parents who should be briefed on the rationale for the use of hypnosis would include not only other physicians, but very importantly, the nursing staff and any others who are in a position to influence the patient on an ongoing basis.

INDICATIONS FOR HYPNOSIS

Before considering the use of hypnosis with any youngster, the therapist must first establish a clear diagnostic formulation of the problem. Ideally, this should be based on a review of the historical information available, as well as on a direct assessment of the patient, and if possible, of the parents. An overall treatment strategy then should be devised aimed both at modifying pathogenic influences in the patient's life circumstances and at augmenting the youngster's capacity for mastery of intrapsychic areas of conflict.

Hypnosis has been used commonly with adults as a diagnostic aid to promote uncovering repressed material. Examples of this would include abreaction of past traumatic experiences and more protracted exploration in "hypnoanalysis." Clinical experience suggests that these approaches are not as useful with children and adolescents. The more prevalent, conventional methods of individual and family assessment, including structured or semistructured interviewing, mutual story telling, and free discussion seem better suited to fostering spontaneous expression in younger patients.

One diagnostic application of hypnosis with youngsters that can often be helpful, however, is the use of a clinical trial of hypnosis focused on symptom-alleviation, where psychogenic factors in the genesis of a physical symptom are suspected but not yet confirmed. In such cases, early and sustained symptom alleviation with hypnosis can help clarify the role of psychogenicity in symptom genesis, as well as become part of a plan of therapy for consolidation of the early therapeutic gains.

In actual treatment application, hypnosis can increase therapeutic leverage by tapping the patient's capacity to participate in the therapeutic experience in a more intense and concentrated way. An atmosphere of receptivity is purposely and dramatically engendered that enhances the youngster's propensity for change. Inherent in this process as well is the generation of a sense of mastery in the patient, which can facilitate the more rapid relief of disabling symptoms (Williams and Singh 1976). Once a treatment plan has been developed, hypnosis can serve to focus attention on key dynamic elements in a welter of complex environmental and intrapsychic variables. By so doing, hypnosis can enable the therapist to present a direct, sound, and palatable route by which the patient can relinquish with honor a symptom complex to which he has retreated under duress. Thus, if the therapeutic strategy has been judiciously formulated, the patient can, under the supportive authority of the hypnotherapist, incorporate a healthier perspective of adaptation into his coping repertoire.

Clinical experience has suggested that hypnosis can play a useful role in treating patients with a wide range of diagnoses. Those that have been found most commonly responsive include somatic pain (Hilgard and Hilgard 1975), somatoform disorders (Williams 1985), dissociative disorders (Bliss 1984), phobias (McGuinness 1984), psychological factors affecting a physical condition, adjustment disorders, anxiety disorders, and some other disorders with physical manifestations (e.g., stuttering, functional enuresis, and functional encopresis) (Gardner and Olness 1981). In contrast to the above enumerated categories, youngsters with clear-cut psychosis or substantial organic brain damage generally lack the necessary capacity for sustained concentration and the associated ego strengths needed to utilize hypnosis effectively. For some patients with borderline conditions or minimal brain dysfunction, hypnosis may be of value and may be combined with appropriate psychotropic medication (Spiegel 1980). It should be emphasized, however, that circumscribed therapeutic changes achieved with severely disturbed patients using hypnosis are unlikely to be sustained unless accompanied by the associated supportive measures that their overall condition requires.

Hypnosis is most often introduced as an adjunct within the larger framework of ongoing individual and/or family therapy. Expertise in these broader areas is clearly a prerequisite for the effective use of hypnosis. With that caveat in mind, some representative scenarios can be sketched wherein hypnosis may play a useful adjunctive role:

Pain Control. Although this is one of the best established applications of hypnosis, an understanding of the neurophysiological processes involved remains elusive. It has been documented that hypnotic analgesia is clearly different from placebo in highly hypnotizable subjects and is significantly more effective for them (McGlashan et al. 1969). Several excellent sources delineate applications of hypnosis for pain control in children and adolescents (Gardner and Olness 1981; Zeltzer and Le Baron 1982; Kellerman et al. 1983).

When Symptomatic Behavior Has Become an Established Habit. Hypnosis may be helpful when such behavior persists on a self-perpetuating basis after having lost its original emotional significance (Kaffman 1968; Gardner and Olness 1981). The augmented sense of mastery afforded by hypnosis can catalyze escape from a previously semiautomatic repetitive pattern in which the patient had felt trapped, yet had lacked the confidence or motivation to break out.

Inadequate Progress in Ongoing Psychotherapy. Hypnosis may be helpful when inadequate progress has been made in the conversion of insight into changed behavior, despite the existence of potential psychodynamic resources for clinical improvement, as judged by the therapist. Introduction of hypnosis affords the therapist an opportunity to "shift gears" from a more exploratory to a more actively directive approach.

At the Beginning of a Therapeutic Relationship. This presupposes that initial evaluation has furnished the therapist sufficient psychodynamic data on both the presenting problem and the child's and family's capacities for change to justify the application of hypnosis. Such an approach is particularly appropriate in crisis intervention, though it need by no means be restricted to such situations. The "ripple effect" of relief and increased self-confidence generated by initial symptomatic improvement can produce a more conducive atmosphere for further psychotherapeutic endeavor (Spiegel 1969).

ASSESSING HYPNOTIZABILITY

A variety of procedures can be used to identify hypnotic trance capacity and to induce trance states. Actually, the particular induction technique used is almost inconsequential in the genesis of the trance, as long as it is esthetically and emotionally acceptable to the patient. Of great importance, however, is the expectation of both the patient and therapist that the ceremonious transaction between them will engender a change in the patient's subjective experience. The operation signaling this change may involve any one of a myriad of disciplined tasks that involve concentration, with the associated tacit anticipation that this will lead to the patient's heightened state of receptivity to the therapist's further comments or suggestions. Space limitations preclude detailed delineation of hypnotic induction procedures here, but several scales commonly used with children will be referred to for measurement of hypnotizability and additional references will be cited for treatment application.

London developed a test called the Children's Hypnotic Susceptibility Scale (London 1963), based on the items in the Stanford Hypnotic Susceptibility Scale, Form A (Weitzenhoffer and Hilgard 1959), which is commonly used with adults. The Children's scale contains twenty-two items, proceeding from the easier to the more difficult. The more items the subject passes, the higher the hypnotizability score obtained. This scale requires forty-five to sixty minutes to administer. Consequently, although valuable for research purposes, it is too time-consuming for general clinical use.

Morgan and Hilgard (1979) developed a shorter scale, the Stanford Hypnotic Clinical Scale for Children (SHCS-Child), which can be administered in twenty minutes. This scale includes one form for children 6 to 16 years old and another for children 4 to 8 years old. The form for older children is based on an eye closure-relaxation induction followed by seven test items. The form for younger children is based on an active imagination induction, since younger children often are resistant to suggestions for eye closure. This form then contains six test items. The SHCS-Child is easy to administer and to score with a minimum of training.

The Hypnotic Induction Profile, developed by Spiegel (Spiegel and Spiegel 1978), is also known as the eye roll, arm levitation method of hypnotic induction. It is particularly useful in clinical settings, as it can be administered in five to ten minutes. The wording of its instructions can readily be modified according to the age and cognitive level of a given child or adolescent. This method affords a quick, convenient, semiquantitative and reproducible way of measuring hypnotizability; consequently it has advantages for both clinical and research purposes. Although standardized norms have not yet been established for children and adolescents, this method has been demonstrated to have satisfactory statistical correlation with existing standardized adult scales that are laboratory based, but that are considerably more cumbersome and time consuming (Frischholz et al. 1980).

The Hypnotic Induction Profile provides a method of measuring and correlating the patient's pattern of response to instructions for eye roll, dissociation, posthypnotic arm levitation, and posthypnotic subjective experiences. These individual measurements are then combined to convey a composite index of the patient's relative ability to maintain a disciplined level of concentration and cooperation in a relaxed, dissociated state. In clinical scoring, degrees of hypnotizability are designated on a scale of 0 to 4, with 0 indicating nonhypnotizability and 4 indicating maximal responsibility.

Written description can provide only a basic frame of reference for any psychotherapeutic technique. Clinical experience is needed for the therapist to cultivate and refine an effective clinical methodology. A growing number of didactic workshops are held periodically at continuing medical education forums around the country to convey this initiating personal exposure.

In addition to ascertaining hypnotizability of the patient, measuring the patient's hypnotizability has another advantage. It provides the patient with a "practice exposure" in which to experience hypnosis without immediate concern about its therapeutic applications. Once this "practice" initiation has been accomplished, the documented hypnotizability of the patient stands as a potential new resource with which to tackle the problem in question. Aside from being a confidence-building maneuver, this approach is empirically supported by recent findings that effective hypnotizability is associated with relative mental health (Spiegel et al. 1982). Specifically, 115 chronically and severely ill adult psychiatric patients were found to be significantly less hypnotizable than a nonpatient comparison group. Finding effective hypnotizability in a patient thus becomes a prognostically relevant indicator of relative intactness and capacity to respond to therapeutic suggestion.

As long as the patient is hypnotizable to some degree, it is reasonable to proceed to the use of hypnosis in treatment. In adults, greater hypnotizability tends to be associated with greater psychotherapeutic responsivity (Spiegel and Spiegel 1985). In children and adolescents, insufficient data are available to establish such a relationship. At least as important as the youngster's degree of hypnotizability, however, would appear to be the patient's constellation of other ego strengths, family resources, and the skill of the therapist in integrating these into an effective treatment strategy.

TREATMENT TECHNIQUES

Having formulated a diagnostic impression as well as the outline of a treatment plan and having ascertained the patients hypnotizability, the therapist can now explain to the patient and parents how hypnosis will be used in treatment, if hypnosis is indeed appropriate. In lay terminology, hypnosis can often best be explained as a "relaxation exercise" that can help the patient concentrate on a new approach to dealing with his problems. It is advisable to combine this with a brief dynamic formulation of the presenting problem and description of the proposed overall treatment plan. If there is general acceptance of these proposals, then an appropriate rapport has been established that constitutes the springboard for effective intervention with hypnosis. The therapist should then see the patient alone and guide him back into the trance state. Attention is focused on postulated causes of the presenting problem and emphasis is placed on the patient's capacity to reorient his own contribution to it by directing thoughts and efforts along new lines. From a psychodynamic perspective, a symptom often evolves as a patient's symbolic expression of unresolved intrapsychic conflict. This is interpreted to the patient at a level he can understand; concomitantly, the therapist offers a more felicitous adaptive metaphor with which the patient can confront his life situation. This "restructuring" by the therapist sets the stage for the patient to incorporate a more "grown-up" or "mature" coping strategy, while implicitly or explicitly favoring symptom attenuation and relinquishment.

For adolescents or older children, these thoughts can be summarized in a dialectical format of two or three short statements that convey the crux of the new orientation. Alternatively, particularly for younger children or those with less verbal ability, a visual or experiential image can be used to convey the sense of mastery that is central to the desired therapeutic reorientation. The child can be induced, for example, to imagine a scene in which his favorite television or sports hero provides support and encouragement for a new approach to overcoming the presenting problem.

A very helpful way of maintaining the momentum of this procedure is to teach the patient self-hypnosis so that the therapeutic message can be reinforced autonomously at home. The therapist can make this easier by having a set of general instructions for self-hypnosis printed, with room left to insert the particular message for each patient. (This will be illustrated in a clinical example below.) For younger or more dependent children, parents may be recruited as surrogate hypnotherapists to administer the exercise at home. Even in these instances, however, it is better to do initial hypnotic induction and self-hypnosis instruction to the patient without the distracting presence of the parents, since the initial emotional impact should accentuate the pivotal role of the patient-therapist relationship in the reorientation process. Once this is done, the parents can be brought back into the room to observe a review of the self-hypnosis format, so that they, with the help of the written instructions, can administer it at home. Alternatively, a tape recording of instructions and suggestions for self-hypnosis can be used for this purpose.

Further discussion of hypnotic techniques with children and adolescents, along with a variety of case summaries demonstrating specific applications of this approach in therapy, are available in the volume by Gardner and Olness (1981). Here only a brief clinical vignette will be used to illustrate the role of hypnosis in facilitating therapeutic reorientation.

CASE VIGNETTE

Lois, aged 13, was transferred to our medical center with episodic jerking movements, involving primarily the axial musculature. Three weeks previously, she had been treated for a documented streptococcal throat infection, cough, and wheezing with an antibiotic, cough medication, and a bronchodilator. Lois developed dizziness and tremors, following which the bronchodilator medication was discontinued. Nevertheless, the tremors became more pronounced, taking the form of episodic jerking movements. These recurred every couple of hours and lasted for twenty to sixty minutes, with apparent progressive increase of intensity and duration. After several days, Lois was admitted to a local hospital, where multiple studies were performed, including a CAT Scan and an EEG, both of which were normal. With the persistence of the symptoms in the absence of a clear diagnosis, she was transferred to our medical center. Differential diagnostic possibilities included a myoclonic seizure disorder versus psychogenic seizures.

Past medical history was noncontributory. Review of family history disclosed that Lois's parents had been divorced one and a half years previously after a stormy separation and that Lois's mother had remarried one year later. Observation of one of the "seizure" episodes revealed that Lois retained full consciousness during the jerking and thrusting movements of her body, including fully coherent speech and the ability to perform complex motor activities with her hands. An EEG performed during one of these episodes was completely normal, as was the rest of the neurological examination. A preliminary diagnosis of psychogenic seizures prompted psychiatric consultation.

On initial psychiatric interview, Lois was alert, cooperative, and articulate in reviewing the history, appearing to be of above-average intelligence. There was no thought disorder and no bizarre or inappropriate behavior.

Mood was subdued, but not depressed. She reported being an A to B student at school and noted having many friends. She acknowledged a history of stormy conflict between her parents before and after their divorce, as well as some adjustment frictions in her mother's new marriage. She could see no connection between these stresses, however, and her presenting symptoms, about which she expressed remarkably little overt concern.

Independent consultations with each parent supported the impression that Lois had been in many ways a "model child," who excelled in all spheres of activity and was never the source of behavior difficulty. This contrasted with both her older siblings, who had particularly vociferous conflicts with the father during adolescent development. On the other hand, Lois didn't confide in either parent and seemed to internalize her feelings about turbulent family events.

The psychiatrist presented a tentative psychodynamic formulation to Lois and her parents along the following lines:

In the setting of physical illness and the use of several other medications, the addition of a bronchodilator with sympathetic nervous system stimulatory effects had probably generated tremor and anxiety in Lois. This was compounded not only by her own and her parents' anxiety about her physical condition, but also by preexisting suppressed feelings of conflict about multiple family changes. Faced with her mother's remarriage, her father's new girlfriend, and her older siblings' departure from the home, Lois's model behavior pattern and self-contained pattern of emotional expression had yielded not much more than benign neglect by other family members who were caught up with meeting their own needs. Lois's physical illness and the secondary emergence of her dramatic seizurelike symptom, most probably as an unconscious symbolic expression of distress about her overall condition, had succeeded in shifting the spotlight of family concern onto Lois. The secondary gain of attention and support from parents and others then tended to reinforce the symptom, while it gratified Lois's long-suppressed dependency needs.

The psychiatrist then explained to Lois and her parents the importance of expediting symptom relinquishment so that Lois could return promptly to school and other regular activities, while the associated emotional concerns could then be worked on in outpatient psychotherapy. He suggested that hypnosis, as a form of "relaxation and concentration," could possibly facilitate this process and allow early discharge from the hospital. Lois and her parents were receptive.

On formal testing, Lois obtained a score of 2 on the Hypnotic Induction Profile, indicating moderate hypnotizability. The therapist noted this to be a favorable prognostic sign for treatment responsiveness and then guided Lois back into the trance state while she was seated comfortably in an armchair.

The following instructions for a self-hypnosis exercise were offered by the therapist:

1. Look up toward the top of your head.
2. Close your eyes and take a deep breath in.

3. Let your breath out, let your eyes relax, and let your body float. As
you feel yourself floating, let one hand or the other feel like a big
ballon and let it float upward. When it reaches this upright position,
this becomes your signal to go into a deeper state of relaxation in
which you concentrate on the following three points:
1. Worried feelings can cause tension.
2. Tension can bring on seizures.
3. By relaxing this way, I can reduce the tension and overcome the
seizures.
After reviewing these important thoughts, you then bring yourself
out of this state of self-hypnosis by counting backwards as follows:
3. Get ready.
2. With your eyes closed, take a deep breath in.
1. Let your breath out and let your eyes open slowly. Then when
your eyes are back in focus, make a fist with the hand that is up
and let your hand float down to the side of the chair. That is the
end of the exercise, though you may continue to have a pleasant
feeling of this floating.

The self-hypnosis exercise was subsequently reviewed in a supportive
conjoint session with Lois and her mother, with advice that Lois continue
to practice it at home several times a day.

Lois was discharged the same day, with a plan for her return to school
two days later, and to have a psychiatric follow-up session ten days later.
At follow-up, Lois noted that she had had one brief and mild "seizure"
episode on the day of discharge and another one the following day, but had
had no subsequent recurrences. She had some premonitory sensations on
subsequent days, but had been able to avoid their progression by use of the
self-hypnosis exercise, which she had been practicing three times a day. She
had returned to school without incident and with no subsequent absences.
The psychiatrist offered supportive reinforcement of the observed gains and
advised additional follow-up sessions despite Lois's lack of enthusiasm for
this endeavor.

The pattern of improvement was observed to be sustained at additional
follow-up one month later, at which time Lois noted that the premonitory
sensations had totally ceased and that she no longer felt the need for the
self-hypnosis exercise. Since Lois's functioning was now fully normal in all
spheres, and since she opposed continuing in ongoing psychotherapy, provision was made that Lois and her parents could call for another appointment on an as-needed basis.

After a symptom-free period of eight and a half months, her mother
called to report that Lois experienced fainting spells, memory difficulties,
and the recurrence of "seizure-like episodes" in the setting of an upper respiratory infection with associated fever and headache. These persisted over
a three-day period, and Lois asked to see the psychiatrist about them. Prompt
office consultation disclosed that Lois had had a good social and academic
adjustment over the intervening eight and a half months. Yet Lois expressed

resentment of her father's lack of sustained involvement with her, coupled with his also making suggestive comments about her attractive physical maturation. Three sessions were held over a week's time, during which Lois's conflicted feelings about her father and about her emerging physical and emotional development were discussed in both individual sessions with Lois as well as conjoint sessions involving her mother and stepfather. The therapist interpreted the symptom recurrence as a call for help by Lois based on unresolved emotional conflicts and precipitated by a recent encounter with her father and a concomitant respiratory infection. Her mother now disclosed for the first time that she herself had experienced violent "stomach spasms" several years earlier, which she now recognized retrospectively to have been a similar symbolic expression of her inability to handle troubled feelings about her first husband's labile and inconsistent behavior.

The psychiatrist again offered Lois the opportunity to use self-hypnosis as an aid in reestablishing control and normal functioning. He also reemphasized that symptom relinquishment needed to be combined with more understanding and direct verbal expression of conflicted feelings, which were now being more fully articulated in individual and conjoint family sessions. Her mother called after the third session to report that all the symptoms had cleared and that Lois therefore felt no need for any additional sessions. Lois confirmed this by telephone, but noted that her mother hadn't tried very hard to persuade her to keep any further appointments. Efforts by the psychiatrist to convince each of them of the need for additional sessions to consolidate therapeutic gains were unavailing. The option was therefore again left open for the family to call on an as-needed basis.

Follow-up contact by the psychiatrist two and a half years later disclosed no further symptom recurrence or symptom substitutions. Lois continued to do well both socially and academically without any further psychotherapeutic assistance.

PRECAUTIONS, CONTRAINDICATIONS, AND LIMITATIONS

When used with reasonable clinical judgment in an appropriately goal-directed manner, hypnosis is a remarkably safe therapeutic resource. Nevertheless, every therapeutic tool can be misused, and there are some precautions to be noted. Since hypnosis has particular value and frequent application in treating somatoform disorders and psychological factors affecting physical conditions, it is crucial to consider the possible presence of undiagnosed organic pathology before launching headlong into a psychotherapeutic endeavor (Williams 1985). It is often possible to elucidate plausible dynamics to rationalize the diagnosis of conversion disorder, for example, when a primary organic lesion is actually responsible for the presenting symptom. Hypnosis would have only transient effect, if any, in suppressing symptoms in such a situation, but such mistreatment may have embarrassing and even dangerous consequences in delaying appropriate medical intervention.

Conversely, the presence of a documented organic disorder such as epilepsy by no means precludes the coexistence of pseudoseizures as a secondary somatoform disorder, a factitious disorder or malingering (Williams et al. 1978, 1979; Williams and Mostofsky 1982). In cases where the diagnosis is initially unclear, it may well be justified to pursue a clinical trial of psychotherapeutic intervention, including hypnosis, while maintaining close liaison with cotreating medical colleagues. Such a team approach will be most likely to ascertain whether the presenting problem is primarily organic, primarily psychogenic, or some combination of the two.

Another important caveat, in cases of psychodynamically based symptomatology, is the contraindication to using hypnosis coercively in an overzealous attempt to remove a symptom without adequately considering the consequences for the patient. It is clearly inappropriate to try to deprive a patient of a symptom that has been serving a defensive function unless one can help restructure his perspective for alternative and more adaptive coping strategies. Attempts at blindly removing such symptoms through hypnosis or any other suggestive method not only will fail, but will undermine the patient's confidence in the therapist. These pitfalls can be avoided by taking into account existing individual and family psychodynamics, the patient's self-esteem, and his capacity to achieve designated goals.

There are popular misconceptions about symptom recurrence or symptom substitution necessarily following the use of hypnosis for symptom removal (Spiegel 1967). One common cause of such untoward sequelae is heavy-handed or otherwise inappropriate technique on the part of the therapist, such as that of a coercive approach, noted above. Furthermore, symptoms may recur even when appropriately removed with hypnosis, if excessive adverse life stresses reappear, or if the psychotherapeutic support needed to consolidate gains is terminated prematurely. This observation is no more characteristic of hypnosis, however, than of other therapeutic modalities.

Another limitation of note is the problem of unrealistic expectations about hypnosis on the part of patients or parents, which provides a set-up for disappointment and disillusionment. The growing number of references to hypnosis in the media in recent years has attracted self-referrals and sometimes misguided medical referrals based on the fallacious belief that hypnosis will provide a panacea for complex life problems. The patient and parents seen by a therapist in such a context obviously must be given some clarification, after the presenting problem and relevant background have been elucidated, as to what hypnosis can and cannot realistically be expected to accomplish. Such clarification can then be the starting point for exploration of supplementary or alternative treatment approaches, when needed. If the presenting problem is circumscribed and resolvable with a short-term intervention using hypnosis, all concerned may be readily gratified. If more protracted supportive therapy, medication, or other approaches are required, educating the patient and family about these constitutes an important service for the therapist to render.

Besides the already-noted prerequisite that hypnosis be incorporated into a comprehensive individual and/or family therapy framework, integration of hypnosis with other treatment modalities also warrants mention.

A therapeutic strategy oriented towards symptom relief must deal with secondary gain features of the symptom. Children and adolescents particularly may have difficulty in appreciating long-range therapeutic benefits as adequate compensation for the loss of immediate secondary gain. It therefore becomes the therapist's responsibility to orchestrate the diminution or elimination of any secondary gain; indeed, this is critical if the symptom's removal is to be sustained. Such orchestration often can be achieved by means of parental counseling, environmental manipulation, or a behavior modification program. The therapist's capacity to influence skillfully the operating contingencies of reinforcement is vital to the success of any psychotherapeutic strategy, including those involving hypnosis.

For some patients, appropriate psychotropic medication use may be necessary if the youngster is to be accessible to hypnosis. This may include the use of stimulants with patients having attention deficit disorders, antidepressant medication with those having significant depression or separation anxiety, and tranquilizing medication for those with more severe forms of generalized anxiety (Wiener 1985).

Definitive guidelines cannot reasonably be delineated regarding optimal frequency or duration of application of hypnosis as a therapeutic adjunct. These will vary widely, depending on the clinical features that are unique in each case. However, if one sees no therapeutic change in a hypnotizable patient after two to three sessions of treatment with hypnosis, there has been some error or omission in either diagnostic assessment, treatment plan formulation, or appreciation of the role of secondary gain factors. A review and reformulation of these areas is then in order.

For some patients, only a few sessions may be needed to achieve fully the desired therapeutic results. For others, there may be a valid role for continued or periodic use of hypnosis within the context of a more conventional and extended therapeutic format. A decision on this matter should be determined by the individual patient's needs. Even when therapeutic intervention has been quickly and dramatically successful, however, it is generally wise to schedule some follow-up sessions to reinforce therapeutic gains. Clinical experience suggests that it takes some time for a youngster and family to assimilate all the ramifications of a new strategy of adaptation.

Accelerating the impact of psychotherapeutic intervention with hypnosis clearly has significant economic and public health implications. It is obvious that a therapist should have a sophisticated grasp of the complex factors that operate in the diverse intrapsychic, interpersonal, and environmental domains that involve his patient. It is by no means necessary, however, that each patient attain a sophisticated level of insight in order to achieve effective therapeutic results. Extended analytic working through may certainly add new dimensions of self-understanding to those with the resources to utilize that approach. Yet, for the many patients for whom a protracted and costly approach is simply not possible, hypnosis may afford an opportunity to achieve certain therapeutic results more rapidly. Actively helping a patient to surmount a developmental obstacle is clearly different from gradually assisting him to overcome it by greater reliance on his own efforts. It behooves the well-trained therapist to have both of these approaches in his armamentarium, so that either or both can be applied when clinically indicated.

CONCLUSION

Hypnosis has had a checkered history in adult and child psychiatry, characterized by extremes of overenthusiastic, uncritical, and nonselective use by some practitioners and equally unreasonable global dismissal by others. Systematic recent studies have clarified that the capacity for hypnosis exists in the majority of the population and that children are generally more hypnotizable than adults. It is a relatively straightforward task for an otherwise well-qualified child therapist to master the basics of assessing a patient's hypnotizability by using any one of a number of standardized scales.

A basic prerequisite for using hypnosis effectively in treatment, as with any other psychotherapeutic technique, is the initial, thorough diagnostic assessment. This will clarify whether an appropriate diagnostic indication and an adequate therapeutic rapport for hypnosis exist. If so, and if the patient is hypnotizable as well as receptive to using hypnosis as part of a process of therapeutic change, a potentially powerful facilitator is available to help implement the treatment plan. The effectiveness of hypnosis in such a context depends on several variables, including the capacities of the patient and family to respond to therapeutic suggestions, the severity of pathogenic environmental stressors, and the skill of the therapist in integrating hypnosis with other elements of a well-formulated treatment plan to foster a more healthy mode of adaptation.

REFERENCES

Bliss, E. L. (1984). Spontaneous self-hypnosis in multiple personality disorder. *Psychiat. Clinics North Amer.* 7(1):135–48.

Frankel, F. H. (1976). *Hypnosis: Trance as a Coping Mechanism.* New York: Plenum Medical Press.

Freud, S. (1919). Lines of advance in psychoanalytic therapy. In *Standard Edition,* Vol. 17. London: Hogarth, pp. 157–68.

———. (1925). An autobiographical study. In *Standard Edition,* Vol. 20. London: Hogarth, pp. 3–74.

Frischholz, E. J., et al. (1980). The relationship between the hypnotic induction profile and the Stanford Hypnotic Susceptibility Scale, Form C: A replication. *Amer. J. Clin. Hypnosis* 22:185–96.

Gardner, G. (1974). Hypnosis with children. *Int'l. J. Clin. Experiment. Hypnosis* 22:20–38.

———, and Olness, K. (1981). *Hypnosis and Hypnotherapy with Children.* New York: Grune and Stratton.

Gill, M., and Brenman, M. (1959). *Hypnosis and Related States.* New York: International Universities Press.

Hilgard, E. R. (1965). *The Experience of Hypnosis.* New York: Harcourt, Brace and World.

———, and Hilgard, J. R. (1975). *Hypnosis in the Relief of Pain.* Los Altos, Calif.: William Kaufmann.

———, and Lauer, L. W. (1965). *Hypnotic Susceptibility.* New York: Harcourt, Brace and World.

Kaffman, M. (1968). Hypnosis as an adjunct to psychotherapy in child psychiatry. *Arch. Gen. Psychiat.* 18:725–38.

Kellerman, J., et al. (1983). Hypnosis for the reduction of the acute pain and anxiety associated with medical procedures. *J. Adoles. Health Care* 4:85–90.

Kelly, J. (1985). Cranial nerve nuclei, the reticular formation and biogenic amine containing neurons. In E. R. Kandel and J. H. Schwartz (Eds.). *Principles of Neural Science.* 2d ed. New York: Elsevier, pp. 539–61.

London, P. (1963). *Children's Hypnotic Susceptibility Scale.* Palo Alto, Calif.: Consulting Psychologists Press.

McGlashan, T., Evans, F., and Orne, M. (1969). The nature of hypnotic analgesia and placebo responses to experimental pain. *Psychosom. Med.* 31:227–46.

McGuinness, T. P. (1984). Hypnosis in the treatment of phobias: A review of the literature. *Amer. J. Clin. Hypnosis* 26:261–72.

Morgan, A. (1973). The heritability of hypnotic susceptibility in twins. *J. Abnorm. Psychol.* 82:55–61.

———, and Hilgard, E. (1973). Age differences in susceptibility to hypnosis. *Int'l. J. Clin. Experiment. Hypnosis* 21:78–85.

———, and Hilgard, J. R. (1979). The Stanford Hypnotic Clinical Scale for Children. *Amer. J. Clin. Hypnosis* 21:148–55.

Putnam, F. W. (1984). The physiological investigation of multiple personality disorder. *Psychiat. Clinics North Amer.* 7(1):31–41.

Spiegel, D. (1980). Hypnotizability and psychoactive medication. *Amer. J. Clin. Hypnosis* 22:217–22.

———, Detrick, D., and Frischholz, F. (1982). Hypnotizability and psychopathology. *Amer. J. Psychiatry* 139:431–37.

———, and Spiegel, H. (1984). Hypnosis. In T. B. Karasu (Ed.). *The Psychosocial Therapies* Washington, D.C.: *American Psychiatric Association*, pp. 701–36.

———, and ———. (1985). Hypnosis. In H. Kaplan and B. Sadock (Eds.). *Comprehensive Textbook of Psychiatry.* 4th Ed. Vol. 2. Baltimore: Williams and Wilkins, pp. 1389–402.

Spiegel, H. (1967). Is symptom removal dangerous? *Amer. J. Psychiatry* 123:1279–83.

———. (1969). The "ripple effect" following adjunct hypnosis in analytic psychotherapy. *Amer. J. Psychiatry* 126:53–58.

———. (1972). An eye-roll test for hypnotizability. *Amer. J. Clin. Hypnosis* 15:25–28.

———, and Spiegel, D. (1978). *Trance and Treatment: Clinical Uses of Hypnosis.* New York: Basic Books.

Weitzenhoffer, A. M., and Hilgard, E. R. (1959). *Stanford Hypnotic Susceptibility Scale, Forms A and B.* Palo Alto, Calif.: Consulting Psychologists Press.

Wiener, J. (Ed.) (1985). *Diagnosis and Psychopharmacology of Childhood and Adolescent Disorders.* New York: Wiley.

Williams, D. T. (1979). Hypnosis as a psychotherapeutic adjunct. In J. D. Noshpitz and S. I. Harrison (Eds.). *Basic Handbook of Child Psychiatry,* Vol. 3. New York: Basic Books, pp. 108–16.

————. (1985). Somatoform disorders. In D. Shaffer, A. Ehrhardt, and L. Greenhill (Eds.). *The Clinical Guide to Child Psychiatry.* New York: Free Press, pp. 192–207.

Williams, D. T., and Singh, M. (1976). Hypnosis as a facilitating therapeutic adjunct in child psychiatry. *J. Amer. Acad. Child Psychiatry* 15:326–42.

————, Spiegel, H., and Mostofsky, D. I. (1978). Neurogenic and hysterical seizures in children and adolescents: Differential diagnostic and therapeutic considerations. *Amer. J. Psychiatry* 135:82–86.

————, et al. (1979). The impact of psychiatric intervention on patients with uncontrolled seizures. *J. Nerv. Mental Dis.* 167:626–31.

————, and Mostofsky, D. I. (1982). Psychogenic seizures in childhood and adolescence. In T. Riley and A. Roy (Eds.). *Pseudoseizures.* Baltimore: Williams and Wilkins, pp. 169–84.

Zeltzer, L., and Le Baron, S. (1982). Hypnosis and nonhypnotic techniques for reduction of pain and anxiety during painful procedures in children and adolescents with cancer. *J. Pediat.* 101:1032–35.

Name Index

Subject Index